Osborne **McGraw-Hill**

MICROSOFT® WORD
SECRETS, SOLUTIONS, SHORTCUTS

Tom Sheldon

Covers Version 4

Microsoft ® Word:
Secrets, Solutions, Shortcuts

Tom Sheldon

Osborne **McGraw-Hill**
Berkeley, California

Osborne **McGraw-Hill**
2600 Tenth Street
Berkeley, California 94710
U.S.A.

For information on translations and book distributors outside of the U.S.A., please write to Osborne **McGraw-Hill** at the above address.

A complete list of trademarks appears on page 739.

Microsoft® Word: Secrets, Solutions, Shortcuts

1234567890 DODO 898

ISBN 0-07-881349-2

Jeffrey Pepper, Acquisitions Editor
Martin Matthews, Technical Reviewer
Madhu Prasher, Project Editor
Michael Paul, Production Coordinator

Contents

To Jim, Beth, and Ryan. Special thanks to Jeff Pepper and Madhu Prasher of Osborne/ McGraw-Hill. Thanks for all your support.

Preface

Microsoft Word is a tool that you can use to create and print high-quality documents. Word contains all the features that you need to plan, organize, write, edit, format, print, and save any form of text. Because of its many features, Word helps you be creative by freeing you from the drudgery associated with older methods of document preparation. The tools provided by Word and the process that you will go through when using them to prepare your documents fall into the realm of word processing. This book will help you become more familiar with the methods of word processing using Microsoft Word.

Microsoft Word is unique among the many word processing programs currently offered in that it is designed for the creation of both small and large documents. Word supports almost every printer on the market and was one of the first to fully support the multi-font capabilities of laser printers such as the Hewlett-Packard LaserJet. Word also supports PostScript printers such as the Apple LaserWriter as well as larger typesetting machines like those made by Linotronic.

The most important feature of Word at the time of its introduction was its approach to "menuing" commands and options for the user. Word has a unique command area below the typing area of the screen. The command names on the menu are names for sets of commands. You can "open" a set of commands by placing the highlight on the command name and pressing the ENTER key or by typing the first letter of the command name. When a "top level" command is executed, a subset of commands is usually displayed. This "second-level" set of commands may contain many options that you can select to have Word perform a specific task. Thus all of Word's features are easy to find and use. This menuing system converted a lot of people to Word and won Microsoft an award for its design several years ago.

Word takes a slightly different approach to document formatting, which is the way that users specify the font, type style, page layout, paragraph indents, alignments, and other features that can be added after the actual text is typed to enhance the appearance of the document when printed. Microsoft allows the user to simply "light up" the block of text to be altered and then choose the alteration or style from a menu of options. Choosing the block of text is a process referred to as highlighting or selecting and can be done in a single stroke with a mouse pointing device or with special keys on the keyboard.

With the keyboard keys, you can highlight a word, sentence, paragraph, or the entire document in one keystroke. This differs from such programs as Word-Star, which force the user to flag both the beginning and ending portions of text to be formatted. The user can even assign often used formatting "styles" to special keycodes that Word recognizes so that the style can be used again in the current document or other documents.

Last, but not least, Microsoft provides full support for the Microsoft mouse pointing device as well as for those from other manufacturers. At the time of Word's introduction, the mouse was considered a nonessential trinket, but today most people wouldn't do without one.

Like everything else, Word is not perfect. There are so many features, concepts, and things to remember that many users simply don't bother to learn them. Many seasoned Word users still use the menu, even though they know that faster keystroke methods are available. Does Word's menuing system actually inhibit new users from learning advanced techniques? This is sometimes the case. To become a truly efficient Word user, you should force yourself to learn the key-stroke combinations and advanced features right away and use them on a regular basis. If you forget a keystroke, don't resort to the old, slow method. Take the time to look up the keystroke and remember it.

Word comes with keyboard templates that list the actions performed by various keystroke combinations. Mount one of these templates on your keyboard or in a convenient place, such as the bottom of your screen. This book also contains a quick reference card in the back.

Another problem with Word is that users become confused by the many features and concepts and don't even know which menu items to look under to perform a specific task. For instance, style and format both have something to do with how a block of text appears on the printed page. In addition, a gallery holds blocks of text that can be instantly inserted in your document, whereas a macro holds a set of commands that cause Word to perform a task automatically. As you can see, you will need to become familiar with many terms. The first part of this book will help you in this area by presenting Word concepts in easy-to-understand, graphical form.

About This Book

This book is about Microsoft Word version 4, which means that it covers the fourth major revision to Word since its introduction. The operation of Word has remained much the same through the revisions. If you are moving up to version

4, or if you are reading this book and using an older version, don't worry; the major differences between the older versions and version 4 will be pointed out in the text.

If you are new to Word, this book will lead you through the learning process in a step-by-step manner. Plenty of examples and illustrations will help you understand the basic concepts underlying Word's operation. There is a learning process that you should go through in order to maximize your understanding of the many features of the program. First, you should learn the basic steps involved in typing a document. These essentials are covered in the first part of this book. If you don't understand something, make a note and review the section later or refer to the Word manuals, but don't disregard it. If you learn Word's essential features and commands now, you will be well on your way to becoming a Word power user.

If you are just beginning with Word, don't worry about the advanced features covered in the last sections of the book until you need them. But don't let that stop you from reading the sections if you really want to understand Word. As new concepts are introduced, try to relate them to things that you will be doing with Word.

The *Tip* and *Trap* flags scattered throughout this book will guide you to a proficient use of Word. Trap flags will help you avoid time-consuming mistakes that many users have fallen into, while Tip flags will offer suggestions to help make your time with Word more efficient. You will find these throughout the text, with a wrap-up at the end of each chapter.

How to Use This Book

This book uses many examples to help you learn Word. Therefore, a number of symbols are used to differentiate what you are to type and what Word displays on its screen. There are also some special key combinations that you will use.

If an instruction says press ENTER, simply press the ENTER key or a carriage return. This usually executes a command or displays a menu. Word has a number of keystroke combinations that allow you to bypass the menu system, assuming that you know the key codes.

If an instruction says press CTRL+F6, hold down the CTRL (Control) key and then press the F6 key. Other keys used in combinations with the function keys are ALT (Alternate) and SHIFT. Be sure to place your keyboard template near your machine so that you can begin learning the best keystroke combinations for the type of work that you will be doing.

This book uses many screen examples that are printouts from real Word screens. Because of this, you can easily follow the text even if you are not at the computer. However, it is highly recommended that you use this book while at a computer. Your Word skills will increase faster if you treat the reading in a hands-on manner.

The typing area of the screen normally surrounded by the border will be referred to as the *edit window*. The *command area* is the lower part of the screen that contains the Word commands. Press the ESC key to toggle between these two areas. The cursor in Word is usually called the *highlight*. Press ESC to move the highlight to the command area or back to the edit window.

Menu selections will usually be shown in their full description, for example, ESC Format Tab Clear. In other words, you would press the ESC key, select Format from the menu, select Tab from the second-level menu, and then select Clear from the final options menu. Remember that the ESC key toggles between the edit window and the command area.

Prewritten Forms, Files, and Document Layouts Available on Disk

A supplemental disk available from the author, contains premade forms, letters, tables, and page layouts. It is designed to save Word users hours of tedious typing and document creation.

You can learn valuable tips and techniques from the files on the disk and integrate them into your everyday activities. You can easily alter the files to fit your needs, and you'll be able to try various forms, files, and layouts without spending a lot of time creating them.

The selection of business forms includes invoices, statements, purchase orders, and common accounting forms. Many of these forms are automated with the Word merge and macro features. Page layout examples include newsletters, premade tables, and other paragraph formats. You'll also find layouts for directories, catalogs, books, and reports.

To order the disk, fill in the order form that follows this introduction and return it with a check for $25.00 plus $2.00 shipping and handling, to the address shown. California residents should add $1.50 for sales tax. Please, no purchase orders.

Word Supplemental Disk
Sheldon Publishing
P.O. Box 90524
Santa Barbara, CA 93190-0524

Name: _____

Address: _____

City, St., ZIP: _____

Phone number: _____

Please bill my:　　☐ Visa card # _____

　　　　　　　　☐ Mastercard # _____

　　　　　　　　☐ Check enclosed

Card holder signature: _____

Type of system: _____

Disk size (5.25″ or 3.5″): _____

Any special requirements: _____

_____

Comments on Word: Secrets, Solutions, and Shortcuts:

_____

_____

_____

This is solely the offering of the author. Osborne/McGraw-Hill takes NO responsibility for the fulfillment of this offer.

I

Introduction

Part I introduces the basic features of Word including the keyboard, function keys, and editing techniques. In it, you'll learn how to load, save, and print files. You'll also learn about the structure of Word documents and be introduced to some of the advanced features that are covered in more detail in later sections.

Part I is meant to be a hands-on tutorial. You will learn more if you work at the computer and try out the examples. This approach is not essential, however. Most of the illustrations and examples will give you a good idea of how Word works even if you are reading without a computer at hand.

1

Installation and
Setup

This chapter will help you install Word on your floppy-drive or hard-drive system. You must first determine what equipment you will need to run Word and then learn how to install the software on the equipment.

What You Will Need

The following equipment is required to run Microsoft Word. Some of it, such as the system unit, base amount of memory, and display, is essential. Other components, such as the mouse, are optional.

The System Unit

To run Microsoft Word, you will need a DOS (disk operating system) based machine such as the IBM Personal Computer, IBM AT Personal Computer, or the new IBM Personal System/2 machines. Word also works with machines compatible with these IBM systems. Two floppy drives or one floppy and one hard drive are required. Word version 4 comes complete with either 3 1/2-inch or 5 1/4-inch diskettes to accommodate either size drive.

Memory

It's best to have a full complement of memory in your machine (640K), though Word will operate with as little as 256K of memory. The extra memory allows Word to operate much faster and work with larger documents. If you plan to run the Help Tutorial, you will need at least 320K of memory.

 Tip: *Word will operate faster and more efficiently if you have more than 320K of memory.*

The Display System

Microsoft Word supports a wide range of display types but looks and operates best with an enhanced graphics monitor and adapter or VGA (video graphics array standard in IBM Personal System/2) because of their better resolution. Word is also compatible with Hercules graphics adapters that use black and white (monochrome) displays, as well as monochrome displays with standard video (nongraphics) adapters and IBM CGA (color graphics adapters). The EGA, VGA, and Hercules adapters all support a special 90-character by 43-line mode (as opposed to the standard 80-character by 25-line mode). Various ways to start Word, depending on the type of monitor you have, are discussed in Chapter 2.

DOS

You can use any version of DOS higher than version 2.0, as well as Operating System/2 in the DOS compatibility mode. If your system uses only floppy drives, you must make a copy of DOS to start your system for Word. This procedure is covered in the next section. Hard-disk users should have a hard drive that starts DOS at boot-time.

 Tip: *It's a good idea to have a few blank diskettes ready before you start.*

The Mouse

You can use either the Microsoft bus mouse, which comes with its own interface card, or the Microsoft serial mouse, which connects to a serial port on the back of your machine. You can also use a mouse from another manufacturer, such as Logitech or Mouse Systems.

 Tip: Make sure that you have a free slot for a bus mouse or an extra serial port for a serial mouse.

 Tip: If your mouse has three buttons, the middle button probably performs the same action as pressing both buttons on a two-button mouse.

The Printer

Word will work with just about any printer on the market. The SETUP program described under "Installing Word" in the next section will help you select the appropriate printer.

The Word Package

The Word package comes with two sets of diskettes. One set is for systems that use the new 3 1/2-inch diskettes, such as the IBM Personal System/2 series and various lap-top machines like the Toshiba 3100. The second set is for systems that use 5 1/4-inch diskettes. The 3 1/2-inch disk set contains fewer diskettes because the options listed below can be combined on higher-capacity disks. The following diskettes make up the 5 1/4-inch disk set.

- Word Program disk
- Word Utilities disk
- Spell disk
- Thesaurus disk
- Word Printer disks (two)
- Learning Word disks (three)

The Learning Word disk set consists of a beginning disk for both mouse and keyboard systems, an advanced disk for mouse, and an advanced disk for keyboard.

Installing Word

The Microsoft SETUP program supplied on the Word Utilities disk should supply you with all the help you'll need to start Word for the first time, with the exception of the tips and traps discussed here. Refer to the section that matches your system.

Floppy-Drive Systems

Once you have Word set up on a floppy-based system, you normally first start DOS and then start Word. Systems with higher-capacity diskettes, such as the IBM Personal System/2, allow you to place both DOS and Word on the same disk.

To begin SETUP on a floppy-drive system, first make sure that you have the system booted with DOS. At the DOS A> prompt, remove the DOS disk and place the Word Utilities disk in the drive. Type **SETUP** and press ENTER. Once the SETUP program is running, you can follow the instructions on the screen. The SETUP program will allow you to format diskettes, so you needn't have formatted diskettes prepared before you start SETUP.

If you have a non-Microsoft mouse, you may not be able to use the mouse drivers that the SETUP program will attempt to install. If you have installed your mouse on the diskette before installing Word, your correct mouse driver will be overlaid by the one installed by SETUP. Refer to your mouse owner's manual for installation instructions.

 Trap: *Do not use the mouse installation routine in the Microsoft SETUP program if you have a non-Microsoft mouse. Instead, use the software that comes with your mouse.*

Prepare a Data Disk   You may want to prepare several data diskettes to hold your files. Each one can hold a different type of file. For example, you could have a disk for personal files and another for business files to help you keep track of your Word documents. To format new diskettes from DOS, first make sure that the DOS disk with the program FORMAT.COM is in drive A. Then place a blank disk in drive B and type the following command:

FORMAT B:

Hard-Drive Systems

Installation on hard-drive systems is simple with the Word SETUP program. Simply place the Word Utilities disk in floppy drive A, type **A:SETUP** from the DOS prompt, and follow the instructions displayed on the screen. SETUP will ask if you want to copy the Word files to a directory called WORD. You should answer Yes unless you are using a special directory.

   If you have a non-Microsoft mouse, you probably cannot use the mouse drivers that the SETUP program will attempt to install on your hard drive. If you have installed your mouse on the hard drive before installing Word, your correct mouse driver will be overlaid by the one installed by SETUP. Refer to your mouse owner's manual for installation instructions.

 Trap: *Do not use the mouse installation routine in the Microsoft SETUP program if you have a non-Microsoft mouse. Instead, use the software that comes with your mouse.*

Prepare an Archive Disk   You may want to prepare several data diskettes to hold copies of the files you create and store on the hard drive. This is merely a backup or archive procedure to ensure that you always have at least two copies of your important files. Procedures for storing to both hard and floppy drives are covered

in Chapter 5. To format new diskettes from DOS, place a blank disk in drive A and type the following command:

FORMAT A:

Further Setup Information for Hard Drives

The Word SETUP program installs the program files, dictionary files, Thesaurus files, and printer driver files in the directory that you specify on your hard disk. This is usually the WORD directory. To run Word, you would move to the WORD directory with the DOS CD (Change Directory) command and then start Word. Unless you specify otherwise, any files that you create and save would then be stored in the WORD directory.

You can use directories other than WORD to store your documents. This helps separate various types of document files and also keeps them separate from the Word program files in the WORD directory. For example, if you are writing a book, you could create a directory called BOOK in which to store the files. You might use a directory called PERSONAL to store your personal files, as shown in Figure 1-1.

There are two ways to have Word store your document files in other directories. The first is to start Word in the normal way and then specify the directory that you wish to load files from and save files to. This technique is covered in Chapter 5. The second method is to start Word after you first move to the directory that will hold your files. This technique requires that you specify the WORD directory in your DOS PATH command. The PATH command is usually placed in the AUTOEXEC.BAT file so that DOS will execute the command every time you boot your system. The new path set by PATH will provide a list of directories on your hard drive to DOS so that it knows where to look when you execute a command. If you execute Word from a directory other than WORD, DOS will check the path and find Word in the WORD directory.

 Tip: *You can run Word from directories other than the one where Word is stored to keep files separate.*

 Tip: *Batch files created in DOS can be used to start Word in various configurations and from specific directories.*

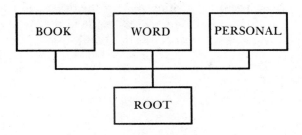

Figure 1-1. Sample directories

Appendix A covers the steps that you must follow to place the WORD directory in your PATH command and to create DOS batch files that will automatically move you to the proper directory and start Word. Various techniques for creating and organizing hard-drive directories are also covered.

Installing Additional Printers

If you add a new printer to your system, you can run through the SETUP program again, selecting the printer installation routines from the menu. A simpler method is to copy the printer driver files from Word's Printer disks to your floppy drive or hard drive. First, list the files on the disks; then determine which driver matches your printer. If you are not sure, use the SETUP method because it describes each printer a little better.

Floppy-Drive Systems

To copy printer drivers with the DOS COPY command, place one Printer disk in drive B and your Word disk in drive A. Type

DIR B:/P

to list the files on the disk; then write down the name of the file you need. If you don't see the file, place the other Printer disk in the drive and perform the same procedure. Use the COPY command to copy the file to the Word disk. For example, this command copies RADIX.PRD to the Word disk.

A>COPY B:RADIX.PRD

Hard-Drive Systems

To copy printer drivers with the DOS COPY command, place one Printer disk in drive A. Type

DIR A:/P

to list the files on the disk; then write down the name of the file you need for the printer you have. If you don't see the file, place the other Printer disk in drive A and perform the same operation.

Use the COPY command to copy the file to the hard drive, making sure to specify the directory that holds your Word files. For example, the COPY command shown below will copy the RADIX.PRD file on the floppy disk in drive A to the WORD directory in drive C.

C:>COPY A:RADIX.PRD \WORD

Word Speedup Techniques for Floppy Systems

You can increase Word's operating speed by using a RAM drive, which is an area of memory in your system that can act like another drive. Because the drive is in memory, access to and from it is almost instantaneous. If Word is running from a RAM drive, you won't have to wait long for it to execute commands and routines.

RAM drives, however, suffer from two problems that make using them a tradeoff. First, a RAM drive must be loaded every time you turn your system on, which means that you must create a batch file that copies the essential Word files to the RAM drive. This loading adds a minute to your startup routine.

The second problem with RAM drives has to do with power outages. When the power goes out, the files that you copied to a RAM drive will be lost. The originals on disk will be intact, but you will have to copy the ones you loaded to the RAM drive when your system comes back up. Because of potential problems due to power losses, you should store document files on a physical disk when using a RAM drive. Then they will not be vulnerable to loss from a power outage. However, you must still save your current work every so often.

All things considered, RAM drives offer enough of a speed increase on floppy-drive systems to make their use advantageous. For more information on RAM drives, refer to Appendix A.

Tips and Traps Summary

What You Will Need

Tip: Word will operate faster and more efficiently if you have more than 320K of memory.

Tip: It's a good idea to have a few blank diskettes ready before you start.

Tip: Make sure that you have a free slot for a bus mouse or an extra serial port for a serial mouse.

Tip: If your mouse has three buttons, the middle button probably performs the same action as pressing both buttons on a two-button mouse.

Installing Word

Trap: Do not use the mouse installation routine in the Microsoft SETUP program if you have a non-Microsoft mouse. Instead, use the software that comes with your mouse.

Word: Secrets, Solutions, Shortcuts

Tips and Traps Summary (*continued*)

Tip: You can run Word from directories other than the one where Word is stored to keep files separate.

Tip: Batch files created in DOS can be used to start Word in various configurations and from specific directories.

2

Getting Started
with Word

This chapter covers the various ways you can start Word, depending on your equipment and the file you want to work on. This chapter also introduces you to the Word screen and leads you through several steps that will alter how Word works, both for your convenience and for the lessons and examples to come.

How to Start Word

Starting Word can be as easy as typing **WORD** on the DOS command line. But there are other ways to start Word. If you have a hard drive, you may first need to move to the WORD directory or another directory. You can also start Word and specify the name of a document that you would like to edit. Or you can specify the document that you worked on in your last session; Word always keeps track of the last file edited, assuming that you may want to use it again next time.

Determining the Display Type

Other ways to start Word will depend on the type of monitor you have. For example, you can start Word in either text or graphics mode. Graphics mode allows you to see character formatting as it normally looks; for example, italics look like italics on the screen. In text mode, however, such characters would appear as highlighted characters because a text mode screen cannot form the slanted characters of italics. There are other benefits to starting in graphics mode if your monitor has this capability. A monochrome system such as the IBM monochrome display cannot work in graphics mode unless you are using a Hercules graphics video card. Let's look at the differences.

Graphics Mode The most important feature of graphics mode is that Word displays characters close to the way they will appear when printed. This display feature is limited to italics, boldface, small capitals, underline, double underline, superscript, subscript, and strikethrough. Other formatting features, such as character size and fonts, will not appear on the screen as they do when printed.

The other important feature of graphics mode is important only if you use a mouse. The mouse pointer — an arrow in graphics mode — changes shape when you move to different parts of the screen. For example, pointing in the top or right bar of the Word display will cause the pointer to change to a box, indicating that you can split a window (this is covered in later chapters). Graphics mode does cause Word to operate a little slower than text mode, however.

 Trap: *Graphics mode slows the operation of Word.*

Text Mode Word will operate much faster in text mode, especially when scrolling through text and executing commands. Instead of showing characters similar to the way in which they are printed, it shows various character formats in colors and intensities if you have a color monitor. Bold appears intensified, and other formats appear in colors set off from the existing background color. If you have a monochrome monitor, formats are shown as underlined, except for bold, which is shown in bold. The mouse appears in this mode as a blinking square.

 Tip: *For fast scrolling and command execution, start Word in text mode.*

90-Character by 43-Line Mode   Word has a special mode that allows you to display 90 characters across and 43 lines down. This is perfect for reviewing documents because the letter size does not reduce so much that it becomes unreadable. You must have a VGA, EGA, or Hercules graphics card and an appropriate display to use this mode. The exact number of lines may differ depending on the type of display adapter that you use, but the Hercules adapter will display the full 43 lines.

Starting Word with Switches and Parameters

A switch or parameter is an option that you type on the DOS command line following the WORD command to specify how you want to start Word. Switches come in two groups. The first is used to specify a file that you want to work on so that it is loaded immediately rather than through the Word menu. The second group is used to specify the display mode as described earlier. You can specify graphics, text, or 90-by-43 mode when you start Word.

Tip: *You don't need to use a switch each time you start Word. Word remembers the switch that you used in the last session and will use it again.*

The following list describes the various methods you can use to start Word.

WORD *filename*	Type **WORD** and the name of the file you want to edit. The document will be loaded for immediate editing.
WORD /L	The L parameter causes Word to load the file that you worked on in your last Word session.
WORD /C	The C (character) parameter starts Word in text mode.
WORD /G	The G parameter starts Word in graphics mode.
WORD /H	The H parameter starts Word in the 90-character by 43-line display mode if you have a Hercules graphics card. If you have a different display adapter, this number may differ.
WORD /M	The M parameter starts Word in high-resolution

monochrome mode if you have an enhanced graphics card with 64K of memory and an enhanced graphics monitor. *Note:* Most non-IBM enhanced graphics cards come with more than 64K, so you will not need this parameter.

The first two options in this list will start Word with a document. The remaining parameters can be used in combination with the first two. That is, you can tell Word to start with the last document and use graphics mode by specifying both the /L and /G parameters. The last four parameters are used to specify the mode of operation for your monitor and are covered below according to the type of display system you may have.

IBM Monochrome Display and Adapter   The only mode for this monitor is text mode. Don't worry about switches; simply type **WORD** to start Word.

IBM Monochrome Display with Hercules or Enhanced Graphics Adapter   Either of these adapters will enhance the performance of the standard monochrome display. You can display graphics characters as well as use the 90-character by 43-line mode. Use the /G, /C, or /H parameter.

Standard Color Graphics Display with Monochrome or Color Monitor   There is really only one mode with either of these combinations—a low-resolution text mode that is hard to look at over long periods of time. However, character formats such as italics will display as they do when printed. If you are using the color monitor, you can use the /C switch to specify text mode, which will provide some enhancement to the characters, but you will lose the on-screen character enhancements.

Enhanced Graphics Adapter   The enhanced graphics adapters provide the modes of operation listed below, assuming that the card has 128K or more of memory. IBM enhanced graphics adapters may have only 64K of memory, which usually provides only two colors in higher-resolution modes. You may want to upgrade the memory on these boards to improve screen resolution.

EGA with Enhanced Graphics Monitor

WORD /G   640 by 350 resolution, 25 lines, 16 colors

WORD /C   text mode, 25 lines, 16 colors

WORD /H   640 by 350 resolution, 43 lines, 16 colors

WORD /H/C   text mode, 43 lines, 16 colors

EGA with Monochrome Monitor

WORD /G   640 by 350 resolution, 25 lines, 2 colors

WORD /C   text mode, 25 lines, 2 colors

WORD /H   640 by 350 resolution, 43 lines, 2 colors

WORD /H/C   text mode, 43 lines, 2 colors

EGA with RGB Monitor

WORD /G   640 by 200 resolution, 25 lines, 16 colors

WORD /C   text mode, 25 lines, 16 colors

You should experiment to see which start mode is best for your needs or more pleasing to your eyes. Some modes promote eyestrain when looked at for a long period of time, even though they may provide the most features. When using color modes, you can change the foreground and background colors with the Windows command in Word. This will often make the screen easier to read.

 Tip: *You can switch between the graphics and text modes from inside Word by using the Options command on the menu.*

Starting Word in Another Directory

If you have Word stored in WORD or some other directory, you must move to that directory before starting Word (unless you choose to start Word from data directories, as covered in Appendix A). To move to another directory while in DOS, use the CD (Change Directory) command. For example, when you start your system, DOS places you in the ROOT directory. To move to the WORD directory, you would type **CD \WORD**. Then you would type the command to start Word as described earlier in this chapter. Remember, you needn't be in the same directory where the Word files are stored to start Word. You can start Word from other directories if the DOS path has been set to point to the directory holding your Word program files. In this way you can have a specific directory to store personal files and another to store business files. Appendix A covers this topic in detail.

Exploring Word's Screen

Start Word by using the method described in the previous section that best fits your system and needs. The screen examples in this book were printed from the output of an enhanced graphics monitor, so you will see graphics mode with characters in their true format and an arrow for the mouse pointer. Upon loading Word for the first time, your screen should look like that of Figure 2-1.

Let's look around the screen so that you can become familiar with Word's features. You might think of this screen as a stage. The large rectangular area is the actual stage where the characters that make up your document will perform. This *window* is called the *edit window*. Below it is the *command area*. The command area is where the stage director and stagehands are standing by to assist in your "presentation." You will type your documents in the edit window and execute Word commands in the command area.

Note the location of the mouse pointer in the edit window. If you are in text mode, the mouse pointer will be shaped like a block rather than the arrow shown in Figure 2-1. Try moving the mouse and note the position of the cursor on the screen. In Chapter 3 you'll try your hand at typing and editing in the Word editing area. For now, let's look further at the screen.

In the upper-left corner of Figure 2-1 is a block with the number 1, which is the number of the window you are currently working with. As you'll find out later in this book, Word allows you to work with several documents at once. Each document has its own edit window which can overlay other windows or be displayed next to other windows if you reduce its size. Just inside the edit window in the upper-left corner is the combination *end mark* and *highlight*. These are actually two objects. The end mark will always designate the end of your document. The highlight is a block that follows your typing, though you can move it to other parts of the document for editing by using the mouse or arrow keys.

Try typing the word **test** now, as shown in Figure 2-2. Notice how the highlight moves to the right as you type. Press ENTER after typing the word and then use either the mouse or your arrow keys to place the highlight in the first *t* in test (press the up arrow, or point to the *t* with the mouse). Figure 2-2 now shows what your screen should look like. Notice the difference between the highlight and the end mark.

Moving to the Command Area

Microsoft Word commands are used for such things as saving or retrieving files, searching and replacing text, or changing the look of text. Most of these com-

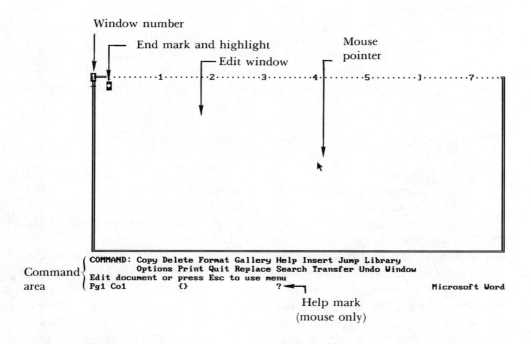

Figure 2-1.   The Word screen

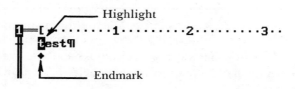

Figure 2-2.   Moving between the edit window and command area

mands are executed from the command area. (In later chapters you will see how to execute many commands with simple keystroke combinations.) To move to the command area from the edit window, simply press the ESC key. A highlight will appear over the word *Copy* in the command area. You can press the spacebar to get to other command selections. As you move between commands, notice how the message line (one up from the bottom of the screen) changes to tell you what each command does. To return to the edit window, press the ESC key again.

Tip: *The ESC key is like a toggle. It switches you between the edit window and the command window.*

You can execute commands in the command area by pressing the first letter of the command that you want to use. Press ESC to get back to the command area. The word *Copy* should be highlighted. Type **O**, which is the first letter of the Options command. Notice how the window shrinks and a large list of new commands appears. This is called a *submenu,* and in this case the options submenu is displayed. Press ESC to close the submenu. Notice that you are back in the typing area. Press ESC again to return to the command area. This time, instead of typing **O** to get to the options menu, press the spacebar eight times. A description of each command is displayed to remind you of what they do. When you get to Options, press ENTER. This is just another way to get to commands in the command area. You can press ESC to return to the edit window. In the next section you'll use the Options command to change some of Word's features.

Trap: *Don't start typing text unless you know that you are in the edit window. Typing in the command area may cause unwanted commands to execute.*

Altering Word's Display

When you start Word for the first time, the screen and various functions are set in a certain way. You can change the way that Word looks and acts by making alterations with various commands. This section will help you learn how to make beneficial changes to Word.

Turning Complete Display On

Word can display symbols for various keys that you press on the keyboard, such as TAB, SPACE, and RETURN, that are normally not displayed. You may want to see where you have pressed these keys when you are editing a document. The Options menu has various settings to alter Word's display mode, including the display of these symbols. Press ESC until the highlight is in the word *Copy* in the command area. Type **O** to get to the options menu. Your display should look similar to that shown in Figure 2-3. Using the mouse, point at *Complete* and press the left button, or use the arrow keys to move to the Visible field, and then type **C** to select Complete. Either way, the Complete selection will be highlighted. Before pressing ENTER to execute the changes, you will also want to turn off the menu bar, so continue reading in the next paragraph.

Turning the Command Menu Off

You needn't display the command area when you are typing. You can tuck it away until it is needed. When it is off, you will have a larger typing area in which to view your documents. Whenever you need to execute commands, simply press the

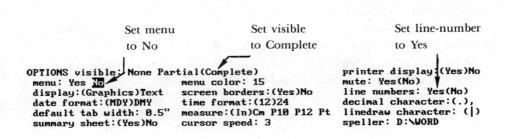

```
          Set menu              Set visible              Set line-number
           to No                to Complete                 to Yes

OPTIONS visible: None Partial(Complete)          printer display:(Yes)No
   menu: Yes No                menu color: 15        mute: Yes(No)
   display:(Graphics)Text      screen borders:(Yes)No   line numbers: Yes(No)
   date format:(MDY)DMY        time format:(12)24    decimal character:(.),
   default tab width: 0.5"     measure:(In)Cm P10 P12 Pt  linedraw character: (|)
   summary sheet:(Yes)No       cursor speed: 3       speller: D:\WORD
```

Figure 2-3. The Options command

ESC key to redisplay the command area. Hiding the command area makes it easier to tell whether you are in the edit window or the command area.

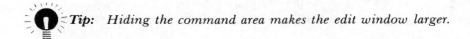

Tip: *Hiding the command area makes the edit window larger.*

Many new users of Word often begin typing, thinking that they are in the edit window when the highlight is actually in the command area. This may cause unwanted commands to execute, so always "look before you type" in Word. Turning off the command area makes it easy to tell that you are in the typing mode. Don't press ENTER yet; you must alter one more option on this menu.

Setting Line Number Display On

While you are still in the Options menu, slide over to the Line Number field and select Yes. This will include the line number in the page and column display in the lower-left portion of the Word screen.

Now press ENTER to make the adjustments to both the Command menu and display options.

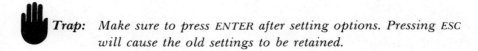

Trap: *Make sure to press ENTER after setting options. Pressing ESC will cause the old settings to be retained.*

Changing the Background Color

The next three options are set in the Window option of the command line. Press ESC to display the command area. Type **W** for the Window commands and then **O** to select Options. Your display should look similar to that shown in Figure 2-4. You can change the background color of a color monitor by changing the number in the Background Color field. Point to the number next to *background color* with the mouse or use the arrow keys to highlight this area. Press the F1 key to see

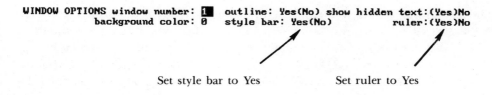

Set style bar to Yes   Set ruler to Yes

Figure 2-4. The Window Options command

a selection of colors and then use the DOWN ARROW key to slide down to the color you want. Don't press ENTER yet; you must set two more options in the next two sections.

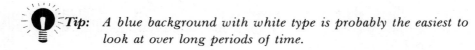

Tip: *A blue background with white type is probably the easiest to look at over long periods of time.*

Setting the Style Bar On

While you are still in the Windows Options menu, use the mouse or the arrow keys to highlight the Style Bar field. Type **Y** for yes. This will cause Word to display codes for various formatting instructions that you will be using in future chapters. Go to the next paragraph before pressing ENTER.

Setting the Ruler On

You should still be in the Window Options menu. Use the mouse or the arrow keys to move to the Ruler field and type **Y** to turn the ruler on. Now press ENTER to execute the menu selections that you have made. Notice that a ruler will appear at the top of the window.

Setting the Printer Type

The last option to set before going on to the next chapter is the printer selection. Press ESC to display Word's command menu and then type **P** to display the Print menu. In the Print menu, type **O** for options. The first selection will be Printer Type. Press the F1 key and you will be presented with a list of printer options. The printer that you will be using will probably be displayed if you used the Word SETUP program to install a printer. If you installed more than one printer, however, you must select the one you want to use. Use the arrow keys to select from the list and then press ENTER to execute the command.

Viewing Microsoft Update Notes

Quitting Word saves all of the changes that you made for the next session (this procedure is described in the next section). However, you must do a few things before wrapping up. First, your Word disk may contain a file with recent updates and comments from Microsoft. You can now load and print this file with the following procedure.

Press ESC to place the highlight in the Word command menu. Type **T** to execute the Transfer menu and then type **L** to select the Load option. Now place the Word Utilities disk in the floppy drive. Type **README.DOC** in the filename field and press ENTER to load the file.

You can use the PGDN and PGUP keys to scroll through and read this file. To print the file, press ESC to get to the Word command menu and then type **P** for Print and **P** again to print the document. Make sure that you have paper in your printer before proceeding.

Many of the topics on the README.DOC file may not apply to you or your system. Some items refer to corrections in the Word manual.

Quitting Word

Now that you have made some changes to the way Word operates, you can save them for future use. Whenever you quit Word, some settings, such as the ones that you made in this chapter, are retained for future sessions. Press ESC to display the Word command menu and type **Q** to quit Word. Word will ask you if you want to save editing changes. You can respond with an **N** because you only typed the word **test** in the edit window. However, Word will save the changes that you made to its operating mode.

 Trap: *Always quit Word by using the Quit command. Do not shut your machine off until you have returned to the DOS prompt. This saves operating changes made to Word.*

Tips and Traps Summary

How to Start Word Word

Trap: Graphics mode slows the operation of Word.

Tip: For fast scrolling and command execution, start Word in text mode.

Tip: You don't need to use a switch each time you start Word. Word remembers the switch that you used in the last session and will use it again.

Tip: You can switch between the graphics and text modes from inside Word by using the Options command on the menu.

Exploring Word's Screen

Tip: The ESC key is like a toggle. It switches you between the edit window and the command window.

Trap: Don't start typing text unless you know that you are in the edit window. Typing in the command area may cause unwanted commands to execute.

Tips and Traps Summary (*continued*)

Altering Word's Display

Tip: Hiding the command area makes the edit window larger.

Trap: Make sure to press ENTER after setting options. Pressing ESC will cause the old settings to be retained.

Tip: A blue background with white type is probably the easiest to look at over long periods of time.

Quitting Word

Trap: Always quit Word by using the Quit command. Do not shut your machine off until you have returned to the DOS prompt. This saves operating changes made to Word.

3

Getting Acquainted
with Word

This chapter will give you a general overview of how text is entered in the edit window of Word. You'll be introduced to important typing concepts as well as some traps to avoid and tips to remember. First, if Word is not loaded, you should start it now. Refer to "How to Start Word" in Chapter 2 for starting instructions. In this chapter you will be typing text from examples that let you see how Word works, so you needn't load a document when you start Word.

Another Look at the Word Screen

Assuming that you have reentered Word after having quit in Chapter 2, let's look over the screen to point out the changes that you made when altering the Options and Window commands in the previous chapter.

Trap: *Word didn't start? Make sure that you are in the proper direc-tory by using the DOS CD (Change Directory) command.*

Larger Edit Window

By answering No in the options menu field, you prevent the Word command menu from being displayed, which gives you an extra three lines of visible typing space. To display the Word command menu, simply press ESC. Note that when you turn the menu off, it becomes easier to determine whether the highlight is in the edit window or the command area. If the command area is displayed, characters that you type will be interpreted as commands, so if you think you are typing normal text in the edit window, commands may execute unnecessarily.

 Tip: *ESC opens the command menu at the bottom of the screen.*

The Ruler Bar

Notice that the ruler displayed in the top bar of the screen indicates the left and right margins as well as the tab settings. The left margin is indicated by a left square bracket in the 0 position on the ruler; the right margin is indicated by a right square bracket in position 6.

 Tip: *Margins are indicated by square brackets in the ruler bar.*

Note that the ruler measures only the typing area. The space from the edge of the paper to the left margin is not shown on the screen. Word starts measuring the left edge of your text at position 0. The right margin is 6 inches from the left margin, which leaves 2 1/2 inches (1 1/4 inches per side) for the space from the left and right margins to the edge of the actual sheet of paper, as shown in Figure 3-1. Later you will learn how to adjust the margins to suit your needs.

 Tip: *The ruler bar will help you keep track of margins and tabs.*

 Tip: *Word's edit window does not show the space from the edge of the paper to the left and right margins.*

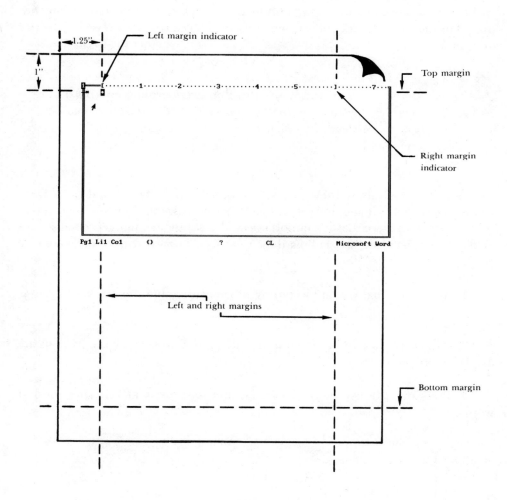

Figure 3-1. The edit screen is a window on a page

Complete Display Mode

With the Options Visible command field set to Complete, you will see dots for spaces, arrows for tabs, and paragraph marks (a backward *P*) for paragraph endings. The paragraph mark appears wherever the ENTER key was pressed at the end of a paragraph.

 Trap: *If you are confused by the space dots, tab arrows, and other symbols displayed by the Options Visible Complete command, you can always turn them back off by responding **N** to the command.*

It is useful to show these symbols, especially the space bar dots between words, which make it easy for you to count spaces or see if too many spaces were typed. Later you'll see that it's important to also see the tab marker, because tabs aren't always the same size. Follow these steps to see how complete display mode works:

1. Make sure that you are in typing mode by pressing the ESC key as necessary.

2. Type **this is a test.** as shown in the illustration to see how the symbols are displayed on your screen.

3. Press the TAB key twice before *test* and then press ENTER after the last word.

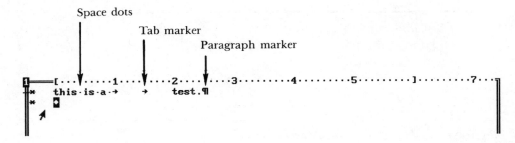

Notice the difference between the dot that represents the period at the end of a line and the dots that represent spaces.

The Style Bar

The *style bar* is a three-character-wide blank area from the left window border to the first character of your text. For now, you won't see much there except the asterisk, as shown in the previous illustration. Later, you will see how this bar will become an important indicator of the type of formatting that your text has.

 Tip: *The style bar can display a character code indicating the type style and paragraph alignment that your text may have.*

Formatting is concerned with the type styles and paragraph alignments that you give your text. The asterisk will change to a code that tells you what styles have been applied. The style bar also serves as a *selection bar* when you are using a mouse. Pointing in the selection bar next to one of your paragraphs or lines will allow you to easily select them for editing or moving.

 Tip: *The style bar and selection bar are one and the same. It displays paragraph formatting codes, or you can click in it with the mouse to select lines or paragraphs.*

The Position Indicator

The position indicator in the lower left corner of the screen keeps track of the current location of the highlight. "Pg" indicates the page number, "Li" indicates the line, and "Co" indicates the column.

 Tip: *The position indicator helps you keep track of the cursor location on the screen and the current page number.*

Typing and Editing

This section will introduce you to typing in Word. To enter your letters, reports, and other documents, you type as you normally would on any typewriter, with a few exceptions.

A typewriter has a carriage return key, but on computers the ENTER key replaces the carriage return and performs other functions as well. For example, ENTER executes commands at the DOS level. In Word ENTER is used to end paragraphs rather than lines of text. The paragraph marker appears (the backward *P*) to indicate the end of a paragraph and the position where ENTER was pressed. This book will refer to all carriage returns as the ENTER key.

If you would like to follow the examples in this chapter, type in the text shown in the illustration below. You needn't press ENTER at the end of each line; Word will automatically *wrap* the text down to the next line. Watch what happens to the word *close* when you approach the right margin. As you type the examples, the entire word will be moved down one line because it doesn't fit on top.

```
This is an example of a paragraph in Word.  As you get close
to the right margin, Word wraps your text to the next line.
There is no need to press the Enter key until the end of the
paragraph.
```

At the end of the paragraph, press the ENTER key. A paragraph marker will appear, and the highlight will jump to the next line down. As you can see, there is nothing special about typing in Word except that you don't need to keep track of where a line ends.

Paragraph Concepts

The paragraph—an important feature in Word—represents a block of text that ends with the ENTER key. If you are a first-time user to electronic word processing, you must make some conceptual changes to how you think about typing. Word (and most other word processors) automatically wraps your text at the end of each line, so you needn't press ENTER at the right margin as you would press a carriage return on a typewriter. Instead, simply keep typing. If it cannot fit the word in the space remaining on the line, Word instantly moves it to the next line.

 Tip: *In Word a paragraph is a continuous block of text as well as the traditional collection of ideas.*

From now on you must consider where the end of your paragraphs will be (not the end of each line), for that is where you will press ENTER. So you must start thinking about what a paragraph is in Word. Like any other paragraph, it contains a collection of similar ideas or statements. A new paragraph usually starts on a new line, possibly with the first word indented. Pressing ENTER only at the end of the paragraph, defines the paragraph as a continuous block of text.

 Tip: *A paragraph is a block of text that you end by pressing ENTER. Press ENTER only at the end of the paragraph.*

 Tip: *Because paragraphs form a continuous and integrated block of text, you can change the type style, indents, line spacing, and tab settings of each paragraph individually.*

Because a paragraph is defined as a continuous block of text, Word will let you perform certain operations on it quickly and easily. For example, you can instantly select a paragraph with the mouse or the function keys and then change its font, margins, indents, and tab settings. Thus individual paragraphs can have different settings, an important reason to separate paragraphs beyond the traditional need to keep ideas together.

Sometimes, such as when you work with tables, you will need to start a new line that you want to keep within the same paragraph. Because lines in tables have the same tab settings, you'll want to maintain their paragraph integrity. Word allows you to start a new line within the same paragraph by using an alternate form of the ENTER key. Instead of ENTER, you press the SHIFT+ENTER key combination. This is called a *soft carriage return,* and it appears on the screen as a down arrow if you have set the Options Visible command field to Complete.

 Tip: *SHIFT+ENTER can be used to start a new line in the same paragraph.*

You can see how this works by typing the example that follows in the edit area of your screen. Here SHIFT+ENTER is used to end lines halfway across the page to make room for photos or artwork. As you type, press the SHIFT+ENTER key combination at the end of every line.

```
This is an example of soft
carriage returns.  You can
maintain paragraph integrity
while starting a new line.
A photo or graph could be
placed in the area to the
right.  Soft returns are
also used to create tables
and lists.
```

Press SHIFT+ENTER at
the end of each line.

In table development you should consider each line of text or numbers as part of the paragraph. If you need to apply formatting or change table alignment, you will probably need to apply it to every line in the table. If you used a hard carriage return (the ENTER key), you would have to apply this formatting to every line individually. Soft carriage returns allow you to apply formatting to all the lines in the table as a group.

If you have a mouse and you typed the text as shown above, you can easily select the entire paragraph by pointing next to it in the selection bar with the mouse and then pressing the right mouse button. Remember, the selection bar is the three-character-wide strip between the window border and the left edge of text. If you don't have a mouse, use the arrow keys to place the cursor anywhere in the paragraph and then press the F10 key. Figure 3-2 shows how you can select the entire paragraph by following these simple steps.

This example illustrates why you will want to maintain paragraph integrity. Easy selection makes applying styles or moving a paragraph to another location a simple task.

 Tip: *You can select paragraphs by pointing to them and pressing F10 or clicking in the selection bar with the mouse.*

Now you can try moving the highlighted text to another location in your document. This will give you an idea of how easy it is to edit with Word. Press the DEL (Delete) key and notice the text between the curly braces at the bottom line of your screen. This area, called the *scrap*, is a temporary holding area for text that you delete with the DEL key. Even though you have deleted the paragraph from the screen, Word retains a copy of it in the scrap until you delete something else, which would then replace the contents of the scrap.

 Tip: *The scrap holds deleted text until you delete something else. The INS (Insert) key can be used to reinsert it elsewhere.*

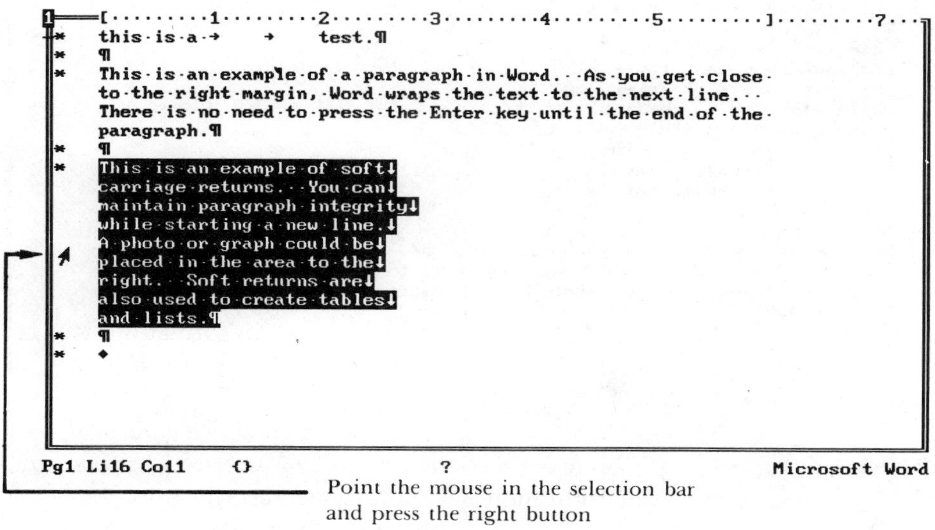

```
┌─────[·········1·········2·········3·········4·········5·········]·········7···┐
│  ※  this·is·a·→      →      test.¶                                            │
│  ※  ¶                                                                        │
│  ※  This·is·an·example·of·a·paragraph·in·Word.··As·you·get·close·            │
│     to·the·right·margin,·Word·wraps·the·text·to·the·next·line.··             │
│     There·is·no·need·to·press·the·Enter·key·until·the·end·of·the·            │
│     paragraph.¶                                                              │
│  ※  ¶                                                                        │
│  ※  This·is·an·example·of·soft↓                                              │
│     carriage·returns.··You·can↓                                              │
│     maintain·paragraph·integrity↓                                            │
│     while·starting·a·new·line.↓                                              │
│     A·photo·or·graph·could·be↓                                               │
│     placed·in·the·area·to·the↓                                              │
│     right.··Soft·returns·are↓                                                │
│     also·used·to·create·tables↓                                             │
│     and·lists.¶                                                              │
│  ※  ¶                                                                        │
│  ※  ♦                                                                        │
│                                                                             │
│                                                                             │
│ Pg1 Li16 Co11      {}                 ?                    Microsoft Word    │
└─────────────────────────────────────────────────────────────────────────────┘
```

Point the mouse in the selection bar
and press the right button

Figure 3-2. Selecting a paragraph

The scrap now holds the deleted text. Let's insert it above the first paragraph as an example.

1. Move the highlight to the *T* in the first paragraph.

2. Press the INS (Insert) key on your keyboard.

3. Press ENTER to place an extra space between the two paragraphs.

Your screen should now look like that shown in Figure 3-3. Notice that Word is still holding a copy of the recently deleted text in the scrap, even though you reinserted it in the previous step. You can use the scrap to insert copies of text at other locations in your document.

For now, press INS twice and then press the PGUP (Page Up) key (located on the 9 key of the numeric keypad). The NUM LOCK (Number Lock) key must be off for you to use PGUP; if it is not, a 9 will be typed. Microsoft Word will display NL

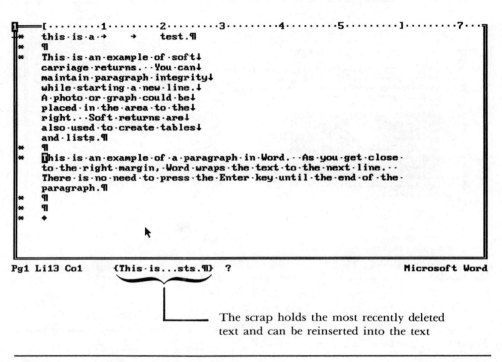

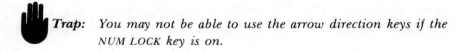

The scrap holds the most recently deleted text and can be reinserted into the text

Figure 3-3. The scrap holds deleted text

in the status line if NUM LOCK is on, and some keyboards have a Number Lock indicator light.

Trap: *You may not be able to use the arrow direction keys if the NUM LOCK key is on.*

The next section will cover the use of the PGUP key in more detail. Your screen should now look like that shown in Figure 3-4. At this point it holds enough text that it will not fit in the edit window.

```
1════[·········1·········2·········3·········4·········5·········]·········7···▪
 ⊁    this·is·a·→      →      test.¶
 ⊁    ¶
 ⊁    This·is·an·example·of·soft↓
      carriage·returns.··You·can↓
      maintain·paragraph·integrity↓
      while·starting·a·new·line.↓
      A·photo·or·graph·could·be↓
      placed·in·the·area·to·the↓
      right.··Soft·returns·are↓
      also·used·to·create·tables↓
      and·lists.¶
 ⊁    This·is·an·example·of·soft↓
      carriage·returns.··You·can↓
      maintain·paragraph·integrity↓
      while·starting·a·new·line.↓
    ↗ A·photo·or·graph·could·be↓
      placed·in·the·area·to·the↓
      right.··Soft·returns·are↓
      also·used·to·create·tables↓
      and·lists.¶
 ⊁    This·is·an·example·of·soft↓
      carriage·returns.··You·can↓
```

Pg1 Li3 Co1   {This·is...sts.¶}   ?   Microsoft Word

Figure 3-4. Text can be inserted from the scrap

A Window on Your Document

The text that you now have in your computer will probably fill a whole sheet of paper. Your screen, however, will display only about 22 lines at a time. Think of the Word edit window as exactly that, a window onto your document. There are several keys on your keyboard that you can use to *scroll* or move through the document. This chapter will cover a few of these keys and Chapter 7 will cover the rest.

 Tip: *The edit window is a window on a large document. Scroll keys on the keyboard move the document up or down through the window.*

The numeric keypad on the right of your keyboard should have a set of direction keys for moving across the screen and through your document. These keys are labeled with directional arrows or names such as HOME, PGUP, END, and PGDN. If you have a newer enhanced keyboard, these keys may form a keypad of their own, so you can leave the NUM LOCK key on and use the keypad for data entry.

 Tip: *If you have a separate highlight movement pad, you can leave the NUM LOCK key on and use the numeric keypad for data entry.*

The Position Indicator

The lower-left corner of the status line in the command area contains a set of numbers that indicate the current position of the highlight in relation to your document, as shown here:

Page, line, and column indicators

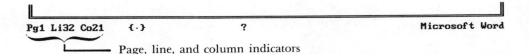

Pg1 Li32 Co21   {·}   ?   Microsoft Word

└───── Page, line, and column indicators

The page number indicator may be incorrect if you have inserted a lot of new text since Word last repaginated your document (document repagination will be covered in Chapter 6). The column indicator shows the current horizontal position of the highlight on the screen, counting from the left edge of the window. The line indicator shows the line number containing the screen highlight, counting from the last page break. This indicator will also show the current division if there is more than one (divisions will be covered in Chapter 6). If you use the 90-character by 43-line mode, where it is often difficult to locate the cursor, you will quickly discover the usefulness of this feature.

The Insertion Point

As you type, the highlight moves just ahead of your characters. This point is called the insertion point. When you move the highlight to previously typed material, the insertion point becomes the point where the highlight rests. If you place the highlight on a character, that character will move to the right when you insert new text.

 Tip: *The insertion point is the current position of the highlight.*

Overtype Mode

The one exception to the rule governing the insertion point occurs when you press the Overtype Toggle (F5) key. When you press F5 to turn Overtype on, an OT indicator lights up at the bottom of your screen. Try this now. In overtype mode the insertion point no longer exists; instead, the highlight becomes the overtype point.

Now move to some portion of the text on your screen with the arrow keys and type a character.

Trap: *If overtype mode is on, you will type over characters.*

Tip: *The F5 Overtype key is a toggle key. Press it once to turn it on; press it again to turn it off.*

Tip: *Overtype's usefulness is limited. To replace a character, it is easier to insert the new character and then delete the old.*

The Highlight Movement Keys

With Word version 4, the keys on the numeric keypad provide a wide range of movements, more than you can probably remember in one sitting. A few important ones will be covered here, and more will be introduced in Chapter 7, which covers how to scroll through your document. Although the highlight is often referred to as the cursor, don't let that confuse you. Microsoft calls it the highlight in all of its manuals.

The Arrow Keys   The arrow keys, the simplest of the direction keys, allow you to move one character left or right and one line up or down. Think of them as a means to move the highlight over your characters so that you can get to various points in your document. They are nondestructive; that is, they will not alter any characters as you move the highlight.

 Tip: *The arrow keys are nondestructive. They cause the highlight to move over the text on your screen.*

    The only peculiarity in arrow movements occurs at the beginning and end of lines when you press the RIGHT or LEFT ARROW key. When you reach the end of a line, pressing the RIGHT ARROW key will drop you down to the first character of the next line. If you press the LEFT ARROW key at the beginning of a line, the highlight will jump to the end of the next line up. Many new users are confused by this. Also, the end of a line may contain spaces, in which case the arrow may be a character or two away from the last visible character. If Options Visible Complete is set, you can see the dots that represent the spaces.

 Tip: *Pressing the LEFT or RIGHT ARROW key at the beginning or end of a line will place you in the previous or next line, respectively.*

The HOME and END Keys   The HOME and END keys are convenient for quickly jumping to the beginning or end of the current line, respectively. Using them in conjunction with the CTRL key allows you to quickly jump to the top or bottom corner of the screen.

The PGUP and PGDN Keys   The PGUP (Page Up) key will move the first two lines of text at the top of the screen to the bottom, displaying everything above it. The PGDN (Page Down) key will move the bottom two lines to the top of the screen, allowing you to see more of the lower part of your document. Try pressing the PGDN and PGUP keys to see how they work.

 Tip: *The PGUP (Page Up) and PGDN (Page Down) keys retain two lines of the previous screen.*

You can also use the PGUP and PGDN keys in combination with the CTRL key to move to either the top (CTRL+PGUP) or bottom (CTRL+PGDN) of the document.

Word and Paragraph Movement Keys   When you use the arrow keys in conjunction with the CTRL key, you can make various jump movements on the screen that will save you time and a lot of "key punching." Holding down the CTRL key and pressing the LEFT or RIGHT ARROW key will move the highlight to the first letter of the word to the left or right, respectively. Holding down CTRL and pressing the UP or DOWN ARROW key will move the highlight to the first character of the previous or next paragraph, respectively. You should remember these key combinations.

Other Keyboard Keys

Other marked keys on the keyboard are designed for various editing purposes. They differ from the arrow and scroll keys in that their actions are sometimes destructive. Therefore, you should use them with care and not get them mixed up with other keys.

The BACKSPACE Key   The BACKSPACE key is used to remove a character to the left of the highlight. Don't use it to move to the left in your text because it is a destructive key and will delete characters as it moves left. This key is most useful when you make a known mistake while typing. Simply press BACKSPACE and type the replacement character.

 Tip: *The BACKSPACE key removes the character to the left and causes all text to the right to shift into the deleted space.*

Trap: *The BACKSPACE key is a "destructive" key. It removes characters without the ability to recover them.*

The INS and DEL Keys   The Insert and Delete keys on your keyboard are often labeled simply INS and DEL. The DEL key will be discussed first because INS is often used to insert text deleted by the DEL key to another location. The DEL key will remove the highlighted character or characters. Note that this action differs from that of the BACKSPACE key in that the current letter is deleted. The DEL key is usually used when you are editing previously typed material. You would use the mouse or arrow keys to move to the character and then press DEL. Deleted text is temporarily stored in the scrap, as mentioned earlier.

The INS key will replace text that has been deleted and placed in the scrap. Be sure to look at the scrap before inserting to make sure that its contents are what you want to insert. You can use the DEL and INS keys to move text from one place to another.

 Tip: *The DEL (Delete) key removes the character under the highlight.*

 Trap: *The DEL (Delete) key is semidestructive; it places removed characters in the scrap so that you can replace them by using the INS (Insert) key.*

 Tip: *The INS (Insert) key will insert deleted text from the scrap to a new location.*

The TAB Key   The TAB key simply places a tab of a set value at the location of the highlight. You can adjust the tab size, as you'll see in Chapter 11. Word's standard tab size is 1/2-inch, though you can change the measure to centimeters or other measurement standards. Think of a tab as being a wider-than-normal space character.

By the way, both the space and tab are considered characters in Word. When you point to and select a tab character or use the arrow keys to move through a tab, the size of the highlight is a block that is determined by your current tab settings. Here is how 1/2-inch tabs look when highlighted.

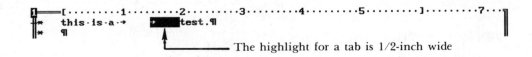

The highlight for a tab is 1/2-inch wide

The Undo Command

You can easily fix a mistake made in Word by using the Undo command, assuming that you catch it immediately after you make it. The Undo command will reverse your most recent editing or formatting action. You can even undo your most recent Undo by using the command again. To correct your most recent mistake, such as deleting a word, press the ESC+U or SHIFT+F1 key combination.

 Tip: *You can undo mistakes with the ESC+U or SHIFT+F1 key combination.*

The Undo command helps you recover from pressing a key accidentally. Usually, you are not looking at the screen and can't tell what happened. For example, pressing INS by accident may insert junk text into the middle of a paragraph, making it hard to separate the junk. Rather than trying to locate and delete the erroneously inserted text, simply Undo.

Making Typing Corrections

As you typed the example text earlier, you may have made mistakes. If you are familiar with word processors, you probably used the BACKSPACE key to fix your mistakes. In a real writing situation, you could rely on Word's built-in spelling checker to catch other mistakes after you typed in the bulk of the text. Though occasional typing corrections are inevitable when you enter a document, this method makes it easy to get your ideas on paper. There are several ways to correct with Word, depending on which keys you use and whether you have a mouse.

If you notice a typing mistake, just press BACKSPACE to erase the wrong character and type in a new one. Let's assume that you want to make a correction or change a word that is several lines away from your current position. In this case you must use the mouse or the arrow keys to move to the location that contains the mistake or the text you want to change.

Moving to Text with Arrow Keys   The arrow direction keys are most commonly used to move to previously typed text that must be altered or deleted. Let's use the previous text examples to illustrate the movements of the arrow direction keys. Assume that you want to change the words *close to* to *near* at the end of the first line of the paragraph. This is how you would proceed:

1. Press the CTRL+PGDN key combination to get to the lower-right corner of your document. Your screen should look similar to that shown in Figure 3-3.

2. Use the UP ARROW key to move to the *t* in the word *to* of the second line of the last paragraph.

3. Now, press the LEFT ARROW key. This will place you at the end of the previous line, as shown here:

```
*    This·is·an·example·of·a·paragraph·in·Word.··As·you·get·close·◄─┘
     ▯o·the·right·margin,·Word·wraps·the·text·to·the·next·line.··
     There·is·no·need·to·press·the·Enter·key·until·the·end·of·the·
     paragraph.¶
```

If it seems odd that the LEFT ARROW key would move you to the end of the previous line, think of a paragraph as being one long single line of text without the line breaks that you see on the screen. It's then easy to see how the LEFT ARROW key will move you to the previous line. Similarly, pressing the RIGHT ARROW key at the end of a line would place you at the beginning of the next line down.

Backspacing to Correct   The BACKSPACE key will delete the character to the right of the highlight. A character deleted with BACKSPACE is not placed in the scrap. The highlight now appears to the right of the *e* in *close*. To remove the word, press BACKSPACE six times. The extra backspace removes one of the spaces from the right of the word *get*. You can see that there are two spaces because the space dots are displayed. Notice how the word *to* follows the highlight up to the current line to fill in the deleted characters.

Removing Characters with the DEL Key   The next task is to remove the word *to* from the line. The BACKSPACE key will not work in this case since it deletes only to the left and the word *to* is to the right of the highlight. You could press the RIGHT ARROW key to move to the right of the word, but it is easier to press DEL three times. As you press DEL, notice that each character is placed in the scrap at the bottom of the screen.

Adding New Text   Having removed the unwanted words, you can simply type in the replacement. Type **near**, preceding it with a space to separate it from the previous word. Notice how Word readjusts the remainder of the line.

Mouse Techniques

This section is for those who have the advantage of using a mouse. Even if you don't have one, you may want to read this section to learn a little of what it does. Most mouse devices are in the $100 range (mail order) and come in two varieties, those with two buttons and those with three. If you have a two-button mouse, some actions may require that you press both buttons at once. With a three-button mouse, you press the middle button instead. That's the only difference other than how the mouse tracks, which may be with a ball or with a light beam on a gridded pad.

 Tip: *On a three-button mouse, pressing the middle button causes the same action to be performed as does pressing both buttons on a two-button mouse.*

If you have a mouse, you may be wondering when it's best to use it and when it's best to use the keyboard for selecting and editing text. The keyboard is usually best for bulk typing and making corrections close to the current insertion point. You can type and worry about editing later because the mouse makes it easy to point to where you want to alter or add more text. Sometimes, however, it is more trouble than it's worth to take your hands off the keyboard and grab the mouse. Try using both until you find the pattern that lets you operate most efficiently. This will eventually become second nature.

The mouse has obvious advantages when you consider that it is easier to select text from the selection bar than with the function keys. It is also easier to select commands in the command line unless you know the keyboard codes to perform a specific task that bypasses the menu. Later, you will see various techniques that demonstrate what an important tool a mouse can be.

Hold the mouse in your hand with the back of your palm resting on the table or mouse pad and extend two fingers to touch the buttons. Resting your palm on the pad will help stabilize the mouse movements. If you don't have a mouse pad, consider getting one. They cost only about $10 and not only improve the accuracy of the mouse movements but also keep the ball from getting dirty.

 Tip: *Never hold your hand up in the air when using the mouse because you will probably find the mouse movement too sensitive and hard to control. Rest the back of your palm on the table top or mouse pad while moving the mouse.*

When you use the mouse to select commands, its left and right buttons have distinct operations. Press the left button when you want to "see what is behind" a command. In other words, pressing on a menu command such as Format will display the Format submenu.

 Tip: *The left mouse button displays the submenus for the commands in the command menu.*

Use the right button when you want to *execute* the command behind the one you are pointing at. In other words, the option that is normally highlighted when you display a submenu is executed. Microsoft placed various options in this highlighted position based on the assumption that they would be the ones most often used. These commands, called the *proposed response* commands, will be covered in Chapter 4.

 Tip: *The right mouse button directly executes the proposed response of a command.*

Using the Mouse to Make Corrections

The mouse makes it much easier to make corrections or replacements. The arrow keys force you into tapping out a beat on the keyboard as you navigate through your text, whereas the mouse takes you directly to the text you want to correct.

Removing a Character   To remove any character, simply point to it with the mouse and press the left button. Then press DEL to remove it to the scrap.

Removing a Word   To remove any word, simply point to the word and press the right button. Then press DEL to remove it to the scrap. Various other movements and selections that you can make with the mouse will be covered in later chapters.

 Tip: *The left mouse button selects a character; the right mouse button selects a word.*

Formatting Characters

Character formatting in Word is the process of applying various type styles and sizes to the characters of your documents. This topic will be covered in detail in Chapter 10.

For now, you can get an idea of how easy it is to change the type style of your text by performing these steps:

1. Highlight the word *paragraph* in the first line of the last paragraph in your text. You can press the CTRL+PGDN key combination to get to the bottom of the text. If you have a mouse, point to the word and press the right mouse button. If you are using the cursor movement keys, press the UP ARROW key until you get to the line; then press F8 until the word is highlighted.

2. Press ALT+I to apply an italic formatting to the character.

3. Move the highlight to see how it looks.

If you have a graphics screen, the text will appear as true italics, as shown in this illustration:

‖*   This·is·an·example·of·a·**paragraph**·in·Word.··As·you·get·close·   ‖

Italic formatting applied

If you have a color screen and are displaying in text mode, the formatted characters will appear in a color other than the background color. If you have a black and white text screen, the characters will be underlined.

 Trap: *Don't get confused by the way that black and white monitors display character formatting. Underlined characters represent all the character formats except bold, which is shown in high intensity.*

Try one last formatting action before clearing your screen. This will illustrate why you want to maintain paragraph integrity, as discussed earlier. If you wanted to double space a paragraph of text that you typed in single-space format, you don't have to go back and add lines between lines.

1. Place the highlight anywhere in the paragraphs on your screen by using the mouse or the arrow keys.

2. Press the ALT+2 key combination to apply the double-spacing format to the entire paragraph.

Thus you can type your document in single-space mode and apply double spacing later on. Because double spacing is a paragraph format, you can select or place the highlight anywhere in the paragraph to apply the double-spacing format. For editing text on the screen, single spacing is usually preferred because you can see more text. For hard-copy editing, double spacing is usually preferred. In Word it's easy to make this change.

 Tip: *You can type documents with single spacing for better viewing of text and later print them as double-spaced with little trouble.*

Clearing and Quitting Word

You're about ready to end this chapter and may be ready to stop for a while. If you simply turn your computer off without saving your text, you will lose what is currently on your screen. It is also not wise to shut your system down while still in Word. Changes or updates that you may have made will be lost because they only become permanent when you quit Word in the proper way.

 Trap: *Quitting Word by shutting off the machine may destroy text and editing changes as well as operational changes. Always quit Word by using the Quit option on the command menu.*

If you want to save the text on the screen for future practice, perform the following steps:

1. Press ESC to get to the command menu.
2. Type **T** to access the Transfer option. The Transfer submenu will appear.
3. Type **S** to access the Save option. Word will ask you for a filename.
4. Type **SAMPLE** and press ENTER.

The file is saved to disk.

Now, you can try clearing the screen before you quit. Although this is not essential to quitting from Word, you will see how to clear text from your screen in case you want to create another document.

1. Press ESC to get to the command menu.
2. Type **T** to access the Transfer option. The Transfer submenu will appear.
3. Type **C** to access the Clear option.
4. Type **A** to select All.

 Tip: *Word will ask if you want to save any typing or editing changes before you clear a screen or quit Word.*

If you had not previously saved your document, Word would ask you if you wanted to save before clearing. Because you've already saved, the screen is cleared and the cursor is placed at the top of the screen. To quit Word, press ESC+Q.

Tips and Traps Summary

Another Look at the Word Screen

Trap: Word didn't start? Make sure that you are in the proper directory by using the DOS CD (Change Directory) command.

Tip: ESC opens the command menu at the bottom of the screen.

Tip: Margins are indicated by square brackets in the ruler bar.

Tip: The ruler bar will help you keep track of margins and tabs.

Tip: Word's edit window does not show the space from the edge oᴉ the paper to the left and right margins.

Trap: If you are confused by the space dots, tab arrows, and other symbols displayed by the Options Visible Complete command, you can always turn them back off by responding **N** to the command.

Tip: The style bar can display a character code indicating the type style and paragraph alignment that your text may have.

Tip: The style bar and selection bar are one and the same. It displays paragraph formatting codes, or you can click in it with the mouse to select lines or paragraphs.

Tip: The position indicator helps you keep track of the cursor location on the screen and the current page number.

Typing and Editing

Tip: In Word a paragraph is a continuous block of text as well as the traditional collection of ideas.

Tips and Traps Summary (*continued*)

Tip: A paragraph is a block of text that you end by pressing ENTER. Press ENTER only at the end of the paragraph.

Tip: Because paragraphs form a continuous and integrated block of text, you can change the type style, indents, line spacing, and tab settings of each paragraph individually.

Tip: SHIFT+ENTER can be used to start a new line in the same paragraph.

Tip: You can select paragraphs by pointing to them and pressing F10 or clicking in the selection bar with the mouse.

Tip: The scrap holds deleted text until you delete something else. The INS (Insert) key can be used to reinsert it elsewhere.

Trap: You may not be able to use the arrow direction keys if the NUM LOCK key is on.

Tip: The edit window is a window on a large document. Scroll keys on the keyboard move the document up or down through the window

Tip: If you have a separate highlight movement pad, you can leave the NUM LOCK key on and use the numeric keypad for data entry.

Tip: The insertion point is the current position of the highlight.

Trap: If overtype mode is on, you will type over characters.

Tip: The F5 Overtype key is a toggle key. Press it once to turn it on; press it again to turn it off.

Tip: Overtype's usefulness is limited. To replace a character, it is easier to insert the new character and then delete the old.

Tip: The arrow keys are nondestructive. They cause the highlight to move over the text on your screen.

Tips and Traps Summary (*continued*)

Tip: Pressing the LEFT or RIGHT ARROW key at the beginning or end of a line will place you in the previous or next line, respectively.

Tip: The PGUP (Page Up) and PGDN (Page Down) keys retain two lines of the previous screen.

Tip: The BACKSPACE key removes the character to the left and causes all text to the right to shift into the deleted space.

Trap: The BACKSPACE key is a ''destructive'' key. It removes characters without the ability to recover them.

Tip: The DEL (Delete) key removes the character under the highlight.

Trap: The DEL (Delete) key is semidestructive; it places removed characters in the scrap so that you can replace them by using the INS (Insert) key.

Tip: The INS (Insert) key will insert deleted text from the scrap to a new location.

Tip: You can undo mistakes with the ESC+U or SHIFT+F1 key combination.

Mouse Techniques

Tip: On a three-button mouse, pressing the middle button causes the same action to be performed as does pressing both buttons on a two-button mouse.

Tip: Never hold your hand up in the air when using the mouse because you will probably find the mouse movement too sensitive and hard to control. Rest the back of your palm on the table top or mouse pad while moving the mouse.

Tips and Traps Summary (*continued*)

> *Tip:* The left mouse button displays the submenus for the commands in the command menu.

> *Tip:* The right mouse button directly executes the proposed response of a command.

> *Tip:* The left mouse button selects a character; the right mouse button selects a word.

Formatting Characters

> *Trap:* Don't get confused by the way that black and white monitors display character formatting. Underlined characters represent all the character formats except bold, which is shown in high intensity.

> *Tip:* You can type documents with single spacing for better viewing of text, and later print them as double-spaced with little trouble.

Clearing and Quitting Word

> *Trap:* Quitting Word by shutting off the machine may destroy text and editing changes as well as operational changes. Always quit Word by using the Quit option on the command menu.

> *Tip:* Word will ask if you want to save any typing or editing changes before you clear a screen or quit Word.

4

Executing
Word Commands

Microsoft designers put a lot of thought into how people use computers when they originally designed their command menu system. Microsoft Multiplan and Chart have the same command menus that Word has. These software packages were designed to be easy to use while also presenting powerful commands to both beginning and experienced users in a helpful way. As you select commands, helpful messages and a complete array of options are displayed. You may never need a reference manual because a complete online Help facility provides even more extensive descriptions of commands.

Accessing Word Commands

You access the command menu by pressing the ESC key, which is like a toggle that moves the highlight between the edit window and command menu. If you set the options menu to No, as discussed in Chapter 2, pressing ESC from the edit window will cause the command line to be displayed. Setting the options menu to Yes causes the command line to appear all the time. The highlight appears on the first command in the command menu and can be scrolled with the SPACEBAR, TAB key, or arrow keys. If you have a mouse, you can point and click in the bottom line of the edit window to display the menu.

 Trap: *The command menu may not always be visible if the Options Menu field is set to No.*

 Tip: *With a mouse, click at the bottom of the screen to display the menu if it is hidden.*

As you move the highlight, a description appears in the message area for each command. When you find the command that performs the action you need, pressing the ENTER key usually causes a submenu of options for that command to be displayed. It is here that you select Options to *customize* the command. In this way Word relieves you of the need to learn extensive parameters and command keywords. After filling in options, you can press ENTER to execute the command or press ESC to cancel it.

 Tip: *Selecting Options allows you to customize commands.*

 Trap: *Press ENTER to execute a command. ESC will back you out of a command without executing it.*

The commands displayed on the main command menu are often only like the tip of an iceberg. Below some of these commands are extensive sets of subcommands. Some submenus even have their own submenus. From now on these submenus will be referred to as *levels* of commands. The top-level main command menu will be referred to as the *Main menu*. The submenu of a Main menu command will be called a *second-level menu,* and further levels will be referred to appropriately. The *option level* of a command refers to the final *endpoint* menu where options are filled in to customize a command. For example, the Transfer command levels are shown in Figure 4-1.

 Tip: *Commands may have several levels of menu selections.*

You can choose any command with the keyboard or mouse. In addition, many commands can be accessed directly by using CTRL, ALT, and SHIFT key combinations. The CTRL, ALT, and SHIFT key combinations make it easy to perform tasks in Word once you become familiar with them and with Word's features. You will probably find yourself learning the key codes for those commands you use the most.

Tip: *You can select commands through the menu, with the mouse, or by pressing keyboard codes.*

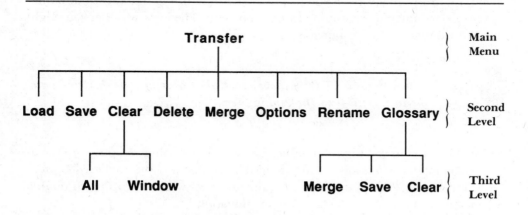

Figure 4-1. Levels of a command

Features of the Command Menu

The actual command menu is only two of the four lines that are displayed on your screen when you press ESC. The bottom line is comprised of various status indicators that will be covered here because they relate closely to the contents of the command menu. The second from the bottom line is a *message line* that explains the current menu selection. Here is the command menu with appropriate labels:

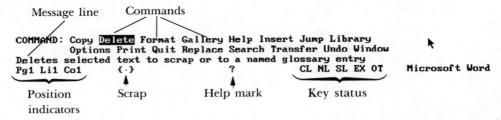

Double Command Line

The top two lines of the menu comprise the commands. In Word version 4, there are 16 commands listed in alphabetical order, not in order of importance. If you have been using an older version of Word, you will notice that the Alpha command is gone. In that version you had to type **A** to return to the edit window after executing a command or escaping from a submenu. The logic was that you might want to execute another command.

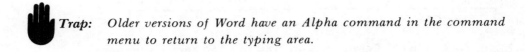

> *Trap:* *Older versions of Word have an Alpha command in the command menu to return to the typing area.*

In Word version 4, you are returned to the edit window after escaping or executing a command. Microsoft finally decided that this was the preferred option. However, if you want to stay in the command window after stepping through a menu option, press the CTRL+ESC key combination.

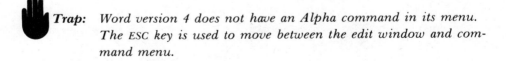

> *Trap:* *Word version 4 does not have an Alpha command in its menu. The ESC key is used to move between the edit window and command menu.*

Tip: *Press* CTRL+ESC *if you are aborting one command to enter another.*

Message Line

Below the double line of commands is the message line, which will always describe the command that the highlight is on or give you some helpful advice. If you are trying to figure out how to perform a task, move the highlight to different commands to see what they do. When you find what you want, press ENTER to get to the command's submenu. The message line will then describe the options in the submenu.

 Tip: *Move the highlight with the* TAB *key to view command description messages.*

Position Indicators

The position indicators were covered in Chapter 3. They help you keep track of the current location of the highlight in the edit window and the current page number. They do not, however, track the highlight in the command menu.

 Trap: *In order for the line number to appear in the status indicator, you must select Yes in the Options Line Number field.*

Scrap

The scrap was also covered briefly in Chapter 3 and will be covered in more detail later on. The scrap holds text deletions for later insertion. It is also used by the Copy command to copy glossary text, as you'll see in Chapters 9 and 15.

The Help Mark

The help mark is useful only if you have a mouse. If you touch on it with the mouse pointer and press a key, it will display help information for the currently highlighted menu command. For example, if you move the highlight to Format and need more information than is available in the message line, simply press the question mark with the mouse. Users who don't have a mouse can press ALT+H instead.

 Trap: *The help mark is useful only to mouse owners.*

Key Status Indicators

In the command menu shown earlier, five key status indicators are on: CL (Caps Lock), NL (Number Lock), SL (Scroll Lock), EX (Extend), and OT (OverType). Normally you won't have this many indicators on at once; but it's important to see their positions on the screen and next to each other. Several other indicators — CS (Column Select), LD (Line Draw mode), RM (Record Macro), ST (Macro Step mode), ZM (Zoom Window), and MR (Mark Revisions) — will overlay some of those shown. CS will usually overwrite EX because they are mutually exclusive. Some status indicators simply take precedence over others.

Selecting Commands

There are several ways to access the commands on the command menu. First, press ESC to get to the menu or, if you have a mouse, press in the bottom line of the edit window to open the menu. When you do, the Copy command is always highlighted first. From there you can use the TAB key, SPACEBAR, or arrow keys to move to each selection. It doesn't make much difference which key you use, but some finer points concerning the mechanics of menu selection with these keys will be covered later. Moving the highlight through the menu allows you to view the descriptions of each command in the message line.

 Tip: *The SPACEBAR, TAB key, and directional arrow keys let you move through the command menu.*

The arrow keys provide up and down movement, so if you want to move to the bottom line, simply press the DOWN ARROW key and then continue to scroll right. The TAB key and SPACEBAR move through the menu *serially* (the same way text is read), making the path to the bottom-right command longer. You can use SHIFT+TAB to move the highlight backward, which is a convenient way to reach the last command in the list when the highlight is in Copy, as shown here:

SHIFT+TAB

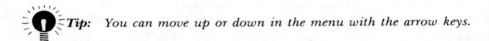

COMMAND: Copy Delete Format Gallery Help Insert Jump Library
Options Print Quit Replace Search Transfer Undo Window

Tip: *You can move up or down in the menu with the arrow keys.*

As you become familiar with Word and no longer need to view the message line for each command, you can make command menu selections by simply typing the capital letter of each one. This will cause the command's submenu or second level of selections to be immediately displayed. The first letter of the command is usually the one to press, though on some submenus the second or third letter may be used because of conflicts with other commands. In the Format Character menu shown here, you type **E** to select sEarch and **L** to select repLace.

FORMAT: Character Paragraph Tab Border Footnote Division Running-head Stylesheet
sEarch repLace revision-Marks

Tip: *Press the capital letter of any command to execute it.*

The Mechanics of Menu Selection

If you run through the following demonstrations, you'll get a good idea of the best way to select commands from Word's menus when using the highlight.

SPACEBAR Method   Press ESC to display the menu. Using the SPACEBAR, highlight the Format command and press ENTER, keeping your finger on the SPACEBAR. Next, space over to Paragraph in the second-level menu and press ENTER.

With your hands still on the SPACEBAR, you can jump between the responses in the Alignment field of the third-level menu. Press CTRL+ESC to return to the Main menu.

TAB Key Method   With the Main menu displayed, press TAB until Format is highlighted and then press ENTER to display the second-level menu. Press TAB once to highlight Paragraph and press ENTER to accept it. In the third-level Paragraph menu, press TAB several times to see how the highlight moves serially through the selections. Press SHIFT+TAB to reverse directions. Press CTRL+ESC to return to the top-level Main menu.

Arrow Key Method   With the highlight in the Main menu, press the RIGHT ARROW key to get to the Format command and press ENTER to display the Format second-level menu. Press the RIGHT ARROW key once to highlight Paragraph and press ENTER. In the third-level Paragraph menu, press the DOWN ARROW key to move to the Keep Together option. Press ESC to exit the menu.

 Tip: *In Word 4 you can use the arrow keys to move up and down as well as left and right in the menu options.*

These exercises illustrate the concept that the key you initially select when choosing commands can be used to make further selections in the second- and third-level menus. For example, if you know that the option you want to change is at the bottom-left of the third-level Format Character menu, you might want to use the arrow keys so that you can easily move to it, as in the previous example.

The TAB key is preferable if you know that you will need to jump to the end of the menu because you can reverse TAB with the SHIFT+TAB key combination. For example, try pressing TAB, TAB, ENTER, ENTER, SHIFT+TAB, and SHIFT+TAB to see how to step through the most direct route to the Font Size option in the Format Character menu.

 Tip: *Get into the habit of finding the direct route to options in sub-menus by using TAB, SHIFT+TAB (reverse), or the directional arrow keys.*

The SPACEBAR is good when you want to select the first field in an options menu. The SPACEBAR toggles the highlight between fields in a single option rather than moving you to another option in the submenu. This first option is often called the *proposed response* of a menu. For example, the Transfer menu opens up with the highlight on Load instead of Save, Clear, Delete, or its other options. The Format menu opens with the highlight on Character. The Format Character menu then opens with a proposed response of Bold set to No (unless you changed it previously).

The proposed response of every command submenu is the response that Word's designers assumed users would need most often, so this is where the highlight will be when you first get to the submenu. As you become familiar with the menu commands, you will begin to remember their proposed responses and be able to use them to advantage, as you'll see next.

Tip: *The proposed response is the most likely choice on a menu and will be highlighted.*

Proposed Response

The proposed response is based on Word's standard settings. If you change the standard response, the new one will often remain from session to session. For example, in Chapter 2 you changed the Ruler Line response in the Window Options menu from No to Yes. When a response is changed, a bracket surrounds the new response. Not all responses are changed permanently in Word from session to session, however. Character and paragraph formatting responses start out with standard setting for each document, or they are automatically set when you apply *style sheets* to your documents. (Style sheets are covered in later chapters.)

Trap: *Be careful when you select commands. The proposed response may not be what you need.*

Figure 4-2 shows the proposed response at various levels in the Format command. At the bottom, the Main menu is displayed with the Format command

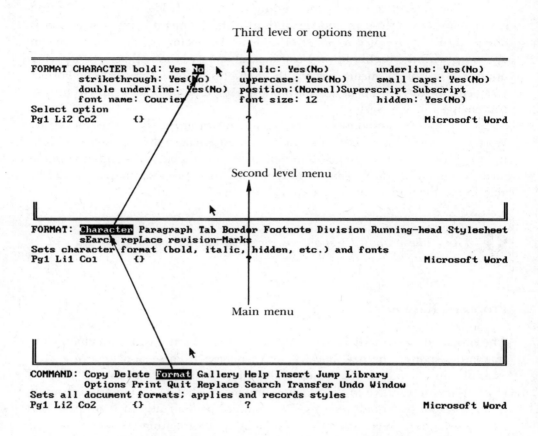

Third level or options menu

```
FORMAT CHARACTER bold: Yes No        italic: Yes(No)         underline: Yes(No)
          strikethrough: Yes(No)     uppercase: Yes(No)      small caps: Yes(No)
          double underline: Yes(No)  position:(Normal)Superscript Subscript
          font name: Courier         font size: 12           hidden: Yes(No)
Select option
Pg1 Li2 Co2        {}                        ?                Microsoft Word
```

Second level menu

```
FORMAT: Character Paragraph Tab Border Footnote Division Running-head Stylesheet
        sEarch repLace revision-Marks
Sets character format (bold, italic, hidden, etc.) and fonts
Pg1 Li1 Co1        {}                        ?                Microsoft Word
```

Main menu

```
COMMAND: Copy Delete Format Gallery Help Insert Jump Library
         Options Print Quit Replace Search Transfer Undo Window
Sets all document formats; applies and records styles
Pg1 Li2 Co2        {}                        ?                Microsoft Word
```

Figure 4-2. Command menu proposed responses

highlighted. Press ENTER to display the second-level menu. The proposed response here is the Character command. Press ENTER again to display the third-level Format Character menu with all of its options. In this menu brackets surround the proposed responses set by Word, or those set previously by a user.

Backing Out of a Command

You have seen how to back out of commands with the ESC key. It will cancel any changes that you made to options in a command and reset them to their previous response. If you are in a command and are making alterations, and you then decide to make an alteration in another command first, you can press CTRL+ESC. This will return you to the top-level Main menu.

Executing Commands

To execute a command, simply press ENTER after setting the preferred menu options. Make sure that you haven't set any options by mistake. Sometimes it is hard to see exactly what the execution of a command has done. You may have inadvertently altered a font size, which is not visible on the screen. You can sometimes use the Undo command to recover from an erroneous command. Press ESC+U (Undo) immediately after the command.

 Trap: *Be sure that all options are set the way you want before pressing ENTER.*

 Tip: *Pressing ESC+U (Undo) may help you recover from some unintentional commands.*

Displaying Alternate Lists

In some Word commands the available selections are so numerous that you will be asked to press the F1 key to display a list. This is the case when you select a printer in the Print Options command or type fonts and sizes in the Format Character command. In older versions of Word you could press the RIGHT ARROW key to see the alternatives. But in Word 4, only the F1 key performs this function. Watch the message area of your screen to see when you should press F1.

 Trap: *In Word 4, only the F1 key displays the list of alternatives. In older versions the RIGHT ARROW key must be used.*

Using the Mouse

The mouse opens up a whole new method of menu selection. With it, you can quickly and easily construct your commands by simply pointing to the options that you want to change. If you have a mouse, you may want to turn the menu back on permanently with the Options Menu command, thus providing quick access to the commands with your mouse. If the menu is hidden, you must first press the ESC key, which adds an extra step to the menu selection process.

 Tip: *Mouse users may want to permanently display the menu for quick access to commands.*

The way that you use the buttons on the mouse can simplify command execution. To select a command with the mouse, simply point to it and press one of the mouse buttons. Which button you press, however, makes a big difference. Press the left button on a command to display that command's second-level menu, at which point you can make another selection. Point at a Main menu command and press the right button to display the third-level command menu of the proposed response, if the command has one.

 Tip: *The right mouse button selects the proposed response of a command, displaying its Options menu.*

For example, you can select Format from the menu with the left button to display the second-level Format menu. Character is highlighted, so you know that this is the proposed response. You can select Character or any other command from this level. Or, you can select Format from the Main menu by pointing and pressing the right button. Because Character is the proposed response for the Format command, the third-level Format Character menu appears. The two mouse selection possibilities are shown in Figure 4-3.

 Tip: *The button you choose to select a menu item has an effect on how the command is executed.*

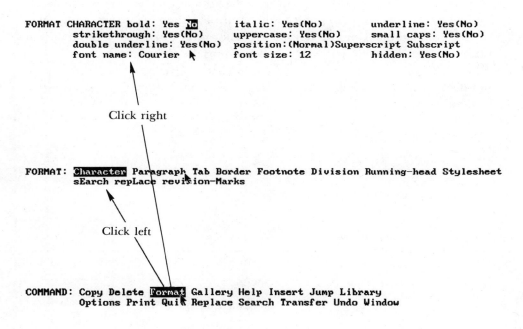

FORMAT CHARACTER bold: Yes █No█   italic: Yes(No)   underline: Yes(No)
              strikethrough: Yes(No)   uppercase: Yes(No)   small caps: Yes(No)
              double underline: Yes(No) position:(Normal)Superscript Subscript
              font name: Courier ▲   font size: 12   hidden: Yes(No)

                    Click right

FORMAT: █Character█ Paragraph Tab Border Footnote Division Running-head Stylesheet
        sEarch repLace revision-Marks

                    Click left

COMMAND: Copy Delete █Format█ Gallery Help Insert Jump Library
         Options Print Quit Replace Search Transfer Undo Window

---

Figure 4-3. Left and right mouse button responses

As you become familiar with the Main menu and its submenus, you will learn the proposed responses for each and eventually will know when to use the correct mouse button to get what you want.

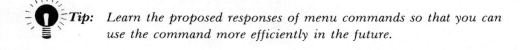

Tip: *Learn the proposed responses of menu commands so that you can use the command more efficiently in the future.*

Table 4-1 lists the proposed responses for each command on the Main Command menu. Because some of these commands are only one level deep, it makes no difference whether you press the left or right button when pointing.

Once you get to an options menu like the Format Character menu shown in Figure 4-3, use the mouse to point to the multiple-choice items that you want to change. Using the left mouse button will allow you to change more than one option because the menu will stay open. Pressing the right button on an option will cause the command to execute. You can change several options with the left button and then use the right one to change your final option, thus executing the changes made in the command.

 Tip: *Select a multiple-choice item with the right mouse button to execute the command.*

Table 4-1. Command Menu Proposed Responses

Command	Response
Copy	Same as left button
Delete	Deletes contents of highlight
Format	Display Format Character options
Gallery	Same as left button
Help	Same as left button
Insert	Scrap at highlight
Jump	Displays Jump Page command
Library	Displays Library Autosort options
Options	Same as left button
Print	Start printing
Quit	Quits and saves file
Replace	Same as left button
Search	Same as left button
Transfer	Displays Transfer Load option
Undo	Same as left button
Window	Displays Window Split option

Occasionally you must type in a response to a menu option. For example, you may need to type the name of a file to load or save, or to select a printer, type style, or type size. Pointing in the Options field and pressing the right mouse button will sometimes display a list of possible selections. The list will appear at the top of the screen. The screen image in Figure 4-4 shows the result of pressing the right button while pointing at the font name in the Format Character menu.

 Tip: *Press the right mouse button in a user response field to display a list of options.*

Other Command Features

You should know about a few other features of Word's command menu system before going on to Chapter 5. These are discussed next.

```
Courier (modern a)              CourForeign (modern b)
LinePrinter (modern h)          HELV (modern i)
TMSRMN (roman a)
```

Clicking the right button on font
name displays a list of font options
at the top of the screen

```
FORMAT CHARACTER bold: Yes(No)       italic: Yes(No)        underline: Yes(No)
         strikethrough: Yes(No)      uppercase: Yes(No)     small caps: Yes(No)
         double underline: Yes(No)   position:(Normal)Superscript Subscript
         font name: Courier          font size: 12          hidden: Yes(No)
Enter font name or press ↰ to select from list
Pg5 Li147 Co53   {options...ble.¶}   ?                       Microsoft Word
```

Figure 4-4. Click with right button (or press F1) to display options

Viewing Menus

You now know how to back out of menus with the ESC or CTRL+ESC key. This is helpful when you want to open submenus and look at their options to see if a command will do what you want. You may also open a command submenu to look at the formatting that has been applied to a particular paragraph. For example, in Figure 4-1 brackets surround various items in the Format Character menu. The brackets indicate the current font and style setting, which is useful if you can't get this information by looking at the screen.

 Tip: *You can open a command menu to view its settings and then back out of it. In this way you can determine format settings for characters and paragraphs.*

Getting Help

To get help with any command, simply highlight it with the arrow, TAB, or SPACE-BAR keys; then press ALT+H or press the question mark at the bottom of the screen if you have a mouse. A help screen will appear with context-sensitive information about the action you are trying to perform. At the bottom of the screen is a menu that looks like that shown in Figure 4-5. You can get additional help by selecting one of these options.

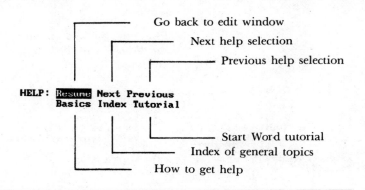

Figure 4-5. The Help menu

Tip: *You can get help for a highlighted command by pressing* ALT+H.

If you choose the Index option, you will see the following list of help options:

```
HELP INDEX: Alignment      File-formats     Macros         Selection
            Character-format  Footnotes      Margins        Spellchecker
            Columns        Form-letters     Mouse          Style-sheets
            Commands       Glossaries       Outlining      Tabs/Tables
            Customize-screen  Indents        Page-numbers   Windows
            Divisions      Keyboard         Printing
            Doc-retrieval  Library-commands Running-heads
            Editing        Load/Open        Save
```

Word's Quick Keys

You can execute many menu options by using various key combinations known as *quick keys*. Though most of these keys will be discussed later, you should know about a few of them now. The best way to keep track of the quick keys is to place the keyboard template that comes with Word on your keyboard. You might want to tape the wide template to the bottom of your screen, assuming it sits on top of your computer, so you can still place reference material on the keyboard lip designed for that purpose.

 Tip: *Quick keys provide a quick entry to command option menus.*

Pressing one important key, F4, repeats your previous command. Many actions, such as applying a type style, must be executed a number of times. Press the F4 key to repeat a formatting operation as you highlight various portions of text. The SHIFT+F4 combination will repeat a text search operation, using the same text entered in the text field of the previous Search command. The ALT+F3 combination will send a copy of any highlighted text to the scrap so that you can insert it somewhere else. This is similar to using the DEL key, but it retains the highlighted text in your document. You can jump to a page with ALT+F5 or check a word in the thesaurus with CTRL+F6. Switching between text and graphics modes is easy with ALT+F9, and saving your work is a snap with CTRL+F10.

Tips and Traps Summary

Accessing Word Commands

Trap: The command menu may not be visible at all times if the Options Menu field is set to No.

Tip: With a mouse, click at the bottom of the screen to display the menu if it is hidden.

Tip: Selecting Options allows you to customize commands.

Trap: Press ENTER to execute a command. ESC will back you out of a command without executing it.

Tip: Commands may have several levels of menu selections.

Tip: You can select commands through the menu, with the mouse, or by pressing keyboard codes.

Features of the Command Menu

Trap: Older versions of Word have an Alpha command in the command menu to return to the typing area.

Trap: Word version 4 does not have an Alpha command in its menu. The ESC key is used to move between the edit window and command menu.

Tip: Press CTRL+ESC if you are aborting one command to enter another.

Tip: Move the highlight with the TAB key to view command description messages.

Trap: In order for the line number to appear in the status indicator, you must select Yes in the Options Line Number field.

Trap: The help mark is useful only to mouse owners.

Tips and Traps Summary (*continued*)

Selecting Commands

Tip: The SPACEBAR, TAB key, and directional arrow keys let you move through the command menu.

Tip: You can move up or down in the menu with the arrow keys.

Tip: Press the capital letter of any command to execute it.

Tip: In Word 4 you can use the arrow keys to move up and down as well as left and right in the menu options.

Tip: Get into the habit of finding the direct route to options in sub-menus by using TAB, SHIFT+TAB (reverse), or the directional arrow keys.

Tip: The proposed response is the most likely choice on a menu and will be highlighted.

Trap: Be careful when you select commands. The proposed response may not be what you need.

Trap: Be sure that all options are set the way you want before pressing ENTER.

Tip: Pressing ESC+U (Undo) may help you recover from some unintentional commands.

Trap: In Word 4 only the F1 key displays the list of alternatives. In older versions the RIGHT ARROW key must be used.

Using the Mouse

Tip: Mouse users may want to permanently display the menu for quick access to commands.

Tips and Traps Summary (continued)

Tip: The right mouse button selects the proposed response of a command, displaying its Options menu.

Tip: The button you choose to select a menu item has an effect on how the command is executed.

Tip: Learn the proposed responses of menu commands so that you can use the command more efficiently in the future.

Tip: Select a multiple-choice item with the right mouse button to execute the command.

Tip: Press the right mouse button in a user response field to display a list of options.

Other Command Features

Tip: You can open a command menu to view its settings and then back out of it. In this way you can determine format settings for characters and paragraphs.

Tip: You can get help for a highlighted command by pressing ALT+H.

Tip: Quick keys provide a quick entry to command option menus.

5

Loading, Saving, and Printing Files

This chapter is important only if you want to print your files, save them for later use, or load an existing file for editing. Because that is what word processing is all about, this chapter is essential material for working with Word. You'll learn about files and how to name them, how to load existing files into the edit window, and how to save your work and print it.

What Is a File?

If you have ever placed a folder of information in a filing cabinet, you are familiar with files. A file in Word is an electronic representation of the characters you type on the screen, saved as a unit with a special *filename* on your floppy or hard disk. You use this filename when you want to call the text back to the screen or copy it to another disk.

 Tip: *A filename is used to load and save files in Word.*

There is a big difference between text on the screen and text that has been saved to a disk file. Text on the screen is impermanent. If you lose power, you will lose the text on the screen and any changes that you made to a file since the last save, so you must save your work to disk on a regular basis.

 Trap: *Text on the screen may be lost unless saved to disk.*

Files stored to disk are relatively permanent. Cassette and video tapes are highly reliable magnetic storage media. Cassettes last for years, and wear usually occurs in the casing first. Files stored to floppy disk are relatively safe as long as you follow the recommended handling procedures. Hard-drive files are even safer because the media is protected inside a sealed case. That does not mean that you shouldn't make extra copies of your files, however. You never know when a piece of electronic hardware will break down, perhaps taking your files with it.

 Trap: *Always make backups of important files. Develop a backup strategy, making backups part of your regular routine.*

Back up your Word files on a regular basis with the help of a standard procedure. You can make backups to floppy diskettes or to tape storage devices if you have a hard-drive system. Refer to your DOS manual or a good book on DOS for a discussion of this topic. For now, this chapter will be concerned with loading, saving, and printing files in Word. Backup procedures are covered in Appendix A, "Working at the DOS Level."

 Tip: *Your backup procedure should comprise a regular daily, weekly, or monthly routine. Set up a schedule now.*

Your computer uses many types of files other than those created in Word.

Loading, Saving and Printing Files

Word creates files commonly referred to as document files, which are normally filled with text. Other types include program files, data files, and miscellaneous files used by your other programs. A program file contains code recognizable only by your computer and cannot be recognizably displayed on the Word screen. The file containing the program code for Microsoft Word is called WORD.COM. Word printer description files use the extension .PRD and have a filename that resembles the name of the printer they define.

Tip: *Your program disk may contain many types of files. Only the document files are of interest in Word.*

When you exit Word, you are at the DOS level, where you can list the files on your diskette or hard drive with the DOS DIR (Directory) command. At this level, you can issue commands to start other programs, or you can perform file operations such as copying files to other diskettes or backing up your hard drive. The DOS level can be considered the service level, where file maintenance is performed. When Word is in use, it is like a plane that flies above this level. Quitting Word is like landing the plane at the DOS airport, where you can perform service on Word or its files.

Tip: *DOS can be considered a service level for your filing system.*

Trap: *Some DOS commands, such as ERASE and FORMAT, can be destructive. Refer to the DOS manual for full instructions.*

Word has the facilities to communicate with DOS while you are running the program. The Run command in the Library menu allows you to issue DOS commands from Word. You can use it to list files in other directories or other disks. For example, if you are trying to locate a file on a set of diskettes, you can place each diskette in the floppy drive and then issue a Library Run DIR A: /P (the paged directory command) command for drive A.

Tip: *DOS commands can be run from Word with the Library Run command.*

You can also format diskettes to be used for backups or run a check of your filing system, as you'll see later in this chapter.

File-Naming Strategies

This section will introduce the rules of naming files and offer some strategies on how to use names to better organize your files. When you first save a document, Word will ask you for a filename in which to save it. You must supply a name that is not more than eight characters long. Word will place the extension .DOC on the filename you supply unless you specify your own extension. The .DOC extension (an abbreviation for document) is a code, used primarily at the DOS level, that helps you organize, delineate, and separate files.

Tip: *Filenames consist of an eight-character filename and a three-character extension.*

Tip: *Word automatically assigns the extension .DOC to your files unless you specify otherwise.*

At the DOS level, you can get a list of files with just the .DOC extension, or you can easily copy all DOC files to another disk by using the extension in a DOS COPY command.

Tip: *DOC files can be grouped and copied together to other disks for backup or transport purposes.*

As mentioned, Word uses the .DOC extension to list files when you want to load a file. Press F1 in the Transfer Load field to produce a list of the DOC files on the current disk or directory. Try this now by selecting Transfer Load and then pressing F1. The F1 key will only list files with the extension .DOC, however. To list files in other directories, you must specify the directory name, covered next.

 Trap: *Press F1 during a load to list DOC files. To see other files, you must specify the directory name.*

 Tip: *Extensions help sort your files into categories and file types.*

 Tip: *Placing a period after the filename will cause Word to not add an extension.*

In addition to the eight-character filename and three-character extension, a file is preceded by a location name, which could be the floppy drive where the file is stored or the directory on a hard drive where it is stored.

 Tip: *An important part of a filename is the drive and directory where the file resides.*

For example, the file A:CHAPTER1.DOC is a document that resides on floppy drive A. The file \WORD\LETTER.DOC is one that resides in the WORD directory of the current drive. If it is on hard-drive C, this file is also known as C:\WORD\LETTER.DOC. A file called D:\BUSINESS\DUNN.DOC is a dunning letter in the BUSINESS directory of drive D.

The drive and directory where a file lives is called the *pathname* of the file. The path is a route that DOS or Word must follow to find the file. For example, the dunning file just described has the path \BUSINESS, which tells DOS or Word what directory to look in for the file.

 Tip: *A pathname points to the location of a file.*

Figure 5-1 depicts a hard-drive directory structure containing WORD, DOS, and BUSINESS directories. Note that this structure also includes a directory called PERSONAL, where you might keep personal Word DOC files.

 Tip: *The full name of a file includes the name of the drive and directory where it resides.*

The importance of file locations becomes evident when you want to save or load a file to another disk or directory. For example, if you are in the WORD directory and want to save the current file to floppy drive A, you would type **A:** in front of the filename. If you are loading a file from a directory other than the current one, you would type the directory name, a backslash, and then the filename.

 Trap: *To load files from another drive or directory, you must tell Word where the file is by specifying its path.*

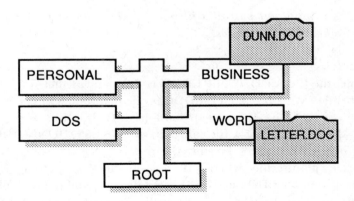

Figure 5-1. Hard-drive directory structure example

Note the use of the backslash and colon in Figure 5-2. The colon separates the drive device name from the filename, while the backslash separates the directory name from the filename.

 Trap: *You must follow the DOS rules for filenames and pathnames when loading files other than DOC files that are not in the current directory.*

Loading Files

You can load files either from the DOS prompt when you start Word or with the Transfer Load command in the Word command menu. The first method was covered in Chapter 2. When you type **WORD** at the DOS prompt, you can specify

Figure 5-2. *A filename consists of a name, extension, drive designator, and, if applicable, a directory*

the name of the file you want to work on. If the file exists, Word brings it into the edit window; if it doesn't exist, Word will display "Enter Y to create file" at the bottom of the screen.

 Trap: *Word may not have been able to find your file if you see the message "Enter Y to create file." Try specifying the pathname of the file.*

From Word, use the Transfer Load command to load an existing file. You would also use this command if you had cleared one file from the screen and wished to edit another. To access Transfer Load, simply place the highlight on the Transfer command and press ENTER or type **T** at the top-level command menu. Because the Load command is the proposed response for Transfer, you can point your mouse at the Transfer command and press the right mouse button to go directly to the Transfer Load option, as shown here:

```
TRANSFER LOAD filename: █                    read only: Yes(No)
Enter filename or press F1 to select from list
```

You can also press CTRL+F7 to access Transfer Load.

 Tip: *Click the right mouse button on Transfer to load a file or press CTRL+F7.*

At the Transfer Load option, Word asks you for a filename. Type in the filename if you know what it is. If not, you can press F1 to see a list. Mouse users can alternately point to the Filename field and click the right button to see the list, as shown here:

```
TRANSFER LOAD filename: ▚
```

 Tip: *Mouse users can click the right button on a filename to list the file.*

If a list of files appears when you press F1, you can use the arrow keys or the mouse to point to the file you want. Then press ENTER to load the file. If unsaved text appears in the edit window, Word will ask you if you want to save it before loading the new file.

 Trap: *Word won't load a new file unless existing text on the screen has been saved or cleared.*

The Transfer Load menu has a Read-Only field that you can use to load a file for viewing only. If this field is set to Yes when you load a file, you will not be able to save an edited or altered version of the file under the same name. When you attempt to save a read-only file, Word will ask you for a new filename. Once a file has been loaded as a read-only file, it maintains this status until changed at the DOS level. (This is covered later in this chapter.)

 Tip: *To protect a file, answer Yes in the Read-Only field of the Transfer Load command when loading.*

 Trap: *Read-only files can only be saved under a different name.*

 Trap: *Read-only files are permanently set that way unless altered with the DOS ATTRIB command.*

A principal reason for protecting files in this way is to create forms and standard document templates for repeated use. The original will always stay intact, while the altered version will be saved as a copy with a different filename.

 Tip: *Protect files that will be used as forms and standard document templates.*

Requesting a Specific File List

You can load any single file by simply typing its filename in the Transfer Load field. If the file is in another directory or drive, you must include the drive letter and directory name with the filename. If the file has an extension other than .DOC, you must use this method to load it because it will not appear on the file listing when you press F1.

Tip: *You can request files from other drives or directories.*

You can request a specific list of files at the Transfer Load command by using special *wildcard* characters or parts of filenames. The wildcard characters are the question mark (?) and asterisk (*). The question mark is used in place of any single character, while the asterisk can be used in place of multiple characters.

Tip: *Wildcard characters can be used to list specific files for loading.*

For example, typing **CHAPTER?** in the Transfer Load field would cause CHAPTER1.DOC, CHAPTER2.DOC, and CHAPTER3.DOC to be displayed if they existed on the drive. You can use the asterisk in place of a filename, part of a filename, or any extension. For example, type **FEB*.*** to display all files that start with FEB and have an extension. Once the list is displayed, you can use the arrow keys or mouse to select a file.

Wildcard characters in filenames are useful if you have a large list of files and want to display only part of it. Wildcards are also useful if you give your files extensions other than .DOC; for example, you can list files with the extension .DAT by typing ***.DAT** in the Transfer Load field.

Loading from Other Drives
and Directories

To view a list of files on another drive, simply type the drive letter with a colon in the Transfer Load field. Then press F1 or point with the mouse and press the right button.

 Tip: *To list files on other drives, type the drive letter in the Transfer Load field and press F1.*

The example shown here would list the files on drive A.

TRANSFER LOAD filename: A:

To view files in other directories and then select one from the list, enter the pathname to the desired directory. For example, to list files in the BUSINESS directory shown in Figure 5-1, you would type the path of the directory in the Transfer Load field and then press F1 or click with the right mouse button, as shown here:

TRANSFER LOAD filename: \BUSINESS

Once a file is loaded, the filename is retained in the Transfer Save field for all future save operations.

 Tip: *The name of a loaded file is retained during an editing session.*

 Trap: *To save an edited file under another name, be sure to change the existing filename so as not to copy over the original.*

Document Retrieval

Word's document retrieval techniques can help you find documents by searching through their text, which is useful if you have forgotten the name of a file but remember specific details about its content.

When a file is first saved, Word asks you to fill out a document summary sheet, assuming that Summary Sheets in the Options menu is set to Yes. When filling out the sheet, you can enter such information as author, operator, creation date, keywords, and comments. This information can then be searched later to help you locate files.

 Tip: *You can locate files with the Library Document Retrieval command.*

The document retrieval commands in Word are sophisticated. For example, you can use *logical operators* in the search routine to specify a date range, say, all files before December 15. You can also list files that contain specific keywords, such as the name of a company or legal case. (Document retrieval is covered in detail in Chapter 20.)

 Tip: *You can use logical operators during a document retrieval to locate files with a specific range of dates.*

Working with Two Files at Once

You can have two files on the screen at once by opening a second window. You can then scroll through one document while referring to another in the other window. You can even copy text from one document to the other. (This topic will be covered in detail in Chapters 7, 9, and 17.)

 Tip: *By using multiple windows, you can view more than one document at a time and copy between them.*

Merging Files

You can use the Transfer Merge command to combine two documents. After loading the first document in the usual way, select Transfer Merge and type in the name of the document you want to merge. This document is then merged into the existing one at the location of the highlight. You can use the merge features to combine blocks of text from separate files into one large file. A block of text might be a standard paragraph that you use in a form, letter, or legal document.

 Tip: *You can combine two files by using the Transfer Merge command.*

Locking Files

You can lock files from further editing or alterations by loading them into Word with the Read-Only field of Transfer Load set to Yes. Or you can lock a file without having to load it by using the DOS ATTRIB command. This command can only be used in the Library Run field because it is a DOS command. For example, to lock the file LETTER.DOC, you would type **ATTRIB +R LETTER. DOC** in the Library Run field.

ATTRIB sets a file's attribute to read-only or read/write. If you specify +R, the file becomes read-only; if you specify −R, the file returns to a read/write status so that it can be edited. The filename is specified after the +R or −R option. Note that you can save a protected file under a different name in order to leave your original file intact.

 Tip: *Protected files can be saved under a different filename, leaving the original intact.*

To unprotect a file, you can issue another ATTRIB command, this time specifying −R to remove the read-only status. You can use ATTRIB −R LETTER. DOC to unprotect files set by both the Transfer Load Read-Only feature and an ATTRIB +R command.

As mentioned, you can protect files that you want to use as standard document templates or as forms. For example, you could create a set of standard business forms for use in an office. Other operators could then enter information to each form but could not change the form itself. The write protection on the file will force other operators to save their edited version under a different name.

 Tip: *Write protection forces other operators to save an edited version of a template file under a different name, thus protecting your original.*

Saving Files

The first time you save a file, you must specify its filename unless you started Word by loading a file. Once a file is loaded, its filename is retained in the Transfer Save field as the proposed response. Word assumes that you want to save the file with the same name you loaded it with. The file save routines are located in the Transfer Save submenu. Type **T** or use the highlight to access the Transfer options. If you have a mouse, use the left button to select Transfer at the top-level command menu and then Save at the second-level menu. You will see the display shown here:

```
TRANSFER SAVE filename: █                    formatted:(Yes)No
Enter filename
```

 Tip: *The filenames of previously loaded files are retained in the Transfer Save field.*

Press CTRL+F10 to save a file under the name specified in the Transfer Save field. Don't use this quick key if you want to save a file under a different name.

 Tip: *Press CTRL+F10 to save a file.*

 Trap: *Don't use the quick key (CTRL+F10) if you want to save a file under a different name.*

If you have a floppy-drive system, Word normally stores files on a data disk in drive B. The SETUP program discussed in Chapter 1 lets you prepare a floppy disk for data storage. You may want to keep several diskettes handy for storing different types of files.

 Tip: *On floppy-drive systems, use different data diskettes to hold different types of files.*

 Tip: *On hard-drive systems, Word lets you organize and separate files into directories.*

On hard-drive systems you can have Word store files in other directories, or you can start Word from another directory (such as the BUSINESS or PERSONAL directory shown in Figure 5-1) and use the files in that directory. Remember that directories are separate storage areas, usually reserved for hard drives, where specific types of files are stored. You can save files in other directories by specifying the directory path in the Transfer Save commands. In the following example, the file LETTER.DOC is saved in the BUSINESS directory. Note that the path to the BUSINESS directory is specified in the filename.

```
TRANSFER SAVE filename: \BUSINESS\LETTER.DOC█        formatted:(Yes)No
```

 Trap: *Files are stored in the current directory unless you tell Word to save them elsewhere.*

Saving Plain Vanilla Files

If you respond No in the Formatted field of the Transfer Save command, the file will be saved as a plain ASCII file with no formatting. All reference to typefaces, type size, paragraph alignments, and margin settings will be lost. You might save a file in this format in order to use it in a word processing system that does not recognize Word's formatting code. You can also send an ASCII file over a phone modem for use on another system.

Word will ask if you are sure before it saves a file as nonformatted. You might want to type a different filename before saving a file in this way. Then you will have two copies, one with Word formats and the other as plain text.

 Trap: *Saving a file as nonformatted will cause all of its format and type style settings to be lost.*

 Tip: *If you need to use a file on another system, you may need to save a nonformatted copy of it.*

Filling Out Document Summaries

If you are saving a file for the first time, Word will display a document summary sheet into which you can enter information that will help you keep track of your files. Later, you can use this information to locate specific files by date, comments, or operator, as shown here:

```
SUMMARY INFORMATION
    title: TEST.DOC                     version number:
    author: TOM SHELDON                 creation date: 1/2/88
    operator: TS                        revision date: 1/2/88
    keywords: WORD BOOK
    comments: THIS FILE IS USED FOR TESTS ONLY█
```

 Tip: If you don't want to use document summaries, set the Options Summary Sheet to No.

 Trap: Use the DOWN ARROW key to get to the selections on the summary sheet, not the ENTER key.

Fill out as much of the information as possible on the summary sheet. You may not consider it useful at first, but after you have stored many files on your system, you will find the document summaries invaluable. Most people, especially hard-disk users, tend to leave files on their disk even after they are no longer useful. When cleanup time arrives, you can print the document summaries into a report that helps you locate files to be deleted.

 Tip: Document summaries are invaluable when it comes time to remove old files.

When to Save

Don't wait until you finish your document to save, unless you are working on a short memo. Save often by using the CTRL+F10 key combination. CTRL+F10 will save you from many headaches because once the file is on disk, it is fairly well protected from accidents of nature and of operators.

    If you live in an industrial area, where large machines turn on and off on a regular basis, save often to protect your documents from power drops and outages. If you have just finished writing a particularly creative passage for your next novel, SAVE! There is no rule about when to save; just do it often.

 Tip: Save often by pressing the CTRL+F10 key combination.

When Word Asks You to Save

When the message "SAVE" appears in the bottom line of your screen, immediately save your document. Word is running out of memory and can no longer manipulate your document properly. If you continue without saving, the "SAVE" message will start to blink. If you run out of memory completely, it may be impossible to save the document. Don't say they didn't warn you!

BAK Files

Every time a file is saved, the previous version is renamed with the extension .BAK instead of .DOC. So you always have the two latest versions of your file on disk, just in case you need the older one for some reason. Perhaps you made some editing changes that you decided you didn't want. You can still use the older version. The File Rename feature discussed next can be used to change the name of a BAK file to a DOC file. A different filename may be appropriate, depending on whether you want to maintain a copy of the most recent update.

 Tip: *The previous version of an edited file is saved with the extension .BAK.*

Though Word protects you by saving the previous version of your files with the .BAK extension, there are tradeoffs for this convenience. After a while, the BAK files begin to take up a lot of disk space, especially on diskettes. You should delete them after you are sure that they are no longer needed. To delete BAK files, type **DEL *.BAK** in the Library Run field.

 Trap: *BAK files tend to fill up your disk, so you should delete them every so often.*

Renaming Documents

The Transfer menu's Rename command allows you to give any file on your disk another name. This command duplicates the function of the RENAME command in DOS, so you can use either one. You may want to rename a file so that it more closely fits a group file-naming strategy, or you may want to rename a BAK file so that you can reuse it, as discussed previously. To rename a file, load it into the edit window, choose the Transfer Rename command, and type the new name in the field. This command also allows you to change the name of a current document if you wish.

 Tip: *You can rename files to fit them into a group file-naming strategy*

You can edit a BAK file by loading it and then using the Transfer Rename command to give it another name.

Managing Disk Space on Floppy-Drive Systems

Users of hard-drive systems seldom need to worry about running out of space, but users of floppy-drive systems must keep a close eye on the contents of their data disks, occasionally cleaning them up and removing unwanted files. The following section is meant for users of floppy drive systems.

Managing the Document Diskette

If you run out of space while saving a file, Word will display the message "Document disk full." This problem is not too serious because you can usually recover without losing a document, but it does cause some headaches. You can make room on the disk by deleting old files with the Transfer Delete command.

It's best to delete BAK files first, so at the Transfer Delete field, type *.**BAK** and press F1 to see a list of BAK files on the disk. Remove those that you no longer need. Also, keep an extra blank, formatted diskette that you can place in the drive if you find that deleting files is not practical.

 Trap: *When a disk becomes full, you cannot save files unless you remove others.*

 Tip: *Use the Transfer Delete command to remove old files.*

The best way to avoid filling up the document diskette is to have several on hand, each for a different type of file. Check the disk occasionally with the DOS CHKDSK command to see how much room is available. This command also performs some diagnostics.

 Tip: *Use the DOS CHKDSK command to check diskettes periodically for capacity and for problems.*

From the DOS level, type **CHKDSK B:** **/F** with the DOS disk in drive A and the Word data or program disk in drive B. You will be presented with a list showing the disk space utilization. Look at the space remaining. If the disk is almost full, either erase unwanted files or start with a new disk. An example of a CHKDSK screen display is shown in Figure 5-3. Notice that 362,496 bytes are on the disk, but only 2048 are available. This disk is out of room. Note that the last two lines of the display refer to the system memory, not the disk memory, and are not important in this discussion.

 Tip: *Floppy-disk users should always keep several formatted disks prepared for use.*

```
C:\>chkdsk b:
Volume PRINTER 1   created Sep 2, 1987 5:31p

  362496 bytes total disk space
       0 bytes in 1 hidden files
  360448 bytes in 57 user files
    2048 bytes available on disk

  655360 bytes total memory
  413760 bytes free
```

Figure 5-3. DOS CHKDSK command display example

Managing the Word Disk

If the Word program disk in drive A becomes full, you've got a little bigger headache. First, you will see the message "Word disk full" or "Scratch file full." To recover, perform the following steps in the order listed.

1. Copy a single character to the scrap. In other words, place the cursor on a space or period and press DEL. This may solve the problem if you had a large amount of text in the scrap.

2. Save all the current documents on the screen.

3. Save the style sheet if you are using one by selecting Gallery, Transfer Save, and then Exit.

4. Save the glossary if you are using one by selecting Transfer Glossary Save.

5. Select Transfer Clear All to clear out all memory; then reload your document and resume editing.

If you have persistent problems with filling up the Word disk, you may want to move the MW.HLP help file to another disk. If you later need help, simply place the disk containing the help file in drive A.

Printing Files

You can print a file at any time by using the Print command in the command menu. The proposed response for Print is to print, so you can select Print with the right mouse button to perform the operation directly. The Print submenu shown here has a range of other options.

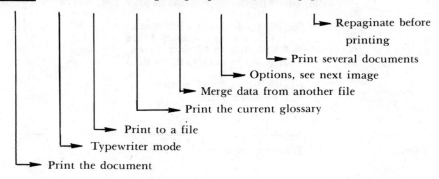

PRINT: Printer Direct File Glossary Merge Options Queue Repaginate

↳ Repaginate before printing

→ Print several documents

→ Options, see next image

→ Merge data from another file

→ Print the current glossary

→ Print to a file

→ Typewriter mode

→ Print the document

Loading, Saving and Printing Files

 Tip: *The Print menu lets you do more than simply print to a printer. You can save to files, merge files, print selected pages or selected text, and more.*

 Tip: *Print Direct lets you use your printer like a typewriter to address envelopes.*

To start printing, press ENTER from the submenu to select the Printer option. You could also "print" to a file by selecting the File option, which directs all output that would normally go to a printer into a file for later printing. Use this option if the printer is not available or if you will take a disk file to another system with a different printer. You can also print directly, as if your keyboard were in typewriter mode. The Options menu looks like this:

This menu lets you specify various options for printing, such as manual or continuous paper feed, the number of copies, and the pages to print, among other features. (The Print command will be covered in more detail in Chapter 19.)

To print a file, first load it into the Word edit window. A good one to print is the README.DOC file that comes with most versions of Word. This file usually contains most of the revisions or notes that should have been added to the manual but didn't make it. Press CTRL+F7 to access the Transfer Load menu and type **README.DOC** in the Filename field. If the file is not found, try another Word disk, or, with hard-drive systems, try specifying the WORD directory. Type **\WORD** in the Filename field and press F1 to see a list of files.

After the file is loaded, execute the Print Printer command by pressing CTRL+F8 or by going through the menu system. If the file does not print properly, you may need to set the correct printer in the Print Options Printer field.

 Trap: *File doesn't print? Make sure that your printer type is selected in the Print Options menu.*

 Tip: *Press CTRL+F8 to start printing a file.*

Tips and Traps Summary

What Is a File?

Tip: A filename is used to load and save files in Word.

Trap: Text on the screen may be lost unless saved to disk.

Trap: Always make backups of important files. Develop a backup strategy, making backups part of your regular routine.

Tip: Your backup procedure should comprise a regular daily, weekly, or monthly routine. Set up a schedule now.

Tip: Your program disk may contain many types of files. Only the document files are of interest in Word.

Tip: DOS can be considered a service level for your filing system.

Trap: Some DOS commands, such as ERASE and FORMAT, can be destructive. Refer to the DOS manual for full instructions.

Tip: DOS commands can be run from Word with the Library Run command.

File-Naming Strategies

Tip: Filenames consist of an eight-character filename and a three-character extension.

Tip: Word automatically assigns the extension .DOC to your files unless you specify otherwise.

Tip: DOC files can be grouped and copied together to other disks for backup or transport purposes.

Trap: Press F1 during a load to list DOC files. To see other files, you must specify the directory name.

Tip: Extensions help sort your files into categories and file types.

Tip: Placing a period after the filename will cause Word to not add an extension.

Tips and Traps Summary (*continued*)

Tip: An important part of a filename is the drive and directory where the file resides.

Tip: A pathname points to the location of a file.

Tip: The full name of a file includes the name of the drive and directory where it resides.

Trap: To load files from another drive or directory, you must tell Word where the file is by specifying its path.

Trap: You must follow the DOS rules for filenames and pathnames when loading files other than DOC files that are not in the current directory.

Loading Files

Trap: Word may not have been able to find your file if you see the message "Enter Y to create file." Try specifying the pathname of the file.

Tip: Click the right mouse button on Transfer to list a file or press CTRL+F7.

Tip: Mouse users can click the right button on a filename to list the file.

Trap: Word won't load a new file unless existing text on the screen has been saved or cleared.

Tip: To protect a file, answer Yes in the Read-Only field of the Transfer Load command when loading.

Trap: Read-only files can only be saved under a different name.

Trap: Read-only files are permanently set that way unless altered with the DOS ATTRIB command.

Tip: Protect files that will be used as forms and standard document templates.

Word: Secrets, Solutions, Shortcuts

Tips and Traps Summary (*continued*)

Tip: You can request files from other drives or directories.

Tip: Wildcard characters can be used to list specific files for loading.

Tip: To list files on other drives, type the drive letter in the Transfer Load field and press F1.

Tip: The name of a loaded file is retained during an editing session.

Trap: To save an edited file under another name, be sure to change the existing filename so as not to copy over the original.

Tip: You can locate files with the Library Document Retrieval command.

Tip: You can use logical operators during a document retrieval to locate files with a specific range of dates.

Tip: By using multiple windows, you can view more than one document at a time and copy between them.

Tip: You can combine two files by using the Transfer Merge command.

Tip: Protected files can be saved under a different filename, leaving the original intact.

Tip: Write protection forces other operators to save an edited version of a template file under a different name, thus protecting your original.

Saving Files

Tip: The filenames of previously loaded files are retained in the Transfer Save field.

Tip: Press CTRL+F10 to save a file.

Trap: Don't use the quick key save method (CTRL+F10) if you want to save a file under a different name.

Tip: On floppy-drive systems, use different data diskettes to hold different types of files.

Tips and Traps Summary (*continued*)

Tip: On hard-drive systems, Word lets you organize and separate files into directories.

Trap: Files are stored in the current directory unless you tell Word to save them elsewhere.

Trap: Saving a file as nonformatted will cause all of its format and type style settings to be lost.

Tip: If you need to use a file on another system, you may need to save a nonformatted copy of it.

Tip: If you don't want to use document summaries, set the Options Summary Sheet to No.

Trap: Use the DOWN ARROW key to get to the selections on the summary sheet, not the ENTER key.

Tip: Document summaries are invaluable when it comes time to remove old files.

Tip: Save often by pressing the CTRL+F10 key combination.

Tip: The previous version of an edited file is saved with the extension .BAK.

Trap: BAK files tend to fill up your disk, so you should delete them every so often.

Tip: You can rename files to fit them into a group file-naming strategy.

Managing Disk Space on Floppy-Drive Systems

Trap: When a disk becomes full, you cannot save files unless you remove others.

Tip: Use the Transfer Delete command to remove old files.

Tip: Use the DOS CHKDSK command to check diskettes periodically for capacity and for problems.

Tip: Floppy-disk users should always keep several formatted disks prepared for use.

Tips and Traps Summary (*continued*)

Printing Files

Tip: The Print menu lets you do more than simply print to a printer. You can save to files, merge files, print selected pages or selected text, and more.

Tip: Print Direct lets you use your printer like a typewriter to address envelopes.

Trap: File doesn't print? Make sure that your printer type is selected in the Print Options menu.

Tip: Press CTRL+F8 to start printing a file.

6

The Structure of
Word Documents

There can be a big difference between how your documents look on screen and how they look when printed. This can be seen in Figure 6-1. Because the type used to print the document differs from that of the Word edit window, it is hard to see on the screen exactly what your document will look like in final form. But Word provides many features that help you know in advance what your documents will look like. Paragraph end markers, tab markers, and soft carriage returns help you see how blocks of text are laid out. Word documents are also divided into elements that help you control page breaks, margins, and headers and footers. In addition, you can select specific text and apply character formats such as type styles and sizes.

This chapter will help you understand the underlying principles and elements of Word documents so that you can begin to use the program more efficiently and create the documents you need. This chapter presents an overview that will prepare you for future chapters where specific details about each element are covered. You can of course jump ahead to the chapters specified if you want to learn more right away.

Word: Secrets, Solutions, Shortcuts

```
[········1········2········3········4········5········]········7···]
Santa·Barbara,·CA·93101¶
¶
Dear·Mr.·Bagley,¶
¶
The·art·of·bonsai·reflects·a·spirit·of·nature.···It·can·take·
you·to·a·moss—carpeted·forest·or·a·spot·under·a·blossoming·
cherry·tree.···Trees·no·more·than·12·inches·tall·may·be·50·or·
100·years·old.···Yet·they·are·trees·that·maintain·their·
natural·dignity.···Bonsai·is·an·art·that·lets·you·bring·out·
the·nature·in·yourself·as·well·as·the·plants·you·cultivate.···¶
¶
You·are·invited·to·a·special·presentation·of·bonsai·on·
December·1·at·the·community·center.···The·schedule·will·begin·
promptly·at·10:00·AM.···Cameras·are·welcome.¶
¶
              10:00→      →     The·Style·of·Bonsai↓
              10:30→      →     Bonsai·Design↓
              11:00→      →     Creating·Your·Own·Bonsai↓
              11:30→      →     Question·and·Answer¶
                     ¶
We·hope·you·can·attend·our·presentation.¶
¶
                                            ═BONSAI.DOC═
Pg1 Li9 Co1        {¶}              ?         Microsoft Word
```

November 3, 1988

Mr. Richard Bagley
246 Ottoman Way
Santa Barbara, CA 93101

Dear Mr. Bagley,

The art of bonsai reflects a spirit of nature. It can take you to a moss-carpeted
forest or a spot under a blossoming cherry tree. Trees no more than 12 inches tall
may be 50 or 100 years old. Yet they are trees that maintain their natural dignity.
Bonsai is an art that lets you bring out the nature in yourself as well as the plants
you cultivate.

You are invited to a special presentation of bonsai on December 1 at the
community center. The schedule will begin promptly at 10:00 AM. Cameras are
welcome.

10:00	The Style of Bonsai
10:30	Bonsai Design
11:00	Creating Your Own Bonsai
11:30	Question and Answer

We hope you can attend our presentation.

Sincerely,

Shin Chin
Santa Barbara Bonsai Club

Figure 6-1.   The Word screen and the printed image

Elements of a Document

A Word document is divided into three basic elements. The largest, called a *division*, may span an entire document. *Paragraphs* make up the second element, and *characters* make up the third. Paragraphs are part of divisions and characters are part of paragraphs. This hierarchy is illustrated in Figure 6-2. Although you could divide just about any written or typed document into these three elements, in Word they are distinct units that you can manipulate with Word's commands. In fact, there are commands in Word's command menu dedicated to each of the elements.

 Tip: *Each element of a Word document has its own special set of Word commands in the command menu.*

The printed pages in Figure 6-2 represent one Word document broken into three distinct divisions. The first division is a cover letter with a 2-inch top margin to accommodate the logo on company stationery. The next two pages form a second division with normal margins for nonlogo stationery. *Running heads* in this division print the page number and date of the letter. The third division is a three-page report set in double-column format with headers at the top of each column describing the document.

The distinction between the division elements concerns the difference in margin size and the fact that the running heads are different for each. Paragraphs fit into the division elements as shown in Figure 6-2. For example, a table has been defined on page 2 of the document with paragraph formats. Character elements are part of paragraphs and can be formatted with type styles and type sizes. Figure 6-3 illustrates some of the variations available in each of Word's document elements.

Use division formatting when you are designing the *layout* of text on the entire page. A division can be either the entire document or a part of it, such as the table of contents, index, or glossary. Division formatting can describe the size of paper and where the text will be placed relative to the edges of the paper, as shown in Figure 6-4.

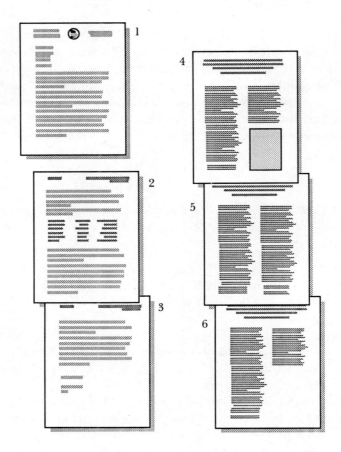

Page 1: Letterhead division
Pages 2 and 3: Letter division
Pages 4 through 6: Column division

Figure 6-2.   A six-page document with three divisions

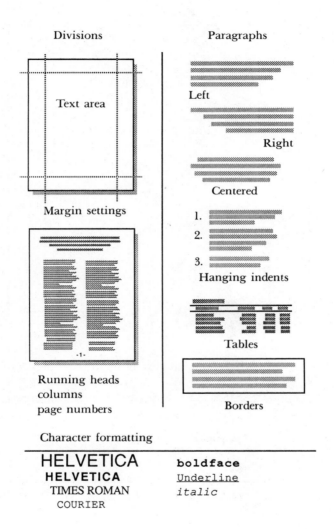

Divisions

Text area

Margin settings

Running heads
columns
page numbers

Character formatting

HELVETICA
HELVETICA
TIMES ROMAN
COURIER

Paragraphs

Left

Right

Centered

1.
2.
3.
Hanging indents

Tables

Borders

boldface
<u>Underline</u>
italic

Figure 6-3. A sampling of division, paragraph, and character elements

Word: Secrets, Solutions, Shortcuts

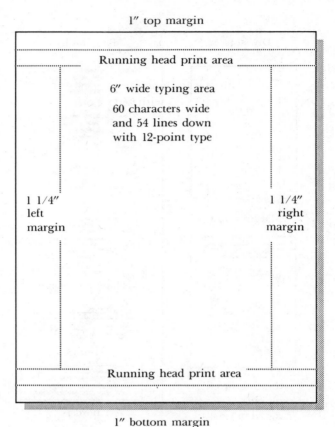

1″ top margin

Running head print area

6″ wide typing area

60 characters wide
and 54 lines down
with 12-point type

1 1/4″
left
margin

1 1/4″
right
margin

Running head print area

1″ bottom margin

Paper size: 8 1/2″ x 11″

Figure 6-4. Page elements determined by division formats

Division formatting can also describe the layout of columns of text. An index, for instance, might be printed in multiple columns. Footnotes and running heads (headers and footers) are set up with the Division Formatting command.

 Tip: *Division formatting describes how text will fit on the pages.*

Paragraph formatting deals primarily with how paragraphs look. Paragraphs are "molded" within the margin setting of the Format Division command, so paragraphs are a subset of divisions. You can justify paragraphs to the left or right or both. You can also center them, add special indents, or alter the line spacing. Finally, you can control where a paragraph will break if it falls near the end of a page. The important thing to remember is that each paragraph can be different. Paragraph elements always end with a paragraph marker, which is displayed when the ENTER key is pressed.

 Tip: *Paragraphs describe how blocks of text are "molded" within the boundaries of the page.*

Character formatting deals with the type fonts, sizes, and styles. Individual characters, words, sentences, paragraphs, and divisions of your document can be enhanced with character formatting.

 Tip: *Character formatting improves the look of text by specifying different type fonts, sizes, and styles.*

Document Divisions

A division represents a group of pages in a document with the same paper size, margins, running heads, column layout, page-numbering scheme, and footnote scheme (refer back to Figure 6-4). Running heads (often called headers and footers) are printed outside of the normal margins and may contain titles, page numbers, dates, and other information.

 Tip: *Running heads are printed outside of the text area defined by the margin settings and may contain page numbers, dates, titles, and other information.*

All documents have at least one division preassigned by Word when you begin. This standard division has preset values that you can view by displaying the Format Division Margins menu, as shown here:

```
FORMAT DIVISION MARGINS top: 1"    bottom: 1"       left: 1.25"  right: 1.25"
                    page length: 11"    width: 8.5"     gutter margin: 0"
                running-head position from top: 0.5"    from bottom: 0.5"
Enter measurement
```

Note the settings for top, bottom, left, and right margins as well as for page size and running-head position.

 Tip: *You can view division formatting by displaying the Format Division Margins menu.*

Changing any feature in the Format Division Margins menu will cause a *division marker* to appear, even if you are using only one division. Figure 6-5 shows what happens when you change both the left and right margins to 2 1/2 inches. Pressing ENTER causes the new changes to execute, and the double line of dots that is the division marker appears. It is important to remember that a division is above the division marker, not below it.

 Tip: *The first time you alter a division setting in a document, the division marker (row of colons) will appear at the bottom of the document.*

 Trap: *Remember that a division is above the division marker, not below it.*

Remember, too, that the division marker holds the formatting information for the division. If you delete it, you will lose the formats.

Trap: *Never delete a division marker unless you are sure that you want to lose division formats.*

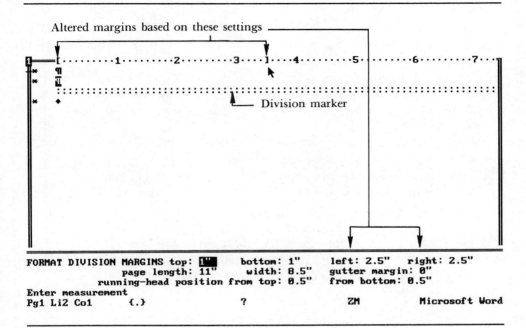

Figure 6-5. A division marker

Most of your documents will probably have only one division. A single-page letter, for example, may only require one division. Remember that a division format defines page layout, so single-page and most multiple-page documents may require only one division.

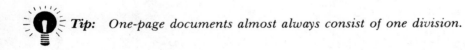

Tip: *One-page documents almost always consist of one division.*

Let's look briefly at the page layout options that you can set with the Format Division command menus. (Chapter 12 covers these topics in more detail.) The options available in the Format Division Margins menu are covered first.

Paper Size

Different paper sizes can be specified in the Format Division Margins menu. You can change to legal-size paper or any special size that you need. Notice that margins are set as the distance from each edge of the paper, so you may not need to change the margin settings every time you change the page size. Figure 6-6 illustrates some standard paper sizes with typical margins (see Chapter 12 for more details).

 Tip: *Margins are set from the edge of the paper. If you change paper size, you may not need to change the margins.*

 Trap: *A page break appears in the edit window as a row of single dots, not to be confused with a division break, which appears as a row of double dots, or colons.*

Margins

You can adjust margins in the Format Division Margins menu by resetting the distance from the edge of the paper or envelope to the edge of the desired printing area. Think in terms of the distance from the text edge to the paper edge rather than the width of the text area. If you must think in terms of the text area, however, subtract its width from the width of the paper and then split this amount for the left and right margin settings. They needn't be equal, of course; you can have a 1-inch left margin and a 1 1/2-inch right margin. Also, begin to think in terms of decimal numbers, not fractions. A 1 1/4-inch margin becomes 1.25 inches; a 1 3/4-inch margin becomes 1.75 inches.

 Tip: *Think about the distance from the paper edge to the text edge, not the width of the text area, when setting margins.*

One reason that Word uses this edge-to-edge distance measure for mai s instead of the width of the typing area is to make it easy to change paper size. Switching to legal-size paper, for example, is a matter of changing the paper length settings in the Format Divisions Margins menu to 14 inches. A 1-inch bottom margin will work fine on either legal- or letter-size paper.

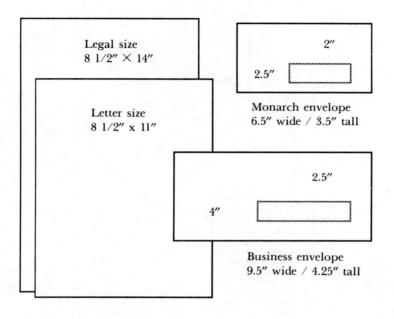

Figure 6-6. Typical paper and envelope sizes

 Tip: *Changing paper sizes requires a paper size adjustment but not necessarily a margin adjustment.*

Binding Space: The Gutter Margin

As shown in Figure 6-7, the *gutter margin* is a space that allows for binding a printed document. If your document will be three-hole punched or bound by some other method, you can allow for the binding by setting an appropriate gutter size. A gutter of 1/2 inch is usually enough for three-ring bindings. You'll only need gutters if your pages will be printed back-to-back, as shown in Figure 6-7. Word automatically places the gutter on the left side for odd-numbered front pages and on the right for even-numbered back pages.

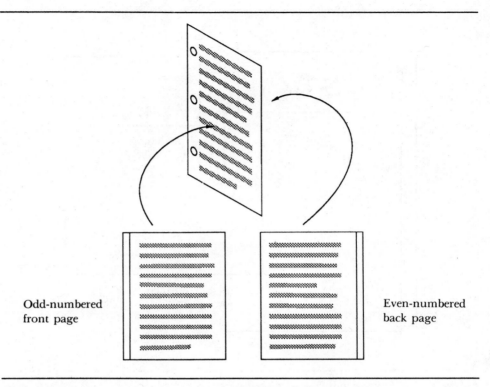

Figure 6-7.   Gutters provide space for binding holes

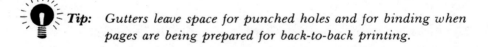

Tip: *Gutters leave space for punched holes and for binding when pages are being prepared for back-to-back printing.*

Keep in mind that a gutter will reduce the width of the printed text. For example, if you set the left and right margins at 1 inch and then set a gutter of 1 inch, normal, nonindented text areas will be 5 1/2-inches wide.

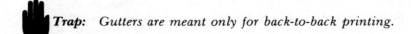

Trap: *Gutters are meant only for back-to-back printing.*

Page Captions: Running Heads

A running head is a line or two of text above or below the text body where titles and page numbers can be placed. These lines are called running heads because once set up, they will print on every page. You can turn printing on the front page off or on depending on whether it is a title page. Running heads can also be staggered left or right on the page depending on whether it is an even- or odd-numbered page. Running heads are often referred to as *headers* or *footers*.

 Tip: *Running heads print on each page of the division except the first, if specified.*

The Format Division Margins menu lets you determine how far from the top or bottom a running head will be placed on the paper.

 Tip: *The exact location of a running head is measured from the left and top edges of the paper.*

You must use the Format Running-Head menu, shown here, to tell Word whether the running head will be at the top or bottom of the page.

```
FORMAT RUNNING-HEAD position: Top Bottom
      odd pages:(Yes)No  even pages:(Yes)No  first page: Yes(No)
```

You can also use the Format Running-Head menu to tell Word that you want the running head to be printed on just the odd pages, just the even pages, or both. In this way left pages can have a document title and page number, while right pages can have a chapter or section title and page number.

You can locate a running head anywhere on the page because running heads are measured from the edge of the paper, not from within the division margins. You can place running heads on the top, bottom, left, or right of a sheet.

 Trap: *Do not measure running heads from within the margins.*

You can place page numbers in a running head by expanding the Page glossary entry. If you do not use a running head, you can insert page numbers by using the Format Division Page-Numbers menu. In Chapters 12 and 15 you'll learn about Word's Glossary feature. It contains glossary entries that can automatically insert the current page number, date, or time when you type the keyword *page, date,* or *time* and then press the F3 glossary expansion key. This will save you some typing. You'll also see how to create your own glossaries to store commonly used text.

Page Numbering

There are two ways to place page numbers in your documents. One method is to use a running head with a page number in it, as discussed earlier. The other method is to use the Format Division Page-Numbers menu. Though both have their advantages, you will probably prefer to place your page numbers using the running-heads method.

 Tip: *Page numbers can be included in running heads or at an exact location on the page*

When using the Format Division Page-Numbers method of placing a page number, the following are true:

- Printing on the first page of a document cannot be suppressed.
- Extra steps must be taken to assign a format such as a type font to the page numbers.
- The location of the page number is not visible until printing.
- Printing alternately on left and right for front and back pages cannot be controlled.

With all these problems, it may seem useless to even consider using the Format Division Page-Numbers menu to set your page numbers. The one redeeming factor is that this method is the quickest way to place a page number, assuming that you don't care about its style and don't need to control first-page and back-to-back printing.

 Trap: *Control of style and layout is limited when you use the Format Division Page-Numbers command to set page numbers.*

To place page numbers with the Format Division Page-Numbers command, you must specify the exact location on the page where the number will appear. The margin settings do not affect the measurements that you supply for the location of the page number. The page number setting, illustrated here, represents its exact location on the paper from the top and left edges (see Figure 6-8).

```
FORMAT DIVISION PAGE-NUMBERS: Yes No    from top: 0.5"    from left: 7.25"
           numbering:(Continuous)Start   at:          number format:(1)I i A a
```

Unlike margin settings, you need only supply two measurements to specify the location of a page number. It is always measured from the left and top edges of the paper. If, for example, you wanted to place a page number in the lower-right corner aligned with a 1-inch right margin, you would type **10.5"** in the From Top field and **7.25"** in the From Left field. Note that a From Left of 7.25 inches was specified instead of 7.5 inches to allow the right side of the printed number to approximately align with the right margin.

 Tip: *Page numbers are measured from the top and left edges of the paper.*

You can also use the page-numbering menu to specify the starting number for page numbers. If your file is part of a group of files that make up a book or report, you may want to start numbering where you left off earlier. You can also specify the type of numbering, such as Arabic, Roman, or alphabetical. (Refer to Chapter 12 for more details.)

 Tip: *Page numbers can begin with any number to account for multiple sections or chapters.*

Chapter 6, Page 15 — Page number as part of running head

15 — Individual page number measured from top and from left paper edge

Figure 6-8.   Page number locations may vary

Footnotes

You handle footnotes in Word much as you would manually. Manually, you might make a numeric note in your manuscript and then write the text on a card. The cards for the footnotes on each page are then assembled and the footnote text is added to the bottom of the page or to the end of the manuscript when it is typed. Word's footnoting capabilities are similar.

In Word the Format Footnote command is used when you want to make a footnote reference at a particular point in your text. Word automatically keeps track of footnote reference numbers and allows you to type the footnote text in a special window. When you have entered the footnote text, Word returns you to your document so that you can continue typing. The whole process can be completely automatic. Figure 6-9 shows how footnotes appear in the edit window and on the printed page.

```
SP  Advances·in·imaging·technology·have·recently·allowed·
    observations·of·galaxies·in·a·very·primitive·stage·of·
    development.···A·new·type·of·infrared·array·detector,·
    developed·at·the·University·of·Arizona,·compresses·more·
    than·4000·individual·detectors·into·one·camera.···One·
    nights·observations·are·equivalent·to·4000·nights·of·
    observations·using·older·single·element·detectors.1·
──[─────────1─────────2─────────3─────────4─────────5───]────6─────────7───
·*  1·D.E.·Thomsen,·"Galaxies·in·a·Primitive·State?"·
    Science·News,·133·(January·23,·1988),·52.
```

Advances in imaging technology have recently allowed observations of galaxies in a very primitive stage of development. A new type of infrared array detector, developed at the University of Arizona, compresses more than 4000 individual detectors into one camera. One nights observations are equivalent to 4000 nights of observations using older single element detectors.[1]

---

[1] D.E. Thomsen, "Galaxies in a Primitive State?" Science News, 133 (January 23, 1988), 52.

Figure 6-9.   Footnotes as they appear on the screen and when printed

 Tip: *Word accumulates footnotes in a special footnote window so that they can be printed at the bottom of each page or at the end of the document.*

Word keeps track of the page that a footnote will print on, even if the footnote reference mark is pushed to a new page by inserted text. The footnote window appears at the bottom of the edit window. The footnote references in this window change as you scroll from page to page. You can print the footnote text at the end of the document by selecting the appropriate field in the Format Division Layout menu as shown here:

`FORMAT DIVISION LAYOUT footnotes:` `Same-page` `End`

Refer to Chapter 12 for more details.

 Tip: *Word moves footnote text to the page where the footnote reference is located.*

Newspaperlike Columns

You can set up newspaperlike multiple columns by making changes to the Format Division Layout menu. An interesting thing happens when you select multiple-column layout, as shown in Figure 6-10. The text visible in the edit window narrows to a width that Word calculates according to the number of columns you choose. The document becomes twice as long in Word's memory, and as you scroll through the text, you will see what appear to be twice as many pages (page breaks are shown as a row of single dots across the screen). Word places two of these screen pages side by side on a printed page.

 Tip: *Newspaperlike columns can be used to create newsletters. Space for pictures and artwork is easy to manage.*

Column layout is handled through the Format Division Layout menu, as shown here:

```
FORMAT DIVISION LAYOUT footnotes:(Same-page)End
         number of columns: 1      space between columns: 0.5"
            division break:(Page)Continuous Column Even Odd
```

Simply select the number of columns and the spacing between them, and Word will handle the column sizing automatically. The bottom line of the menu lets you insert a column break so that a photograph or illustration can be inserted.

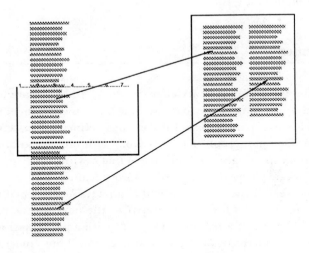

Figure 6-10. Newspaperlike column layouts as they appear on the screen and when printed

Line-Numbering Documents

Legal documents often require line numbers on the left margin of the page. You can number each line, every other line, or use any increment you want. Use the Format Division Line-Numbering menu to select line numbering, as shown here:

```
FORMAT DIVISION LINE-NUMBERS: Yes No        from text: 0.4"
        restart at:(Page)Division Continuous    increments: 1
```

Select Yes; then specify how far the line number will be from the right margin and whether the numbers will be continuous throughout the entire document or restart at 1 for each new page or each new division. (Refer to Chapter 12 for more details.)

Tip: *Line numbers can be printed beside every line or in any increment you wish.*

Paragraph Elements

Paragraphs are the most uncustomary elements in Word. They are blocks of text to which you can apply various formats, such as alignments, indents, line spacing, and spacing between paragraphs. Tabs are also defined for paragraphs, not as part of a division. One paragraph may be a table with tabs set to align columns, while the next paragraph might have tabs set so that outlines or lists can be typed. You can box a paragraph by using Word's Border feature, and you can control where paragraphs break if they are at the end of a page. As discussed previously, a paragraph is a long string of text that "wraps" to the next line as you approach the right margin. The end of a paragraph is "set" with a paragraph marker when you press ENTER. If you think of a paragraph as one long line that has been "folded up," you'll begin to see its significance. For example, you can place the highlight on any character in a paragraph and apply formats such as indents. Pointing in the style bar with a mouse and pressing the right button causes a whole paragraph to be selected.

Table formatting is one of the most important reasons for keeping text together in paragraph form. Moving tab stops assigned to a paragraph is an easy way to move a column of numbers, assuming that each line of the table is also part of the paragraph. To keep separate lines of a table together as part of a single paragraph, you must use a soft carriage return (SHIFT+ENTER).

 Tip: *Tab settings are part of paragraph formatting, not division formatting. Thus each paragraph can have its own tab settings.*

It's important that you don't mix up the features and concepts of paragraphs with those of divisions. You can prevent a lot of headaches and menu "searching" by remembering the elements controlled by divisions and those controlled by paragraphs and the menus where the formatting options for each are located. Let's look at different ways to work with paragraphs, starting with alignment.

 Trap: *Paragraphs are a subcategory of divisions, but they have their own set of formatting commands.*

Aligning Paragraphs

Once you have set your left and right margins, any text that you type will fall in the space between them. How the text aligns to these margins is the topic of this section. Each paragraph of your document can align differently, depending on how you set it. But if you keep typing new paragraphs after assigning a special paragraph alignment format, each subsequent paragraph will retain that formatting until you change it. In other words, the ENTER key continues the previous paragraph's formatting.

 Tip: *Press ENTER to start a new paragraph with the same formats as the last.*

Think of the paragraph marker as the holder of paragraph formats. Figure 6-11 shows how the paragraph marker indicates the paragraph alignment. If you

```
[········1·········2·········3·········4········5···]···6·········7···
This·paragraph·is·flush·with·the·left·margin,··The·
right·margin·is·ragged.¶
¶
This·paragraph·retains·the·same·formatting·as·the·above·
paragraph,··The·paragraph·marker·from·the·previous·
paragraph·carries·the·formatting·to·new·paragraphs.¶
¶
    Alt+R·was·pressed·before·typing·this·paragraph,··It·is·
    aligned·flush·with·the·right·margin·and·ragged·on·the·
                                                  left.¶
                                                     ¶
        Now,·all·new·paragraphs·are·flush·right·until·a·new·
                                  format·is·applied.¶
                                                  ¶
            Alt+C·was·typed·to·center·this·line.¶
                          ¶
                          ¶
```

Figure 6-11. Paragraph alignment examples

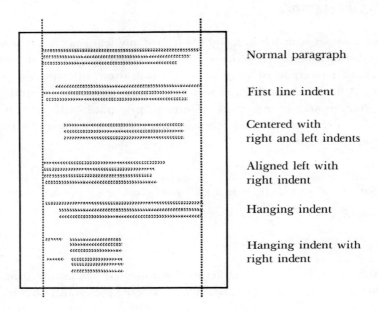

Normal paragraph

First line indent

Centered with
right and left indents

Aligned left with
right indent

Hanging indent

Hanging indent with
right indent

Figure 6-12.   Paragraph indenting examples

insert text on any of the solitary paragraph markers, like those below the bottom line, a new paragraph will be created with the centered alignment of the previous one. However, you can change paragraph alignment whenever you wish. Figure 6-12 shows a few possibilities.

 Tip: *The paragraph marker holds the paragraph formats.*

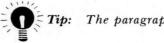 *Trap:*   *Deleting a paragraph marker may cause a loss of formats.*

Aligning with the Menu or with Quick Keys   You can assign alignment formatting to paragraphs in two ways. The fastest and simplest way is to use the keyboard combination keys. For example, ALT+C centers a paragraph, while ALT+J applies left and right justification.

Trap: *You may need to press ALT+X+C or ALT+X+J if a style sheet is attached.*

The other way to assign alignments is through the Format Paragraph menu, as shown here:

```
Paragraph alignment options ──────────┐
                                       │
FORMAT PARAGRAPH alignment: ▐Left▌ Centered Right Justified
    left indent: 0"           first line: 0"        right indent: 0"
    line spacing: 1 li        space before: 2 li    space after: 1 li
    keep together: Yes(No)    keep follow:(Yes)No    side by side: Yes(No)
```

You may prefer this method if you are assigning several formats to a document at once, such as alignments, indents, and page break specifications.

Tip: *Use the Format Paragraph menu if you are assigning several formats at once.*

Indents

Indents can be applied to paragraphs in combination with alignment commands if you wish. Figure 6-12 illustrates several possibilities. Note that some of the hanging indents have the same formats. They just look different because of the text used.

To apply indents to any paragraph, you can use the keyboard direct formatting keys or the Format Paragraph menu as shown here:

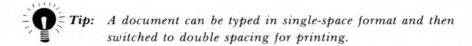

```
FORMAT PARAGRAPH alignment: Left Centered Right Justified
    left indent: 0"          first line: 0"          right indent: 0"
    line spacing: 1 li        space before: 2 li      space after: 1 li
    keep together: Yes(No)    keep follow:(Yes)No     side by side: Yes(No)
```
└─ Paragraph indenting options

The quick keys are best for indenting a paragraph "on the fly." You can start a new paragraph and quickly indent it for emphasis or add a hanging indent for numbered lists. The menu method is best when several options must be set at the same time.

Controlling Line Spacing

You can easily control whether your documents have single, double, or other spacings, as well as the number of spaces before and after a paragraph. Normally, you will want to type documents in single-space format so that you can see more of the text on your screen. When you're ready to print, simply alter the spacing to double-space format or the spacing of your choice.

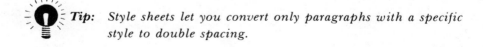

Tip: *A document can be typed in single-space format and then switched to double spacing for printing.*

Problems occur with this method when blocks of text must retain single spacing. You must go back in and individually select and reformat these paragraphs to single spacing.

Another method, called style sheets, allows you to assign codes to each paragraph. Then you can simply change the style code to alter all paragraphs that are assigned a particular code. (Style sheets will be covered in detail in Chapter 16.)

Tip: *Style sheets let you convert only paragraphs with a specific style to double spacing.*

Word will automatically insert spaces between paragraphs. You can specify a line space setting in the Space Before and Space After options of the Format Paragraph menu to separate paragraphs automatically. Then you won't have to press ENTER twice after every paragraph. Word also manages page breaks better when spacing is assigned to the paragraphs rather than entered by the user. The Format Paragraph menu is shown here, with line-spacing options specified in the third line.

```
FORMAT PARAGRAPH alignment: Left Centered Right Justified
      left indent: 0"          first line: 0"        right indent: 0"
     line spacing: 1 li        space before: 0 li    space after: 0 li
      keep together: Yes(No)   keep follow: Yes(No)  side by side: Yes(No)
```
Line-spacing options

Tip: *Word will automatically insert spaces between paragraphs.*

Controlling End-of-Page Breaks

You probably won't ever want to print the first or last line of a paragraph alone on a page. Word will automatically prevent these *widow* and *orphan* paragraph breaks if you set the Print Options Widow/Orphan Control field to Yes. If you wanted to print as many lines on a page as possible, change this option to No.

Tip: *Word can prevent a single line of a paragraph from being printed by itself on another page.*

You can further control how Word breaks pages by setting the Keep Together and Keep Follow options in the Format Paragraph menu, as shown here:

```
FORMAT PARAGRAPH alignment: Left Centered Right Justified
      left indent: 0"          first line: 0"        right indent: 0"
      line spacing: 1 li       space before: 0 li    space after: 0 li
     keep together: Yes(No)    keep follow: Yes(No)  side by side: Yes(No)
```
Paragraph page break controls

The Keep Together option allows you to specify that a paragraph or table be printed completely on one page. Specifying Yes will cause Word to move the paragraph or table to the next page if there is not enough room to print it on the current page, thus leaving a large blank space.

 Tip: *You can ensure that a paragraph or table will be printed completely on one page.*

The Keep Follow field of the Format Paragraph command provides control over how two paragraphs are printed together. Occasionally, you may want to keep part of one paragraph together with a following paragraph if it must be moved to the next page. You can also use this option to make sure that section titles are kept with the first paragraph of the section. Specifying Yes in this option causes Word to print the last two lines of the first paragraph on the second page if the first two lines of the second paragraph do not fit on the first page (see Figure 6-13).

 Tip: *You can ensure that two paragraphs are printed together on a page.*

Printing Side-by-Side Text

You can align blocks of text side by side in Word to show various relationships or print short tables of information. Side-by-side text should not be confused with newspaperlike columns, discussed earlier. In newspaperlike columns most of the text or the whole document is printed as columns on the paper. The side-by-side option is designed for printing short blocks of text next to each other on a page that normally has single-column text.

 Trap: *Don't confuse side-by-side layout with newspaperlike column layout. Side-by-side formatting is for small blocks in the middle of normal text. Newspaperlike columns can run for several pages.*

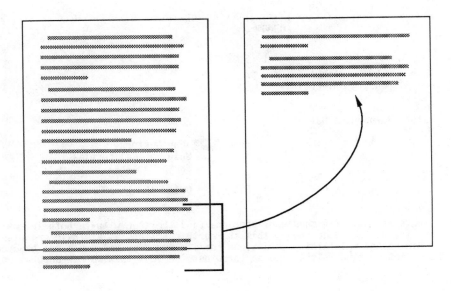

Figure 6-13.   *Word can keep parts of two paragraphs together on a second sheet if they don't fit together on one*

Figure 6-14 shows how side-by-side text is developed on the screen and how it appears when printed. Setting up side-by-side text requires a few steps. First, answer Yes to the side-by-side option in the Format Paragraph menu and type the text of the paragraphs, alternating between the left and right text. Then adjust the right indent to the left for the left text and adjust the left indent to the right for the right text. The indent, especially the one for the right column, determines where on the page the columns will print.

Tip: *In side-by-side text indents determine where on the page each block of text will be printed.*

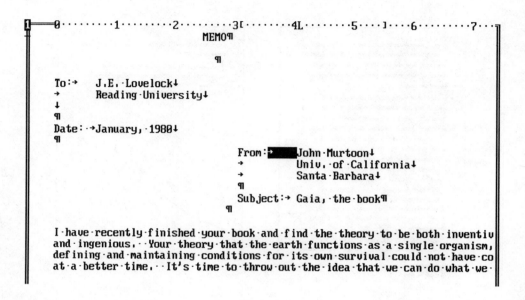

Figure 6-14.   Side-by-side paragraphs as they appear on the screen and when printed

An easy way to set up multiple side-by-side columns is to create a short side-by-side template, apply the necessary formats to it, and then duplicate it as often as needed. Last, add the necessary text to each duplicate to fit your needs. (This will be covered in detail in Chapter 13.)

 Tip: *To make side-by-side text easier to use, set up a small block of side-by-side text and then duplicate it for each set you need.*

Microsoft now supplies a set of styles for setting up double or triple side-by-side paragraphs (see Chapter 13).

Tab Stops and Table Creation

Tabs in Word are similar to what you may be familiar with on typewriters. Pressing the TAB key causes the cursor to jump to one of Word's preset tab stops at 1/2-inch intervals. You can readjust Word's tab stops in order to align paragraphs or create tables. Pressing the TAB key causes a small arrow to be displayed on the screen if you have the Options Visible field set to complete.

 Tip: *Word comes with preset tab stops that you can adjust to fit your needs.*

A table is a group of separate lines that form a paragraph. Special tab settings are normally used to align text or numbers into columns, but you must maintain the integrity of a tabled paragraph so that the tab settings can be adjusted as needed.

 Tip: *Always use tabs when creating tables. Never use the SPACEBAR.*

When a tab setting is adjusted, each line in a column will readjust itself to the new setting, assuming that the lines are part of the paragraph. Word even has a special Column Select feature. You can select a block of text as a column, move it to the other side of another column, adjust its position, or simply delete it. You can even perform math operations on selected columns.

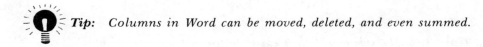

Tip: *Columns in Word can be moved, deleted, and even summed.*

Tabs are set in the Format Tab Set menu, as shown here:

```
FORMAT TAB SET position: ▌
        alignment:(Left)Center Right Decimal Vertical    leader char:(Blank). - _
```

Type the position in the Position field or use the mouse to point to the position in the ruler at the top of the screen and then press the left mouse button.

The five tab alignment possibilities are shown next. Each tabbed item is aligned against the 1-inch tab setting.

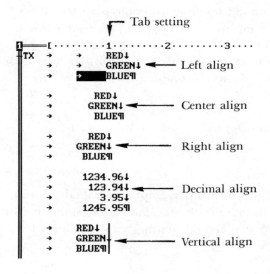

Tab Leaders   Word allows you to specify *leader* characters with your tabs, making it easy to print guide lines to numbers or items in tables or text. Figure 6-15 shows how Word's tab leader characters can be used to print a table of contents, a form, or an agenda.

```
¶                                                  ┌── Dot tab leader
Hiking the Urban Wilderness.....┊.......43¶
Primitive Food Restaurants.............55¶
¶
┴                    ┌── Underscore tab leader
Name: _____┊_____  Age: ____¶
Address: _____¶
City: _____  State: ____¶
¶
¶                    ┌── Dashed tab leader
Section 1 ─────────┊─── Al Stone¶
Section 2 ──────────── Judy Booth¶
Section 3 ──────────── Jim Martin¶
¶
```

Figure 6-15. Tab leader examples

Borders and Boxes Around Paragraphs

You can place borders around your text and tables, assuming two things. First, a border can only be placed around a complete paragraph, so you must use the SHIFT+ENTER (soft carriage return) key combination or word wrap to group all text together that will receive the border.

Trap: A border can only be placed around a complete paragraph.

Tip: Press SHIFT+ENTER to create blocks of text that you want to surround with borders.

Second, your printer must be able to print the border characters produced on the screen. Many dot-matrix printers have a special IBM-compatible graphics mode that can be used when printing borders. If you have a Hewlett-Packard LaserJet Series II printer, you must obtain special printer drivers from Microsoft unless you have the latest version which includes them. The names of the drivers start with H2 instead of HP. (See Chapter 19 for more details.)

Figure 6-16 shows two examples of borders, with the Format Border menu open at the bottom of the screen. The second paragraph uses hanging indents and soft carriage returns to include space between the text and border.

 Tip: *A hanging indent in the first line allows space between text and the left border.*

The Format Border menu includes an option to surround paragraphs with single, bold, or double-line boxes. In addition, lines can be placed on any one side or a combination of sides of the paragraph. Word keeps bordered paragraphs together on the same page when they are printed. (This will be covered in detail in Chapter 11.)

 Tip: *Lines can be placed around any side of a paragraph.*

 Tip: *Bordered paragraphs are never split across pages.*

Character Elements

The last elements of Word documents are the characters themselves. Character elements are part of both paragraphs and divisions, so the need to differentiate between these parts of Word documents diminishes. Single characters, words, and sentences as well as paragraphs, groups of paragraphs, and divisions all take part in character formatting. In other words, you can select any of these groups and apply formatting to it.

You must learn how to apply character formats and keep in mind the difference between how they appear on your screen and how they appear on the printed page. First, character formatting can only be applied to highlighted text.

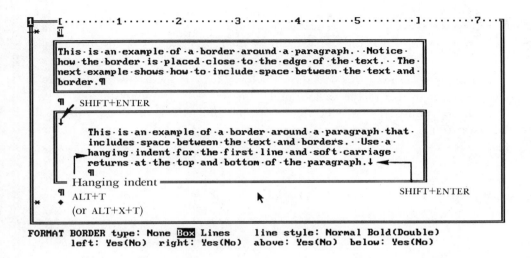

Figure 6-16. Bordered paragraph examples

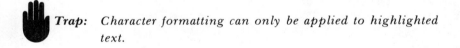

Trap: *Character formatting can only be applied to highlighted
text.*

This differs from applying such paragraph formats as alignment and indents,
where you simply point anywhere in the paragraph. To format a word, you must
move it with the arrow keys and press F7 or F8 to highlight it or right click the
word with the mouse. You can then apply the formatting either with the quick
keys or through a menu. For example, to apply italic formatting, you could press
ALT+I (or ALT+X+I) or use the Format Character menu after selecting the word.

How formatted characters appear on your screen depends on the type of monitor you have and the display mode set in the options menu. If you are in full
graphics mode on a graphics monitor, characters formatted in italics will appear

in true italic form, as shown here:

```
║TX   An·italic·formatted·word·displays·in·italics·on·
║     graphics·screens:··ITALICS,·italics¶                    Highlight the characters
║TX   ¶                                                           to be formatted
```

Other types of monitors will show the formatting either as underlined or in a color other than that of the background window.

Though your screen may be able to display some characters the way they will be printed, this is not true when you apply type fonts and size variations of these fonts.

 Trap: *Fonts and font size variations are not shown on monospaced character screens.*

Most screens display *monospaced* characters that resemble the Courier font. Monospaced characters are all the same width; for example, *i* is as wide as *m*. If you change to a *proportionally* spaced font such as Helvetica or Times Roman, where each character is assigned a special width, you will no longer be able to accurately see on the screen how the final printed document will look. Compare the examples shown in Figure 6-17 to see how characters appear on the screen and how they appear when printed. Here, a Times Roman, 12-point italic font was applied to the text. Notice the difference in appearance and the location of the line breaks on the printed page compared to the screen.

 Trap: *When you use proportional fonts, the screen cannot show how the text will look when printed.*

Figure 6-18 shows how three font styles compare to each other in printed form. Note that the Courier characters are monospaced and closely resemble those on the screen, while the other fonts are proportionally spaced, so each character is of a different width.

Because proportionally spaced fonts create random line widths, you often cannot tell how your document will look until printed. But you can get a rough idea of where line breaks will occur by setting the Options "print display" field to

```
‖TX  ¶
‖TX  This ·paragraph ·will ·be ·printed ·in ·Times ·Roman ·
     12 ·point · italic. · ·Note ·that ·only ·italics ·
     appears ·on ·the ·screen.¶
‖TX  ¶
```

This paragraph will be printed in Times Roman 12 point italic. Note that only italics appears on the screen.

Figure 6-17.   Font styles as they appear on graphics screens and when printed

Yes. This will cause the monospaced fonts on the screen to extend past the margin, showing where line breaks will occur when the text is printed, as shown in Figure 6-19. You can also toggle the print display mode with ALT+F7.

 Tip: *Toggle ALT+F7 to see how text will break when printed.*

If you are setting up columns and plan to print in a proportional font, make sure to use tabs instead of spaces to align your columns. Many users assume that because a column in a table aligns on the screen, it will align on the paper, but look at Figure 6-20. In the first case the operator used the SPACEBAR to align columns. Because characters are of different sizes in proportional fonts (in this case Helvetica), the column can never line up. Always use tabs to align columns.

Courier 12 pt:

i
m
w
I
M
W

Times 12 pt:

i
m
w
I
M
W

Helvetica 12 pt:

i
m
w
I
M
W

Courier 12 pt:	G	I	M	O	W
Times 12 pt	G	I	M	O	W
Helvetica 12 pt	G	I	M	O	W

Figure 6-18.   How proportionally spaced and monospaced fonts compare. Note:
Courier is a monospaced font

Trap: *Spaces will align columns in monospaced font tables but*
not in proportionally spaced font tables.

Another thing to keep in mind is that changing a font type and size will dramatically change how your document is placed on paper. If you are trying

```
[·········1·········2·········3·········4·········5·········]·········7···
You·can·view·where·a·line·of·text,·formatted·in·a·proportionally·spaced·
font,·will·break·on·the·printed·page·by·setting·the·Options·printer·
display·field·to·Yes.··Note·how·the·text·extends·past·the·margin·in·print·
view·mode.¶
¶
This·example·is·printed·in·Times·Roman·14·point·type.·◆
```

You can view where a line of text, formatted in a proportionally spaced font, will break on the printed page by setting the Options printer display field to Yes. Note how the text extends past the margin in print view mode.

This example is printed in Times Roman 14 point type.

Figure 6-19. The screen when Options Print Display is set

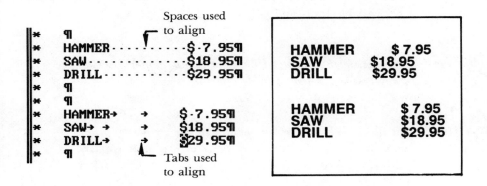

Figure 6-20. Table alignment: spaces versus tabs

to control where a page breaks, choose the break location after changing a font style or formatting the text.

 Tip: *Repaginate a document only after fonts and formats have been assigned.*

The Format Character Menu

To format characters, words, sentences, paragraphs, and other text, you must first select the text. (Selecting text will be covered in detail in Chapter 8.) Then, you can use the quick keys, as shown in Figure 6-21, or you can open the Format Character menu. Access the quick keys by pressing the ALT key in sequence with the designated character code. If a style sheet is attached, you may need to press ALT+X and then the character code.

The Format Character menu is shown here:

```
FORMAT CHARACTER bold: Yes No       italic: Yes(No)        underline: Yes(No)
        strikethrough: Yes(No)      uppercase: Yes(No)     small caps: Yes(No)
        double underline: Yes(No)   position:(Normal)Superscript Subscript
        font name: Courier    ▶     font size: 12          hidden: Yes(No)
```

Through this menu, you can assign formats to selected characters in the same way that you do with the quick keys. However, by using the menu, you can assign several styles to the selected character and change both its font and font size at the same time. Press F1 when the highlight is in the Font Name or Font Size field to produce a list of available fonts and sizes.

 Tip: *When using the Format Character menu, remember that the F1 key displays a list of fonts and font sizes.*

 Trap: *You must pick the proper printer in the Printer Options menu before a list of fonts for your printer will appear.*

Hidden Text

You may have noticed a selection in the Format Character menu for *hidden text*. This format field allows you to hide text typed on the screen from the printed

Bold type style: press Alt + B

<u>Underline type style: press Alt + U</u>

<u>Double underline type style: press Alt + D</u>

Italic type style: press Alt + I

Small Caps type style: press Alt + K

~~Strikethrough:~~--press Alt + S

Super^{script}: press Alt + = (equal or plus)

Sub$_{script}$: press Alt + - (minus)

Note: If a style sheet is attached, press
Alt + X and the character.

An 8 point font size was also applied
to the superscript and subscript text.

Figure 6-21. Direct formatting key combinations

version. In this way you can include comments on your screen that will not be printed on the final document. Hidden text is also used to mark words to be placed in an index and titles to be placed in a table of contents. (The use of hidden text will be covered in detail in Chapter 10.)

Tip: *You can type text or comments on the screen that will be hidden in the background or not printed with hidden character formatting.*

Trap: *Display of hidden text on the screen is controlled with the Window Options Show Hidden Text command. Printing of hidden text is controlled by the Print Options Hidden Text command.*

Other Parts of Your Document

With Microsoft Word, you can tag parts of your document and assemble them in other parts of the document. The table of contents and index are the best examples. As you enter words and titles to be included in the index or table of contents, you can tag them with a special code.

Style sheets are important because they help you format the document for final printing. Word's outlining feature can help you organize and plan a document, and, as you will see in later chapters, it can be used to move through the document, create the table of contents, and reorganize at any time.

Table of Contents and Index

It is easy to create a table of contents and an index for your document with Word. Each title or subheading that is to appear in the table of contents is marked with a special code that can be hidden with the hidden text format. Each word that is to appear in the index is also labeled with a special code that can be hidden. When your document is complete, you can use the Library Index and Table commands to compile these sections. One of the best features of these two commands is that they can be executed at any time. If you add to your document, you can recompile the table of contents or index.

 Tip: *Entries destined for the table of contents and index must be tagged with a special code in the text of a document.*

Recall that a document can be divided into divisions, each with its own margins, headers, footers, and column layout. You can place the table of contents and the index as separate divisions in your documents, assigning each its own page layout.

 Tip: *The table of contents and index can have a different division layout from the text.*

Figure 6-22 shows a typical document that has been divided into three sections: the table of contents, the text, and the index. Because the table of contents and the index will probably have different margin settings and running heads, it makes sense to split them into separate divisions. In Figure 6-22 the index division has been formatted to columns, as is normal for an index.

Styles and Style Sheets

Styles and style sheets are the most powerful tools in Word. Although they will be covered in detail later, you should become somewhat familiar with their use now. This chapter has covered many document elements that you are probably familiar

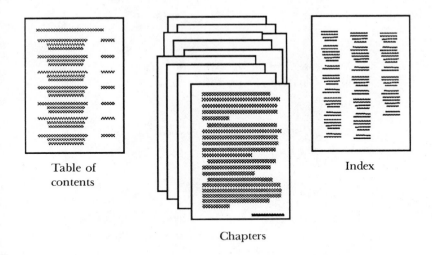

Table of
contents

Index

Chapters

Figure 6-22. A table of contents and index as separate divisions with different margins and running heads

with from using typewriters, but styles and style sheets accomplish tasks that are unique to Microsoft Word.

Briefly, a style is a character, paragraph, or division format that you can apply automatically rather than going through the Word Format command menu. You've already had some experience with styles when you used the ALT+I (italics) and other quick keys to apply formats to text in your documents. ALT+I is a built-in formatting key that applies what will be called *direct* formats to characters. Styles apply *indirect* formats.

 Tip: *Direct formats are applied by Word's built-in formatting keys. Indirect formats are applied by styles.*

The significance of styles is that you can customize a set of formatting commands that you use often and assign them in ALT key sequences, just as the built-in italic and boldface formats are assigned to the ALT+I and ALT+B keys. These custom styles can be saved as a group in a *style sheet,* which has its own filename and is displayed when you select the Gallery command.

 Tip: *You can create formatting styles and assign them to ALT key sequences, just like the built-in formatting keys.*

 Tip: *Custom styles are saved as a collection in a style sheet, which is a file on the disk.*

Think about how you could use these features for a minute. Assume that you are writing a long document that includes numerous long quoted passages. Each quoted passage is to be typed in a separate paragraph that has a left and right indent of 1 inch and an italic type style (see Figure 6-23). Because these passages appear infrequently throughout your document, you would need to change format from normal to quote text each time by using the Format Paragraph menu to set indents or by pressing several quick-key combinations.

Styles make all of this work easy. You can assign the indent and italic formatting sequence to a key combination, say ALT+QT (*QT* is short for quote and helps you remember the keystrokes). Now, before typing the quote, simply press

ALT+Q+T, and the special paragraph will be immediately set up by Word. Of course, you will need another sequence to return to a normal text mode without indents and italics. Word has a standard paragraph format that can be called *TX*, so you would press ALT+T+X to return to the normal paragraph mode.

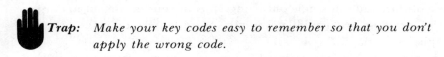 **Trap:** *Make your key codes easy to remember so that you don't apply the wrong code.*

When you apply a style to a paragraph, you assign that paragraph and every paragraph like it the same special code. This code appears in the style bar on the left side of the Word screen. So each quote will have a *QT* next to it in the bar while each normal paragraph will have a *TX* next to it. This can be seen in Figure 6-23.

```
█━━━[········1·········2·········3·········4·········5·········]·········7···┐
║TX   The twentieth century has produced its share of great men.
║     As we move into the twenty first century, who shall we
║     remember most from this century?
║TX
║QT          "Let the word go forth from this time
║            and place, to friend and foe alike, that
║            the torch has been passed to a new
║            generation of Americans— born in this
║            century,"
║TX
║TX   President John Fitzgerald Kennedy spoke these words in his
║     inaugural address.  Spreading the torch, Kennedy continues:
║TX
║QT          "My fellow citizens of the world: ask
║            not what America will do for you, but
║            what together we can do for the freedom
║            of man."
║TX
```

Figure 6-23.   The style bar shows the assigned paragraph style code

Tip: *The style bar displays the style code of a paragraph. The Window Options Style Bar field must be set to Yes to display the style bar.*

Because of this, you can single out paragraphs in your document to do special tasks. For example, you could later use the Word Search command to locate all paragraphs given the *QT* style.

More importantly, you can alter all paragraphs given a particular style by simply changing the definition in the style sheet. For example, you could automatically change all the quote paragraphs in your document from italic to underline with a few keystrokes.

 Tip: *You can instantly change paragraphs that have been indirectly formatted with styles by altering the definition in the style sheet.*

A style in the style sheet can be thought of as the personality of the paragraphs you have assigned it to. When you change the personality of the style, all the paragraphs instantly change in the same way.

Now let's say that you are ready to print your document. The normal text paragraphs (labeled *TX*) should be printed double-spaced, but the quotes (labeled *QT*) should retain their single spacing. Because each paragraph in your document is assigned a style code, you can simply go into the style sheet and change the line spacing for *TX* to double spacing. Every paragraph labeled *TX* will change to double spacing, but every *QT* paragraph will retain its single-spacing format. You can now print the document. If you wish to return to single-spacing format in the *TX* paragraphs, simply return to the style sheet and make the change.

 Tip: *Once a paragraph is given a style code, you can alter the code to alter all paragraphs holding that code.*

Again, once you create a set of styles for a document, you can save them to a style sheet disk file. The next time you need to write a document that requires those styles, you can *attach* the saved style sheet to your new document and use all of the key codes that you previously created.

Tip: *A style sheet holds a collection of style codes and can be saved as a disk file. These codes can then be used with other documents.*

Where Styles Are Created and Stored   Styles and style sheets are created in Word's *Gallery,* which is a special window that opens when you select Gallery on the Word command menu. The gallery window includes an edit window at the top that is similar to the normal Word edit window. At the bottom is a menu like that of the Main command menu, except that only about half the commands are available, as you can see here:

```
‖───────────────────────────────────────────NORMAL.STY─‖
COMMAND: Copy Delete Exit Format Help
         Insert Name Print Transfer Undo
Select style or press ESC to use menu
GALLERY           {}                ?                Microsoft Word
```

The commands in the Gallery menu help you create new style codes.

 Trap: *The gallery window looks similar to the Word edit window. Don't confuse them.*

Creating a style is as simple as typing I for insert, answering a few questions about what type of style it is (character, paragraph, or division), and giving the new style a two-character code name. If the code is used to format characters or paragraphs, you can use the Format command much as you would in the main edit window.

 Tip: *You create styles in the gallery window by inserting a new style code and then formatting it in the same way that characters and paragraphs are formatted.*

A complete description of the style will appear in the edit window, including the type of indents, character size, and other formatting information. A description field allows you to explain what the particular key code will do and where it should be used. This screen image shows what the styles to format quotes (*QT*) and regular text (*TX*) look like in the gallery window.

```
1─0·······[········2········3········4···]··5········6·······7···
 1  QT Paragraph 6                       Quotation formatting
    Courier (modern a) 12 Italic. Flush left, Left indent 1", right
    indent 1".
 2  TX Paragraph 4                       chapter text
    Courier (modern a) 12. Flush left.
```

Notice that the paragraph formatting is described in easy-to-understand terms. To change a format in a style, simply highlight it as shown for the *QT* style and use the Format command as you would for text.

Word retains one style sheet, called NORMAL.STY, that it automatically applies to all new documents you create unless you specify another style sheet. In the screen image just shown, you may have noticed that NORMAL.STY was the name of the style sheet. That means that all new documents will be assigned this style sheet and have access to the *TX* and *QT* styles. You can of course create style sheets for specific purposes, such as writing books, legal documents, forms, letters, and so on.

Tip: *NORMAL.STY is a style sheet that Word attaches to each document you create. It can hold styles that are common among your documents.*

Outline

Word has an Outline feature that can help you plan and create documents. A Word outline allows you to free-flow your ideas into an organized form. Many users ignore the Outline feature because they do not fully understand its capabilities, one of which is that it allows text to be "collapsed" under major headings. You can then easily scroll through a document by moving through the headings. This lets you easily pinpoint various parts of your document without scrolling through a lot of text on the screen.

Tip: *An outline can help you create the divisions, headings, and sections of your document while you collect your ideas.*

Tip: *Outlines allow you to "collapse" text under headings so that you can easily scroll through your document.*

Think of a Word outline as a stack of roll-up window shades. When the shades are rolled up, only the main titles are visible. When the shades are pulled down, you can view subtitles and the text under them. There may be additional headings with collapsed text as second-level headings. You can pull down shades as needed and then collapse them to move on to other editing.

Tip: *You can view only the text you want to edit by pulling down the "window shades" under a heading.*

Word supplies a special style sheet for outlines. With it, you can easily apply font and character styles to the heading levels of your outline. Word also allows you to instantly switch between outline mode and the normal text mode of the Word edit window. In the edit window the entire text of your document is visible, while Outline mode gives you the collapsed heading view. (Outlining is covered in detail in Chapter 18.)

Planning Your Document

Before you start typing large documents, you should do a little planning. The Outline feature can help you get your ideas together, but you should also set up various options and styles before inputting your text.

Set Up the Styles

Consider how the text will look on paper. Will it have titles? What typeface and type style will they be formatted with? Will there be subheads? What size should they be? How many paragraph types will there be? Will some be indented while others are set up as tables? You can build each of these individual styles in a style sheet by using the Gallery command before you begin typing.

Tip: *Think about the different type styles and paragraph formats of your document; then build style codes for them in the gallery before you begin typing.*

If you've created a similar style sheet for another document, you may be able to use it with some alterations. Remember that it is best to give your document elements styles as you type them. To change a style later, you need only change the style definition in the gallery to adjust all the elements given that style.

 Tip: *You may be able to use style sheets created for other documents.*

Plan for Table of Contents and Index

Before typing a long document, consider the table of contents and index. Entries for these divisions of your document must be tagged as you type, unless you want to tag them later during a reread and edit.

 Tip: *You can tag your table of contents and index entries as you type them, rather than search for them later.*

Prepare a Storage Area

Where your documents will be stored is also important. If you are using a hard-drive system, you may want to store your document file in a special directory. For example, if the document is a book, with multiple files for each chapter, you may want to create a directory called BOOK to hold just these files. The same holds for diskette systems. You may want to prepare a new disk just to hold the new files that you will be creating (see Appendix A).

Consider Often Used Text

Word's Glossary feature lets you temporarily or permanently store often used names, addresses, phrases, sentences, paragraphs, and other text to memory for later use. Each *string* of text is given a code name so that when you type it and press the F3 *expand glossary name* key, the text will be retyped by Word. (This extremely convenient feature will be covered in Chapters 9 and 15.)

Tip: The glossary is a place to store often used words, phrases, and other text.

 Tip: The F3 key is used to expand the name of a glossary entry.

Many legal documents, for instance, contain blocks of text that must be repeated verbatim in other documents. Why retype this text for each document when you can save it as a glossary entry for repeated use? When planning a document, you can assemble often used text blocks in advance of the writing, or you can simply type the glossary names in the text and expand them before printing. The Search command makes it easy to perform this step, as you'll see.

Tips and Traps Summary

Elements of a Document

Tip: Each element of a Word document has its own special set of Word commands in the command menu.

Tip: Division formatting describes how text will fit on the pages.

Tip: Paragraphs describe how blocks of text are "molded" within the boundaries of the page.

Tip: Character formatting improves the look of text by specifying different type fonts, sizes, and styles.

Document Divisions

Tip: Running heads are printed outside of the text area defined by the margin settings and may contain page numbers, dates, titles, and other information.

Tips and Traps Summary (*continued*)

Tip: You can view division formatting by displaying the Format Division Margins menu.

Tip: The first time you alter a division setting in a document, the division marker (row of colons) will appear at the bottom of the document.

Trap: Remember that a division is above the division marker, not below it.

Trap: Never delete a division marker unless you are sure that you want to lose division formats.

Tip: One-page documents almost always consist of one division.

Tip: Margins are set from the edge of the paper. If you change paper size, you may not need to change the margins.

Trap: A page break appears in the edit window as a row of single dots, not to be confused with a division break, which appears as a row of double dots, or colons.

Tip: Think about the distance from the paper edge to the text edge, not the width of the text area, when setting margins.

Tip: Changing paper sizes requires a paper size adjustment but not necessarily a margin adjustment.

Tip: Gutters leave space for punched holes and for binding when pages are being prepared for back-to-back printing.

Trap: Gutters are meant only for back-to-back printing.

Tip: Running heads print on each page of the division except the first, if specified.

Tip: The exact location of a running head is measured from the left and top edges of the paper.

Trap: Do not measure running heads from within the margins.

Tips and Traps Summary (*continued*)

Tip: Page numbers can be included in running heads or specified to print in an exact location on the page.

Trap: Control of style and layout is limited when you use the Format Division Page-Numbers command to set page numbers.

Tip: Page numbers are measured from the top and left edges of the paper.

Tip: Page numbers can begin with any number to account for multiple sections or chapters.

Tip: Word accumulates footnotes in a special footnote window so that they can be printed at the bottom of each page or at the end of the document.

Tip: Word moves footnote text to the page where the footnote reference is located.

Tip: Newspaperlike columns can be used to create newsletters. Space for pictures and artwork is easy to manage.

Tip: Line numbers can be printed beside every line or in any increment you wish.

Paragraph Elements

Tip: Tab settings are part of paragraph formatting, not division formatting. Thus each paragraph can have its own tab settings.

Trap: Paragraphs are a subcategory of divisions, but they have their own set of formatting commands.

Tip: Press ENTER to start a new paragraph with the same formats as the last.

Tip: The paragraph marker holds the paragraph formats.

Tips and Traps Summary (*continued*)

Trap: Deleting a paragraph marker may cause a loss of formats.

Trap: You may need to press ALT+X+C or ALT+X+J if a style sheet is attached.

Tip: Use the Format Paragraph menu if you are assigning several formats at once.

Tip: A document can be typed in single-space format, and then switched to double spacing for printing.

Tip: Style sheets let you convert only paragraphs with a specific style to double spacing.

Tip: Word will automatically insert spaces between paragraphs.

Tip: Word can prevent a single line of a paragraph from being printed by itself on another page.

Tip: You can ensure that a paragraph or table will be printed completely on one page.

Tip: You can ensure that two paragraphs are printed together on a page.

Trap: Don't confuse side-by-side layout with newspaperlike column layout. Side-by-side formatting is for small blocks in the middle of normal text. Newspaperlike columns can run for several pages.

Tip: In side-by-side text indents determine where on the page each block of text will be printed.

Tip: To make side-by-side text easier to use, set up a small block of side-by-side text and then duplicate it for each set you need.

Tip: Word comes with preset tab stops that you can adjust to fit your needs.

Tip: Always use tabs when creating tables. Never use the SPACEBAR.

Tip: Columns in Word can be moved, deleted, and even summed.

Tips and Traps Summary (*continued*)

Trap: A border can only be placed around a complete paragraph.

Tip: Press SHIFT+ENTER to create blocks of text that you want to surround with borders.

Tip: A hanging indent in the first line allows space between text and the left border.

Tip: Lines can be placed around any side of a paragraph.

Tip: Bordered paragraphs are never split across pages.

Character Elements

Trap: Character formatting can only be applied to highlighted text.

Trap: Fonts and font size variations are not shown on monospaced character screens.

Trap: When you use proportional fonts, the screen cannot show how the text will look when printed.

Tip: Toggle ALT+F7 to see how text will break when printed.

Trap: Spaces will align columns in monospaced font tables but not in proportionally spaced font tables.

Tip: Repaginate a document only after fonts and formats have been assigned.

Tip: When using the Format Character menu, remember that the F1 key displays a list of fonts and font sizes.

Trap: You must pick the proper printer in the Printer Options menu before a list of fonts for your printer will appear.

Tip: You can type text or comments on the screen that will be hidden in the background or not printed with hidden character formatting.

Tips and Traps Summary (*continued*)

Trap: Display of hidden text on the screen is controlled with the Window Options Show Hidden Text command. Printing of hidden text is controlled by the Print Options Hidden Text command.

Other Parts of Your Documents

Tip: Entries destined for the table of contents and index must be tagged with a special code in the text of a document.

Tip: The table of contents and index can have a different division layout from the text.

Tip: Direct formats are applied by Word's built-in formatting keys. Indirect formats are applied by styles.

Tip: You can create formatting styles and assign them to ALT key sequences, just like the built-in formatting keys.

Tip: Custom styles are saved as a collection in a style sheet, which is a file on the disk.

Trap: Make your key codes easy to remember so that you don't apply the wrong code.

Tip: The style bar displays the style code of a paragraph. The Window Options Style Bar field must be set to Yes to display the style bar.

Tip: You can instantly change paragraphs that have been indirectly formatted with styles by altering the definition in the style sheet.

Tip: Once a paragraph is given a style code, you can alter the code to alter all paragraphs holding that code.

Tip: A style sheet holds a collection of style codes and can be saved as a disk file. These codes can then be used with other documents.

Trap: The gallery window looks similar to the Word edit window. Don't confuse them.

Tips and Traps (*continued*)

Tip: You create styles in the gallery window by inserting a new style code and then formatting it in the same way that characters and paragraphs are formatted.

Tip: NORMAL.STY is a style sheet that Word attaches to each document you create. It can hold styles that are common among your documents.

Tip: An outline can help you create the divisions, headings, and sections of your document while you collect your ideas.

Tip: Outlines allow you to "collapse text" under headings so that you can easily scroll through your document.

Tip: You can view only the text you want to edit by pulling down the "window shades" under a heading.

Planning Your Document

Tip: Think about the different type styles and paragraph formats of your document; then build style codes for them in the gallery before you begin typing.

Tip: You may be able to use style sheets created for other documents.

Tip: You can tag your table of contents and index entries as you type them, rather than search for them later.

Tip: The glossary is a place to store often used words, phrases, and other text.

Tip: The F3 key is used to expand the name of a glossary entry.

7

Moving Through Documents

In order to edit a character or insert new text in your documents, you must move the highlight to the *insertion point* and then type, edit, or delete according to your needs. This chapter explains how to get to the parts of your document that you want to edit.

Moving through a document in Word is fairly straightforward, right? If you know how to use the arrow keys, PGUP and PGDN, and maybe the mouse, you already know how to get to where you want to go. But many users overlook a lot of tricks because they are either satisfied with using the arrow keys or simply don't appreciate the full potential of Word's highlight movement keys. It is easy to overlook many features in Word because the most efficient way of performing a task sometimes requires an extra step or a little extra learning.

I often wonder if any Word users have mastered the complete set of scrolling techniques? For example, pressing the SCROLL LOCK key to use the arrow keys provides some interesting and useful movements. But how many people bother to use SCROLL LOCK? First, you must press SCROLL LOCK before using the arrows, an extra step that many people learn but soon forget because the basic arrow keys get the job done, though sometimes less efficiently. Then you must remember to turn SCROLL LOCK off if you want to use arrows in the command menus. This chapter will explore the advantages of using SCROLL LOCK and other Word scrolling keys. You will find some interesting tips and techniques.

First, the range of movements across the edit window is covered. Next, the range of movements through the pages of a document is discussed. Finally, special techniques, such as jumping, searching, and windowing your way through your documents, are discussed.

Before getting started with the exercises in the chapter, you need a document to work with. Type the text that follows if you want to follow along with the examples in this chapter. This text will then be duplicated a number of times to increase the length of the document. Start Word or, if it is already in use, clear the screen by using the Transfer Clear All command.

The first passage is from "Three Men in a Boat," by Jerome Klapka Jerome. The second is from "The Purple Cow," by Gelett Burgess. Press ENTER twice at the end of the first passage. In the second passage press SHIFT+ENTER to end each line so that paragraph integrity is maintained. At the end of the passage, press ENTER twice.

It always does seem to me that I am doing more work than I should do. It is not that I object to the work, mind you; I like work; it fascinates me. I can sit and look at it for hours. I love to keep it by me; the idea of getting rid of it nearly breaks my heart.

I never saw a Purple Cow,
I never hope to see one;
But I can tell you, anyhow,
I'd rather see than be one.

After typing the passages, select both of them by pressing the SHIFT+F10 key combination. Both paragraphs should now be highlighted, as shown in Figure 7-1. Press DEL (Delete) to insert the text into the scrap; then press INS (Insert) 11 times to insert 11 copies of the text. This will form a document that is three pages long. Press CTRL+PGUP (Page Up) to get to the top of the document. After you have created the text, save it to a disk file for future use. Press ESC and select the Transfer Save command by typing **T** and **S**. Finally, type **PASSAGES** in the Filename field.

```
1━━━[·········1·······2·······3·······4·······5······━━━]·······7··
 *  It·always·does·seem·to·me·that·I·am·doing·more·work·than·I·
    should·do.··It·is·not·that·I·object·to·the·work,·mind·you;·I·
    like·work;·it·fascinates·me.··I·can·sit·and·look·at·it·for·
    hours.··I·love·to·keep·it·by·me;·the·idea·of·getting·rid·of·
    it·nearly·breaks·my·heart.¶
    ¶
 *  I·never·saw·a·Purple·Cow,↓
 *  I·never·hope·to·see·one;↓
    But·I·can·tell·you,··anyhow,↓
    I'd·rather·see·than·be·one.¶
 *  ¶
 *  ◆
```

Figure 7-1.   Highlighted paragraphs, ready for copying

Traversing the Edit Window

Your screen should now display two copies of the paragraphs that you typed previously. There is more text below the edit window that can be scrolled into view, as you will see shortly. For now, the highlight should be in the upper-left corner. You already know how to use the arrow keys to move around in your text. The highlight is moved to various parts of your document so that you can insert or delete characters. You can also move to characters or words in order to apply formatting changes.

Two terms will be used in this and future chapters to describe highlight movements. The first term has been mentioned, to some extent, in previous chapters. It is the *insertion point,* but in the context of this chapter, it will be called the *current insertion point.* This is the point where the highlight is before you move it to another location. The current insertion point may well be the last character of your document because you may be adding new text to the end of it. The *target insertion point* is the point in your document where you want to jump to make editing changes, delete a character, or insert new text. So you will move from the current insertion point to the target insertion point with the highlight movement keys.

Tip: *Move the highlight from the current insertion point to the target insertion point to make editing or formatting changes.*

When using the arrow keys to move about in your document, it is best to localize their movements to within a diamond that includes the next or previous word, or the three closest lines (either up or down), as shown in Figure 7-2. If you need to move further away, you can use the jump keys that will be discussed next. As an example, assuming that the highlight is in the upper-left corner, move to the *u* in *should* on the next line down by pressing the DOWN ARROW key once and the RIGHT ARROW key four times.

 Tip: *Localize the use of the arrow keys within the next or previous word and the three closest lines.*

: · I · can · tell · you, · a

l · rather · see · than · b

·always · does · seem · t

ould do. · · It · is not

e · work; · it · fascina

rs. · · I · love · to · kee

·nearly · breaks · my · h

Figure 7-2. Arrow key highlight movement is best limited to the diamond

Jump Keys

One of the best ways to use the arrow keys is in combination with a *jump* key. The HOME and END keys are good examples of jump keys. Press END now to jump to the end of the current line. From this position, you can then use the arrow keys to highlight a particular letter. Don't move across an entire page with the arrow keys. The jump keys are much better for this, as shown here:

It·always·does·seem·to·me·that·I·am·doing·more·work·than·I·
should·do.···It·is·not·that·I·object·to·the·work,·mind·you;·I
——————————————— END ———————————————

Tip: *Use jump keys to get to a localized area; then use the arrow keys.*

Similarly, you can jump back to the beginning of a line with the HOME key. The CTRL+HOME and CTRL+END keys will jump the cursor to the upper-left and bottom-left of the current edit window, respectively. Figure 7-3 illustrates the CTRL+HOME and CTRL+END key actions.

Tip: *CTRL+HOME and CTRL+END move the highlight to the top or bottom of the screen, not the document. CTRL+PGUP and CTRL+PGDN perform this task.*

Trap: *When SCROLL LOCK is on, HOME and END work the same as CTRL+HOME and CTRL+END without SCROLL LOCK.*

As mentioned, the arrow keys are best used after you jump to an area close to the characters or words that you want to edit. The trick is to get as close as possible to the target point. Three sets of jump keys can be used to close in on the

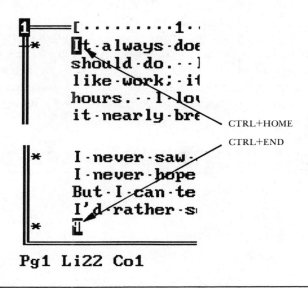

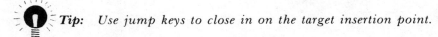

Figure 7-3. CTRL+HOME and CTRL+END actions

target insertion point. The first set jumps you one word at a time and assumes that the target insertion point is somewhere within the same sentence.

Tip: *Use jump keys to close in on the target insertion point.*

Next or Previous Word Jump Keys   Don't confuse the Word jump keys covered here with the Word selection keys covered in Chapter 8. The keys discussed here will jump you to the first letter in either the next or previous word. The word keys discussed in the next chapter highlight the next or previous word so that you can apply formats.

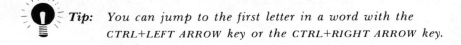

Tip: *You can jump to the first letter in a word with the CTRL+LEFT ARROW key or the CTRL+RIGHT ARROW key.*

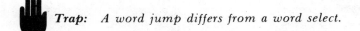

Trap: *A word jump differs from a word select.*

Let's try inserting a word in the Burgess passage. The current highlight should be at the end of the second line. If not, press END now to get there, and then move to the last line by pressing the DOWN ARROW key (a quicker way to get there will be discussed shortly). Notice how the highlight trails the ends of the lines because it started at the end of a line.

When you reach the end of the last line of the Burgess passage, you can try jumping over words. Let's assume that you have just finished typing this last line. The cursor waits at the end of the line for more characters. You then decide to insert the word *one* in front of *than* to alter the author's grammar. At the end of the line, press CTRL+LEFT ARROW three times to get to the target insertion point — the *t* in the word *than*. Type **one** and a space. Now, you can press END to jump back to the end of the line and resume typing. Figure 7-4 illustrates this process.

 Tip: *The* END *key allows you to resume typing where you left off.*

Jumping Over Sentences   Next, we'll change the Jerome passage by contracting the words *It is* in the second sentence to *It's*. For this example, we'll borrow a trick from the next chapter. The SHIFT+F7 key combination lets you highlight previous sentences. Instead of placing the highlight on the first letter of the previous sentence, however, it highlights the whole sentence. Pressing CTRL+RIGHT ARROW

CTRL+LEFT ARROW

I'd·rather·see·than·be·one.···◆

I'd·rather·see·one·than·be·one.···◆

END

Figure 7-4. Jumping over words

lets you select the *i* in *is*. This time, SHIFT+F7 is used just to close in on the target edit point.

 Tip: *SHIFT+F7 moves the highlight to previous sentences; SHIFT+F8 moves the highlight to subsequent sentences.*

 Trap: *Pressing an arrow key after selecting a sentence causes a character in the next or previous sentence to be selected.*

First, move the highlight to the end of the first paragraph by pressing UP ARROW. Then, press SHIFT+F7 four times to move the highlight four sentences up. Now you can press CTRL+RIGHT ARROW to land on the *i* in *is*. Delete it, backspace, and then type an apostrophe. To get back to the bottom of the paragraph, press CTRL+DOWN ARROW and then the LEFT ARROW. Figure 7-5 shows the steps in this operation. The CTRL+DOWN ARROW is covered next.

 Tip: *Determine the most efficient path between the current insertion point and the target insertion point.*

Jumping Over Paragraphs   This example will encompass most of the highlight movement commands you've already tried. CTRL+DOWN ARROW and CTRL+UP ARROW are used to move between paragraphs. Assume that you want to move the highlight to the *w* in the word *work* on the top line. With the highlight at the end of the paragraph, press CTRL+HOME to get to the upper-left corner of the screen. Next press END. Now press CTRL+LEFT ARROW three times. From here you could edit or add text, but don't bother for now. Press CTRL+DOWN ARROW three times to see how the highlight jumps between paragraphs. Figure 7-6 shows these processes.

 Tip: *CTRL+DOWN ARROW jumps to paragraphs beneath and CTRL+UP ARROW jumps to paragraphs above the current insertion point.*

SHIFT+F7 (four times)

> It·always·does·seem·to·me·that·I·am·doing·more·work·than·I·
> should·do.··It·is·not·that·I·object·to·the·work,·mind·you;·I·
> likes·work;·it·just·facinates·me.···I·can·sit·and·look·at·it·
> for·hours.···I·love·to·keep·it·by·me;·the·idea·of·getting·rid·
> of·it·nearly·breaks·my·heart.··¶
> ¶

CTRL+RIGHT ARROW

It·always·does·seem·to·me·that·I
should·do.··It·is·not·that·I·obj
likes·work;··it·just·facinates·me
for·hours.···I·love·to·keep·it·by
of·it·nearly·breaks·my·heart.·¶
¶

CTRL+DOWN ARROW   LEFT ARROW

Figure 7-5. Jumping over sentences

You may have noticed that the highlight landed on the paragraph marks between paragraphs. This is natural because a paragraph mark represents a paragraph without text. In Chapter 11 you'll learn how to include spaces above or below paragraphs as part of the paragraph formatting rather than inserting a blank paragraph marker as a separator.

Trap: *Don't separate paragraphs by using the ENTER key to insert paragraph markers. Use the Format Paragraph Space Before or Space After options instead.*

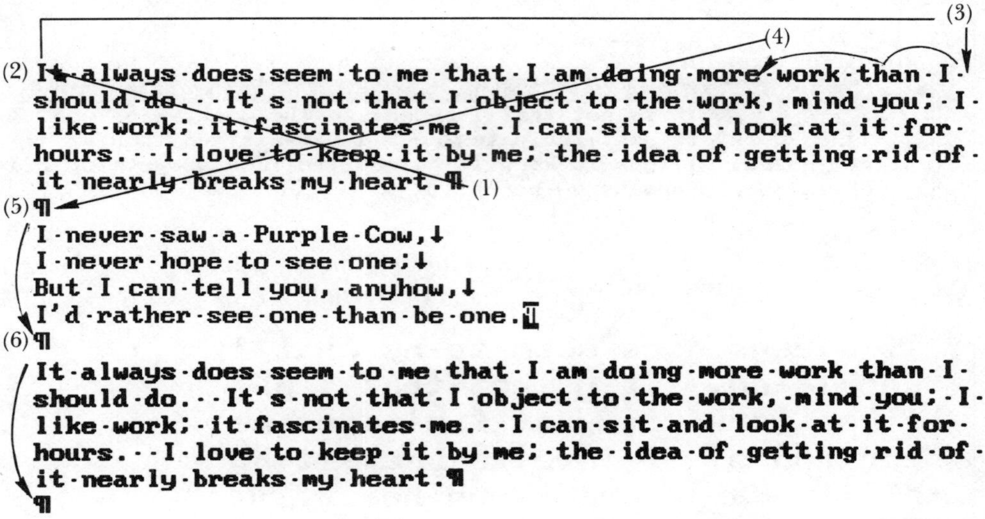

(2) It·always·does·seem·to·me·that·I·am·doing·more·work·than·I·
should·do.··It's·not·that·I·object·to·the·work,·mind·you;·I·
like·work;·it·fascinates·me.··I·can·sit·and·look·at·it·for·
hours.··I·love·to·keep·it·by·me;·the·idea·of·getting·rid·of·
it·nearly·breaks·my·heart.¶ (1)

(5)¶
I·never·saw·a·Purple·Cow,↓
I·never·hope·to·see·one;↓
But·I·can·tell·you,·anyhow,↓
I'd·rather·see·one·than·be·one.¶

(6)¶
It·always·does·seem·to·me·that·I·am·doing·more·work·than·I·
should·do.··It's·not·that·I·object·to·the·work,·mind·you;·I·
like·work;·it·fascinates·me.··I·can·sit·and·look·at·it·for·
hours.··I·love·to·keep·it·by·me;·the·idea·of·getting·rid·of·
it·nearly·breaks·my·heart.¶
¶

(1) CTRL+HOME
(2) END
(3) CTRL+←(3 times)
(4) CTRL+↓
(5) CTRL+↓
(6) CTRL+↓

Figure 7-6. Moving around the screen

Active Window Mouse Techniques

The mouse is most useful when you need to move the highlight to another location on the screen. Simply point and press. The current insertion point moves to the target point, where you can make your changes. When done, simply point back to where you were. In the next section you'll see how to use the mouse to scroll through documents.

Traversing Documents

Looking at the text currently displayed on your screen, it's hard to get a good idea of the size and extent of your document. Word provides a convenient measuring device, called the *thumb,* in the left border of the edit window. The thumb is a short horizontal line that moves up and down in the left window border. If you think of this border as a ruler that represents the page length of your documents, the thumb indicates your current location in the document. Press the PGDN (Page Down) key three times. The text will scroll through the edit window until you are approximately in the middle of the text, and the thumb will move to the middle of the left border. A comparison of your three-page document next to the border containing the thumb is shown in Figure 7-7.

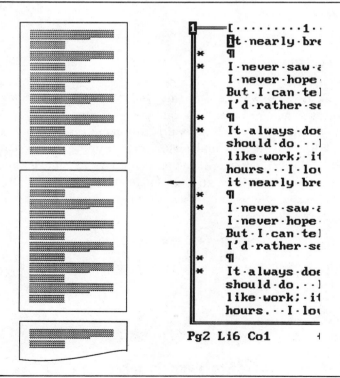

Figure 7-7. The thumb in relation to a document

Tip: *The thumb indicates the position of the highlight in rela-*
tion to the entire document.

The measure of the thumb border automatically adjusts relative to the size of your document. If you are working with 10 pages of text, the border represents 10 pages of text. Note that the movement of the thumb is proportional to the size of the document and is harder to detect on large documents.

 Trap: *The document measure bar readjusts as your document*
grows.

 Tip: *Look at the thumb to determine where you are in your*
document.

Showing Page Breaks

When scrolling through your documents, you often want to see exactly where pages will break when printed. You can preview page breaks by executing a repagination command. Not only does this command insert a row of dots where page breaks will occur, it also updates the page number in the command line indicator. Select the Print Repaginate command (type **P** and **R**) and then press ENTER. Now you can scroll through your document, watching for the page breaks in the text and noting the page numbers in the page indicator at the bottom-left corner of your screen.

 Tip: *Repaginate to view page breaks and update the page*
indicator.

This screen image shows how the Print Repaginate command looks.

`PRINT REPAGINATE confirm page breaks: Yes` **No**

The proposed response is No. If you answer Yes, Word will show you the location of each page break and allow you to adjust it to prevent pages from breaking in unnatural locations.

Beware that the page number indicator may not always be accurate. First, you must repaginate at least once before the number in the page indicator will show anything but 1. Then, if you insert text in the middle of your document, the page indicator will not know that a page has "grown" until you repaginate again. Until then, the number in the page indicator will be inaccurate. Printing will also repaginate a document automatically.

 Trap: *The numbers in the page indicator are accurate only if you have repaginated at least once and have repaginated since adding text.*

Paging Techniques

You've already seen how the PGDN and PGUP keys let you scroll through your document. You should keep in mind exactly how much text scrolls by when you press either of these keys. If your document is single-spaced and the menu is off, pressing PGDN will cause 20 more lines from the lower part of your document to be displayed. Two lines from the previous screenful of text remain at the top. Pressing PGUP has the opposite effect; two lines from the previous screen remain displayed at the bottom. Paging up and down with the PGUP and PGDN keys is one of the most efficient ways to view your document for editing. Because the keys are not part of a sequence, you don't have to hold down another key while using them, which makes them even more convenient. Figure 7-8 shows how text scrolls through the edit window with these keys.

 Tip: *Using the PGUP and PGDN keys leaves two lines from the previous screen at the bottom and top, respectively.*

Press CTRL+PGUP or CTRL+PGDN to place the highlight at the top or bottom of the document, respectively. The CTRL+PGDN combination is a good way to get back to the bottom of your document to resume typing after editing in previous pages.

 Tip: *Press CTRL+PGUP or CTRL+PGDN to place the highlight at the beginning or end of a document, respectively.*

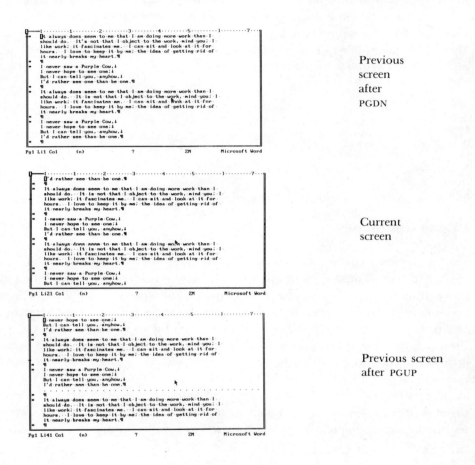

Previous screen after PGDN

Current screen

Previous screen after PGUP

Figure 7-8. Effects of scrolling with PGUP *and* PGDN

Scroll Lock Movements

Pressing the SCROLL LOCK key produces some interesting effects with the cursor movement keys. When you press SCROLL LOCK, an indicator light will come on if you have an AT-style keyboard, and "SC" will appear at the bottom of your screen. Because SCROLL LOCK interferes with the use of the arrow keys in the

command menu, it's good to know when this key is on. You cannot use the
HOME, END, or arrow keys in the command menu when SCROLL LOCK is on.

 Trap: *You cannot use the HOME, END, or arrow keys in the menu*
when SCROLL LOCK is on.

The basic feature of scrolling with SCROLL LOCK on is that the highlight
maintains its position on the screen relative to the borders. The text slides under it
as you press the arrow keys. Try this test. Move the highlight to the middle line of
your screen, press SCROLL LOCK, and watch the highlight as you press the UP or
DOWN ARROW key. The highlight will maintain its position as the text scrolls
under it.

 Tip: *The function of the arrow keys is altered when SCROLL*
LOCK is on; the HOME and END keys take on the functions
of CTRL+HOME and CTRL+END.

Try pressing the RIGHT ARROW key. The screen will shift horizontally to the left.
This is for viewing documents that have wide margin settings.

 Tip: *Scrolling horizontally is useful for viewing documents with*
wide margins.

 Trap: *The RIGHT and LEFT ARROW keys will not move one*
character left and right when SCROLL LOCK is on.

Using SCROLL LOCK to scroll through a document has advantages over both
the arrow keys and the PGUP and PGDN keys. Consider what happens when you
use the DOWN ARROW key to move through your document. If the highlight is in
the middle of the screen, you must first "bump" it against the bottom border
before text starts scrolling. Try this now. Make sure that SCROLL LOCK is off and
then press the DOWN ARROW key. As the highlight hits the bottom, the text starts
to scroll.

Now let's say that you are looking for a particular word to edit. If it pops up from the bottom of the window, you probably won't see it until the line has moved several lines above the cursor in the bottom line. You will have to use the UP ARROW key to get to the word that has scrolled past the highlight. With SCROLL LOCK set, you can leave the highlight in the middle of the screen. As text appears in the bottom of the edit window, it moves up with the lines to meet the highlight.

The one failure of the SCROLL LOCK key is that most people can't get into the habit of using it. The arrow keys are usually more useful in their non-SCROLL LOCK position for moving one character at a time. You will find yourself doing the "SCROLL LOCK shuffle" as you press the key on and off. The CTRL+RIGHT ARROW and CTRL+LEFT ARROW combinations, however, still operate correctly when SCROLL LOCK is on. If you have a mouse, you may as well set SCROLL LOCK on because you can use the pointer for all functions normally performed by the arrow keys.

 Tip: *If you have a mouse, use it instead of the arrow keys. Then you can leave SCROLL LOCK on to take advantage of its superior scrolling capabilities.*

Horizontal Scrolling

Horizontal scrolling is primarily for working with documents that have margins wider than will fit on the screen. If you are using 14-inch-wide computer paper, for instance, the right margin will be set to 11 1/2 inches on the ruler bar. If your SCROLL LOCK key is on, you can press the RIGHT ARROW key twice to get to the right margin. Press the LEFT ARROW key twice to return to the left margin. Of course, HOME and END without SCROLL LOCK achieve the same thing with one keystroke.

 Tip: *Wide paper will have wide margins that you can only view with horizontal scrolling.*

 Tip: *Pressing the RIGHT ARROW key with SCROLL LOCK on causes one third of the screen to scroll left.*

With SCROLL LOCK off, you can use the END key or the arrow keys to scroll to the right margin. As an example, execute Format Division Margins in the command menu. Type **14** in the Paper Width field and press RETURN. Now try scrolling to the right with the END key. Press HOME to scroll back to the left margin, but make sure that the highlight is in a line that extends to the right margin before doing so. Press SCROLL LOCK, the RIGHT ARROW key, and then the LEFT ARROW key to see its effect. Figure 7-9 shows these effects.

Mouse Techniques for Traversing Documents

If you own a mouse, you have a powerful tool for scrolling through your documents. The left bar of the edit window is your scroll bar for moving up and down through documents.

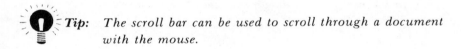 *Tip:* *The scroll bar can be used to scroll through a document with the mouse.*

By pointing in the bar and pressing either the left or right mouse button, you will scroll the text the distance from the pointer to the top of the bar.

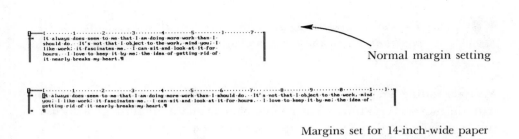

Normal margin setting

Margins set for 14-inch-wide paper

Figure 7-9. Horizontal scrolling displays text in wide right margins

Tip: *Press the scroll bar with the left button to move the top line of text next to the pointer.*

 Tip: *Press the scroll bar with the right button to move the adjacent text to the top line.*

If you press both buttons at once, or the middle button if you have a three-button mouse, the scroll bar becomes the measuring stick and places you in your document relative to where you pressed in the measuring stick. For example, if you press in the middle of the measuring stick, you will be placed in the middle of your document.

 Tip: *Pressing both mouse buttons at once in the scroll bar places you in the part of your document that corresponds to the measuring stick position.*

Horizontal Scrolling with the Mouse   Place the mouse pointer in the lower edit window bar to scroll the mouse horizontally. If your document's margins are wider than the screen, point to the lower-right window bar until a double arrow appears. Press the right button to scroll right and the left button to scroll back to the left. Pressing both buttons while pointing at the bottom border will move you to the horizontal position in the text relative to the location in the horizontal scroll bar.

 Tip: *You can use the mouse to move horizontally by pressing both buttons in the horizontal scroll bar at the bottom of the screen.*

Mouse Scrolling Trap   You may run into the following problem when scrolling with the mouse. It confuses many people. When you thumb through a document, the highlight stays in its original position, even if it scrolls out of the edit window. When you get to the section that you want to edit, you must click it with the mouse to move the highlight to this new position. If you press an arrow key, the screen will go through a confusing display that can devastate novice users.

 Trap: *After thumbing to a section of your document, point to a target insertion point with the mouse. Do not use the arrow keys.*

What happens is not really that confusing if you understand how Word handles its highlight. As you thumb through the document, the highlight retains its position. If you press an arrow key, the highlight, which is not visible on your screen, moves one line up. Word insists on displaying the part of the text where highlight movement is occurring, so the place that you scrolled to will be lost as Word redisplays the screen containing the highlight. This happens in a flash, so many users are not sure what went on. If this does happen, just thumb back to your target position and select a character on that screen with the mouse.

Page Jumping Through Documents

Once you have paginated a document, you can move to any page within it by using Word's Jump command. Access this command from the menu by pressing the Jump Page command on the menu.

 Tip: *You can use the Jump command to jump to any page in your document.*

However, a better way to access the Jump command is to press ALT+F5.

 Tip: *Press ALT+F5 to activate page jump mode.*

You'll run into a problem with the Jump command if you haven't paginated your document. Pagination, discussed earlier, places page breaks at the appropriate places, updates the page indicator at the bottom of the page, and allows you to perform page jumps.

 Trap: *The document must be paginated with the Print Repaginate command before a page jump can occur.*

Remember, if you add text to your document after running the Print Repaginate command, you will need to run the command again to get accurate page breaks. Word does not adjust page breaks as you add text. Instead, a page grows beyond normal size until you repaginate.

Search Jumping Techniques

Another way to get around in your document is to use the Search command. If the arrow keys can be compared to walking, the PGUP and PGDN keys to running, and the CTRL+ARROW combinations to jumping, then the Search routines can be compared to flying. With Search you can pinpoint a target insertion point in one step, depending on how good your search criteria are.

 Tip: *Search is the fastest way to move to a target insertion point that is far away.*

Try searching through the document on your screen. Press ESC+SEARCH to display the Search menu, as shown here:

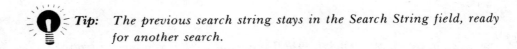

```
SEARCH text: █
        direction: Up(Down) case: Yes(No) whole word: Yes(No)
```

Type in the letter *I* because it appears often in the passages. Make sure to select Down in the Direction field if you are at the top of the document. Press ENTER. An *I* or *i* should be highlighted. To narrow the search, press ESC+SEARCH and answer Yes in the Case field. This will search for only those instances that match the case of the Search String field, here a capital *I*. Press ENTER and the next *I* should be highlighted.

 Tip: *The previous search string stays in the Search String field, ready for another search.*

 Tip: *The search begins at the current location of the highlight.*

 Tip: *You can search up or down through a document.*

Now, press SHIFT+F4. This quick key will repeat the search using the contents previously specified in the Search String field. Press SHIFT+F4 as many times as you wish.

Tip: *SHIFT+F4 will repeat a search using the string of the last search.*

Narrowing a Search   Performing a search that locates many undesired strings is not beneficial. You can specify various parameters of the Search command to narrow your searches. For example, the Whole Word field specifies that Word should not show a string if it is only a part of another word.

 Tip: *You can narrow searches by selecting different Search options.*

For example, press CTRL+PGUP to get to the very top of your document. Press ESC+SEARCH to open the Search menu and type **it** in the Search String field. Press ENTER and then press SHIFT+F4 several times. Word will find *It's, it,* and *sit.* Now press CTRL+PGUP to get to the top of text again; then press ESC+SEARCH and select Yes in the Whole Word field. Press ENTER and SHIFT+F4 several times. This time, Word finds only *It's* and *it* because they are the word itself and not a part of another word. Note that Word is smart enough to ignore the contraction in *It's.*

 Tip: *The Whole Word field eliminates strings inside other words that match your search string.*

You can also narrow a search if the string contains some capital letters. Select Yes in the Case field to highlight only those strings that match your upper/lowercase criteria.

 Tip: *You can limit searches by specifying upper/lowercase matches.*

The longer a search string is, the more specific the match. For example, look at the first two lines in the Burgess passage. The first line reads "I never saw" and the second reads "I never hope"; so, to place the cursor on the second line, type **never hope** in the Search String field.

 Tip: *The longer your search string, the more specific the match.*

If your document has titles, you can move from one title section to another by typing the title names in the Search String field. You can also place codes in your title or text that can be searched for. For example, you could type **S1** after a title for section 1 of a document. You could then search for S1 whenever you want to return to that section. Occasionally, you may want to jump up to another section of your document and then resume your typing where you were. You could type an uncommon code, like ******* or **@@@**, as a marker in your current edit area. When you're ready to return, simply specify the code in the Search String field.

 Tip: *Placing search codes throughout your document makes it easy to return to specific parts with the Search command.*

Window Techniques

The use of windows provides an interesting way to move to different portions of your document. Windows are covered in detail in Chapter 17, but they are covered here briefly so that you can see their usefulness in viewing different parts of your document.

 Tip: *Windows can be opened on different parts of a document so that you can move or copy text from one part of your document to another.*

When a window is open on another part of your document, you needn't scroll to that section. Simply point in the window with the mouse or press F1 to make the window active. The F1 key is a toggle that makes one or the other of two windows active. If there are more than two windows, each window is made active in order.

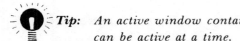

Tip: *An active window contains the highlight. Only one window can be active at a time.*

To open a window, press in the middle of the right edit window border with the mouse or select Esc Window Split Horizontal (or Vertical if you prefer) and enter 11 as the window split line. Two windows will appear on your screen. Although the editing area for each is reduced, you can move between them and edit different parts of your document. Figure 7-10 shows a split window on the Burgess and Jerome passages.

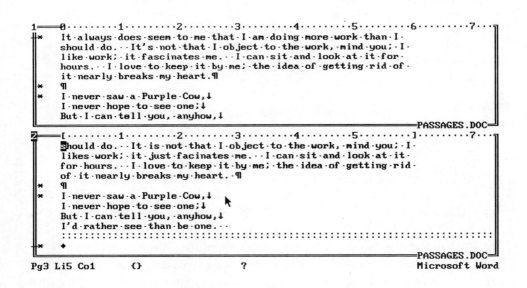

Figure 7-10. *It's easy to move to other parts of a document with two windows active: the top of the document is in window 1; the bottom is in window 2*

Let's say that while working in a later part of your document, you discover that you must make changes to an earlier part based on what you just typed. You will need to see the most recent text while editing the previous text. Opening two windows will let you do this. In the second window, simply scroll to the earlier part of the text to be edited while leaving the first window intact with your text.

 Tip: *Splitting a document with windows does not create two documents. You are working on two different parts of the same document at the same time.*

When you are through with a window, you can close it to make more room in the typing area. Up to eight windows can be open in Word, and a portion of each can be displayed on the screen at the same time. But this is not practical because it is hard to manage the edit window with portions of up to eight windows displayed.

 Trap: *Having too many windows open can make the edit window hard to manage.*

However, Word's special Window Zoom feature makes managing up to eight windows more practical. When you zoom a window, it takes up the whole screen. Other windows remain available "behind" the current window, and you can zoom each one. Then your windows will form layers that you can scroll through like a Rolodex with the F1 key. Why have so many windows? Assume that your document has eight major sections or title headings. By stepping through the stack of windows, you can easily get to the section you want in a few keystrokes, as shown in Figure 7-11.

 Tip: *Windows can be zoomed to fill the whole screen and then stacked in layers. Use the F1 key to step through the stack. Each window can point to a different section of your document.*

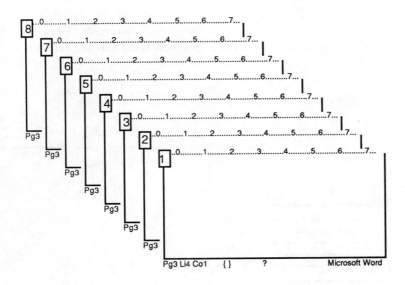

Figure 7-11. Windows can be stacked and each window can hold the sections or titles of your document

Outline Mode Jumps

When you create documents with the outline mode, two possible views are available. One is the normal text mode that shows all typing, titles, and subtitles. The second, the outline mode, can show the document in collapsed form, as shown on the right in Figure 7-12. In collapsed form you can scroll through just the titles. When the highlight is in the appropriate section, you can jump back into regular text mode for editing. The SHIFT+F2 combination makes it easy to toggle between the two modes. (Chapter 18 will cover outlining in detail.)

 Tip: *If a document is outlined, you can scroll through the collapsed titles in outline mode, and then return to the selected section in text mode.*

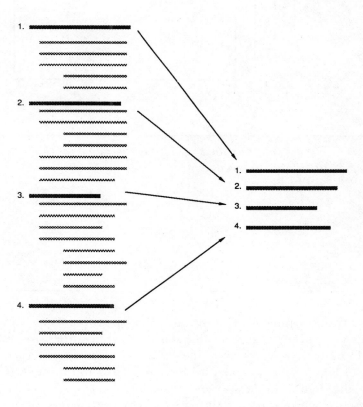

Figure 7-12. *Scrolling through a collapsed outline is a quick way to move through a document*

Tips and Traps Summary

Traversing the Edit Window

Tip: Move the highlight from the *current insertion point* to the *target insertion point* to make editing or formatting changes.

Tip: Localize the use of the arrow keys within the next or previous word and the three closest lines.

Tip: Use *jump* keys to get to a localized area; then use the arrow keys.

Tip: CTRL+HOME and CTRL+END move the highlight to the top or bottom of the screen, not the document. CTRL+PGUP and CTRL+PGDN perform this task.

Trap: When SCROLL LOCK is on, HOME and END work the same as CTRL+HOME and CTRL+END without SCROLL LOCK.

Tip: Use *jump* keys to close in on the target insertion point.

Tip: You can jump to the first letter in a word with the CTRL+LEFT ARROW key or the CTRL+RIGHT ARROW key.

Trap: A word jump differs from a word select.

Tip: The END key allows you to resume typing where you left off.

Tip: SHIFT+F7 moves the highlight to previous sentences; SHIFT+F8 moves the highlight to subsequent sentences.

Trap: Pressing an arrow key after selecting a sentence causes a character in the next or previous sentence to be selected.

Tip: Determine the most efficient path between the current insertion point and the target insertion point.

Tip: CTRL+DOWN ARROW jumps to paragraphs beneath and CTRL+UP ARROW jumps to paragraphs above the current insertion point.

Trap: Don't separate paragraphs by using the ENTER key to insert paragraph markers. Use the Format Paragraph Space Before or Space After commands instead.

Tips and Traps Summary (*continued*)

Traversing Documents

Tip: The *thumb* indicates the position of the highlight in relation to the entire document.

Trap: The document measure bar readjusts as your document grows.

Tip: Look at the thumb to determine where you are in your document.

Tip: Repaginate to view page breaks and update the page indicator.

Trap: The numbers in the page indicator are accurate only if you have repaginated at least once and have repaginated since adding text.

Tip: Using the PGUP and PGDN keys leaves two lines from the previous screen at the bottom and top, respectively.

Tip: Press CTRL+PGUP or CTRL+PGDN to place the highlight at the beginning or end of a document, respectively.

Trap: You cannot use the HOME, END, or arrow keys in the menu when SCROLL LOCK is on.

Tip: The function of the arrow keys is altered when SCROLL LOCK is on; the HOME and END keys take on the functions of CTRL+HOME and CTRL+END.

Tip: Scrolling horizontally is useful for viewing documents with wide margins.

Trap: The RIGHT and LEFT ARROW keys will not move one character left and right when SCROLL LOCK is on.

Tip: If you have a mouse, use it instead of the arrow keys. Then you can leave SCROLL LOCK on to take advantage of its superior scrolling capabilities.

Tip: Wide paper will have wide margins that you can only view with horizontal scrolling.

Tip: Pressing the RIGHT ARROW key with SCROLL LOCK on causes one third of the screen to scroll left.

Tips and Traps Summary (*continued*)

Tip: The scroll bar can be used to scroll through a document with the mouse.

Tip: Press the scroll bar with the left button to move the top line of text next to the pointer.

Tip: Press the scroll bar with the right button to move the adjacent text to the top line.

Tip: Pressing both mouse buttons at once in the scroll bar places you in the part of your document that corresponds to the measuring stick position.

Tip: You can use the mouse to move horizontally by pressing both buttons in the horizontal scroll bar at the bottom of the screen.

Trap: After thumbing to a section of your document, point to a target insertion point with the mouse. Do not use the arrow keys.

Page Jumping Through Documents

Tip: You can use the Jump command to jump to any page in your document.

Tip: Press ALT+F5 to activate page jump mode.

Trap: The document must be paginated with the Print Repaginate command before a page jump can occur.

Search Jumping Techniques

Tip: Search is the fastest way to move to a target insertion point that is far away.

Tip: The previous search string stays in the Search field, ready for another search string.

Tip: The search begins at the current location of the highlight.

Tip: You can search up or down through a document.

Tip: SHIFT+F4 will repeat a search using the string of the last search.

Tip: You can narrow searches by selecting different Search options.

Tips and Traps Summary (*continued*)

Tip: The Whole Word field eliminates strings inside other words that match your search string.

Tip: You can limit searches by specifying upper/lowercase matches.

Tip: The longer your search string, the more specific the match.

Tip: Placing search codes throughout your document makes it easy to return to specific parts with the Search command.

Window Techniques

Tip: Windows can be opened on different parts of a document so that you can move or copy text from one part of your document to another.

Tip: An active window contains the highlight. Only one window can be active at a time.

Tip: Splitting a document with windows does not create two documents. You are working on two different parts of the same document at the same time.

Trap: Having too many windows open can make the edit window hard to manage.

Tip: Windows can be zoomed to fill the whole screen and then stacked in layers. Use the F1 key to step through the stack. Each window can point to a different section of your document.

Outline Mode Jumps

Tip: If a document is outlined, you can scroll through the collapsed titles in outline mode, and then return to the selected section in text mode.

8

Text Selection
Techniques

When it comes time to apply various formats to your documents, such as bold-face, italics, and type fonts, you must *select* the text in your documents that will receive these formats. If you need to move a word, sentence, paragraph, or other string of text to another part of your document, or if you need to simply delete text, you must first select it. This chapter covers the various ways in which you can select text in Word with either the keys on your keyboard or a mouse.

Basics of Text Selection

At the visual level, text selected on the screen is highlighted. Selected text will appear as if it were a large cursor or an extended version of the single-character highlight that normally appears at the insertion point. Only one, contiguous block of text can be selected at a time. You cannot pick a block in one paragraph and another in a second paragraph at the same time. Each block must be selected separately. In the example shown here, a sentence in the middle of the paragraph is highlighted.

```
It·always·does·seem·to·me·that·I·am·doing·more·work·than·I·
should·do.··It's·not·that·I·object·to·the·work,·mind·you;··I·
like·work;·it·fascinates·me.··I·can·sit·and·look·at·it·for·
hours.··I·love·to·keep·it·by·me;··the·idea·of·getting·rid·of·
it·nearly·breaks·my·heart.¶
```

 Tip: *Selected text is covered by a large highlight.*

 Tip: *Highlighted text must be a single, contiguous block of text.*

In most cases you will select text before performing an action or command in Word. For example, if you want to change a word somewhere in the text, scroll to the word to make it visible on the screen and then highlight it with the selection keys or the mouse. Once the proper text is highlighted, you can execute the Word command or edit action you want. Highlighted text can scroll off the screen, so be careful when you apply formats. Always try to keep the text that you are formatting visible on the screen.

 Trap: *Highlighted text that has scrolled off the screen can still be formatted.*

There is an important difference in the way text is selected that depends on the size of text block that you are selecting. To select a single character, you must place the highlight directly on that character. To select a word, however, you can place the highlight anywhere in the word and press the selection key that selects words. Sentences, paragraphs, and whole divisions can be selected in a similar way: you can point anywhere in them and press a key designed to select that size text block. If you want to be very specific about the text selected, however, you must use the arrow keys or a mouse to highlight exactly what you want.

 Tip: *You can select text in blocks by pointing anywhere in the block and using the proper block select key.*

Because spaces, tabs, paragraph markers, and other special keys are such an integral part of sentences and paragraphs, you can also select them in Word. In fact, when you press the appropriate key to select a single word, the space to the right of it is also selected.

 Tip: *Spaces, tabs, and paragraph markers may be highlighted for editing.*

Word assumes that all words include a space to separate them from the next word. If you select a sentence, the space following that sentence is automatically selected. The period at the end of a sentence is Word's cue for sentence selection. If you place two spaces between the period and the beginning of the next sentence, Word will select both spaces. If you select a paragraph, Word will automatically include the paragraph marker at the end of the paragraph. Because Word includes these "characters," you must have the Options Visible command set to Complete, as was done in Chapter 2. This will help you see where space characters, tabs, paragraph markers, and other characters are located so that you can see when they are included as part of a selection.

 Trap: *Words and sentences also include the space or spaces after them when they are highlighted.*

Be careful when you delete paragraph markers. Deleting a paragraph marker may cause the paragraph below to move up and assume the format of the previous paragraph. This will be covered shortly in this chapter and also in later chapters.

 Trap: *Be careful when you delete paragraph markers.*

A principal reason for selecting text is to format characters. You may be wondering, however, whether you should apply formats while typing or after you have finished. For example, if you are typing a sentence and want to put a word in boldface, you can simply press ALT+B (or ALT+X+B if a style sheet is attached) to turn on boldface typing. After the word is typed, press ALT+SPACEBAR to turn boldfacing off. The alternative method is the selection process described in this chapter, which is used to apply formats after text has been typed.

 Tip: *You can apply formats while typing or after typing a document.*

After you have worked with Word for a while, you will find the method that is best for you. You may want to format as you type if you don't like the idea of later searching for words that will need special formatting. These "hunt and format" sessions, however, can be beneficial if you include them as part of your reread and editing sessions. Some users want to get their thoughts on the screen as fast as possible. For them, stopping to press the ALT key sequences to change formatting is a bother. If you have a mouse, however, it is easy to format characters, words, and sentences because highlighting is much simpler.

 Trap: *Formatting after text is typed may require considerable hunting through text.*

 Tip: *You can include formatting in your reread and editing sessions.*

If you will be using style sheets in Word, you'll probably format as you type. Remember that style sheets contain formatting codes that you design to fit the type of documents you create. For example, you might create a style that aligns paragraphs with 1-inch left and right indents and sets an italic type style. Normally you would have to type several key combinations to set this paragraph format. Instead, you can assign all the formats to a single key combination of your choice. From then on, you just press the formatting key combination before you begin typing the paragraphs.

 Tip: *If style sheets are in use, it is best to apply paragraph format styles while typing.*

You highlight text not only to format it but also to edit it. You can move a block of highlighted text to another location, copy it, or delete it. The mouse is almost essential for editing in Word because it makes these operations a snap. So, if you don't yet have a mouse, you should consider getting one. Base this consideration on how you use Word and how much editing you do. If you write long documents that require rereading and editing, or if you like to move blocks of text around in a document after typing, a mouse can save you countless hours.

 Tip: *Text is highlighted so that it can be both formatted and edited.*

 Tip: *A mouse is best for editing operations because it can save you time in highlighting, deleting, copying, and removing text.*

You know about selecting text for formatting or editing. Now let's look further at what can be highlighted in your Word documents and at some special cases of what happens when you highlight.

The Selection Keys

This chapter will concentrate on formatting and editing a document after it has been typed. If a document isn't already on the screen, use the Transfer Load command to load the PASSAGES.DOC file created in Chapter 7 into your computer.

Points About Highlight Behavior

The highlight has a certain behavior that you will become accustomed to through use. This section will demonstrate how the highlight works in several situations.

The Highlight Shadow   Whenever you select text, keep in mind the exact location of the insertion point. If the highlight is on a single character, the insertion point is just to the left of that character. If the highlight is on an entire word, the insertion point is just to the left of that word. The same holds true with a highlighted sentence or paragraph. Try this now: move the highlight or point with the mouse into the second sentence of the first paragraph in your document; then press the SHIFT+F7 combination to highlight the sentence. Type **Now** and you will see that Word places the new characters in front of the sentence.

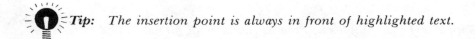 ***Tip:*** *The insertion point is always in front of highlighted text.*

When the highlight surrounds more than a single character, try to see it as a single-character highlight with an extended shadow. That is, the leftmost character of the highlight is the actual highlight, and the following characters are part of the shadow of the highlight (see Figure 8-1).

Although the first character of highlighted text is the insertion point, highlight movement resumes at the end of the current highlight if you press the RIGHT or DOWN ARROW key. Try pressing SHIFT+F7 to select a paragraph; then press the RIGHT ARROW key and notice how the highlight moves to the next character.

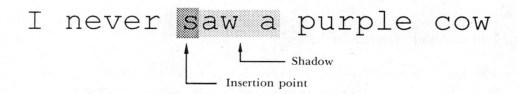

Figure 8-1. A highlight consists of an insertion point and its shadow

The Anchor Point   Don't confuse the function of the first character of a high-light with the *anchor point*, which concerns the ability to "extend" the highlight away from a certain point as you press the arrow keys or other cursor movement keys. The F6 key is the Extend key; when you press it, the EX keycode appears at the bottom of your screen. By using the anchor point method, you can select very specific groups of characters, such as those that are part of a word or part of a sentence.

 Tip: *The F6 (Extend) key lets you choose very specific groups of characters.*

The character that the highlight is on when you press F6 becomes the anchor point. As you move away from the anchor point with an arrow key, all characters between your current position and the anchor point become highlighted. You can move left, right, up, or down with the arrow keys, or you can use the PGUP and PGDN keys to select large blocks of text.

 Tip: *The character that the highlight is on when you press the F6 key becomes the anchor point for the extend operation.*

Experiment with the anchor point by selecting any point in the text and then pressing F6 (watch the EX code appear in the bottom of the screen) and the arrow keys. Try moving right and then down. Notice how the highlight follows the cursor movement, including all text between it and the anchor point. You must press F6 again to turn Extend off. Do this now; then try the next experiment.

 Trap: *Be sure to turn Extend off by pressing F6 when you have finished making your text selection.*

With Extend off, press an arrow key to return the highlight to single-character width. Now press F6 again and then press the RIGHT ARROW key several times. Next, press the LEFT ARROW key until the highlight shrinks back to the anchor point and then begins to expand to the left of it. With this experiment, you can see how the anchor point gets its name (see Figure 8-2). Press F6 again to turn Extend off.

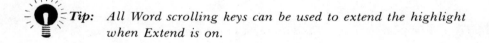 ***Tip:*** *You can move back over the anchor point and select text on the opposite side of it.*

All the keys that you normally use to move through a document can be used with Extend. For example, with Extend off, press CTRL+HOME to return to the upper-left corner of your document. Press F6, press F8 (Next Word) several times, press SHIFT+F8 (Next Sentence) several times, press F10 (Next Paragraph) several times, and then press PGDN. As you can see, the highlight follows the movement of text as you scroll, maintaining its anchor on the first word of the document. If you want to select the entire document, you could press CTRL+PGDN or, more simply, press SHIFT+F10.

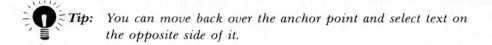 ***Tip:*** *All Word scrolling keys can be used to extend the highlight when Extend is on.*

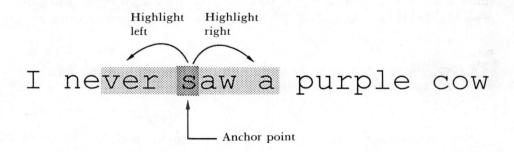

Figure 8-2. *The highlight extends from an anchor point when Extend is on*

The Extend Direction   You should keep in mind which way you are extending the highlight and what effect the cursor movement keys have. If you are extending to the right of the anchor point, you add characters to the highlighted block with the RIGHT ARROW key and remove them with the LEFT ARROW key. If you are highlighting backward, the LEFT ARROW key adds new characters to the high-light, while the RIGHT ARROW key removes them.

Using the Mouse with Extend   If you have a mouse, you can use Extend (F6) to increase its capabilities. For example, make sure that Extend is off and then move the highlight with an arrow key to return it to single-character size. Press F6 and then click at another point in your text. All text between the anchor and the mouse click point will be highlighted, as shown here:

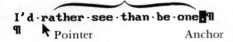

I'd·rather·see·than·be·one█¶
¶ ⸜ Pointer   Anchor

When you are done, press F6 to turn Extend off.

 Tip: *The mouse can be used to extend highlights when Extend is on.*

Selecting Characters

Selecting single characters is nothing new. You have already done this by placing the highlight on the target character with the arrow keys or a mouse. Use of the F6 (Extend) key is the primary method for selecting more than one character. With Extend, you can anchor the highlight and then select any number of characters that you want to the left, right, up, or down. Remember that you can use the highlight to select an odd group of characters, such as those in the middle of a word.

Tab stops, spaces, and paragraph markers are considered single characters, and you can highlight them with the arrow keys.

Selecting Words

Selecting whole words in Word is fairly easy. You will normally select a whole word to format it (say, to convert it to italic or bold) or to delete it. To do so, locate the word by using the arrow keys and then press F7 or F8 to highlight it, or point to it with the mouse and press the right button to select it. When a word is selected, the space to the right of it is included in the highlight, as shown here:

I·never·saw·a·**Purple·Cow**,↓

                └── A word selection includes the space after it

> **Tip:** *The F7 and F8 keys are used to select words. The space to the right is always included as part of the word.*

You may notice that F7 and F8 do the same thing when you are on a word. This is normally the case when the highlight is on a single character. Word simply assumes that you want to select the current word. Press F7 again to select the next word to the left and F8 to select the next word to the right.

> **Tip:** *The F7 and F8 keys both select the current word. Press them again to select a word to the left or right, respectively.*

If you press the F6 (Extend) key, you can continue to include whole words in your current selection, either to the right or left. But pressing the LEFT ARROW or UP ARROW key will cause the currently selected word to drop out of the selection. The first character of the word becomes the anchor point as the highlight moves to the left or up. You should place the highlight in the last letter of the word before selecting to the left or up.

> **Trap:** *Highlighting up or to the left from the current word selection removes the word from the selection.*

Selecting Lines

You can use the SHIFT+F9 combination to select the current line of text. Pointing in the selection bar with a mouse and pressing the left button will also select a line. Users select this option primarily when working with tables or selecting single-line titles. It makes little sense to select a line of text because it may include part of a sentence or paragraph.

The next example shows how a line of a table is selected with the mouse.

```
*    Phone·Numbers↓
     ↓
     Dianne·Shale→    687-9874↓
     John·Jones→      687-9375↓
     Mary·Millet→     963-2456¶
```

Notice that the entire table is a single paragraph, as indicated by the down arrows at the end of the line. Use the SHIFT+F9 combination or mouse method for selecting single lines in multiple-line paragraphs.

Selecting Sentences

A sentence is a group of words that ends with a period and either one space or two. When you select a sentence with the mouse, SHIFT+F7, or SHIFT+F8, the period and spaces are also selected. The sentence selection keys are similar to the word selection keys in that the current location of the highlight is selected first. Press SHIFT+F7 or SHIFT+F8 to highlight the previous or next sentence, respectively.

 Tip: *Sentence selection includes the period and spaces that follow the sentence.*

If you have a mouse, point anywhere in the sentence and press both buttons at once to select it. If you have a three-button mouse, press both right and left buttons or the middle button.

🖐 *Trap:*   *On a three-button mouse, press both the right and left buttons or just the middle button to select a sentence.*

Selecting Paragraphs

Selecting paragraphs is as simple as pressing either the F9 or F10 key. If you have a mouse, simply press the right button in the selection bar next to the paragraph. When a paragraph is selected, the paragraph marker is selected as well.

 Tip: *Select paragraphs by pressing F9 or F10 or by clicking the right button of a mouse in the selection bar.*

Selecting the Document

You can select the entire document by pressing SHIFT+F10 or by clicking both mouse buttons in the selection bar. For example, you may want to select the entire document to change its type style or to convert it to double spacing.

 Tip: *Press SHIFT+F10 or click with both mouse buttons in the selection bar to select the whole document.*

Other Selections

You must keep a few other things in mind when making selections with Word. The TAB key and SPACEBAR are considered characters, just like A and B, as discussed earlier. Because Word allows for flexible tabs, a tab character may be from one to five or more characters wide. This often confuses novice users. In the example shown here,

```
 ▌═[·········1·········2·········3·····
 │    J.·Hill→   →   524-0875¶
 ▐*   John·Hamilton▌678-2345¶
```

tabs are set to the standard 1/2-inch settings. In the top line notice that two tabs are used to place the phone number in the 1.5-inch position. In the second line a single tab aligns phone number with the one above. This tab has shrunk to two characters wide. Word allows characters to infringe on the tab domain until it is filled. Then the characters to the right of the tab move to the next tab stop with a new, five-character-wide tab between.

Trap: *The size of a tab will shrink or grow according to the text around it.*

When you work with tables, Word allows you to select a single column of information, as shown here:

```
Phone·Numbers↓
↓
Dianne·Shale→   687-9874↓
John·Jones→     687-9375↓
Mary·Millet→    963-2456↓
J.·Hill→   →    524-0875↓
John·Hamilton→  678-2345¶
```

Use SHIFT+F6 to toggle Column Select on and off. Here the highlight was placed in the number 6 of the top phone number. Column Select was toggled on, and the arrow keys were used to move the highlight down to the lower-right corner. When you select a column, you can move, format, or delete it. (Column selection is covered in detail in Chapter 11.)

 Tip: *You can select a column to format, move, or delete it.*

Selecting with the Mouse

The mouse is by far the most convenient way to select text. You select a character by pointing to it and pressing the left button. You can point to a word and press the right button to select it. Press both buttons to select a sentence, or press in the selection bar to select a line, paragraph, or the whole document. The mouse is also best for selecting odd groups of text. You can point anywhere in the text and "drag" the selection to any other point you want by simply holding down the left button. In addition, the mouse can be used with the F6 (Extend) key.

When using a mouse, it is easy to mistakenly select and delete the markers that separate two paragraphs with different formats. For example, you might drag the mouse from the paragraph end marker of one sentence and into the characters of another. Pressing DEL will remove not only the characters but also the paragraph marker that separates the formats of the two paragraphs. The upper paragraph will assume the formatting of the lower one. That is, if the lower paragraph has both left and right indents, the upper paragraph will be assigned these same indents.

One advantage of the mouse is that it is easy to select blocks of text larger than the screen. When you are dragging the mouse during a selection and hit the walls of the edit window, the text will begin to scroll so that you can continue to select further up, down, or horizontally in the document.

 Tip: *The mouse lets you actively scroll through the document while you are selecting text.*

Search Techniques for Selecting Text

Word is so versatile that you can use the Search command to help highlight text. Let's say that your document is split into sections labeled Section 1, Section 2, Section 3, and so on. Now let's assume that you want to remove Section 2. You can place the highlight on the first character of Section 2, press the F6 (Extend) key, and then use the Search command to find the title "Section 3." When Word finds it, simply use the LEFT ARROW key to remove the highlight from the title and then press DEL. This removes all text highlighted by the extended search.

 Tip: *The Search command can be used to extend the highlight.*

Try this with the text in the **PASSAGES.DOC** file. Press CTRL+PGUP to get to the first paragraph of the document. Now, press the F6 (Extend) key and then press ESC+S to open the Search command. Type **i** and press ENTER; the highlight should extend to the second *I* in the first sentence. Press SHIFT+F4 (Repeat Search) six times to get to the last *I* in the third line. Then press the LEFT ARROW key to move off the *I*. At this point, you can delete the text under the highlight. This routine may seem cumbersome, but keep it in mind as you use Word. You never know when you may need to use search to make selections.

Tips and Traps Summary

What Is Text Selection?

Tip: Selected text is covered by a large highlight.

Tip: Highlighted text must be a single, contiguous block of text.

Trap: Highlighted text that has scrolled off the screen can still be formatted.

Tip: You can select text in blocks by pointing anywhere in the block and using the proper block select key.

Tip: Spaces, tabs, and paragraph markers may be highlighted for editing.

Trap: Words and sentences also include the space or spaces after them when they are highlighted.

Trap: Be careful when you delete paragraph markers.

Tip: You can apply formats while typing or after typing a document.

Trap: Formatting after text is typed may require considerable hunting through text.

Tip: You can include formatting in your reread and editing sessions.

Tip: If style sheets are in use, it is best to apply paragraph format styles while typing.

Tip: Text is highlighted so that it can be both formatted and edited.

Tip: A mouse is best for editing operations because it can save you time when highlighting, deleting, copying, and moving text.

Tips and Traps Summary (*continued*)

The Selection Keys

Tip: The insertion point is always in front of highlighted text.

Tip: The F6 (Extend) key lets you choose very specific groups of characters.

Tip: The character that the highlight is on when you press the F6 key becomes the anchor point for the extend operation.

Trap: Be sure to turn Extend off by pressing F6 when you have finished making your text selection.

Tip: You can move back over the anchor point and select text on the opposite side of it.

Tip: All Word scrolling keys can be used to extend the highlight when Extend is on.

Tip: The mouse can be used to extend highlights when Extend is on.

Tip: The F7 and F8 keys are used to select words. The space to the right is always included as part of the word.

Tip: The F7 and F8 keys both select the current word. Pressing them again selects a word to the left or right respectively.

Trap: Highlighting up or to the left from the current word selection removes the word from the selection.

Tip: Sentence selection includes the period and spaces that follow the sentence.

Trap: On a three-button mouse, press either both the right and left buttons or just the middle button to select a sentence.

Tip: Select paragraphs by pressing F9 and F10, or by clicking the right button of a mouse in the selection bar.

Tip: Press SHIFT+F10 or click with both mouse buttons in the selection bar to select the whole document.

Trap: The size of a tab will shrink or grow according to the text around it.

Tip: You can select a column to format, move, or delete it.

Tips and Traps Summary (*continued*)

Selecting with the Mouse

Tip: The mouse lets you actively scroll through the document while you are selecting text.

Search Techniques for Selecting Text

Tip: The Search command can be used to extend the highlight.

9

Editing
Techniques

In this chapter, you will learn the full spectrum of Word commands used to edit documents. Editing includes not only adding and deleting new characters but copying and moving them to other locations. It also includes the use of various Word tools, such as the dictionary, thesaurus, and sorting capabilities to alter existing text.

The Writing Process

There are basically five steps to creating any document in Microsoft Word:

- Enter the text.
- Revise and edit the text.
- Format the text.
- Print the document.
- Save the document for future use.

The first two steps are often combined. Writers accustomed to using typewriters naturally correct typing mistakes and grammatical problems as they enter a document. Other writers, who have become accustomed to electronic word processing, may type their documents as quickly as possible, attempting to get down as many ideas as they can. Later, they may go back through the document to copy and move text blocks, fix mistakes, and so on. This does not imply that you should adopt this method as you become accustomed to your system. The best way to work with Word is the one that is most comfortable for you, which you will discover over time.

You can take care of such formatting tasks as boldfacing, italicizing, paragraph aligning, and indenting as you type or later, after the document has been entered. Again, you needn't follow the steps to creating a document in any particular order. You should write in a way that is most comfortable for you or that is most applicable to the document you are creating. If a style sheet is attached (as discussed earlier and in detail in Chapter 16), you may want to apply preset styles as you type paragraphs. It is sometimes easier to apply character formats as you type because applying them later may require a search of the text. On the other hand, you can combine this search with a reread of the document. Printing and saving are the last two steps, which are, of course, optional. Printing may be postponed until a final version is prepared, which means that you must save the document to disk for a later editing session. Some documents don't need to be saved. Quick memos and letters may simply be printed and then erased from the screen.

The Editing Process

Editing a document goes beyond spell checking, deleting duplicate words, and inserting new text. A document is often completely rearranged before final printing, and the editing process can sometimes be considered the "construction phase" of document creation. For example, a professor, doctor, or scientist might need to prepare a report or professional paper. As the research is performed, notes, tables, and other text are collected in a file or several files. From these files, a kind of blueprint or outline of the final document is constructed, which will later be prepared by a research assistant. In this draft, notes and comments to the assistant are included as "hidden," nonprintable text. The assistant then has everything needed to finish the construction of the document.

Editing Techniques

This chapter will concentrate on the text entry and revision process, which can be broken down into a number of steps that constitute the topic headings of this chapter. Almost all editing and revision techniques in Word, including mouse techniques, can be grouped into one of these categories:

- Inserting and adding text
- Deleting text
- Copying text blocks
- Moving text blocks
- Replacing text blocks

The process of inserting and adding text is *nondestructive* to existing text. It is the normal text entry process that you go through when first entering text or when adding new text to a document. Note that text is not always entered from the keyboard. You will see how to insert previously typed text blocks from other parts of your document, from the glossary, and even from other files. The glossary is a short- or long-term memory location in Word where you can place often used text.

 Tip: *Text can be inserted not only from the keyboard but also from a glossary or from another file.*

Deleting text is a *destructive* process that can become more involved than you might think at first. You can delete text into oblivion; into a kind of limbo area, where it can be recalled into another part of your document; or into a permanent area for use at a later time or in another document.

 Trap: *Deleting is a destructive process that can cause permanent loss of text.*

Don't confuse *copying* text blocks with *moving* text blocks, as discussed next. When you copy a block of text, a duplicate is made in another location and the original stays intact. When you move a block of text, the original is deleted and reinserted somewhere else. You can copy text by using the mouse, by inserting a duplicate in the glossary for later use, or even by deleting and then reinserting it in various places.

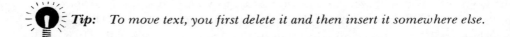

Trap: *Don't confuse copying text with moving text. Copying makes a duplicate of the highlighted text.*

Moving text blocks involves deleting text from its current location and inserting it in another location. So the move process involves a combination of deleting and inserting. A mouse can be used to perform a text move in a few simple keystrokes, as you'll see.

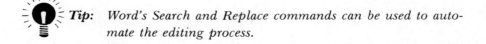

Tip: *To move text, you first delete it and then insert it somewhere else.*

Many editing tasks can be automated with Word's Search and Replace commands. For example, you may discover that a name is spelled incorrectly throughout a document. You can use Search and Replace to locate the incorrect version and replace it with the correct one in the whole document. In a standard letter that you print often, you can use Search and Replace to substitute a new name for one used in the previous version. You can also plan to search and replace ahead of time. For example, you could type the abbreviation of your company name and then search and replace it with the longer name later on.

Tip: *Word's Search and Replace commands can be used to auto-mate the editing process.*

In addition to the major editing features described so far, text revision and editing include the following topics:

- Moving and copying between documents
- Automatic spelling check

- Word substitution with the thesaurus

- Rearranging lists with the Sort command

Using windows, you can open two or more documents at once and then cut and paste between them. If you need text from one document, figures from another, and notations from still another, you can easily jump between the windows with the F1 key or the mouse to copy text and insert text blocks. You can also open several windows on one document to copy text between different parts of it.

 Tip: *Windows can be used to copy text between different parts of a document or between two or more documents.*

Spell checking was once one of the most tedious parts of document editing, especially when typewriters were in widespread use. Word's built-in spell checker flags all words that it doesn't recognize. Although many of these words may be spelled correctly, they are unfamiliar to Word. You can add them to the spell checker, however, thus building a library of words that are specific to your use. Because spell checking is such an important part of the editing process, it is covered briefly here and in more detail in Chapter 20.

 Tip: *Spell checking is performed by Word. You can add your own special words to the dictionary.*

Word's built-in Thesaurus is another editing tool at your disposal. As you type a document, you can look up an alternate word. Or, while rereading the document, you may notice that an often used word begins to sound repetitive. You can use the Thesaurus to find a substitute.

 Tip: *Using Word's thesaurus is a convenient way to substitute repetitive words in a document.*

Sorting a list of names, numbers, or other text is another important part of the editing process. You can type in a table of information without worrying about alphabetical or numerical order. Later, you'll sort some text; for now, additional editing features of Word need to be covered.

 Tip: *Word's Sort feature lets you type text or tables in any order and then sort them later.*

As you make changes to your text, Word automatically readjusts it into the margins. If you are adding text, Word readjusts all text below the insertion point. At times, this may not only be confusing but may also slow the operation of Word. If you are inserting a large amount of text, you may want to temporarily insert a paragraph marker (press ENTER) to move the lower text out of the way. Then you can add text without having to wait for Word to wrap each line below. When you are done, rejoin the paragraphs by removing the temporary paragraph marker.

 Tip: *Word automatically readjusts text to the margins when you insert or delete.*

 Trap: *Word's automatic word wrap may cause Word to become sluggish during text insertion. Insert a temporary paragraph marker for the text ahead of the insertion point; then rejoin the paragraph when done.*

If you work with large documents, it will become increasingly clear to you that outlining is an essential part of creating and editing documents. When a document has an accompanying outline, you can quickly jump from one place to another in the document by repositioning the highlight in the outline mode, which shows only the headings. You can also rearrange blocks of text in outline mode by moving just the headings. For example, you can simply move a heading before or after another one to rearrange the entire block of text under that heading.

 Tip: *Outline mode lets you quickly rearrange whole sections of documents, as well as letting you quickly jump between sections of your document.*

All large documents that will require editing or rearranging should initially be created in outline mode. Outline mode isn't just a tool for organizing your ideas. It is much more than that. Once you have your ideas on the screen in outline form, you can rearrange them with little effort. After the major portion of your text is entered, outline mode can help you move text and headings around or find your way through all the text by displaying only the headings.

Creating a Work Document

To get the most out of this chapter, follow the exercises on the screen as you read to get a feel for how Word works and see how to use its features in real situations. At this point, you should type in the sample document shown in Figure 9-1. You can make one change, however, that you will find useful as you use Word. In place of Easy Ledger Software's name and address at the top, type in your own company name or personal name and address. Later, you'll see how to save it in the glossary so that it can be used in other documents.

Figure 9-2 shows the letter of Figure 9-1 with some marks for editing changes. In the remainder of this chapter you'll see how to make these changes to the letter you typed.

The Scrap and Glossary

The *scrap* and the *glossary* are memories where you can store text, both temporary and permanent. Recall that the scrap, or at least a small portion of it, is visible as

```
Easy Ledger Software
3000 Journal Drive
Santa Barbara, CA 93105


November 29, 1988


Mr. John Jones
Norton Engineering
3991 State Street
Santa Barbara, CA 93101

Dear Mr. Jones,

It was a pleasure to talk with you the other day
concerning your office automation needs.  I am sure
that we can help you establish a computerized
accounting system to fit your needs.  It will be our
pleasure to assist you.  Based on our initial meeting,
we recommend the following software packages.


EL General Ledger              $350
EL Accounts Receivable         $495
EL Accounts Payable            $495
EL Payroll                     $595
EL California tax module       $100

Our service rate is $60 per hour.  We estimate
installation should take 8 hours.  If you wish to
proceed, please call.


Sincerely



Alexander Halliburton
Marketing Manager
```

Figure 9-1. Letter to Jones for chapter exercises

a left and right bracket on the bottom line of your screen. When you delete text with the DEL (Delete) key, it is placed in the scrap. You can also use other keys to place text in the scrap, as you'll see later.

Whenever you delete a character, a word, or other text block, the contents of the scrap are replaced by the newly deleted text, so you must be careful about what you are deleting.

 Trap: *Text in the scrap can be overwritten by a new deletion.*

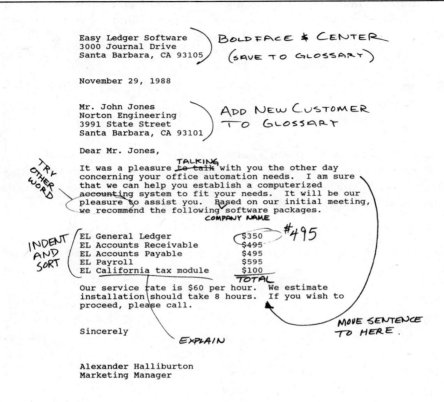

Figure 9-2. Editing marks and changes in Jones letter

A glossary is a more permanent version of the scrap. If you know that you will need a block of text at a later time, one that either needs to be deleted or is highlighted on the screen, you can use the Delete or Copy command to copy it to the glossary as a glossary entry.

 Tip: *Text highlighted on the screen can be saved for later use in a glossary with the Copy or Delete command.*

The Insert command is used to insert the glossary entry into another part of the text. Think of the glossary as another window behind the edit window that holds glossary entries, as shown in Figure 9-3.

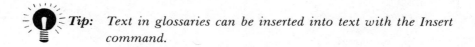

Tip: *Text in glossaries can be inserted into text with the Insert command.*

Each glossary entry is given a name. For example, the address that you typed in the letter of Figure 9-1 will be saved to a glossary entry called ADDRESS (or any other name you choose). The glossary can hold a number of these named text entries, which can then be saved in a Word *glossary file.*

Tip: *A set of glossary entries can be saved to a disk file for later use.*

Word automatically attaches a glossary called NORMAL.GLY (not to be confused with the NORMAL.STY style sheet) to each document that you create, unless you attach another glossary. Word allows other glossary files because you

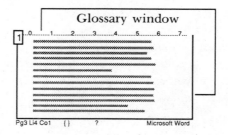

Figure 9-3.   Glossaries are stored in a separate window

may want to create specific glossary entries for specific types of work, such as personal and work-related glossaries.

 Tip: *You can create several glossary files to use with different types of documents.*

 Trap: *Word automatically attaches NORMAL.GLY to every new document.*

One way to think about how the scrap and glossaries work is to relate them to how you use and remember phone numbers. Studies show that the brain has a built-in temporary notepad where short-term memories, such as phone numbers, are stored. You remember a phone number long enough to dial it. New information usually replaces the phone number almost immediately. If you want to remember a phone number for a few days, you might write it on a matchbook. If you want to remember it for a long time, you might write it in a phone directory book.

The Word scrap and glossary system work in the same way. The contents of the scrap, like those of the brain's temporary storage area, are not permanent. The contents of the scrap, which you can insert elsewhere if you want, are copied over by the next deletion.

 Tip: *Text in the scrap can be inserted elsewhere with the INS key.*

If you need to delete text from its current location but use it later in the document, you can commit it to a glossary entry, just as you might write a phone number to a matchbook.

 Tip: *Text can be committed to a glossary entry with the Delete menu command.*

Like phone numbers on matchbooks, glossary entries are not necessarily permanent. As you might throw away an empty matchbook, glossary entries are discarded when you quit Word, unless you save them to a disk file. If you save a glossary that has new entries, you can use the entries when you next use Word.

 Trap: *You must save a glossary file if you want to keep the entries added in a Word session for a future session.*

Figure 9-4 shows how the scrap, glossary, and glossary file work in relation to each other. Text can be deleted to the scrap for immediate insertion elsewhere. It can be deleted or copied to a glossary for later use in the same document, or it can be saved with the glossary for use in another document.

Creating Glossary Entries

As mentioned, you can create glossary entries by either copying highlighted text with the Copy command or deleting highlighted text into the glossary with the Delete command. When you want to use the text later on, use the Insert command to replace it in the document at the location of the highlight. When you attempt to either Copy or Delete, the scrap brackets will always appear in the command field, as shown here:

COPY to: {}

Enter glossary name or press F1 to select from list

Word is proposing the scrap as the destination for the copy or delete. Press ENTER to place the highlighted text in the scrap. You could perform the same function by pressing DEL or the ALT+F3 key combination, which sends a copy of the highlighted text to the scrap.

 Tip: *You can use either the Copy command or ALT+F3 to copy highlighted text to the scrap.*

 Tip: *You can use either the Delete command or the DEL key to remove highlighted text to the scrap.*

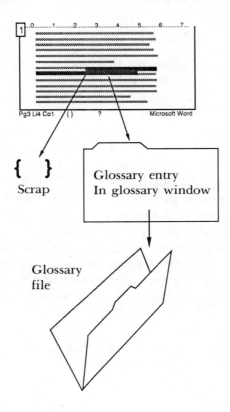

Figure 9-4. *Highlighted text can be placed in the scrap, glossary, or glossary file*

If you press F1 after executing Copy, Insert, or Delete, a list of current glossary entries will be displayed. You can use this list to determine existing entries so that you don't copy over them, or you can use it to determine the name of a glossary entry to copy over. Occasionally you may want to update a glossary entry by inserting the new entry with the name of the old.

Tip: *You can update glossary entries by specifying the existing name when using Copy or Delete.*

It's time to try creating a glossary entry. For this example, use the company name that you typed in the letter of Figure 9-1. If you used your own company name and address or your home address, you will be able to use this glossary entry in future sessions.

Move the highlight to the top line of the address and press the HOME key if it is not on the leftmost character. Press the F6 (Extend) key and then press the DOWN ARROW key until the paragraph marker under the address is highlighted. It is OK to include the extra paragraph marker because you will probably always want to include a space under the address. Before inserting this name in the glossary, press ALT+C to center it and then ALT+B to boldface it. If a style sheet is attached, you may need to press ALT+X+C and ALT+X+B.

Press ESC to get to the Word command menu and then execute the Copy command. Because the highlight is already on Copy, you can simply press ENTER. Word proposes the scrap as the destination for the highlighted text. Instead, type **address** in the Copy field. Finally, press ENTER to execute the command.

 Trap: *Word proposes the scrap as the destination for Copy and Delete. You can simply type over this with a glossary name.*

It will appear that nothing has happened at first. The command menu disappears and the screen looks normal. At this point, you can look at the current glossary. Press ESC, execute the Insert command, and press F1 to see a list of glossary entries. Your screen should look like the one shown here unless you have taken steps to add more than the standard glossary entries. Notice that the Address glossary entry is included on the screen, along with other glossary entries that will be discussed in the next section.

```
page                            footnote
date                            dateprint
time                            timeprint
address
```

Editing Techniques

Try inserting the Address entry just to see how Insert works. Use the arrow keys to move the highlight to Address and, then press ENTER. The edit window will reappear, and you will see two copies of the address. That's how simple it is to retype previously typed text. For now, press ESC+U to undo the insert.

 Tip: *Press ESC+U to undo glossary inserts.*

Using Glossary Entries

It's one thing to place blocks of text in the glossary file but another to reinsert them at the appropriate locations. Word provides two ways of doing this, one of which is to use the Insert command as you just did. Alternatively, you can insert a glossary entry by first typing its name and then pressing the F3 (Glossary Expand) key.

 Tip: *Glossary entries can be inserted with the Insert command or the F3 (Glossary Expand) key.*

 Trap: *Enter the name of the glossary entry before pressing the F3 (Glossary Expand) key.*

 Tip: *Use the Insert command if you can't remember the name of a glossary. Press F1 to see a list.*

At this point, try using the F3 (Glossary Expand) key to insert the Address glossary entry. Type **address** anywhere in your document and then press F3. The boldfaced, centered address should appear immediately. Because this is only an example, press ESC+U (Undo) to remove it. This example should show you how easy it is to have Word type text for you.

Supplied Glossary Entries

Microsoft supplies a set of predefined glossary entries that are attached to every document you create. They are quite convenient and sometimes essential. To see the list of supplied entries, press ESC, execute the Insert command, and then press F1. Six entries are available unless you use Microsoft Windows, in which case a Clipboard entry is also listed. Word's supplied glossary entries are described next.

Page   The *Page* glossary entry is used to insert the special (page) entry in your text. This entry automatically inserts the current page number when the document is printed. Typically (page) is placed in a running head. (See Chapter 11 for more details.)

Footnote   The *Footnote* glossary entry can be used to reinsert a footnote that may have been deleted. (See Chapter 13 for more details.)

Date   The *Date* glossary entry automatically inserts the current date into the text at the position of the highlight. This date is the one set at the DOS level of your system. You can try this now. First, select the date on the letter and delete it. The deleted text appears in the scrap. Next, type **date** and press the F3 (Glossary Expand) key. The current date is typed, assuming that it is properly set in your computer.

Dateprint   The *Dateprint* glossary entry differs from the Date entry. Dateprint will print the current date only when the letter is printed. So you can create a standard form letter to be printed at any time. Then, when you do print it, the correct date is used. Try this now. Replace the current date on the letter with the Dateprint glossary entry. First, highlight the date and delete it. Next, type **dateprint** and press F3. "Dateprint" will appear between round brackets, indicating that the dateprint glossary entry is in this location.

Time   The *Time* glossary entry works like the Date entry, except that the current time is inserted in the text.

Timeprint   The *Timeprint* glossary entry works like the dateprint entry, except that the current time is printed when the document is printed.

Clipboard   If you are running Microsoft Windows, you can insert text from the *Clipboard* of the Windows program. The clipboard is a special holding area where text or graphics from other programs running in the Windows environment can be placed while you move between applications.

Inserting and Adding Text

There is more to adding and inserting text than was covered in the section on the scrap and glossary. True, when you add text to a document or insert at the current highlight, you will often use the scrap or glossary as your source. But these are not the only sources of text.

The keyboard is the most obvious source of new text, though you can import text from other parts of the same document or even other documents. You can also merge data from mailing lists or databases into Word documents when special fields in the text are assigned to receive that data. The thesaurus and calculator are other sources of new text. Figure 9-5 illustrates these different sources, which are covered next.

Copy to Scrap; Insert Elsewhere

You can "borrow" text from one part of your document and insert elsewhere. You may have noticed that the scrap is a great place to perform cut-and-paste type operations. You can quickly copy or delete text into the scrap and then insert the scrap somewhere else in a document.

The edited version of the letter to Mr. Jones (Figure 9-2) requests an explanation of why the California tax module is needed. Type the following sentence at the end of the last paragraph: **The California tax module is required to run the Payroll package in California.** You can borrow the phrase "California tax module" in the last line of the product pricing table by highlighting it and then pressing ALT+F3 to copy it to the scrap, as shown here:

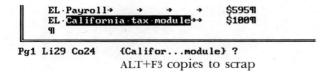

```
EL·Payroll→    →    →    →    $595¶
EL·California·tax·module→→    $100¶
¶
```

Pg1 Li29 Co24   {Califor...module} ?
                 ALT+F3 copies to scrap

Because this is a copy, the original text remains in the paragraph. Notice that only the first and last parts of the text are visible in the 16-character-wide scrap.

 Tip: *The ALT+F3 key combination places a copy of the highlighted text in the scrap.*

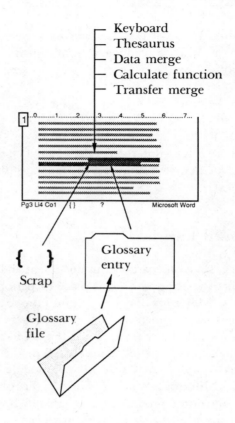

Figure 9-5. Text can be inserted and added from many sources

Next, start typing the new sentence. Position the cursor at the end of the paragraph, type a couple of spaces and the word **The**, and press the INS key. The text in the scrap is inserted. You can then finish typing the new sentence.

Insert Text to Glossary; Then Expand Elsewhere

The next change to make on the letter is to insert the company name into what is now the second to last sentence of the first paragraph. You could just move the cursor to that location and type the company name, but in this case we'll again borrow text from another location. This time, however, the borrowed text will first be placed in the glossary because the company name is a good thing to have on hand in the glossary.

Highlight the company name in the logo at the top of the letter. It doesn't matter if you typed your own company name here. Be sure to highlight only the company name, not the paragraph marker (the reason why will be covered next). Once the text is highlighted, press ESC and execute the Copy command. In the To field, type **coname** and press ENTER. Now, move to the *s* in *software* in the target sentence, type **coname**, and press the F3 (Glossary Expand) key. The company name is inserted, but notice that the word *software* is repeated. Enter a space to separate the words, press F8 to highlight the second word, and then press the DEL key.

Inserting Paragraph Markers

If you need to split a paragraph in two, move the highlight to the desired break point and press ENTER. A paragraph marker will be inserted, and the rest of the paragraph will move down as a new paragraph.

 Tip: *Insert a paragraph marker to split an existing paragraph in two.*

Be careful when inserting text that may contain paragraph markers from the scrap and glossary. If you insert text with paragraph markers in the middle of another paragraph, the existing paragraph will be split in two. Further, a paragraph marker contains formatting information, so the existing paragraph will take on the formatting of the inserted one. Press ESC+U to undo such a situation.

Trap: *Paragraph markers inserted from the scrap or glossary may carry formats that alter existing paragraph formats.*

Inserting Calculation Results

Word will perform automatic calculations on any numbers that are within the boundaries of a highlight; that is, the numbers can be anywhere in the highlight. The F2 key is used to perform the calculation. Addition is always performed unless you insert symbols to specify other types of calculations. The result of the calculation is placed in the scrap so that you can insert it at an appropriate place in your text, as shown in Figure 9-6. (Math operations will be covered in Chapter 20.)

To highlight the entire price table, place the cursor on the left of the first line, press the F6 (Extend) key, and move the cursor under the bottom line. Then press F2. The sum of all numbers within the highlighted area will appear in the scrap. You can then insert a new line at the bottom of the table called "Total," tab to the right, and press INS to insert the total.

Numbers to be calculated should not usually be selected with the normal highlight. Word has a special column select mode that can highlight numbers in columnar form like those in a table. In this way you can more easily select just the numbers you want to calculate.

Deleting Text

There are a number of ways to delete text in Word. Some are obvious; others are not. You must learn how to distinguish among the many ways of deleting so that you use the best one for a particular situation. This section divides deletion into two types. Those that do not preserve a copy of deleted text (unless you execute an immediate Undo command) are *destructive deletions* and are covered first. *Recycled deletions* preserve a copy of deleted text in either the scrap or the glossary. They are covered in the following section.

Keep in mind that all deletions can be recovered if you execute the Undo command immediately. Press ESC+U or SHIFT+F1 to recover deleted text, assuming that you have not performed other deletions or commands since the deletions.

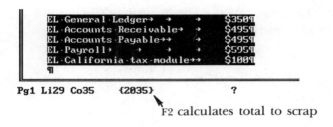

F2 calculates total to scrap

Figure 9-6. Calculation results are placed in the scrap

Do not delete a paragraph marker unless you are sure that it is not needed. If you delete a paragraph marker that separates two paragraphs with different formats, the first paragraph will take on the formatting of the second as they merge.

 Trap: *Deleting paragraph markers may cause paragraphs to take on formats of other paragraphs.*

Destructive Deletions

Destructive deletions cause a permanent loss of text, by either copying over text or throwing it out completely. In this section you'll see a number of ways to alter the Jones letter.

BACKSPACE You've had some experience with the BACKSPACE key, which is used primarily to delete a mistake made during typing. The character typed over with the backspace is lost. Note that the scrap is not altered by a backspace deletion.

SHIFT+F1: Delete, Not to Scrap   The SHIFT+F1 (Delete) key combination is more important than you might think at first. Pressing this key sequence will cause highlighted text to be removed though not to the scrap. The scrap remains untouched. This is important if you are using the scrap to temporarily hold text that is to be inserted elsewhere.

 Tip: *To perform a delete but retain the contents of the scrap, use SHIFT+F1.*

For example, assume that you are working on a 10-page document and decide to move a paragraph on page 3 to page 5. You highlight the paragraph and press DEL to delete the paragraph to the scrap. You then begin to scroll down the text to page 5, where you plan to insert the paragraph from the scrap into text. While scrolling, you notice a word typed twice, so you stop scrolling and highlight the word with the intention of deleting it. *Watch your step in this situation.* Remember that the scrap holds the deleted paragraph from page 3, making it vulnerable to complete loss because you no longer have a copy of it in the text. If you delete the currently highlighted word with the DEL key, you will overwrite the paragraph in the scrap. Instead, use SHIFT+F1 to remove the extra word.

Overtype   Overtype mode allows you to turn off the insertion of text at the highlight. If the highlight is located on previously typed text, that text will be overwritten and lost. Overtype is rarely useful unless you need to replace characters or words with new text of the same length.

In the first sentence of the Jones letter, the phrase "to talk" should be replaced with the word *talking*. Move the highlight to the *t* in *to* and press the F5 (Overtype) toggle key. Notice that the OT keycode appears in the bottom of the screen. Now type **talking** over the old text.

 Tip: *Overtype types over existing text.*

Overtype has limited use, and it is often easier to simply stay in insert mode, type in the new text, and then remove the unwanted text. Because Overtype is a toggle key, you must remember to turn it off when done. Many users forget this, which often leads to lost text as typing continues.

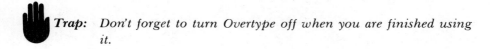

Trap: *Don't forget to turn Overtype off when you are finished using it.*

There is another place in the Jones letter that needs editing in overtype mode. Move the highlight to the 3 in the $350 price for the EL General Ledger package. With overtype on, change the price to $495.

Thesaurus Replacement   The thesaurus offers a quick way to change an over-used word. You can also use it while entering text to display alternate words. Simply place the highlight anywhere on the word to be altered and press CTRL+F6. The thesaurus window appears, and you can use the arrow keys to move the highlight to the word you want. If you are typing, press CTRL+F6 immediately after typing the word to display the thesaurus window. (For more information on the thesaurus, see Chapter 20.)

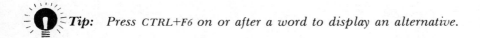

Tip: *Press CTRL+F6 on or after a word to display an alternative.*

The thesaurus is destructive in that it copies over the highlighted word with the one you select from the thesaurus listing. You can see how this works by changing a word in the letter.

Move the highlight to the word *pleasure* in the third sentence of the first paragraph. You can place the highlight anywhere in the word. Press CTRL+F6 and choose a word from the list that suitably replaces *pleasure*.

SHIFT+INS: Copy Over Text with Scrap   Normally, text in the scrap has been copied or deleted from another location. You can then move elsewhere in your document to insert it. Thus, you can think of the scrap as a kind of clipboard that holds blocks of text while you find a place to put them. You may sometimes want to completely replace a block of text with the text in the scrap. Use SHIFT+INSERT to replace any highlighted text with the scrap.

Tip: *Press* SHIFT+INSERT *to replace highlighted text with the contents of the scrap.*

Earlier you changed the price of the General Ledger package to $495, so the total at the bottom is now wrong. Highlight the price table again by using the F6 (Extend) key and arrow keys. Do not highlight the line labeled "Total." Press F2 to calculate the total. The result is placed in the scrap. Now highlight the old total and press SHIFT+INSERT. The new total copies over the old one.

Deleting Tabs   Tabs are often confusing because of how they change size and because of what they do to paragraphs that have their indents adjusted. In Figure 9-7, you'll see how inappropriate tab settings can cause paragraph alignment to become jumbled. In the following exercise, you'll see how to correct tab problems for aligned columns in paragraphs.

First, highlight the entire price table in the Jones letter. Place the cursor on the upper left character, press the F6 (Extend) key, and move the highlight down with the arrow key. Next, press ALT+N to indent the paragraph to the first tab stop.

Because the total calculated earlier does not align properly with the rest of the numbers, it will be helpful to use a decimal tab to align all of the numbers on the decimal point. With the entire table still highlighted, press ALT+F1 to display the Format Tab Set menu and type 4 as the tab setting. Then press the DOWN ARROW key to get to the alignment option and select Decimal. When you press ENTER, the table should look like the one shown in Figure 9-7.

Your task now is to remove the excess tabs. Each of the arrows represents a tab stop. Notice how the first tab jumps to the new 4-inch setting. Two of the lines have enough excess tabs that the line breaks into two. You can remove the excess tabs by using the arrow keys to highlight them and pressing DEL to remove them. Remember to leave one tab in each line.

 Trap: *Excess tabs may cause needless line breaks.*

The tabs are now set up to properly align the column of numbers. Notice that the $2035 total is right-justified with the rest of the numbers. You can use the arrow keys to move to each number and insert ".00" to make the numbers look better, but it is easier to use the Word Replace command, which will be covered in a later section. For now, leave the table as it is.

Figure 9-7. *Excess tabs cause table misalignment after setting tabs*

Recycled Deletions

A recycled deletion is a delete that is still available for use in another part of the current document or even in other Word sessions, depending on what you do with the deletion.

Delete to Scrap   As mentioned, the scrap is where text deleted by the DEL key is placed until another delete occurs. You can recycle this deleted text by using the INS key to place it somewhere else in the text.

Be careful when using the scrap to temporarily hold text. The DEL key is used so often that it's easy to press it without realizing that the text you were trying to preserve in the scrap has just been lost.

 Trap: *Don't use the DEL key while text is being held in the scrap.*

If you need to hold a block of text longer than you can maintain it in the scrap, delete it to the glossary, as described in the next section.

Tip: *Delete text to the glossary if you need to keep it for an extended period.*

Note that Word's Delete and Insert commands perform the same operations as the INS and DEL keys in relation to the scrap. In addition, these keys allow you to work with the glossary.

Delete to Glossary   If you are deleting a block of text to be used later in your document, delete it to the glossary with the Delete command. Note that the DEL key will not allow you to place text in the glossary.

If you have text that must be placed in other documents, you can use the glossary to hold these text blocks while you load the new documents. If saved to disk, the glossary will also hold text blocks from one Word session to another. In other words, if you shut down your machine, the text blocks will be retained in the glossary until the next session. If a glossary entry is to be used in another Word session, you must save the glossary to disk before exiting Word.

 Tip: *If you need a glossary entry for another document, save the glossary to disk.*

For example, assume that you are organizing the text for a chapter of a book and then decide that some blocks of text are better placed in another chapter. Save these blocks to the glossary, giving them a name that closely relates to their contents and the chapter they are targeted for.

Copying and Moving Text

Text can be copied to other parts of your document in several ways. Remember that copying differs from moving text. In a text move the original version of the text is deleted and reinserted in another location. In a text copy a duplicate is made of the highlighted text in another location.

 Tip: *Copying text and moving text are not the same. Copying keeps the original block of text intact, while moving text deletes the original.*

Editing Techniques

Text Copy and Move Techniques

There are three methods for moving and making copies of text. If text is already in the scrap, you can use the INS key to insert it at a target location. You can also insert text from the glossary. Mouse users can make quick copies and text block moves by using special mouse pointing techniques.

Copying and Moving Text with the Scrap   As discussed earlier, the scrap can hold a block of text that is to be inserted elsewhere. But you must first get the text into the scrap. If you are moving text, simply press DEL to place the highlighted text in the scrap.

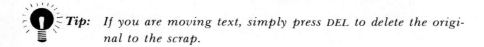 *Tip:*   *If you are moving text, simply press DEL to delete the original to the scrap.*

If you are copying text, there are two ways to get text in the scrap. You can press the DEL key, which deletes the highlighted text to the scrap but removes the original text from the screen. Second, you can press INS to reinsert the text in its original position. This two-step process is used often because it is more intuitive.

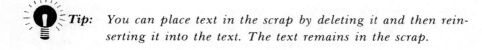 *Tip:*   *You can place text in the scrap by deleting it and then reinserting it into the text. The text remains in the scrap.*

When copying text, it is better to use the ALT+F3 key combination. This copies the highlighted text to the scrap, leaving the original intact, which is exactly what you want. You can then move to the destination and press the INS key.

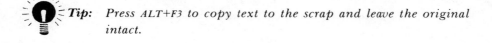 *Tip:*   *Press ALT+F3 to copy text to the scrap and leave the original intact.*

You can always use the Copy and Delete commands to copy text to the scrap for copies and moves. These commands always propose the scrap as the destination in their fields. A more practical use for the Copy and Delete commands involves the use of glossaries, as described next.

If you don't have a mouse, you can try the following block move exercise. If you have a mouse, perform the exercise under the mouse section discussed shortly.

Place the highlight anywhere in the second sentence of the Jones letter and press SHIFT+F7. Notice that the period and the space before the next sentence are also highlighted. This is important because you must know where to place the highlight in order to insert the paragraph later. Because this sentence must be moved, press DEL. The content of the sentence appears in the scrap.

Next, move the highlight to the *I* in the word *If* of the last sentence. Because the sentence to be moved already has spaces at its end, you should place the highlight on the first letter of the sentence that will follow the inserted sentence. Press INS to insert the contents of the scrap.

Copying and Moving Text with the Glossary   Highlighted text can be either copied or deleted to the glossary for later use with the Copy or Delete menu commands. All glossary entries have a name, so you can type the glossary name at the new insertion point and press the F3 (Glossary Expand) key to reinsert the text at the new location. The text block is automatically typed.

Copying and Moving Text with the Mouse   The mouse is a perfect tool for either copying or moving text. To copy a text block with the mouse, highlight the text to be copied, point to the new insertion point, and press the left mouse button while holding down the SHIFT key. To move text, you follow the same procedure except that you hold down the CTRL key while pressing the left button.

 Tip: *To copy text, highlight it, point to the new location, and press SHIFT and the left button on the mouse.*

 Tip: *To move a block of text, highlight it, point to the new insertion point, and press CTRL and the left button on the mouse.*

If you have a mouse, you can move the second sentence in the Jones letter to the bottom paragraph. First, point anywhere in the sentence and press both mouse buttons at once to highlight the entire sentence. Next, point to the *I* in *If* of the last sentence in the letter and, holding down the CTRL key, press the left button on the mouse. The sentence is moved to the new location.

Transposing Text with the Mouse   Word offers an interesting and convenient way to transpose characters, words, and sentences if you have a mouse. If you type two letters backward, simply highlight the right letter, point to the left letter, and press the left mouse button while holding down the CTRL key.

 Tip: *Transpose two letters by highlighting the right letter, pointing to the left letter, and then left clicking with the mouse.*

To transpose two words, make sure that the second word is highlighted by right clicking on it. Then point to the first letter of the previous word and hold down the CTRL key while pressing the right button.

 Tip: *Transpose two words by holding down the CTRL key and pressing the right mouse button.*

To transpose two sentences, highlight the second sentence by clicking on it with both mouse buttons. Then point to the first letter of the previous sentence and hold down the CTRL key while pressing both mouse buttons.

 Tip: *Transpose two sentences by holding down the CTRL key and pressing both mouse buttons.*

Window Techniques   Many times, the destination for text to be moved or copied is off the screen. This is no problem if the text is in the scrap. Simply scroll to the new location and insert it. If you want to use the mouse, however, you must open windows on your document because the mouse does not use the scrap for copying or moving operations.

 Tip: *The mouse does not affect the scrap when copying or moving text.*

Splitting a document is a convenient way both to see two parts of the document at once and to copy or move text from one part to another. For example, assume that you need to compile a list of quotes, titles, or other information from the text of your document and place it at the end. You could open a second window and scroll to the bottom of the document in it. You could then use the top window to scroll through the whole document, searching for the desired text to be copied to the lower window. You could copy with the mouse or use ALT+F3 to copy to the scrap and then insert in the bottom window. Pressing F1 moves the highlight between windows.

 Tip: *Windows can be used to open several views on a document for easy copying and moving of text.*

Replacing Text

One way to edit a document is to do a mass search and replace on specific words or codes. For example, if you discover a misspelled company name in a long document, you can search for it and replace it with the correct name.

 Tip: *Search and replace techniques can alter common mistakes throughout a document.*

You can also place codes in your document while typing that become targets for later search and replace operations. For example, instead of typing out the entire city name Poughkeepsie many times in your document, you could simply type **PK**. Later, when the document is finished, you could search for **PK** and replace it with Poughkeepsie. (You could also make Poughkeepsie a glossary entry, of course.)

The Replace command, illustrated here, is very similar to the Search command except that a field is supplied for the replacement text. The Confirm field will cause Word to stop at each location and confirm replacement. When words or parts of words are similar, it is a good idea to use this field.

```
REPLACE text: PK                     with text: Poughkeepsie█
       confirm:(Yes)No  case: Yes(No)  whole word: Yes(No)
```

For example, consider the word *it,* which is part of *city, hit, bitten,* and many other words. You would get some unusual words if you let Word replace every instance of *it* with *them.*

Trap: *The Replace command will replace all instances of the replace text unless you ask for confirmation.*

The Case field of the Replace command allows you to narrow the search by specifying that capitalization of a word must match the search field exactly. For example, if you specify *Zoo, zoo* will not be located, only *Zoo.*

Tip: *Specifying a case match in a Replace command narrows the search to words that exactly match the upper/lowercase criteria of the search word.*

If you select No in the Case field, Word will replace the target word with a capitalized version of the replacement word if the original begins with a capital letter. For example, if you are replacing *airplane* with *helicopter* and Word finds *Airplane,* it will replace it with *Helicopter.*

Tip: *Word will replace words with capitalized versions where necessary.*

The Whole Word field lets you specify that only those words that exactly match the one you are searching are replaced. For example, in the case of *it,* you could specify a whole word to find only the word *it.*

Word: Secrets, Solutions, Shortcuts

 Tip: *In searching and replacing you can specify a whole word match only.*

There are two opportunities to search and replace in the letter to Mr. Jones. First, you can replace the abbreviations in the price table with the full company name by specifying "EL" as the search and "Easy Ledger" as the replacement. Press ESC and execute the Replace command. Type **EL** in capital letters in the Search Text field and **Easy Ledger** in the Replace Text field. Select Yes in the Case field to prevent searches for words that contain "el" in them. The command is shown here.

```
REPLACE text: EL                          with text: Easy Ledger
        confirm:(Yes)No   case: Yes No  whole word: Yes(No)
```

Type **Y** to each replacement response from Word. Notice that the decimal tab must be moved to the right to make room for the newly inserted text. To readjust the tabs, first highlight the entire table with the arrow keys and the F6 (Extend) key or by using a mouse. Next, clear the old tab setting by pressing ESC Format Tab Reset-All. Finally, press ESC Format Tab Set, type **4.5** in the Position field and select Decimal in the Alignment field.

As long as the price table is highlighted, you can perform another search and replace. The goal is to place ".00" after the numbers in the price table. The problem, however, is that there doesn't appear to be a common block of text to search for. But all of the numbers in the table do have one thing in common — the paragraph marker. Fortunately, Word lets you both specify a paragraph marker in a search and limit the search to the highlighted area. That is, you can search only the table for paragraph marks and replace each one with a paragraph mark that has the string ".00" attached to it.

The table is still highlighted from the previous exercise, so execute the Replace command as shown here. Note that the replacements will only occur in the highlighted area. Type ^p in the Replace Text field. The ^ (caret) is the symbol above the 6 on the keyboard. Type .00^p in the Replace With Text field. This specifies a decimal point, two zeros, and a new paragraph marker. When you press ENTER, Word asks for confirmation before each replacement. Just type y and watch Word do the typing for you.

```
REPLACE text: ^p                          with text: .00^p
        confirm:(Yes)No   case:(Yes)No  whole word: Yes(No)
```

Searching for Special Characters

A number of special characters can be searched for in Word. They represent the special characters in Word that do not normally have printable characters.

 Tip: *Word allows you to search and replace special characters such as paragraph markers, tabs, and spaces.*

The paragraph marker is a good example. It appears on the screen as a backward *P* but never prints on the paper; instead, it performs a function. The special symbols are listed below, the first of which is an all-purpose symbol.

^w   This character represents a space, tab, newline marker, paragraph marker, division marker, forced page breaks, and nonbreaking space. It cannot be used in the Replace With Text field because it represents so many different characters. In the Search Text field, however, it can be combined with other text to provide a powerful search technique that allows you to narrow your searches.

Each of the special characters can be searched specifically with the following characters:

^s   Search for nonbreaking space.

^t   Search for tab characters. This would have been a handy way to eliminate the excess tabs in the previous example. Specifying nothing in the Replace With Text field would have deleted the tab character.

^p   Search for paragraph marker. If you use hard carriage returns when creating tables and later wish you had used soft carriage returns so that tables can be formatted as one paragraph, you can search for this character and replace it with the newline character below. This is covered in the next example.

^n   Search for newline character. Newline markers are often used to generate tables. You can search for this marker to locate lines in those tables.

^_   Search for optional Hyphen.

^d | Search for division mark or page break character. Searching for either of these is a quick way to get to different sections of pages.

Throughout the exercises, you have highlighted the price table by using the arrow keys and F6 (Extend) key because it comprised six separate lines with paragraph markers. You can convert the paragraph markers in each line to newline characters by executing the Replace command as shown here. Type ^p in the Replace Text field and ^n in the With Text field. Answer Yes to each response except the last. The last line must contain a paragraph marker so that the paragraph won't take on the formatting of the next paragraph.

```
REPLACE text: ^p                      with text: ^n█
         confirm:(Yes)No  case:(Yes)No  whole word: Yes(No)
```

Moving and Copying Between Documents

You can move and copy blocks of text between documents either by using windows or by saving the text to move or copy in a glossary. The window technique is the easiest because you can use the scrap as a bridge for text to cross between the documents in the windows.

 Tip: *The scrap can be considered a bridge for text between windows.*

Open the first document; then split a window and open the second document. Use the F1 key or a mouse to move between the documents. Scroll to the area containing the text that you want to move or copy and press DEL to move text or ALT+F3 to copy text to the scrap. Then press F1 to move to the other window, scroll to the insertion point, and press INS. Figure 9-8 shows two documents on the screen in separate windows.

If you have a mouse, copying between documents follows the same rules for mouse copying and moving described earlier. (See Chapter 17 for more information on windows.)

```
1═══[········1········2········3········4········5········6····]····7··┐
    doing,·"I·will·not·do·them·wrong.···I·rather·choose⁄·To·wrong·the·
    dead,·to·wrong·myself·and·you,⁄·Than·I·will·wrong·such·honorable▪
    men³."··Again,·as·he·delivers·his·final·blow·which·incites·the·
    citizens·to·mutiny,·Anthony·hints·that·"I·fear·I·wrong·the·
                                                        ═════JCAESAR.DOC═
2═══0········1········2········3········4········5········6········7···┐
    Perhaps·Anthony's·most·effective·technique·is·the·constant·
    repetition·and·eventual·juxtaposition·of·the·two·adjectives·
    "honorable,"·to·describe·the·conspirators·and·"ambitious"·the·
    accusation·against·Caesar.··Anthony·clearly·states·the··
    assumption·that·"Brutus⁄·Hath·told·you·Caesar·was·ambitious",·and·
                                                        ═════JCAESAR.DOC═
```
(9140224·bytes·free)

Figure 9-8. Documents can be viewed by splitting windows

Tip: *The mouse can be used to copy text between documents in separate windows just as text is moved in a single document.*

Rearranging Text with Sort

Word has a sorting capability that falls under the category of text editing. You can sort columns of information or tables in ascending, descending, alphabetical, or numerical order. The Library Autosort command, shown here, is used to perform sorting. (See Chapter 20 for more details.)

```
LIBRARY AUTOSORT by: Alphanumeric Numeric   sequence:(Ascending)Descending
           case:(Yes)No                  column only: Yes(No)
```

```
Easy·Ledger·General·Ledger→        $495.00↓
Easy·Ledger·Accounts·Receivable→   $495.00↓
Easy·Ledger·Accounts·Payable→      $495.00↓
Easy·Ledger·Payroll→               $595.00↓
Easy·Ledger·California·tax·module→ $100.00↓
Total→                            $2180.00¶
```

Figure 9-9. Column Select lets you select a column to sort on

You can sort the price table in the Jones letter in alphabetical order. First, place the highlight on the G in "General Ledger" and press SHIFT+F6 to turn on Column Select. This will allow you to move the cursor down one column of letters, as shown in Figure 9-9. The first letter of each software package name will constitute the sort criteria, as you can see in the figure. After the column is selected, select the Library Autosort command and press ENTER. The price table will be rearranged in order.

Tip: *Use SHIFT+F6 (Column Select) to select a specific column of text or numbers for a sort.*

Tip: *A sort can be undone with the Undo command.*

Transfer Merge

Word allows you to merge text into the current document from other documents. This special technique will be covered in detail in Chapter 23, but briefly, you can leave blank fields in your text where names, addresses, comments, and other information can be merged from another file.

Tip: *Blank fields can be left in text so that text can be merged from other documents.*

The source of this information is referred to as a *data file* and is usually a mailing list, product file, or some other type of data file. Data files contain structured information, as shown in Figure 9-10. When information is structured, a *field* represents a piece of information such as a name, an address, or a city. A set of fields forms a *record,* and many of these records together constitute a data file.

Each field in a data file is either tagged with a name or has a specific location so that it can be pinpointed and copied to the target document. The target document specifies which fields it needs from the data file and where the information in the field should be printed.

Hidden Text and Revision Marks

Word provides several techniques to make the editing process easier for you and for others who might be working with your documents. You can place notes in documents, mark text that has been added, and strikeout text that needs to be deleted. The usefulness of the latter two techniques goes beyond editing. In legal documents text additions and deletions must be marked. A text deletion is one that is simply struck out but is never removed from the document completely.

Hidden Text

You can make notes to yourself or others by using hidden text, which can be hidden on the screen or displayed. In addition, hidden text can be printed or suppressed from the printing process. A teacher, for example, could create a test with the answers formatted as hidden text. In the copy printed for the students the hidden text would be suppressed, but in the personal copy the hidden text would be printed.

The use of hidden text is an excellent way to make notes to yourself or someone else as a document goes through editing. Some documents may have contributions from several different people or groups of people. Each group can leave

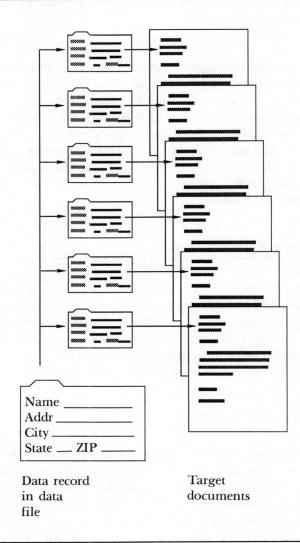

Data record
in data
file

Target
documents

Figure 9-10.   A structured data document

special hidden text notes containing vital information for the next group that should not be printed in the final copy. Of course hidden text can be printed with the document to assist in the editing process. (See Chapter 10 for details on working with hidden text.)

 Tip: *Hidden text can be used in documents to create nonprinting notes to yourself or others.*

Revision Marks

Revision marks help you track changes in a document as it moves through an editing process. You can also track the changes made between two versions of the same document. Legal documents, in particular, require revision marks in printed versions. Changes or deletions are specifically marked, while the original text of the document remains. Formatting, spelling, and sorting changes are not marked, however.

 Tip: *Legal documents require a record of all additions, deletions, and changes. Word's revision mark features are well suited to this task.*

The Format Revision-Marks menu shown here lists four options. Type **F** and then **M** to get to this menu. Figure 9-11 shows what the Jones letter would look like if the Revision Marking feature had been on for some of the editing changes.

FORMAT REVISION-MARKS: `Options` Remove-marks Undo-revisions Search

The options menu shown on the next page lets you turn Revision Marking on or specify the types of revision marks to use. Inserted text can have a mark under it and also a bar next to it in the margin as a secondary indicator, or flag.

```
                    Easy Ledger Software
                    3000 Journal Drive
                    Santa Barbara, CA 93105

| November 29, 1988 January 18, 1988

  Mr. John Jones
  Norton Engineering
  3991 State Street
  Santa Barbara, CA 93101

  Dear Mr. Jones,

  It was a pleasure to talktalking with you the other day
  concerning your office automation needs.  I am sure
  that we can help you establish a computerized
  accounting system to fit your needs.--It will be our
  pleasure to assist you.  Based on our initial meeting,
  we recommend the following software packages.  The
  California tax module is required to run Payroll in
  California.

          EL General Ledger           $495.00
          EL Accounts Receivable      $495.00
          EL Accounts Payable         $495.00
          EL Payroll                  $595.00
          EL California tax module    $100.00

  Our service rate is $60 per hour.  We estimate
  installation should take 8 hours.  I am sure that we
  can help you establish a computerized accounting system
  to fit your needs.  If you wish to proceed, please
  call.


  Sincerely


  Alexander Halliburton
  Marketing Manager
```

Figure 9-11. The Jones letter with revision marks

"MR" appears in the status line when Revision Marking is on.

Tip: *"MR" appears in the status line when Revision Marking is on.*

```
FORMAT REVISION-MARK OPTIONS
     add revision marks: Yes No
     inserted text: Normal Bold(Underlined)Uppercase Double-underlined
     revision bar position:(None)Left Right Alternate
```

When you use Word's Revision Marking feature, actual editing changes are not made to a document until you specify them. In the case of legal documents, instead of actually marking the changes, you might print all documents with the revision marks. In other cases an editor may use revision marks to make changes to your document and then return the document to you. After you have made additional changes, you can "accept" the revisions.

 Trap: *Actual revisions to text are not made until you specify them in the Format Revision-Marks command.*

Accepting revisions with the Remove Marks option removes all text that is marked with strikeouts. The marks applied to text that has been added to the document are removed, and that text becomes a permanent part of the document. You can accept revisions for the entire document, or you can accept a specific part by highlighting the desired section.

 Tip: *You can finalize revisions in selected text by highlighting that text.*

You can remove revision marks without actually changing the text by using the Undo-Revisions option. In this case all text that was inserted is deleted, strike-through marks are removed, and the revision bars are removed.

 Tip: *Revisions can be undone with the Undo-Revisions option.*

The Search option can be used to quickly move the sections in a document where text has been revised. This is convenient when changes have been made to a large document by someone else.

Editing in the Outline Mode

If you have created a document using an outline, you can quickly move whole sections of text by using the Outline Organize option. Press SHIFT+F5 in outline mode to execute the Organize option. You can then select headers and move them to other locations. (The Outline Organize option will be covered in more detail in Chapter 18.)

Tips and Traps Summary

The Editing Process

Tip: Text can be inserted not only from the keyboard but also from a glossary or from another file.

Trap: Deleting is a destructive process that can cause permanent loss of text.

Trap: Don't confuse copying text with moving text. Copying makes a duplicate of the highlighted text.

Tip: To move text, you first delete it and then insert it somewhere else.

Tip: Word's Search and Replace commands can be used to automate the editing process.

Tip: Windows can be used to copy text between different parts of a document or between two or more documents.

Tip: Spell checking is performed by Word. You can add your own special words to the dictionary.

Tip: Using Word's thesaurus is a convenient way to substitute repetitive words in a document.

Tip: Word's Sort feature lets you type text or tables in any order and then sort them later.

Tip: Word automatically readjusts text to the margins when you insert or delete.

Trap: Word's automatic word wrap may cause Word to become sluggish during text insertion. Insert a temporary paragraph marker for the text ahead of the insertion point; then rejoin the paragraph when done.

Tips and Traps Summary (*continued*)

Tip: Outline mode lets you quickly rearrange whole sections of documents, as well as letting you quickly jump between sections of your document.

The Scrap and Glossary

Trap: Text in the scrap can be overwritten by a new deletion.

Tip: Text highlighted on the screen can be saved for later use in a glossary with the Copy or Delete command.

Tip: Text in glossaries can be inserted into text with the Insert command.

Tip: A set of glossary entries can be saved to a disk file for later use.

Tip: You can create several glossary files to use with different types of documents.

Trap: Word automatically attaches NORMAL.GLY to every new document.

Tip: Text in the scrap can be inserted elsewhere with the INS key.

Tip: Text can be committed to a glossary entry with the Delete menu command.

Trap: You must save a glossary file if you want to keep the entries added in a Word session for a future session.

Tips and Traps Summary (*continued*)

Tip: You can use either the Copy command or ALT+F3 to copy highlighted text to the scrap.

Tip: You can use either the Delete command or the DEL key to remove highlighted text to the scrap.

Tip: You can update glossary entries by specifying the existing name when using Copy or Delete.

Trap: Word proposes the scrap as the destination for Copy and Delete. You can simply type over this with a glossary name.

Tip: Press ESC+U to undo glossary inserts.

Tip: Glossary entries can be inserted with the Insert command or the F3 (Glossary Expand) key.

Trap: Enter the name of the glossary entry before pressing the F3 (Glossary Expand) key.

Tip: Use the Insert command if you can't remember the name of a glossary. Press F1 to see a list.

Inserting and Adding Text

Tip: The ALT+F3 key combination places a copy of the highlighted text in the scrap.

Tip: Insert a paragraph marker to split an existing paragraph in two.

Tips and Traps Summary (*continued*)

Trap: Paragraph markers inserted from the scrap or glossary may carry formats that alter existing paragraph formats.

Deleting Text

Trap: Deleting paragraph markers may cause paragraphs to take on formats of other paragraphs.

Tip: To perform a delete but retain the contents of the scrap, use SHIFT+F1.

Tip: Overtype types over existing text.

Trap: Don't forget to turn Overtype off when you are finished using it.

Tip: Press CTRL+F6 on or after a word to display an alternative.

Tip: Press SHIFT+INSERT to replace highlighted text with the contents of the scrap.

Trap: Excess tabs may cause needless line breaks.

Trap: Don't use the DEL key while text is being held in the scrap.

Tip: Delete text to the glossary if you need to keep it for an extended period.

Tip: If you need a glossary entry for another document, save the glossary to disk.

Tips and Traps Summary (*continued*)

Copying and Moving Text

Tip: Copying text and moving text are not the same. Copying keeps the original block of text intact, while moving text deletes the original

Tip: If you are moving text, simply press DEL to delete the original to the scrap.

Tip: You can place text in the scrap by deleting it and then reinserting it into the text. The text remains in the scrap.

Tip: Press ALT+F3 to copy text to the scrap and leave the original intact.

Tip: To copy text, highlight it, point to the new location, and press SHIFT and the left button on the mouse.

Tip: To move a block of text, highlight it, point to the new insertion point, and press CTRL and the left button on the mouse.

Tip: Transpose two letters by highlighting the right letter, pointing to the left letter, and then left clicking with the mouse.

Tip: Transpose two words by holding down the CTRL key and pressing the right mouse button.

Tip: Transpose two sentences by holding down the CTRL key and pressing both mouse buttons.

Tip: The mouse does not affect the scrap when copying or moving text.

Tip: Windows can be used to open several views on a document for easy copying and moving of text.

Tips and Traps Summary (*continued*)

Replacing Text

Tip: Search and replace techniques can alter common mistakes throughout a document.

Trap: The Replace command will replace all instances of the replace text unless you ask for confirmation.

Tip: Specifying a case match in a Replace command narrows the search to only words that exactly match the upper/lowercase criteria of the search word.

Tip: Word will replace words with capitalized versions where necessary.

Tip: In searching and replacing you can specify a whole word match only.

Tip: Word allows you to search and replace special characters such as paragraph markers, tabs, and spaces.

Moving and Copying Between Documents

Tip: The scrap can be considered a bridge for text between windows.

Tip: The mouse can be used to copy text between documents in separate windows just as text is moved in a single document.

Tips and Traps Summary (continued)

Rearranging Text with Sort

Tip: Use SHIFT+F6 (Column Select) to select a specific column of text or numbers for a sort.

Tip: A sort can be undone with the Undo command.

Transfer Merge

Tip: Blank fields can be left in text so that text can be merged from other documents.

Hidden Text and Revision Marks

Tip: Hidden text can be used in documents to create nonprintable notes to yourself or others.

Tip: Legal documents require a record of all additions, deletions, and changes. Word's revision mark features are well suited to this task.

Tip: "MR" appears in the status line when Revision Marking is on.

Trap: Actual revisions to text are not made until you specify them in the Format Revision-Marks command.

Tip: You can finalize revisions in selected text by highlighting that text.

Tip: Revisions can be undone with the Undo-Revisions option.

II

Formatting and Style Sheets

You have learned how to move through documents, select text, and edit. You have saved and printed documents. Now it is time to learn about the steps that you can take to make your documents more visually appealing and easy to read.

Formatting has to do with applying typefaces and type styles to the text of your document. The next four chapters will describe each of the formatting types that you can apply. As discussed in Chapter 6, these formatting enhancements are divided into the following groups.

Character Enhancements. Chapter 10 will cover the various character styles and typefaces (fonts) that you can apply to the individual characters and text of your documents. You will see how to apply boldfacing, underline, italics, and many other character styles.

Paragraph Enhancements. Chapter 11 deals with the paragraphs — that all-important block of text that you can mold into many different shapes and sizes. You'll see how to indent, add spacing, and control line breaks; how to create tables, running heads, and lists; and how to apply other paragraph styles for use in letters, reports, charts, statements, and other documents.

Page Enhancements. In Chapter 12 you will see how to adjust the paragraphs of your documents to fit on a page in just the right spot. Page size and margin alterations and other page-related subjects will also be discussed.

Additional Page Enhancements. Chapter 13 covers additional page enhancements that are a part of some documents but not all. These include running heads, line numbering, footnotes, and newspaperlike columns. In addition, border and line-drawing features will be discussed.

Style Sheets and the Formatting Process

The use of *styles* is vitally important in the formatting process. Recall from Chapter 6 that a style is a convenient way to save a particular set of formatting instructions so that you can use them at a later date. However, in its manuals Microsoft does not cover the use of styles and style sheets with formatting. This book takes a different approach. As you learn about formatting, you will learn how to use styles and style sheets in relation to the topic at hand. This approach is designed to give you the most effective introduction to document formatting. Styles and style sheets will be covered in detail in Chapter 16.

In the next four chapters you will be creating a number of formatting examples as you read through the text. Each one is a format that you will probably find useful during normal day-to-day operations with Word. With styles and style sheets, you can "record" these formats so that they will always be available.

For instance, in Chapter 11 you will see how to format a paragraph so that it properly aligns side-by-side text. This process requires quite a few steps that are easy to forget, which means that you'll have to refer to the manuals if you want to set up another side-by-side format. However, by using styles and style sheets, you can record all the steps and then repeat them whenever you wish.

What's Important to Know About Style Sheets

Many new users are confused by style sheets because they can't borrow equivalent concepts from the use of typewriters. If you think of a style as a sort of recipe for a particular format and the style sheet as a collection of those recipes, it becomes easier to understand their use. Just as you might have a collection of fish and chicken recipes, you can have a collection of styles in Word for a particular purpose. There are many ways to format words, paragraphs, and pages, and you can assign these recipes to styles. You can then collect and save these styles to their own disk file just as you might collect Oriental recipes in one box and Mexican recipes in another.

 Tip: *Styles can be thought of as a collection of recipes that define how text is formatted.*

How to Name a Style

All styles are given a one- or two-character keycode name. This code is what you type when you want to apply a style to a selected paragraph. The codes should be meaningful in some way. For example, all table styles could be named with a code that starts with *T*, such as TC for a centered table or TD for one that has decimal tabs for aligning numbers.

 Tip: *Styles are given keycode names, which you use when you apply the style to a block of text.*

Assigning a Usage to a Style

Styles have different usages, which Word will ask you for when you are creating a style. These are character, paragraph, and division usage, as described here:

- Character usage styles are designed for applying such character formats as boldface, underline, and italics as well as the type font and type size.

- Paragraph usage styles perform the full range of paragraph alignments and can also include character formatting.

- Division styles are designed for page layout formatting such as margins, columns, and page numbering.

Using Character Formats in Paragraph Styles

Because paragraph usage allows both character and paragraph formats to be defined, you can create paragraph styles that also change the font and character style of a paragraph. In this case, you don't need to highlight the exact characters to be given the character formatting. Word assumes that you want to assign the designated character format to the entire paragraph.

 Tip: *Paragraph styles can also define the type font and type style of the paragraph.*

Global Style Changes

A global change is a change that occurs over an entire document for each use of a particular style. If you decide to surround all T1 titles with a border, you can add the border to the T1 style definition in the gallery. The border will then be added to all T1 formatted items in the text. You can use this type of global format alteration on any paragraph assigned to a style. The power of this feature alone makes Microsoft Word the most dynamic word processor on the market today.

 Tip: *When you change a style, global changes are made automatically over an entire document.*

How to Create and Use Styles

Almost every paragraph with special formats used more than once should be assigned to a style so that you can easily use it again in the same document. The Gallery command in the Word command menu is used to manage styles. If you open the gallery now by pressing ESC and typing **G**, you will see a separate window that normally remains "hidden" in the background as you work with Word. This window is the filing cabinet for styles.

 Tip: *If a paragraph format change will be used more than once in a Word session, it should be assigned a style code in the style sheet.*

There are two ways to create a style:

- You can create styles in the edit window by using a previously formatted block of text as an example. Microsoft calls this method "creating styles by example."

- You can open the gallery and "build" styles by using the commands in the gallery. You can then apply these styles to text.

When a style is created, Word asks you for a special one- or two-character *key-code* that will be the name that you use when you later apply the style. All styles, along with their code names and format descriptions are stored in the gallery.

The styles in the gallery are available for use during the editing session in which they were created, or you can save the gallery as a *style sheet* so that you can use the styles at a later date.

For now, styles will be stored in a style sheet called NORMAL.STY. Word automatically attaches this style sheet to every document that you create unless you attach a different style sheet. Be aware that sets of styles designed for specific types of documents can be grouped into other style sheets. To use a style sheet other than NORMAL.STY, you would use the Format Stylesheet Attach command. Other style sheets might contain groups of specific styles, like those used for legal documents, contracts, or forms.

 Tip: *Style sheets other than NORMAL.STY, designed for special use, can be attached to documents.*

When to Create Styles

You can create styles "on the fly" as you create and write your document, or you can create them beforehand by planning the structure of your documents. Planning is always best, though it does take some thinking ahead about what you will need. If you are writing and you define a special paragraph format that you know you will need later in the document, add it to the gallery. If you know that you might need it at some later date, save it with the style sheet.

Planning a document involves considering how many special paragraph formats you will have. Think about the tables, quotes, and other types of paragraphs that you will use in the document; then design their layout and create the styles in the gallery. Creating styles ahead of time ensures a consistent format throughout your entire document.

Where to Create Styles

You can create styles by example if you highlight a previously formatted block of text and press ALT+F10. You can also build styles in the gallery by using the Gallery commands.

 Tip: *You can create paragraph styles "by example" or by building them in the gallery.*

From the Edit Window by Example

Press ALT+F10 while highlighting a paragraph to open the Format Stylesheet Record menu. This is the same menu displayed by the Gallery Insert command, and it performs the same function. Simply enter the code for the style, its usage (character, paragraph, or division), the variant, and a remark to record the new style. It will be added to the gallery window.

 Tip: *When you create a style by example, many of the options will have already been selected.*

In the Gallery

You can go into the gallery window to create styles. Use the Gallery Insert command to add a new style, the Gallery Copy command to make a copy of an existing style for alteration, or the Gallery Delete command to remove a style. The Transfer option lets you save the current styles in a style sheet.

Creating new styles in the gallery is a two-step process. First, you define the style code, usage, variant, and remark by using the Insert command. Then you use the Format command to apply the formats just as you would apply formats to paragraphs in the edit window. This differs from creating styles by example. In that method Word automatically assigns the formats of the highlighted paragraph to the style.

In the next four chapters you will be creating most styles by the example method.

Built-in Styles

Just as you can create a few styles of your own to keep around for later use, Word has default styles that it uses whenever you fail to assign a style to a particular block of text. For example, Word will assign its own paragraph style to every paragraph that you type unless you specify a new style. The important point here is that you can change this standard or default paragraph style to fit your own needs. The *standard paragraph* is left-aligned with no indents and is single spaced. However, you might want all your paragraphs to have a first-line indent of 1/2 inch. If so, simply change the default paragraph style so that Word automatically assigns the indent.

 Tip: *Word automatically applies default or built-in styles to various elements of your document. However, you can change these default styles to fit your needs.*

Standard formats are also assigned to other elements of Word documents, including footnotes, running heads, headings, line numbers, and page numbers. You will be able to create new formats for special use in addition to these or change the default settings.

In the next four chapters you'll be introduced to the simplest and quickest way to use styles. This should get you up and running with their use. Don't forget, you can always jump ahead to Chapter 16 if you would like to learn more.

Direct and Indirect Formatting

Once you attach a style sheet, several things will change concerning the way that Word is used. First, the character and paragraph formatting keys must be typed with an *X*; for example, to boldface a word, you would press ALT+X+B. This is a minor inconvenience compared to the benefits of the tradeoff. The major change has to do with the hierarchy of formats, which are now referred to as direct and indirect formatting.

The difference between the two formatting actions is simple to understand. Their combined results are often confusing. A direct format is any format that you apply to a character, word, paragraph, or block of text with the ALT key or through the Format menu system. An indirect format is any style that you apply with the style sheet.

Direct formats are chiseled in stone. They become a permanent part of your document, and cannot be altered when you apply a style from the style sheet. The following rules apply to the way Word handles direct and indirect formats when both are applied.

- If you apply direct *character* formatting on top of a style designed for *character formatting*, Word adds the formatting and breaks the link that the selected text has with the style sheet. The same applies for paragraph and division usage.

- If you apply direct *character* formatting on top of *paragraph* or *division* formats previously applied by a style sheet, the formatting is added to the highlighted text within the paragraph or division. The style sheet link is maintained.

- If you use direct formatting on top of a style, only the selected text is altered.

- Word always uses the most recently applied formatting. If a style is applied on top of regular formatting, the style is used.

The significance of this hierarchy may not mean much now, but as you go through the next few chapters, you may want to refer to these rules for reference.

Before Continuing

Before continuing, you should add the SIDEBY.STY style sheet to your current style sheet. This style sheet is supplied by Microsoft on the Utilities disk. The styles in this style sheet have specific names that must be reserved; therefore, it should be merged before you continue. This will prevent you from creating styles that might fill the reserved spots of the SIDEBY.STY style sheet.

Press ESC and open the Gallery menu. Press ESC again, select the Transfer Merge command, and type **SIDEBY.STY** in the Filename field. You may need to place the Word Utilities disk in the floppy drive. Once the file is merged, select Transfer Save (type **T** and **S**). Make sure that the Filename field is set to NORMAL.STY and press ENTER.

10

Type Style
Formatting

Formatting has to do with how your document will look when printed. The visual appeal of the pages will depend a lot on the typefaces and type styles that you choose to use. When you type a document, you are creating its content; when you format a document, you are designing its look and readability. Although typing and editing may seem to be the most important steps in creating documents with Word, formatting is a step that can make your documents stand out above the rest.

This chapter begins a four-chapter exploration into the layout and design of printed documents. This chapter covers character formatting. In the next chapter you will learn how to design paragraph layouts, and in the following two chapters you will learn how to control the layout of text on the printed page. If you recall, topics such as centering, indenting, and justification are related to paragraphs and thus are covered in the next chapter.

In a way formatting concerns Word's ability to control your printer and its features. When you select a special character style, such as italic or boldface, Word sets up special printer commands that tell it to turn these special print modes on and off. The significance of Word's ease of use in this area may only be realized by the word processing pioneers of the world who remember the inconvenience of early software and systems.

Typefaces and Type Styles

This chapter actually deals with two closely related types of formatting. The first concerns the *style* of a block of text. Style formatting is used to apply italic, bold-face, underline, superscript, and other styles to your text. You can apply these styles *directly* from the keyboard by using the quick keys or the Format Character menu. You can apply them *indirectly* with style sheets.

The second type of formatting has to do with applying *typefaces*. Typeface refers to the printed design of a character, for instance, whether it is rounded or straight, or has serifs or not (serifs are small lines at the points of characters, used to enhance appearance). A typeface may also be called a *font set*. You apply type-faces either directly by using the Format Character menu or indirectly by using style sheets. There are no quick keys for applying typefaces.

Many typefaces are available, such as Helvetica, Times Roman, and Courier, depending on whether your printer supports them. Style formatting is actually a subset of typeface formatting. For example, you can apply the Helvetica typeface to your entire document and then go back to apply individual character styles such as bold and italic. Conversely, you can apply the character styles as you type and alter the font of the entire document later.

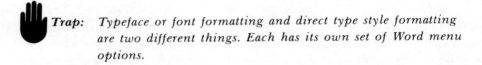 *Trap:* *Typeface or font formatting and direct type style formatting are two different things. Each has its own set of Word menu options.*

Keep in mind that you do not have to apply a typeface to your documents every time. You may sometimes have only one choice anyway, depending on the quality of your printer. If you start Word and begin typing without assigning any special typeface, Word will automatically assign the Courier font to your text. When you print the document, the printer will use its default typeface, usually a 10-character-per-inch Courier or Pica typeface. Courier is the closest approxima-tion to the typeface available on most typewriters, and because it is monospaced, it is equivalent to the typeface displayed on the screen.

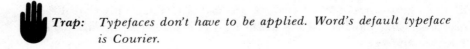 *Trap:* *Typefaces don't have to be applied. Word's default typeface is Courier.*

Character formatting is in fact completely optional. If all of your documents will be printed in normal 10-character-per-inch type style, with no character enhancements, you may want to skip this chapter altogether. However, if your printer can print various typefaces and styles, you should take the time to learn how easy it is to use them.

Figure 10-1 illustrates a comparison between two documents. Both were printed on a Hewlett-Packard LaserJet printer, so the quality of the printout on both is exceptional. However, the overlapping letter was printed with the Times Roman typeface, while the other letter was printed with the standard Courier typeface. It's not hard to decide which is more visually appealing. Font variations of this type are now available on most printers, especially the 24-pin variety that uses NLQ (near letter quality) mode.

Figure 10-2 is a LaserJet printout that shows the various character formats available with the Times Roman typeface. Several character styles have been grouped together. Note also that several point sizes are available.

Figures 10-3 and 10-4 show the same printout with the Helvetica and standard Courier typeface, respectively. All these fonts are available when you use the special Microsoft Word Z font cartridge developed by Hewlett-Packard in conjunction with Microsoft. Many printers use font cartridges to define fonts just as you might change the type ball or print wheel on a typewriter.

 Tip: *Printer font cartridges are analogous to typewriter print wheels and type balls. A font cartridge contains a set of fonts.*

There are a few anomalies in the printouts that you should notice. Bold and italic cannot be mixed if you use these fonts on the Hewlett-Packard LaserJet. Also, the Courier font prints in 12-point type only, so the superscript and subscript type size cannot be controlled. Your printer may have similar problems with printing certain type styles. This chapter will help you determine its abilities by developing a sample printout that has many font and type style variations.

 Trap: *Some type styles cannot be mixed.*

For comparison, look at the Epson FX-86e printout in Figure 10-5. This

Soaring Technologies
101 West Montecito Street
Santa Barbara, CA 93101

June 16, 1988

Mr. John Jones
870 Stone Drive
Palmdale, CA 93500

We are pleased to announce that our new line of Cloud
Nine hang gliders will be presented on July 1, 1988.
Our records indicate that you presently own a Mark Ten.
We would like to invite you to our showroom on June 30,
1988 for an advanced showing. Refreshments will be
served.

If you are unabl[...]
contact us to mal[...]
at your convenie[...]

Sincerely,

Dan Lane
President

SOARING TECHNOLOGIES
101 West Montecito
Santa Barbara, CA

June 16, 1988

Mr. John Jones
870 Stone Drive
Palmdale, CA 93500

Dear John,

We are pleased to announce that our new line of Cloud Nine hang gliders
will be presented on July 1, 1988. Our records indicate that you presently
own a Mark Ten. We would like to invite you to our showroom on June 30,
1988 for an advanced showing. Refreshments will be served.

If you are unable to attend the June 30 showing, please contact us to make
arrangements for a private showing at your convenience.

Sincerely,

Dan Lane
President

Figure 10-1. Fonts and styles make documents more visually appealing

---

TIMES ROMAN

Times Roman 8 point
Times Roman 10 point
Times Roman 12 point
Times Roman 14 point

normal   **bold**   *italic*

<u>underline</u>   <u>double underline</u>   ~~strikethrough~~

<u>bold/underline</u>   *<u>italic/underline</u>*

<u>bold/double underline</u>   *<u>italic/double underline</u>*

~~**bold/strikethrough**~~   *~~italic-strikethrough~~*

superscript normal size subscript

SMALL CAPS TYPE

NOTE: Superscripts and subscripts are formatted in 8 point type.

Figure 10-2.   Times Roman font and style test from LaserJet

printer will print a number of variations in its NLQ (near letter quality) mode. Bold, italics, underline, superscript, and subscript can be mixed on the same line. However, note that the superscript underline does not print directly under the characters. The Epson has five other typefaces, each with various type sizes that can be controlled by Microsoft Word. When you combine these typefaces and sizes with such special character formats as italic and bold, hundreds of font possibilities become available.

The Epson examples in Figure 10-5 were produced by a dot-matrix printer, where each character is formed by a set of pins and printed with an inked ribbon. Most dot-matrix printers use a print head that has 9 or 24 pins stacked on top of

---

HELVETICA

Helvetica 8 point
Helvetica 10 point
Helvetica 12 point
Helvetica 14 point

normal   **bold**   *italic*

underline   double underline   ~~strikethrough~~

bold/underline   *italic/underline*

bold/double underline   *italic/double underline*

~~bold/strikethrough~~   *~~italic strikethrough~~*

superscript normal size subscript

SMALL CAPS TYPE

NOTE: Superscripts and subscripts are formatted in 8 point type.

Figure 10-3.   Helvetica font and style test from LaserJet

each other. Obviously, the more pins that the printer has, the better the print resolution will be. Still, most dot-matrix printers lose print quality because they must use inked ribbons rather than the carbon-film-type ribbons used on many business typewriters and hammer-type printers.

Laser printers excel in quality because of their higher resolution and use of toner printing "ink." Standard laser printers will print at 300 dots per inch, a greatly improved resolution. Further, these printers also use a powdered toner similar to that used in copying machines, so the material used to produce the printout is capable of better resolution.

COURIER 12 POINT

normal   **bold**   *italic*

underline   <u>double underline</u>   ~~strikethrough~~

<u>bold/underline</u>   *<u>italic/underline</u>*

<u>bold/double underline</u>   *<u>italic/double underline</u>*

~~**bold/strikethrough**~~   ~~*italic-strikethrough*~~

superscript normal subscript

Figure 10-4.   Courier font and style test from LaserJet

About the Exercises in This Chapter

One reason for producing the printouts shown in Figures 10-1 through 10-5 is to help determine which typefaces and character styles are available for a specific printer. The Hewlett-Packard LaserJet printers and some printers from other manufacturers have font test modes that print a sample of all currently available fonts. If your printer does not have such a test (and even if it does), you will be interested in the exercises presented in this chapter. Initially you will create a font and character format sample page like those shown in Figures 10-1 through 10-5 to use in testing your printer. Then you will make font changes to the sample page in order to test the font capabilities of your printer.

This chapter will help you determine which combinations of character formats and type styles are available and are best to use for the type of system you have.

EPSON NLQ 12 PITCH (MODERN E)
EPSON NLQ 16 PITCH

normal **bold** *italic*

underline double underline ~~strikethrough~~

bold/italic **bold/underline** *italic/underline*

bold/italic/underline

bold/italic/double underline

bold/italic/underline/strikethrough

superscriptnormalsubscript

BOLD superscriptnormalsubscript

ITALIC superscriptnormalsubscript

UNDERLINE superscriptnormalsubscript

BOLD ITALIC UNDERLINE superscriptnormalsubscript

Figure 10-5. Epson Near Letter Quality (NLQ) print mode

Setting Up Your Printer

Because formatting has so much to do with controlling your printer, you must make sure that Word understands how to talk to your printer before going further. Almost every printer on the market is different. Word must send a special control code to the printer to turn boldfacing or italic on and then another to turn it off. Different printers have different control codes to set these various modes; therefore, special printer description (PRD) files are needed for almost every printer used by Word. In addition, some printers use special font cartridges, so a subset of font description files may be available for use with specific font cartridges. This is the case for the Hewlett-Packard LaserJet.

Tip: *Printer description (PRD) files tell Word how to communicate with your printer.*

Microsoft is one of the better software manufacturers when it comes to making sure that their software works with most of the printers on the market. Word has two diskettes full of printer description files with names that closely match those of the printers they support. For example, the IBM Quietwriter uses the **IBMQUIET.PRD** file, and the Epson FX-80 series uses the **EPSONFX.PRD** file. If you own a Hewlett-Packard LaserJet, a whole series of description files is available for the various fonts used by the printer.

Trap: *If a description file is not available for your printer, contact Microsoft or use the TTY.PRD file. TTY.PRD only supports single-font, nonformatted printing, however.*

You must select the proper printer description file before you can use your printer to its full capacity. If you select the wrong file, garbled characters may show up in the printing.

Trap: *Selecting the wrong printer description file may result in garbled printing.*

The selection of fonts available under the Format Character Font Name option is completely dependent on the printer description file, which is why it is important to choose the proper printer now. Of course, if you choose the wrong description file, some font selections may not print properly on the printer, even though Word lets you select them. In most cases, however, Word will substitute the most likely matching font.

Tip: *The selection of available fonts depends on which printer description file is selected and on whether it properly describes
your printer.*

Printer description files are available on the printer diskettes supplied with
Word. You probably copied the file you need when you ran the Word SETUP
program in Chapter 1. If you use more than one printer or move a portable computer between several printers, you may have several PRD files on your Word disk
or directory. Some printers have available memory where additional fonts can be
placed. These fonts are usually *downloaded* from a disk file to the printer
memory. In this way many fonts are made available to the printer for the price of
the disk file and the time that it takes to transfer the font descriptions to the
printer each time you want to use them.

 Tip: *Some printers have additional memory designated for downloadable fonts.*

To select a printer description file, start Word, open the Print command
menu, and type **O** to select Options. In the menu illustrated here the printer
description file for Epson FX series printers is displayed.

```
PRINT OPTIONS printer: EPSONFX                    setup: LPT1:
        copies: 1                                 draft: Yes(No)
        hidden text: Yes(No)                      summary sheet: Yes(No)
        range:(All)Selection Pages                page numbers:
        widow/orphan control:(Yes)No              queued: Yes(No)
        feed: Manual(Continuous)Bin1 Bin2 Bin3 Mixed
```

To select a printer or font description file, press F1 while the highlight is in the
Printer field. You will be presented with a list of printers or font sets. Only **PRD**
files that you copied automatically with the SETUP program or manually with
the DOS COPY command will be displayed. For example, the screen shown in
Figure 10-6 appears on a system that has the description sets for Hewlett-Packard
font cartridges and downloadable fonts.

Trap: *Only printer description files copied to the Word disk or directory are available for selection.*

 While in the Print Options menu, take a quick look at the options available. (They will be covered in detail in Chapter 19.) You can control the number of copies, whether hidden text is printed, and the range of pages to copy in a multiple-page document. In this case you can print all the pages, specific pages, or just the selection that is highlighted on the screen. You can also choose manual or continuous feed paper, the bins of a sheet feeder, draft-quality, high-speed printing (available on selected printers), and queued printing. Queued printing allows you to "stack up" several print jobs to be printed one after the other.

 Use the arrow keys to highlight a printer selection and then press ENTER to select it. (For more information on setting up and controlling your printer, refer to Chapter 19.)

```
HPDWNCNP          HPDWNPRP          HPLASER1          HPLASPS
HPDWNGAP          HPDWNR8L          HPLASER2          HPLASRMN
HPDWNHLP          HPDWNR8P          HPLASER3          HPLASTAX
HPDWNLGL          HPDWNSFL          HPLASLAN          HPPCCOUR
HPDWNLGP          HPDWNSFP          HPLASMS           TTY
HPDWNPRL          HPDWNZHP          HPLASMSL
```

```
PRINT OPTIONS printer: HPLASMS              setup: LPT1:
        copies: 1                           draft: Yes(No)
        hidden text: Yes(No)                summary sheet: Yes(No)
        range:(All)Selection Pages          page numbers:
        widow/orphan control:(Yes)No        queued: Yes(No)
        feed: Manual(Continuous)Bin1 Bin2 Bin3 Mixed
Enter printer name or press F1 to select from list
Pg1 Co1          {}                    ?                      Microsoft Word
```

Figure 10-6. *Pressing* F1 *in Printer field displays printer options*

Downloadable Fonts

Fonts are either *hard-wired* or *downloadable*. Hard-wired fonts are built into the printer and are always available for printing. They are coded into the microchips of your printer. Cartridge fonts, like those used by the IBM Quietwriter and HP LaserJet, are also considered hard-wired fonts.

 Tip: *Built-in or* hard-wired *fonts are always available for use.* Downloadable *fonts must be copied from the computer to the printer before use.*

Downloadable fonts must be transferred from a disk file on your computer to the memory of your printer. Some printers support both hard-wired and downloadable fonts. To use a downloadable font, you must send a font description file to the printer before you attempt to print. This usually happens in the background, as long as you have the font description file on your disk. You need only select the downloadable font from the Font Name field in the Format Character command.

 Tip: *Word handles all font download functions in the background. You need only select the font set to download.*

Font Substitutions

If you assign a font that is not available on your printer (by using the wrong printer driver or setting character styles that are not supported), Word or the printer will substitute the next most likely font. For example, if you assign italics to characters and your printer doesn't support them, Word will usually substitute underlining. If you are using the Hewlett-Packard LaserJet, a font that is not on the current cartridge or download set will be replaced with one that most nearly matches the one requested. Font substitution is covered in more detail in the next section.

 Trap: *Word may select a substitute for a font that you assign if the printer can't print your assigned font.*

A Brief Typography Discussion

Fonts are collections of characters that have a similar typeface, style, and size. Fonts are often available in a wide variety of sizes to suit various printing requirements. For example, Figure 10-7 illustrates the Helvetica typeface available on a Hewlett-Packard LaserJet with the Microsoft Word Z font cartridge installed. To select any of these formatting options, you must specify a combination of the font size and boldfacing or italic style in the Format Character menu.

Type Characteristics

The characters that make up fonts have various characteristics that you must consider to some extent when formatting your documents. The most important of these is character spacing. In addition, characters have a certain pitch, point size, style, and typeface.

Helvetica 8 point typeface

Helvetica 10 point typeface

Helvetica 10 point italic typeface

Helvetica 10 point bold typeface

Helvetica 12 point typeface

Helvetica 12 point italic typeface

Helvetica 12 point bold typeface

Helvetica 14 point bold typeface

Figure 10-7. Helvetica font comparison

Word: Secrets, Solutions, Shortcuts

Character Spacing   A font set is either monospaced or proportionally spaced. In a monospaced font all characters have the same width, whether the character is a *W* or an *i*. The Word edit window displays characters in a monospaced font. Proportionally spaced fonts assign a special width to each character to increase its readability and visual appeal. Figure 10-8 illustrates the difference between monospaced and proportionally (also called variable) spaced fonts.

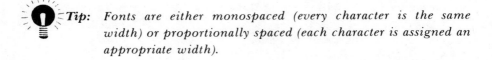 *Tip:*   *Fonts are either monospaced (every character is the same width) or proportionally spaced (each character is assigned an appropriate width).*

Each type of spacing has its advantages. While variable fonts may look more appealing, they are sometimes awkward to work with. Because the edit window displays characters in monospaced fonts, it is sometimes hard to tell how your printouts will look when you assign a proportionally spaced font to them. Monospaced fonts are convenient when you are trying to line up characters or columns

Figure 10-8.   Monospaced and proportionally spaced fonts compared

without using tabs. It is also easy to count characters across in a monospaced font, if the need should arise.

 Tip: *Monospaced fonts are easier to work with when spacing or counting characters.*

 Tip: *Proportionally spaced fonts are easier to read and are visually more appealing.*

Character Pitch The pitch of a character relates directly to how many characters can be placed in a horizontal inch of text. Monospaced fonts use a specific pitch size that indicates how many characters are printed per inch. Proportionally spaced fonts do not define characters with pitch: because each character is a different size, there is no way to measure how many will fit in an inch unless you are measuring the same character. Figure 10-9 shows an example of the Courier monospaced font in different pitch sizes.

---

6 pitch
8 pitch
10 pitch
12 pitch

Figure 10-9.   Character pitch

Tip: *Monospaced fonts are described in terms of pitch, which determines the number of characters that can be placed horizontally in an inch of text.*

 Trap: *Proportionally spaced fonts can never be measured accurately in characters per inch because the characters differ in size.*

Character Point Size   Point size is a measure of the height of a character and is often used to specify the type size for proportionally spaced fonts. Figure 10-10 illustrates different point sizes in Times Roman. The larger the point size, the larger the character width.

 Tip: *The point size of a character measures its height and is therefore a measure of the overall size of the character.*

Times Roman 8 point type
Times Roman 10 point type
Times Roman 12 point type
Times Roman 14 point type

Figure 10-10.   Point size determines overall font size

Character Style and Typeface   Character style has to do with a change in the slant (italics), weight (bold), or other characteristics of a character within a font set. The face of a character has to do with the design of the letters. The characteristics of a font design will be discussed in the next section. The differences in character font styles and typefaces can be seen in Figures 10-2 through 10-5. You should remember that once a typeface has been assigned, type styles can still be applied. Also, a typeface can be applied after character style formatting has been applied.

 Tip: *Think of character style and typeface formatting as masks placed over the characters of your text. They can be mixed, and either can be applied before the other.*

Typeface Groups

According to Microsoft, fonts fall into six groups. The name of a font represents its intended use to some extent. The importance of font groups in Word goes beyond a simple classification of typefaces. When a font is part of a group, Word will often substitute that font for another within the same group if a particular printer does not support the font. This will be covered in the next section. The six groups are as follows:

Modern	Modern fonts are designed with uniform thickness, either without serifs (*sans-serif*) or with serifs of the same line quality. Most typewriter fonts belong to this group.
Roman	Roman fonts are of classical design with serifs and strokes of varying thickness.
Script	Script fonts are slanted characters formed from curved lines.
Foreign	Eight foreign font sets are defined by Word, including such sets as Hebrew, Greek, and Kana.

Decor   Decor fonts can be used for titles and for such nonbusiness printing needs as posters and invitations. Old English and calligraphic fonts are examples.

Symbol   Symbol fonts consist of large groupings of mathematical symbols, printer's symbols, and publishers symbols.

Each font set has a number of variations that are given character names such as "a" or "b." For example, Helvetica is Modern i and Avant Garde is Modern j. You will always see font group names listed with a character variation.

 Tip: *Each font group has a subset of variations, each of which is given a character code.*

Figure 10-11 shows a listing of fonts for the IBM Quietwriter III, many of which must be downloaded to the Quietwriter before use. Note the variety of fonts and the font group name given to each. In the next section you'll see how to put these to use.

```
Courier (modern a)          Courier-WP (modern b)
Prestige (modern c)         Prestige-WP (modern d)
LetterGothic (modern e)     LetterGothic-WP (modern f)
Gothic-WP (modern g)        DualGothic-WP (modern h)
ModernPS (modern i)         ModernPS-WP (modern j)
Artisan (modern k)          TitlePS (modern l)
Presentor-WP (modern m)     APL-WP (modern n)
Artisan-WP (modern o)       TitlePS-WP (modern p)
BoldfacePS (roman a)        BoldfacePS-WP (roman b)
Bookface-WP (roman f)       Adjutant-WP (roman g)
Advocate-WP (roman h)       Delegate-WP (roman i)
Script-WP (script b)        Courier-ML (foreign a)
Prestige-ML (foreign b)     LetterGothic-ML (foreign c)
ModernPS-ML (foreign d)     Artisan-ML (foreign e)
BoldfacePS-ML (foreign f)   Title-ML (foreign g)
Orator-WP (decor a)         OldeWorld-WP (decor e)
Symbol-WP (symbol a)
```

Figure 10-11. Fonts available for IBM Quietwriter III

Font Substitution Strategies   One reason that Word gives fonts the group names just described is so that it can use a suitable font substitute when printing the document on another printer. When Microsoft builds a printer description file for a specific printer, it assigns a font group name to each font available on that printer. Although the font may not be exactly like that of another printer, Word considers it a close enough match to use as a substitute for existing font assignments.

 Tip: *Font group names assist Word in performing font substitutions.*

Font substitution is very helpful when you have access to two printers. Assume that you have an Epson printer (with a low-quality, high-speed, dot-matrix printing mode) and an IBM Quietwriter (which prints at a slower rate but at a higher quality). You would use the high-speed printer to produce draft-quality printouts of your document. Because it allows some font variations and style changes, you format and print the document using those font names. When choosing the font names, you carefully match the font group names between the two printers so that similar fonts will be printed on both. The illustrations here show the font groups for the Epson and the Quietwriter.

`Pica (modern a)`	`PicaD (modern b)`
`Elite (modern c)`	`EliteD (modern d)`
`NLQ (modern e)`	`NLQD (modern f)`
`PS (roman a)`	`PSD (roman b)`

Epson fonts

`Courier10-slot1 (modern a)`	`Prestige12-slot2 (modern c)`
`Prestige15-slot2 (modern d)`	`BoldfacePS-slot2 (roman a)`

IBM Quietwriter fonts

Assume that you use PS (Roman a) and Elite (Modern c) when formatting the document to be printed on the Epson. When the document is finally edited and ready for high-quality printing on the Quietwriter, Word will substitute BoldfacePS (Roman a) and Prestige12 (Modern c).

You can also use this strategy if you are sending documents on disk to other users. If you know what kind of printer they have, you can format your documents in typefaces that will match the fonts on their printer while retaining a style you prefer to print on yur printer.

Tip: *Font substitutions can be used to advantage when you are printing on several printers.*

Introducing Formatting Techniques

The rest of this chapter will introduce you to the techniques used to format your documents. Menus and quick keys can be used to apply character styles. But applying typefaces requires the use of the Format Character menu, and this section will show you an easy way to get there. Style sheets will also play an important part in the creation of your documents, as you will see at the end of this chapter and in later chapters.

The Format Character Menu

All character formatting is done in the Format Character menu unless you use the quick keys or a style sheet. However, uppercase conversion can only be done through the menu, which is shown here.

```
FORMAT CHARACTER bold: Yes No      italic: Yes(No)         underline: Yes(No)
           strikethrough: Yes(No)   uppercase: Yes(No)      small caps: Yes(No)
           double underline: Yes(No) position:(Normal)Superscript Subscript
           font name: Courier       font size: 12           hidden: Yes(No)
```

The Format Character menu is not only used to set styles and typefaces. It is often necessary to open it to check on the style or typeface applied to a particular format. This is especially true of typeface formats because they do not appear on the screen as printed. You must place the highlight somewhere in the block of text formatting that you are checking.

Tip: *To check the format applied to a block of text, place the highlight somewhere in the block and open the Format Character menu.*

If you have a monochrome (noncolor) monitor, bold will appear as boldfaced text, but other styles will appear as underlined characters unless you have a Hercules graphics card. If you use a color monitor in text mode, bold will appear in bold type and other styles will appear highlighted in a color other than the background color. You can open the Format Character menu to check on the applied style of the characters by placing the highlight somewhere in the character style.

Quick Keys

The quick-key method is the easiest way to assign styles to selected text. Hold down the ALT key while pressing the appropriate key for the style. The letter on the key representing the style is the first letter of its description except for hidden text and the superscript or subscript style. Type **B** for boldface, **I** for italics, and so on. If a style sheet is attached, you must press ALT+X+B or ALT+X+I.

ALT+F8

The ALT+F8 combination is the "back door" method of getting into the Format Character menu. The highlight appears on the Font Name field when the menu appears, making font changes a snap. Simply press F1 to see a list of fonts.

 Tip: *ALT+F8 is a quick way to get to the Format Character Font Name field.*

Style Sheets

Style sheets are a convenient way to assign both character styles and typefaces (as well as paragraph and division formats, as discussed in the next few chapters). If you need to apply an often used style that normally requires several quick-key keystrokes, you can assign it your own ALT key code combination. For example, you could assign bold and underline to the ALT+B+U keys.

 Tip: *You can assign often used quick-key combinations to their own ALT key sequence by using a style sheet.*

The formatting of a common heading throughout a document or report is another example. You could assign the Helvetica 12-point typeface plus a bold style to the ALT+H+E key combination.

 Tip: *You can assign formats for common headings, titles, and other often used fonts and styles to ALT key combinations by using a style sheet.*

If you need a foreign character not available in the font set that you are using, you must select a symbol font set to make the character available. Then you must decide which key on your keyboard you will use to display or print the symbol from the symbol set and then apply that character. The steps involved in performing this task make it a good candidate for the style sheet.

When to Format

You can apply formats as you type or after you type, and if you use style sheets and outlines, you can even apply styles before you type the body text of your documents. If you don't like to be interrupted as your thoughts cascade into the computer, do the formatting when you edit.

After you've used Word for a while, you will settle on your own style of formatting, which may be a combination of all the methods described earlier. You should format a character on the spot if you feel that you might forget to format it later. If a document is long, it is easy to miss or forget words or blocks of text that require specific formats.

If you are formatting a single character, note that Word needs to know whether you want to format a single character or turn on a character format for characters that you will be typing. When the selection is a single character, press the ALT key twice to apply a format to just that character.

 Trap: *To format a single character, press the ALT key twice.*

Applying Character Styles

The smallest unit in any document is a single character. Word's character style formatting applies styles to these individual characters or to groups of them, depending on where you place the highlight. This section will lead you through exercises to create a print sample sheet to test the type style capabilities of your printer.

Start Word in the normal way or, if you are already in Word, clear the current screen to start a new document.

Built-in Styles

Because character style formatting is usually applied often in the course of creating a document, the styles are built into Word and easy to get to when needed. Pressing the quick keys is one of the fastest ways to apply character formatting. The following sections describe each of the 10 built-in styles that are available with Word. Keep in mind that many of these styles can be combined.

The ALT+SPACEBAR combination returns formatted text to normal. If the selected text is a single character, you must press ALT+SPACEBAR twice to return to normal.

 Tip: *The ALT+SPACEBAR combination returns formatted text that is highlighted back to the normal type style.*

Normal   Normal is the default typeface and style used by Word when you start typing a document, unless you have assigned fonts and styles beforehand, or have attached a style sheet. At the top of the screen, type **normal** and press TAB three times to get to the 2-inch tab mark. This will serve as an example of normal typing on the print test sheet.

Bold   Use boldface type to make a particular letter, word, or block of text stand out on the page. Press ALT+B to apply boldface to selected text or to turn boldface typing on. For this example, type **BOLD** at the current highlight location and press TAB three times to get to the 3.5-inch tab position. Now press F7 four times to move the highlight back to the word and press ALT+B (ALT+X+B if style sheets are used). The character is converted to boldface and appears as boldface on the screen. In this example you applied character formatting after the text was typed. In the next example you will apply it beforehand.

 Tip: *Text formatted to bold is printed as characters with more weight or in double-strike mode on many printers. Press ALT+B to format selected text as bold.*

 Tip: *Text formatted to bold is displayed on the screen in double-intensity mode.*

Italics   Use italics to emphasize text. Press the END key to move to the paragraph mark at the end of a line. Next, press ALT+I (ALT+X+I if style sheets are used) to turn italic typing on and then type **italic text**. Your screen may display the text as slanted, underlined, or highlighted in a color. Before moving to the next example, press ALT+SPACEBAR to turn italic typing off.

 Tip: *Italic characters are displayed on the screen as slanted, underlined, or highlighted in a color.*

Underline   Underline is often used with titles and in accounting applications. Underlined text will extend through blank spaces created by tab characters, as shown here:

<u>Itinerary</u>   **<u>Date</u>**
Carnegie Hall   1/10

Press ENTER to start a new line and then type **underline**. After the last character, press F7 to highlight the word and then press ALT+U (ALT+X+U if style sheets are used). The characters appear as underlined or highlighted. Press the LEFT ARROW key and then press the TAB key twice.

 Tip: *Tabs and spaces are considered characters that can be underlined, just like any other text.*

Double Underline Double underline is often used to underscore totals in accounting applications. In this example turn double-underline mode on before typing the text by pressing ALT+D (ALT+X+D if style sheets are used). Type **double underline** and then press ALT+SPACEBAR to turn the mode off. Press the TAB key once for the next exercise.

Strikethrough Strikethrough is used to strike out sections of contracts that are no longer valid. The original text remains in the document, though in the strikeout format. Type **strikethrough** at the tab stop and then press F7 to highlight the word. By now you can see that it doesn't matter whether you format characters by first turning on the style or by highlighting them after you type. The same number of keystrokes are involved. Press ALT+S (ALT+X+S if style sheets are used) to strike through the word. Press END and then ENTER to move to the next line.

 Tip: *Strikethrough is used to strike out sections of text in contracts that are no longer valid.*

Superscript and Subscript Superscript and subscript are used in various technical papers, chemical formulas, and mathematical formulas. You will usually want to apply a smaller type size to characters that are formatted to superscript or subscript. (This will be covered later in this chapter.)

 Trap: *On some printers the type size of superscript or subscript characters must be reduced.*

Type **superscript normal subscript** on the line. Then press F7 three times to return to the word *superscript*. Press ALT+PLUS (or ALT+X+PLUS); that is, hold down the ALT key and press the plus (or equal) key on the keyboard. Press F8 twice to highlight the word *subscript* and then press ALT+MINUS to subscript the word.

It is easy to remember superscript and subscript keycodes if you remember that the plus sign raises the text and the minus sign lowers it. Press the END key and then press ENTER twice to move to a new line.

Certain printers may not place the underline directly under superscript or subscript characters. The following illustration shows the effect of underlining superscript and subscript on a Hewlett-Packard LaserJet printer (top sample) and a Star Micronics Radix type printer (bottom sample). Note how the underline is below the superscript and actually strikes through the subscript in the lower print sample.

<u>superscript</u>
        <u>subscript</u>

superscript
──────── subscript

Combination Styles   You can combine styles to get special effects. In these examples you will create several combinations of type styles. Remember, if you have a style sheet attached, you must type **X** with the style codes.

1. Press ALT+B and ALT+I to turn on bold and italic. Type **bold+italic** and press ALT+SPACEBAR to return to normal style.

2. Tab once and then press ALT+B and ALT+U for bold and underline. Type **bold+underline** and press ALT+SPACEBAR to return to normal style.

3. Tab once and then press ALT+I and ALT+U for italic and underline. Type **italic+underline** and press ALT+SPACEBAR to return to normal style.

4. Press ENTER to start a new line.

Next, try several triple type style combinations. This will give your printer a real test.

1. Press ALT+B, ALT+I, and ALT+U to turn on bold, italic, and underline at the same time. Type **bold+italic+underline** and press ALT+SPACEBAR to return to normal style.

2. Press the TAB key and then press ALT+B, ALT+I, and ALT+D to turn on bold, italic, and double underline. Type **bold+italic+double underline** and press ALT+SPACEBAR to return to normal style. Press ENTER twice to start a new line.

Now, add the strikethrough style to your lineup.

1. Press ALT+B, ALT+I, ALT+U, and ALT+S to turn on bold, italic, underline, and strikethrough. Type **bold+italic+underline+strikethrough** and press ALT+SPACEBAR to turn the modes off.

2. Before moving to the next line, press SHIFT+F9 to highlight the current line. Press ALT+F3 to copy the text to the scrap.

3. Move to the next line by pressing END and ENTER (twice if necessary); then press INS to insert a copy of the scrap into the line.

For the next example, you'll add superscript and subscript to the end of the line formatted with bold, italic, underline, and strikethrough. However, you must use a special formatting trick to format text added to the end of the line in the previous format. To see why you need a trick, do the following:

1. With the cursor on the last line, press the END key. This is the point where you want to type the new text.

2. Type **su.**

Notice that the text you are typing is not formatted with the styles of the previous text. In order to apply them to your new text, perform the following "odd" trick.

1. Press BACKSPACE twice to remove the characters that you just typed. The highlight is just to the right of the *h* in the line.

2. Press the LEFT ARROW key and then type another **h.**

3. Now type **+superscript+subscript.**

4. At the end of the line, press DEL to remove the extra *h.*

By moving into the previously formatted text, you were able to "pick up" the formatting and continue typing. The extra character simply gets deleted at the end of the line. By the way, deleting the character places the highlight on the paragraph marker, automatically returning the formats to normal text. For future reference, this trick will be referred to as the Sheldon Format Capture (SFC) routine. Not really, but at least that might help you remember it.

 Tip: *You can capture previous formats by moving the insertion point into the characters and typing. However, at least one character must be retyped.*

Finally, you must convert the superscript and subscript characters to their proper format. Press F7 three times and then press ALT+PLUS to raise the word *superscript.* Then press F8 twice and press ALT+MINUS to lower the word *subscript.* Press END and ENTER twice.

Small Caps   Small caps can be used for footnotes, tables, or special labels. If the formatted text contains capital letters, they are printed in the normal text size. If the letters are lowercase, they are printed as reduced-size capital letters.

 Tip: *Small caps style converts lowercase letters to a reduced font size in all capitals.*

If your printer cannot support a font size smaller than the one you are using for normal type, text formatted to small caps is printed in normal type in all capital letters.

 Trap: *If your printer does not have a smaller type size, Word uses the normal size and converts lowercase letters to uppercase.*

Try this to see if your printer supports small caps.

1. On the new line, press ALT+K and type **Small Caps**.
2. At the end of the line, press ALT+SPACEBAR.

On graphics monitors the lowercase letters should appear as small capital letters. This illustration shows how text in small caps is printed on a Hewlett-Packard LaserJet using the Microsoft Word Z font cartridge.

`This is normal Courier.   THIS IS SMALL CAPS`
This is normal Times Roman. THIS IS SMALL CAPS
This is normal Helvetica. THIS IS SMALL CAPS

Uppercase   Uppercase formatting will convert lowercase letters to capital letters. This formatting option is only available through the Format Character menu. In addition, if you remove the formatting from the characters by pressing ALT+SPACE-BAR, the lowercase letters will return. This is something to consider if you save a file with the Transfer Save Unformatted option. All characters formatted for uppercase will revert to lowercase in the disk file.

Hidden Text   In Chapter 9 you learned how to use hidden text during editing to place notes that are not printed and are available only to the author or editor of the document. You can display or hide hidden text at any time, and you can print it if you want.

 Tip: *Hidden text can be displayed on the screen or not, and it can be printed with the document if you wish.*

Consider the editing process for a minute. When you create a document, you might write hidden notes or reminders to yourself that you can hide when the document is printed. If the document is being passed to several people during the editing process, as is true for many technical and corporate documents, you can include hidden notes for others. These people can include notes of their own. In the last stage of editing, you can apply the notes or comments to the document and then print it with hidden text turned off.

To apply hidden text formats, press ALT+E. Presumably, you will want to do this before you start typing the notes or comments. However, you can apply hidden text formats to those parts of the document that you don't want to print. To remove these formats, press ALT+SPACEBAR, but be aware that ALT+SPACEBAR will also remove any other formats applied to the text.

To show or hide hidden text, use the Window Options command and select the appropriate option in the Show Hidden Text field. If you start Word in graphics mode, hidden text that is made visible on the screen is displayed with dotted underlines. On color monitors running in text mode, visible hidden text is displayed in another color.

 Tip: *You can make hidden text visible by selecting the Show Hidden Text field in the Window Options command.*

Never paginate a document with hidden text made visible unless you intend to print the visible hidden text. Word will include the hidden text with the rest of the text and insert page breaks around it. If you then print the document without the hidden text, the page breaks will be in the wrong places.

 Tip: *Never paginate a document with visible hidden text unless you plan to print the visible hidden text.*

When the Options Visible field is set to either partial or complete, and hidden text is not visible on the screen, a double-arrow symbol indicates the location of hidden text.

 Tip: *A double-arrow symbol indicates the location of hidden text when partial or complete display mode is on and hidden text is invisible.*

Printing the Type Style Sample Sheet

Your screen should now look like the one shown in Figure 10-12 if you have a graphics monitor. At this point, you can print out the text on your screen to see how your printer reacts to it. Use the Print option in the Print menu. When the document is printed, inspect each character style and style combination. Do bold and italic print when combined, or do they print in just italic, just bold, or maybe as underlined text? Where does the underline fall in the underline superscript and subscript example? Some printers will automatically reduce the size of characters used for superscript and subscript. If so, does the underline fall directly under the

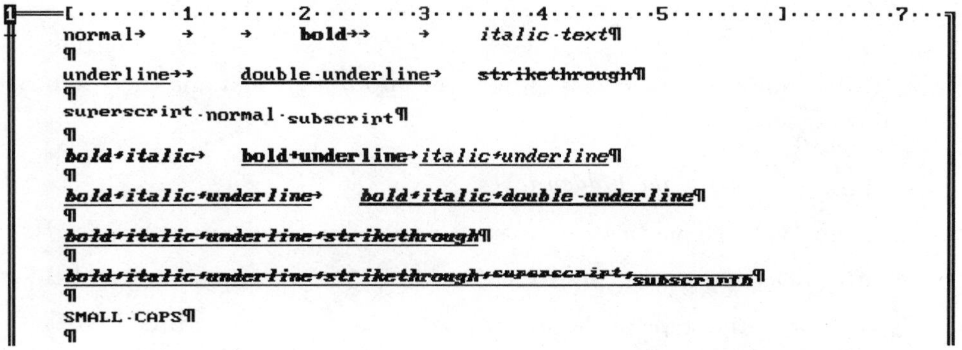

Figure 10-12. A type style printer test sample

superscript characters, or does it remain in the bottom of the line with the rest of the underlined characters? Did small caps print in small caps? Look for all these things so that you can effectively use character styles in the future.

Saving the Type Sample Sheet

Save the type sample sheet for use later in the chapter and for whenever you want to test the printing capabilities of another printer. Select Transfer Save and type **FONTTEST** in the Filename field.

Applying Typefaces

This section will deal primarily with the selection of different fonts and sizes through the Format Character menu. You should select the text to be formatted before opening the menu, and you should get into the habit of using ALT+F8 to get to the menu when changing or viewing fonts. This key combination will place the cursor directly on the Font Name menu option. From there, you can press F1 to see a selection of fonts.

Word: Secrets, Solutions, Shortcuts

 Tip: *Use ALT+F8 whenever possible when changing or viewing type-faces and sizes.*

To set a font or a font size, highlight the appropriate text and then perform the following steps:

1. Press ALT+F8.

2. In the Font Name field, press F1 to display and select a typeface.

3. After selecting a font, press the TAB key to jump to the Font Size field.

4. You can either type in the size or press F1 to see a list of available sizes for the font selection currently displayed in the Font Name field.

5. Press ENTER to perform the font change.

If you want to change the font of an entire document but don't get around to it until you've finished typing, simply press SHIFT+F10 to select the entire text. Even if parts of the document have varying font sizes, you may want to initially select the entire document to change the typeface. Then you can go through and change the font size of specific paragraphs or text blocks.

 Tip: *Press SHIFT+F10 to select and format an entire document.*

If your document has several different typefaces, you can format the entire document to the dominant typeface and then scroll through to select sections that must be changed to other typefaces. Of course, planning ahead and using style sheets will eliminate these problems by making it easy to change fonts as you type.

Changing Fonts

If you need to change a font, simply highlight the appropriate characters and press ALT+F8. You can then alter the font. Be aware, however, that if you highlight an area containing two different font types and then display the Format Character menu, all fields will be blank. This is because two different sets are ounder the highlight and Word can't display the fonts for both.

Trap: *If the highlight is over two font types, the Format Character menu will contain blank fields because two selections cannot be displayed at once.*

Printer Selection and Available Fonts

As discussed earlier, the fonts available to you when you are formatting a block of text completely depend on the printer description file selected in the Print Options Printer field. To view the options, press ALT+F8 and then press F1.

It is possible to select an incorrect printer description file and use its fonts to print on your printer, but this is rare. Garbage usually results. Note that fonts for incorrect description files still appear in the Format Character menu. Because printer description files describe the operating characteristics of a particular printer, they are seldom interchangeable.

If your printer allows multiple font cartridges or downloadable fonts, like the Hewlett-Packard LaserJet, you can use font sets other than the ones that specifically describe the font you have in your printer, assuming that the set you select has a typeface with the same name as the one in your printer. For example, Helvetica in one font description file on a LaserJet works with any cartridge that supports Helvetica.

 Tip: *Some printers that support cartridges and downloadable fonts allow crossovers among font description files.*

Testing the Fonts of Your Printer

You can test the type fonts of your printer by performing the following steps:

1. If the file FONTTEST is not on the screen, recall it with the Transfer Load command.

2. Press SHIFT+F10 to select the whole document.

3. Press ALT+F8 to display the Format Character menu.

4. With the highlight in the Font Name field, press F1 to display the fonts available for your printer. The objective is to print the highlighted text once for each of the fonts now displayed at the top of your screen. Most likely the first font displayed is standard Courier, which you have already printed.

Word: Secrets, Solutions, Shortcuts

    5. Slide down or across to the next font and press ENTER.

The new font will be applied to the highlighted font. Use the Print command to print the printer test sheet with this new font.

    Repeat the above steps for each font listed on your screen. Remember that some printers use cartridges and downloadable fonts, so some of the selections on your screen may not be available. For example, the font description file HPLASER1.PRD defines 29 fonts that can be printed when the correct cartridges or downloadable fonts are available. In reality only a few of these fonts can be printed at any one time. Microsoft simply grouped a large number of fonts into one file for convenience.

Differences Between Screen and Printout

If you are using a monospaced font such as Courier, the screen displays text alignment and line breaks just as they will be printed. When you use a proportionally spaced font, a few problems arise that may not be apparent until you print your documents.

Print Display Mode   The print display mode can help you see where lines will break when you use proportionally spaced fonts. To display line breaks on the screen as they will break on the printout, press ALT+F7 or select Yes in the Printer Display field of the Options command. Figure 10-13 shows how text appears on the screen and how it will appear when printed. Notice that even in print display mode, the edit window cannot fully display the text.

 Tip: *Set the print display mode on (ALT+F7) to view line breaks when you use proportionally spaced fonts.*

Tabs and Proportional Fonts   The first time you work with tabbed columns and attempt to print them in proportionally spaced type, you will be in for a surprise. The columns may not align properly, even though they seem to on the screen.

```
TX  Although·there·was·only·a·two·month·gap·between·the·writing·of·Mozart's·F·
    Concerto·and·his·D·Minor·Concerto,·the·two·compositions·are·as·different·a
    and·white.··The·F·Major·Concerto·is·bright·and·full·of·life,·whereas·the·D
    concerto·is·dark·and·gloomy,·but·moving.¶
```

Although there was only a two month gap between the writing of Mozart's F Major
Concerto and his D Minor Concerto, the two compositions are as different as black
and white. The F Major Concerto is bright and full of life, whereas the D Minor
concerto is dark and gloomy, but moving.

Figure 10-13. Print display mode shows line breaks

Trap: *Tabbed columns may not align properly when you use a pro-*
portionally spaced font.

Note in this illustration that the columns appear properly aligned in the
screen image. Tabs were used to set up the column alignments.

```
TX  Cho—Liang·Lin↓
    ↓
    Itinerary→→    →     →     →     Date↓
    Carnegie·Hall→ →     →     →     1/10↓
    Music·Hall·at·Fair·Park→ →       1/15↓
    Dallas,·TX→    →     →     →     1/17↓
    Meyerhoff·Symphony·Hall→ →       1/21↓
    Baltimore,·MD→ →     →     →     1/22↓
    Symphony·Hall,·Boston→     →     1/28↓
```

Now look at the printed result on the next page. Obviously, there is a problem.
Because characters are different sizes in proportionally spaced fonts, the screen
image does not accurately show where columns will align.

Cho-Liang Lin

Itinerary	Date
Carnegie Hall	1/10
Music Hall at Fair Park	1/15
Dallas, TX	1/17
Meyerhoff Symphony Hall	1/21
Baltimore, MD	1/22
Symphony Hall, Boston	1/28

One way to solve this problem is to turn print display mode on.

Tip: *Set print display mode on (ALT+F7) to display column alignments when you use proportionally spaced fonts.*

The table will then appear as shown here. You can see where an extra tab is
required to align a column.

```
TX  Cho-Liang·Lin↓
    ↓
    Itinerary→→    →    →    →   Date↓
    Carnegie·Hall→   →    →    →   1/10↓
    Music·Hall·at·Fair·Park→→1/15↓
    Dallas,·TX→→    →    1/17↓
    Meyerhoff·Symphony·Hall→→1/21↓
    Baltimore,·MD→   →    →   1/22↓
    Symphony·Hall,·Boston→→  1/28↓
    ¶
```

The best way to solve the problem is to set special tabs when you create
tables. In the illustration shown here, a single tab stop at the 3-inch mark was set
with the Format Tab Set command.

```
═[········1········2········L········4··
  Cho-Liang·Lin↓
  ↓
  Itinerary→              Date↓
  Carnegie·Hall→          1/10↓
  Music·Hall·at·Fair·Park→  1/15↓
  Dallas,·TX→             1/17↓
  Meyerhoff·Symphony·Hall→  1/21↓
  Baltimore,·MD→          1/22↓
  Symphony·Hall,·Boston→   1/28↓
  ¶
```

This method has two benefits. First, all text will align properly because there is only one tab stop to align with. Second, you don't have to type a lot of tab spaces. Notice the tab marker (L) in the 3-inch position of the ruler.

 Tip: *The best way to work with tables and proportional fonts is to set specific tab stops with the Format Tab Set command.*

Fonts and Superscript/Subscript Characters   When you work with superscript and subscript characters, you should format the characters to a smaller size unless your printer does this automatically.

 Tip: *If your printer supports it, reduce the font size of superscript and subscript characters to improve their appearance.*

Highlight the characters and then press ALT+F8 to display the Format Character menu. Tab to the Size option and select an appropriate size. It is often best to assign such formatting to style sheets, as you'll see shortly.

 Tip: *It's best to use a style sheet for character formatting routines that require several keystrokes and menu options.*

Determining an Existing Font

If you have a style sheet attached and are formatting your document as you type, you can easily determine the typeface and size you are using if you know what the style code in the style bar represents. This assumes that you left the style bar on after setting it in Chapter 2. If the style bar is not active, use the Window Options command and answer Yes in the Style Bar field.

 Tip: *The style code in the style bar is a clue to the typeface and size of the text in a paragraph.*

Figure 10-14 shows several of the styles used in writing this book. The T styles are used for titles, so T1 is a first-level heading formatted to the Helvetica 14-point typeface. T2 and T3 are second- and third-level headings, respectively. The TX style is body text, formatted to standard Courier.

If you are not using style sheets, you can open the Format Character menu by pressing ALT+F8 to get a quick glance at the formats set for the text at the current highlight position. This is the only way you can determine the font of a text block embedded within a paragraph.

Quick Formatting Techniques

You've already seen how to perform some formatting routines quickly. Now you can add the following techniques to your formatting repertoire.

Repeating Formats

Use the F4 key to repeat the last format you applied. For example, assume that you have just applied boldface to a word in your text. You can move to another word with either the highlight movement keys or the mouse, press F7 or F8 to highlight

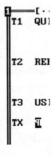

Figure 10-14.   Type style codes in the style bar

it, and then press F4 to apply boldfacing.

Tip: *The F4 key provides a convenient way to jump through your document and apply a common format to titles, tables, paragraphs, or other blocks of text.*

Keep in mind that F4 repeats the most recent action. Assume that you format a word to bold, then scroll through the text looking for other words to boldface with the F4 key. Along the way, you notice a character that you want to delete. If you do so, Delete will become the new command executed by the F4 key, not boldfacing.

Trap: *When using F4 to repeat formatting commands, you must perform the anticipated commands one after the other. Other commands will replace the formatting routines remembered by the F4 key.*

Remember, too, that Word will apply only the last format used in a double-format operation. If you apply bold and then underline to a block of text, and you then select another block for formatting, Word will repeat only the underline when F4 is pressed.

Copying Formats with the Mouse

The mouse can be used to copy both character and paragraph formats. First, select the characters, words, or other text that you want to format; then point to the character format that you want to copy and press the left button while holding down the ALT key.

Tip: *To copy a format with the mouse, highlight the target text, point to the previously formatted text, and click the left button while holding down the ALT key.*

Using Windows with the Mouse   If you need to copy formats with the mouse that cannot be displayed on the screen at one time, open a window on the screen with the Windows Split Horizontal command. You can then leave the formatted text stationary in one window, scrolling through the other window, and point from one window to the other to copy formats.

 Tip: *Use windows when you copy styles with a mouse over large documents.*

Glossaries to Establish Formats

You can insert glossary entries into your text to establish formats. For example, the glossary entry Table could be a *template* for a table. You would type **table** and then press the F3 (Glossary Expand) key. This would type the template shown here:

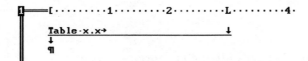

Once the template is in your document, you can simply fill in the blanks to create a table. The template helps establish the formats for the table, such as typeface and size, character style, and tab settings. As a result, all of your tables will retain a similar look and format and will be easier to create and read.

 Tip: *Templates for tables and other blocks of text with both charac-ter and paragraph changes can be stored as glossary entries.*

A filled-in table created in this way might look like the one shown in Figure 10-15.

Table 3.1	Famous Sculptures
The Great Sphinx	Giza, Egypt
Charioteer of Delphi	Delphi, Greece
Michelangelo Buonarroti	St. Peter's, Rome
Virgin of Paris	Notre Dame Cathedral
Auguste Rodin: The Thinker	New York, New York

Figure 10-15. A table developed from a glossary template

Searching and Replacing Formats

There are two ways to use the Search command with character formatting. You can search for specific formats, such as those used to format section titles and headings, figure text, and notes. If you are searching for titles or headings, the Search command is a convenient tool for jumping to different sections of your document. Often the format is all that headings or titles have in common, so searching for the format is an efficient way to locate them.

 Tip: *You can search for formats to find specific portions of a document, such as headings, titles, and tables, by using the Format sEarch command.*

You can also use the search facilities to search for and replace a specific format. Formats applied with quick keys or style sheet codes can be searched and replaced. You cannot, however, search for combined character and paragraph formats unless they are part of a style sheet code, in which case you would search for the code instead of the format.

The commands to search and replace formats are located in the Format menu, as shown here. Type **E** to search for formats and **L** to replace them.

```
FORMAT: Character Paragraph Tab Border Footnote Division Running-head Stylesheet
        sEarch repLace revision-Marks
```

If you want to search only a specific area of your document, highlight that area before you execute the commands. When you type either **E** to search or **L** to replace, Word asks if you want to search for character formats, paragraph formats, or styles. If you select Character or Paragraph, Word displays a menu of selections similar to the Format Character or Format Paragraph menu, respectively. You can then select the option to search on and specify the direction, either up or down.

 Tip: *You can limit searches to a highlighted area, and you can choose to search up or down through text.*

For example, to search for text formatted in italic and underline, you would fill out the Format sEarch Character menu as shown here. Italic and underline are selected, and the search direction is down, assuming that the highlight is at the top of the text to be searched.

```
FORMAT SEARCH CHARACTER direction: Up(Down)
       bold: Yes No              italic:(Yes)No        underline: Yes No
       strikethrough: Yes No     uppercase: Yes No     small caps: Yes No
       double underline: Yes No  position: Normal Superscript Subscript
       font name:                font size:            hidden: Yes No
```

If you select Styles from the Format sEarch command, Word asks you for the style code. This is the code that you used when applying the style to the selected text. If you are searching paragraphs, it is the style code in the selection bar that represents the format selection from the style sheet.

To repeat a search or replace action, simply press SHIFT+F4. This makes repeated searching or replacing through an entire document easy. If you have a mouse, you can repeat a format search or replace by clicking on the word *command* in the command area of the Word screen.

 Tip: *You can repeat searches by clicking on the word* command *in the command area at the bottom of the screen.*

Style Sheets

This section will give you a quick look at style sheets and their use in applying character styles and type fonts. A style must first be created before it can be used to format text. When a style is created, a description of it "lives" in the gallery. There are basically two ways to use styles. You can build a style description in the gallery, or you can add a new style to the gallery by copying the formats applied to text in your documents.

Creating Styles by Example

In this section you'll see how to add a character style group that you've created in the text of a document as a new selection to the gallery. Once the new style is part of the gallery, you will be able to apply it to other documents. If the FONTTEST file created earlier is not displayed on your screen, load it now with the Transfer Load command. Use the arrows or mouse to move the highlight anywhere in the block of text that reads "bold+italic+underline."

When the highlight is anywhere in the block, the character and font formats for that block are active. You can now add this triple character style combination to the style sheet. Microsoft calls this method "creating a style by example" because an existing style is simply added to the style sheet.

 Tip: *Creating a style by example is an easy way to retain styles as you create them during text entry.*

You can use the Format Stylesheet Record menu option or simply press ALT+F10 to record the new style.

1. Press ALT+F10 to display the menu shown here.

```
FORMAT STYLESHEET RECORD key code: █        usage: Character(Paragraph)Division
            variant: 1                     remark:
```

The Keycode field is where you type the code to use when applying the style to text blocks. It would be useful to call the bold/italic/underline format "biu," but

Word only allows two-character codes, so type **bu** in the Keycode field.

2. In the Usage field select Character because this is a character format. Don't worry about the Variant field for now.

3. In the Remark field you can type a short description of what this format does. Type **bold+italic+underline** and press ENTER.

 Trap: *Style codes can only be two characters wide, so try to make them as descriptive of the style as possible.*

It won't appear that anything has happened, but if you open the Gallery menu by selecting Esc Gallery, you will see an entry called BU. The complete description of the style used by Word appears in the bottom line. Notice that the Courier font is displayed unless you altered the font at some point.

The bold/italic/underline style is now available to quickly format other text in your documents. Simply highlight the target text and press ALT+BU. If you want to use this style in other documents, you must save the gallery. Use the Transfer Save command in the Gallery menu to save the current gallery as a style sheet. Select the proposed response of NORMAL.STY in the Filename field by pressing ENTER.

 Tip: *Once a style is added to the gallery, you can use it throughout a document or in other documents by saving the style sheet.*

The Gallery

Another way to create styles is to build them in the gallery. While still in the Gallery menu, type **i** to execute the Gallery Insert command. The gallery insert screen will appear, which looks similar to the one shown earlier.

 Tip: *You can create new styles "from scratch" while in the gallery.*

To create a format to use for titles, perform the following steps. This format should use a large type font and be boldfaced.

1. In the Keycode field, type **ti** as the keycode to represent title formatting.

2. Tab over to the Usage field and select Character.

3. Don't worry about the Variant field.

4. In the Remark field type **Title formatting** and press ENTER.

The new style should now be inserted on top of the BU style. At this point, you can apply formats to the style just as you apply character and font formats by using the Format Character menu. As in the edit window, the style in the gallery must be highlighted before you can apply formats to it. Perform the following steps to apply character styles.

1. Highlight the style by using the arrow keys.

2. Press ALT+B to apply boldfacing.

3. Press ALT+F8 to open the Format Character menu.

4. With the highlight on the Font Name field, press F1. Select a font from the list on your screen that is suitable for titles.

5. Press the TAB key to move to the Font Size field. Press F1 and select a font size suitable for titles.

6. When done, press ENTER.

In the example shown here, Helvetica 12-point bold was selected as the format for the TI code.

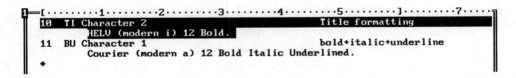

You can now use the title style by typing ALT+T+I on any text that you want to format with the styles and fonts assigned to it. A big advantage of using styles is that you can instantly change all text formatted with a particular style by altering the style's format in the gallery.

Tip: *Altering the format of a style in the gallery will alter the format of all text that the style has been applied to.*

For example, assume that you create a document with five sections and thus five heading titles. Each title has been formatted with the TI style. Now assume that you want to add underlining to each title. You don't have to scroll to each one and apply underlining individually. Simply open the gallery, highlight the TI style, and either press ALT+U or use the Format Character command in the Gallery menu.

Note that you can change any style with the Format Character command in the Gallery menu in the same way that you change text directly when working in the edit window. You can now save the gallery for later use by using the Transfer Save command. If you attempt to quit Word after making any changes to the gallery, Word will ask if you want to save the gallery.

In the next chapter you will see how to use the Format Paragraph command to alter the paragraph formatting of styles.

Entering Special Characters

Each font set has up to 256 printable characters. Your keyboard allows you to type only the lower 128 of these characters. In order to display any of the upper 128 characters, which include foreign characters, math symbols, printer's symbols, and other characters, you must hold down the ALT key while typing the character's ASCII code on the numeric keypad. You cannot use the numbers along the top of the keyboard, only the numeric keypad.

To determine the ASCII code of a character, refer to Appendix C. For example, try pressing ALT+171 or ALT+172. You may find these characters, along with some of the others listed in the ASCII table, to be of use.

Note that your printer must support the displayed character in order for it to print. Sometimes another character will be printed instead of the one displayed. This is the case when certain math and foreign language fonts are used on some printers. You will need to determine the ASCII number of the character that you want to print and then use the ALT sequence to enter that number on the screen. The actual symbol may not appear on the screen, but it will print on the printer.

Tips and Traps Summary

Typefaces and Type Styles

Trap: Typeface or font formatting and direct type style formatting are two different things. Each has its own set of Word menu options.

Trap: Typefaces don't have to be applied. Word's default typeface is Courier.

Tip: Printer font cartridges are analogous to typewriter print wheels and type balls. A font cartridge contains a set of fonts.

Trap: Some type styles cannot be mixed.

Setting Up Your Printer

Tip: Printer description (PRD) files tell Word how to communicate with your printer.

Trap: If a description file is not available for your printer, contact Microsoft or use the TTY.PRD file. TTY.PRD only supports single-font, nonformatted printing, however.

Trap: Selecting the wrong printer description file may result in garbled printing.

Tip: The selection of available fonts depends on which printer description file is selected and on whether it properly describes your printer.

Tip: Some printers have additional memory designated for downloadable fonts.

Trap: Only printer description files copied to the Word disk or directory are available for selection.

Tips and Traps Summary (*continued*)

Tip: Built-in or *hard-wired* fonts are always available for use. *Downloadable* fonts must be copied from the computer to the printer before use.

Tip: Word handles all font download functions in the background. You need only select the font set to download.

Trap: Word may select a substitute for a font that you assign if the printer can't print your assigned font.

A Brief Typography Discussion

Tip: Fonts are either monospaced (every character is the same width) or proportionally spaced (each character is assigned an appropriate width).

Tip: Monospaced fonts are easier to work with when spacing or counting characters.

Tip: Proportionally spaced fonts are easier to read and are visually more appealing.

Tip: Monospaced fonts are described in terms of pitch, which determines the number of characters that can be placed horizontally in an inch of text.

Trap: Proportionally spaced fonts can never be measured accurately in characters per inch because the characters differ in size.

Tip: The point size of a character measures its height and is therefore a measure of the overall size of the character.

Tip: Think of character style and typeface formatting as masks placed over the characters of your text. They can be mixed, and either can be applied before the other.

Tips and Traps Summary (*continued*)

Tip: Each font group has a subset of variations, each of which is given a character code.

Tip: Font group names assist Word in performing font substitutions.

Tip: Font substitutions can be used to advantage when you are printing on several printers.

Introducing Formatting Techniques

Tip: To check the format applied to a block of text, place the highlight somewhere in the block and open the Format Character menu.

Tip: ALT+F8 is a quick way to get to the Format Character Font Name field.

Tip: You can assign often used quick-key combinations to their own ALT key sequence by using a style sheet.

Tip: You can assign formats for common headings, titles, and other often used fonts and styles to ALT key combinations by using a style sheet.

When to Format

Trap: To format a single character, press the ALT key twice.

Applying Character Styles

Tip: The ALT+SPACEBAR combination returns formatted text that is highlighted back to the normal type style.

Tips and Traps Summary (*continued*)

Tip: Text formatted to bold is printed as characters with more weight or in double-strike mode on many printers. Press ALT+B to format selected text as bold.

Tip: Text formatted to bold is displayed on the screen in double-intensity mode.

Tip: Italic characters are displayed on the screen as slanted, underlined, or highlighted in a color.

Tip: Tabs and spaces are considered characters that can be underlined, just like any other text.

Tip: Strikethrough is used to strike out sections of text in contracts that are no longer valid.

Trap: On some printers the type size of superscript or subscript characters must be reduced.

Tip: You can capture previous formats by moving the insertion point into the characters and typing. However, at least one character must be retyped.

Tip: Small caps style converts lowercase letters to a reduced font size in all capitals.

Trap: If your printer does not have a smaller type size, Word uses the normal size and converts lowercase letters to uppercase.

Tip: Hidden text can be displayed on the screen or not, and it can be printed with the document if you wish.

Tip: You can make hidden text visible by selecting the Show Hidden Text field in the Window Options command.

Tip: Never paginate a document with visible hidden text unless you plan to print the visible hidden text.

Tip: A double-arrow symbol indicates the position of hidden text when partial or complete display mode is on and hidden text is invisible.

Tips and Traps Summary (*continued*)

Applying Typefaces

Tip: Use ALT+F8 whenever possible when changing or viewing typefaces and sizes.

Tip: Press SHIFT+F10 to select and format an entire document.

Trap: If the highlight is over two font types, the Format Character menu will contain blank fields because two selections cannot be displayed at once.

Tip: Some printers that support cartridges and downloadable fonts allow crossovers among font description files.

Tip: Set the print display mode on (ALT+F7) to view line breaks when you use proportionally spaced fonts.

Trap: Tabbed columns may not align properly when you use a proportionally spaced font.

Tip: Set print display mode on (ALT+F7) to display column alignments when you use proportionally spaced fonts.

Tip: The best way to work with tables and proportional fonts is to set specific tab stops with the Format Tab Set command.

Tip: If your printer supports it, reduce the font size of superscript and subscript characters to improve their appearance.

Tip: It's best to use a style sheet for character formatting routines that require several keystrokes and menu options.

Tip: The style code in the style bar is a clue to the typeface and size of the text in a paragraph.

Quick Formatting Techniques

Tip: The F4 key provides a convenient way to jump through your document and apply a common format to titles, tables, paragraphs, or other blocks of text.

Tips and Traps Summary (*continued*)

Trap: When using F4 to repeat formatting commands, you must perform the anticipated commands one after the other. Other commands will replace the formatting routines remembered by the F4 key.

Tip: To copy a format with the mouse, highlight the target text, point to the previously formatted text, and click the left button while holding down the ALT key.

Tip: Use windows when you copy styles with a mouse over large documents.

Tip: Templates for tables and other blocks of text with both character and paragraph changes can be stored as glossary entries.

Tip: You can search for formats to find specific portions of a document, such as headings, titles, and tables, by using the Format sEarch command.

Tip: You can limit searches to a highlighted area, and you can choose to search up or down through text.

Tip: You can repeat searches by clicking on the word *command* in the command area at the bottom of the screen.

Style Sheets

Tip: Creating a style by example is an easy way to retain styles as you create them during text entry.

Trap: Style codes can only be two characters wide, so try to make them as descriptive of the style as possible.

Tip: Once a style is added to the gallery, you can use it throughout a document or in other documents by saving the style sheet.

Tip: You can create new styles "from scratch" while in the gallery.

Tip: Altering the format of a style in the gallery will alter the format of all text that the style has been applied to.

11

Paragraph
Formatting

When you create long documents, it is often necessary to include tables, lists, indented paragraphs with bullets or numbers, and even side-by-side blocks of text. This chapter will delve into the topics and techniques of paragraph development.

The Significance of Paragraphs

As learned in Chapter 6, the paragraph is a critical element in Word documents. Paragraphs are text blocks that comprise the smallest elements of a Word document (characters, words, and sentences) and together make up the largest elements (pages and divisions). A paragraph is always selected and formatted as a block, and paragraphs have their own set of commands in the command menu.

If you wish, you can format every paragraph in your document differently. One paragraph might have special indents, another might have special tab settings for aligning columns, and others might have double or even triple line spacing. You can even surround a paragraph with a box or place lines on any side — left, right, top, or bottom.

Consider the difference between character and paragraph formatting. If you select a word in the middle of a paragraph, you can assign it any font or character style, and only the highlighted characters will receive the font or style formatting. If you select a character or word and apply paragraph formatting, however, the formatting is applied to the entire paragraph. This is because paragraph formatting options have no meaning at the character, word, and sentence level (unless your paragraph consists of just a single character, word, or sentence).

 Tip: *Any character or word within a paragraph can be selected to format the paragraph.*

For example, what significance is there to applying a double-spacing format to a word in the middle of a sentence? Why would you ever need to center a single character in the middle of a sentence? As you can see, when you use a paragraph format, Word applies it to the entire paragraph. Because of this, you can place the highlight anywhere in a paragraph and use paragraph formats.

The Paragraph Mark

Every time you press ENTER, you generate a paragraph mark, which has the all-important purpose of carrying the formatting information from one paragraph to another. You could press ENTER several times to create a number of paragraph markers, each with the paragraph formats of the original paragraph. This information carries not only the character fonts and styles last used but all of the paragraph formats described in this chapter.

 Tip: *The paragraph mark carries the formatting information of a paragraph.*

You can change the formats of any paragraph by formatting the paragraph mark with the paragraph format commands described here. You can even delete a paragraph mark and insert it elsewhere in your text if you want to reuse the formatting it holds.

 Tip: *Paragraph markers can be copied to carry formatting information to other areas of the document.*

Because the paragraph mark contains the formatting information for a paragraph, you must be careful not to delete it unless you have a reason to.

 Trap: *Deleting a paragraph mark may remove the paragraph formatting from a paragraph.*

Look at the two paragraphs shown here. The top paragraph is indented and centered, while the second is a normal paragraph with no indenting.

```
█━━[·········1·········2·········3·········4·········5·········]··
                    This·paragraph·is·formatted·for·1·inch·
                    left·and·right·indents·and·centering.¶
            This·paragraph·is·set·for·normal·paragraph·alignment·with·no·
            indents.¶
```

If you delete the paragraph mark of the first sentence, the two paragraphs will join and the formats of the existing paragraph mark will be retained. In this case the top paragraph will take on the left and right margins of the bottom paragraph, as shown here:

```
█━━[·········1·········2·········3·········4·········5·········]··
            This·paragraph·is·formatted·for·1·inch·left·and·right·
            indents·and·centering.█his·paragraph·is·set·for·normal·
            paragraph·alignment·with·no·indents.¶
```

Deleting the paragraph mark is actually a common mistake that novice users make. Because the paragraph alteration happens so fast, these users become confused and are not sure what they did. If this happens to you, simply press SHIFT+F1 to undo the mistake.

What Constitutes a Paragraph

A paragraph can be as small as a single sentence, word, character, or even the paragraph mark itself. When you create tables, you may want to define each line as a separate paragraph. In this way you could set different tabs for each line (remember, tab settings are applied to an entire paragraph, and they can differ from one paragraph to another).

Titles and headings are often separate, one-line paragraphs that you can center, left- or right-justify, and format to special typefaces and type styles.

A normal paragraph is left-justified with a "ragged" right margin. It is not indented, and it aligns to the margin settings specified by the Format Division Margins command. The line spacing is single, and there are no lines before or after a paragraph. You can change these settings whenever you wish. In fact you can permanently change Word's normal paragraph setting by changing the standard in the NORMAL.STY style sheet, which Word automatically attaches to every document that you create.

 Tip: *You can permanently change Word's preset standard paragraph format by using the gallery.*

Selecting Paragraphs

Before applying formats, you must select the paragraph or paragraphs by placing the highlight anywhere in the appropriate paragraph. For example, this illustration shows how three paragraphs can be selected. The F6 (Extend) key is pressed, and the DOWN ARROW key extends the selection from the top paragraph into the third paragraph.

```
[········1········2········3········4········]·····
As·we·look·across·the·reaches·of·space,↓
we·see·ancient·things·in·a·different·place↓
The·light·from·distant·worlds·of·the·past↓
touches·our·world-·at·last,↓
Light·is·history¶

If·you·could·somehow·be·placed·many·millions·of·
miles·from·earth,·then·look·back,·you·might·be·
able·to·see·your·past·(with·a·strong·telescope).¶

Someday,·we·may·look·upon·the·beams·of·light·from·
the·beginning·of·this·world.¶
```

Note that the highlight simply has to "touch" each paragraph. You needn't highlight the whole thing. If you have a mouse, slide it against the left of each paragraph while pressing either button.

Paragraph Width

Paragraph width is initially determined by the settings in the Format Division Margins menu. All paragraphs will fall in the text area defined by these settings unless a left or right indent or both are specified.

The Role of Style Sheets
in Paragraph Formatting

Almost every paragraph with special formats that you will use more than once should be assigned a style code in the style sheet so that you can easily use the style again in the same document. If the style will be used in other documents, the style sheet should be saved to disk with the new styles. Styles and style sheets are even more important in paragraph development than in character formatting, because setting up a paragraph format often involves several steps. When you set up a paragraph format, you will often want to save it as a style so that you never have to do it again.

 Tip: *If a paragraph format change will be used more than once in a Word session, it should be assigned a style code in the style sheet.*

How Styles Will Be Created
in This Chapter

This chapter will describe the various paragraph types available in Word. As you work with the examples, you'll be able to save them in a style sheet for future use and thus familiarize yourself with the process of creating a style sheet. For now, the styles that you create will be stored in the NORMAL.STY style sheet that Word automatically attaches to all your documents. Note that when a style sheet is attached, the direct formatting key must be preceded by an x. This will be shown as ALT+X+C or ALT+X+R in the case of centered or right aligned text.

A particular type of paragraph will be described along with its normal use. You will use the Word quick keys and Format menu to assign various formats to the paragraph. Before going on, you will use the ALT+F10 (Record Style) combination to record the style to the style sheet for future use. Note that you can also use the Format Stylesheet Record command from the menu, which is illustrated here:

```
FORMAT STYLESHEET RECORD key code: ▮        usage: Character(Paragraph)Division
                        variant: 1           remark:
```

Occasionally, you will use the gallery and its commands to create paragraph styles, but detailed discussion of the gallery will be left to Chapter 16.

Using Character Formats in Paragraph Styles

When you format paragraphs with style sheets, the style can also apply a character format such as boldface, italic, type fonts, or type sizes to the paragraph. You needn't highlight the exact characters to be given the character formatting. Instead, Word assigns the designated character format to the entire paragraph.

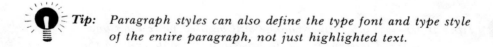 *Tip:* *Paragraph styles can also define the type font and type style of the entire paragraph, not just highlighted text.*

Word's Standard Paragraph Styles

Although Word's style sheet facility is designed to allow you to create your own special styles, Word reserves a few standard styles that are automatically used for paragraphs, footnotes, running heads, and other specific parts of a Word document. For example, when you start Word and type the first paragraph, Word uses a default set of parameters to define how that paragraph looks. A standard default paragraph is single-spaced with no indents.

Now let's say that you want all your documents to have paragraphs with 1/2-inch first-line indents—a common paragraph format. You could simply create a new style for this type of paragraph and save it with the style sheet for future use. But then you'd have to apply it at least once whenever you started a new document. To have Word automatically apply the 1/2-inch indent to all paragraphs, you must change its default paragraph style, which is called Standard in the Variant field for paragraphs.

The gallery is used to change Word's Standard paragraph, or any other reserved style, such as the ones for footnotes and running heads. To display a list of paragraph types to which Word applies standard defaults, select Gallery Insert. Tab to the Usage field and select Paragraph; then tab to the Variant field and press F1.

 Tip: *You can see a list of paragraph types by pressing F1 in the Variant field.*

Note that the Usage field must be paragraph mode. The following illustration shows only a portion of the Variant listing because only the top five lines are important here. Press ESC to close the Insert command.

Standard	Footnote	Running Head	Heading level 1
Heading level 2	Heading level 3	Heading level 4	Heading level 5
Heading level 6	Heading level 7	Index level 1	Index level 2
Index level 3	Index level 4	Table level 1	Table level 2
Table level 3	Table level 4	1	2
3	**4**	5	6

In the Variant listing note the types of paragraphs that Word uses for defaults. The "Heading level" selections are used for outlines and will be covered in Chapter 18. These selections can also be used to create titles and headers. The "Index level" selections are used for indexing, and the "Table level" selections are used for table of contents development.

Changing the Standard Paragraph   The following exercise will help you learn to use the gallery for making changes to paragraph styles. The gallery is used here because a style that already exists must be altered. In this example you will change the first-line indent of the default paragraph to 1/2-inch. Even if you don't want your paragraphs to default to this setting, you can still perform the exercise and later delete the format change with the Gallery Delete command.

1. To open the gallery window, press ESC and select Gallery from the edit window.

2. Type **i** for the Insert command.

3. The Insert menu will appear with the highlight on the Key Code field. Type **SP** (for Standard Paragraph).

4. Select Paragraph in the Usage field.

5. Tab to the Variant field and press F1.

6. The list of variants appears, with "Standard" highlighted.

7. Accept Standard by tabbing to the Remark field.

8. In the Remark field type **Altered to first line indent** and press the ENTER key. The Insert command should appear, as shown here:

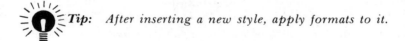

```
INSERT key code: {}                      usage: Character(Paragraph)Division
         variant: Standard              remark: Altered to first line indent█
```

The new entry will appear in the gallery window, as shown here:

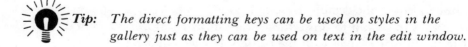

```
1        Paragraph Standard                   Altered to first line indent
         Courier (modern a) 12. Flush left.
```

Remember, creating a style in the gallery requires two steps, one to insert it and another to define what it will be. Your next step is to apply the indenting format to this entry.

> 💡 *Tip:* *After inserting a new style, apply formats to it.*

If the new entry is not highlighted, use the arrow keys until it is. To make the 1/2-inch formatting change, simply press the ALT+X+F ("Indent first line to next tab") quick key.

> 💡 *Tip:* *The direct formatting keys can be used on styles in the gallery just as they can be used on text in the edit window.*

The process just described is what you will go through when changing either default styles or styles that you have previously created. You can now exit the gallery with the Gallery Exit command and then type a few lines of text in the edit window to see how Word applies the first-line indent. If you want to remove the alteration to your standard paragraph, choose Gallery from the command menu, highlight the standard paragraph entry just created, and press DEL.

The rest of this chapter will concentrate on creating styles by example while working in the edit window. You will apply formats to paragraphs by using the direct formatting keys or the Format Paragraph and Format Character menus; then you will add the formats as a style to the style sheet in the gallery by using the ALT+F10 (Record Style) command.

Create Extra Paragraph Markers

When you first start a document, it's often a good idea to enter several extra paragraph markers. If you change styles on the last paragraph marker, you must often go through extra steps to return to the standard style unless you leave yourself a few extras at the bottom of the text. Simply press ENTER three or four times and then move back to the top of the text and start typing.

Tip: *Create an extra buffer of paragraph markers before you start typing a document.*

Format Paragraph Menu
and Direct Formatting Commands

The Format command in the edit window has a number of selections, as shown here. Of these, Paragraph, Tab, and Border are covered in this chapter, along with Stylesheet, to some extent.

```
FORMAT: Character Paragraph Tab Border Footnote Division Running-head Stylesheet
        sEarch repLace revision-Marks
```

Open the Format Paragraph menu to display the menu shown here. This menu is used to create and change most of the paragraph types discussed in this chapter.

```
FORMAT PARAGRAPH alignment: Left Centered Right Justified
     left indent: 0"           first line: 0"          right indent: 0"
     line spacing: 1 li        space before: 0 li      space after: 0 li
     keep together: Yes(No)    keep follow: Yes(No)    side by side: Yes(No)
```

The menu allows you to select several options at once by using the TAB key to jump to each. In the following sections, you will see how each option is used.

The quick keys allow you to format directly from the keyboard while in the edit mode. They will apply the specified format directly to the paragraph that the highlight is in, overriding any formats previously applied by a style. Table 11-1 shows a list of these keys.

Types of Formatting

Paragraph formats are divided into several groups in this chapter, the first of which concerns the alignment of a paragraph. Will it be flush left, flush right, or both left- and right-justified? Paragraphs can also be centered. Hyphenation is also covered so that you can better control a ragged right margin.

The second group deals with indents. Indents come in all varieties, including whole paragraph indent, first-line-only indents, left and right indents, and hanging indents used for numbered or bulleted lists.

The third group of paragraph formats concerns spacing, either in the paragraph itself or in its relation to other paragraphs. You can have Word insert one or more spaces either before or after a paragraph.

Table 11-1. Paragraph Direct Formatting Keys

Format	ALT Key	When Style Sheet Is Attached
Centered	ALT+C	ALT+X+C
Justified	ALT+J	ALT+X+J
Left Flush	ALT+L	ALT+X+L
Right Flush	ALT+R	ALT+X+R
Indent First Line	ALT+F	ALT+X+F
Increase Indent	ALT+N	ALT+X+N
Decrease Indent	ALT+M	ALT+X+M
Hanging Indent	ALT+T	ALT+X+T
Space Before	ALT+O	ALT+X+O
Double Spacing	ALT+2	ALT+X+2
Normal Paragraph	ALT+P	ALT+X+P

Paragraph formatting also lets you control the location of page breaks. You can keep a paragraph together or keep it with two lines of the previous paragraph. In the case of titles, you can keep a title with the next paragraph.

Paragraph formatting also includes side-by-side paragraph development, border control, and tabs and table development. These topics are covered in the last section of this chapter.

Alignments

Aligning paragraphs is a task that you will find most useful as you become more familiar with Word. If you are a novice user, or if you are not used to such a powerful word processing program as Microsoft Word, you may not yet be able to fully use and appreciate the paragraph alignment capabilities of the program.

Paragraph alignment and paragraph indenting are very similar. Alignment concerns lining up text with the left margin, right margin, or both. Indents have to do with the adjustments of left or right margin. Left- or right-aligned text will still align the same within an indented paragraph. Keep in mind that margins are set by the Format Division command and generally stay the same throughout your document.

 Tip: *Paragraph alignment has to do with blocking or centering a paragraph, while indenting has to do with reducing its width.*

Left, Right, Centered, or Justified Paragraphs

You can use the Format Paragraph menu to select the type of alignment you prefer, as shown here. Use the TAB key or spacebar to select any of the options.

FORMAT PARAGRAPH alignment: Left Centered Right Justified

You can also use the quick keys to select alignments. If you are starting a new sentence, simply press the appropriate key combination (See Table 11-1); then press ALT+X+P to return to normal paragraph mode. Flush left text is the most

---

```
                              The Brookings Company
                                   123 Wardlow Drive
                          Santa Barbara, CA 93105




November 27, 1988

Department of Physics
University of California
Santa Barbara, CA 93106
```

Figure 11-1. Letterhead with company name flush right

common type of alignment, while flush right is used for headings and sometimes for the closing of a letter. Figure 11-1 shows a letterhead with the company name flush right.

You can center paragraphs by pressing ALT+X+C and both left- and right-justify them by pressing ALT+X+J. Centered paragraphs are often used for company headings, quotes, announcements, invitations, and even poems. Justified paragraphs are often used to obtain a special column type of look. The problem with justifying paragraphs is that extra spaces are distributed between words, sometimes unevenly, causing an unnatural look to the text. Justification is best used with proportionally spaced type fonts. However, hyphenation helps to alleviate some spacing problems, as you'll see later.

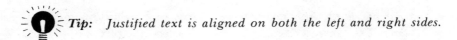 ***Tip:***   *Justified text is aligned on both the left and right sides.*

Trap: *Odd spacing between words may result when you justify text. Use a proportionally spaced font or hyphenate the text for best results.*

You can best deal with most alignment situations by using the direct formatting keys rather than styles. However, if you plan to create a document with many centered paragraphs that you might later want to convert to another alignment, you could assign the centered key to a style. Then you could use the global application of styles to change all centered text in your document to the new alignment.

Occasionally you might want to add special formatting to a centered, justified, or flush right paragraph. For example, you can create a company letterhead that is right-justified and boldfaced or one that has a special type font such as Helvetica or NLQ Boldface.

 Tip: *You can create alignment styles that have special type fonts and sizes.*

Right-Justified, Bold Heading for Company Logo   For this example, first type your company name, address, and other pertinent information using soft carriage returns at the end of each line to maintain paragraph integrity. Then perform the following procedure:

1. Select the paragraph that contains your company name.

2. Press ALT+X+R to right-justify it.

3. Press ALT+X+B to boldface the entire selection.

4. To change the type font, press ALT+F8 and make a selection appropriate to your printer. Make sure that the entire block of text is highlighted when you assign a font.

Your company logo may look something like the one shown in Figure 11-2, formatted in Times Roman 14-point type. Next, record the style for later use.

1. Press the ALT+F10 (Record Style) command. The following display will appear:

```
FORMAT STYLESHEET RECORD key code: █        usage: Character(Paragraph)Division
            variant: 1                       remark:
```

2. In the Key Code field you must type the name to use for applying this style to text. Type **RH** (for Right Heading).

3. The Usage field should have Paragraph selected. If not, tab to it and select Paragraph.

4. Tab through the Variant field and use the variant that Word suggests.

5. In the Remark field, type **LOGO, FLUSH RIGHT.** Your screen should look similar to the one shown here:

```
FORMAT STYLESHEET RECORD key code: RH        usage: Character(Paragraph)Division
                       variant: 11           remark: LOGO, FLUSH RIGHT█
```

6. Press ENTER. The logo should now have the "RH" code listed in the style bar, as shown here:

```
1━━━━[·········1·········2·········3·········4·········5····]····6
║RH                                          The·Brookings·Company↓
║                                             123·Wardlow·Drive↓
║                                          Santa·Barbara,·CA·93105¶
║
```

The Brookings Company
123 Wardlow Drive
Santa Barbara, CA 93105

November 27, 1988

Department of Physics
University of California
Santa Barbara, CA 93106

Figure 11-2.   The company logo

To see that the style has been added to the gallery, press ESC and type **G**. You may need to scroll through the listing with the arrow keys. The new RH style should look similar to the one shown here. In this example the Times Roman 14-point font is listed as "TMSRMN (roman a) 14/12," and "Flush right" is listed to indicate right alignment.

```
16  RH Paragraph 11                        LOGO, FLUSH RIGHT
        TMSRMN (roman a) 14/12. Flush right.
```

Centered Company Logo   In the following exercise, you can use the same company logo to create a new style. This time the logo will be centered.

1. Select the logo and press ALT+X+P to return the paragraph to normal flush left alignment.

2. Press ALT+X+C to center the paragraph.

If you applied a special font or type size to the text block in the previous example, it should still be active. Press ALT+F8 to find out. If not, or if you want to apply a different font for this block, do so in the Font menu.

1. Press ALT+F10 to display the Record Style menu.

2. Type **CH** (for Centered Heading) in the Key Code field.

3. The Usage field should be in Paragraph.

4. Use Word's suggested variant.

5. The Remark field should read "LOGO, CENTERED."

The CH keycode should appear in the style bar. You can check the gallery if you want to see the new style listed.

Centered Italic Remarks   You can use the following style to place remarks in your text that are automatically centered and in italics. Or you can apply underline or boldface if you prefer. You don't have to type text before creating a style. Instead, you can press ENTER to create a new paragraph mark and then just format the paragraph mark. After the formats are applied, you can create the style. Try this now.

1. Press ENTER to create a new paragraph mark.

2. Press ALT+X+C to center the marker.

3. Press ALT+X+I to select italic (or any other format).

4. Press ALT+F10 to display the Record Style menu.

5. Fill it in as shown here. CR (for Centered Italic) is the style code. Use the suggested variant and be sure that the Usage field is set to Paragraph.

```
FORMAT STYLESHEET RECORD key code: CR      usage: Character(Paragraph)Division
                     variant: 1            remark: CENTERED ITALIC REMARK█
```

Hyphenation

Use hyphenation to better align your paragraphs, especially if they are justified. Hyphenation reduces the number of extra spaces that produce unsightly gaps between words in justified text. It can also help to reduce the jagged edge look of flush right or flush left paragraphs.

 Tip: *Hyphenation reduces extra spaces left in justified text and can help reduce jagged edges when text is flush right or left.*

 Trap: *Hyphenation may not be visually appealing and is seldom needed on centered text.*

(For a complete discussion of Word's hyphenation feature, refer to Chapter 20.)

Indents

Indenting reduces the width of a paragraph without changing the margins. Never change the margins unless you have definite division boundaries, such as a table of contents, body text, and an index. You never need to change margins in the body of a document, unless you have a special section that contains many paragraphs of reduced width. If you are creating only one or two paragraphs of reduced width, use the indenting keys or, better yet, create indent styles.

 Trap: *Never change a margin to adjust the width of a single paragraph within a document. Use indenting.*

First-Line Indents

The most obvious and often used indent is the first-line indent, shown here. Notice the vertical indent marker in the ruler bar.

```
▌━━━━[···¦···1········2········3·······4········5···]···6·
         Your·order·of·October·17,·1988·has·been·delayed·
      until·we·December·15,·1988.··We·will·be·happy·to·send·
      you·a·substitute,··if·you·so·desire.▌
```

If you prefer to always use a first-line indent, you will want to make it the default style, as described earlier. If not, you can still indent paragraphs for any document by pressing ALT+X+F or by using the First Line option of the Format Paragraph menu, as shown highlighted here:

```
FORMAT PARAGRAPH alignment:(Left)Centered Right Justified
      left indent: 0"          first line: █▌      right indent: 0"
      line spacing: 1 li       space before: 0 li   space after: 1 li
      keep together: Yes(No)   keep follow: Yes(No)  side by side: Yes(No)
```

After indenting a paragraph, create extra paragraph markers by pressing ENTER several times. This will duplicate the indented paragraph format so that you can use it throughout your document.

Indenting a Whole Paragraph

You can indent a whole paragraph, on the left, the right, or both sides. Press ALT+X+N to move the left indent for an entire paragraph to the next tab stop. If you have changed the tab stops, the first stop on the left will be used. You can press ALT+X+N several times to further increase the indent.

Tip: *ALT+X+N increases the indent of an entire paragraph to the next tab stop. You can press it more than once.*

Using the Format Paragraph menu, you can adjust the left or right indent to any specification. However, you must use the menu to adjust the right indent.

Tip: *The Format Paragraph menu must be used to set right indents.*

The following illustration shows the indent fields of the Format Paragraph menu, with the Left Indent field set to 0.8 inch. The Right Indent field can also be adjusted to center an indented paragraph between the current margin settings.

```
FORMAT PARAGRAPH alignment:(Left)Centered Right Justified
    left indent: .8█          first line: 0"          right indent: 0"
    line spacing: 1 li        space before: 0 li      space after: 1 li
    keep together: Yes(No)    keep follow: Yes(No)    side by side: Yes(No)
```

The most common method is to indent a paragraph about 1/2 inch to type quotes or special comments.

Close of a Letter Style   Figure 11-3 shows a close for a standard letter that you might want to include in your style sheet. This close is placed at the 3-inch mark. Though you could use the ALT+X+N (Increase Left Indent) key combination to get the same effect, that would require pressing the key combination seven times, assuming that the tabs are set for 1/2-inch intervals.

   1. To create the style, first place the highlight on a blank paragraph marker or a name in a letter.

   2. Open the Format Paragraph menu and type **3** in the Left Indent field; then press ENTER.

```
        Your order of October 17, 1988 has been delayed
until December 15, 1988.  We will be happy to send you
a substitute, if you so desire.

                        Sincerely,


                        Barry Beanhead
```

Figure 11-3.   A standard letter close

Next, assign the indented close to the style sheet. Use the key code name CI (for Close Indented).

1. Press ALT+F10 to open the Record Style menu.

2. In Key Code field type **CI**. Make sure that the Usage field is set to Paragraph. Use Word's suggested variant.

3. In the Remark field type **INDENTED CLOSE FOR LETTER**.

Left and Right Indents

Right indents are usually used in conjunction with left indents to center a quote or other block of text between margins. To set both left and right indents, you must use the Format Paragraph menu. Figure 11-4 shows an example of left- and right-indented text under a paragraph with normal settings. The Format Paragraph menu used to set the margins is illustrated here. Note that both the Left Indent and Right Indent fields are set to 1 inch.

Consider the following excerpts from *Nineteen Eighty-Four*, by English journalist, critic and novelist, George Orwell.

> War is Peace, Freedom is Slavery, Ignorance is Strength.

> Doublethink means the power of holding two contradictory beliefs in one's mind simultaneously, and accepting both of them.

Figure 11-4. Left- and right-indented text

```
FORMAT PARAGRAPH alignment:(Left)Centered Right Justified
        left indent: 1"           first line: 0"        right indent: 1"
        line spacing: 1 li        space before: 0 li    space after: 1 li
        keep together: Yes(No)    keep follow: Yes(No)  side by side: Yes(No)
```

Because the setup of this paragraph requires the use of the Format Paragraph menu, it is a good candidate for a style code.

Text Block, Left and Right Indented   To create a style that indents a block of text 1 inch on both the left and right sides, as shown in Figure 11-4, perform the following steps:

1. Select a block of text or blank paragraph marker.

2. Press ALT+X+P to clear any existing formats.

3. Enter the Format Paragraph menu, type 1 in the Left Indent and Right Indent fields, and press ENTER.

4. Press ALT+F10 to record the style. In the Key Code field type **CB** (for Centered Block). Make sure that Paragraph is selected in the Usage field. Accept the variant and type 1 **INCH LEFT & RIGHT INDENT** in the Remark field.

You can create a number of variations on this indented block in the gallery. For example, you might create a similar block that formats the text to italic. In the discussion of before and after spacing, you'll see how to ensure that the indented blocks are preceded and followed by at least one space.

Decreasing Paragraph Indents

You can decrease a paragraph's left indent by using ALT+X+M. Basically, this key combination is used to return paragraph indent to normal after you have typed a quick indented paragraph. It is not used to return paragraphs with both the left and right indents to normal.

There are several ways to return to a normal indent. First, you can press ALT+X+P, but that will also remove other paragraph formats that you may have set unless they are assigned to the default. Second, you can have a style for standard paragraphs. Typing its style code on the next line will restore normal paragraphs.

 Tip: *A style for normal paragraphs can be used to restore nonin-dented paragraphs.*

You can also restore normal paragraphs by using the Format Paragraph command to remove the indents. If you type a few extra paragraph markers ahead of the one that is assigned indents, you need only use the DOWN ARROW key to move to one of those markers to resume normal paragraph style.

 Tip: *Before applying an indent format to a paragraph, type a few extra paragraph markers ahead so that you can easily get back to normal paragraph formats.*

Hanging Indents

Hanging indents are certainly the most interesting and useful type of indenting. Look at the examples shown in Figures 11-5 through 11-7. In Figure 11-5 a numbered list prints the numbers in the left hanging indent. All text starting in the

---

THE BLIND SPOT TEST

1. Draw a plus sign with thick bars about 1 inch wide on a sheet of paper using a felt tip or similar pen.

2. Hold the sheet of paper about fifteen inches away from you.

3. Cover your left eye and stare at the cross.

Does the cross "suddenly" disappear? This blind spot is the area of the retina where the optic nerve emerges.

Figure 11-5.   A numbered list

```
DOS has from 40 to 50 commands, some of
which are used to handle the following
file functions:

♦ LISTING FILES.  The DIR command can be
  used to list files in either a paged
  format or a wide listing.

♦ VIEWING FILES.  The TYPE and MORE
  command will display the contents of
  files.

♦ COPYING FILES.  COPY is a
  comprehensive DOS command that can be
  used to move files between disks and
  directories.
```

Figure 11-6.   A bulleted list

second line of each item is aligned with the first character in the top line. When you create a numbered list, you must leave enough room to accommodate two-digit numbers, if the list will be that long.

In Figure 11-6 a bulleted list uses a first-line, left hanging indent. In this case the space to the edge of the indented text is small because only one character must be accommodated in the hanging portion. Figure 11-7 is just the opposite. A wide hanging indent is required to allow space for titles of unknown length. Note that you must set a tab at the location of the indent with the Format Tab Set command.

Numbered Lists   Setting up a hanging indent for a numbered list is as easy as pressing ALT+X+T, which will indent the text 1/2 inch. You must use a tab after typing the number, but you do not need to set special tabs. If you want more control over a numbered list, such as a reduced indent or a right indent, you must use the Format Paragraph menu.

EDUCATION

May, 1975   Bachelor of Science Degree in Marketing and
                            Management, University of Oregon

EMPLOYMENT

1980-Present   Berlitz Manufacturing
                            Sands, Arizona
                            Marketing Manager

1978-1980   Automated Technologies
                            Wrangler, New Mexico
                            Marketing Assistant

Figure 11-7.   A wide hanging indent

Tip: *Use the ALT+X+T (Hanging Indent) key combination to create 1/2-inch hanging indents. For more control over indent size, use the Format Paragraph menu.*

In the following exercise you will create the hanging indent list of Figure 11-5. Because the type used is proportionally spaced Times Roman, a smaller indent can be used, 0.3 inch to be exact. If you are using a monospaced font, the minimum tab size that you can use is 0.4 inch. This allows a two-digit number, a period, and a space to fit in the hanging indent. After setting the indents, use the Format Tab Set command to set a tab at the same ruler location as the indent.

Tip: *When you create numbered lists, allow enough room for two-digit numbers.*

Place the highlight on a normal paragraph or press ALT+X+P to reset a paragraph to normal. Type a number, a period, and then a tab. Type some example text or use the text shown in Figure 11-5. Open the Format Paragraph menu and fill in the Left Indent, First Line, and Right Indent fields as shown here. If you want to adjust the indent to fit your needs, you may do so.

```
FORMAT PARAGRAPH alignment: Left Centered Right Justified
     left indent: 0.3"        first line: -0.3"      right indent: 1.5"
     line spacing: 1 li       space before: 0 li     space after: 1 li
     keep together: Yes(No)   keep follow: Yes(No)   side by side: Yes(No)
```

You must also set a new tab to accommodate the new indent setting. Select Format Tab Set and type the same number in the Position field that you typed in the Left Indent field of the Format Paragraph command. Remember, you can change the type font and type size to fit your needs. You can apply any type style changes at this point by using the Format Character command or ALT+F8.

Tip: *Don't forget to set a corresponding tab when you use indents.*

Press ALT+F10 to open the Record Style menu. Call this style NL (for Numbered List). Make sure that the Usage field is set to Paragraph and accept the default variant. In the Remark field type **NUMBERED LIST**.

Bulleted Lists   The bulleted list, as shown in Figure 11-6, is just like the numbered list, but the indent is smaller. On monospaced typefaces, such as Courier, the indent can be as small as 0.3 inch. This allows one space for the bullet and another between it and the text. For the diamond bullet, press ALT+4, where the 4 is on the numeric keypad. Other bullets include a dot (ALT+7) and a small square (ALT+254). You must use the numbers on the numeric keypad, not those along the top of the keyboard. However, these symbols may not print on certain printers.

Tip: *You can create bulleted lists with hanging indents.*

Tip: *A diamond, dot, square, or other ASCII character can be displayed with the ALT key and a number or combination of numbers from the numeric keypad.*

Labeled Lists   The labeled list, as shown in Figure 11-7, is just like the previous two, except that a large indent is required to accommodate text labels that may be more than one word long. Such a list is often readjusted after all the labels are inserted so that the indent can fit snug to the largest label. Don't forget to set a corresponding tab.

 Tip: *Determine the width of the widest label before setting the indent in a labeled list.*

This illustration shows the settings used to produce the labeled list in Figure 11-7. Note that there is no setting in the Right Indent field. You can create this hanging indent format in the same way that you produced the numbered list. While you're at it, you may want to make type style changes to the labeled list format. If you want to save it to a style sheet, use the name TL (for Text List) and type **TEXT LIST** in the Remark field.

```
FORMAT PARAGRAPH alignment: Left Centered Right Justified
        left indent: 2"          first line: -2"          right indent: 0"
        line spacing: 1 li       space before: 0 li       space after: 1 li
        keep together: Yes(No)   keep follow: Yes(No)     side by side: Yes(No)
```

Nested Indents

Nested indents are simply a series of indents applied one after the other to text. Each new indent moves further to the right, as shown in Figure 11-8. Nested indents are often used for outlining or for several levels of classification. Use ALT+X+N to increase indents and ALT+X+M to reduce them.

 Tip: *Nested indents can be used to create outlines.*

Double Spacing

You can double space a highlighted paragraph by pressing ALT+X+2. To return to normal single spacing, press ALT+X+P. For a different line spacing, use the Format Paragraph menu. The principal reason for double spacing is to print manuscripts

---

1.   **A planet**
        Earth

    2.   **A continent**
                North America

        3.   **A country**
                        The United States

            4.   **A state**
                                of mind: California

Figure 11-8.   A nested indent

and other documents that will receive editing marks. You will usually want to create your documents in single space on the screen and then print them in double space. This is where the importance of style sheets and the Standard paragraph come in.

 Tip: *Documents can be created in single-space mode and then printed in double-space mode.*

If all the text in your document must be double-spaced, select the entire text with SHIFT+F10 and then press ALT+X+2. If only certain parts should be altered, you've got a problem unless you used styles. With styles, as discussed, you can simply alter the style in the gallery to double spacing to change all paragraphs formatted with that style. When you are finished printing, you can return the paragraph style to single-space mode.

 Tip: *Use SHIFT+F10 to select the entire document to apply double spacing.*

Before and After Spacing — Open Paragraphs

Open paragraph mode makes Word insert spaces either before or after designated paragraphs. One reason for this is to eliminate unnecessary paragraph markers between paragraphs that require space between them. Extra paragraph markers can also be a problem when it comes to keeping paragraphs and titles together.

 Tip: *Open spacing instructs Word to place blank lines between paragraphs for readability.*

For example, you would rarely want to print a title as the last item on a page. It is best to leave a blank spot and print the title on the following page, where its body text is located. Word allows you to keep two paragraphs together, but if the text for a title is separated by a paragraph marker, Word will assume that the paragraph marker being used as a spacer is the paragraph you want to keep with the title. Open paragraph spacing helps solve this problem by making a space part of the title or paragraph.

 Tip: *Open spacing helps prevent the unnecessary separation of paragraphs meant to stay together.*

Use ALT+O to place a single space above the designated paragraph. Of course, if you choose this option in one paragraph, all following paragraphs will retain open spacing until you change it. With the Format Paragraph menu, you can specify how many spaces you want above or below a paragraph. You may want to place two lines before titles and headings to ensure plenty of space between them and the previous text.

 Tip: *Titles are often assigned multiple spacing above and below.*

Adding Space After Standard Paragraphs

Because the open spacing option is so important to improving the quality of your documents and eliminating unnecessary paragraph markers, you may want to modify some of the styles that you've created to include open spacing. For existing styles, this is easily done in the gallery. You can also alter the Standard paragraph so that it includes a line after each paragraph to separate it from the next. Let's try changing a few so that you can see how to use the gallery for this purpose.

First, let's change the Standard paragraph to include a following space. Press ESC and type **G** to open the gallery. The screen should list the styles that you just assigned and may look like the illustration shown here:

```
═╡··········1········L········3········4········5····]···6·········7·····╗
  16  RH Paragraph 11                        LOGO, FLUSH RIGHT
         TMSRMN (roman a) 14/12. Flush right, space after 1 li.
  17  CH Paragraph 12                        LOGO, CENTERED
         TMSRMN (roman a) 14/12. Centered, space after 1 li.
  18  CR Paragraph 1                  CENTERED ITALIC REMARK
         Courier (modern a) 12. Centered, space after 1 li.
  19  CI Paragraph 2                       INDENTED CLOSE
         Courier (modern a) 12. Flush left, Left indent 3", space after 1
         li.
  20  CB Paragraph 3              1 INCH LEFT & RIGHT INDENT
         TMSRMN (roman a) 12. Flush left, Left indent 1", right indent 1",
         space after 1 li.
  21  NL Paragraph 4                        NUMBERED LIST
         TMSRMN (roman a) 12. Flush left, Left indent 0.3" (first line
         indent -0.3"), right indent 1.5", space after 1 li. Tabs at: 0.3"
         (left flush).
  22  TL Paragraph 5                          TEXT LIST
         TMSRMN (roman a) 12. Flush left, Left indent 2" (first line indent
         -2"), space after 1 li. Tabs at: 2" (left flush).
                                                    ═NORMAL.STY═
      Copy Delete Exit Format Help
      Insert Name Print Transfer Undo
```

Scroll through the list with the arrow keys to locate and highlight the Standard paragraph. It should be labeled "Paragraph Standard" and will be in the list if you created the first-line indent earlier in this chapter. If you can't find the entry, type **i** to insert one. Do not enter a key code. Tab to the Usage field and select Paragraph. In the Variant field press F1. "Standard" should appear in the field. Tab to the Remark field to add a remark if you wish, or just press ENTER.

Now that the style is highlighted, use the Format Paragraph command and type 1 in the Space After field.

Open Space the Company Logos

The company logo, created earlier, can use both a space before and a space after, especially if you have letterhead with a special logo that requires extra spaces from the top of the sheet. If the RH and CH styles are together, you can use the F6 (Extend) key to highlight both of them. If not, you can delete one to the scrap and reinsert it above or below the other.

Once the two styles are highlighted, open the Format Paragraph command in the gallery. On the third line in the Space Before field, enter the number of lines needed to clear the logo on your letterhead, if any. In the Space After field enter the number of lines needed between the company name and other parts of the letter. In this illustration, two lines are used for each.

```
FORMAT PARAGRAPH alignment:(Left)Centered Right Justified
    left indent: 0"          first line: 0"          right indent: 0"
    line spacing: 1 li       space before: 2         space after: 2█
    keep together: Yes(No)   keep follow: Yes(No)    side by side: Yes(No)
```

Open Space the Indented Block

Whenever you create an indented block such as a quote with the CB style, you'll probably want a space before and after it. However, because standard paragraphs now include a space after, you might end up with two spaces between the indented block and a previous paragraph if you include a space before the paragraph. Instead, use the Format Paragraph menu to include one space after the indented block.

Page Break Control

Word has several options for controlling where a page will break in a document. These controls are designed to prevent your paragraph from being divided over two pages in unusual ways. You can choose to keep a paragraph together on a page; that is, the entire paragraph is moved to the next page if it won't fit on the current page. You can also choose to bring two lines from the previous page over to the next page with a paragraph.

 Tip: *Word has controls to keep paragraphs from being split in unusual places over page breaks.*

A *widow* is a single line of text from the previous paragraph that prints at the top of the next page. An *orphan* is a single line at the bottom of a page from a paragraph printed on the following page. The Page Break option in the Format Paragraph menu helps prevent these situations. You can control whether Word will prevent widows and orphans by selecting Yes in the Widow/Orphan Control field in the Print Options menu. If you want to print as much on one page as possible, choose No.

 Tip: *The Widow/Orphan Control field in the Print Options menu can be used to control page breaks in the first or last line of a paragraph.*

Print Paragraph Entirely on the Same Page

To ensure that a paragraph is printed entirely on one page, choose Yes in the Keep Together option of the Format Paragraph command. You may want to make this change to paragraphs that are tables or lists. When the document is printed, Word may move the entire paragraph to a subsequent page if it won't fit on the current one, thus leaving a large blank space on the current page.

 Tip: *You can keep tables and lists entirely on one page by using the Keep Together option in the Format Paragraph command.*

 Trap: *The Keep Together option may leave large blank spaces on pages by moving paragraphs entirely to other pages.*

Printing a Paragraph with Part of Another

The Format Paragraph menu's Keep Follow option will keep at least some of a previous paragraph with a paragraph that must be printed on another page. This option improves the look of the paragraphs. If the first two lines of the second paragraph do not fit at the bottom of the page, Word will print the last two lines of the first paragraph on the next page.

Tip: *You can keep parts of two paragraphs together to enhance their appearance by using the Keep Follow option.*

 Tip: *You may want to add the Keep Follow option to your Standard paragraph style in the gallery.*

 Tip: *You can keep two entire paragraphs together by choosing Yes in both the Keep Together and Keep Follow fields.*

Titles and Headings

Titles and headings are good candidates for both open paragraph spacing and the Keep Together option, as well as for character formatting options. When you start a new section of a document, its title or heading should usually be placed at least two lines from the previous paragraph. In addition, a title should be tied to the next paragraph so that it doesn't print at the bottom of a page by itself.

The Print Repaginate command lets you view where pages will break when printed, and you can often adjust these breaks to accommodate titles. However, it is best to have Word automatically handle titles to make sure that one never falls by itself at the bottom of a page.

 Tip: *Print Repaginate can help you adjust page breaks.*

 Tip: *It's best to let Word automatically control page breaks by using the page break controls in the Format Paragraph menu.*

Word uses seven standard or default titles, mainly in the outline facility. When you use the outliner, titles are automatically assigned to up to seven levels of indented headings. Because you can apply character formats, you can essentially design the format structure of your document in the outline mode, down to the type font of the titles.

Tip: *Word uses seven default title variants for outlining. Use*
these titles whenever possible so that you can create an out-
line of your document after it is typed.

Once you have assigned fonts and other paragraph formats to titles, you can use them in regular edit mode whenever you wish. Using the default outline titles allows you to create an outline of your document after it has been typed, even if you didn't use the outline facility previously. Word will remember the hierarchy of the titles and allow you to collapse text under them to produce title lists and even a table of contents.

Let's try assigning paragraph open spacing, page break control, and character formatting to several of the default titles. Press ESC and type **G** to get into the gallery. Type **I** to insert a new style.

1. In the Key Code field, type **T1**.

2. Tab to the Usage field and select Paragraph.

3. Tab to Variant and press F1. The possible variants are listed, as illustrated here. Word's default variants are listed at the top. Notice heading levels 1 through 7.

```
Standard               Footnote          Running Head       Heading level 1
Heading level 2        Heading level 3   Heading level 4    Heading level 5
Heading level 6        Heading level 7   Index level 1      Index level 2
```

4. Tab to Heading Level 1 in the list and press the TAB key.

5. In the Remark field type **MAIN HEADING**.

Perform the same steps for a second heading level, filling out the Gallery Insert menu as shown here. The Key Code field should be T2, the Usage field should be Paragraph, and the Variant field should be Heading Level 2, which you can pick from the list by pressing F1. In the Remark field type **SUBTITLES**.

```
FORMAT STYLESHEET RECORD key code: 2      usage: Character(Paragraph)Division
           variant: Heading level 2       remark: SUBTITLES
```

Create a third-level heading by filling out the Gallery Insert menu as shown here. The Key Code field should be T3, Usage should be Paragraph, and Variant should be Heading Level 3, which you can pick from the list by pressing F1. In the Remark field type **SUB-SUBTITLES**.

```
FORMAT STYLESHEET RECORD key code: 3      usage: Character(Paragraph)Division
      variant: Heading level 3            remark: SUB-SUBTITLES█
```

The next step is to begin applying the formats to the titles. The open spacing and the Keep Follow option are the same for all titles, so you can press F6 (Extend) or use the mouse to select all three. Then open the Gallery Format Paragraph menu and fill in the options, as shown here:

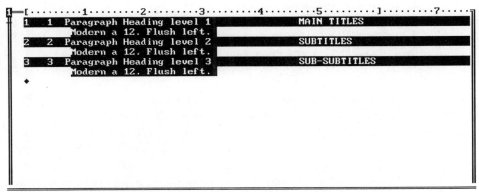

```
1═[·········1·········2·········3·········4·········5·········]·········7·····┐
│1   1  Paragraph Heading level 1              MAIN TITLES                   │
│       Modern a 12. Flush left.                                             │
│2   2  Paragraph Heading level 2              SUBTITLES                     │
│       Modern a 12. Flush left.                                             │
│3   3  Paragraph Heading level 3              SUB-SUBTITLES                 │
│       Modern a 12. Flush left.                                             │
│ ◆                                                                          │
│                                                                            │
│                                                                            │
│                                                                            │
└────────────────────────────────────────────────────────────────────────────┘
FORMAT PARAGRAPH alignment:(Left)Centered Right Justified
      left indent:            first line:          right indent:
      line spacing:           space before: 2      space after: 1
      keep together: Yes No   keep follow: Yes No   side by side: Yes No
```

Type 2 in the Space Before field and 1 in the Space After field. Answer Yes in the Keep Follow field and press ENTER. The three titles should now look like the ones shown here:

```
1═┌────────────────────────────────────────────────────────────────────────┐
  │1   1  Paragraph Heading level 1              MAIN TITLE                  │
  │       Courier (modern a) 12. Flush left, space before 2 li, space after 1│
  │       li (keep with following paragraph).                               │
  │2   2  Paragraph Heading level 2              SUBTITLES                   │
  │       Courier (modern a) 12. Flush left, space before 2 li, space after 1│
  │       li (keep with following paragraph).                               │
  │3   3  Paragraph Heading level 3              SUB-SUBTITLES               │
  │       Courier (modern a) 12. Flush left, space before 2 li, space after 1│
  │       li (keep with following paragraph).                               │
  └────────────────────────────────────────────────────────────────────────┘
```

The last step is to assign individual character formats to each title. These formats will depend entirely on your printer's capabilities. You may want to refer to the print sample produced in Chapter 10 to determine the best type fonts and sizes to use for your titles. The examples that follow use 14-point Helvetica font for the main title, 12-point Helvetica bold for the subtitle, and 10-point Helvetica for the sub-subtitle.

Highlight each title and then use ALT+F8 to assign the appropriate fonts. Remember, you can press F1 to see a list of fonts and font sizes. You can create other levels of title headings at any time. There are four default titles left that you can use in the outline mode. You might want to assign one to figure headings, for example. When you are finished, the styles should appear as shown here:

```
1    1   Paragraph Heading level 1               MAIN TITLES
         HELV (modern i) 14/12. Flush left, space before 2 li, space after 1
         li (keep with following paragraph).
2    2   Paragraph Heading level 2               SUBTITLES
         HELV (modern i) 12 Bold. Flush left, space before 2 li, space after
         1 li (keep with following paragraph).
3    3   Paragraph Heading level 3               SUB-SUBTITLES
         HELV (modern i) 10/12. Flush left, space before 2 li, space after 1
         li (keep with following paragraph).
```

Once the formats are created, you can begin using them right away. Press ALT+T1 to type main titles, ALT+T2 to type subheadings, and ALT+T3 to type third-level headings. When they are applied to text in the edit window, "T1," "T2," or "T3" will appear in the style bar to indicate which heading has been selected. Figure 11-9 shows an example of the use of titles and headings. Note that blank paragraph markers were inserted to produce the spacing between titles and text.

Borders

Borders are a welcome new feature of Word 4. The titles from Figure 11-9 are shown with borders in Figure 11-10. With the Format Borders command, you can surround titles, paragraphs, quotes, imported art, and other material with normal, bold, or double-lined boxes, assuming that your printer supports this feature.

 Tip: *Use the Format Borders command to surround blocks of text with single, bold, or double-line borders. You can also place horizontal or vertical bars in the text.*

 Trap: *If you have a Hewlett-Packard series II LaserJet, you will need to obtain the H2 printer description files from Microsoft.*

A PLANET CALLED EARTH

The Earth is the third planet from the Sun. It circles in a belt that is considered ideal for the development of planetary life, neither too hot or too cold...

A CONTINENT CALLED AMERICA

In the northern hemisphere of the planet is the American continent...

A COUNTRY CALLED THE UNITED STATES

The United States extends from the Atlantic Ocean to the Pacific Ocean ...

Figure 11-9.   Titles and headings

You can also place bars in a side-by-side column or in a table of numbers, as shown in Figure 11-11. In this section you'll learn how to set up the title borders. In a later section you'll see how to include lines in tables, and in Chapter 13 you'll see how to apply borders to side-by-side paragraphs.

Note that Word's borders feature is not the same as the line-drawing feature, which is covered in Chapter 20. Line-drawing mode allows free-form drawing anywhere on the screen, whereas the Format Borders command is a paragraph element and is restricted to paragraph use.

Trap: *Borders and Line Draw are not the same. Line Draw allows free-form drawing, while borders are restricted to paragraphs.*

A PLANET CALLED EARTH

The Earth is the third planet from the Sun. It circles in a belt
that is considered ideal for the development of planetary life,
neither too hot or too cold. . .

A CONTINENT CALLED AMERICA

In the northern hemisphere of the planet is the American
continent. . .

A COUNTRY CALLED THE UNITED STATES

The United States extends from the Atlantic Ocean to the
Pacific Ocean . . .

Figure 11-10.   Titles with borders

The Format Border menu is illustrated here. Before using it, you must highlight the paragraph that is to receive the border. Use the Type field to specify the
type of border. If you choose Box, the lower part of the menu is not used. If you
choose Lines, the line is set in the lower part of the menu, on the left, right,
above, or below a paragraph. Use the Style field to specify the line type.

```
FORMAT BORDER type: None Box Lines      line style:(Normal)Bold Double
            left: Yes(No)  right: Yes(No)   above: Yes(No)   below: Yes(No)
```

Keep in mind that certain printers won't print all of the line types, or will
substitute other line types. For the following exercise, first type **TI** to set up a style
for a first-level title.

Slot machine dial symbols

Symbol	Dial 1	Dial 2	Dial 3
Bar	1	3	1
Bell	1	3	3
Plum	5	1	5
Orange	3	6	7
Cherry	7	7	0
Lemon	3	0	4

Gaia Theory
The Gaia theory, proposed by James Lovelock, states that the earth's living matter- air, ocean, and land surfaces- forms a complete system that has the capacity to keep our planet a fit place for life.

Conventional Theory
The conventional theory states that life is passive in the face of threats to its existence and is a product of the environment.

Figure 11-11. Bars in a table of numbers and between columns

Trap: *Some printers may print only one kind of border; others may not support them at all.*

Type anything in the title or the text shown here:

```
 1═══[· · · · · · · · ·1· · · · · · · · ·2· · · · · · · · ·3· ·
 ┃
 ┃T1   THIS·IS·A·SAMPLE·TITLE¶
```

Next, select the Format Border command and fill in the options as shown here. Select Box in the Type field and Double in the Line Style field. Because this is a box, you needn't select a line position.

```
FORMAT BORDER type: None(Box)Lines     line style: Normal Bold Double
              left: Yes(No)  right: Yes(No)  above: Yes(No)  below: Yes(No)
```

The box will appear as shown here:

```
[·········1·········2·········3·········4·········5····]····6··

 THIS·IS·A·SAMPLE·TITLE¶
```

You can select anywhere in the text of the box and press ALT+X+C to enter it, as shown here:

```
[·········1·········2·········3·········4·········5····]····6···

      THIS·IS·A·CENTERED·SAMPLE·TITLE¶
```

You can also reduce a box in size by changing the left or right indent, or both. Here both the left and right indents were set to 1 inch.

```
[·········1·········2·········3·········4·········5····]····6·

     THIS·IS·A·CENTERED·SAMPLE·TITLE¶
```

An interesting problem arises when text is typed in a box. Look at how the text butts up against the left wall of the box in this illustration.

```
[·········1·········2·········3·········4·········5····]····6·

 This·is·a·sample·of·text·within·a·border·line.··As·you·
 can·see,·the·border·is·placed·directly·against·the·edge·
 of·the·text.¶
```

You can make space between the text and the borders of a box by creating a hanging indent and using a blank line at both the top and bottom of the text, as shown here:

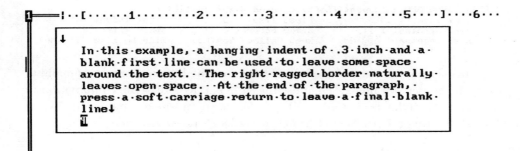

The first-line hanging indent moves the text away from the left box border. Because the first line is blank (a soft carriage return was used to maintain paragraph integrity), the top line is blank and provides spacing from the border. The same holds true of the bottom line.

Tip: *A hanging indent can be used to provide space around a bordered paragraph.*

If a bordered paragraph falls near the bottom of a page, Word may break it over two pages, which may or may not be desirable. You can prevent Word from breaking a bordered paragraph by setting the Keep Together field in the Format Paragraph menu to Yes.

Trap: *Word breaks bordered paragraphs across pages unless you set the paragraph to Yes in the Keep Together field.*

Bordered Paragraph with Indents

You can save the hanging indent border box to the style sheet in the following way. Position the highlight on a blank paragraph marker and press ALT+X+P to clear any previous formats. Open the Format Paragraph menu and set the options as shown here. Remember to set before and after line spacing to 0 and the Keep Together option to Yes.

```
FORMAT PARAGRAPH alignment:(Left)Centered Right Justified
        left indent: .3           first line: -.3          right indent: 0"
        line spacing: 1 li        space before: 0 li       space after: 0
        keep together: Yes No     keep follow: Yes(No)     side by side: Yes(No)
```

After setting the indents and line spacing, use the Format Border command to apply the border you prefer. Then use the ALT+F10 (Record Style) combination to save it to the style sheet. Call it BI (for Bordered Indented paragraph). In the Remark field type **BOX WITH SPACE INDENTS,** as shown here:

```
FORMAT STYLESHEET RECORD key code: BI        usage: Character(Paragraph)Division
                     variant: 9              remark: BOX WITH SPACE INDENTS
```

The Importance of Soft Carriage Returns

The importance of maintaining paragraph integrity becomes evident when you work with borders and tables, as you'll see shortly. If you want to keep text together within a box but need to start a new line, you must use SHIFT+ENTER (soft carriage return); otherwise, a new box is begun, as shown here:

```
 ═══[········1········2········3········4········5···]···6··
    │This·is·an·example·of·a·paragraph·formatted·with·a·   │
    │single·line·border.··The·paragraph·does·not·have·"space·│
    │before"·or·"space·after"·settings.¶                   │
    │                                                       │
    │Pressing·the·Carriage·will·start·a·new·box.··If·you·   │
    │need·to·start·a·new·line,·press·a·soft·carriage·return·│
    │where·the·line·should·start↓                           │
    │Here·is·the·new·line·within·the·same·box.¶             │
```

When you work with tables, you can move a tab to readjust all lines in the column of the tab.

Tip: *When you use borders, maintain paragraph integrity by using soft carriage returns.*

Tabs and Tables

There isn't much difference between working with tab stops in Word and working with them on a typewriter. Think of a line of text as a street and tab stops as stoplights. Each intersection can be compared to the distance from one character to the next, so the street has a lot of intersections (usually 65), and you can place a stop light at any one of them.

Use the TAB key to jump ahead to the next tab stop, and if the Visible field in the Options command is set to Complete, a right arrow will appear for each tab.

Tabs are considered characters, like a space or any letter, and you can apply character formatting to them. For example, you can apply underlining if you want to extend an underline to another tab stop.

 Tip: *Tabs are considered characters and can be formatted.*

Word has a standard tab setting of every 1/2 inch (depending of course on the unit of measure that you have set in the Options Measure field). You can change the standard tab stop by altering the Default Tab Width field in the Options menu. Word will use this tab for all paragraphs unless you change the tabs for a specific paragraph.

 Tip: *You can change Word's standard tab size in the Default Tab Width field of the Options menu.*

It's important to understand that Word lets you customize tabs stops, but they are relevant only for the paragraph they are set in. Other paragraphs will maintain their own tab stops.

 Tip: *Each paragraph can have its own tab settings.*

This illustration shows how each line can have a completely different set of tabs.

```
1═[···L···1·L····L·2·········3········4·······5···]····6·
  RED→ GREEN→     BLUE→BLACK→    WHITE¶
  RED→      GREEN→  BLUE→    BLACK→  WHITE¶
  RED→ GREEN→ BLUE→ BLACK→ WHITE¶
  RED→              GREEN→  BLUE→    BLACK→ WHITE¶
```

The top line uses the standard 1/2-inch tab settings, while the other lines have custom tabs. Note that special tab adjustments were added to the highlighted line in order to space each word two characters apart.

Each tab can be assigned a specific alignment so that text in the columns under it is placed a specific way. Figure 11-12 shows a table created with various tab stops. The part numbers are left-aligned, the description column is centered, the weight column is right-aligned, and the price column is aligned on the decimal point of the numbers.

Tip: Tabs can align text left, right, centered, or on the decimal point of numbers.

Tabs can also have leader characters. For example, you can fill a tab space with dots, underscores, or hyphens for developing a table of contents, price list, or other forms. Figure 11-13 shows an example of these tab leaders.

Part Num.	Description	Weight	Price
234	Condenser	123	798.00
1-2345	Spent fuel rack	150	1084.00
34	Reactor pump	3000	7045.00
9823	pressurizer	376	2056.00
Left-aligned	Centered	Right-aligned	Aligned on the decimal

Figure 11-12.   A table created with tab stops

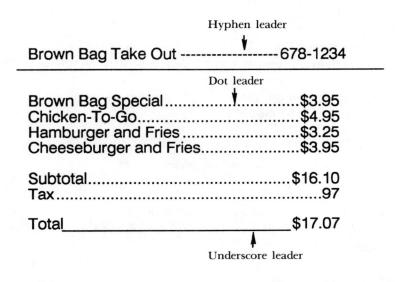

Hyphen leader

Brown Bag Take Out --------------------678-1234

Dot leader

Brown Bag Special.............................$3.95
Chicken-To-Go.................................$4.95
Hamburger and Fries $3.25
Cheeseburger and Fries.......................$3.95

Subtotal...$16.10
Tax..97

Total_____$17.07

Underscore leader

Figure 11-13. An example of tab leaders

How Tab Stops Are Used

The Format Tab menu has options for setting, clearing, and resetting all tabs for the paragraph that the highlight is in. If the highlight is in more than one paragraph, the tabs are set for each paragraph. You can change tabs for the entire document by pressing SHIFT+F10 to select them.

 Tip: *Tabs can be set for the entire document, groups of paragraphs, or individual paragraphs.*

The ruler is helpful when you are setting tabs, and it is displayed when the Format Tab Set or Format Tab Clear command is used. If you have a mouse, you can point to the ruler and click the left button to set tabs or point and hold the right button to move them, but only when the Format Tab Set menu is open.

Trap: *The ruler shows the position and type of tab only when custom tabs are set.*

Setting a Single Custom Tab When you create a set of custom tabs for a paragraph, the preset tabs are removed to the left, which saves you the trouble of pressing the TAB key an excessive number of times to get to the tab that you specifically set. In fact you can place only the number of tabs that you need for a particular paragraph in the tab ruler.

 Trap: *Setting custom tabs removes preset tabs to the left.*

To set a tab, you can use the Format Tab Set command or, preferably, ALT+F1. Position the highlight on a blank paragraph marker, press ALT+F1, and this menu will appear.

```
FORMAT TAB SET position: 3"
        alignment:(Left)Center Right Decimal Vertical   leader char:(Blank). - _
```

Setting a tab is as simple as scrolling to the proper position with the highlight on the ruler bar and pressing ENTER to set the tab for that position.

1. The highlight appears in the ruler bar. (Note that you may need to press F1 if you used the Format Tab Set command.)

2. Use the RIGHT or LEFT ARROW key to move the highlight to the position where you want the tab. As an example, try the 3-inch setting.

3. Press ENTER.

Type a short word and press the TAB key. The highlight jumps to the 3-inch mark, where you can type more text.

Setting More Than One Tab and Moving Tabs You can set more than one tab at a time. You enter the Format Tab Set menu with the ALT+F1 key, move the highlight to the position where you want the tab, and press INS. Then you can move to a second position and do the same thing.

The INS and DEL keys are important for moving and removing tabs. These keys perform the same tasks that they perform in the edit window. You can delete a tab, placing it in the scrap, and then move to another position in the ruler bar and reinsert it.

With the highlight on the paragraph used previously, press ALT+F1 to display the Format Tab Set menu.

1. Use the highlight to move to the tab marker in the 3-inch position. (Note that you may need to press F1 first.)

2. Press DEL to remove the tab marker to the scrap.

3. Move back to the 2-inch position and press INS.

4. Move the highlight to the 3.2-inch position. Notice that the measure of the line appears in the Position field. The ruler bar should look like this.

5. Press INS to insert another tab in this location; then press ENTER to accept the tab settings.

You may have noticed that the text in the line readjusts to the new tab settings.

Setting Tab Leaders and Alignment   Tab leaders were shown in Figure 11-13. You can use leader characters to fill up the blank space produced by the tabs and help lead the eye to the proper row in a column of text. Tab alignments (see Figure 11-12) are used according to the type of text in the column under the tab. You set both leaders and alignment in the Format Tab Set menu when you set the tab position.

After highlighting the desired position with the arrow keys, press the TAB key to get to either the Alignment or Leader Char field. After making a selection in one or both of these fields, press INS to set the tab. This leaves the menu open so that you can set other tabs.

For this example, first create a new paragraph marker by pressing ENTER. Because the tab settings of the previous paragraph are carried over, use the Format Tab Reset-All command to return them to their original settings.

Next, open the Format Tab Set menu by pressing ALT+F1. In this example you'll set a decimal-aligned tab with dot leaders at the 3-inch position.

1. Move the highlight to the 3-inch position with the arrow keys.

2. Press the TAB key to move to the Alignment field and select Decimal.

3. Press the TAB key to the Leader Char field and select the dot.

4. Press INS to accept the tab.

Before pressing ENTER to accept these changes, set another tab by performing the following steps:

1. Press F1 to display the highlight in the ruler.

2. Move it to the 4.5-inch position.

3. Press the TAB key to move to the Alignment field and select Right.

4. Press the TAB key to the Leader Char field and select Blank.

5. Press ENTER because no more tabs are required.

Now you can enter some text into the new tab settings. Type a word and tab to the decimal tab position, type a number with a decimal point and tab to the right-aligned tab, and type some text. You may not see the tab leaders. To view them, select Partial or None in the Visible field of the Options command. Tab leaders will print, however, whether or not they are displayed.

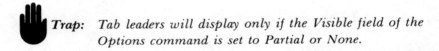 **Trap:** *Tab leaders will display only if the Visible field of the Options command is set to Partial or None.*

Setting Tabs with a Mouse   If you have a mouse, it's easy to set tabs. Simply open the Format Tab Set menu with ALT+F1 and select the options you want by pointing in the menu. For example, if you want a right-aligned tab with dots, press on the fields to select. Then point to the ruler bar and press the left button in the position where you want the tab.

To move a tab with the mouse, simply point to it and hold down the right button while you move the tab stop.

How Tabs Are Displayed in the Ruler   A tab's alignment and leader are displayed on the ruler line in the position of the tab. A left-aligned tab is displayed with an L and a centered tab with a C, while a leader is displayed in front of the tab character, as shown here.

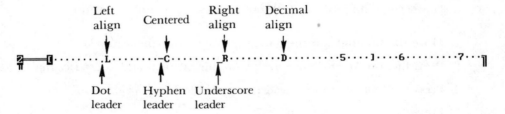

Clearing Single Tabs   The Format Tab Reset-All command is used to clear all custom tabs. To clear individual tabs, follow the steps described earlier, but press DEL to remove a tab marker from the ruler line.

Tab Weirdness   This section will explain tab phenomena that may puzzle you when you first use Word's tabs. The first concerns what happens when you approach and then exceed a tab setting. First, start a new line by pressing ENTER and then use the Format Tab Reset-All command to clear any custom tab stops. Now type **RED GREEN BLUE**, making sure to press the TAB key after the first two words.

Notice how GREEN aligned to the 1/2-inch tab two characters from the end of RED. This is what you would expect because there is a tab every five characters. But look what happened to BLUE. Because GREEN is a five-character word, it exceeds the second tab position, where you might at first think that BLUE would be typed. Instead, BLUE is typed in the next tab spot.

Of course, this is fine because you wouldn't want to type directly next to the previous word anyway, but it does demonstrate what happens when tabs are exceeded. Now type **RED BLUE GREEN**, tabbing after the first two words as before. This demonstrates how the placement of different-sized words can make a difference in tables set up with tabs.

Another tab phenomenon will be experienced by those who work with proportionally spaced typefaces. Because proportionally spaced characters are of different sizes and the text on your screen is monospaced, the screen cannot accurately display how tabular material will align. Look at the following table, taken from a Word screen image.

```
▌▆━━[ · · · · · · · · ·1· · · · · · · · ·2· · · · · · · · ·3· · · · · · · · ·4· · · · ·

    Numbers·of·petals·on·certain·flowers¶
    ═══════════════════════════════════════════

    Some·irises·and·lilies→   →     3·petals↓
    Buttercups→       →       →     →   5·petals↓
    Larkspurs·(delphiniums)→  →      8·petals↓
    Corn·marigolds→→          →      →   13·petals↓
    China·asters→    →        →      →   21·petals¶
    ═══════════════════════════════════════════

    ¶
```

Now look at the following printout, produced on a Hewlett-Packard LaserJet II with proportionally spaced Times Roman type font.

Numbers of petals on certain flowers

Some irises and lilies	3 petals
Buttercups	5 petals
Larkspurs (delphiniums)	8 petals
Corn marigolds	13 petals
China asters	21 petals

Some varieties may differ
Interestingly, the numbers form a Fibonacci sequence

There is nothing wrong with the printer. The problem has to do with the number of tab stops used to align the column on the screen and is similar to the phenomenon discussed earlier.

There are two ways to avoid this problem. First, you can create this table with one tab stop set at an appropriate location. Alternatively, because the table was created with multiple tab stops, you can set the printer display mode on. Word will then show as best it can how text will be aligned when printed. Pressing the ALT+F7 (Print Display On) key combination will produce the following screen. You can then add or remove tabs as needed to align columns.

```
[·········1·········2·········3·········4·········5·

Numbers·of·petals·on·certain·flowers¶


Some·irises·and·lilies→→3·petals↓
Buttercups→→    →    5·petals↓
Larkspurs·(delphiniums)→→8·petals↓
Corn·marigolds→→   →   →   13·petals↓
China·asters→→  →   21·petals¶

¶
```

 Tip: *When using proportionally spaced fonts, be sure to use custom tabs and set the printer display mode on.*

Table Development

This section is closely linked to the previous one because the main task in setting up tables is setting the tabs. It's helpful to have the print display mode on (press ALT+F7) when you are developing tables with standard tabs; however, this section will deal primarily with tables that have custom tabs.

It is most important to maintain paragraph integrity when typing tables by pressing SHIFT+ENTER at the end of each line. As you'll see later, you can select columns of text for movement to other locations. This is much easier when the lines in the column belong to the same paragraph.

Tip: *It is important to maintain paragraph integrity when developing tables. Use SHIFT+ENTER to end lines.*

There is one exception to this rule. The column titles for your tables will often need a slightly different alignment. For example, the title over a column of decimal-aligned numbers will look better when centered at a specific point that may not be the same point as the decimal tab. This will be covered as you work with the examples.

Tip: *Column titles for tables should be part of a separate paragraph so that they can be adjusted to fit properly above the columns.*

Planning Tables

If you plan your tables, you will usually come up with better results the first time you print. Consider the columns. Will they need to be centered or decimal tabbed? What will be the width of the widest text?

Tip: *When planning tables consider the alignment and maximum width of each column.*

It is common to set the tabs beforehand based on the information that you accumulated when planning the table. Then, after you enter the text, you can adjust the tab settings (if necessary) by using the Format Tab Set menu.

 Tip: *Table development often involves presetting the tabs, typing the table, and then adjusting the tabs.*

Test Printing Tables   You can go through a number of calculations to determine the optimum alignment for your tables. However, it is often easier to "eyeball" a table and then print a sample to see how it looks. The Print command has an option that lets you print only highlighted text.

 Tip: *You can test print a table by highlighting it and setting the Print Options Range field to Selection.*

Highlight the entire table; then open the Print Options menu and choose Selection in the Range field to print just the highlighted text. Remember, however, to reset this option to All when you're ready to print the entire document. If Selection is still chosen and the highlight is on a paragraph mark, space, or tab, a blank sheet will be printed.

 Trap: *Don't forget to reset the Print Options Range field to All when you're ready to print your document.*

Simple Table Development   The table shown in Figure 11-14 was produced using the tab stops discussed here. This table has two parts. The upper part—the table heading—was simply centered between the left and right margins with the ALT+XC key combination. The lower part is the table body. Its margin settings can be seen in the ruler because the highlight is in the table. Notice that it forms

Paragraph Formatting

one paragraph; soft carriage return markers appear at the end of each line except the last, where the table ends.

```
1 ══[·········1·········2·········3·········R·········5·········R·····
                        EMBASSY·IMPORTS¶
                              ¶
                        1988·Sales¶
                              ¶
          →                 Division·A→           Division·B↓
      Quarter·One→            432,237→              345,926↓
      Quarter·Two→            397,430              330,534↓
      Quarter·Three→          413,524→              352,953↓
      Quarter·Four→           455,254→              395,834¶
```

Type this table in now so that you can perform the exercises that follow.

1. Insert a new paragraph marker and use the Format Tab Reset-All command to clear any existing tabs.

EMBASSY IMPORTS

1988 Sales

	Division A	Division B
Quarter One	432,237	345,926
Quarter Two	397,430	330,534
Quarter Three	413,524	352,953
Quarter Four	455,254	395,834

Figure 11-14. A sample table

2. Type the first title and press ALT+X+C to center it. Press ENTER twice and type the other title.

3. Press ENTER to make a space and set the tabs for the table by pressing ALT+F1.

4. Place right-aligned tabs at the 4-inch and 6-inch positions following the method described earlier. Press ENTER.

You can now enter the text of the table, pressing the TAB key where appropriate and SHIFT+ENTER at the end of all but the last line. On the last line, press ENTER.

Adjusting Tables   You may notice that the table in Figure 11-14 seems too wide. Look at a revised version in Figure 11-15. It is both more visually appealing and easier to read because the columns are closer together. To reduce the width of a table but still keep it centered on the page, place indents on both the left and right sides and then adjust the tab settings to fit within the new indented paragraph. Because the indents will be equal for both sides, the center will be the same, so you won't need to indent the headings.

                     EMBASSY IMPORTS

                       1988 Sales

                           Division A   Division B
        Quarter One   432,237   345,926
        Quarter Two   397,430   330,534
        Quarter Three   413,524   352,953
        Quarter Four   455,254   395,834

Figure 11-15.   A revised table

Tip: *To reduce the width of a table, use the Format Paragraph indent settings.*

 Trap: *To reduce the width of a table, you may have to adjust the tab settings.*

Perform the following steps to adjust the table that you just typed in:

1. Place the highlight in the table.

2. Choose Format Paragraph and type 1 in both the Left Indent and Right Indent fields. Press RETURN.

3. Notice that the tab markers must be adjusted. Press ALT+F1 and delete and reinsert the right tab markers at the 3.7-inch and 5-inch positions. Press ENTER.

Your table should now look like the one shown here:

```
1    0·······[········2········3····R·4········R········6·
                    EMBASSY·IMPORTS¶
                          ¶
                    1988·Sales¶
                          ¶
            →            Division·A→   Division·B↓
     Quarter·One→          432,237→    345,926↓
     Quarter·Two→          397,430→    330,534↓
     Quarter·Three▶       413,524→    352,953↓
     Quarter·Four→         455,254→    395,834¶
```

Be careful when you are reducing the width of tables; they won't all be as simple to fix as the one in these exercises. If a table has a combination of centered, decimal, and right- or left-aligned tabs, along with column headings that are set to different tabs, you could be faced with a big job. You must readjust each column and set of tabs. This is more easily done with monospaced fonts than with proportionally spaced fonts.

 Tip: *It is better to plan tables beforehand than to readjust them later.*

Reorganizing Tables
with Column Selection

Tables often must be reorganized. You may decide that one column of information is more important than another and that it should become the first column. Or you may want to remove a column entirely. For example, you might want to remove the cost column from a sales bid before sending it to a customer. This section describes how to make changes in tables by *selecting columns*. Before you go further, make sure that the Visible field of the Options command is set to Complete so that you can better see the tab characters that make up tables.

 Tip: *You can reorganize a table by selecting an entire column and moving, copying, or deleting it.*

Column selection allows you to highlight a block of numbers that extend over several lines, without including other parts of the line to the right or left, as is the case with normal selection. Try this in the sales table that you just created. Place the highlight on the first number in the left column and press the F6 (Extend) key. Move the highlight down by pressing the DOWN ARROW key three times. Your display should look like the one shown here:

```
1───■──0····[····1·········2·········3····R··4·········R····]····6·
                        EMBASSY·IMPORTS¶
                               ¶
                        1988·Sales¶
                               ¶
            →           Division·A→  Division·B↓
        Quarter·One→            432,237→     345,926↓
        Quarter·Two→            397,430→     330,534↓
        Quarter·Three→          413,524→     352,953↓
        Quarter·Four→           455,254→     395,834¶
```

Now place the highlight back on the 4 in the top of the left column. Make sure that Extend is off by pressing F6 if necessary ("EX" should not appear in the key status area of the screen). Press the SHIFT+F6 (column select) combination; then press the DOWN ARROW key three times and the RIGHT ARROW key seven times.

Tip: *Use SHIFT+F6 to select columns.*

Your display should look like the one shown here:

```
1══0····[····1·········2·········3·····R··4········R····]···6·
                        EMBASSY·IMPORTS¶
                        ¶
                        1988·Sales¶
                        ¶
            →           Division·A→   Division·B↓
         Quarter·One→    432,237→     345,926↓
         Quarter·Two→    397,430→     330,534↓
         Quarter·Three→  413,524→     352,953↓
         Quarter·Four→   455,254→     395,834¶
```

With a column of numbers highlighted in this way, you can apply character formats, perform math calculations, copy it, or delete it. If you delete the column, it is placed in the scrap so that you can insert it elsewhere.

 Tip: *Column select allows you to format, copy, delete, and perform calculations on a column.*

Moving columns can sometimes be confusing, especially if the column is uneven, as is often the case with the last column in a table. In the following illustration the column select extends over paragraph markers and line breaks.

```
1══[·········1·········C·········3·C······]········5·
   Engine→          Cylinders→    (kg)→¶
   ─────────────────────────────────────────────
   Webra·Speedy→       1→        0.135↓
   Webra·Speed·20→     1→        0.25↓
   Webra·40→           1→        0.27↓
   McCulloh·M2-10→     1→        3.5¶
   ¶
```

When the column is deleted, the markers and line breaks stay where they are, but when it is reinserted in front of the Cylinders column, as shown on the next page, the table becomes a mess. Notice the ones for the Cylinders column are butted up against the back of the kg column.

```
┃═══[········1········C········3·C······]········5··
┃   Engine→          (kg)→    Cylinders→   ¶
┃
┃   Webra·Speedy→         0.1351→      ↓
┃   Webra·Speed·20→       0.251→       ↓
┃   Webra·40→             0.271→       ↓
┃   McCulloh·M2-10→       3.51→        ¶
```

One way to fix this is to column-select the tabs and insert them in front of the ones that are supposed to be under the Cylinders column. To do this, you can temporarily right-align the first column. This will line up the tabs, as shown here:

```
┃═══[········1········R········3D·······4········5··
┃   Engine→          (kg)→    Cylinders→   ¶
┃
┃   Webra·Speedy→ 0.1351→            ↓
┃   Webra·Speed·20→0.251→            ↓
┃   Webra·40→      0.271→            ↓
┃   McCulloh·M2-10→ 3.51→            ¶
```

Once the tabs are selected, they are deleted and then reinserted in front of the column of ones, as shown here:

```
┃═══[········1········R········3D·······4········5··
┃   Engine→          (kg)→    Cylinders→   ¶
┃
┃   Webra·Speedy→  0.135→        1↓
┃   Webra·Speed·20→ 0.25→        1↓
┃   Webra·40→       0.27→        1↓
┃   McCulloh·M2-10→ 3.5→         1¶
```

Adding a new column is as simple as moving the highlight to the upper-left corner of the column in front of which the new column will be inserted. Press SHIFT+F6 to select columns and move the arrow down the left side of the entire column; then press the TAB key. Word will insert a new column down all the rows.

Calculating Columns

Word's math capabilities will be covered in Chapter 20. This brief discussion will introduce you to the features and link them to the column select mode. In the sales table that you created earlier, place the highlight on the upper-left character in the first column. Press SHIFT+F6, arrow down to the bottom-right corner of the column, and press F2. The total for the number in the highlight is placed in the scrap.

 Tip: *You can perform math operations on columns selected with SHIFT+F6 (Column Select).*

You can create a total line by moving to the paragraph marker at the end of the table and pressing ENTER. In the next section you'll apply a special line format to the total line, so it must be a separate paragraph. Type **Total for Year** and press the TAB key; then press INS to insert the total from the scrap.

 Tip: *The total from a calculation is inserted into the scrap.*

You can repeat the previous steps on the second column and insert the result in the position of the second tab. Your screen should look like the one shown here:

```
█───0···[····1········2········3·····R··4········R····]···6··
                       EMBASSY·IMPORTS¶
                       ¶
                       1988·Sales¶
                       ¶
           →           Division·A→   Division·B↓
     Quarter·One→           432,237→      345,926↓
     Quarter·Two→           397,430→      330,534↓
     Quarter·Three→         413,524→      352,953↓
     Quarter·Four→          455,254→      395,834¶
     Total·for·Year→      1,698,445→    1,425,247█
```

Table Metamorphoses

In this section you'll see how to enhance the appearance of tables by adding lines and changing type styles. To add a line above the Totals in the sales table, highlight the line and open the Format Borders menu. Choose Lines in the Type field, Normal in the Line Style field, and answer Yes in the Above field. A line should appear above the Total line.

In some accounting applications the Total line is underscored twice. To do this, open the Format Borders menu and select a double lower line. Before pressing ENTER, answer No in the Above field; a double line above this line is not needed. To replace the single line removed by this step, place the highlight in the table paragraph above and use the same procedure to specify a lower single line. Your table should now look like the one shown in Figure 11-16.

The table would also look better if a single line were placed below the Division A and Division B column headers. However, because these headers are part of the table paragraph, you cannot apply a border under them. You must separate this line from the rest of the table. Place the highlight on the upper left *Q* of the word *Quarter;* press the BACKSPACE key, and then press ENTER. The column titles now constitute a separate paragraph. Because this line was part of the table paragraph formatted with a lower line, the format is retained in the new paragraph.

EMBASSY IMPORTS

1988 Sales

	Division A	Division B
Quarter One	432,237	345,926
Quarter Two	397,430	330,534
Quarter Three	413,524	352,953
Quarter Four	455,254	395,834
Total for Year	1,698,445	1,425,247

Figure 11-16. A double underline is included

You can also place a line over the column titles by highlighting the initial tab of the line and pressing ENTER. You can remove the extra space under the main headings by deleting the paragraph marker, but don't delete the one above the column headings that holds the line. You can also change fonts for the table by highlighting it and pressing ALT+F8.

In addition, the headings can be boldfaced or assigned a larger font size. A completed table printed on a Hewlett-Packard LaserJet II is shown in Figure 11-17. The results that you obtain from your printer will depend on which fonts your printer supports.

Table Examples

Tables can be divided into several categories defined by the type of paragraph and the formatting available from Word. For example, you can place borders around tables or have lines printed on the top and bottom or even the left and right. Tables can have mixed left, right, centered, and decimal tabs. They can also have Keep Together instructions as well as automatic before-and-after spacing.

EMBASSY IMPORTS

1988 Sales

	Division A	Division B
Quarter One	432,237	345,926
Quarter Two	397,430	330,534
Quarter Three	413,524	352,953
Quarter Four	455,254	395,834
Total for Year	1,698,445	1,425,247

Figure 11-17. The completed table

Word: Secrets, Solutions, Shortcuts

The tables described here will usually comprise three or more separate paragraphs with different tab settings. Many of the settings are not standard and are therefore not useful when saved as a style. The few cases where a paragraph tab setting is useful as a style will be covered individually.

Table of Contents   A table of contents usually aligns page numbers on the right and titles on the left. The screen image illustrated here shows a standard table of contents with the tab setting shown in the ruler line above.

```
[··L··L··1··········2········3········,R········5····
          List of Tables.....................i¶

          Introduction......................1¶

       1. Problem Definition.................5↓
              What is the problem?..........6↓
              Stating scope and objectives....9¶

       2. The Feasibility Study.............12↓
              Is there a feasible solution?...14↓
              Cost/benefits analysis........17¶

       3. Design and Implementation.........25↓
              Solving the problems.........28↓
              Implementation of solutions....40
```

Note that the space to the first tab is for chapter numbers. The second tab is for indenting subtitle headings, which are single-spaced with SHIFT+ENTER. The page number is aligned on the right.

Tabs: Left-align at 0.3 and 0.6 inch; right-align with dots at 4 inches

Spacing: Double, except for subtitles (use SHIFT+ENTER)

Borders: None

Figure 11-18 shows another type of table of contents, which is highly formatted. The top line of each chapter entry is formatted with a line above and three tab stops. The lower portion is indented 1.2 inches on the left and 1 inch on the right. Also, a smaller type font is used.

CHAPTER 6	MANUAL ACCOUNTING SYSTEMS Control Accounts and subsidiary ledgers, 183; Special Journals, 185; The General Journal, 192	182
CHAPTER 7	INTERNAL CONTROLS The law, 196; Elements of internal control, 200; Other Considerations, 210	195

Figure 11-18. A table of contents

Tabs:	Left-align at 1.2 inches; right-align at 5.5 inches
Spacing:	Single spacing with space before in top paragraph
Borders:	Upper single line
Indents:	Lower portion indented 1.2 inches on the left and 1 inch on the right, with no hanging indent

Because this table comprises two paragraphs, you could create a style for each to make table development easier. You could call the top portion with bar and tabs HC (for Header for Contents) and the bottom portion BC (for Bottom of Contents). On the other hand, you could create a template, as shown here, which could be duplicated for the number of chapters and then filled in with the text for each one. (See the section on glossaries at the end of this chapter for more details.) In this illustration note the style codes HC and BC in the style bar for the two parts of the paragraphs.

```
  [·········1·········2·········3·········4·········5·········]·····
    ____________________________________________________________
HC  CHAPTER 6   MANUAL ACCOUNTING SYSTEMS             182¶
BC              Control accounts and subsidiary
                ledgers, 183; Special Journals, 185;
                The General Journal, 192¶
BC              ¶
    ____________________________________________________________
HC  CHAPTER x   title here¶
BC              subtitles here¶
```

Five-Column Table   A five-column table is shown in Figure 11-19. Its tabs are all right-aligned and are illustrated in the ruler shown here. This table comprises a table paragraph, a column heading paragraph, and two centered main heading paragraphs. The table paragraph has a line above it.

```
▯──[········1········2···R···3···R···4···R···5···R···]········7···▯
▯                                                                ▮
```

Tabs: Right-align at 2.5, 3.5, 4.5, and 5.5 inches

Spacing: Single spacing with space before in top paragraph

Borders: Line above table paragraph

Indents: None

Lined Table   The lined table shown in Figure 11-20 comprises two decimal tab columns. Almost every line of the table is a separate paragraph so that border lines can be placed under each. The exception is the column heading table, which has stacked headings. SHIFT+ENTER was pressed after the word *Daily* to type the text on the next line. The right indent for all paragraphs was set at 3.75 inches to keep the border lines from extending across the page.

Tabs: Title headings: centered at 1.2 and 1.9 inches
           Table data: decimal tabs at 1.2 and 1.9 inches

FOUR-YEAR SUMMARY OF INCOME STATEMENT DATA

(in thousands of dollars)

	1982	1981	1980	1979
Net Sales	$600	$400	$300	$250
Cost of Goods Sold	384	244	187	145
Income Before Taxes	18	16	12	10

Figure 11-19. A five-column table

Shreveport, LA

Month	Daily High	Daily Low
January	56.6	37.8
February	60.4	40.6
March	67.3	46.2

Figure 11-20. A lined table

Spacing	Single spacing
Borders:	Top line: double border line All others: single line
Indents:	Right indent set to 3.75 inches

You can also surround the table with a box, as shown in Figure 11-21. To do so, select the entire table; then open the Format Borders menu and select Box in the Type field and Normal in the Line Type field.

Mixed Tables   Figures 11-22 and 11-24 illustrate examples of mixed tables. These tables have several paragraphs, each with different tab settings, but when combined form the whole table. The table in Figure 11-22 consists of four separate paragraphs, as shown in Figure 11-23. The tab types and tab positions are shown in the figure. Note also that some portions of the table are underlined.

Tabs:	See Figure 11-23
Spacing:	Single spacing with space before in top paragraph
Borders:	None

Shreveport, LA		
	Daily	Daily
Month	High	Low
January	56.6	37.8
February	60.4	40.6
March	67.3	46.2

Figure 11-21.   A table in a box

Jones and Radue

	Dollars (in thousands)		Percentage	
	1982	1981	1982	1981
Net Sales	$600	$400	100.0%	100.0%
Cost of Goods Sold	384	244	64.0	61.0
Income Before Taxes	18	16	36.0	39.0

Figure 11-22.   A sample table

C 3.9" } 1

C 2.8"
C 2.8"   **C 4.8"** } 2

R 2.5"   **R 3.5"**   **R 4.5"**   **R 5.5"** } 3

Net Sales	R 2.5"	R 3.5"	D 4.3"	D 5.3"	} 4
Cost of Goods Sold	R 2.5"	R 3.5"	D 4.3"	D 5.3"	
Income Before Taxes	R 2.5"	R 3.5"	D 4.3"	D 5.3"	

Figure 11-23.   The four paragraphs

CITY	TYPICAL WEATHER	AVERAGE TEMPERATURE		
		MONTH	HI	LO
Santa Barbara	Mild year-round	January	62.7	38.3
		July	71.8	52.4
Seattle	Wet but mild	January	43.4	33.0
		July	75.1	53.8
Oklahoma City	Hot summers	January	47.6	26.0
	Mild winters	July	92.6	70.4
Miami	Sub-tropical	January	75.6	58.6
	Hurricanes	July	89.1	75.5

Figure 11-24.   Mixed alignments, borders, and other features

CITY	C 2.3" C 2.3"	L 3.4"		
		L 3.4"	D 4.7"	D 5.3"
		L 3.4"	D 4.7"	D 5.3"

Figure 11-25. The layout

Indents: None

Fonts: The lower portion of the table uses a reduced size font to fit within the margins

Figure 11-24 shows a table with mixed alignments, borders, and other interesting features. The layout for this table is shown in Figure 11-25. When you enter data to this table, you press tabs on the second line of each entry to move to the Month column. The top double line is part of the TYPICAL paragraph; the second line down is part of the CITY paragraph; the third line is part of the MONTH paragraph; and the bottom line is formatted as part of the table.

Tab Macros

Word version 4 now comes with a set of macros that you can use to automaticall set up tab stops. (Macros will be discussed in detail in Chapter 23.) TABLE.MAC is a macro that sets tabs for a table by prompting for the first tab position and the distance between consecutive tabs. TABS.MAC sets tabs at positions that you specify. The macro prompts you for desired alignments.

Quick Formatting Techniques

You've already seen how to quickly perform some formatting routines. Now you can add the following techniques to your formatting repertoire. Most of them are exactly the same as those used in Chapter 10, so they are covered only briefly here.

Repeating Formats

You can use the F4 key to repeat the last format that you applied. For example, if you just applied left and right indents to a paragraph, you can point to another paragraph and press F4.

 Tip: *You can copy paragraph formats by using F4.*

Keep in mind that F4 repeats the most recent action. If you delete the character, the Delete command will become the new command executed by the F4 key, not the formatting command.

 Trap: *When you use F4 to repeat formatting commands, you must perform the anticipated commands one after the other. Other commands will replace the formatting routine held by F4.*

Remember, too, that Word will only apply the last format used in a double-format operation. If you apply an indent and then apply a font change, only the font change will be repeated when you press F4.

Copying Formats with the Mouse

If you have a mouse, follow these steps to copy paragraph formats.

1. Place the highlight in the paragraph that is to be formatted.

2. Point in the selection bar next to the paragraph with formats that need to be copied.

3. Hold down the ALT key.

4. Click the right button.

 Tip: *To copy a format with the mouse, highlight the target text; then point to the formatted text and click the right button while holding down the ALT key.*

Using Windows with the Mouse   If you need to copy formats from other parts of the screen to the current location, you can open a window on the screen with the Windows Split Horizontal command. You can then leave the formatted text stationary in one window while scrolling through the other window. Point from one window to the other to copy formats.

 Tip: *You can use windows when copying styles with a mouse over large documents.*

Glossaries To Establish Formats

You can insert glossary entries into your text to establish formats. For example, you can copy into a glossary entry any of the paragraphs or tables discussed in this chapter that require special setup. Entries that include all relevant information except the text you need are called templates. You simply type the text in the template after inserting it with the F3 (Glossary Expand) key. For example, the table of contents template shown here could be included in the glossary with a name such as TOC. Then it becomes a simple matter to establish all the formats required to put together the table.

```
CHAPTER·x→   type·title·here,·tab·to·page·number·—>¶
             subtitles·go·here,·indents·are·on·the·
             left·and·right.¶
```

The template helps establish table formats such as type font and character style because you can assign them to the template before inserting it into the glossary. The advantage of using templates is that all your tables will retain a similar look and format, and they will be easier to create and read.

 Tip: *Templates for tables or other blocks of text with both character and paragraph changes can be stored as glossary entries.*

A filled-in table created with templates can be seen in Figure 11-18.

Searching and Replacing Formats

There are two ways to use the Search command with paragraph formatting. You can search for specific formats, such as those used in section titles and headings, figure text, or notes. If you are searching for titles or headings, the Search command is a convenient way to jump to different sections of your document. The format is often all that headings or titles have in common, so searching for the format is an efficient way to locate them.

 Tip: *You can search for paragraph formats to find specific portions of a document, such as headings, titles, and tables, with the Format sEarch command.*

You can also use the search facilities to search for and replace a specific format. Formats applied with the quick keys or with style sheet codes can be searched for and replaced. But you cannot search for a combination of character and paragraph formats unless they are part of a style sheet code, in which case you would search for the code instead of the formats.

 Tip: *You can search for formats and replace them with other formats with the Format repLace command.*

Tip: *Style sheet codes can be searched for and replaced.*

The commands to search and replace formats are located in the Format menu. Type **E** to search and **L** to replace formats.

To search a specific area of your document, you can select or highlight that area before executing the commands. When you type either **E** to search or **L** to replace, Word asks if you want to search for character formats, paragraph formats, or styles. If you select Character or Paragraph, Word will display a menu of selections similar to those of the Format Character menu or Format Paragraph menu, respectively. You can then select the option to search on and specify the direction, either up or down.

 Tip: *You can limit searches to a highlighted area, and you can choose to search up or down through text.*

For example, if you are searching for text formatted in italic and underline, you would fill out the Format sEarch Character menu. If you select Styles from the Format sEarch command, Word asks you for the style code. This is the code that you use when applying the style to the selected text. If you are searching paragraphs, the style code in the selection bar represents the format selection from the style sheet.

If you want to repeat a search and replace action, simply press SHIFT+F4. This makes repeated search and replacements through an entire document easy. If you have a mouse, you can repeat a format search or replace by clicking on the word *command* in the command area of the Word screen.

 Tip: *You can repeat searches by clicking on the word* command *in the command area.*

Tips and Traps Summary

The Significance of Paragraphs

Tip: Any character or word within a paragraph can be selected to format the paragraph.

Tip: The paragraph mark carries the formatting information of a paragraph.

Tip: Paragraph markers can be copied to carry formatting information to other areas of the document.

Trap: Deleting a paragraph mark may remove the paragraph formatting from a paragraph.

Tip: You can permanently change Word's preset standard paragraph format by using the gallery.

The Role of Style Sheets in Paragraph Formatting

Tip: If a paragraph format change will be used more than once in a Word session, it should be assigned a style code in the style sheet.

Tip: Paragraph styles can also define the type font and type style of the entire paragraph, not just highlighted text.

Tip: You can see a list of paragraph types by pressing F1 in the Variant field.

Tip: After inserting a new style, apply formats to it.

Tip: The direct formatting keys can be used on styles in the gallery just as they can be used on text in the edit window.

Tips and Traps Summary (*continued*)

Create Extra Paragraph Markers

Tip: Create an extra buffer of paragraph markers before you start typing a document.

Alignments

Tip: Paragraph alignment has to do with blocking or centering a paragraph, while indenting has to do with reducing its width.

Tip: Justified text is aligned on both the left and right sides.

Trap: Odd spacing between words may result when you justify text. Use a proportionally spaced font or hyphenate the text for best results.

Tip: You can create alignment styles that have special type fonts and sizes.

Tip: Hyphenation reduces extra spaces left in justified text and can help reduce jagged edges when text is flush right or left.

Trap: Hyphenation may not be visually appealing and is seldom needed on centered text.

Indents

Trap: Never change a margin to adjust the width of a single paragraph within a document. Use indenting.

Tip: ALT+X+N increases the indent of an entire paragraph to the next tab stop. You can press it more than once.

Tip: The Format Paragraph menu must be used to set right indents.

Tips and Traps Summary (*continued*)

Tip: A style for normal paragraphs can be used to restore non-indented paragraphs.

Tip: Before applying an indent format to a paragraph, type a few extra paragraph markers ahead so that you can easily get back to normal paragraph formats.

Tip: Use the ALT+X+T (Hanging Indent) key combination to create 1/2-inch hanging indents. For more control over indent size, use the Format Paragraph menu.

Tip: When you create numbered lists, allow enough room for two-digit numbers.

Tip: Don't forget to set a corresponding tab when you use indents.

Tip: You can create bulleted lists with hanging indents.

Tip: A diamond, dot, square, or other ASCII character can be displayed with the ALT key, and a number or combination of numbers from the numeric keypad.

Tip: Determine the width of the widest label before setting the indent in a labeled list.

Tip: Nested indents can be used to create outlines.

Double Spacing

Tip: Documents can be created in single-space mode and then printed in double-space mode.

Tip: Use SHIFT+F10 to select the entire document to apply double spacing.

Tips and Traps Summary (*continued*)

Before and After Spacing — Open Paragraphs

Tip: Open spacing instructs Word to place blank lines between paragraphs for readability.

Tip: Open spacing helps prevent the unnecessary separation of paragraphs meant to stay together.

Tip: Titles are often assigned multiple spacing above and below.

Page Break Control

Tip: Word has controls to keep paragraphs from being split in unusual places over page breaks.

Tip: The Widow/Orphan Control field in the Print Options menu can be used to control page breaks in the first or last line of a paragraph.

Tip: You can keep tables and lists entirely on one page by using the Keep Together option in the Format Paragraph command.

Trap: The Keep Together option may leave large blank spaces on pages by moving paragraphs entirely to other pages.

Tip: You can keep parts of two paragraphs together to enhance their appearance by using the Keep Follow option.

Tip: You may want to add the Keep Follow option to your Standard paragraph style in the gallery.

Tip: You can keep two entire paragraphs together by choosing Yes in both the Keep Together and Keep Follow fields.

Tips and Traps Summary (*continued*)

Titles and Headings

Tip: Print Repaginate can help you adjust page breaks.

Tip: It's best to let Word automatically control page breaks by using the page break controls in the Format Paragraph menu.

Tip: Word uses seven default title variants for outlining. Use these titles whenever possible so that you can create an outline of your document after it is typed.

Borders

Tip: Use the Format Borders command to surround blocks of text with single, bold, or double-line borders. You can also place horizontal or vertical bars in the text.

Trap: If you have a Hewlett-Packard series II LaserJet, you will need to obtain the H2 printer description files from Microsoft.

Trap: Borders and Line Draw are not the same. Line Draw allows free-form drawing, while borders are restricted to paragraphs.

Trap: Some printers may print only one kind of border; others may not support them at all.

Tip: A hanging indent can be used to provide space around a bordered paragraph.

Trap: Word breaks bordered paragraphs across pages unless you set the paragraph to Yes in the Keep Together field.

Tip: When you use borders, maintain paragraph integrity by using soft carriage returns.

Tips and Traps Summary (*continued*)

Tabs and Tables

Tip: Tabs are considered characters and can be formatted.

Tip: You can change Word's standard tab size in the Default Tab Width field of the Options menu.

Tip: Each paragraph can have its own tab settings.

Tip: Tabs can align text left, right, centered, or on the decimal point of numbers.

Tip: Tabs can be set for the entire document, groups of paragraphs, or individual paragraphs.

Trap: The ruler shows the position and type of tab only when custom tabs are set.

Trap: Setting custom tabs removes preset tabs to the left.

Trap: Tab leaders will display only if the Visible field of the Options command is set to Partial or None.

Tip: When using proportionally spaced fonts, be sure to use custom tabs and set the printer display mode on.

Table Development

Tip: It is important to maintain paragraph integrity when developing tables. Use SHIFT+ENTER to end lines.

Tip: Column titles for tables should be part of a separate paragraph so that they can be adjusted to fit properly above the columns.

Tip: When planning tables consider the alignment and maximum width of each column.

Tip: Table development often involves presetting the tabs, typing the table, and then adjusting the tabs.

Tips and Traps Summary (*continued*)

Tip: You can test print a table by highlighting it and setting the Print Options Range field to Selection.

Trap: Don't forget to reset the Print Options Range field to All when you're ready to print your document.

Tip: To reduce the width of a table, use the Format Paragraph indent settings.

Trap: To reduce the width of a table, you may have to adjust the tab settings.

Tip: It is better to plan tables beforehand than to readjust them later.

Tip: You can reorganize a table by selecting an entire column and moving, copying, or deleting it.

Tip: Use SHIFT+F6 to select columns.

Tip: Column select allows you to format, copy, delete, and perform calculations on a column.

Tip: You can perform math operations on columns selected with SHIFT+F6 (Column Select).

Tip: The total from a calculation is inserted into the scrap.

Quick Formatting Techniques

Tip: You can copy paragraph formats by using F4.

Trap: When you use F4 to repeat formatting commands, you must perform the anticipated commands one after the other. Other commands will replace the formatting routine held by F4.

Tip: To copy a format with the mouse, highlight the target text; then point to the formatted text and click the right button while holding down the ALT key.

Tips and Traps Summary (*continued*)

Tip: You can use windows when copying styles with a mouse over large documents.

Tip: Templates for tables or other blocks of text with both character and paragraph changes can be stored as glossary entries.

Tip: You can search for paragraph formats to find specific portions of a document, such as headings, titles, and tables, with the Format sEarch command.

Tip: You can search for formats and replace them with other formats with the Format repLace command.

Tip: Style sheet codes can be searched for and replaced.

Tip: You can limit searches to a highlighted area, and you can choose to search up or down through text.

Tip: You can repeat searches by clicking on the word *command* in the command area.

12

Page Enhancements

You've seen how to format characters, align paragraphs, and set up tables. Now you will learn how to bring all those elements together on a page. Page layout—the subject of this chapter—concerns the overall appearance of text on a printed page. The number of columns and the positions of the page number, titles, running heads, and margins as well as the placement of various types of artwork are all page layout topics.

The Printed Page

As discussed in Chapter 6, Word calculates the position of all page elements according to the size of the paper being used. Once you specify a particular paper size in the Format Division Margins menu, Word handles the placement of text with default settings (see Figure 6-4).

These default settings include top and bottom margins of 1 inch and left and right margins of 1 1/4 inches. The default settings provide space for the text that is 6 inches wide and 9 inches long. If you are using a Pica or Courier 12-point type (which is monospaced and has fixed-size letters) and 8 1/2- by 11-inch paper, that translates to 60 characters per line and 54 lines per page.

 Tip: *Word's default margin settings print 60 characters per line and 54 lines per page when you use 8 1/2- by 11-inch paper.*

You can of course alter the default settings to fit your needs. A legal-size sheet of paper, 8 1/2 by 14 inches, is 3 inches longer than standard (see Figure 6-6). To use this paper size, simply change the appropriate settings in the Format Division Margins menu. Once the paper size is specified, Word uses its default margin settings to determine how text will be placed on the page.

Note that the default settings work just as well on legal-size paper as they do on letter-size paper. The top and bottom margins remain at 1 inch and the right and left margins at 1 1/4 inches from the edges of the paper.

You can change the margins to fit your needs. If you want to print as much text on a page as possible, you could reduce all margins to 1/2 inch, thus increasing the size of the text area. Some laser printers may not print any closer to the edge of the paper than 1/2 inch, by the way.

 Trap: *Some laser printers may not print less than 1/2 inch from the edge of the paper.*

Once the page size and margins are set, paragraph formatting determines where text is printed on the page (see Figure 6-12). Paragraph indents can place a paragraph 1 or 2 inches from the margins. Just keep in mind that the margin settings determine the placement of text on each page in the entire document (unless you add a new division). Paragraph formatting is used to alter individual elements within the entire text.

 Tip: *Once the page size and margins are set, text placement is under the control of paragraph formatting.*

Page Enhancements

After setting up the paper specifications, you can focus on the other elements of page design and layout, two of which are page numbers and running heads. Running heads (often called headers and footers) usually hold such information as the chapter or section name or number, the name of the author, or a date.

 Tip: *Running heads print the same text on every page.*

Word allows a great deal of control over how both page numbers and running heads are placed on the page. Page numbers can be printed by themselves in a specified location on the page or can be included with the running head (seen in Figure 6-8).

Word makes an important distinction concerning running heads and text placement on the page that depends on whether you eventually plan to reproduce the pages output by your printer as single-sided or as double-sided documents (see Figure 12-1). (Note that a document file may, in some cases, be used as input to a typesetting machine.)

If you intend to use your printed sheets as the final product or to reproduce them as single-sided documents, your tasks are relatively few. If, however, you are planning to have your pages professionally printed or photocopied in a back-to-back style for insertion in a three-ring binder or book, you have more to consider. The key concept here is "back-to-back" printing. When you realize all that this implies, you will see why Word offers so many controls over the placement of text, page numbers, and running heads on a page. For example, Word makes it easy to stagger headers and gutter margins (the inside margin for bindings) left to right.

 Tip: *Running heads can be staggered left and right for even- and odd-numbered pages.*

Word gives you full control over the position of running heads, whether they are for pages printed only on the front or for camera-ready back-to-back documents. You can specify that a header be printed at the top or the bottom; you can have different headers for the top and bottom; or you can even have several headers in the same corner of a page.

Page numbers can be printed anywhere on a document or can be included in

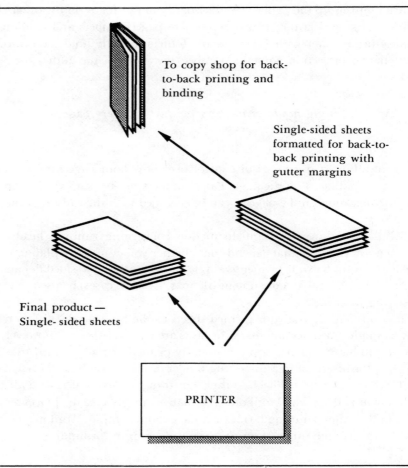

To copy shop for back-to-back printing and binding

Single-sided sheets formatted for back-to-back printing with gutter margins

Final product — Single- sided sheets

PRINTER

Figure 12-1.   Pages from the printer can be used as finals or as camera-ready copy for back-to-back printing

the running heads to print staggered left and right, either at the bottom or top of the page.

 Tip: *Page numbers can be printed separately or with running heads.*

Documents printed on both sides usually require a space for the binding or for three-ring hole punches. The *gutter* is a nonprinting zone placed on the left for odd-numbered pages and on the right for even-numbered pages (see Figure 6-7). Gutters are important only when you print back-to-back sheets because Word staggers the nonprinting zone left to right. If you are binding single-sided sheets, you need only specify a wide left margin.

 Tip: *Gutters provide a staggered nonprinting zone for sheets that will be printed back to back. They are not used for single-sided printing.*

Word will also print multiple newspaperlike columns on a page. Up to three columns will fit comfortably on a page, though you can specify more if necessary. You can adjust the space between these columns and control where they break. For example, if you are printing a newsletter, you could break a column before the bottom of a page to make room for a picture, an illustration, a table, or a graph. (Multiple-column formatting will be covered in Chapter 13).

Divisions and Pages

Even though the page layout is defined in the Format Division menus, there is a big difference between divisions and pages. A division usually defines how a group of pages will look, but each page is not itself a division. (Actually a division can be smaller than a page and a page can have several divisions, though some limitations exist as to how multiple divisions will print on a single page.) When a new division is defined, a page break will usually occur, but you can control this also.

Most of your documents will consist of one division. You define a new division when you need to make a major alteration in the placement of text on a page that will continue for several pages or when you need to change the location of the running head or page number.

 Tip: *Think of a division as a page layout change that continues for several pages.*

Many people are confused by the way that margins work in Word because they are used to adjusting them on a typewriter in order to reduce the width of text. Margins *can* be used to reduce text width, but this is only practical if the width is reduced over a number of pages. As you'll recall from Chapter 11, paragraph indenting is used to reduce the text width of paragraphs within the margin settings of the division.

 Tip: *Altering the width of text for blocks smaller than a page is best done with paragraph indenting.*

The following are several cases in which you might want to start a new division or change Word's standard division settings.

Letterhead Stationery

If you print letters on stationery that has a company logo at the top (or even at the sides or the bottom), you can adjust the margin to accommodate it. Usually only the top sheet is printed on letterhead paper; therefore, the first page will need different margin settings than the remaining pages, which calls for two divisions.

The first division defines the margins for the front page with the company logo; the second division defines normal margins for normal pages. The best way to do this is to use two different division styles from a style sheet. One style could be called LD (for Logo Division); the other could be Word's standard division for regular paper (which you will label SD later in this chapter).

Be sure to specify manual paper feed in the Print Options Feed field so that you can easily change paper types in between the front and following pages.

Tip: *When a document requires a switch in paper type, specify Manual feed in the Print Options Feed field.*

Envelope Division

You can create a division style that defines the margin settings for company envelopes. You can even add the division to the end of your letter and press ALT+F3 (copy to scrap) to copy the address in the body of the letter to the envelope division.

Labels and Special Forms

When you print on continuous labels, you must adjust the margins according to the size of the label. The settings will depend on whether the labels are single, double, or triple wide. (See Chapter 21 for more details.) Special forms may require that you adjust both the paper size and the margins. (Chapter 22 covers both creating forms from scratch and matching existing forms.)

Special Printer Divisions

Some printers may require an alteration to the page size. For example, the Hewlett-Packard LaserJet printer cannot print within 0.25 inch of the edge of the paper, so you must adjust margins or running heads accordingly. Set the page width to 8 inches and the running head position to at least 0.25 inch from the top edge of the paper and 0.40 inch from the bottom edge (0.55 if you have a line or box under the footer).

Documents with Table of Contents and an Index

A document that contains a table of contents and an index can consist of three separate divisions. The table of contents might have special margin settings without running heads. The body of the document might have running heads, page numbers, and normal margin settings. The index could be a multiple-column layout.

Documents with Exhibits

Some documents and reports have complete sections set aside for exhibits, charts, artwork, illustrations, and so on. These sections might require that special margins be set or that the running head be turned off.

Screen Division

A screen division has nothing to do with printing. Instead, it sets the margins so that the maximum amount of text displays on your screen. When you're ready to print, the standard division is reapplied.

The Format Division Command

You make alterations to pages by using two submenus of the Format command. The Format Division command, shown here, has four submenus that allow alterations to the features listed.

FORMAT DIVISION: **Margins** **Page-numbers Layout line-Numbers**

The Format Division Margins menu contains most of the options for setting up the page size and typing area of Word documents. You can also specify the placement of the running head and gutter. Running heads are also controlled under the Format Running-Head menu.

In the Format Division Margins menu you control the following:

- *Page size* Specify the width and length of the paper.

- *Margin settings* Specify the width of each margin from the edge of the paper. Each margin is measured from its own edge of the paper.

- *Position of running head* You can alter the preset running head position.

- *Size of gutter* You can set the width of the gutter to make room for page bindings.

In the Format Division Page-Numbers menu you control the following:

- *Page number position on page* You set the location of the page number from the top and from the left.

- *Continuous or new starting number* Use a number continuing from the last division or start with a new number.

- *Format of number* Specify one of the following formats: 1 I i A a.

In Format Division Layout you control the following:

- *Location of footnote* Specify footnotes on the same page or in the back of the document.

- *Column setup options* Specify the number of columns, the space between them, and how they will break on the page.

In Format Division Line-Numbers you control the following:

- *Line number setup options* You can specify line numbering, common for legal documents.

The Division Mark

The division mark is to divisions what the paragraph mark is to paragraphs: it holds the formatting information for the division. The division mark does not appear when you first open a Word document; it only appears if you make changes to the division. The division mark is the row of double dots in the illustration shown here:

```
┌────[·········1·········2·········3·········4·········5·········6·········]···┐
│SP   This·is·division·1.··The·left·and·right·margins·are·set·at·
│     1.25·inches.·
│     ::::::::::::::::::::::::::::::::::::::::::::::::::::::::::::::::::::::::::::
│
│SP   This·is·division·2.··The·left·and·right·
│     margins·are·set·at·2·inches·each.
│     ::::::::::::::::::::::::::::::::::::::::::::::::::::::::::::::::::::::::::::
└─────────────────────────────────────────────────────────────────────────────┘
```

The division mark always appears as the last item in a division. To create a new division, press CTRL+ENTER. The new division marker will appear directly under the location of the highlight.

Once a division is inserted, you can place the highlight anywhere within it and use the Format Division commands to alter its features. Be careful not to delete a division mark; this will either return the division to Word's standard settings or the division will take on the setting of the one below it.

When more than one division is present in a document, the division indicator is visible in the position indicators at the bottom-left of the screen. Division 2 in indicated in the following illustration as D2:

P1 D2 Li12 Co15

Page Size Alterations

Word's standard page size is 8 1/2 by 11 inches, and you will seldom need to alter this setting. However, if you need to print on other paper sizes (see Figure 6-6), use the Format Division Margins menu to adjust the paper size, as shown here:

```
FORMAT DIVISION MARGINS top: 1"      bottom: 1"      left: 1.25"  right: 1.25"
                        page length: 11"    width: 8.5"    gutter margin: 0"
                 running-head position from top: 0.5"    from bottom: 0.5"
```

Type the length of the page in the Page Length option and the width in the Width option.

 Tip: *Do not include the pin-hole stripe on tractor-feed paper in your page measurement.*

With certain printers, Word may not seem to print in the margin positions that you have set on the page. Centered text will not appear centered on the page. These printers have a nonprinting zone on the edges of the paper that you must subtract from the normal page size in the Format Division Margins fields. You must also reduce the margin settings. These problems are common in laser printers. Figure 12-2 illustrates the Hewlett-Packard LaserJet page layout.

Tip: *To calculate the value for left and right margin settings on some laser printers, subtract the size of the nonprinting zone from the actual margin size.*

Margin Settings

Margins in Word are always set from the edge of the paper (except in the special case of Hewlett-Packard LaserJets, as just described). The left margin is a measure from the left edge of the paper, and the right margin is a measure from the right edge of the paper (not from the left, as is done on typewriters).

 Trap: *The right margin is not a measure of the distance from the left edge of the paper, as is often done on typewriters. It is a measure from the right edge.*

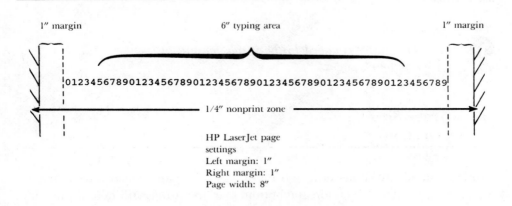

Figure 12-2. HP LaserJet page settings

Don't confuse this with how you calculate the page number position. Because there is only one page number position, it is always measured from the top and left edge (while the four different margins are calculated from the four edges of the paper).

You can alter margin settings in the Format Division Margins menu. Use decimal numbers when specifying margin settings that are increments of an inch. For example, 1.25″ 1.5″ and 1.75″ are used to represent quarter-inch increments.

The Gutter Margin

When you need to make room for bindings or three-hole punching, set the gutter margin in the Gutter Margin field of the Format Division Margins command. Gutters are rarely used for other than camera- or photocopy-ready pages for back-to-back printing.

Calculating gutter margins is a matter of determining how much space must be added to an existing margin to make room for binding or punch holes.

Of course a gutter margin will reduce the width of the typing area. For example, if you have 1 1/4-inch margins on 8 1/2-inch-wide paper, your typing area is 6 inches. If you add a 1/2-inch gutter, the typing area becomes 5 1/2 inches. You add the gutter to the "inside" margin, which is on the left for odd-numbered pages and on the right for even-numbered pages when you are printing back to back.

 Tip: *The gutter is added to the inside margin of even- or odd-numbered pages.*

Special Page Sizes and Orientations

Word automatically knows how to print on legal-size paper when you change the page size alone. The 1-inch top and bottom margin settings still hold for the new sheet size. But printing envelopes can open up a whole new can of worms unless you know some tricks.

First, whenever you are printing a document that requires you to insert one sheet of paper at a time, specify Manual in the Print Options Feed field so that Word will ask you for each sheet or envelope in succession. Of course, if you have an envelope feeder, this is not necessary.

 Tip: *To hand-feed envelopes, specify Manual in the Feed field of the Print Options command.*

Printing on Business Envelopes

To print a 9 1/2- by 4-inch business envelope on a standard platen-feed-type printer, set the left margin at the 4-inch mark and the right and top margins at 0. Printing will start on the line where the print head is located instead of advancing the envelope. Set the bottom margin at 0 because you want the envelope to feed out of the printer. You do not need to adjust the page size.

Printing Envelopes on Laser Printers

If you have a Hewlett-Packard LaserJet printer, the procedure to print an envelope is different. You must set the printer to manual feed and then select a font in the Printer Options command that supports landscape mode. These landscape fonts have names like HPLASLAN and HPLEGLAN.

 Trap: *You must select a landscape font to print in sideways mode on envelopes in the Hewlett-Packard LaserJet and similar printers.*

To print an address in the standard location on the envelope, set the top margin at 4.5″, the bottom and right margins at 0, and the left margin at 5.75″. Then set the page length to 8″ and page width to 11″ to accommodate the landscape mode on the LaserJet.

When you feed the envelope into the printer, insert it lengthwise into the middle of the manual paper feed slot. This is no problem with the LaserJet II. Simply move the manual feed guides until they are snug against the top and bottom of the envelope.

 Tip: *When you print envelopes on a Hewlett-Packard LaserJet,*
feed the envelope through the middle, not against the edge,
of the manual feed slot.

Because the page size is altered, the LaserJet II may flash the message "PC LOAD." Just press the CONTINUE key. This message states that the printer received a request for a paper size that is not currently loaded.

To print a return address as well as a destination address on an envelope, use the following settings. They print the return address in the upper-left corner of the envelope, but not close enough to cause the toner to smear or print incorrectly. Set the top margin at 2.5", the bottom and right margins at 0, and the left margin at 2.5". Then set page the length to 8" and page width to 11" to accommodate the landscape mode on the LaserJet.

After typing the return address, perform the following to type the destination address. Space down 10 lines (assuming 12-point type). Next, indent to the 3.25" mark either by using ALT+N (Increase Left Indent) or by setting the left indent in the Format Paragraph menu. Then type the address.

Don't forget that you can save any of these page layout settings to a style in a style sheet. In the previous example, however, the paragraph formatting would have to be an extra style. Instead, you may want to save the entire layout, including the 10 spaces and the paragraph indents, to a separate file called ENV.DOC.

 Tip: *Special page divisions, such as those to print envelopes, can*
be saved to a style sheet, file, or glossary for future use.

You could also highlight and save the entire section as a glossary entry. The formatting is saved with the glossary if you save the paragraph markers. Be sure to specify the landscape printer font before printing. (Chapter 15 covers the topic of glossaries and envelope printing in more detail.)

Microsoft supplies four macro utilities for printing on either monarch-size or business-size envelopes with the Hewlett-Packard LaserJet Series II printer. The macros send a special code to the LaserJet that initializes a special envelope print mode. Because a TTY print driver is used, you cannot set special fonts, but you can choose them on the printer front panel before printing. (See Chapter 23 for more details.)

Laser Printer Landscape Modes

Landscape mode on laser printers offers a way to print text lengthwise on a document. When you use this mode, reverse the page length and page width settings of the Format Division Margins command. In other words, a standard sheet in landscape mode would have a length of 8 inches and a width of 11 inches.

 Tip: *Landscape mode on laser printers provides a way to print text in wide format or tables with numerous columns.*

 Tip: *When you use landscape mode, swap the page length and width settings.*

With this setting, the right margin will not appear on the screen. You will need to set the SCROLL LOCK key on and use the LEFT and RIGHT ARROW keys to move horizontally in your text.

Landscape mode provides a way to print the maximum amount of information on a sheet. For example, when you select the LinePrinter font on a Hewlett-Packard LaserJet, up to 176 characters can be printed across a normal 11-inch page, assuming that the margins are set for 0.25 inch. You may want to use landscape mode to print financial documents or tables with numerous columns.

Controlling Where Pages Break

There are a number of ways to control where pages break. If you need to break pages early on every sheet, specify a larger bottom margin in the Format Division

Margins menu. To selectively break pages as you type text, press CTRL+SHIFT +ENTER. This places a single row of dots across the screen where the page break will occur.

 Tip: *Use CTRL+SHIFT+ENTER to add page breaks to text.*

You can also set page breaks (and determine where Word will place them) with the Print Repaginate command, as shown here:

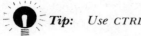

PRINT REPAGINATE confirm page breaks: Yes No

The command will ask you if you want to confirm. If you answer No, Word recalculates the page breaks according to its own rules. You can watch the page numbers as they are recalculated to get an idea of how long your document is.

 Tip: *The Print Repaginate command calculates the current page breaks and inserts page break markers.*

If you choose Yes in the Print Repaginate command, Word allows you to adjust its proposed page break. However, you can only move the page break up in the page by using the arrow keys. Word won't let you add more lines to its proposed break.

Print Repaginate is useful for determining if Word will break pages in improper places. For example, if a break will occur after a heading, move the break just above the heading so that it will print with its body text on a new page.

Once you have repaginated a document, the page break markers in the text are accurate. When you start adding new text, however, the markers become incorrect until you repaginate again.

Trap: *If new text is added inside the document, the page breaks become inaccurate. Another repagination is required to set new page breaks.*

Controlling Where Divisions Break

You can control how a division will break by using the Format Division Layout command. A division can break in several ways, as shown in Figure 12-3 and the following list:

Page	The default setting for division breaks is to start a new division on a new page.
Continuous	The new page format starts on the next page. (Note: This may not work on some laser printers.)
Column	Word breaks a column of text at the specified location and prints it in the next column on the same page or the first column on the next page.
Even	Word starts printing the new division on an even-numbered page and may leave a blank page.
Odd	Word starts printing the new division on an odd-numbered page and may leave a blank page. The odd-numbered format can be used when breaking from, say, a table of contents division to the chapter or section division. The starting page would then be the next right odd-numbered page. The same holds true when you break from the chapters to the index division.

Page Numbering

There are two ways to print page numbers in Word. You can use the Format Division Page-Numbers command, or you can include the page number in a running head. There are advantages to the second method.

If you are not using running heads, you can only print page numbers with the Format Division Page-Numbers command. If you are using running heads, you can include the page number in the running head or print it as a separate item. The logic here is that if you are already setting up one running head, you may as well set up another one with a page number or include the page number in the running head.

Word: Secrets, Solutions, Shortcuts

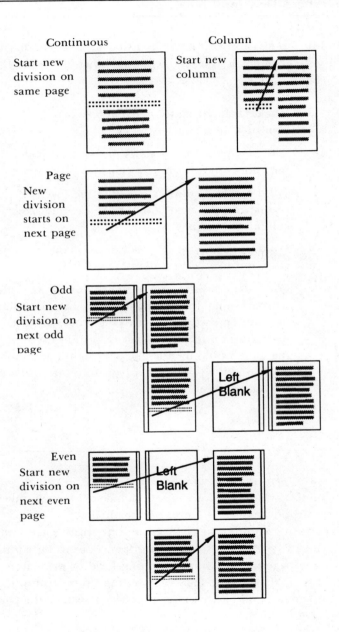

Figure 12-3. How divisions break

Page Enhancements

Tip: *Set page numbers with the Format Division Page-Numbers command only if you are not using running heads.*

Tip: *If you are using running heads, include the page number in the running head or create a separate running head for the page number.*

Using the Format Division Page-Numbers method has several disadvantages and is not recommended unless you absolutely do not want to use running heads. The disadvantages are as follows:

- It is hard to specify a character format for the number. You must insert and format the "page number" default character in the gallery.

- You can't see the location of the number anywhere on the screen. You must open the menu to find out where it is.

- You cannot turn off the number for the first page.

Printing numbers as part of the running head offers the following advantages:

- You can turn off page numbers for the first page of a division.

- You can alternate page numbers from left to right, depending on whether the page is odd or even.

- The page number position is visible on the screen as (page).

- You can easily format the page number with normal formatting commands.

If you must use the Format Division Page-Numbers method, the rest of this section describes how to use the options. If you use running heads, skip ahead to the next section.

Adding Page Numbers

The Format Division Page-Numbers menu is shown here.

```
FORMAT DIVISION PAGE-NUMBERS: Yes No      from top: 0.5"    from left: 7.25"
        numbering:(Continuous)Start       at:      number format: 1 I i(A)a
```

Turn on page numbering by answering Yes in the first field. You can specify where on the page the numbers will be printed by calculating the distance for the top and left of the page. To place a number in the bottom margin, you would type a number greater than 10. Keep in mind that this measuring method differs from that used to set margins.

Tip: *When you use the Format Division Page-Numbers option, page numbers are measured from the top and left edge of the paper.*

Because you can specify a location from the top-left edge of the paper, page numbers can be printed anywhere on the sheet, including the areas outside of the margin settings but within the printing zone of your printer. If you want the page numbers to align with one of the margins and the edge of text, specify the same width as the margins.

Trap: *Be careful not to set page numbers in the text area or outside the printing zone of your printer.*

In the Numbering field select Continuous to continue the page numbers from where they left off in the previous division. If you specify Start, the numbers will start with the number that you specify in the At field.

You can specify the format of the page number in the Number Format field. The options are standard Arabic numerals, Roman uppercase and lowercase, and alphabetic uppercase and lowercase. By the way, the Number Format field is also used to specify the numbering format of the page number used in a running head.

Running Heads

A *running head* is a paragraph that ends with a paragraph marker and can be formatted just like a paragraph. Running heads, however, differ from normal text paragraphs in that they are printed on almost every page of a document, are printed outside the normal text area, and can be staggered between left and right pages. Running heads are rarely printed on the first page of a document, and with Word first-page printing can be suppressed.

A running head can print the title, author name, company name, or any other information that is the subject of a document. A book, for instance, could have chapter titles printed on each page or the book title on the left page and the chapter title on the right page. You can also include page numbers, dates, and times in the running head. You can even use the Dateprint and Timeprint glossary entries to print the most current date and time.

Running heads are often referred to as headers and footers because you can control whether they are printed at the top or bottom of the page. You can also control whether they are printed to the left, centered, or to the right.

Because running heads print outside the normal text area defined by the margin settings, they can print close to the edge of the paper. A running head can hang to the left or right of the left or right margin, if you wish.

Think of running heads as another form of paragraph that is formatted with most of the same commands used to format paragraphs, and you will find them easy to set up.

The Running Head Commands

The running head commands are located in the Format menu under Format Running-Head and Format Division Margins commands. Use the Format Running-Head command to assign a paragraph as a running head and adjust the position of the running head in the Format Division Margins Running Head Position fields.

Selecting the Page Location The Format Running-head command, shown here, is used in the same way that the Format Paragraph command is used. Select the paragraph that is to be formatted as the running head; then open the running head menu and select the options. When ENTER is pressed, the paragraph is assigned as a running head.

```
FORMAT RUNNING-HEAD position: Top Bottom
     odd pages:(Yes)No  even pages:(Yes)No  first page: Yes(No)
```

The top line of the command assigns the paragraph to either the top or bottom of the page. The bottom commands are used to control even- and odd-numbered pages for back-to-back printing and to control the printing of the first page.

Note that besides the front-page control, the command lets you assign four running head positions: the top and bottom of odd pages and the top and bottom of even pages. Beyond these four positions, the look and design of the running head is controlled by regular paragraph formatting. For example, you assign centering or right alignment with the Format Paragraph command.

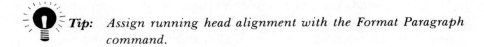

Tip: *Assign running head alignment with the Format Paragraph command.*

Adjusting the Page Position   The Format Division Margins command contains two fields that let you adjust the vertical location of a running head. You can use them when a running head contains more than one line and is overlapping the text at the top or is printing too low at the bottom.

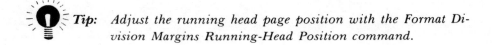

Tip: *Adjust the running head page position with the Format Division Margins Running-Head Position command.*

The running head commands in the Format Division Margins menu are shown in the bottom line of the following illustration and are covered later in this section.

```
FORMAT DIVISION MARGINS top: 1"      bottom: 1"     left: 1"     right: 1"
                 page length: 11"     width: 8"      gutter margin: 0"
          running-head position from top: 0.5"       from bottom: 0.5"
```

The Running Head Position Indicators

When the style bar is on, a code will appear to the left of a running head that indicates its position on a printed page. You set the style bar in the Window Options command by answering Yes to the Style Bar option. The codes displayed in the style bar are as follows:

Top Running Heads:

t   Prints on odd- and even-numbered pages and possibly the
            first page

tf   Prints on the first page only

to   Prints on odd-numbered pages and possibly the first page

te   Prints on even-numbered pages

Bottom Running Heads:

b   Prints on odd- and even-numbered pages and possibly the
            first page

bf   Prints on the first page only

bo   Prints on odd-numbered pages and possibly the first page

be   Prints on even-numbered pages

Creating the Running Head

It is usually best to create running heads before you start typing the text of your document. If you decide to create them later, move to the top of your document and place the running heads as the first lines of text. This makes them easy to find and change if necessary.

You should know about one trick to creating running heads. You should format the running head before you type its text. This will make it easier to align the components of your running heads. Look at the running head examples in Figure 12-4. Note that the text and page number of the top one are right-justified, while the page number in the middle one is centered. To set the tabs for these components, use the ruler at the top of the Word screen.

Tip: *Apply the running head format to a blank paragraph before you type the text of the running head.*

However, keep in mind that running heads do not use the margin settings of the Format Division Margins commands. They are measured from the edge of the paper, which means that the ruler for normal text will be different than the ruler for running heads. Thus it is best to apply the running head style to a paragraph before you attempt to set tab settings and type the text.

The procedure to set up a running head is outlined in the following steps,

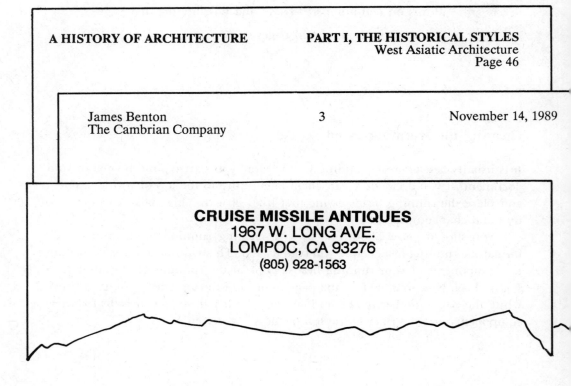

Figure 12-4. Running head examples

assuming that body text already exists.

1. Move to the top of the document.

2. Insert a blank paragraph marker.

3. Highlight the paragraph marker and then execute the Format Running-Head command.

4. Choose the position and pages for the running head and press ENTER.

5. The running head code will appear, and the ruler margin settings will change to reflect the size of the paper.

6. Set tab stops according to the style you prefer, samples of which are shown in Figure 12-4.

7. Type the text of the running head.

If you follow this procedure, you should not have trouble placing the components of your running head the first time you do so. Occasionally, though, you may want to run a print test to see if everything is properly set.

You can set all the running heads at once if you prefer. Placing them at the top of the document helps you keep track of them, and the code in the style bar helps you differentiate among them.

The Format Running-Head Options   To set the running head, place the highlight on the paragraph marker that will be the running head and open the Format Paragraph menu. In the Position field specify whether the running head will be at the top or bottom of the page. In the next fields, specify whether the running head will appear only on odd pages, only on even pages, or on both (answer Yes in both fields). If the running head is to appear on the first page, answer Yes in the First Page field. If the first page is a title page, you will probably want to answer No here.

When you press ENTER, a caret (^) will appear to the right of the running head, and if the style bar is on, the running head code will appear.

Speed formatting can be performed by pressing CTRL+F2 for headers and ALT+F2 for footers. The running head will have the default settings in the Format Running-Head menu (top on even and odd pages). If a style sheet is attached, the formatting style set in the gallery for the Running Head Standard option will be set (this will be covered later).

Tip: *Speed formatting of running heads can be performed with CTRL+F2 (top) and ALT+F2 (bottom).*

Trap: *Speed formatting uses the default settings in the Format Running-Head command or the format of the running head style in the style sheet.*

Formatting the Running Head

Once the running head is set and its code appears in the style bar, you can begin to format the running head text. This is a matter of applying character and paragraph styles. In the logo shown at the bottom of Figure 12-4, centered paragraph formatting was used. In the top example a flush right format was used, with an indent of 1 1/4 inches from the edge of the paper. This indent aligns the right edge of the running head with the right margin setting.

In some cases you may want the running head to hang out from the right or left of the body text. If so, simply set the indents with the Format Paragraph command, keeping in mind that they are measured from the edge of the paper.

 Tip: *Running heads can "hang" over the normal margins.*

If you want running heads to align with the body text, you can set either indents or tabs. Use tab stops if several components of a running head align in different ways at different positions, as shown in the middle example of Figure 12-4. Three tab stops are set in this running head: the first is left-aligned at the 1.25″ mark; the second is centered at the 4.25″ mark (the middle of an 8 1/2-inch-wide sheet); and the third is right-aligned at the 7 1/4-inch mark. The right and left tabs are at the same settings as the division margins. Of course you could decrease the left setting and increase the right one if you wanted the running heads to hang out beyond the text margins.

Use indents if your running head is to align with body text and will be either flush left or flush right. This is also important if the running head contains more than one line of text. When you use indents, you needn't press the TAB key to move the highlight to the position where the running head will align with the text.

If you use a laser printer, remember that most of them will not print within 1/4 inch of the left and right edges of the paper, which essentially makes an 8 1/2-inch-wide paper setting 8 inches wide.

Including Page Numbers, Dates, and Other Information

You can use any of the standard glossary entries such as Page, Date, Time, Date-print, and Timeprint in your running heads. Remember that Dateprint and Timeprint will print the date and time that is current at the time of printing. The date and time will not appear in the text on the screen.

 Tip: *Glossary entries such as Page, Dateprint, and Timeprint can be included in running heads.*

You can format glossary entries in running heads with any character formatting available to regular text. If page numbers are used, five different formats are available in the Number Format field of the Format Division Page-Number command. You can select Arabic, Roman, or numeric formats.

Don't forget that you can place any type of text before a page number or other glossary entry. For example, type **Page page** F3 to print the word *Page* followed by the page number. You can also use formats that include the chapter and page numbers, such as 1-1, 1-2, and 1-3, or the document title and the page number.

When Running Heads Don't Fit

Word automatically places running heads 1/2 inch from the top and bottom of the paper, which is fine when a running head consists of one line but poses problems when more than one line is used. With standard 12-point type, six lines of type are printed per inch. If the top margin is 1 inch and the top running head is placed 1/2 inch from the top, that leaves three lines for the running head from the top of the text, as shown in Figure 12-5. Because you need at least one space to separate the running head from the text, the top running head can be two lines at most unless you adjust the vertical position.

 Trap: *Running heads of more than one or two lines may overlap the text in top running heads or be pushed off the page in bottom running heads.*

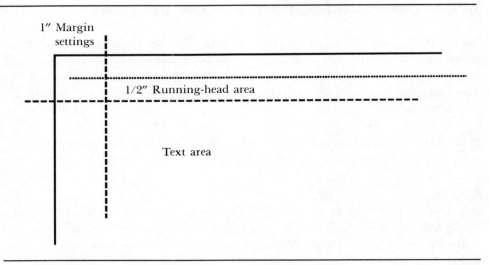

Figure 12-5. Allocated running head space

The footer is a different story. Word places it 1/2 inch from the bottom edge of the paper and won't print anything under that on some printers. So if you want a two-line bottom running head, you must adjust its vertical position.

Vertical Adjustments of the Top Running Head   You make vertical position adjustments in the Format Division Margins Running-Head Position From Top and From Bottom fields. Let's look at the company logo at the bottom of Figure 12-4 to see how the top running head can be adjusted. It starts at 1/2 inch from the top of the paper and contains four lines, so it intrudes into the text area by one line.

To make room for this running head, you could set the Running Head Position From Top field to 0.25 inch. This would allow the necessary space but will place the first line unattractively close to the top of the sheet. It is better to lower the top margin. In this case the top margin was reset to 1.5 inches and the running head position was left at 0.5 inch.

 Tip: *Lowering the top margin is one way to get multiple-line running heads to fit at the top of a page.*

Vertical Adjustments of the Bottom Running Head   When you set the bottom running head, remember that its first line starts printing at 1/2 inch from the bottom of the page. If there are additional lines, Word will attempt to print them below this line and closer to the edge of the paper. This is usually unattractive, and in the case of some laser printers, the bottom lines of the running head will not even print.

The solution is to adjust the Running-Head Position From Bottom field to a setting greater than 1/2 inch, depending on the number of lines in the running head. If the running head contains so many lines that it interferes with the text of the page, you should increase the bottom margin to accommodate it.

Trap: *Bottom running heads with multiple lines may "vanish" off the page if the Running Head Position From Bottom field is set too low.*

Back-to-Back Running Heads

When back-to-back printing is desired, you may need to stagger the running heads. For example, the document title may be on the even-numbered pages and the chapter title may be on the odd-numbered pages.

Tip: *To print running heads for back-to-back printing, format a running head as an odd or even page but not both.*

If page numbers are to be printed on the outside of every page, as shown in Figure 12-6, you must set up separate running heads. The following illustration shows how the running heads shown in the figure were set up.

```
 ┌═══[·········1··L·····2·········3···········4········5·········6·········7·R·┐
 │te ^→          (page)→                  THE·CARE·AND·FEEDING·OF·THE·MIND¶   │
 │to ^→        The·Nervous·System→                                   (page)¶  │
```

The top running head is labeled "te" and includes the glossary reference Page on the left. The book title is flush right. The running head was formatted with the

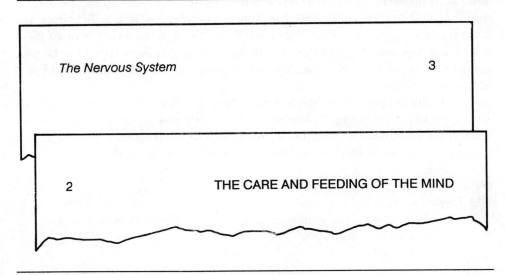

The Nervous System   3

2   THE CARE AND FEEDING OF THE MIND

Figure 12-6. Staggered running heads

Format Running Head Even Pages field set to Yes. The second running head has the Page glossary reference on the right with the chapter title on the left. It was formatted with the Format Running-Head Odd Pages field set to Yes.

Suppressing First Page Running Heads   Few documents require a header or footer on the first page. If this is the case, simply specify No in the First Page field of the Format Running-Head command when you format the even and odd page running heads.

Converting a Running Head Back to Regular Text

To convert a running head back to normal text, highlight the running head; then open the Format Running Head command and answer No to the Even Pages, Odd Pages, and First Page fields. If you delete the paragraph marker at the end of the running head, the paragraph will take on the formatting of the one below it. Press ENTER to then separate the two paragraphs. You can also simply delete the running head by highlighting it and pressing the DEL key.

Creating a Division Style

Style sheets play an important role in division formatting. You can change the standard settings so that all divisions will have the changes you make, or you can create special divisions for letterhead stationery, envelopes, and other uses, as discussed earlier.

Changing the Standard Division

Recall that Word automatically attaches the style sheet NORMAL.STY to every new document. Within this style sheet, you can make changes to the Standard Division automatically applied by Word. You may need to alter the Standard Division to accommodate a particular paper, company style or letterhead, or, in the case of Hewlett-Packard LaserJet printer owners, the width of the paper.

To change the Standard Division, go to the gallery and use the Insert command to create a new style. Call it SD in the Key Code field, choose Division in the Usage field, and choose Standard Division in the Variant field. Once the style is inserted, you can use the Format Division command in the gallery to alter the margins or other features to fit your needs.

Creating New Division Styles

To create new division styles, follow the normal gallery insert and format procedures just described. Use the variant that Word supplies and give the division styles names that relate to their purpose.

For example, create a division style that will use the entire screen to display the text. Margins set at 1/2 inch on the left and right sides will allow you to see as much of your document as possible when you are typing and editing. To print the document, you would apply the Standard Division or one that is especially defined for printing.

As an example, go to the gallery and use the Insert command to insert a new entry. Call it WD (for Wide Division) in the Key Code field. In the Usage field select the Division format. Use Word's suggested variant and enter an appropriate remark in the Remark field.

Using the Format Division command, change the left and right margins to 1/2 inch and press ENTER. Then exit the gallery, press ALT, and type **WD** to apply the new division style. To reapply the Standard Division at any time, type its key code name with the ALT key anywhere in the division.

Tips and Traps Summary

The Printed Page

Tip: Word's default margin settings print 60 characters per line and 54 lines per page when you use 8 1/2- by 11-inch paper.

Trap: Some laser printers may not print less than 1/2 inch from the edge of the paper.

Tip: Once the page size and margins are set, text placement is under the control of paragraph formatting.

Tip: Running heads print the same text on every page.

Tip: Running heads can be staggered left and right for even- and odd-numbered pages.

Tip: Page numbers can be printed separately or with running heads.

Tip: Gutters provide a staggered nonprinting zone for sheets that will be printed back-to-back. They are not used for single-sided printing.

Divisions and Pages

Tip: Think of a division as a page layout change that continues for several pages.

Tip: Altering the width of text for blocks smaller than a page is best done with paragraph indenting.

Tip: When a document requires a switch in paper type, specify Manual feed in the Print Options Feed field.

Page Size Alterations

Tip: Do not include the pin-hole stripe on tractor-feed paper in your page measurement.

Tips and Traps Summary (*continued*)

Tip: To calculate the value for left and right margin settings on some laser printers, subtract the size of the nonprinting zone from the actual margin size.

Margin Settings

Trap: The right margin is not a measure of the distance from the left edge of the paper, as is often done on typewriters. It is a measure from the right edge.

Tip: The gutter is added to the inside margin of even- or odd-numbered pages.

Special Page Sizes and Orientations

Tip: To hand-feed envelopes, specify Manual in the Feed field of the Print Options command.

Trap: You must select a landscape font to print in sideways mode on envelopes in Hewlett-Packard LaserJet and similar printers.

Tip: When you print envelopes on a Hewlett-Packard LaserJet, feed the envelope through the middle, not against the edge, of the manual feed slot.

Tip: Special page divisions, such as those to print envelopes, can be saved to a style sheet, a file, or glossary for future use.

Tip: Landscape mode on laser printers provides a way to print text in wide format or tables with numerous columns.

Tip: When you use landscape mode, swap the page length and width settings.

Tips and Traps Summary (*continued*)

Controlling Where Pages Break

Tip: Use CTRL+SHIFT+ENTER to add page breaks to text.

Tip: The Print Repaginate command calculates the current page breaks and inserts page break markers.

Trap: If new text is added inside the document, the page breaks become inaccurate. Another repagination is required to set new page breaks.

Page Numbering

Tip: Set page numbers with the Format Division Page-Numbers command only if you are not using running heads.

Tip: If you are using running heads, include the page number in the running head or create a separate running head for the page number.

Tip: When you use the Format Division Page-Numbers option, page numbers are measured from the top and left edge of the paper.

Trap: Be careful not to set page numbers in the text area or outside the printing zone of your printer.

Running Heads

Tip: Assign running head alignment with the Format Paragraph command.

Tip: Adjust the running head page position with the Format Division Margins Running-Head Position command.

Tip: Apply the running head format to a blank paragraph before you type the text of the running head.

Tip: Speed formatting of running heads can be performed with CTRL+F2 (top) and ALT+F2 (bottom).

Tips and Traps Summary (*continued*)

Trap: Speed formatting uses the default settings in the Format Running-Head command or the format of the running head style in the style sheet.

Tip: Running heads can "hang" over the normal margins.

Tip: Glossary entries such as Page, Dateprint, and Timeprint can be included in running heads.

Trap: Running heads of more than one or two lines may overlap the text in top running heads or be pushed off the page in bottom running heads.

Tip: Lowering the top margin is one way to get multiple-line running heads to fit at the top of a page.

Trap: Bottom running heads with multiple lines may "vanish" off the page if the Running Head Position From Bottom field is set too low.

Tip: To print running heads for back-to-back printing, format a running head as an odd or even page but not both.

13

Additional Page Enhancements

This chapter will cover additional methods for placing text on the pages of your documents. Not all users will need these techniques, however, and you may want to skip this chapter until you do.

Side-by-side paragraphs are covered first; then multiple-column text mode is discussed. Although these formats may seem similar, they are not. Side-by-side paragraphs are formatted with the Format Paragraph command, and multiple columns are set up in the Format Division Layout command. In addition, side-by-side paragraphs are meant for brief or temporary use, whereas multiple columns are meant for layouts extending over several pages.

Following these discussions, you will learn about footnote, line-numbering, and line-drawing techniques.

Side-by-Side Paragraphs

Side-by-side paragraph formatting may seem confusing at first, and it's easy to forget how to do it. Word 4, however, offers five styles that can help you set up two or three side-by-side columns. This section will also show you how to manu-ally set up columns not covered by the preset styles.

 Tip: *Word 4 comes with five premade styles to make side-by-side column formatting easy.*

Side-by-side paragraphs are two or more paragraphs that are indented to a certain width and then aligned at the top with other paragraphs. Figure 13-1 shows an example of triple side-by-side paragraphs. Notice how they are aligned at the top. When typed on the screen, however, these paragraphs look quite a bit different, as illustrated here:

```
▐──0·······1·····[·2········3····]···4·······5·······6·······7···
  This·is·a·standard·paragraph·with·left·and·right·margins·set·
  at·the·standard·1.25·inches.··The·typing·width·is·6·inches.¶
  ¶
  This·is·the·
  left·paragraph.··
  The·left·indent·
  is·0·and·the·
  right·indent·is·
  4.5·inches.¶
              This·is·the·
              middle·paragraph.··
              The·left·indent·
              is·1.8·inches·and·
              the·right·indent·
              is·2.5·inches.¶
                          This·is·the·right·
                          paragraph.··The·left·
                          indent·is·3.8·inches·
                          and·the·right·indent·
                          is·0.¶
  ◆
```

Take a look at this illustration. The top paragraph is of normal width. It is 6 inches wide and fits within the boundaries of left and right margins set at 1.25 inches. Now look at the middle paragraph. Because it is highlighted, the indented margin settings are visible in the ruler. The left indent is 1.8 inches, and the right indent is 2.5 inches.

The left, middle, and right paragraphs were formatted with the Format Paragraph command. This command, with the settings for the middle paragraph, is shown in the following illustration. The settings for the left and right indents are shown, and the side-by-side field has been set to Yes.

```
FORMAT PARAGRAPH alignment: Left Centered Right Justified
     left indent: 1.8"      first line: 0"        right indent: 2.5"
     line spacing: 1 li      space before: 0 li     space after: 1 li
     keep together: Yes(No)  keep follow: Yes(No)   side by side:(Yes)No
```

Setting the Format Paragraph command options is all you have to do to set up side-by-side paragraphs. The rest of the work involves calculating the following criteria, which you must establish before you set the options.

1. How many side-by-side columns will there be?

2. How wide will each column be?

3. How much space is required between each column?

Once you know these factors, you can enter the indent values for each paragraph in the Format Paragraph command. This is quite easy, as you'll see later on.

This is a standard paragraph with left and right margins set at the standard 1.25 inches. The typing area is 6 inches wide. Space between columns is 0.3 inches.

This is the left paragraph. The left indent is 0 and the right indent is 4.5 inches.	This is the middle paragraph. The left indent is 1.8 inches and the right indent is 2.5 inches.	This is the right paragraph. The left indent is 3.8 inches and the right indent is 0.

Side-by-side paragraphs usually look better when a proportionally spaced font is used, since more text will fit in a column. The columns above were formatted with a smaller font size.

Figure 13-1. Side-by-side paragraphs in printed form

Things To Know About
Side-by-Side Paragraphs

Side-by-side paragraphs will never appear side-by-side style on the screen. Instead, you type the paragraphs in order, and each one goes on top of the other. When you have finished typing, you can apply the side-by-side formatting. However, there are easier ways to apply this formatting than using the Format Paragraph menu for each paragraph. They will be discussed at the end of this section.

 Trap: Side-by-side paragraphs never display side by side on the screen, but they print correctly.

 Tip: Type side-by-side paragraphs in succession so that they appear one after the other on the screen.

When the side-by-side formatting is applied, each paragraph assumes a position on the screen relative to where it will print on the paper but not next to the previous paragraph, as was seen in the screen illustrated earlier. If a set of side-by-side paragraphs won't fit on one page, Word will move them to the next page. Note that you can apply side-by-side formatting to footnotes and running heads.

 Tip: If side-by-side paragraphs don't fit on one page, Word will move them to the next.

You can have multiple paragraphs in any one column, as shown in figure 13-2. Simply format the paragraphs with the appropriate indents for the column you want them to fall in. If the tops are to align with other columns, you may need to insert additional line spaces. To start a new set of side-by-side paragraphs, simply set the indents for the leftmost column.

Word supplies side-by-side styles that you can use if you want each column to be the same width. If you need to customize column width, you must calculate and format your columns with the Format Paragraph command. However, you can apply the supplied Word styles and then alter them to fit your needs.

This is the left paragraph. The left indent is 0 and the right indent is 4.5 inches.	This is the middle paragraph. The left indent is 1.8 inches and the right indent is 2.5 inches.	This is the right paragraph. The left indent is 3.8 inches and the right indent is 0.
	This is a second middle paragraph.	This is a second right-hand paragraph. An additional space was inserted to align it with the top of the second middle paragraph.
		This is a third right-hand paragraph.
This is the left paragraph of a new side-by-side paragraph set.	This is the middle paragraph of a new set.	This is the right paragraph of a new set.

Figure 13-2. Side-by-side paragraphs with multiple paragraphs per column

The Side-by-Side Styles

Word 4 supplies five side-by-side styles to facilitate paragraph formatting. These styles are available only if the SIDEBY.STY style sheet was merged with the NORMAL.STY style sheet. Merging has been described in the introduction to Part II. Each column is of equal width, with a 0.5-inch space between. The styles are as follows:

Two-column side-by-side paragraphs:

ALT+2+L   Formats the left paragraph with a 0.5-inch space between it and the right paragraph.

ALT+2+R   Formats the right paragraph.

Three-column side-by-side paragraphs:

ALT+3+L   Formats the left paragraph, leaving a 0.5-inch space between it and the center paragraph.

ALT+3+C   Formats the center paragraph, leaving a 0.5-inch space between it and the right paragraph.

ALT+3+R   Formats the right paragraph.

You can type each paragraph and apply the styles as needed, or you can apply the styles as you type. Remember that you can have several paragraphs in any one column. Simply apply the style for that column as often as needed or continue to create new paragraphs after the style has been applied. Each new paragraph will retain the formatting for that column until you apply another.

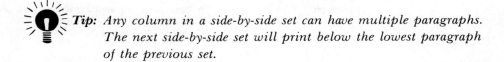 **Tip:** *Any column in a side-by-side set can have multiple paragraphs. The next side-by-side set will print below the lowest paragraph of the previous set.*

Creating Styles Manually

You must create side-by-side paragraphs manually when you need to customize column widths. To determine the column widths, follow these steps.

1. Determine the space between each column and multiply it by the number of spaces required, except for two-column formats. For example, three columns with 0.5-inch spacing between will require 1 inch of total space between columns.

2. Subtract this quantity from the normal text width, which is usually 6 inches if you have the margins set with Word's default settings.

3. Divide this leftover amount according to the width required for each column in the side-by-side paragraphs.

For example, three columns with a 0.5-inch space between in a 6-inch typing area will leave 5 inches of workable space. Assume that the first column will be 1.5 inches wide. Its left indent will be 0 and the right indent will be 4.5 inches. Remember, the right indent is measured from the right margin.

The middle column will have a left indent of 2 inches (the 1.5 inches of the left column plus the 0.5-inch space between). Of the 5 inches available for the columns, 3.5 inches remain. Assume that you want the middle column to be 2 inches wide. You must set the right indent at 2 inches from the right margin (the 4-inch mark).

The right column will have a left indent of 4.5 inches and a right indent of 0, giving it a width of 1.5 inches.

You can of course adjust these numbers in any way you want, but remember to consider the space between columns in the calculation. It is often easier to type the paragraphs and then adjust the column width by using a trial-and-error method with the Format Paragraph command. This method can be useful when you want to manually adjust columns in order to fit text a certain way.

 Tip: *It is often helpful to adjust columns by using a trial-and-error method when column widths must vary.*

You can use hyphenation to improve the appearance of your columns and make the text fit better inside them. You can also use proportionally spaced type fonts or smaller point sizes, as shown in Figure 13-1.

 Tip: *Hyphenation and the use of proportional fonts can improve the appearance and layout of side-by-side columns.*

Saving Side-by-Side Styles

Once you have established a custom set of side-by-side paragraphs, you may want to create a style for each, just as Microsoft has done with the styles supplied in the SIDEBY.STY style sheet. Keep in mind that each column must have its own style, so a three-column set will have three styles.

To speed the development of side-by-side columns that will have consecutive paragraphs, you can set up the column formats without text and then insert all three into the scrap and reinsert them as often as necessary.

 Tip: *A set of side-by-side paragraphs can be copied to the scrap and reinserted as a template for other sets.*

For example, if you need to create five consecutive sets of side-by-side paragraphs, first create the formats without text. Then highlight all three paragraphs and copy them to the scrap using ALT+F3. Next, press the INS key five times to insert five sets of blank, side-by-side formatted paragraphs. Then you can move back up to the top paragraph and start typing the text for each column.

You can even copy this set of side-by-side paragraphs to the glossary so that it is available when you need it. This method is superior to using style sheets because you don't have to apply three different styles. When copying formatted paragraphs to the glossary, be sure to include the paragraph marker because it contains the formatting information.

Memo Style Example   A sample memo is shown in Figure 13-3. Its two side-by-side columns appear on the screen, as shown in the following illustration:

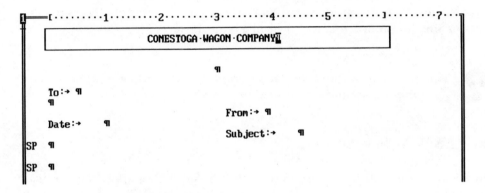

The columns are of the same width, with a 0.5-inch space between. Note that each paragraph is also formatted with hanging indents and tab stops so that text typed in the fields of each category will align. The box around the title was formatted with the Format Border command. The settings for each paragraph are shown in the next four illustrations when the Times Roman font and a Hewlett-Packard LaserJet printer are used. Except for the hanging indents and tab settings, which may differ, the indents will be the same for other printers.

The "To:" category:

```
FORMAT PARAGRAPH alignment: Left Centered Right Justified
        left indent: 0.5"       first line: -0.5"      right indent: 3.25"
        line spacing: 1 li      space before: 0 li     space after: 0 li
        keep together: Yes(No)  keep follow: Yes(No)   side by side:(Yes)No
```

```
┌─────────────────────────────────────────────────────────┐
│              CONESTOGA WAGON COMPANY                     │
└─────────────────────────────────────────────────────────┘
```

To: **JAMES JONES**   **From:**   **MICHAEL SMITH**
        OVERLAND TRAVEL CO.

Date: **NOVEMBER 18, 1848**   **Subject:** **Bid dated October 10 for 56
                                                    wagons.**

Figure 13-3. Side-by-side running heads for a memo

A tab is also set at the 0.5-inch mark.

The "From:" category:

```
FORMAT PARAGRAPH alignment: Left Centered Right Justified
    left indent: 3.9"        first line: -0.7"      right indent: 0"
    line spacing: 1 li       space before: 0 li     space after: 0 li
    keep together: Yes(No)   keep follow: Yes(No)   side by side:(Yes)No
```

A tab is also set at the 3.9-inch mark.

The "Date:" category:

```
FORMAT PARAGRAPH alignment: Left Centered Right Justified
    left indent: 0.5"        first line: -0.5"      right indent: 3.25"
    line spacing: 1 li       space before: 0 li     space after: 0 li
    keep together: Yes(No)   keep follow: Yes(No)   side by side:(Yes)No
```

A tab is also set at the 0.5-inch mark.

The "Subject:" category:

```
FORMAT PARAGRAPH alignment: Left Centered Right Justified
    left indent: 3.9"        first line: -0.7"      right indent: 0"
    line spacing: 1 li       space before: 0 li     space after: 0 li
    keep together: Yes(No)   keep follow: Yes(No)   side by side:(Yes)No
```

A tab is also set at the 3.9-inch mark.

Multiple-Column Layout

Multiple-column layout differs from side-by-side formatting in that the columns may extend over several pages. You can set up a complete document to print in this way. If you select two columns per page, Word will fill the first column on a page, then the second, and then start printing the next page.

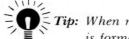 *Tip:* *When multiple columns are selected, the entire text of a division is formatted into columns.*

You can break columns before the end of a page to insert pictures or artwork. You can also place banners over multiple-column text by using running head formats. Note that column layout is a division command; that is, all text within the current division will be formatted to column mode.

 Tip: *Columns can be broken early on a page to leave white space for photographs and artwork.*

Commands for Setting up Multiple Columns

The multiple-column commands are found in the Format Division Layout menu, as shown in the following illustration. The bottom three options in this menu are used. In the Number of Columns field specify two or three (more than three are not recommended unless you are printing on wide paper or in small point sizes). You control the space between the columns by setting the Space Between Columns field. Use the Division Break field to break a column early.

```
FORMAT DIVISION LAYOUT footnotes: Same-page End
        number of columns: 1       space between columns: 0.5"
        division break:(Page)Continuous Column Even Odd
```

The Space Between Columns field uses a preset value of 0.5 inch unless you change it. When you press ENTER, the text in the current division is formatted to column mode and displayed on the screen as a single column of text (see Figure 6-10 for an example). When a Print Repaginate is performed and the style bar is on, Word will display a column break symbol beside each column break. The number of each column is displayed with this break symbol.

 Tip: *The column break symbol indicates which column is displayed on the screen for each page.*

Controlling Column Breaks

You can control where a column will break in order to leave white space for a picture or artwork. Follow these steps to break the column. In the Format Division Layout command, select Column in the Division Break field and press ENTER. Move the highlight to the break position and press CTRL+ENTER to insert a new division mark.

Adding a Full Line of Text Above Columns

You can use a running head to insert a full line of text above multiple columns. To do so, you must move the top margin of each column down to accommodate the running head, which can be several lines long.

 Tip: *Use a running head to insert a full-measure block of text above a multiple-column layout.*

The running head can be placed at the top of the first page only or on all pages. If the running head is to appear on the first page only, you must create a division break where the second page begins and reset the margins in the second division to exclude the running head.

 **Tip:** *To exclude the running head from subsequent pages, create a new division without it.*

To create the running head for the first page, first determine how much space it will need and how much the top margin must be adjusted down to accommodate it. Remember that 1 inch of text is equal to six lines of 12-point type. The default running head allows for three lines of text, so a six-line running head would require an extra 0.5 inch of space, plus a few lines to spare. For a six-line running head, you might want to set the top margin at 2 inches to start and then adjust it to fit.

After determining the proper top margin, you can format the text for multiple columns. To turn the running head off on the second page, first repaginate the document with the Print Repaginate command to locate the page breaks. At the break for page 2, insert a new division by pressing CTRL+ENTER. Use the Format Division command to restore the original top margin.

Line Numbering

Line numbering is mainly used in legal documents to position reference numbers in the left margin. The numbers do not appear on the screen but will be printed. If the Line Number field in the Options command is set to Yes, the current line number is displayed in the status line of the Word edit window. Line numbering in Word follows these rules:

- Only the body text of a document is included in line numbering. Running heads are not included.

- If you use the Space Before and Space After fields to include blank lines before and after paragraphs, they are not included in the line counts. Spaces between double- and triple-spaced lines of text are not counted either. Word only counts lines that have text or paragraph markers.

- Each horizontal line in side-by-side paragraphs is counted as one line.

- If line numbers exceed three digits, Word may truncate them to two digits if there is not enough room in the margin.

- Word will start renumbering on each page or at each new division.

- Line numbers can be continuous between divisions.

- If Print Selection is used, only the selected text is printed, and the first line is numbered 1.

- If a range of pages is printed, the numbers assigned to the lines on the printed pages are calculated from the first page of the document, even though that page may not be printed.

- Line numbering can be incremented to 5, for example, so that every fifth line is numbered.

The Format Division Line-Numbers command is shown here:

```
FORMAT DIVISION LINE-NUMBERS: Yes No          from text: 0.4"
        restart at:(Page)Division Continuous   increments: 1
```

Choose Yes to turn line numbering on and use the From Text field to adjust the position in the left margin where numbers will print. The numbers can be as large as the left margin, though you should leave at least 0.4 inch for the revision bars and paragraph borders. The numbers are right-aligned.

Use the Restart At field to specify whether line numbering will restart on each new page or at the beginning of the division. If you select Continuous, line numbering continues from the number in the previous division. You can insert a nonnumbered division between two numbered divisions. However, Word will continue numbering where it left off in the last numbered division.

Use the Increments field to specify the increment of lines that will be numbered. The default is 1, but you can alter it to 5 or 10 if necessary.

Footnote Techniques

In Word footnotes are more than just numbers in the document and notes at the end of the page. Word footnotes are dynamic. If a footnote is bumped to the next page because text has been added, the footnote text follows it and is printed at the bottom of the new page. If a footnote reference mark is deleted, the footnote text is also deleted.

As you can see, the footnote reference mark and the footnote text are linked. You can automatically jump to the text of a footnote by placing the cursor on the footnote number and selecting the Jump Footnote command. Similarly, you can jump from the footnote text to its reference mark in the body text by using the same command.

 Tip: *The footnote reference mark and the footnote text are dynamically linked.*

 Trap: *Deleting a footnote reference mark also deletes the footnote text.*

 Tip: *Use the Footnote Jump command to jump back and forth between footnote reference marks and their corresponding text.*

You can make footnotes visible on the screen by opening a footnote window. This lets you see some of the footnotes for the current page. As you scroll through the document, the footnotes for each page are listed in the window. You can also "zoom" the window to view footnotes that don't appear on the page.

 Tip: *A footnote window makes the footnotes for the current page visible. As new pages are viewed, the contents of the footnote window change accordingly.*

Footnotes can be printed at the bottom of the page on which their reference mark appears or at the end of the document. Word prints a line over the footnote text if it is printed at the bottom of a page.

 Tip: *Footnotes can be printed at the bottom of each page or at the end of the document.*

You can control the type fonts and styles of footnote reference marks and text with standard styles called Footnote and Footnote Ref in the gallery. If you change the format of these styles, all footnotes and footnote reference marks will take on the new format. For example, you might want to change the footnote reference mark to superscript text.

Tip: The gallery contains the standard Footnote and Footnote Ref styles that are used to set default fonts and character styles for footnotes and reference marks.

Footnote reference marks do not have to be numbers. You can use special symbols, such as the asterisk and dagger, as is common when simple notes are used to make additional points about a topic in the text.

Tip: You can footnote notes and comments with symbols other than numbers, such as the asterisk and dagger.

The Footnote Commands

There are only four footnote commands in the Word menu system, but because they are found in various menus, they can be confusing. The first command, Format Footnote, is used to create a footnote reference mark and the footnote text. It is illustrated here:

FORMAT FOOTNOTE reference mark: █

Use this command when you insert a footnote. If you don't specify a number, Word will insert the next available footnote number. The number 1 is used if you are formatting the first footnote.

Tip: Word will number footnotes automatically.

Use the Jump Footnote command to jump back to the body text after typing the footnote text, or to jump to the footnote text when the footnote number is highlighted. The command is shown here:

```
JUMP to: Page  Footnote
```

The next footnote command is in the Window Split command, shown here:

```
WINDOW SPLIT:  Horizontal  Vertical Footnote
```

You can create a footnote window by selecting Footnote. Word will ask you for the line number on which to split the window but will suggest the line of the highlight.

The last command is in the Format Division Layout command, as illustrated here:

```
FORMAT DIVISION LAYOUT footnotes:  Same-page  End
```

Use the Footnotes field to specify whether footnotes will appear on the same page or at the end of the document.

Changing the Style of the Footnote

In addition to the footnote commands, the glossary holds the two standard footnote styles, one for the footnote reference and one for the footnote text. You may now want to change the character formatting of these styles so that all your footnotes will be formatted in the proper way.

Enter the gallery by pressing ESC and typing **G**. Execute the Insert command and proceed to fill out the options. You needn't enter anything in the Key Code field because all footnotes will automatically be given this style. Choose Paragraph in the Usage field. In the Variant field press F1 and choose Footnote Ref to ensure that all footnote reference marks receive this style. You can fill in the Remark field as you wish. Press ENTER to insert the style.

Next, choose Format and the Format Character menu will appear automatically because this is a character style. Choose Superscript in the Position field. In the Font Name field choose a suitable font that will allow superscript formatting and a small typeface. In the Font Size field choose an 8-point type or something close to it, if available. Press ENTER when you are done.

To format the footnote text, choose the Gallery Insert command to insert a paragraph style. You needn't fill out the Key Code field. Choose Paragraph in the Usage field. In the Variant field press F1 and select Footnote. Fill out the Remark field as you wish and press ENTER to insert the new style.

At the gallery menu, select Format Character to assign the character format to the footnote text style. In the Font Name and Font Size fields select the same options that you used in the footnote reference style if you want them to look the same.

The Footnote Creation Process

The footnote creation process is like a loop that first assigns a footnote number, then drops you down to the footnote window to type the footnote text, and then brings you back up to the text so that you can continue typing.

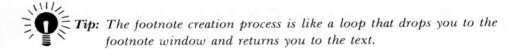 *Tip: The footnote creation process is like a loop that drops you to the footnote window and returns you to the text.*

At the place in the text where you want to insert a footnote, execute the Format Footnote command. If you press ENTER immediately, Word will insert the next available footnote number and place the highlight in the footnote window so that you can type the text. You can, however, insert your own code. You may want to enter an asterisk or another character to create a "note" at the bottom of the page.

When Word moves the highlight to the footnote window, it automatically inserts the correct footnote reference. You need only type the text of the footnote. (An example of the Word footnote window was shown in Figure 6-9.)

After you type the text, execute the Jump Footnote command to jump back to the body text to continue typing. That's all there is to it. Word handles the numbering and placement of footnotes automatically. If a footnote reference is moved to another page because new text is inserted, Word automatically updates the location of the footnote text.

Tip: *If footnotes are moved, Word automatically renumbers all the footnotes.*

Tip: *To jump to a footnote, place the highlight on the footnote number and execute the Jump Footnote command.*

If you need to change the text of a footnote, open the footnote window by selecting the Window Split Footnote command. You can enter the number of the location where the footnote window should be placed, or you can use a mouse to point to the split location in the right border of the Word edit window. Press ENTER to open the window.

A footnote window will appear with a line of dashes across the top. To edit text in the window, use the same procedure that you use to edit any other text in Word.

You can zoom the footnote window to cover the entire screen by pressing CTRL+F1 when the highlight is in the footnote window. To close a footnote window, choose Window Close when the highlight is in the footnote window.

Tip: *To zoom the footnote window, press CTRL+F1 when the highlight is in the window.*

Another method of editing a footnote, and a convenient way to get to the footnote window, is to place the highlight on the reference number for the footnote to be formatted and use the Jump Footnote command. The footnote window opens immediately, and you can edit the footnote.

To delete a footnote, simply place the highlight on the footnote reference mark and press the DEL key. To print the footnotes at the end of a document, choose the Format Division Layout command and select End in the Footnotes field.

Vertical and Horizontal Line Drawing

Line drawing on pages is covered here because it is one technique that you can use to enhance the appearance and readability of your documents. You've already seen how to draw boxes and lines around paragraphs in Chapter 11. That chapter also covered the use of the underline tab leader for creating form lines. Word also has line-drawing techniques that let you use the arrow keys to draw lines anywhere on the page.

Your printer may not support these techniques, or it may need to be switched to a different font set that does support them. Look at ASCII codes 176 through 223 in Appendix B. These are the line-drawing characters that your printer must support. In the printer manual, find a font set that includes these characters and select it either by setting dip switches or by making a front panel selection.

 Tip: *You may need to adjust dip switches to allow your printer to support line-drawing characters.*

Owners of Hewlett-Packard LaserJet Series II printers must obtain the font sets that have H2 in their name. For example, H2LASMS.PRD is the Z cartridge font set that supports line draw characters. Early releases of Word did not include these drivers, so you may need to contact Microsoft.

 Tip: *The H2 fonts are required on Hewlett-Packard LaserJet Series II printers for line draw character support.*

You can use line drawing in a number of ways, the most important of which is the creation of forms. You can use the underline tab leader to create fields on forms that are to be filled in, as shown in Figure 13-4, and you can use the

```
Name Last: _____  First: _____

Address: _____

City: _____  State:___  Zip: _____
```

Figure 13-4. Underscore tabs example

vertical line tab to create vertical column separators, as shown in Figure 13-5.

Word's line-drawing feature was used to create the product survey form shown in Figure 13-6. The boxes were created first, and then the text was typed in. Figure 13-7 shows an office floor plan with the names of office occupants and their phone extensions.

With the line-drawing techniques, you can of course create many types of charts, forms, flowcharts, and diagrams. (Chapter 23 deals with the creation of forms using many of the line-drawing techniques discussed here.)

Underlined Forms

The underline tab, covered in Chapter 11, is reviewed here for those putting together forms or other documents that require lines. To set underline tabs, choose the underline in the Format Tab Set Leader Char field. Press the TAB key to draw the horizontal line to the tab marks. If the underline characters do not appear on the screen, set the Visible field of the Options command to Partial. They will print either way, however.

Vertical Tabs

The vertical tab will insert a vertical line in the position specified. It is not, however, a tab stop on which you can type text. Instead, the vertical tab stop should be positioned before or after the tab stop that you use to align a column.

```
   Employee            Birth Date        Hire Date

   Ann Hoffman         February 8        7/16/79
   Jim Theis           November 12       1/23/80
   Judy Sacks          December 3        10/14/85
   Tom Anders          June 15           5/18/83
```

Figure 13-5.   Vertical tab example

```
                    P R O D U C T    S U R V E Y

                Did you enjoy our product?         [ ]

        Did it perform the way you expected?       [ ]

            Do you feel the price was fair?        [ ]

        Would you recommend it to your friends?    [ ]
```

Figure 13-6.   Line draw examples

In Figure 13-5 vertical tab stops were set at the 0, 2-, and 4-inch positions on the ruler. The text columns were then aligned at the 0.5-, 2.5-, and 4.5-inch positions.

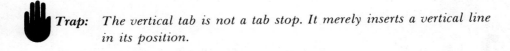 ***Trap:***   *The vertical tab is not a tab stop. It merely inserts a vertical line in its position.*

Jim x234	Jane x236	Joe x230
Office Phone Extension Numbers		
Bob x231	Ann x233	Kay x232

Figure 13-7. Line draw examples

You set vertical tabs in the same way that you set horizontal tabs (discussed in Chapter 11). Remember to press SHIFT+ENTER at the end of each line if you want to continue the paragraph with vertical tabs.

Drawing Keys

Enter the line-drawing mode for Word by pressing CTRL+F5. When you are in this mode, the highlight will move in unfamiliar ways until you get the hang of it. If you need lines around text, it's best to draw the lines first because line-drawing mode either deletes or readjusts text in odd ways.

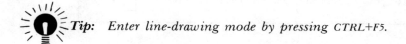 *Tip:* *Enter line-drawing mode by pressing CTRL+F5.*

Use the arrow, HOME, and END keys to move the highlight around the screen. As it moves, the highlight draws the line that you selected in the Options Line-draw Character field. Word will automatically create corner characters if you "turn a corner" with the highlight. For example, if you are drawing a box and start at the upper-right, Word will draw horizontal lines as you move left. When you move down, Word will automatically insert a corner bracket and then start inserting vertical lines as the highlight moves down.

 Tip: *Word creates corner brackets when you change directions with the arrow keys.*

There are a few things that you should know about line-drawing mode.

- Draw the lines before you type the text associated with them. Plan the appearance of the box and text beforehand.

- Use only monospaced fonts when you print. The monospaced font on the screen lets you see how boxes and text align, and printing with a proportional font will throw this alignment off. You can draw boxes around proportional type, but that requires a lot of of trial and error.

- Avoid paragraph formatting and styling such as indents, centering, and above and below spaces.

- Use only the arrow, HOME, and END keys when drawing. Never use ENTER to start a new line of text.

Changing the Line Character   The default line in Word is the single line. To choose other line types, open the Options menu and press F1 with the highlight on the Linedraw Character field. The menu is illustrated here:

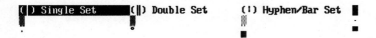

The first three sets — Single, Double, and Hyphen/Bar — will automatically insert corner brackets when you "turn a corner," as described earlier. The other sets are full blocks that, when selected, will type only the character shown.

      Trap: *Some line draw characters are single characters only, not sets.*
                 Word will not insert corners when they are used.

Line Draw Examples   Open a blank edit window to experiment with the line-drawing characters. It's not important to have any particular design in mind. Just draw with the arrow keys to get a feel for how they work.

Press CTRL+F5 to enter line-drawing mode. The line draw flag LD will appear in the status line. Try creating a box by pressing each of the arrow keys, and watch what happens as you create corners. Try pressing HOME and END to create lines that stretch to the beginning and end of lines.

Press ESC to exit line-drawing mode; then open the Options menu and change the line draw character to the Double Set or Hyphen/Bar Set. Press CTRL+F5 to reenter line-drawing mode and experiment further.

Deleting Lines and Inserting Characters   When you have finished drawing lines, press ESC to return to the normal edit mode. You can now try typing and deleting characters. Normally, when you type characters between other characters, the characters to the right are adjusted to the right. However, this is not desirable when lines have been drawn. You must turn on overtype mode by pressing F5. You can then move to a box or another shape and type characters. Be careful not to type over lines. If you do, simply delete the characters, place the highlight on the line position, press CTRL+F5 to return to line-drawing mode, and re-create the line.

Trap: *Use overtype mode when you type characters on a screen that has lines. Insert mode will move lines out of position.*

To delete lines, use the same editing techniques that you use to delete normal text. When Word draws lines, it automatically creates a paragraph marker at the end of the line. This paragraph marker will be adjusted as parts of lines are removed.

Tip: *If you delete a line, you may need to insert a blank space to re-align characters to the right.*

Tips and Traps Summary

Side-by-Side Paragraphs

Tip: Word 4 comes with five premade styles to make side-by-side column formatting easy.

Trap: Side-by-side paragraphs never display side by side on the screen, but they print correctly.

Tip: Type side-by-side paragraphs in succession so that they appear one after the other on the screen.

Tips and Traps Summary (*continued*)

Tip: If side-by-side paragraphs don't fit on one page, Word will move them to the next.

Tip: Any column in a side-by-side set can have multiple paragraphs. The next side-by-side set will print below the lowest paragraph of the previous set.

Tip: It is often helpful to adjust columns by using a trial-and-error method when column widths must vary.

Tip: Hyphenation and the use of proportional fonts can improve the appearance and layout of side-by-side columns.

Tip: A set of side-by-side paragraphs can be copied to the scrap and reinserted as a template for other sets.

Multiple-Column Layout

Tip: When multiple columns are selected, the entire text of a division is formatted into columns.

Tip: Columns can be broken early on a page to leave white space for photographs and artwork.

Tip: The column break symbol indicates which column is displayed on the screen for each page.

Tip: Use a running head to insert a full-measure block of text above a multiple-column layout.

Tip: To exclude the running head from subsequent pages, create a new division without it.

Tips and Traps Summary (*continued*)

Footnote Techniques

Tip: The footnote reference mark and the footnote text are dynamically linked.

Trap: Deleting a footnote reference mark also deletes the footnote text.

Tip: Use the Footnote Jump command to jump back and forth between footnote reference marks and their corresponding text.

Tip: A footnote window makes the footnotes for the current page visible. As new pages are viewed, the contents of the footnote window change accordingly.

Tip: Footnotes can be printed at the bottom of each page or at the end of the document.

Tip: The gallery contains the standard Footnote and Footnote Ref styles that are used to set default fonts and character styles for footnotes and reference marks.

Tip: You can footnote notes and comments with symbols other than numbers, such as the asterisk and dagger.

Tip: Word will number footnotes automatically.

Tip: The footnote creation process is like a loop that drops you to the footnote window and returns you to the text.

Tip: If footnotes are moved, Word automatically renumbers all the footnotes.

Tip: To jump to a footnote, place the highlight on the footnote number and execute the Jump Footnote command.

Tip: To zoom the footnote window, press CTRL+F1 when the highlight is in the window.

Tips and Traps Summary (*continued*)

Vertical and Horizontal Line Drawing

Tip: You may need to adjust dip switches to allow your printer to support line-drawing characters.

Tip: The H2 fonts are required on Hewlett-Packard LaserJet Series II printers for line draw character support.

Trap: The vertical tab is not a tab stop. It merely inserts a vertical line in its position.

Tip: Enter line-drawing mode by pressing CTRL-F5.

Tip: Word creates corner brackets when you change directions with the arrow keys.

Trap: Some line draw characters are single characters only, not sets. Word will not insert corners when they are used.

Trap: Use overtype mode when you type characters on a screen that has lines. Insert mode will move lines out of position.

Tip: If you delete a line, you may need to insert a blank space to realign characters to the right.

III

Productivity Tools

You have already been introduced to many of the features covered in this part of the book. This part will provide additional information and more details on how to take advantage of features that can help you be more productive and make Word easier to use.

Chapter 14 starts out by organizing the control features of Word into one chapter. These features are used to set various modes or change the display of the screen.

In Chapter 15 you'll learn how to manage glossaries and get some practical tips and glossary examples. Chapter 16 then covers style sheets, which were used extensively in Part II to make paragraph formatting easier. You'll see how glossaries and style sheets can work together.

Chapter 17 explains how windows are used, a subject often confusing to novice users. You'll see how to best use them in your day-to-day tasks. Chapter 18 explains Word's outlining facility, a feature that you will want to use when you create and write documents that have several sections and more than a few pages.

Chapters 19 and 20 cover printing and such Word tools as the spelling checker, thesaurus, hyphenation, document summaries, and others.

14

Controlling Word's Features

This chapter will help you in several ways. It contains information that will enable you to customize Word by altering the appearance of the screen, the unit of measure, and the way Word operates, among other things. This chapter also combines information about many of the feature alterations covered in previous chapters, so you can use it as a quick reference in the future.

In this chapter you'll see how to control various screen, typing, and printing options. For example, you can change the background color, turn off the window borders, alter the menu display, change default tab sizes, and do a number of other things. These changes can then be saved in a special file called MW.INI that Word uses to remember the settings from the last Word session. The options saved in this file are listed in Table 14-1, which also lists most of the options covered in this chapter. To save these settings, exit Word properly with the Quit command.

 Trap: *To save current settings for the next session, you must exit Word in the proper way with the Quit command.*

459

Table 14-1. Options Saved with the Quit Command

Options

visible:	None Partial Complete
printer display:	Yes or No
menu:	Yes or No
menu color:	F1 to select color options
mute:	Yes or No
display:	graphics or text mode
screen borders:	Yes or No
line numbers:	Yes or No
date format:	MDY or DMY
time format:	12 or 24
decimal character:	period or comma
default tab width:	preset to 0.5″
measure:	In Cm P10 P12 Pt
linedraw character:	press F1 to select
summary sheet:	Yes or No
cursor speed:	preset to 3
speller:	location of dictionary

Print Options

printer:	press F1 for list
setup:	press F1 for list
draft:	Yes or No
hidden text:	Yes or No
widow/orphan control:	Yes or No
feed:	Manual Continuous Bins Mixed

Window Options

show hidden text:	Yes or No
background color:	press F1 for list
style bar:	Yes or No
ruler:	Yes or No

Quit also records the following:

- The name of the document in window 1. When Word is started again with the /L parameter, this file is loaded.

- The default directory/path in Library Document Retrieval.

- The document's position in the window.

- The document's read-only status.

- The status of the overtype mode.

Using Several Versions of Word

There is a good chance that you will need to use Word in several different ways and thus need to alter various options at different times. For example, you may prefer to work with a 10-pitch measure sometimes and a 12-pitch measure at other times. Or you may want a screen without borders when you write programs, whereas you may want the scroll bar capabilities of the left border when you work with long documents.

You may want to start Word in different ways, which you can do by creating several versions of Word's startup parameter file. This file is normally called MW.INI, but through special DOS batch files, you can have several versions on hand to install Word the way you want, depending on the work you are doing.

Tip: *Word's startup parameter file is called MW.INI.*

MW.INI is created or altered every time you use the Quit command to exit Word, which means that any changes made to options during a session are saved in the file for the next session. For example, the name of the file you were working on is saved. If you start Word again with the /L option, the file will be reloaded. If you want to revert to Word's original default settings, simply delete MW.INI at any time. Word does not require this file in order to start; it simply creates a new one at the end of a session for future reference.

Trap: *Removing MW.INI removes alterations to Word's operating environment. Word will revert to its default settings.*

To have different sets of options, say, one for programming and one for writing documents and letters, you can create two or more versions of MW.INI by using a special DOS batch file trick. This trick involves having several INI files on hand with different filenames. You then use batch files to rename one of the "standby" files MW.INI before starting Word and then restore its original name when quitting Word.

This trick will be covered in the last section of this chapter. First, each option and setting will be discussed so that you can determine which ones are best for your use.

The Options, Windows, and Print Menus

Almost all the settings used to change the look and feel of Word are set in three menus: the Options menu, the Windows menu, and the Print menu. All three are shown here:

```
OPTIONS visible: None Partial Complete          printer display: Yes(No)
  menu: Yes(No)          menu color: 7          mute: Yes(No)
  display: Graphics(Text) screen borders:(Yes)No line numbers:(Yes)No
  date format:(MDY)DMY   time format:(12)24     decimal character:(.),
  default tab width: 0.5" measure:(In)Cm P10 P12 Pt linedraw character: (|)
  summary sheet:(Yes)No  cursor speed: 3        speller: C:\WORD
```

```
WINDOW OPTIONS window number: 1    outline: Yes(No) show hidden text:(Yes)No
              background color: 0  style bar:(Yes)No          ruler:(Yes)No
```

```
PRINT OPTIONS printer: H2LASMS              setup: LPT1:
  copies: 1                                 draft: Yes(No)
  hidden text: Yes(No)                      summary sheet: Yes(No)
  range:(All)Selection Pages               page numbers:
  widow/orphan control:(Yes)No             queued: Yes(No)
  feed: Manual(Continuous)Bin1 Bin2 Bin3 Mixed
```

The Transfer Options menu, which lets you change the default directory used by Word to store files, is not illustrated.

Each option in these menus is covered in this chapter, though not necessarily in the order that is shown in the menu. Instead, this chapter is divided into topics that cover operating parameters, screen appearance, typing features, and printer options.

Operating Parameters

The operating parameters let you control the sound, ruler, measure, and other features that are shared by other Word commands or used throughout the system.

The Measure of Word

The default measure in Word is inches. Other units of measure include centimeters, 10-pitch characters, 12-pitch characters, and points. If you switch to other units of measure, Word automatically converts existing measures and changes the measure of the ruler at the top of the edit window.

Remember that 10-pitch type is often called 12-point type, and 12-pitch type is often called 10-point type. Points are usually used to measure a character's size, whereas pitch is used to measure the number of characters per inch. There are 10 characters per inch for 10-pitch, 12-point Pica type and 12 characters per inch for 12-pitch, 10-point Elite type.

 Tip: *Ten-pitch type, often called Pica, has 10 characters per inch.*

 Tip: *Twelve-pitch type, often called Elite, has 12 characters per inch.*

Each of the measures is described here:

Inches	Choose In in the Options Measure field to select inch measuring. Inch measurements are then displayed with the quotation mark ("). The ruler accurately displays inches in this mode.
Centimeters	Choose Cm in the Options Measure field to select centimeter format. There are 2.54 centimeters per inch. Centimeter measurements are indicated with the "cm" marker. The relation of the ruler to inches is accurate, although the numbers in the ruler have no relation to the centimeter measure. However, they can be used to count the number of characters.

Pica(P10)	Choose P10 in the Options Measure field to select Pica 10-pitch characters. Pica measures are indicated with "p10." Pica 10-pitch characters are displayed accurately on the screen. The ruler accurately displays inches in this mode.
Elite(P12)	Choose P12 in the Options Measure field to select Elite 12-pitch characters. The "p12" indicator will then be used in all measure fields. The numbers on the ruler no longer represent inches but can be used to count characters. Word will show sentence and paragraph line breaks accurately.
Points	Choose Pt in the Options Measure field to select point sizing. There are 72 points per inch. The "pt" indicator will be used in all measure fields.

Setting the measure can be confusing if you are not familiar with different settings. However, those familiar with different forms of measure will probably already know how to make use of them and may want to skip this section.

What happens when a different measure is set is not always readily apparent. One reason for changing the measure is to do paste-up work or to create files for precision typesetting machines. Specific measurements that correspond to the measurements used on pasteboards are required to properly align text in Word.

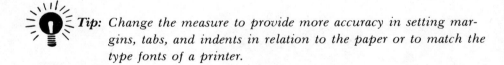 *Tip: Change the measure to provide more accuracy in setting margins, tabs, and indents in relation to the paper or to match the type fonts of a printer.*

Typesetters and graphics artists may balk at working with inches and increments of inches. They usually prefer more exact measures. Points provide the most accurate unit of measure in Word and should be used if you are preparing a document for a typesetting machine.

If you have a daisy wheel printer or a printer that supports both 10- and 12-pitch fonts, the measure can be changed to support 12-pitch Elite-type wheels. You can then view line breaks on the screen the way they will print. The ruler bar also changes, as described in the next section.

Changing the unit of measure changes the settings in all Word options that use a measurement. For example, an indent of 1.2 inches set in the Format Paragraph menu will change to 3.05 when you select centimeters, to 86.4 when you select points, and to 12 when you select Pica(P10). More to the point, you can specify a measure in these options that relates exactly to the measure on the paper you are working with.

 Tip: *Word calculates the conversions when you switch to other measure formats.*

The Pica(P10) setting is most convenient when you use the standard Courier 10-pitch type style. The measure will then represent the number of characters, which is helpful when you set tabs to fit columns and indents that hang.

 Tip: *The Pica(P10) setting is best when you work with 10-pitch monospaced fonts. Elite(P12) is best for 12-pitch monospaced fonts.*

The Ruler

For some reason, the default settings of Word do not include a ruler in the upper edit window border. You should include the ruler as soon as possible. It is used to set tabs and is helpful when you are setting indents and typing characters in Word. To turn the ruler on, set the Window Options Ruler field to Yes.

The ruler will show the tab stops for the current paragraph, as well as normal or indented margin positions, as shown here.

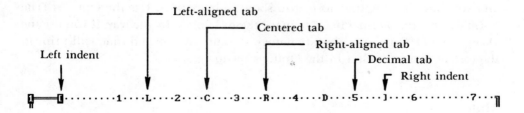

Word: Secrets, Solutions, Shortcuts

The left square bracket is the position of the left indent, and the right square bracket is the position of the right indent. Normally these rest on the margin settings. Tab stops are indicated by *L* for left-aligned, *C* for center-aligned, *R* for right-aligned and *D* for decimal-aligned. If tab leaders are set, the type of leader (dot, hyphen, or underline) is shown next to the tab stop.

The ruler attempts to show the measure of the type pitch you are using, whether it is 10- or 12-pitch. If you are using monospaced 10-pitch fonts, the ruler will accurately show the characters per inch. If you are using a 12-pitch font, each dot on the ruler still represents a character, but the numeric indicators no longer represent inch marks. When the P12 measure is selected, the right margin extends farther out, and the numbers in the ruler represent the number of characters, not the measure of the line. Line breaks for 12-pitch characters will show on the screen as they will break on the printed page.

 Trap: *When you use the P12 measure, the numbers on the ruler no longer represent inch marks.*

You can turn off the ruler by clicking both mouse buttons (or the center button on a three-button mouse) in the upper-right corner of the screen. Click either button to turn it back on. The ruler will always display when you are setting options such as tabs.

Date and Time Formats

The default settings for time and date in Microsoft Word are the standard American date format (month-day-year) and 12-hour time format. You can change the date format to an international style that displays or prints the day-month-year, and you can alter the time format to show 24-hour time. Use the Options Date Format and Time Format fields to make these changes. By the way, if you use the Dateprint and Timeprint glossary names, the current date and time will print in the format that you select in the Options menu.

Mute

Word will beep annoyingly if you make a mistake, try to execute a command incorrectly, or try to type text at an inappropriate time such as when a menu is displayed. This beep is sometimes helpful, but you can turn it off by selecting Yes in the Options Mute field if you need quiet.

Default Directory

The default directory is the hard-drive directory where Word loads and stores your files automatically, unless you change it by specifying another location in the Transfer Load or Transfer Save command. The use of directories for storing files is usually limited to hard-drive users. Floppy-drive users format other diskettes as alternative storage areas.

You can alter the default directory for each Word session by changing the Transfer Options Setup command to the directory you want to use. This directory only stays active during the current session, and the alteration made to the Setup field is not saved when you exit Word with the Quit command. (The use of directories is covered in Appendix A.)

 Trap: *Changing the default directory with the Transfer Options Setup field only alters the directory for the current Word session.*

Screen Appearance

The appearance of the screen can be altered to suit your personal taste or a particular task that you may be doing. The screen is divided into the edit window and the command area, each of which has special options that can be altered.

Background Color

If you have a color monitor, you have a choice of background colors. If you have an RGB monitor, you must start Word with the /C option to be able to select different background colors. If you have an Enhanced Graphics Display, you can start Word in any mode to choose colors.

Word's standard background color is black; however, studies have shown that blue has a relaxing effect on humans, so you may want to choose it. Your choice may depend on the type of lighting that you have in your office. For example, fluorescent lighting tends to be green, so you might want to choose an opposite color such as amber. If your office has incandescent lighting, which tends to be orange, you may want to choose a green background. Either way, your personal preference is all that matters.

Set the background color in the Window Options Background Color field. Press F1 to see a table of colors and use the arrow keys to move through them.

The Style Bar

The style bar displays the type of style attached to a particular paragraph. When the style bar is turned on, the style code appears just to the left of the first line of a paragraph in a two-character-wide bar that runs down the left side of the edit window, just inside the window border.

 Trap: *If you are using style sheets, turn the style bar on to properly display the current style codes.*

The style bar also shows the type of running head assignment. These codes are "t" for top running head, "b" for bottom, "e" for even pages, "o" for odd pages, and "f" for front page. Two of the codes may be combined. Turn the style bar off to get two extra characters of display if you are using a wide-margin format and need to see as many horizontal characters as possible.

Turn the style bar on or off by setting the Window Options Style Bar field to Yes or No.

Window Borders and Scroll Bars

The borders of the edit window can be removed to allow an extra two lines of text and an extra two characters per line to appear on the screen. The trade-off, however, may not be worth it if you have a mouse. Mouse users will lose the ability to scroll in the left window border and the ability to split and close windows in the right and bottom borders.

 Trap: *If borders are removed, you cannot use the mouse for scrolling and window control.*

Turn window borders off and on with the Options Screen Borders command. If window borders are turned off and a window is split with the Windows Split command, the borders will reappear if you place one of the windows in full-screen mode by using the Zoom feature (CTRL+F1) or if you close one of the windows.

Command Area

There are several ways to display and control the command menu.

Menu Off and On   Set the command menu on or off with the Options Menu command. If the menu is off, an extra three lines of text are visible on the screen, which is preferable. Press ESC to display the menu at any time.

   If you have a mouse, you will not be able to select directly from the menu if it is turned off. Instead, you must first press the ESC key to select it or, better, click anywhere in the bottom line of the screen to display the menu. You can then click on the menu selection you want. After you execute a command, the menu will disappear. If you do not execute a command, however, you must press the ESC key to turn the menu off.

 Tip: Mouse users can click in the bottom line of the screen to display the menu instead of pressing the ESC key.

Menu Color   Select the menu color in the Options Menu Color field. Press F1 to see a selection of colors. Only the color of the command names and fields will change, but this separation can help you distinguish between the different options in the menus.

Key Status Indicators   The key status indicators are displayed in the bottom line of the screen when a particular key is depressed or an option is selected. Toggle keys are keys that you press once to turn a mode on and press again to turn it off. When the mode is on, the key status appears. The key status codes are listed in Table 14-2.

   The codes appear next to each other in the status line of the screen. Some keys are mutually exclusive and will overwrite each other, such as the EX and CS codes. Other keys have precedence over keys sharing the same status line position.

 Trap: Some key status indicators may overlap others.

Line and Column Numbering   The line-numbering option is used to print pages with numbers before each line, which is often done for legal documents. The Options Line Numbers field will display the line number of the highlight in the status indicators at the bottom-left line of the screen. You can use this to

Table 14-2. Key Status Codes

Code	Key/Commands	Meaning
CS	SHIFT+F6	Column select mode
EX	F6	Extend highlight mode
NL	NUM LOCK	NUM LOCK key on
SL	SCROLL LOCK	SCROLL LOCK key on
CL	CAPS LOCK	CAPS LOCK key on
OT	F5	Overtype mode on
LD	CTRL+F5	Line draw mode on
RM	SHIFT+F3	Macro record mode on
ST	CTRL+F3	Macro step mode on
ZM	CTRL+F1	Windows are zoomed
MR	ESC+F+M	Revision marking is on

determine which line of a page you are on. Keep in mind that this line number does not account for space before, space after, and double-spaced lines.

 Trap: The line number in the status line does not account for space before, space after, and double-spaced lines.

Typing Area Options

A number of typing area options can be selected. Special characters can be displayed to show spaces, tabs, and paragraph markers. In addition, display modes can be set to optimize the typing area.

Graphics/Text Mode

You can switch between graphics and text modes if you have an appropriate monitor by pressing ALT+F9 or by setting the Options Display field to either Graphics or Text. You can take advantage of an increase in scrolling speed by using the text mode. In text mode, however, certain character formatting does not appear as it will when printed, as it does in graphics mode. Instead, highlights are used to display character formatting.

The mode selected will be stored in the MW.INI file, so the next Word session will start in that mode unless you change it. Remember that you can start in graphics mode by using the /G option and in text mode by using the /C option. If the MW.INI file is removed, Word starts in text mode.

With some graphics cards, you may not be able to properly switch between modes. For example, when you start the Hercules graphics card with the /H option for 43-line mode, you will not be able to switch to text mode because that is a 25-line mode.

Printer Display Mode

If you are using monospaced printing fonts, you don't need to use printer display mode. If you are using proportionally spaced fonts, however, this mode can help you align tables and determine where lines will break.

Word cannot properly display on the screen how proportional fonts will print. Instead, printer display mode is a tradeoff that at least lets you see the line breaks. In addition, you can determine tab alignments when you are developing tables.

 Tip: Use printer display mode to show line breaks and tab alignments when you are using proportional fonts.

In printer display mode lines may extend past the margins, but they won't print past the margins. Word has predetermined how the proportional characters will fit on the paper and simply shows where the lines will break. You may need to scroll horizontally to see the ends of the lines.

To select printer display mode, press ALT+F7 or use the Options Printer Display field. The ALT+F7 key combination makes it convenient to switch between the two modes for editing.

A Wide Screen Division

If you want to see as much text on the screen as possible, change the margins in the Format Division Margins menu to a smaller size, say 0.75 inch. This will set the ruler indent marks at the 0- and 7-inch positions. When you are ready to print, you can convert the division margins back to the original setting. (Chapter 12 discusses how to create a division style for both the wide screen and normal print modes.)

Tabs

The normal tab setting in Word is 1/2 inch. If you set tab stops in the Format Tab Set menu, all tabs to the left of your custom tab stops are removed, but the default 1/2-inch tabs to the right remain. You can change the default tab stops to other values by altering the Options Default Tab Width field.

Invisible Characters

The following illustration shows six special characters used by Word that can indicate the presence of normally nondisplayable characters, such as spaces, carriage returns, tabs, and hyphens. Hidden text can also be displayed as a symbol.

```
Newline·character↓
Paragraph·markers¶
Space·····dots¶
Tabs→→      ¶
Op-tion-al·hyph-enation¶
Hidden·↔·text¶
```

The display of character symbols is controlled by the Options Visible Command field. Three options are available: None, Partial, and Complete. If None is selected, no special characters are displayed, and the screen appears uncluttered. When Partial is selected, the paragraph, newline, and optional hyphen characters are displayed in the text. When Complete is selected, all characters are displayed. Although the tab mark is displayed, the tab leader characters are not. However, they will still print. You can tell which leader is used by looking in the ruler bar at the tab mark, which will display a dot, hyphen, or underline before it.

It is recommended that you use the Complete setting because you will be able to determine excess space characters and tabs. Complete is also useful for table development because it displays the tabs and the newline character.

When a paragraph is left- and right-justified, Word may insert spaces between words. When Complete is set, these Word-inserted spaces will show as blank spaces, while spaces that you type will still show as dot characters. Thus you can determine where Word is placing its spaces and alter the setting by removing your own if necessary.

The Partial option is for those who find the space and tab marks too confusing. The screen does look less cluttered with this setting, so you may prefer to use it.

Hidden text is displayed as the double arrow shown in the illustration. However, the symbol is only visible if hidden text is actually hidden. The other option is to show the hidden text on the screen, which you can select in the Window Options menu. When hidden text is displayed on the screen, a dotted line will appear under it to show that it is hidden during printing.

Printer Options

You can set a few options with the Print Options menu. These are covered next.

Printer Type and Setup

The printer type selected in the Print Options menu has an important effect on the type fonts, sizes, and styles available to you in the Format Character menu. Make sure that the printer description file selected is the one for your printer. If it is not, expect unpredictable printing results.

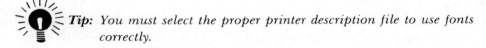

Tip: You must select the proper printer description file to use fonts correctly.

In the Print Options menu press F1 in the Printer field. Choose your printer from the list or, if it doesn't appear, copy the printer description file from the Word Printer disks with the DOS COPY command or the Word SETUP program, as discussed in Chapter 1.

Number of Copies

You can print multiple copies of each page by entering the appropriate number in the Print Option Copies field. Word prints one copy before starting the next so that the pages are properly paginated.

Hidden Text

You can print hidden text for your own use or for others to read by selecting Yes in the Print Options Hidden Text field.

Range

The print range has to do with how much of a document you want to print. You can highlight a specific paragraph or block of text and print just that block by choosing Selection in the Print Options Range field. If you choose Selection, it will stay active until you change the Range field back to All. This can cause problems when you decide to print the entire document and the highlight is on a paragraph marker, for example. A page will be ejected with nothing on it! Don't forget to set this option back.

Trap: Alterations to the Print Options Range field stay active during Word sessions until altered. If a document doesn't print correctly, check this field.

The Pages option of the Range field is tied to the Page Numbers field. If you choose Pages, you must specify the numbers of the pages you want to print. If you want to print one page, type its number in this field. If you want to print specific non-contiguous pages, such as pages 1, 5, and 7, separate the page numbers with commas. If you want to print a continuous range of pages, such as 5 through 10, use a hyphen. For example, type **5-10** in the field to print pages 5 through 10.

 Trap: *In the Print Options Page Number field use commas to select individual pages and hyphens to select ranges of pages.*

You can mix commas and hyphens. For example, type **1,2,5-10,16-18** to print pages 1, 2, 5 through 10, and 16 through 18. You can also print specific divisions by specifying the division number preceded by a *d*. For example, to print pages 2 and 3 in division 1 and pages 10-15 in division 2, you would type **2,3d1,10-15d2.**

Pages specified in the Page Numbers field will remain intact during a Word session. If you want to print the entire document at some point, make sure to select All in the Range field. The page numbers will be removed when All is selected.

Widow/Orphan Control

The Widow/Orphan Control field in the Print Options menu lets you control whether Word will print a single line of a paragraph by itself on a new page. Answer No to this option if you want to print as much text on the page as possible. However, a more visually appealing document is produced when this option is set to Yes. (Chapter 12 covered this subject in detail.)

Feed

You can control how Word will feed paper as it prints. The options are listed here:

Manual   This mode, which allows you to insert the sheets of paper manually, is handy if the top sheet is letterhead stationery and the second sheet is not.

Continuous   The printer will print continuously in this mode. Tractor-feed paper is assumed.

Bin1   The printer will feed paper from bin 1 of a sheet feeder for all pages.

Bin2   The printer will feed paper from bin 2 of a sheet feeder for all pages.

Bin3   The printer will feed paper from bin 3 of a sheet feeder for all pages.

Mixed   The printer will feed from bin 1 for the first sheet and bin 2 for the second sheet, which is handy when the first sheet is letterhead stationery.

Batch File for Changing Word Parameters

As discussed earlier, you can create a batch file that allows you to have several versions of Word available for use. You can set up Word with any of the options discussed in this chapter and then exit with the Quit command to create a new MW.INI file. You then rename this file with a special standby name that pertains to the type of setup you have. Then you can reenter Word and create other setup options, quitting and saving them as other MW.INI files to be renamed.

You can then create a batch file at the DOS level that temporarily renames one of the standby setup files to MW.INI and then starts Word. Word then executes with the parameters of that file. When you exit Word, the batch file resumes and restores the standby name to the file so that you can use others.

For example, assume that you create a special set of options for Word that are to be used when you write program code. After setting the options in the Word command menus as described in this chapter, you exit Word with the Quit command. At the DOS level, MW.INI is renamed PROG.INI. You then create a batch file called PROG.BAT that executes the commands shown in the following illustration:

```
RENAME MW.INI TEMP.INI
RENAME PROG.INI MW.INI
WORD
RENAME MW.INI PROG.INI
RENAME TEMP.INI MW.INI
```

To start Word using the setup file for programming, type **PROG** to run the PROG.BAT batch file. You can create other setup routines and batch files in the same way. The batch files would have the same lines, but the names of the standby files would be different.

Here's how the program works. It first saves any existing MW.INI file as a temporary file called TEMP.INI. It then renames the standby file PROG.INI to MW.INI. When you start Word, it will use the setup parameters of this file. When you exit Word, the batch file resumes execution at the fifth line. The MW.INI file is renamed PROG.INI, placing it in standby status, and then the temporary file TEMP.INI is restored to its original MW.INI status.

To create this batch file, use Microsoft Word and save the file with the Transfer Save Formatted field set to No. If you are using subdirectories, keep in mind that the MW.INI file is stored in the WORD directory. This is the directory where you must place your standby files.

Tips and Traps Summary

Trap: To save current settings for the next session, you must exit Word in the proper way with the Quit command.

Using Several Versions of Word

Tip: Word's startup parameter file is called MW.INI.

Trap: Removing MW.INI removes alterations to Word's operating environment. Word will revert to its default settings.

Tips and Traps Summary (*continued*)

Operating Parameters

Tip: Ten-pitch type, often called Pica, has 10 characters per inch.

Tip: Twelve-pitch type, often called Elite, has 12 characters per inch.

Tip: Change the measure to provide more accuracy in setting margins, tabs, and indents in relation to the paper or to match the type fonts of a printer.

Tip: Word calculates the conversions when you switch to other measure formats.

Tip: The Pica(P10) setting is best when you work with 10-pitch monospaced fonts. Elite(P12) is best for 12-pitch monospaced fonts.

Trap: When you use the P12 measure, the numbers on the ruler no longer represent inch marks.

Trap: Changing the default directory with the Transfer Options Setup field only alters the directory for the current Word session.

Screen Appearance

Trap: If you are using style sheets, turn the style bar on to properly display the current style codes.

Trap: If borders are removed, you cannot use the mouse for scrolling and window control.

Tip: Mouse users can click in the bottom line of the screen to display the menu instead of pressing the ESC key.

Trap: Some key status indicators may overlap others.

Trap: The line number in the status line does not account for space before, space after, and double-spaced lines.

Tips and Traps Summary (*continued*)

Typing Area Options

Tip: Use printer display mode to show line breaks and tab alignments when you are using proportional fonts.

Printer Options

Tip: You must select the proper printer description file to use fonts correctly.

Trap: Alterations to the Print Options Range field stay active during Word sessions until altered. If a document doesn't print correctly, check this field.

Trap: In the Print Options Page Number field use commas to select individual pages and hyphens to select ranges of pages.

15

Automatic Typing
with Glossaries

Glossaries are the equivalent of shorthand in Microsoft Word. You can create abbreviations for long words, sentences, and other blocks of text. Word does the typing for you if you type the abbreviation and press the F3 (Glossary Expand) key. Instructing Word to type the contents of a glossary entry is referred to as *expanding* the glossary. So this chapter is really about the F3 (Glossary Expand) key and about how you can manage the glossary features of Word to your benefit.

Entries in glossaries are sometimes referred to as *boilerplates*. You could conceivably type a complete contract or proposal by just using single-word glossary names. The F3 key would expand the glossary names into the standard paragraphs that you normally use to word the contract or proposal.

Every time you type a glossary name and expand it with the F3 key, the exact text placed in the glossary is typed again. This helps to eliminate typing mistakes and promote consistency within documents. Glossary entries can be used to set up standard text blocks for proposals, contracts, forms, form letters, and other such documents.

The glossary creation and expansion process is shown in Figure 15-1. You type the text for glossaries in the edit window, highlight it, and then either copy

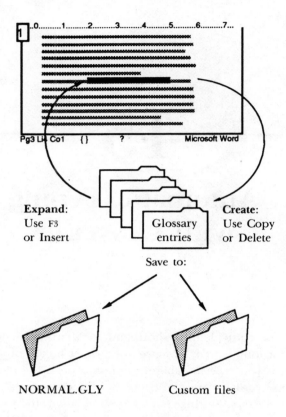

Figure 15-1.   The glossary creation and expansion process

or delete it to the glossary. The glossary can be saved as a disk file after new entries have been added. Later, you can expand glossary entries into the text with the Word Insert command.

The Glossary as a Storage Place

Any word, phrase, sentence, or other block of text that must be typed again is a candidate for inclusion in the glossary. Getting one of these blocks of text in the glossary is simple. You use the Copy command in the Word command menu.

The glossary can be considered another type of scrap. Unlike the normal scrap, which loses its contents if something else is deleted, the glossary can hold onto a block of text much longer. Text inserted in the glossary will be retained throughout a Word session, and you can save it permanently by saving the glossary before exiting Word.

 Tip: *Copy text to the glossary instead of the scrap if it must be saved for a long period.*

Think of the glossary as a sort of clipboard. You can copy or cut text from its current location and place it in this clipboard until you find another place in the text to insert it. You can have as many glossary entries as you want at any one time, and you can create more than one complete glossary. You might have one glossary for legal documents, another for business documents, and a third for personal documents.

 Tip: *Because each glossary entry has its own name, any number of them can be stored at a time.*

Most glossary entries will be stored in the standard glossary called NOR-MAL.GLY. Word will attach this glossary to all your documents unless you specify that another glossary should be used. Switching to another glossary is easy with the Word commands. If you think that you will need more than one glossary, consider which text blocks will be stored in NORMAL.GLY and which will be stored in other, special-purpose glossaries.

Tip: *NORMAL.GLY is attached to all documents unless you specify another file.*

The Glossary Commands

The glossary commands are located in the Copy, Delete, Insert, and Transfer options in the Word Command menu. Copy, Delete, and Insert are not really menus because they are used exclusively for moving text in and out of either the glossary or the scrap. The Copy, Delete, and Insert commands are illustrated here:

COPY to: {}

Enter glossary name or press F1 to select from list

DELETE to: {}

Enter glossary name or press F1 to select from list

INSERT from: {}

Enter glossary name or press F1 to select from list

Notice that each command recommends the scrap, indicated by the curly brackets. You can, however, enter a glossary name for each command or press F1 to see a list of glossary entries.

The Transfer Glossary Command menu is also used when you work with glossaries. This menu allows two glossaries to be merged and also allows glossaries to be saved and cleared. It is illustrated here:

TRANSFER GLOSSARY: Merge Save Clear

In addition to these commands, the Print Glossary command will print a list of glossary names and the expanded text that goes with them.

Creating Glossary Entries

Create glossary entries by first typing the text on the screen and then either copying or deleting it to the glossary. The steps that you use depend on what you intend to do with the text. If you have just typed a passage that you decide should be placed elsewhere in the text, use the Delete command to delete the passage to the glossary. If you want to have a duplicate of the passage elsewhere in the text or in another document, use the Copy command.

 Tip: *A glossary can hold a block of text that you decide to place elsewhere in your document at a later time.*

You can create glossary entries "on the run" as you type. In this way you can build a large repertoire of glossary entries. Users often create glossary entries ahead of time by opening a Word file and typing the text blocks that go in the glossary. In this case either Copy or Delete can be used to place the text in the glossary. If you use Copy instead of Delete, the screen will still hold the text blocks, which can be saved as a backup file for the glossary.

The Delete Process

To delete a block of text to the glossary, highlight it, press DEL and type a suitable name for the entry. If the name already exists, Word will prompt you with "Enter Y to overwrite glossary, or Esc to cancel." The ESC key allows you to try a different name.

The Copy Process

Use the Copy command to copy the highlighted text block to the glossary. The original block stays intact within the text. The previous paragraph explains the message that Word displays if you attempt to give a glossary entry a name that is already in use.

Naming Glossaries

Though glossary names can be up to 31 characters long, only one word is allowed, so you may need to use underscores or hyphens for spaces if you want names composed of two or three words. Typically, glossary names are two or three characters or short words, like the built-in Word glossary entries Date, Time, and Page.

Trap: *Glossary names must be one word long, but you can use hyphens or underlines to simulate spaces.*

Use unique names for your glossary entries that both describe the text and are easy to remember. You may want to develop a coding system if you will have a lot of glossary entries. For example, text blocks for proposals and contracts could have numbers that relate to their normal position in the proposal or contract. It may be helpful to create a table of contents for the glossary entries that includes the glossary name plus a short description of the text in the glossary.

Trap: *The more glossary entries you have, the harder they are to remember. Use unique names or develop a coding system.*

Saving the Glossary

If you save a glossary with a name already in use, Word will overwrite the existing glossary entry. However, Word will ask you if you want to copy over the existing entry before it does so. You can review your glossary entry names by selecting Insert, Copy, or Delete and pressing F1. This will display a list of the current entries.

Trap: *You cannot use a glossary name more than once within the same glossary file.*

If you attempt to quit Word when entries have been made to the glossary but have not been saved, Word will ask you if you want to save the entries in the glossary file. This procedure will be covered shortly.

Retrieving Glossary Entries

When you open a new file, NORMAL.GLY is automatically attached to it, and all the entries in the normal glossary are available for your use. If you need to use another glossary file, you can use the Transfer Glossary Clear and Transfer Glossary Merge commands. The process of retrieving glossary entries is called "expanding the glossary" because the text referred to by the glossary name is typed.

You can use the F3 (Glossary Expand) key or the Insert command when retrieving glossary entries. Both can be used to perform the same task, but they have specific functions. Use the F3 (Glossary Expand) key if you know the name of the glossary entry that you want to use. Simply type the name and press F3 in the text location where you want the glossary to be typed. If you don't know the name of the glossary, use the Insert command from the Word command menu. You will see the display illustrated here:

INSERT from: {}

Enter glossary name or press F1 to select from list

Press F1 to see a list of possible glossary choices. Your screen may appear as shown in the following illustration, with the standard glossary entries supplied by Word. If other glossary entries have been created or another glossary has been merged, you will see other entries.

page	footnote
date	dateprint
time	timeprint

When the glossary list is displayed, use the arrow keys to move the highlight to the entry you prefer. Press ENTER to then insert the contents of that glossary entry into the text at the location of the highlight. Make sure that the highlight is positioned exactly where you want the glossary text before you execute the command.

Word's Built-in Glossary Entries

Word's six built-in glossary entries are listed below with a short description of their use.

Page	Use the Page glossary entry to insert page numbers into the text, either in a running head or in any position where the glossary is expanded. Type **page** and press F3. Word will insert (page) into the text. During printing, Word will insert the proper page number.
Footnote	Use the Footnote glossary entry to insert a footnote reference mark for one that was accidentally deleted. Word will insert a new footnote number in the proper order.
Date	Word will type the date currently set in your computer system if you type **date** and press F3.
Dateprint	Dateprint will print the current date at the time a document is printed in the position of the glossary expansion.
Time	Word will type the time currently set in your computer system if you type **time** and press F3.
Timeprint	Timeprint will print the current time at the time a document is printed in the position of the glossary expansion.

Leaving Entries Unexpanded

One way to use glossary entries is to leave them unexpanded until you are ready to print. This will keep documents uncluttered and reduce their scroll length until the last minute. When you are ready to print, simply place the highlight to the right of the glossary entry name or press the F7 or F8 key to highlight the entire glossary entry; then press F3.

 Tip: *You can leave glossary names unexpanded until the last minute to keep the document uncluttered and take up less memory space.*

You can use the Search command to search for the glossary entries that you want to expand in your text. When an entry is found, Word highlights the entire word. Press F3 to expand the entry.

Managing Glossary Files

This section covers how to make changes to an existing glossary, whether it is the normal glossary or one that you have customized. You can edit or delete any entry in a glossary.

Finding Out What's in a Glossary

You will need to know what is in a glossary so that you do not duplicate entry names and you know what is available for expansion. To view the contents of a glossary, select Copy, Delete, or Insert and press F1 to see the list.

You can print a glossary by executing the Print Glossary command. The current glossary is printed. The glossary entry name is printed on the left and the text of the glossary entry is printed below and indented 1/2 inch. Page breaks in the entries are shown as <Page>, and division breaks are shown as <Division>.

Editing Glossary Entries

To edit a glossary entry, first place the highlight on a blank line in your document or open a new window. Press INS in the command menu and type the name of the glossary entry. The entry is typed in the edit window. You can make any changes that you want by using the normal editing process. When done, use the Copy or Delete command to place the edited text back in the glossary. Word will ask if you want to overwrite the existing version, to which you can answer Yes.

 Trap: *Edited glossary entries will copy over the original unless you give the edited version a new name.*

Deleting Glossary Entries

Glossary entries are deleted with the Transfer Glossary Clear command. But you must be careful when using this command. It is designed to accept a list of glossary entries to remove from the current file. Each entry is typed and separated from the next by a comma. If you press ENTER without typing any entries, Word will attempt to delete the entire glossary, though it will prompt you before doing this.

 Trap: *Pressing ENTER without specifying an entry will delete all entries when you are using the Transfer Glossary Clear command.*

Glossaries tend to become cluttered over time as entries outlive their usefulness, and eventually you need to do a little housecleaning on a glossary file. Use the Print Glossary command to produce a list of the glossary contents and the expanded text under each entry. You can then delete entries by typing each name in the field of the Transfer Glossary Clear command.

Discarding Session Entries

When you are working with Word, you may create glossary entries for use only during that session. If you don't want to save these entries for later use, simply quit Word without saving the glossary. When Word prompts you to save the glossary, answer No.

 Tip: *You can choose not to save your most recent glossary entries by quitting Word without saving the glossary.*

A problem occurs if you want to save some glossary entries but not others. In this case you must use the Transfer Glossary Clear command to selectively delete the unwanted entries before saving the glossary file.

Changing Glossary Files

Changing to a different glossary file in Word is a little awkward because you must clear the current list of entries before loading a new list. In some cases you may want to merge the entries in another file with those in your current list. You can accomplish both of these tasks with the Transfer Glossary Merge command. The former, however, requires clearing the screen beforehand.

Removing the Current Glossary Entries   To remove the current glossary entries in order to make room for another set, use the Transfer Glossary Clear command. Press ENTER at the field response to clear all entries in the current file. If you want to save some of the entries, selectively delete the ones you don't want.

Loading and Saving Glossary Files   Use the Transfer Glossary Merge command to load a new glossary file after another set of entries has been deleted, as just described, or to merge a new set with the current one, as described next.

   If you want to create an entirely new file, clear off the current set and begin creating the new entries. When the set is the way you want it, use the Transfer Glossary Save command to save the new set under a new glossary filename. This filename should reflect the type of entries in the file; for example, LEGAL, MED-ICAL, OFFICE, and PERSONAL are appropriate names for glossary files. Word will supply the .GLY extension to saved glossary files.

 Tip: *To create a new set of glossary entries, clear the old set, type the new set, and save the file under a different name.*

Combining Two Glossary Files   Word lets you merge some of your existing files with a new set. As discussed previously, you can delete some entries in your current glossary file and then merge another glossary file to create a new file that combines the entries of both. After merging the two files, use the Transfer Glossary Save command to save the combined file under a new name.

   When you merge glossary files, entries with similar names will be replaced by the entry in the merged file. Existing entries with the same names in the glossary are removed. To prevent entries from being overwritten, expand them into the edit window and then copy them back into the glossary with a name that is not in the glossary list being merged.

 Trap: *When you merge glossaries, the new glossary copies over entries with similar names.*

Using Glossaries Instead of Styles

Styles are a powerful feature in Word. However, complex text blocks may require the use of many different styles. A table, for example, may require a style for the title, another for the column headings, and still another for the columns. This is where glossary entries can help.

Glossary entries can be thought of as a style enhancement feature. They can store a combination of styles into a *template* that can be expanded and then filled in by the user. For example, here is a table with three distinct paragraphs, each formatted with a different style and tab settings.

The combined table was stored in a glossary entry called INC_STAT_DATA. The expanded and filled-in version is shown in its final printed state in Figure 15-2.

Tip: *Glossaries can store a combination of styles, making them more convenient than individual styles from the style sheet.*

FOUR-YEAR SUMMARY OF INCOME STATEMENT DATA

(in thousands of dollars)

	1982	1981	1980	1979
Net Sales	$600	$400	$300	$250
Cost of Goods Sold	$384	$244	$187	$145
Income Before Taxes	$18	$16	$12	$10

Figure 15-2.   A filled-in table template from the glossary

In this example, an equation produced with special character formatting is saved to a glossary.

```
▌━━[········1········2·····L·3········4········5·········]········7···▐
▌  Odds·in·favor·of·an·event·=→number·of·favorable·ways↓
▌  →                          number·of·unfavorable·ways▓
```

It produces the printout shown in Figure 15-3. All the text is formatted to Times Roman 12-point type. The statement "number of favorable ways" is formatted as underlined text in superscript mode. The statement "number of unfavorable ways" is also formatted in superscript mode but is placed on the next line down. This type of equation obviously takes a number of steps to set up, but you can save it to a glossary as a template without the text.

Glossary Examples

This section will serve two purposes. First, it should give you some ideas for your own glossary entries. Second, you may be able to use some of the entries described here for your own use.

Tables such as the one shown in Figure 15-2 make it apparent that glossaries are not just for long-winded text blocks. You will often need to apply multiple

$$\text{Odds in favor of an event} = \frac{\text{number of favorable ways}}{\text{number of unfavorable ways}}$$

Figure 15-3. An equation with multiple formats from the glossary

formats to characters and paragraphs, making the application of styles from a style sheet only one step of the formatting process. However, you can use glossaries to type blocks of text, complete with the proper formats in template form, and then simply fill in the blanks.

Simple Glossaries

Figure 15-4 shows the simplest type of glossary entries. These are entries that are typed often and may require a font or format change.

Multiple-Line Glossary Entries

The examples shown in Figure 15-5 illustrate a number of other useful types of glossaries. Many of the parts of a standard letter, such as the opening and closing, can be inserted in the glossary. Your name and address, as well as those of people to whom you often send letters, are also good candidates for the glossary.

The disclosure and reminder paragraphs in Figure 15-5 are good examples of boilerplate text blocks that can make letter creation a snap. Boilerplates promote consistency and reduce mistakes.

Notes and Memos

Many notes and memos are typed so often and are so similar in content that the complete document can be inserted in the glossary. In the memo shown in Figure 15-6, for example, all that changes from quarter to quarter for this memo are the date and meeting location, which you can fill in before printing.

Glossary Name	Expanded Glossary Text
uc	University of California
tc	Thomas Carlyle, Ph.D.
pp	plaster of paris
ww2	World War II
water	H_2O

Figure 15-4. Simple glossary entries

Addresses   Glossary name: **addr**

Kenneth Murray
1425 Oceanview Court
Ventura, CA 93102

Letter close   Glossary name: **close**

Sincerely yours,

Leslie Whitmore
Customer Relations Manager

Disclosures   Glossary name: **bid_cond**

This bid is subject to conditions on the face and reverse side. No changes may be made without written permission of the purchasing agent.

Reminders   Glossary name: **overdue**

```
This is a reminder that your current balance of
$(amount) is overdue.  Please make arrangements to pay
this amount immediately.  If there is a problem, you
can call our office between 8:00 and 5:00 at 964-3102.
```

Figure 15-5. Boilerplate glossary entries

MEMORANDUM

To: Department Managers   **From:** John Adams

Subject: Quarterly Meeting   **Date:** (date)

This is to confirm our next staff meeting, to be held on (date) at (place). Please be prepared for the topics and agendas listed on the attached sheet.

Figure 15-6.   Multiple-style glossary entry

This memo also represents a multitude of style and format changes. The word *memorandum* is centered and typed in a large bold font. The "To/From" heading is formatted as side-by-side paragraphs with two type fonts used. The bottom portion is a normal type.

Forms

Figure 15-7 shows the skeleton of a resume. It represents a combination of indents, borders, font changes, and tab settings, all of which are set up in advance and added to the glossary. You simply fill in the blanks. Figures 15-8 and 15-9 illustrate other components of forms that you may need on a regular basis.

Document Titles and Headers

Figures 15-10 and 15-11 show a few types of document titles and headers, each using borders and lines. These would be good candidates for glossaries if you were writing a book or report. One important thing that a glossary can provide is a consistent look to your titles and headers.

E D U C A T I O N

(date)   (degree)

E M P L O Y M E N T

(date)   (employer)

R E F E R E N C E S

(names and addresses)

Figure 15-7.   Glossary template for resume

Q1   (first question)   ☐

Q2   (second question)   ☐

Figure 15-8.   Glossary template for questionnaire

```
Signature: _____     Date:_____

Print name:_____

Witness: _____     Date:_____

Print name:_____
```

Figure 15-9. Glossary template for signature line

Chapter x, (title)

Chapter x

(Chapter title)

Figure 15-10. Glossary templates for titles

(name)	(page)	(date)
(company name)		

Figure 15-11. Glossary template for running head

Tips and Traps Summary

The Glossary as a Storage Place

Tip: Copy text to the glossary instead of the scrap if it must be saved for a long period.

Tip: Because each glossary entry has its own name, any number of them can be stored at a time.

Tip: NORMAL.GLY is attached to all documents unless you specify another file.

Creating Glossary Entries

Tip: A glossary can hold a block of text that you decide to place elsewhere in your document at a later time.

Trap: Glossary names must be one word long, but you can use hyphens or underlines to simulate spaces.

Tips and Traps Summary (*continued*)

Trap: The more glossary entries you have, the harder they are to remember. Use unique names or develop a coding system.

Trap: You cannot use a glossary name more than once within the same glossary file.

Retrieving Glossary Entries

Tip: You can leave glossary names unexpanded until the last minute to keep the document uncluttered and take up less memory space.

Managing Glossary Files

Trap: Edited glossary entries will copy over the original unless you give the edited version a new name.

Trap: Pressing ENTER without specifying an entry will delete all entries when you are using the Transfer Glossary Clear command.

Tip: You can choose not to save your most recent glossary entries by quitting Word without saving the glossary.

Tip: To create a new set of glossary entries, clear the old set, type the new set, and save the file under a different name.

Trap: When you merge glossaries, the new glossary copies over entries with similar names.

Using Glossaries Instead of Styles

Tip: Glossaries can store a combination of styles, making them more convenient than individual styles from the style sheet.

16

Style Sheets

Style sheets let you quickly apply a character or paragraph format that you use often. This formatting information is tailored to fit your needs and can be applied with just a few keystrokes. You can save styles for subsequent use, which promotes a consistency in the look and design of your documents.

How Styles Fit into the Big Picture

You've already seen how to use styles to apply character formats (Chapter 10), paragraph formats (Chapter 11), and division formats (Chapter 12). This chapter will cover the details of style and how to develop and manage style sheets.

It is important to look at the steps used in developing a Word document to see how style formatting fits into the big picture. One way to write is to type and edit a document and then format it with the direct formatting keys or the styles in the style sheet. The other way to create Word documents is through templates, which let you create a blank form to be filled in later. The form contains the styles in the appropriate places, but no text.

Writing with Templates

A template is a prewritten block of text that can be used in many different ways. The parts of the template that change are usually left blank or have a code corresponding to the type of information that should be inserted there. Chapter 15 demonstrated the use of templates by inserting prewritten running heads, titles, and forms into the glossary.

> *Tip:* *Templates are glossary or disk files that are filled in when needed. Various styles are already applied.*

Templates are more than text with blanks, however. A template can be a combination of styles. Some tables, for instance, might require one style for the header, another for the column heads, and one or two for the table itself. In setting up a table template, you might apply the four styles to four separate paragraph markers and then save them in that simple form to the glossary. Later, when you insert the template with styles in the text, you can fill in the table.

Another important type of template is a disk file with a combination of styles. Such a file does not contain text; instead, paragraph markers with specific style formatting are combined, as shown in Figure 16-1. This file was created with the styles in the SEMI.STY style sheet supplied with Word 4.

> *Tip:* *Templates can be saved in the glossary or as a disk file.*

The key codes next to each paragraph are a clue to the type of text that should be typed, whether that is the address, salutation, the body of the text, or the closing. Note that the letter is a semiblock style. In other words, the date, closing, name, and title are partially indented. The indents, paragraph alignments, and space before and after are already applied with the styles in the sheet. The text between brackets, as shown in Figure 16-1, can be included in the template to further clarify the components.

Important Things to Know About Style Sheets

You should know a few things about style sheets, including where styles are kept as well as which style sheet is in use. You should also understand the process of

```
┌──────────────────────────────────────────────────────────────┐
│LH  (letter head)                                               │
│                                                                │
│DA                              (date)                          │
│IA  (inside address)                                            │
│SA  (salutation)                                                │
│SP      (body of letter)                                        │
│CL                              (closing)                       │
│                                                                │
│NA                              (name)                          │
│TI                              (title)                         │
│RI  (reference initials)                                        │
│                                               ═LET-TEMP.DOC═   │
└──────────────────────────────────────────────────────────────┘
```

Figure 16-1.   A template file is a combination of styles saved to disk; text is added later

switching and combining style sheets as well as the style creation process. This section will briefly cover some of these topics.

The Gallery

Styles are stored in a style sheet that can be viewed and edited in the gallery. To enter the gallery, execute the Gallery command in the Main menu. To get back to the Word edit window, execute the Gallery Exit command.

Think of the gallery as a room, like a library of a house, where the references to the format styles in your document are described. When you start Word for the first time, the gallery is empty. But as soon as you begin to create styles or merge another style sheet, entries will appear, as shown in Figure 16-2. This gallery contains the SEMI.STY style sheet supplied with Word 4. You should use it when you create semiblock letters, as shown in Figure 16-1. Semiblock letters are those with partial indents for the date, closing, name, and title.

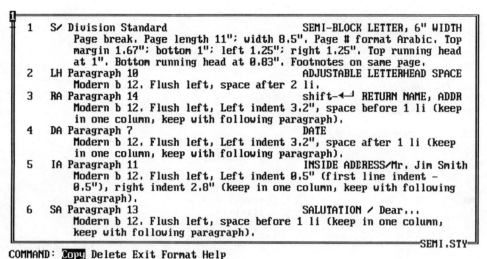

Figure 16-2.   Styles in the gallery window

Applying Styles

Once a style sheet contains entries, you apply them by using the ALT key or the Format Stylesheet command after highlighting the text to be formatted. When you use the ALT key, hold it down while pressing the key code of the style.

The Style Bar

The style bar runs along the left side of the screen and displays the codes of paragraph and division styles. It does not display the codes for character styles. Turn on the style bar by answering Yes in the Window Options Style Bar field.

Single or Multiple Sheets

Word normally attaches a style sheet called NORMAL.STY to all new files. But you can create additional style sheets, each with its own name and purpose. For example, you could have style sheets for legal documents, letters, books, and contracts.

Word 4 comes with several style sheets of its own. One of these, which is called FULL.STY, is designed for creating full-block letters. These are letters that block all text, salutations, and closings on the left. Another style sheet, called SEMI.STY, is designed to help you create semiblock letters — letters with partial indents. Still another, called SIDEBY.STY, contains six styles for creating side-by-side paragraphs.

Figure 16-1 shows a template for semiblock letters. Attached to this template is the SEMI.STY style sheet. Similarly, you could create another template for full-block letters and attach the FULL.STY style sheet. You may want to merge the SIDEBY.STY style sheet with each of your other style sheets because the styles in this sheet are useful in many different applications.

As you can see, style sheets can stand alone for specific applications or can be merged into other style sheets. This chapter will discuss both of these techniques.

The NORMAL.STY Style Sheet   When you create a new document, Word will always attach the NORMAL.STY style sheet to it, even if the style sheet contains no entries. As entries are created and saved with the NORMAL.STY style sheet, a family of styles is assembled for use with other documents. Because NORMAL.STY is attached to all new documents, you should include only styles that are common and useful for all of your "normal" documents. Styles specific to certain types of documents, such as contracts and reports, should be assembled in their own style sheets.

 Tip: *Word always attaches NORMAL.STY to new documents.*

If you are creating a new document, you can override the NORMAL.STY style sheet by "attaching" a new style sheet.

Word's Existing Style Sheets

Word 4 comes with five premade style sheets, three of which were discussed earlier. These style sheets are listed here, with a brief description of their use.

SAMPLE.STY — This is a combination style sheet. It has styles for developing a numbered list, titles and subheads, hanging indented lists, running heads, and side-by-side paragraphs. You may want to merge this style sheet with NORMAL.STY because the styles are so useful.

FULL.STY — This style sheet, covered earlier, is used to create a full-block letter. It contains styles for formatting the address, salutation, body text, closing, and other features. It is best used with a template.

SEMI.STY — This style sheet, also covered earlier, is used to create semiblock letters.

SIDEBY.STY — This style sheet contains six styles for developing side-by-side paragraphs. You can create two-column or three-column side-by-side paragraphs with equal column widths. Merge SIDEBY.STY with NORMAL.STY as soon as possible if you plan to create side-by-side paragraphs.

OUTLINE.STY — This style sheet can be used in conjunction with Word's outline facility. Although Word will automatically add indents to various levels of heads and subheads when outlining, this style sheet also adds character formats to each heading level, such as bold, italic, and others. You may want to alter this style sheet to conform with the title formatting conventions that you use. In other words, you can convert the heading levels to apply the type fonts and styles that you prefer.

Word's Preset Styles

Just as Word automatically attaches the NORMAL.STY style sheet to every document, it attaches built-in styles to various parts of your document. The built-in styles are divided into three groups: character, paragraph, and division styles.

They define formats for individual components of your document, such as paragraphs, running heads, page numbers, and divisions, when you do not assign special formats yourself.

 Tip: *Built-in or standard styles are automatically applied to various elements of Word documents.*

The built-in formats are visible in the gallery. (If you refer ahead to Figures 16-3 and 16-4, you can see the preset formats as the nonnumbered entries at the top of the listings.) Because Word automatically applies these styles to their respective document components, you can alter them to automatically change the format of all of your documents.

 Tip: *You can alter built-in styles to fit your needs.*

For example, you can change the Standard Paragraph to include a first-line indent and assign a different type font to it, such as Times Roman instead of Courier. From then on, all documents that use the style sheet where the standard formats were changed will reflect this formatting change. If you make the changes in NORMAL.STY, Word will automatically apply the formatting changes to all documents unless you change the style sheet.

Making a Direct Format a Style

Word's *direct formatting* keys, as discussed in Chapters 10 and 11, are always available for use, even if a style sheet is not attached. These keys include ALT+U for underline, ALT+B for bold, ALT+C for centering, and so on. However, when a style sheet is attached, you can no longer use these keys in the same way. Instead, you must type an **X** with the keystroke so that Word knows you want the direct formatting keys instead of a style from the style sheet (which may not exist).

 Tip: *To avoid having to first type **X** when you use direct formatting keys, create styles for them in the style sheet.*

To get around this problem, you can create styles in the style sheet that perform the same functions as the direct formatting keys. For example, you can create a style called B for bold, I for italic, U for underline, and so on. Unfortunately, however, you won't be able to create any other codes that start with the letter you assign to single-character key codes. That is, if you create a B style for bold, you cannot have a BI or BT style because the bold formatting style will execute when you type **B**. To get around this, you can assign double characters to the styles, such as BB for bold and II for italic. You may not have enough styles to worry about using the B, I, U, and other characters as style codes.

An added bonus to using styles for the direct formatting keys is that you can alter all characters and paragraphs formatted with these styles by changing the style in the gallery. For example, you could globally change all boldfaced text to underlined or italic text.

 Tip: *When you make direct formatting keys into styles, you can globally alter them by changing the style in the style sheet.*

Coordinating Other Style Sheets

A document is not limited to one style sheet. You can attach another at any time. But this can create some problems unless you understand what happens when a style sheet is attached to a document that has already been assigned styles with a different style sheet.

Assume that your documents go through two phases. The first phase is editing. You print out the document on a high-speed printer with a low-quality draft mode that is fine for producing copy that you can edit. After editing is complete, the document goes into a formatting and printing phase. You use a high-quality laser printer or even a type-setting machine to print in this phase.

You can use two completely separate style sheets to prepare this document. Call the first one EDIT.STY. Listed here are a few of the styles that it defines:

- A division style that uses as much of the screen as possible to display text. Margins are set at 0.5 inch.

- Paragraph styles with single spacing and no indents. There is no space before or after paragraphs so that as much text as possible can fit on the screen.

- Character formatting styles use standard 10-point monospaced fonts.

The second style sheet is attached when the document is ready for phase 2. The styles in this style sheet are as follows:

- Paragraph styles are set for the actual margins required in the final printout.

- Paragraph styles contain spaces after and are first-line indented.

- Character styles define the fonts and styles for titles and text as required in the final document.

When you switch from the first style sheet to the second, there obviously must be some coordination between the two. You have applied style codes to paragraphs and characters, but Word must match up the codes with those of the second style sheet. This matchup, surprisingly, is done not with the style code but with the variant, as discussed next.

Tip: *You can use two style sheets when you create documents. The first makes editing easy; the second changes the text for printing.*

The Role of the Variant   The style variant is what Word locks onto when a new style sheet is attached. It is the key that tells Word which styles should be matched to which text. For example, assume that a paragraph is formatted with a style from the first style sheet called TL (for Text List). This code is designed to give the paragraph a hanging indent wide enough to accommodate a word or phrase that hangs out in the first line. The usage of the style is Paragraph, and the variant is 5.

Now it's time to apply the second style sheet, which must contain a style with a variant of 5 that has the formatting required for this type of paragraph. If a style with variant 5 doesn't exist, unpredictable results will occur. Therefore, the formats that you want to match between style sheets must contain the same variant number in the style. Once again, the key codes don't matter, though you should also make them consistent to avoid confusion.

Trap: *In order to match styles between different style sheets, the variant must be the same.*

An interesting part of this two-step document preparation process is that the styles in the first style sheet needn't have any special formatting properties. All the styles may look the same in order to maximize the use of the screen. The reason for applying the styles in this phase is to assign the variant code to the paragraphs and characters so that they can be converted with the styles in the second style sheet when it is attached in phase 2.

Variant- and Style-Naming Conventions   If you will be attaching other style sheets to your documents, as discussed earlier, you must be concerned with the names of your styles and the variants applied to them in order to avoid conflicts and unpredictable results when switching style sheets. One way to do this is to develop variant- and style-naming conventions.

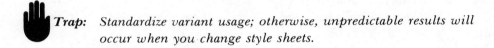 *Trap:*   *Standardize variant usage; otherwise, unpredictable results will occur when you change style sheets.*

Figures 16-3 and 16-4 list the variants available for character and paragraph usage, respectively. The character variants include 4 predefined and 25 user-defined variants. The paragraph variants include 18 predefined and 56 user-defined variants available for styles of your choice.

Page number	Line Number	Footnote ref	Summary Info
1	2	3	4
5	6	7	8
9	10	11	12
13	14	15	16
17	18	19	20
21	22	23	24
25			

Figure 16-3. Character variants

Standard	Footnote	Running Head	Heading level 1
Heading level 2	Heading level 3	Heading level 4	Heading level 5
Heading level 6	Heading level 7	Index level 1	Index level 2
Index level 3	Index level 4	Table level 1	Table level 2
Table level 3	Table level 4	1	2
3	4	5	6
7	8	9	10
11	12	13	14
15	16	17	18
19	20	21	22
23	24	25	26
27	28	29	30
31	32	33	34
35	36	37	38
39	40	41	42
43	44	45	46
47	48	49	50
51	52	53	54
55	56		

Figure 16-4. Paragraph variants

You can use Table 16-1 to develop a variant number strategy for assigning various types of character and paragraph styles. Note that if you have existing styles in your style sheets that do not follow this format, you can use the Glossary Name command to assign them different variants.

 Tip: *You can use the Glossary Name command to alter variants and key code names to match a numbering scheme.*

Style Sheet Commands

Most of the commands for working with styles are located in the gallery. You can access a few commands, however, from the menu or by using the quick keys. The Format Stylesheet command, illustrated on the next page, contains commands for

Table 16-1. Variant-Numbering Schemes

Character Variant Use Strategies

1-16	Use variant 1-16 to create duplicates of the direct formatting keys as discussed in the text.
17-25	Use 17-25 for special comminations or font changes.

Paragraph Variant Use Strategies

1-5	Miscellaneous paragraph variations
6-9	Boxed and lined paragraphs
10-14	Indented paragraphs
15-18	Numbered and bulleted lists
19-21	Worded lists
22-30	Side-by-side paragraphs
31-35	Paragraphs with special tab settings
36-43	Running heads
44-50	Table formats
51-56	Special titles
Built-in:	Outlines, titles, and subtitles: Use built-in Heading level 1-7. (Headings should be developed in the Word outline mode.)
Built-in:	Indexes: Use built-in Index level 1-4.
Built-in:	Tables of contents: Use built-in Table level 1-4.

---

attaching a new style sheet (this can also be done in the gallery).

FORMAT STYLESHEET: Attach Character Paragraph Division Record

You can also apply character, paragraph, and division formatting to text by using this menu instead of pressing ALT and the key code. The advantage of using this menu is that it will list the available styles in a format similar to the listing illustrated here:

```
SP Paragraph Standard (line after, oth)NP Paragraph 10
P1 Paragraph 9 (PARAGRAPH, NOT OPEN)   TP Paragraph 7 (tips and traps)
IL Paragraph 8 (FIGURE LEGENDS)        NU Paragraph 6 (numbered paragraphs)
T1 Paragraph Heading level 1 (Chapter) T2 Paragraph Heading level 2 (Chapter)
T3 Paragraph Heading level 3 (Chapter) RH Paragraph Running Head (Chapter tit)
```

The Format Stylesheet Record command is shown here:

```
FORMAT STYLESHEET RECORD key code: T1        usage: Character(Paragraph)Division
           variant: Heading level 1          remark: Chapter Main Headings
```

This command lets you create a style from the formatting just applied in the text by using the standard Format Character, Paragraph, or Division commands. The command menu is similar to the Gallery Insert Command menu. You can also press ALT+F10 to display this menu.

The Gallery menu, shown here,

```
COMMAND: Copy Delete Exit Format Help
         Insert Name Print Transfer Undo
```

contains commands for inserting, copying, or deleting styles. You can also rename a style or its parts, print the style sheet, and use the Transfer command to load or merge a style sheet or save the existing style sheet. The Format command in the Gallery menu lets you format styles in the same way that text is formatted in the edit window.

Components of Styles

You must first create a style before you can apply it to your text. Creating a style can be as easy as copying one that you have already applied to text with the standard formatting commands in the Word Format menu. This is called "creating a style by example."

Creating a style is a two-step process that can be done in the gallery or by example. In the gallery an entry is made to define the key code name, usage, and variant of a style. Formatting is then applied to this entry in the same way that formats are applied to text in the edit window, except that the Format command in the Gallery menu is used. Creating a style by example performs these same steps in reverse. First, you apply the formatting to some block of text in your document; then create the entry in the gallery from these formats. In this way you can create styles without ever going into the gallery.

A style comprises four components: the key code, usage, variant, and remark. Two of these components, the usage and variant, are essential to every style. The key code is sometimes essential, and the remark is useful for keeping track of what the style does but is not essential.

Key Code

The key code—an abbreviated name for a style—is what you type in the edit window with the ALT key. The key code also appears in the style bar of the edit window, next to paragraphs formatted with styles. The key code for divisions appears to the left of the division marker. Character style key codes do not appear on the screen.

 Tip: *Styles don't need a key code, but it makes their use a lot easier.*

The key code can be either one or two characters long, but it's best to use two characters so that you'll have more options to work with. You might want to set up a naming strategy. For example, all titles could start with a *T* and use a number in the second position to indicate the level of the title. T1 would then be a major title, and T2 would be a subtitle.

You cannot create styles that start with an *X* because this conflicts with the way that Word defines how the quick formatting keys work when a style sheet is attached.

 Trap: *Don't use X in a key code name.*

Usage

Style usage can be Character, Paragraph, or Division. A main reason that Word breaks styles down in this way is to determine which variant list to use and how to place the key code. Once you select the usage, you can then select the variant displayed for that usage.

The Usage option separates Word's document elements in the same way discussed throughout this book. The three options and a short description follow.

Character   Character formats are fonts and styles applied to single characters or blocks of characters. Character formats also apply to page numbers, line numbers, and footnote references.

Paragraph	Paragraph formats apply to all paragraph alignments, indents, tabs, footnotes, running heads, indexes, table of contents entries, outlines, and borders.
Division	Division formats apply to margins, page number positions and type of numbering, multiple-column layouts, running head positions, footnote positions, and line number positions.

Variant

As described earlier, the variant is important if you are attaching other style sheets to the documents to which you have already applied styles. The variant, not the key code, is the code that Word uses to match styles between these style sheets. If you are not planning to attach other style sheets, you need not be too concerned with the variant.

There are up to 29 character variants, 73 paragraph variants, and 22 division variants. These numbers include the built-in variants, which are listed in Table 16-2 according to their usage.

If you do not supply a variant when you create a style, Word will automatically supply the next available variant for the type of style usage.

Description or Remark

The remark is optional but can be an important indicator of what a style does. It becomes increasingly important as you create more and more styles. You can type up to 28 characters in the field. Type remarks in capital letters to make them more visible in the gallery.

Creating Styles

As mentioned earlier, there are several ways to create styles. First, you can select text in your documents that has already been formatted and use ALT+F10 to record the styles. The second and third methods require the use of the gallery. You can

Table 16-2. Built-in Standard Variants

Usage	Variants
Character	Page Number
	Footnote reference
	Line number
	Document summary
	1-25 (user defined)
Paragraph	Standard
	Footnote
	Running head
	Heading levels 1-7
	Index levels 1-4
	Table levels 1-4
	1-56 (user defined)
Division	Standard
	1-21 (user defined)

use the Gallery Insert and Copy commands to create a new entry, and then use the Format commands to alter its function.

Before recording any style, make sure that the style sheet in which you want to place the style is attached. If you have started a new document, the NORMAL.STY style sheet will be attached. If you want to attach a different style sheet, use the Format Stylesheet Attach command to remove the existing style sheet and attach a new one. To create a new style sheet, use the Gallery Clear command to clear the current style sheet and leave the Gallery window blank. Working with style sheets is covered later in this chapter.

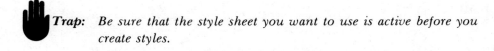

Trap: *Be sure that the style sheet you want to use is active before you create styles.*

After adding or creating any styles, remember to save the gallery if you want to use the styles in other Word sessions. Word will ask if you want to save an altered style sheet if you quit Word with the Quit command. You can also save a style sheet at any time by using the Gallery Transfer Save command.

Creating Styles by Example

To record a style by example, follow these steps:

1. Place the highlight on the text that has the formatting you want to use. If it is a character format, place the highlight on the exact character that holds the format. If it is a paragraph or division format, place the highlight anywhere within these document elements.

2. Press ALT+F10 (or Format Stylesheet Record).

3. Enter the key code. Remember to use a coding scheme that will help you remember the style.

4. In the Usage field select Character, Paragraph, or Division.

5. In the Variant field enter the variant number according to Table 16-1 so that your style can be coordinated with other style sheets.

6. Enter a remark in capital letters to describe this style. In this way the remark becomes a title that is easy to see when you view the entire style sheet list.

7. Press ENTER.

Word will add the style to the gallery. You can enter the gallery to see for yourself. Word will usually add the style to the bottom of the list. To scroll to the bottom, press CTRL+PGDN, just as you would scroll to the bottom of a text document.

Creating Styles in the Gallery

When you create styles in the gallery, you can use the Insert command to create an entirely new style or the Copy command to copy an existing style that you can then alter. When you use Copy, you must also use the Gallery Name command to rename the style and its variant.

Trap: *Don't forget to rename a copied style by using the Galley Name commmand.*

Creating styles in the gallery is a two-step process. First, you make a style entry with the Insert or Copy command; then you use the Format commands to alter the style to your needs. Use the following steps to create a new style with the Insert command.

1. Position the highlight in the gallery where you want the new style to be inserted.

2. Type **I** to insert a new entry.

3. Enter the key code, usage, variant, and remark as per your requirements. The Variant field should follow a coding scheme like that shown in Figure 16-1.

4. Press ENTER.

You can create styles from existing styles and save yourself a few steps in the formatting process. The reason for using the Gallery Copy command is to make styles from existing styles, except with minor changes. For example, an existing style to format titles might be copied and altered for use with subtitles.

To copy a style, follow these steps.

1. Highlight the style that you want to copy in the Gallery command.

2. Press the Gallery Copy command. The style will be inserted in the scrap.

3. Highlight the style that you want to insert the new style in front of and press the keyboard INS key, not the Gallery Insert command. The style will be inserted in the gallery.

4. Use the Gallery Name command to change the key code and variant of the style to follow your coding scheme (see Figure 16-1).

5. Change the format of the style with the Gallery Format command.

Removing a Style from the Gallery

To remove a style from the gallery, simply place the highlight on the style and press the keyboard DEL key. Keep in mind that removing a style will affect text in documents that are coded for that style.

 Trap: *If you remove a style, the text in a document dependent on that style may not be formatted properly.*

Applying Styles to Documents

You apply styles to the text of your documents by using the ALT key or the Format Stylesheet command. To apply a style with the ALT key, you must know the key code of the style. Simply select the text to be formatted and hold down the ALT key while typing the key code.

To use the Format Stylesheet command, highlight the text to be formatted and execute the command. Choose Character, Paragraph, or Division and then press F1 to see a list of available styles. Use the arrow keys to make a selection and then press ENTER to execute it. This method is the best when you can't remember the name of a style.

Viewing the Style Type

If the style bar is on, the key code will appear to the left of paragraphs. If a division format is applied, the key code will appear to the left of the division marker at the bottom of the division. Key codes do not appear for character styles. You can, however, place the highlight on the characters and press ALT+F8 at any time to see which character formats have been applied.

 Tip: *Sometimes you can only determine character styles by pressing ALT+F8 to see the Format Character menu.*

Removing Styles from Text

To remove a style from text, highlight the text and press ALT+X+P to remove paragraph styles or ALT+SPACEBAR to remove character styles. Remove division styles by deleting the division marker.

Creating and Attaching New Style Sheets

You could use only one style sheet, NORMAL.STY, for all your work with Word. If so, you won't need to attach other style sheets because NORMAL.STY will include all the styles you need. Eventually, however, you may find that your single style sheet begins to grow so large that it is hard to manage. In addition, you may begin to run out of variants, and if you are following the variant-coding strategy in Table 16-1, you may begin to run out of variants for specific types of styles.

 Tip: *If a style sheet becomes unmanageable, break it down into several special-purpose style sheets.*

When this occurs, you will need to subdivide your large style sheet into groups of styles designed for specific documents. For example, you may need to break out the styles used to create letters or those used to create reports and contracts. You can create new style sheets in two ways. The first method involves making copies of the existing style sheet, while the second involves creating entirely new styles from scratch.

Copying and Revising Existing Style Sheets

You can use the following method to reduce the size of an existing style sheet by moving some of its entries into new style sheets. Follow these steps.

1. Execute the Gallery Transfer Save command to make a copy of the existing style with a new style sheet name.

2. The old style sheet is still on the disk under its original name. The new style sheet is in the gallery with its new name in the lower-right corner.

3. Highlight the entries in the style sheet that you don't need and press DEL.

4. Use the Gallery Transfer Save command again to save the completed style sheet.

Creating Entirely New Style Sheets

You can create a new style sheet from scratch. Follow these steps.

1. Clear off existing gallery entries by using the Gallery Transfer Clear command.

2. Create new entries by using the methods described earlier in this chapter.

3. Use the Gallery Transfer Save command to save the new style sheet with a name that is appropriate for the type of entries.

Merging Styles from Other Style Sheets

You may want to merge styles from other style sheets in order to build a collection of styles. Use the Transfer Merge command to do this. All styles from the merging style sheet are inserted into the existing style sheet, so you may want to delete the ones that you don't want. In addition, a new problem will occur if styles from the merged style sheet have the same key codes and variants as styles in your existing sheet. How to handle this is covered next.

Merging Style Sheets

Use the Gallery Transfer Merge command to merge another style sheet into the existing style sheet. You can press F1 to see a list of possible style sheets.

When two style sheets are merged, a potential problem exists if two styles have the same key code and variant. Word will allow the two sheets to merge, but you won't be able to get out of the gallery until the conflicts are resolved. Resolving conflicts between styles is the purpose of the Gallery Name command.

 Trap: *When two style sheets are merged, you cannot leave the gallery or save the sheet until duplicate style conflicts are resolved.*

To resolve the conflicts, highlight one of the conflicting styles and use the Gallery Name command to give it a different key code or variant. Note that you may only need to change the variant. When assigning a new variant, use the numbering scheme in Table 16-1 to help avoid future conflicts.

You may want to print the style sheet with the Gallery Print command in order to see all the entries. This will make it easier to find the conflicting entries.

One trick that you can use to make Word highlight conflicting entries is to attempt to exit with the Gallery Exit command. Word will beep and highlight a conflicting style. You can then use the Gallery Name command to change its key code or variant. Keep trying to exit in this way until all conflicting styles are resolved.

 Tip: *Word will highlight conflicting entries when you try to exit the gallery with the Gallery Exit command. You can then edit this style.*

The following example will show you how to merge two or more style sheets and how to resolve conflicting entries. In this example the SAMPLE.STY and SIDEBY.STY style sheets will be merged. If you wish, you can then merge entries from your NORMAL.STY style sheet to create an entirely new NORMAL.STY style sheet.

First, open a new document and remove the NORMAL.STY style sheet. Then follow these steps.

1. Use Gallery Transfer Clear to clear the gallery.

2. Use Gallery Transfer Load and type **SAMPLE** to load the SAMPLE.STY style sheet. (Note: if the style sheet didn't load, it may be in another directory or on another disk. Specify the correct directory in the field or change diskettes.)

3. Merge the SIDEBY.STY style sheet by using the Gallery Transfer Merge command. Type **SIDEBY** in the Name field.

The styles from both sheets are now in the gallery. Try exiting the style sheet. Word will beep and highlight the first conflicting style. At this point, you should print out the style sheet to help resolve the conflicts. This printout is shown in Figure 16-5.

Styles 1 through 5 are the side-by-side styles merged from the SIDEBY.STY style sheet, while styles 6 through 16 are from SAMPLE.STY. Note that styles 12 and 13 are duplicates of styles 1 and 2, except for the fonts. Shortly, you will delete styles 12 and 13. Save this for last because deleting styles alters the style numbers, which you need to direct this example.

Note the variant conflicts between styles 1 and 9, 2 and 6, 3 and 7, 4 and 12, and 5 and 13. You can simply alter the variants to another number, but it is best to change all the variants to fit into the numbering scheme of Table 16-1. In this way you will be able to better manage future style sheet merges. Use the following steps to alter the variants in the style sheets. Note that there are no key code conflicts, so there will be no need to change them.

```
1    2L Paragraph 1                          LEFT
        Courier (modern a) 12. Flush left, right indent 3.25". Place side
        by side.
2    2R Paragraph 2                          RIGHT
        Courier (modern a) 12. Flush left, Left indent 3.25". Place side by
        side.
3    3L Paragraph 3                          LEFT
        Courier (modern a) 12. Flush left, right indent 4.3". Place side by
        side.
4    3C Paragraph 4                          CENTER
        Courier (modern a) 12. Flush left, Left indent 2.15", right indent
        2.15". Place side by side.
5    3R Paragraph 5                          RIGHT
        Courier (modern a) 12. Flush left, Left indent 4.3". Place side by
        side.
6    NL Paragraph 2                          NUMBERED LIST
        TMSRMN (roman a) 10/12. Flush left, Left indent 0.4" (first line
        indent -0.4"), right indent 0.4", space before 1 li, space after 1
        li (keep in one column).
7    TI Paragraph 3                          TITLE
        HELV (modern i) 14/12 Bold. Centered.
8    SH Paragraph 7                          SUBHEAD
        HELV (modern i) 12 Bold Underlined. Flush left.
9    LE Paragraph 1                          LIST ENTRY
        TMSRMN (roman a) 10/12. Flush left, Left indent 1" (first line
        indent -1"), right indent 0.4", space after 2 li (keep in one
        column). Tabs at: 1" (left flush).
10   SP Paragraph Standard                   STANDARD PARAGRAPH
        TMSRMN (roman a) 10/12. Flush left.
11   RH Paragraph Running Head               RUNNING HEAD
        TMSRMN (roman a) 10/12 Italic. Centered.
12   L1 Paragraph 4                          LEFT SIDE-BY-SIDE
        TMSRMN (roman a) 10/12. Flush left, right indent 3.25". Place side
        by side.
13   R1 Paragraph 5                          RIGHT SIDE-BY-SIDE
        TMSRMN (roman a) 10/12. Flush left, Left indent 3.25". Place side
        by side.
14   H1 Paragraph Heading level 1            HEAD LEVEL 1
        HELV (modern i) 14/12 Bold. Flush left, space after 1 li (keep with
        following paragraph).
15   H2 Paragraph Heading level 2            HEAD LEVEL 2
        TMSRMN (roman a) 10/12 Bold. Flush left, space before 2 li, space
        after 1 li.
16   H3 Paragraph Heading level 3            HEAD LEVEL 3
        TMSRMN (roman a) 10/12 Italic Underlined. Flush left.
```

Figure 16-5. Styles available after merging SAMPLE.STY and SIDEBY.STY

1. Highlight style number 1, which is coded 2L. This is a side-by-side paragraph format, so its variant number should be 22 through 30.

2. Select the Gallery Name command and change the Variant field to 22.

3. Highlight style number 2, execute the Gallery Name command, and change its Variant field to 23.

4. Perform step 3 for styles 3, 4, and 5, using variants 24, 25, and 26, respectively.

You must also change the variant numbers of styles 6 through 9 in order to fit them into the numbering scheme of Table 16-1. Note that all conflicts are now resolved, and you can exit the style sheet. However, it is best to change the variant in 6 through 9 for future use. Highlight style 6 through 9 in turn and use the Gallery Name command to change the variant as follows:

Style 6: change to variant 15 (numbered list).

Style 7: change to variant 51 (title).

Style 8: change to variant 52 (subtitle).

Style 9: change to variant 19 (worded list).

The rest of the styles in the style sheet use Word's built-in styles. You can now change the typeface, type style, or paragraph formatting of any of the styles in the style sheet to fit your needs. Save the style sheet with an appropriate name by using the Transfer Save command.

You now have a style sheet with some very common styles, such as the side-by-side and title styles. At this point, you may want to consider making this sheet the standard NORMAL.STY style sheet. You can either remove the existing NORMAL.STY style sheet or merge this new style sheet with NORMAL.STY. If you decide to merge, you must remove duplicate entries and rename some of the variants in the existing sheet. You can do this to NORMAL.STY before or after merging the new sheet.

Tips and Traps Summary

How Styles Fit into the Big Picture

Tip: Templates are glossary or disk files that are filled in when needed. Various styles are already applied.

Tip: Templates can be saved in the glossary or as a disk file.

Tip: Word always attaches NORMAL.STY to new documents.

Tip: Built-in or standard styles are automatically applied to various elements of Word documents.

Tip: You can alter built-in styles to fit your needs.

Tip: To avoid having to first type **X** when you use direct formatting keys, create styles for them in the style sheet.

Tip: When you make direct formatting keys into styles, you can also globally alter them by changing the style in the style sheet.

Tip: You can use two style sheets when you create documents. The first makes editing easy, the second changes the text for printing.

Trap: In order to match styles between two different style sheets, the variant must be the same.

Trap: Standardize variant usage; otherwise, unpredictable results will occur when you change style sheets.

Tip: You can use the Glossary Name command to alter variants and key code names to match a numbering scheme.

Tips and Traps Summary (*continued*)

Components of Styles

Tip: Styles don't need a key code, but it makes their use a lot easier.

Trap: Don't use X in a key code name.

Creating Styles

Trap: Be sure that the style sheet you want to use is active before you create styles.

Trap: Don't forget to rename a copied style by using the Gallery Name command.

Trap: If you remove a style, the text in a document dependent on that style may not be formatted properly.

Applying Styles to Documents

Tip: Sometimes you can only determine character styles by pressing ALT+F8 to see the Format Character menu.

Creating and Attaching New Style Sheets

Tip: If a style sheet becomes unmanageable, break it down into several special-purpose style sheets.

Merging Style Sheets

Trap: When two style sheets are merged, you cannot leave the gallery or save the sheet until duplicate style conflicts are resolved.

Tip: Word will highlight conflicting entries when you try to exit the gallery with the Gallery Exit command. You can then edit this style.

17

Working with Windows

Word's window feature allows you to view more than one part of your document or two different documents at once. If two or more windows are "open" on the same document, you can read the text from one section while typing new text in another. If windows are open on two documents, you can copy text between them.

If you are using hidden text, you can display a document with hidden text in one window while you work with the document in the normal way in the other window. You can also open a window to write notes in while creating or editing a document in another window. You can open up to eight windows at one time, although that number may be a little hard to manage.

 Tip: *You can open up to eight windows at one time.*

You can remove a text block from a document in one window and place it in another window, where it can then be saved as a separate file. This is helpful when you decide to reduce the size of a file by splitting it in two. The document in the current window remains open, so you can continue to add or edit text.

Windows are simple to use, especially if you have a mouse. The borders of Word's edit window are sensitive to the mouse pointer. By pointing to the upper or right border and clicking, you can split new windows. Copying text between windows is easier with a mouse because the number of keystrokes is reduced.

You can size windows so that only a small part is showing at one time. Reducing the size of a window is not always advantageous for editing, but it does leave the window visible on the screen, as shown in Figure 17-1. In this way you can quickly point to it and *zoom* it to full size. Zooming is a special window operation that you can do with the mouse or from the keyboard.

Tip: Zoom a window to display it in full-size mode.

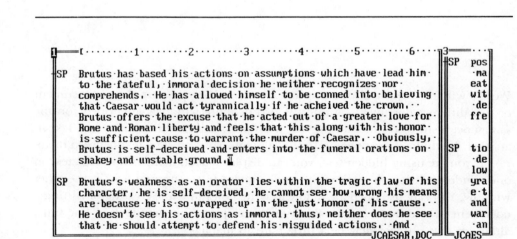

Figure 17-1.   Three windows on the same document allow you to zoom in on different parts of it

When you are finished editing in a window, you can reduce it and zoom another window, or you can leave all windows in full-screen zoomed mode, forming window layers. You can bring each layer to the front by pressing F1 or by selecting the number of the window to display. (This was illustrated in Figure 7-11.)

Working with different documents in two windows is the same as if you were working in two entirely different editing sessions. Changes made in one window do not affect changes made in another. Each window can have its own style sheet, margin settings, window colors, and so on.

The Window Commands

The window commands are located in the Window option on Word's command menu, as shown in the following illustration. The Window Split command lets you split a window horizontally or vertically or open a footnote window. Use the Window Close command to remove a window from the screen.

WINDOW: **Split** Close Move Options

Use the Window Move command to resize a window, although this is best performed with a mouse if you have one. The Window Options menu is illustrated here. With this menu, you can control which window is visible, switch to outline view, show hidden text, change the background color, and set the style bar or ruler on or off.

WINDOW OPTIONS window number: **1** outline: Yes(No) show hidden text: Yes(No)
background color: 1 style bar:(Yes)No ruler:(Yes)No

Opening a Window

You can open a new window by *splitting* a current window into two parts. Do this by using the Window Split command, illustrated here, or by using the mouse, which is covered shortly.

WINDOW SPLIT: **Horizontal** Vertical Footnote

As you can see, the Window Split command lets you split a window either horizontally or vertically. You can also open a window to view footnotes.

Tip: *When a window is split into two parts, text from the current document is still visible in both.*

The menu for splitting a window horizontally is illustrated next. Word will suggest that the window be split on the line position of the highlight. You can type another number in this location. Use the Clear New Window field to clear text from the new window if you want to load another document. If you don't select Yes in this field, you can still clear the window with the Transfer Clear Window command.

```
WINDOW SPLIT HORIZONTAL at line: 5   clear new window: Yes(No)
```

 Tip: *Answer Yes in the Clear New Window field if you want to load another file in the new window.*

 Trap: *When you clear a window, make sure to select Transfer Clear Window instead of Transfer Clear All, which clears all windows currently open.*

To split a window with the mouse, simply point in either the upper or right border of an existing window and click the left button. Clicking in the top border will split a vertical window, while clicking in the right border will split a horizontal window. All windows are split at the click location. If you click in an area that doesn't give Word enough room for a window, the message "Not a valid window split" will be displayed.

 Tip: *The top and right borders are sensitive to the mouse pointer. Clicking there will split a window at the click point.*

If you don't have a mouse, use the Window Split Vertical command to split side-by-side windows. Each vertical window must be large enough to display the borders, the selection bar, the style bar, and at least one character. Turn the style bar off when you split vertical windows if you need to gain extra characters.

Trap: *Word may not let you split a window if it is too small.*

Once a window is split, you use the F1 key to move between it and other windows. If you have a mouse, you can simply point in the other window. You can also type the desired window number in the Window Options Window Number field.

 Tip: *Use F1 to jump between windows.*

Note that window borders are important when you are working with multiple windows. If only one window is open and window borders are turned off, Word will include borders if you split a window. Borders are controlled in the Screen Borders field of the Options command.

 Trap: *Turning window borders off eliminates the use of the mouse for splitting windows.*

If you need to view the text in a window in its full width, split a window horizontally. Splitting a window vertically is useful for leaving a portion of the window on the screen so that it can be easily selected, as shown in Figure 17-1. For example, there is often about an inch of blank space on the right side of the edit window unless you are using a full-screen typing mode. If there is, you can split a vertical window in this area to make it easy to get at.

 Tip: *Leave a portion of a window open on the right side or in the lower-right corner so that you can easily select it.*

Zooming Windows

Zoom allows you to convert a small window into one that uses the entire screen. Place the highlight in the window to be zoomed and press CTRL+F1 or click the right mouse button in the upper-left corner of the window. When windows are zoomed, "ZM" will appear in the status line. To move between zoomed windows, press F1 or click in the upper-left corner with the left mouse button.

You can press SHIFT+F1 to zoom to the previous window. If you press CTRL+F1 again, the window will be restored to its original size. If you have a mouse, hold down the SHIFT key while clicking the left button on the window number to zoom the previous window. Click the right button on the window number to restore a window to its original size.

 Trap: *When windows are in zoomed mode, you cannot create new windows, except for the footnote window. Footnote windows zoom with the windows they are displayed in.*

Clearing and Closing Windows

You can clear a window with the Transfer Clear Window command, as discussed previously. If the text in the window has not been saved, Word will ask you if you want to save it. Be careful not to select Transfer Clear All because this command clears all windows. The Transfer Clear Window command is often used to clear the text of the current document from a window so that new text can be added. Whenever a window is split on a current document, Word keeps the text in both windows unless you clear one of them.

 Trap: *To split a window with the mouse, you may need to clear the new window. Select Transfer Clear Window with the highlight in the correct window. Don't select Transfer Clear All.*

If you use the mouse to split windows and want to load a new document, simply make sure that the highlight is in the new window and execute the Transfer Load command. The new text is loaded and the old text removed.

To close a window, select the Window Close command and enter the number of the window to close. If you have a mouse, press both buttons when the pointer is in the right border of the window.

Copying Between Windows

One of the main reasons for using windows is to copy text between them. For example, you can open another window on your document and then scroll through the main text in the top window and copy selected paragraphs or other text blocks to the other window to build up a document summary at the end of the document.

You can also display two different documents in order to copy a text block from one document to the other. For example, you can create a document of excerpts from another document or "borrow" text that you've already typed.

You can copy between windows through the keyboard or with the mouse. The steps for both methods are listed next, assuming that two windows are open, either on the same document or on different documents.

Copying with the Keyboard

1. Press F1 until the highlight is in the window containing the text to be copied.

2. Highlight the text block and press ALT+F3 to copy it to the scrap or DEL to remove it to the scrap.

3. Press F1 to jump to the other window.

4. Move the highlight to the insertion point and press INS.

Copying with the Mouse

1. Select the text to be copied or moved.

2. Point to the insertion point in the other window. You may need to scroll to this position first.

3. To copy the text, hold down the CTRL key and press the left button. To move the text, hold down the SHIFT key and press the left button.

Tips and Traps Summary

Tip: You can open up to eight windows at one time.

Tip: Zoom a window to display it in full-size mode.

Opening a Window

Tip: When a window is split into two parts, text from the current document is still visible in both.

Tip: Answer Yes in the Clear New Window field if you want to load another file in the new window.

Trap: When you clear a window, make sure to select Transfer Clear Window instead of Transfer Clear All, which clears all windows currently open.

Tip: The top and right borders are sensitive to the mouse pointer. Clicking there will split a window at the click point.

Trap: Word may not let you split a window if it is too small.

Tip: Use F1 to jump between windows.

Trap: Turning window borders off eliminates the use of the mouse for splitting windows.

Zooming Windows

Tip: Leave a portion of a window open on the right side or in the lower-right corner so that you can easily select it.

Tips and Traps Summary (*continued*)

Trap: When windows are in zoomed mode, you cannot create new windows, except for the footnote window. Footnote windows zoom with the windows they are displayed in.

Clearing and Closing Windows

Trap: To split a window with the mouse, you may need to clear the new window. Select Transfer Clear Window with the highlight in the correct window. Don't select Transfer Clear All.

18

Outlining
Techniques

You should create any document that has more than one section and uses titles to separate those sections with Word's outliner. Period. Forget your old notions of how to perform word processing on a computer. You will no longer just start typing text or rummage through a stack of paper notes. From now on, begin to think of Word's outliner just as you would any other commonly used Word tool, such as the scrap or the formatting keys. The outliner integrates the research and writing phases of document preparation.

Outlining in Word is much more valuable than the pencil and paper outlines you are used to. Because Word's outliner is computerized, it handles many important tasks automatically. Title numbering, outline reorganization, and title-only document views are just a few of the features available with the outliner. Most important, the outline becomes a part of your document that changes and actively grows with it.

This chapter will first introduce the concepts of outlining documents in Word and then cover the outline commands, including their description, use, and operation.

What Is the Outline Mode?

The outline mode allows you to view and organize your documents by compressing the text normally seen in the edit window into just titles and subtitles. An outline actually appears in another window, while the normal document view remains in the edit window.

 Tip: *The outline of a document is displayed in another window.*

Use SHIFT+F2 to switch between edit mode and outline view. The outline view is similar to the gallery in that it is always present in the background while you work on a document in the edit window. More important, an outline is part of the document, not a separate file in another window.

 Tip: *An outline is a part of your document and is saved with it in the disk file.*

You can develop outlines before you start writing or after your document is written, although it's best to create them beforehand. The lines typed in an outline will normally become the titles and subtitles of a new document. You can type text in outline mode, but it is recommended that you type most of the text in the edit window after the outline is complete. Actually, because its purpose is to allow you to easily reorganize at any time, your outline is never really complete until you are fully satisfied with it.

 Tip: *The outliner enables you to develop the titles and subtitles of your documents.*

Outlining gives you both another way to view and organize your documents and a new way to think about them. You can collect and record ideas in Word's outliner much more conveniently and efficiently than you can on paper. Word's outliner is like a file box for ideas. Even though the outliner is used primarily for displaying and organizing the titles and subtitles of a document, you can still type in normal text, such as notes to yourself, references, and other material.

The outliner is a powerful research tool. As you collect information and research notes, you can place references in the outline under the appropriate headings and later integrate them as your writing progresses.

 Tip: *You can use Word's outliner as a research tool for collecting, organizing, and saving ideas, notes, and reference material.*

Outlining Concepts

This section will introduce the features of outline mode, its terms, and some of its rules. First, look at Figure 18-1, which shows (a) the outline of the document in the outline window, (b) the document in the edit window, and (c) the printed version. Of course the document is not really complete. Much more text can be added. You can see, however, that the outline window offers a compressed view of the document.

In the edit window view shown in Figure 18-1, text has been added under each heading, and the headings are shown with the special character and paragraph formats assigned in the style sheet, as shown in Figure 18-2. The printed copy in Figure 18-1 shows how the formatting differentiates the status of the headings in the document.

 Tip: *A style sheet can contain formats for the heading levels of an outline.*

Heading Levels

When you are creating an outline like the one shown in Figure 18-1, you select various heading levels by *lowering* or *raising* the headings. When a heading is lowered, Word automatically indents it in the outline window. You will not see this indent in the edit window or in the final document unless you format it that way as part of normal character and paragraph formatting.

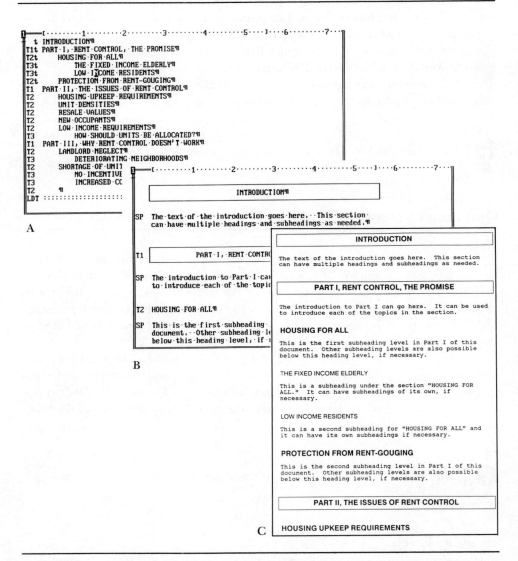

Figure 18-1. Steps in the outline process: a) outline view, b) edit window, and c) printed document

Tip: *When you are typing an outline, you select various heading levels by* raising *and* lowering *the headings.*

 Trap: *The indents you see in the outline mode are not printed; they are used only to display heading levels.*

Every line in a document is assigned one of the seven automatic styles in the style sheet according to how far you lower it. These styles are Heading Levels 1 through 7 in the Paragraph Variant list, as discussed in Chapter 16. Normally Word does not assign any special character or paragraph styles to these heading levels except to indent them and treat them as heading levels in the outline mode. You can, however, apply any special formatting that you need (an example of which is shown in the style sheet of Figure 18-2). The resulting format changes will appear in the normal edit window and in the printed version, as shown in Figure 18-1.

 Tip: *The automatic paragraph styles Heading Levels 1 through 7 are used to format each heading level.*

To lower a heading and thus assign a lower heading level style to it, press ALT+0. To raise a heading back up one level, press ALT+9 in outline mode. When you lower headings, the line is assigned a heading level one below the current level.

Collapsing and Expanding Text

Once the headings of an outline are typed and assigned their proper levels in the outline mode, text can be added in the edit window, as shown in Figure 18-1. If you need to return to outline mode to view or reorganize the document, the text will also be displayed, which is seldom desirable. In this case you should *collapse* the text under the headings so that you can see just the outline view.

```
┌─0·········[·········2·········3········4····]···5········6·········7····┐
│ 11  T1 Paragraph Heading level 1            CHAPTER MAIN HEADINGS       │
│        HELV (modern i) 14/12, Centered, space before 1 li, space after 1│
│        li (keep with following paragraph), Box,                         │
│ 12  T2 Paragraph Heading level 2            CHAPTER SUB-HEADINGS         │
│        HELV (modern i) 14/12, Flush left, space before 1 li, space after 1│
│        li (keep with following paragraph),                              │
│ 13  T3 Paragraph Heading level 3            CHAPTER SUB-SUB-HEADINGS     │
│        HELV (modern i) 12, Flush left, space before 1 li, space after 1 li│
│        (keep with following paragraph),                                 │
└────────────────────────────────────────────────────────────────────────┘
```

Figure 18-2. Formatted headings in a style sheet

 Trap: *Text added under a heading in the edit window will be visible under the heading in outline view until you collapse it under the heading.*

Text is only collapsed in the outline view. If you jump back to the edit window, the full document will be visible. In addition to collapsing text under its headings, you can collapse subheadings under headings, as shown in Figure 18-3. This provides a greatly reduced view of the document.

 Tip: *Collapsing headings and text only affects the document in outline view.*

```
┌─[·········1·········2·········3········4·········5···]···6·········7···┐
│  t INTRODUCTION¶                                                        │
│ T1+ PART·I,·RENT·CONTROL,·THE·PROMISE¶                                  │
│ T1+ PART·II,·THE·ISSUES·OF·RENT·CONTROL¶                                │
│ T1+ PART·III,·WHY·RENT·CONTROL·DOESN'T·WORK¶                            │
└────────────────────────────────────────────────────────────────────────┘
```

Figure 18-3. An outline showing only main headings (subheadings have been collapsed under them)

Reorganizing a Document

When an outline is on the screen, you can switch to a special outline organize mode that lets you quickly rearrange the titles of your document. At first, you might think that this is easily done by deleting a heading to the scrap and then inserting it elsewhere. Remember, however, that an outline heading may contain collapsed text under it. The power of the outline mode lies in its ability to move all subheadings and text with a heading when you move it elsewhere.

 Tip: *When you move a heading, all subheadings and text under it also move.*

For example, look at Figure 18-4. The writer wants to move the heading LANDLORD NEGLECT below the heading SHORTAGE OF UNITS. LAND-LORD NEGLECT has a subheading that must also move. By switching to outline organize mode, you can highlight the title as shown in Figure 18-4 and delete it to the scrap. Figure 18-5 shows how the screen looks after the deletion. The

```
=[·········1·········2·········3·········4·········5···]···6·········7···
   t  INTRODUCTION¶
T1+  PART·I,·RENT·CONTROL,·THE·PROMISE¶
T1+  PART·II,·THE·ISSUES·OF·RENT·CONTROL¶
T1   PART·III,¶
T1   WHY·RENT·CONTROL·DOESN'T·WORK¶
T2       LANDLORD·NEGLECT¶
T3           DETERIORATING·NEIGHBORHOODS¶
T2       SHORTAGE·OF·UNITS¶
T3           NO·INCENTIVES·TO·BUILD·NEW·UNITS¶
T3           INCREASED·COMPETITION·FOR·EXISTING·UNITS¶
T2t      ¶
```

Figure 18-4. A heading highlighted for moving

```
T1   WHY·RENT·CONTROL·DOESN'T·WORK¶
T2       SHORTAGE·OF·UNITS¶
T3           NO·INCENTIVES·TO·BUILD·NEW·UNITS¶
T3           INCREASED·COMPETITION·FOR·EXISTING·UNITS¶
T2t      ¶
```

Figure 18-5. The heading and its subheading temporarily moved to the scrap

subheading is automatically deleted with the heading. Figure 18-6 shows the heading inserted below the previous section and the subheading inserted with it. Note that if this section contained any text, it also would be moved.

Using the outline organize mode is an excellent way to move large amounts of text around in a document. The heading-only view of the outline mode lets you see exactly where the block is and where it will be moved.

```
T1   WHY·RENT·CONTROL·DOESN'T·WORK¶
T2       SHORTAGE·OF·UNITS¶
T3           NO·INCENTIVES·TO·BUILD·NEW·UNITS¶
T3           INCREASED·COMPETITION·FOR·EXISTING·UNITS¶
T2       LANDLORD·NEGLECT¶
T3           DETERIORATING·NEIGHBORHOODS¶
T2t      ¶
```

Figure 18-6. The heading and its subheading reinserted in another location

Jumping Through the Document

Assume that the document outlined in Figure 18-1 is near completion and has a number of pages. You are working in Part III but need to go back to look at a section in Part I. This is easy to do in outline mode. Simply place the highlight on the specific heading of the section in Part I to which you need to jump; then press SHIFT+F2 to go back to edit mode. Part I will then be displayed on the screen.

 Tip: *To quickly jump to other parts of a document, select the desired location in outline view and then return to document view.*

Heading Level Adjustments

Not only can you easily move a heading and all of its subheadings and text to another part of a document with a few keystrokes, you can also adjust the level of a heading. When a heading is lowered or raised, all of its subheadings are lowered or raised with it.

For example, assume in Figure 18-7 that you want to include the Part II heading as a subheading of the first part. When you select the Part II heading, all the subtitles and text under it are collapsed. You then use ALT+0 to lower the heading. The text "Part II" will be removed, and the headings will be expanded.

 Tip: *You can raise or lower a heading and all of its subheadings one level at a time.*

As you can see in Figure 18-8, all the subheadings were lowered to reflect the adjustment that you made to the main heading. Note also that the last heading, HOW SHOULD UNITS BE ALLOCATED?, has been reduced to a fourth-level heading. The style bar displays an asterisk to its left because a style has not yet been defined for fourth-level headings. You can create this style in the gallery.

```
⌐━━[·········1·········2·········3·········4·········5···]···6·········7···┐
   t  INTRODUCTION¶
T1t PART·I,·RENT·CONTROL,·THE·PROMISE¶
T2t      HOUSING·FOR·ALL¶
T3t          THE·FIXED·INCOME·ELDERLY¶
T3t          LOW·INCOME·RESIDENTS¶
T2t      PROTECTION·FROM·RENT-GOUGING¶
T2+      PART·II,·THE·ISSUES·OF·RENT·CONTROL¶
T1  PART·III,·WHY·RENT·CONTROL·DOESN'T·WORK¶
T2       SHORTAGE·OF·UNITS¶
T3           NO·INCENTIVES·TO·BUILD·NEW·UNITS¶
T3           INCREASED·COMPETITION·FOR·EXISTING·UNITS¶
T2       LANDLORD·NEGLECT¶
T3           DETERIORATING·NEIGHBORHOODS¶
T2t       ¶
```

Figure 18-7. You can lower all subheadings under a heading by collapsing them under the heading and then lowering the heading

```
T1t PART·I,·RENT·CONTROL,·THE·PROMISE¶
T2t      HOUSING·FOR·ALL¶
T3t          THE·FIXED·INCOME·ELDERLY¶
T3t          LOW·INCOME·RESIDENTS¶
T2t      PROTECTION·FROM·RENT-GOUGING¶
T2       THE·ISSUES·OF·RENT·CONTROL¶
T3           HOUSING·UPKEEP·REQUIREMENTS¶
T3           UNIT·DENSITIES¶
T3           RESALE·VALUES¶
T3           NEW·OCCUPANTS¶
T3           LOW·INCOME·REQUIREMENTS¶
*                HOW·SHOULD·UNITS·BE·ALLOCATED?¶
```

Figure 18-8. The lowered heading and its subheadings now grouped under the first-level heading

Automatic Numbering

In Figure 18-9 the headings have been numbered according to their level in the outline. Word automatically performs this task when you select the Library Number command. Here a legal number format was used, but you can use Arabic numbers or Roman numerals in either uppercase or lowercase. If you add headings or move them around, Word will automatically renumber your outline.

Outlining Techniques

This section will introduce specific keys, commands, and techniques used to develop, organize, and utilize outlines.

```
[··········1·········2·········3·········4·········5···]···6·········7···]
T1    INTRODUCTION¶
T1t  1.·RENT·CONTROL,·THE·PROMISE¶
T2t     1.1·HOUSING·FOR·ALL¶
T3t        1.1.1·THE·FIXED·INCOME·ELDERLY¶
T3t        1.1.2·LOW·INCOME·RESIDENTS¶
T2t     1.2·PROTECTION·FROM·RENT-GOUGING¶
T2      1.3·THE··ISSUES·OF··RENT·CONTROL¶
T3         1.3.1·HOUSING·UPKEEP·REQUIREMENTS¶
T3         1.3.2·UNIT·DENSITIES¶
T3         1.3.3·RESALE·VALUES¶
T3         1.3.4·NEW·OCCUPANTS¶
T3         1.3.5·LOW·INCOME·REQUIREMENTS¶
*             1.3.5.1·HOW·SHOULD·UNITS·BE·ALLOCATED?¶
T1   2.·WHY·RENT·CONTROL·DOESN'T·WORK¶
T2      2.1·SHORTAGE·OF·UNITS¶
T3         2.1.1·NO·INCENTIVES·TO·BUILD·NEW·UNITS¶
T3         2.1.2·INCREASED·COMPETITION·FOR·EXISTING·UNITS¶
T2      2.2·LANDLORD·NEGLECT¶
T3         2.2.1·DETERIORATING·NEIGHBORHOODS¶
T2t     ¶
```

Figure 18-9. Numbered headings

The Outline Screen

To get to the outline screen, press SHIFT+F2 or select Yes in the Outline field of the Window Options command. Once you are in outline view, many of the operations that you are familiar with in the edit window are no longer valid. For one thing, editing is limited to a single line or paragraph. You can't select more than one paragraph with the highlight and you can't delete the line unless it is just a paragraph marker.

 Trap: *You can select only one line at a time in outline view; to select more, use outline organize mode.*

One way to tell if you are in the outline window is to watch the prompt in the lower-left corner of the screen. It will display either "Level #" or "Text," depending on whether the highlight is on a heading or on text. The number in "Level #" indicates the heading level assigned to it.

When you jump into outline mode, what you see on the screen will depend on the stage of development that your document is in. If you are starting a new document and jump directly into outline view without typing text in the edit window, the outline window will be blank. If you create an outline, go to the edit window to add text, and then jump back into outline view, the screen will at first seem confusing because of the amount of text.

For example, look at the outline view of the document shown in Figure 18-10, where the writer has not yet collapsed the text that was added under each heading. (Note that outline view does not display space before and space after blank lines for the titles, so the text is right up against the titles.) When you have added text to an outline, you must collapse it in the outline view if you don't want it to be visible. This will be covered shortly.

Outline View Symbols   A few symbols appear in the style bar when outline view is active. You are already familiar with some of them. Look at the text and titles shown in Figure 18-11. The symbols T1 and T2 are the key codes for styles

```
█━━[········1········2········3········4········5···]···6········7···]
║T1  INTRODUCTION¶
║T1  1.·RENT·CONTROL,·THE·PROMISE¶
║SPT The·introduction·to·Part·I·can·go·here.··It·can·be·used·
║    to·introduce·each·of·the·topics·in·the·section.¶
║
║T2      1.1·RENT·HOUSING·FOR·ALL¶
║SPT This·is·the·first·subheading·level·in·Part·I·of·this·
║    document.··Other·subheading·levels·are·also·possible·
║    below·this·heading·level,·if·necessary.¶
║
║T3          1.1.1·THE·FIXED·INCOME·ELDERLY¶
║SPT This·is·a·subheading·under·the·section·"HOUSING·FOR·
║    ALL."··It·can·have·subheadings·of·its·own,·if·
║    necessary.▊
```

Figure 18-10.   Uncollapsed text under a heading

```
█━━[········1········2········3········4········5···]···6········7···]
║T1  INTRODUCTION¶
║T1  1.·RENT·CONTROL,·THE·PROMISE¶
║SPT The·introduction·to·Part·I·can·go·here.··It·can·be·used·
║    to·introduce·each·of·the·topics·in·the·section.¶
║
║T2+ 1.1·HOUSING·FOR·ALL¶
║T2t 1.2·PROTECTION·FROM·RENT-GOUGING¶
```

Figure 18-11.   Symbols of an outline (see the text for an explanation)

assigned to the Heading Level 1 and Heading Level 2 automatic styles in the style sheet. The SP key code in the third line designates a Standard Paragraph.

The third character (T) in the third line is exclusive to the outline mode. A capital *T* in outline mode means that a full paragraph is displayed as it would be displayed in the edit window. Now look at title 1.1, HOUSING FOR ALL. The style bar displays the T2 second-level style indicator and a plus sign. The plus sign means that both text and subtitles are collapsed under this heading. (If you look again at Figures 18-9 and 18-10, you can see the subtitles and text under this heading.) Title 1.2, PROTECTION FROM RENT-GOUGING, is also a second-level heading (T2). The lowercase *t* means that body text only is collapsed under this heading. The outline symbols are as follows:

T   Text (not headings) displayed uncollapsed

+   Subheadings and body text collapsed

t   Body text collapsed below the heading

Establishing the Title Styles

Although the style of the headings and subheadings is not important to the outline process, you may want to establish how they will look when printed. This will help you coordinate the different levels of the outline. Figure 18-12 shows a few examples of how you might format heading levels. These styles will of course depend on your printer and its font capabilities.

 Tip: *When you apply styles to the heading levels, they become more visible in the edit window.*

If you don't alter the heading styles in the style sheet, Word will give all titles the same style. It will, however, maintain and remember the heading level status of each title. Thus you can go back in to add or alter heading level styles at any time. Word will automatically apply the new styles to the heading levels as you

---

HEADING LEVEL 1 (CENTERED AND BOXED)

HEADING LEVEL 2, HELVETICA 14pt

HEADING LEVEL 3, HELVETICA 12pt BOLD

HEADING LEVEL 4, HELVETICA 12pt NORMAL

HEADING LEVEL 5, HELVETICA 10pt BOLD

HEADING LEVEL 6, HELVETICA 10pt NORMAL

HEADING LEVEL 7, HELVETICA 10pt ITALIC

HEADING LEVEL 1 (CENTERED AND BOXED)

HEADING LEVEL 2, HELVETICA 12pt BOLD WITH LINE UNDER

HEADING LEVEL 3, HELVETICA 12pt BOLD

HEADING LEVEL 4, HELVETICA 12pt ITALIC

HEADING LEVEL 5, HELVETICA 10pt ITALIC

Figure 18-12. An example of heading level styles

create them. Whenever you lower or raise a heading, Word applies a style to it according to its heading level and the definition for that heading level in the style sheet.

 Tip: *Word automatically changes styles whenever you raise or lower a heading.*

To alter a heading level style, open the gallery window and execute the Insert command. In the Key Code field type a code that you want to use for your titles. Titles like T1 and T2, which reflect the title status and heading level, are recommended. In the Usage field select Paragraph. In the Variant field press F1 and select one of the automatic heading level variants, such as Heading Level 1 or Heading Level 2. In the Remark field you can include a brief description of the format or the heading level status, as illustrated here:

```
INSERT key code: T1              usage: Character(Paragraph)Division
         variant: Heading level 1   remark: FIRST LEVEL TITLE█
```

After inserting the style entry, use the standard formatting procedures to change the styles of each of the headings according to your needs. There are two important formats that you will probably want to give to each of your titles:

- Use the Format Paragraph command to assign space before and space after lines to your titles to automatically separate them from previous text and the first paragraph of the new section. You may want to include two lines in the Space Before field.

- Answer Yes in the Format Paragraph Keep Follow field to ensure that titles are not printed by themselves at the end of each page. Keep Follow will ensure that they are printed on the next page with the first paragraph of the new section.

 Tip: *Add space before and space after lines to titles and keep them together with the first paragraph of the section that they represent.*

The use of two different style sheets at different stages in the development of a document was discussed in Chapter 16. You may want to consider doing this with titles and headings. Here's why. The use of such formats as paragraph boxes, underlines, and boldfacing makes titles easier to see as you scroll through your document in the normal edit window. You may want to have one style sheet that formats all titles with a box for visibility. Then, just before printing, you could use the second style sheet to format the title levels (see the examples shown in Figure 18-12).

Tip: *You can use two style sheets to apply formats to titles, depending on the development stage of the document.*

Word 4 comes with a style sheet called OUTLINE.STY that you may want to alter. It is recommended that you change the key code names to two-letter codes such as T1 and T2 to avoid confusion. You may also want to change the font types and sizes to fit your printer's capabilities. To attach the style sheet, use the Format Stylesheet Attach command as discussed in Chapter 16.

Creating an Outline

To begin creating an outline, switch to the outline mode by pressing SHIFT+F2. If you are outlining a new document, you will see a blank screen. If you are outlining an existing document, the screen will probably be filled with normal text. The process for outlining an existing document will be covered shortly.

Keep in mind that you can type more than just titles in outline mode. You can type normal paragraph text if you want. This is where the style sheet assignments discussed earlier come in handy. You can press the ALT key codes to change title formats and to switch to typing text. If a style sheet is not attached, Word will indent each line according to its level but will not apply formats.

Typing the lines of an outline is no different than typing in the normal edit window. Word will not let you indent the first line. You must first type a title or text at this first level.

Normally Word will suggest that the first-line format be text. If a style sheet is attached, press ALT+T+1 (assuming that first-level headings have the key code T1) to assign the first-level heading formats. Now everything that you type will retain the title formats until you switch back to normal paragraph mode by typing ALT+X+P. Remember that body text should be typed in the normal edit mode, not in the outline mode.

Tip: *You can develop outlines without title formatting and assign the formatting later.*

To lower a heading, press ALT+0. This is also the right parenthesis key, which can help you remember that the key is used to lower headings. When you lower a heading, Word automatically applies the heading level formats for that heading. The style code in the style bar will change to reflect the heading level.

To raise a heading, press ALT+9. The left parenthesis on this key should help you remember its function. As with lowering a heading, the style sheet format is automatically applied according to the heading level.

If you need to insert headings between existing ones, place the highlight on the first letter of the heading that the new heading is to be inserted in front of and press ENTER. You may need to change the heading level. You can do this by pressing ALT+0 or ALT+9, or by typing the style code with the ALT key.

Outlining an Existing Document

Working with an existing document is easier when you can view it in an outline format. If you are editing a document, especially one written by someone else, an outline is especially useful and can help you reorganize blocks of text with which you are not intimately familiar.

Load the document and switch to the outline mode. All text blocks will have the standard text format, indicated by a "T" in the style bar. Select each title and apply the appropriate heading style to it. If you haven't already established heading styles, refer to the earlier section in this chapter called "Establishing the Title Styles." After applying the titles, you can collapse the text to see the outline view and reorganize the text as needed. These topics are discussed next.

Collapsing and Expanding Headings

You collapse and expand the subheadings and body text of headings in the outline mode (or in the outline organize mode, covered next). The text, the headings, or both may be collapsed or expanded. Remember that the current (highlighted) heading is the one that will be expanded or collapsed, so you don't necessarily need to be on a level 1 or 2 heading.

Tip: *The heading that you highlight is the one that will be expanded or collapsed.*

Collapsing Text and Headings   You can collapse text, subheadings, or both under a heading. To collapse both headings and text under the selected heading, press the MINUS key (− on the numeric keypad). You can also press ALT+8 if your keyboard doesn't have a numeric keypad, press F11 on an expanded keyboard, or press both buttons on a mouse when pointing to the heading.

To collapse just the text under a heading, press SHIFT+MINUS (− on the numeric keypad), SHIFT+ALT+8, or SHIFT+F11.

Remember that when text is collapsed, a lowercase *t* appears in the style bar. When both text and subheadings are collapsed, a plus sign (+) appears in the style bar next to the heading.

Expanding Text and Headings.   There are several ways to expand the text and subheadings under a heading. You can place the highlight on the collapsed heading and press the ASTERISK (or PRTSC) key to expand all subheadings under a heading.

To expand only the next lower-level headings, press the PLUS key (+ on the numeric keypad) or press F12 on an expanded keyboard. You can also press ALT+7 or click with the right button on the mouse while pointing at the heading. To expand text, press SHIFT+PLUS (+ on the numeric keypad), SHIFT+ALT+7, or SHIFT+F12.

Expanding and Collapsing Highlighted Text   You can highlight specific blocks of text in the outline organize mode (covered next) and use the keys just mentioned to either expand or contract the text. Press SHIFT+F10 to select the entire text. When the entire text is collapsed, only the first-level headings will remain.

Reorganizing Outlines

You can reorganize a document by selecting a heading in the outliner and moving it elsewhere. All subheadings and text under that heading will move with it. To reorganize an outline, you must be in the outline organize mode, which you access by pressing SHIFT+F5 while in the outline mode. The word *organize* will appear in the lower-left corner of the screen when you are in this mode.

 Tip: *Use the outline organize mode to rearrange an outline.*

Reorganizing a document is as easy as highlighting the heading that you want to move and deleting it to the scrap. You can move the highlight to a new insertion point and press the INS key. If you determine that certain subheadings should not be moved with that heading, raise them to the same level as the heading that you are moving and then move the heading. This will seldom cause a problem because any headings left behind will presumably form a new heading of their own.

 Tip: *To move some but not all subheadings, select the ones that you don't want to move and raise their heading level.*

You can sort headings with the Library Sort command. The trick is to specify a number before each heading that designates what its new place should be in the sorted headings. For example, simply type **1**, **2**, and **3** before collapsed headings because all subheadings and body text move with a sorted list.

Numbering Outlines

The headings in an outline can be numbered and renumbered as needed. The number format that Word uses places Roman numerals first, then capital letters, then Arabic numbers, then lowercase letters, and so on. The legal numbering scheme illustrated in Figure 18-9 is also possible.

To number a entire outline, simply select the Library Number command, illustrated here:

```
LIBRARY NUMBER: Update Remove          restart sequence:(Yes)No
```

This command lets you update (or add) or remove numbers. Choose Update and select Yes in the Restart Sequence field. If you want a different numbering sequence, such as the legal one, type a number in front of the first heading. The number must be a 1 followed by a period and a space or tab.

You can renumber an outline after it has been reorganized. First, remove any existing numbers with the Library Number command by selecting the Remove option. Select the first character in the first heading or type a number, period, and space in this position if you want legal numbering. Choose Update in the Library Number command and press ENTER. You can also renumber selected portions of an outline by highlighting the portion to be renumbered. This is often the case when you just reorganize one section of your document. Remember that you must be in outline organize mode to select more than one line.

Tips and Traps Summary

What Is the Outline Mode?

Tip: The outline of a document is displayed in another window.

Tip: An outline is a part of your document and is saved with it in the disk file.

Tip: The outliner enables you to develop the titles and subtitles of your documents.

Tip: You can use Word's outliner as a research tool for collecting, organizing, and saving ideas, notes, and reference material.

Outlining Concepts

Tip: A style sheet can contain formats for the heading levels of an outline.

Tip: When you are typing an outline, you select heading levels by *raising* and *lowering* the headings.

Tips and Traps Summary (*continued*)

Trap: The indents you see in the outline mode are not printed; they are used only to display heading levels.

Tip: The automatic paragraph styles Heading Levels 1 through 7 are used to format each heading level.

Trap: Text added under a heading in the edit window will be visible under the heading in outline view until you collapse it under the heading.

Tip: Collapsing headings and text only affects the document in outline view.

Tip: When you move a heading, all subheadings and text under it also move.

Tip: To quickly jump to other parts of a document, select the desired location in outline view and then return to document view.

Tip: You can raise or lower a heading and all of its subheadings one level at a time.

Outlining Techniques

Trap: You can select only one line at a time in outline view; to select more, use outline organize mode.

Tip: When you apply styles to the heading levels, they become more visible in the edit window.

Tip: Word automatically changes styles whenever you raise or lower a heading.

Tip: Add space before and space after lines to titles and keep them together with the first paragraph of the section that they represent.

Tips and Traps Summary (*continued*)

Tip: You can use two style sheets to apply formats to titles, depending on the development stage of the document.

Tip: You can develop outlines without title formatting and assign the formatting later.

Tip: The heading that you highlight is the one that will be expanded or collapsed.

Reorganizing Outlines

Tip: Use the outline organize mode to rearrange an outline.

Tip: To move some but not all subheadings, select the ones that you don't want to move and raise their heading level.

19

Printing Techniques

Microsoft Word's Print command, in its most basic form, will print your documents using the formats that you applied during editing. But just as a videocassette recorder will do more than just play back movies, Word's powerful set of optional printing features will do much more than just produce a hard-copy printout. These tools let you fully control how the printer handles your document when printing. For example, you can print specific pages or blocks of text, or you can use the printer as if it were a typewriter. You can "stack" several documents in a queue to be printed in succession, or you can print multiple copies and merge information from a data file as you print. All of the topics that involve printing are discussed or reviewed in this chapter.

The Print Commands

Word's print commands are shown here and on the next page:

`PRINT: `**`Printer`**` Direct File Glossary Merge Options Queue Repaginate`

The command that Word proposes when you enter the Print menu is Printer. When you type **P** twice at the Word Main menu, the document in the edit window is printed.

The commands in the Print menu are listed and described here:

Printer	Print the current document.
Direct	Type directly to the printer from the keyboard.
File	Direct the printing to a file for later printing or printing on another printer.
Glossary	Print the glossary.
Merge	Merge fields from a data file into the current document while printing.
Options	Change the print options.
Queue	Print one or more documents while continuing to work in Word.
Repaginate	Preview and change page breaks before printing.

The Print Options command, illustrated here, contains many important commands that you will use to print documents in various ways.

```
PRINT OPTIONS printer: H2LASMS              setup: LPT1:
          copies: 1                         draft: Yes(No)
          hidden text: Yes(No)              summary sheet: Yes(No)
          range:(All)Selection Pages        page numbers:
          widow/orphan control:(Yes)No      queued: Yes(No)
          feed: Manual(Continuous)Bin1 Bin2 Bin3 Mixed
```

All of Word's print commands are covered in the following sections. The Print Options command is covered first because it is used in a number of ways to control how documents print. If your printer has not yet been set up or installed, refer to the section called "Printer Setup" later in this chapter.

Setting Print Options
and Printing a Document

As mentioned earlier, printing the current document is as simple as typing **P** twice in the Word Main menu. This will execute the Printer command in the

Print menu and begin printing. If windows are open to different documents, the highlight must be in the window of the one that you want to print before you execute the command.

 Trap: *If more than one window is open, only the document in the current window is printed.*

There is a slight delay before Word starts printing your document. You will see the message "Formatting page 1 of *filename*," where *filename* is the name of your document. Word determines the page break and sets the fonts and type styles for the first page; then it moves on to the next page and continues in that way until the document is printed.

If the document doesn't print the first time, several things could be wrong. The printer may not be on, the paper may not be loaded (or may be jammed), or the cable may not be connected (refer to the last section, "Printing Problems," for more details). If the printer prints, but the printing is garbled, the wrong printer description file is probably loaded (refer to the "Printer Setup" section for more details).

 Trap: *Garbled printing usually indicates an improper printer description file.*

If only certain sections or pages print, or if multiple copies print, check the settings in the Print Options command. Certain fields in this command do not reset to their defaults after a document is printed, and these settings may be adversely affecting the printing of your current document.

Stopping the Printer

You can stop the printer by pressing the ESC key. This will produce the message "Enter Y to continue or Esc to cancel." You may need to quickly change paper types, answer the phone, or whatever. When you type **Y**, printing will resume at the exact point where it was stopped. If you press ESC a second time, printing will stop altogether and the current sheet will be ejected from the printer.

Tip: *You can temporarily pause printing by pressing* ESC *and then resume at any time.*

You will want to stop the printer if you notice that the first sheet is not formatted properly or you forgot to set double spacing or some other options. If that is the case, you must make your corrections and start printing all over.

Recorded Print Settings

Word saves some, but not all, of the Print Option settings. Some settings are saved only during the current Word session, while others are saved from session to session if you quit Word with the Quit command.

 Tip: *When some of the print options are set, they remain so from one Word session to the next.*

The following settings are saved from one session to the next if they are altered during a session:

Print Options Printer
Print Options Setup
Print Options Draft
Print Options Hidden Text
Print Options Widow/Orphan Control
Print Options Feed

The following fields are saved only during the current Word session:

Print Options Copies
Print Options Hidden Text
Print Options Range
Print Options Page Numbers
Print Options Queued

Selecting the Number of Copies

Select the number of copies of a document that you want to print in the Print Options Copies field. Word prints an entire document before it starts printing the next, which ensures proper collation of the documents.

Draft Mode and Microspace Justification

Select draft mode printing by answering Yes in the Print Options Draft field. It will speed up printing and produce a lower-quality printout of a document that you can use for editing or revising.

You might think that the draft mode would print a nonformatted, straight text document, ignoring font and type style changes in order to speed up the printing. This is not the case. Draft mode is designed for printers that use microspace justification. It speeds up printing by ignoring the calculations required to microspace. If your printer does not do this, you may not notice a difference in printing modes.

 Trap: *You may not notice a difference in speed if your printer does not use microspace justification in draft mode.*

When a paragraph is both left- and right-justified, microspace justification places extra space between words to produce a visually appealing alignment. Extra character-size spaces are subdivided into microspaces, which are then allocated over the whole line.

 Tip: *To print a nonformatted version of a document, create a second style sheet and change the font of all styles to a draft-quality font.*

Printing Hidden Text

You can print hidden text whether it is visible in the edit window or not. Simply choose Yes in the Print Options Hidden Text field. You can print the notes that you included in your text with a document, or, if you are using footnotes and table of contents entries, you can print them with the document for editing.

Printing the Summary Sheets

If you are using summary sheets to create synopses of your documents, select Yes in the Print Options Summary Sheet field to print the summary sheet for the current document. This topic is also covered in the next chapter.

Printing Specific Pages

You can print only a specific page or range of pages. Thus, if you need to change paper types or have edited a certain section, you are not forced to reprint the entire document. Two options are used to select specific pages. First, choose the Pages option in the Print Options Range field. Then tab to the Page Numbers field and select the pages to print, using the following formats:

- To print individual or noncontiguous pages, type the page number or separate multiple page numbers with a comma. For example, type **3,5,10** to print pages 3, 5, and 10.

- To print contiguous groups of pages, separate the page numbers with a colon or hyphen. For example, type **3:11** or **3-11** to print pages 3 through 11.

- To print a division or pages within a division, type **d** followed by the division number. For example, type **5-7d2** to print pages 5 through 7 in division 2.

You can combine most of these options in a number of ways. For example, type **3,5,7-10,3d2** to print pages 3, 5, and 7 through 10 in division 1 and page 3 in division 2.

If you select Pages in the Print Options Range field and press ENTER, the highlight will jump to the Pages field and request page numbers first.

Remember that the settings in the Range and Pages fields will stay active during a Word session. If you decide to print the entire document, select All in the Print Options Range field.

Trap: *Options set in the Range field stay active during a Word session, affecting future printing. Don't forget to change them.*

Printing Highlighted Text Only

To print just a specific portion of your document, choose Selection in the Print Options Range field, highlight the text that you want to print, and select the Print menu's Printer command. You can use this option to run a test print of tables or other selections to check alignment or fonts and type styles.

 Tip: *You can test table alignments or font changes by printing just the highlighted selection.*

You can also use this feature to print a quick note while you are in the middle of creating a document. Simply type the text of the note, highlight it, choose Selection in the Print Options Range field, and print it. After printing, press DEL to remove the highlighted note from the document.

Controlling the Paper Feed on the Printer

You can control the way your printer feeds paper with the Print Options Feed command. The selections are as follows:

Manual
: Select Manual to feed sheets one at a time. Use this option if the first sheet differs from the rest or if a sheet feeder is not present. Word prompts for each sheet when this option is set.

Continuous
: Set this option when continuous tractor-feed paper is used.

Bin1,2,3
: Set Bin1, Bin2, or Bin3 when a sheet feeder with multiple bins is attached to a printer. Select the bin with the paper type that you want to use for a print job.

Mixed
: Use this option to print on two different types of paper. Word will select the first sheet from Bin1 and all other sheets from Bin2. Use this option when you want to print on company letterhead.

 Tip: *To print mixed company letterhead and second sheets, use the Manual print feed setting, or use the Mixed setting if a dual-bin sheet feeder is attached.*

Queued Printing

A *queued* document is one that prints while you continue to work in Word. You can set up several documents in the queue at once so that you can use it to start and continue a large print job while you are doing something else. In this way you do not need to stand by to start the printing for other documents.

 Tip: *Placing a document in a queue lets you continue to use Word. You can also queue several documents for printing and then leave the computer unattended.*

To set up a queued printing job, set the Print Options Queued field to Yes and choose the Print Printer command to start printing. The print queue requires some disk space because Word creates a print file for the document being printed. As the document prints, you can load other documents and place them in the queue.

 Tip: *The number of documents in the print queue is limited by available disk space.*

Use the Print Queue command illustrated here,

PRINT QUEUE: `Continue` Pause Restart Stop

to control the queue once it is set in motion. This command lets you continue printing after the queue has been paused, restart the printing of a document from its beginning, and completely stop the print queue.

Typewriter Mode

The Print Direct command echoes what is typed on the keyboard at the printer. This command is most useful for printers with a platen that allows single envelopes or notes to be inserted. It is not commonly used on laser printers because you must be able to see where the printer will print, just as you do when typing on a typewriter.

With some printers, the Print Direct command is awkward to use because the printer does not always directly respond the way that a typewriter responds when you press a key. Some characters do not print until you press ENTER, and tab and space characters may not print until you type a "normal" character. Because of this, it is sometimes hard to align the print head at the intended place on the sheet or envelope.

You can perform direct printing at any time, even while a document is loaded in the edit window. Characters typed in typewriter mode are not added to the text in the edit window or saved to disk in any way. They are sent directly to the printer. Also, Word will not ask you if you want to save the characters.

 Trap: *Characters that you type with the Print Direct command are not added to the document in the edit window.*

The printer will usually begin printing in the leftmost resting position of the print head. You must line up the paper or envelope according to this point. If you need to space in further, press the TAB key or the SPACEBAR. When you have finished printing directly, press ESC to return to normal edit mode.

 Tip: *The margin settings are not applicable when you are using the Print Direct command to print directly.*

Printing to a File

Printing to a file may seem confusing at first, but there are good reasons for doing this. When a document is printed to a file, all the text and all the commands used to format that text on your printer are saved with the file. You can then print the file outside of Microsoft Word.

 Tip: *Print a file to disk for later printing or for printing on another computer.*

Several reasons why you may want to use print files are listed here:

- You can use print files on systems that do not have Word installed but do have a printer that you want to use. Use the printer description file for that printer when you print to the file.

- You can also use print files to take advantage of the DOS PRINT command, which allows queueing of files much as the Word Queue command does. You can use the DOS queue if you need to do work outside of Word or to print on a system that does not have Microsoft Word installed.

- Finally, you can use print files to send formatted documents on disk to other users who may not have Word.

You can print the print files at any time. Use the DOS COPY command to copy them to other diskettes.

 Tip: *Files printed to disk do not require the Word program in order to print.*

Printing the Glossary

You can print the current glossary with the Print Glossary command. The glossary entry name is printed on the left, and the text is indented and printed under it. Page breaks print as <Page>, and division breaks print as <Division>. You may want to use this command occasionally to print the glossary as a reminder or to clean up the glossary, as discussed in Chapter 15.

Merged Printing

Merged printing is used to create form documents that coordinate information in data files with a document file. You can insert names and addresses from a data file, or you can insert account balances, first names, product information, historical information, or any other text that you might keep track of in a data file. (Chapter 21 covers the merge process in detail.)

Controlling Page Breaks

You can preview or alter the way that Word breaks pages. Word does not automatically recalculate page breaks while you add text. But you can use the Print

Repaginate command to reset the page breaks any time after text has been added. You can oversee the page breaks by selecting Yes in the Confirm Page Breaks field, as illustrated here:

PRINT REPAGINATE confirm page breaks: Yes **No**

You can also select the Print Repaginate command by pressing CTRL+F9.

If you choose not to confirm page breaks, Word will quickly recalculate them. As it does so, the page numbers will show in the status line, allowing you to see the new number of pages in your document. Word will also insert the page break symbol (a single row of dots) at all page breaks in the document.

 Tip: Use the Print Repaginate command to quickly determine the number of pages in a document or update the page indicator in the status line after text has been added.

Keep in mind that any additions or deletions of text after a Print Repaginate will offset the page breaks. However, the page break symbols will not adjust to new positions. You must repaginate. Note that printing will repaginate a document, but you will not be able to view where it breaks pages.

Recall from Chapter 11 that you can control how Word will break paragraphs and section titles by selecting the Keep Together and Keep Follow fields in the Format Paragraph command. You can keep a section title together with the paragraph that follows it, thus preventing Word from printing a title by itself at the bottom of a page.

 Tip: You may not have to manually check page breaks if you use the Keep Together and Keep Follow settings in the Format Paragraph command.

Confirming Page Breaks

If you choose Yes in the Print Repaginate Confirm Page Breaks field, Word will change the screen to printer display mode and scroll through the document, displaying page break symbols at the appropriate places. You can then adjust the page breaks up if necessary. You cannot add additional lines; you can only shorten the amount of text on a page.

Tip: *Word's suggested page breaks can be adjusted up but not down.*

If you confirm a page break, Word quickly moves to the next one. If you adjust a page break, Word inserts the page break in the position that you select and begins to calculate the next page. If Word comes to a page break that was inserted when the text was typed, the message "Enter Y to confirm or R to remove" will appear. The page break is highlighted. Type **R** to remove it, and Word will recalculate the current page.

 Trap: *Page breaks adjusted during a previous pagination will appear in the new pagination. However, Word allows you to remove them because they may no longer be valid.*

A good reason to answer Yes in the Confirm Page Breaks field is to ensure that pages do not break in odd places, such as immediately after a title or in the last line of a paragraph. You can, however, control this automatically and eliminate the need to confirm page breaks by setting the Keep Together and Keep Follow fields in the Format Paragraph command, as discussed earlier.

Commands That Affect Printing

Beyond the commands covered here, the format commands covered in Chapters 10 through 13 are used to control how the document is printed. These topics are summarized here.

Controlling Fonts and Type Styles

You control the fonts and type styles for your printer with the Format Character command. Chapter 10 discussed how you can test the fonts and styles on your printer by printing out a sample test sheet. Some printers allow control of the printer font from the front panel, but it is usually better to do this through the format commands unless a proper printer description file is not available for your printer.

When you change fonts on impact (daisy wheel) printers, you may see the message "Enter Y after mounting," followed by a font name. Word is signaling that it has come to a font change in the text and is requesting that the print wheel be changed.

Page Layout

You determine how the text is placed on the printed page with page layout commands. They cover paper-size settings as well as the margins and running heads. Use the format division commands, covered in Chapters 12 and 13, to set these parameters.

Printer Setup

This section covers the installation and setup of a printer. If you are setting up the printer for the first time, you must make sure that the correct cable is connected to the proper port and that the Print command is set to recognize this port. You must also select the correct printer description file, paper size, and margins.

Setting Up the Printer

The printer must be unpacked and set up according to the printer manual. Make sure to remove all packing ties; otherwise, the printer may not work properly. Install the printer ribbon or toner cartridge.

Feed in the paper. On printers that use tractor-feed paper, make sure that the sprockets are in the correct position to align the edge of the paper with the paper edge mark on your printer. Your manual should explain this procedure. The edge of the paper is to the right of the sprocket holes at the tear-off point.

 Tip: *Adjust the sprockets on pin-feed printers to align the paper edge with the print head.*

If you are using a laser printer, place the paper in the tray. Some paper has a special print side, so make sure it is in the proper direction. If you are using legal paper, you must use the appropriate tray which activates switches inside the printer to accommodate the longer sheets.

 Trap: *Make sure that you know which way is "up" in the paper tray so that the printing side of the paper is up.*

 Trap: *Most paper has a natural curl. Make sure that the paper curl follows the curled path of the paper through the printer; otherwise, paper jams may occur.*

The Printer Interface

Some printers may have two printer cable ports. One of these is usually a Centronics-type parallel printer interface, and the other is usually a serial printer interface. The serial interface port will be smaller and have a 25-pin female-type connector. You may need to set switches inside your printer to select the interface you need. On some printers this is done on the front panel.

The interface type that you use will depend on the port of your computer. In most cases it is much easier to use the parallel printer port. However, if you must place the printer more than 10 to 12 feet away from the computer, consider using the serial interface because it can carry signals over a longer distance with fewer errors.

 Tip: *Use the serial interface if your printer must be more than 12 feet from the computer.*

The Printer Cable

If the printer cable is parallel, it should not be much longer than 12 feet. Signals in parallel cables tend to go out of synchronization over long distances, producing garbled output.

If the cable is serial, it may need to be specially designed for the computer and printer you are using. A discussion of serial interfacing is beyond the scope of this book. You should check with an appropriate dealer or electronics firm for a cable that fits your needs. Your printer manual will have a chart that lists the serial pinouts. If the cable will extend over some distance or be strung near fluorescent lighting, make sure that it is shielded.

Establishing a Serial Connection

If a serial connection is being made, you must add a few commands to the startup file of your computer system. This is the AUTOEXEC.BAT file, which should be located in the ROOT directory of your system. If it doesn't exist, you must create one. Using Microsoft Word, execute the Transfer Load command and type **\AUTOEXEC.BAT** in the field.

 Tip: *The AUTOEXEC.BAT file, which executes automatically every time the computer starts, can contain commands to set up the serial printer port.*

If the file exists, it will be displayed on the screen. If it doesn't exist, type **Y** to create it. Add the following line to the file:

MODE COM1:9600,n,8,1,p

This command will initialize the COM1 serial communications port to a baud rate of 9600, no parity, eight data bits, and one stop bit for printing. Your printer must match these settings, or you can alter them to match your printer. Refer to your printer manual for its current settings or for instructions in how to adjust the printer.

 Trap: *The baud rate and other settings in the computer must match those of the printer, which you may be able to adjust with printer dip switches.*

 Trap: *You may need to reduce the baud rate if garbled printing occurs.*

After establishing the printer connection, you can try printing by pressing the PRTSC key while in DOS. If nothing happens, you may need assistance from a qualified technician in order to set up your printer.

Selecting the Printer Description File

Once the printer has been connected, you must copy the printer description file for that printer from the Word printer disks to your working disk or hard-drive directory. Once the correct description file is installed, you must select it in the Print Options Printer field.

The procedure for copying the printer driver to your Word disk was covered in Chapter 1. You can use the SETUP program to install both Word and the printer driver. You can also use the DOS COPY command to copy the printer description file from the Word printer disks to your Word disk or directory. The COPY command is often used to copy a different printer description file after Word has already been set up.

First, locate the printer description file on one of the Word printer disks and copy it to the disk in the other drive or to the WORD directory on your hard drive. A COPY command to copy the Epson FX printer driver to the WORD directory on a hard drive is shown here.

```
COPY A:EPSONFX.PRD C:\WORD
```

The next step is to start Word in the normal way. Open the Print Options menu and press F1 with the highlight in the Printer field. Choose the printer description file that you want to use and press ENTER. There may be only one description file or there may be several, depending on the printers available.

Selecting the Printer Port

Use the Print Options Setup field to select a different printer port. A *port* is a connection on the back of a computer to which a cable can be attached and run to an external printer. Some systems may have two printers connected and so will use two of these ports. To use one or the other printer, you will need to change the port description in the Print Options command.

Tab to the Setup field and press F1 to see the listing illustrated here:

`COM1:` `LPT1:` `LPT2:` `LPT3:`
`COM2:`

There are three LPT ports and two COM ports. The LPT ports are line printer ports that support standard parallel Centronics printers. The COM ports are communications ports that support serial interfacing. Note that your system may not physically have all these ports available.

A single parallel printer is normally connected to LPT1. If you have two parallel printers, the second will be connected to LPT2. If you have a serial printer, the first one will be connected to COM1. You can even have a parallel printer connected to LPT1 and a serial printer connected to COM2. Simply select the port of the printer that you want to use.

If you followed the procedure earlier for installing a serial printer with the AUTOEXEC.BAT file, COM1 may already be selected in the Setup field.

Setting the Paper Size and Margins

Once all of the connections and settings have been made, you can start printing. You may need to adjust the paper size and margins by using the format division commands discussed in Chapter 12.

Printing Problems

When the printer doesn't print, the solution is sometimes as simple as making sure that it has power or that the printer ribbon is correctly installed. This section will discuss a few of the more common printer problems.

Centering Text on the Page

This problem, which has been discussed more than once in this book, has to do with the inability of some printers (especially laser printers) to print near the edges of the paper. If you have this problem with a normal impact or dot-matrix printer, simply move the paper further to the right or left. With laser printers, you must reduce the paper size in the Format Division Margins command to accommodate the nonprinting areas. (Refer to Chapter 12 and Figure 12-2 for a discussion on properly setting up the Hewlett-Packard LaserJet printers.)

Garbled Printing

When the printer prints unknown and garbled characters, an incorrect printer description file is probably loaded. Use the Print Options Printer field to select another printer. You may need to try a different printer description file from the Word printer disks. The procedure for copying another file was discussed earlier.

If a printer description file is not available for your printer, try other description files for printers from the same manufacturer. If all else fails, use the TTY file on the printer disks. You will be able to print standard text, but Word character and paragraph formats may not print properly. Contact Microsoft for a printer description file that works with your printer.

 Tip: *When all else fails, you can usually use the TTY printer description file to print on an undefined printer.*

For those with a knack for programming, Word offers a program called MAKEPRD that allows printer manufacturers and advanced users to create a description file for any printer. This program is covered completely in the printer information manual supplied with Word.

Printing Starts Too Low or Too High

When the printer doesn't print in the proper place, the most common culprits are the margin settings and the paper size. Some printers with automatic sheet feeders may automatically feed the paper a certain distance to accommodate a top margin. If a top margin is also set in Word, these two top margins will be placed on the paper. You can make adjustments in the Format Division Margins command to correct the problem.

Printer Doesn't Print

If the printer just doesn't print, check for power at the printer and make sure that the cables are connected and that a paper jam hasn't occurred. Word will sometimes flash a message after a few seconds that a paper jam has occurred. The printer ribbon may have broken, or the ribbon may be at the end of its reel.

When the printer is a serial device, you must check the following areas:

- Make sure that one of the COM ports is selected in the Print Options Setup field.

- Make sure that the correct baud rate and other communications options are set by using the MODE command at the DOS level (a command for doing this was described earlier).

- Make sure that the printer cable is connected to one of the serial ports on your computer and to the serial port on your printer.

- Make sure that the printer is set up to use the serial adapter. Some printers have both serial and parallel plugs, so you may need to set dip switches to activate the serial plug on the printer.

- If all else fails, the problem is almost certainly in the wiring of the cable. Try reversing pins 2 and 3 on one side of the cable. If that doesn't work, call in a technician.

It is often helpful to try printing from DOS rather than Word to isolate the problem to the printer or the printer connection. Printer problems can rarely be traced back to Word as long as the correct printer description files and ports are set. Try using the PRTSC key to print the current screen on the printer. If this test doesn't work and you have checked the other possible solutions, you may need to call a technician. It is possible that the printer port is defective, the cable is wired incorrectly, or the plug on the printer is defective.

Tips and Traps Summary

Setting Print Options and Printing a Document

Trap: If more than one window is open, only the document in the current window is printed.

Trap: Garbled printing usually indicates an improper printer description file.

Tip: You can temporarily pause printing by pressing ESC and then resume at any time.

Tips and Traps Summary (*continued*)

Tip: When some of the print options are set, they remain so from one Word session to the next.

Trap: You may not notice a difference in speed if your printer does not use microspace justification in draft mode.

Tip: To print a nonformatted version of a document, create a second style sheet and change the font of all styles to a draft-quality font.

Trap: Options set in the Range field stay active during a Word session, affecting future printing. Don't forget to change them.

Tip: You can test table alignments or font changes by printing just the highlighted selection.

Tip: To print mixed company letterhead and second sheets, use the Manual print feed setting, or use the Mixed setting if a dual-bin sheet feeder is attached.

Queued Printing

Tip: Placing a document in a *queue* lets you continue to use Word. You can also queue several documents for printing and then leave the computer unattended.

Tip: The number of documents in the print queue is limited by available disk space.

Typewriter Mode

Trap: Characters that you type with the Print Direct command are not added to the document in the edit window.

Tip: The margin settings are not applicable when you are using Print Direct command to print directly.

Tips and Traps Summary (*continued*)

Printing to a File

Tip: Print a file to disk for later printing or for printing on another computer.

Tip: Files printed to disk do not require the Word program in order to print.

Controlling Page Breaks

Tip: Use the Print Repaginate command to quickly determine the number of pages in a document or update the page indicator in the status line after text has been added.

Tip: You may not have to manually check page breaks if you use the Keep Together and Keep Follow settings in the Format Paragraph command.

Tip: Word's suggested page breaks can be adjusted up but not down.

Trap: Page breaks adjusted during a previous pagination will appear in the new pagination. However, Word allows you to remove them because they may no longer be valid.

Printer Setup

Tip: Adjust the sprockets on pin-feed printers to align the paper edge with the print head.

Trap: Make sure that you know which way is "up" in the paper tray so that the printing side of the paper is up.

Trap: Most paper has a natural curl. Make sure that the paper curl follows the curled path of the paper through the printer; otherwise, paper jams may occur.

Tips and Traps Summary (*continued*)

Tip: Use the serial interface if your printer must be more than 12 feet from the computer.

Tip: The AUTOEXEC.BAT file, which executes automatically every time the computer starts, can contain commands to set up the serial printer port.

Trap: The baud rate and other settings in the computer must match those of the printer, which you may be able to adjust with printer dip switches.

Trap: You may need to reduce the baud rate if garbled printing occurs.

Printing Problems

Tip: When all else fails, you can usually use the TTY printer description file to print on an undefined printer.

20

Word Tools

This chapter discusses various tools that Word makes available to facilitate document creation. You can control how words are hyphenated to improve the appearance of paragraph alignments, and you can sort lines in special orders. The thesaurus and spelling checker can dramatically reduce the time and effort that you put into editing.

Many of the tools discussed in this section are found in the Library command of the Word main command menu.

Hyphenation Techniques

Hyphenation improves the appearance of jagged margins by breaking words either at a position that you specify or at a position automatically picked by Word. Hyphenation is especially useful when the right margin is justified because it reduces the number of leftover spaces placed between words to align the text.

 Tip: *Hyphenation is most useful when paragraphs are justified.*

583

Hyphenation is performed either manually, while you type, or automatically by Word when the document is near completion. You can place three types of hyphens while you type. In some cases hyphenating while you type is the only way to print the type of hyphen required for the word. The three types of hyphens are listed here:

Normal	Hyphen key on keyboard.
	Some words already contain hyphens, such as *round-about* or *leisure-class*. You type these hyphens with the normal hyphen symbol. If the words fall at the end of a line, Word may break the line on the hyphen that you specified.
Optional	CTRL+HYPHEN.
	The optional hyphen is used when you want to specify where a word should break if it falls at the end of a line. The optional hyphen is used when Word automatically hyphenates a document, but you can insert your own.
Nonbreaking	CTRL+SHIFT+HYPHEN.
	The nonbreaking hyphen is used for words that require hyphens but should not be split over two lines at the hyphen. For example, names such as Alexandra Liley-Sheldon can be kept together with nonbreaking hyphens.

You can use each of these hyphens while typing the text of a document to better control the hyphenation process. Note that optional hyphens will not appear on the screen unless you set the Options Visible field to Partial or Complete. To delete such a hyphen, set the Visible field on so that the hyphens are visible; then press DEL to delete the hyphen as you would any other character.

 Trap: *To delete hyphens, set the Options Visible field to Partial or Complete and then use the DEL key.*

Automatic Hyphenation

The Hyphenation command is found in the Library menu and shown below. By selecting Yes in the Confirm field, you can control how Word inserts hyphens. Use the Hyphenate Caps field to designate whether words in all caps should be hyphenated or not.

```
LIBRARY HYPHENATE confirm: Yes No        hyphenate caps:(Yes)No
```

The following rules apply when you use the Hyphenate command.

- Word hyphenates from the current highlight down through the document.

- You can select the portion of the document that you want to hyphenate.

- You can insert optional hyphens with the automatic hyphenation routine.

- Word only inserts hyphens in words that fall at the end of a line.

- Word inserts hyphens according to positions specified in a standard dictionary; therefore, it will always insert correct hyphens.

- You can alter Word's predetermined hyphen position by selecting Yes in the Library Hyphenation Confirm field.

- Word switches to printer display mode as it hyphenates a document if you select Yes in the Confirm field.

To hyphenate a document, move to the top by pressing CTRL+PGUP, or start hyphenating at the location of the highlight. Select the Library Hyphenate command and choose Yes in the Confirm field if you want to control how Word hyphenates the document.

When Confirm is selected, Word will stop at each word and display the message "Enter Y to insert hyphen, N to skip, or use direction keys." In the first choice, Word suggests the hyphen position in the word; simply type **Y** to accept it. Type **N** if you don't want to hyphenate the word.

 Trap: *Hyphenation starts at the highlight location. Press CTRL+PGUP if you want to automatically hyphenate the whole document.*

You can use the direction keys in the following way to move the hyphen to another location in the word.

UP ARROW: The highlight jumps to the next suggested hyphen point to the left.

DOWN ARROW: The highlight jumps to the next suggested hyphen point to the right.

LEFT ARROW: Choose a hyphenation point to the left.

RIGHT ARROW: Choose a hyphenation point to the right.

Use the Confirm field if you suspect that Word will hyphenate words incorrectly. Often, however, there aren't enough suspect words to make the confirm process worthwhile. Instead, you can place an optional hyphen at the end of a word by using CTRL+HYPHEN. Word will not break the word with a hyphen during automatic hyphenation.

Tip: *Place an optional hyphen at the end of a word to prevent it from being hyphenated.*

The Spelling Checker

Word's spelling checker, SPELL, can check and correct words in your document to help eliminate one of the most tedious tasks of editing. Access the spelling checker through the Library command at the main menu. When SPELL is running, the current file is checked. Word is temporarily exited and the spelling program is run outside of Word.

The spelling checker highlights all the words that are not in its dictionary. Words like *NASA, Fred,* and various brand names will be highlighted as unrecognized. You can choose to add certain words to the dictionary, thus customizing SPELL as you use it. Eventually, your dictionary can contain most of the words that you use on a regular basis.

Tip: *Think of the spelling checker as a tool that locates "unknown" words, rather than misspelled words.*

SPELL also checks for misspellings, plural forms of words that are normally singular, possessive forms of words and names, and repeated words such as *the the*. Hidden text words are checked as well.

Trap: *Be careful when you correct repeated words. One of them may be the heading of a list that is repeated in the explanation.*

If a word is spelled correctly but is not in the dictionary, SPELL will prompt you to ignore the word, correct it, or add it to the dictionary. Once you have taken one of these actions, SPELL will remember it throughout the rest of the spell check. Other occurrences are automatically handled in the same way.

Tip: *SPELL remembers the actions taken on words in a spelling check session and repeats them for similar words.*

The SPELL program can be customized in the various ways listed here:

- You can add your own special words to the standard spelling dictionary.
- You can add special words to a separate dictionary used for specific documents, say, legal or medical documents.
- You can mark a word or passage and then return to it in normal edit mode with the Search command. As you run the spell checker, you may come across a passage that you want to edit further. Marking the passage allows you to quickly return to it when you return to document mode.
- SPELL will normally list alternatives when you request a correction. You can turn this mode off in order to retype the words yourself. This is common when the words you are using are specialized medical or scientific terms.
- SPELL capitalizes the corrected word according to the capitalization that was in place for the original word. You can turn this mode off.
- SPELL can ignore words in all caps.

Tip: *Occasionally a single word will be mistakenly spaced and will appear as two words. Word finds each as a different word. You must mark the words and make the corrections in the edit window.*

Using the Spelling Checker

After typing and editing or loading a document, choose the Library Spell command from the Word command menu or press ALT+F6. The spelling checker selected in the Speller field of the Options command is loaded. This field should normally point to your Word diskette or the Word directory on a hard drive. If necessary, you can select another dictionary by choosing the Dictionary command.

To proceed with the spell check using the standard dictionary, choose Proof from the Spell menu. As SPELL finds unknown words, they appear on the screen with parts of the text that surround them so that you can check their context. You can choose one of the following options:

Correct   If you choose to correct the word, SPELL produces a list of alternatives. Use the arrow keys to select the alternative that you want and press ENTER. SPELL inserts the new word and moves on to the next unknown word.

Add   If the word is spelled correctly and is a word that you use often, you can add it to the standard dictionary or to a special dictionary.

Ignore   Choose Ignore if the word is spelled correctly but you do not wish to add it to the dictionary.

Mark   Mark the word if you want to go back to it in normal edit mode to make changes.

When the spelling check is complete, the message "Enter Y to process, N to discard changes" will appear. To update the document and add the new words to the dictionary, type **Y**.

 Tip: *Build up a dictionary of words that you commonly use by using the Add command as much as possible. This will make future spelling checks run much faster.*

Controlling Alternatives   When SPELL corrects a word, it displays a list of alternatives that may take a few seconds to look up. This can be a nuisance if you just want to retype it, especially if you know that the word is a special term and is not in the dictionary anyway. You can set the word lookup off so that you can make corrections manually by changing the Alternatives field in the Options command to Manual. In the manual mode press F1 to display the options; otherwise, make corrections by typing them on the correction line.

 Tip: *If you have many specialized words that are not in Word's dictionary, set the Alternatives field to Manual.*

Changing the Marking Character   If you mark a word, SPELL places an asterisk next to it in the document. You can then use the Search command to locate marked words for editing. If you use the asterisk character for other things, select the Library Spell Options and change the marking character in the Marking Character field.

 Trap: *Word's asterisk marking character may interfere with other text in your documents. If necessary, change this character to fit your needs.*

Reviewing Previous Corrections   You may decide that a change made to a previously correct word is inappropriate. Use the Previous command to back up during a spelling check session. As you back up to each word, the action that you took is displayed. You can change the action by selecting from the menu as you normally would.

Adjusting Capitalization   SPELL normally corrects words by giving them the same capitalization as the incorrect word. For example, *Tha* is corrected to *The*, not *the*. You can choose not to adjust the case while correcting the word by selecting No in the Library Spell Proof Correct command's Adjust Case field.

Ignoring Capitalized Words   It is often convenient to ignore words in all uppercase letters, such as NASA and FBI. Choose the Library Spell Options command and select Yes in the Ignore All Caps field. Keep in mind that setting this option will cause SPELL to ignore other text that you may have in all capital letters such as titles and table listings.

 Trap: *Setting Ignore All Caps on will cause SPELL to ignore all capitalized words, including titles and table entries.*

Using the Thesaurus

You can use the thesaurus to replace words that are used too frequently or that begin to sound repetitive. To check a word in the thesaurus, perform the following steps:

1. Highlight a word or place the highlight immediately after the word.

2. Press CTRL+F6.

3. The thesaurus window opens, and a list of alternative words is displayed.

4. Use the arrow keys to move to different words.

5. Press ENTER to select a word. It replaces the word in the text, and the thesaurus window closes.

If the word is not in the thesaurus, Word displays a list of alternative words from which you can choose. One trick for getting closer to the word you want is to have the thesaurus look up several times. In the first lookup choose a word that is close to the one you want. Press ENTER to accept the word; then press CTRL+F6 again to look up the new word.

 Tip: *It is sometimes useful to select a word from the thesaurus and then look that word up in the thesaurus to get closer to the word you want.*

In the thesaurus window you may need to press the PGUP or PGDN key to move through the list. If you decide not to replace a word, simply press ESC.

Working with Document Summaries

The Library Document Retrieval command is used to locate documents on a disk that contains many different types of documents. You can search through the document summaries (assuming that you have been filling them out) for author names, dates, and other information that was typed into the summaries when the files were first saved.

 Tip: *The Library Document Retrieval commands are used to locate documents whose contents have been forgotten.*

The use of document summaries depends on the setting of the Options Summary Sheets field. If you selected Yes in this field, Word will present a blank document summary the first time that you attempt to save a new file. The information in the document summaries can then be searched.

The Library Document Retrieval commands are shown here. When you enter the Document Retrieval menu, you will also see a list of files on the current disk or in the current directory.

COMMAND: Query Exit Load Print Update View

The document retrieval process involves the following steps:

1. Fill out the document summary sheets when you save new documents. Make sure that the summaries include enough information about the contents of the file to perform a search later.

2. Search for files with the Library Document Retrieval Query command, which lets you specify the search criteria for the file that you are looking for.

3. The documents that satisfy the criteria of the query are displayed. You can then choose the document that you want to work with.

Filling Out Document Summaries

Chapter 5 covered how to fill out document summaries. Make sure to use the arrow keys when moving from field to field in the summary sheet. Press ENTER to execute the save, and the summary sheet will be removed from the screen with the changes made so far. Note that summary sheets are only saved if the Options Summary Sheets field is set to Yes, and the document is saved with the Formatted field set to Yes.

 Tip: *The Options Summary Sheets field must be set to Yes to create document summaries.*

You can update a summary sheet at any time after the initial save by selecting Library Document Retrieval. A list of available documents will be displayed. Use the arrow keys to highlight the document that you want to update and then choose the Update command. You will be presented with the summary sheet for editing.

 Tip: *You can update summary sheets by selecting the document in the Library Document Retrieval command and choosing Update.*

Searching for Documents

To search for documents, fill out the Library Document Retrieval Query command, illustrated here, with the criteria that match the document you are searching for.

```
QUERY path: █
  author:
  operator:
  keywords:
  creation date:                        revision date:
  document text:
  case: Yes(No)
```

The fields of the Query command are discussed next.

Path   Type in the path of the directory that you want to search. You can specify several paths by separating them with commas. If you are familiar with the DOS path-naming guidelines, you can specify many different types of paths and file-names within paths.

Tip: *Specifying specific groups of files within the Path field will cut down on the search time.*

The following examples illustrate different paths that you can type in the Path field.

\WORD	The WORD directory branching from the ROOT directory is searched.
\BUSINESS\RPT*.DOC	Search through all files in the BUSINESS directory that start with RPT and end with DOC.
\WORD, \BUSINESS	Search both the WORD and BUSINESS directories.

In general the wildcard file-naming shorthand used in DOS can also be used in the Path field.

Logical Operators   The remaining fields in the Query command can use logical operators. These operators are used to make specific searches based on the relation of items in the lists.

Tip: *You can use logical operators to narrow a search among the files selected in the Path field.*

, (comma)	OR. A search is made for either of the items in the list. For example, Microsoft,Word tells Word to locate files with Microsoft or Word

& or space	AND. Word locates files that contain all of the items but not just one or the other. For example, Microsoft&Word tells Word to locate files only if the two words appear in the same file.
~ (tilde)	NOT. Search for but do not include items. For example, soft~Microsoft tells Word to search for soft but not Microsoft.
<	LESS THAN. This operator works on dates only. You can use it for dates earlier than the specified date. For example, <1/2/87 searches for dates earlier than January 2, 1987.
>	GREATER THAN. This operator searches for dates greater than the specified date. For example, >1/2/87 searches for dates later than January 2, 1987.
?	Use this character if you are not sure of a single character. This wildcard character will assume that any character can work in its place.
*	You can use the asterisk to replace more than one character or word.

Author, Operator, and Keywords Fields   Specify the appropriate information in each of these fields; however, the information is not required to perform the search. You can use logical operators in the fields.

Creation Date and Revision Date   You can use the logical operator to locate ranges of dates before or after a specific date, or you can specify a single date.

Document Text   You can specify up to 256 characters in the Document Text field. This text can include words and passages from the document. You can separate the words and passages with the logical operators discussed earlier. If you need to include quotes in a string, place a double set of quotes around the string.

Case   The Case field allows you to specify that searches for the text specified in the Document Text field should match upper- and lowercase.

Choosing a Document

Once a list of documents that meet the criteria of the Query command is displayed, you can use the arrow keys to select them. The Library Document Retrieval View command provides three ways to view the document listed on the screen. In the short view you will see the name and path of the files. In the long view you will see the author and title. In the full view the complete summary sheet will appear in a separate window for the highlighted document. You can also sort the document list by using the Sort By field in the Library Document Retrieval View command.

Printing a Document Summary

You can print the summary sheet with the document by selecting the Summary Sheet field in the Print Options command. To print a summary sheet for a single document, highlight the document and select the Document Retrieval Print command. Select Summary, Document, or Both; then choose Selection in the Range field. To print the summaries or summaries and documents for the complete list, choose the Document Retrieval Print command and select All in the Range field.

The Autosort Command

The Autosort command is used to rearrange portions of your text in alphabetical or numerical order. The command can be used to sort a list of items in either ascending or descending order or to sort a numbered list.

You can use Autosort in an outline to sort the headings or use it in data documents to sort records of information in a specific order. Lines in columns or tables and paragraphs can also be sorted.

The Autosort command is shown on the next page. You can specify a sort in alphanumeric or numeric order and in ascending or descending order. The Case field allows you to sort uppercase before lowercase letters, and the Column Only

Word: Secrets, Solutions, Shortcuts

field allows you to sort items in a column without sorting the rest of the lines.

```
LIBRARY AUTOSORT by: Alphanumeric Numeric    sequence:(Ascending)Descending
                case: Yes(No)              column only: Yes(No)
```

The sort rules are as follows:

- Numeric sorts sort numbers.
- Alphanumeric sorts sort letters before numbers.
- Ascending sequences sort smallest to largest.
- Descending sequences sort largest to smallest.
- Paragraphs and lines are sorted in the following manner: punctuation marks first, followed by numbers, then letters.
- Uppercase letters come before lowercase if Case is set on.
- Accents, umlauts, and so on are ignored.
- International characters are sorted as they appear in the alphabet.

To sort paragraphs, insert a number at the beginning of each paragraph. Number the paragraphs in the order that you want them to appear in the sorted order, highlight the numbered paragraphs, and then execute the Library Autosort command. Choose Numeric in the By field and press ENTER. When done, use the Library Number command to remove the numbers. To undo the sort, select the Undo command on the Word command menu.

 Tip: *You may need to place temporary numbers in front of paragraphs and lines to sort them in the order that you want.*

Table sorting is unique in that you can sort just a column of numbers, leaving the lines intact, or you can move each line in the table with the column you are sorting. If you select the whole table, the order of the sort is based on the first character. To select a column to sort on, such as a part number column, use the column select mode (SHIFT+F6). Once the column is selected, choose the Library Autosort command and fill in the fields as required.

 Tip: *Use the column select mode (SHIFT+F6) to select and sort columns in tables.*

Running External Programs

The Library Run command can be used to run programs outside of Word. In the Command field type the command name to be run and press ENTER. Word is temporarily exited, and control passes to DOS or the external program. When the outside program finishes, the message "Press any key to resume Word" is displayed. Word will resume where you left off when you press a key.

You can run a number of useful DOS commands by using this method. For example, you can format diskettes or list directories on other diskettes. You can run the CHKDSK command to check the disk, or you can use COPY to copy files to different directories or diskettes.

 Tip: *Diskette-based systems must have COMMAND.COM on the Word disk.*

 Trap: *You may not be able to run memory-resident programs with the Library Run command. Such DOS commands as ASSIGN, GRAPHICS, MODE, and PRINT will also not run.*

 Tip: *Never delete files that you are working on by using the Library Run command.*

Word's Calculator

Word's built-in calculator allows you to quickly add, subtract, multiply, divide, and calculate percentages for numbers within a highlighted area. The calculator works on integers and decimals and computes to 14 significant digits. Word's calculator can be used to quickly add up a table or compute totals in a form, as covered in the next few chapters.

 Tip: *Calculation results are placed in the scrap, from which they can be inserted elsewhere in the text.*

Use the F2 key to calculate the numbers within the highlighted area. The results are placed in the scrap, from which they can be inserted in the text. Normally Word will add any numbers that it finds anywhere within a highlighted area. Use the following symbols to perform other types of calculations.

 Trap: *All numbers within a highlighted area are included in the calculations.*

Subtraction	— (or parentheses around a number)
Multiplication	*
Division	/
Percent	%

Follow these guidelines when you use the calculator:

- Numbers in parentheses (not expressions) are treated as negative numbers.

- Calculations are performed in floating-point arithmetic with a two-decimal-place result unless numbers in the expression have more than two decimal places.

- Numbers can be embedded within text. Word will still add them in the calculations, as the following illustration demonstrates. Notice that the scrap holds the results of the addition.

Pg13 Li36 Co18   {300}

- Commas are included in the results if a number in the expression contains a comma.

- The calculation order is as follows: percentages, multiplication or division (depending on the level of parentheses), then addition and subtraction (depending on the level of parentheses).

- Word's column select mode (SHIFT+F6) can be used to select columns in a table for calculation.

Notice the paragraph in the next illustration and the calculation result in the scrap. There are two problems with this calculation. First, the date of July 6th was included in the highlight and so was inadvertently added into the calculation. Second, the numbers, pounds, and price were added when they should have been multiplied.

```
On July 6th, 100 pounds of beans were shipped.   The beans
are priced at $1.25 per pound.¶

Pg1 Li22 Co19    {107.25}         ?              EX      Microsoft Word
```

In the next illustration the date is not included in the highlight, and a multiplication symbol is typed after the 100 to perform the proper calculation. The scrap holds the proper results, which can then be inserted elsewhere in the paragraph.

```
On July 6th, 100* pounds of beans were shipped.   The beans
are priced at $1.25 per pound.¶

Pg1 Li22 Co19    {125.00}         ?              EX      Microsoft Word
```

Tip: *Be sure to include an operator symbol next to the number to indicate the type of calculation to be performed.*

Trap: *Use parentheses to alter the order of calculation. If an operator is not specified, the numbers are treated as negative.*

Indexing and Table of Contents

The creation of both an index and a table of contents can be automated with Word. Basically, you place a special character code before each word or heading that is to be inserted in the index or table of contents. These are then compiled with special Word commands into the appropriate list.

To designate a word as an index entry, place the code .i. before the word and a semicolon (or paragraph mark or division mark) after the word. These are then formatted as hidden text. For table of contents entries, place the code .c. at the beginning of the entry and end with a semicolon (or paragraph mark or division mark). Interestingly, you can create other types of entries to compile into tables or lists of your own choice. Simply use different letters in the table-coding scheme.

 Tip: *Use the codes .i. and .c. to designate index and table of contents entries, respectively. You can create other table entries by supplying your own codes.*

Once index and table of contents entries have been designated in the text, compile them with the Library Index and Library Table commands, discussed later in this section.

Designating Entries

You can type the codes before and after each entry and then format them as hidden text, or you can create glossary entries for the codes to make them easier to type. The best way to designate entries, however, is to use the index_entry.mac and toc_entry.mac macros supplied with Word 4. To designate an index entry, simply highlight the word and press CTRL+I+E. To designate a table of contents entry, highlight the entry and press CTRL+T+E. Word will automatically insert the proper code and format it to hidden text.

 Tip: *Use the index and table of contents macros to designate entries.*

Designating Levels   When an index or table of contents is compiled, many entries become subentries under main entries. These can be coded as the entries are designated. Use a colon to designate each sublevel entry to be lowered. The use of colons to designate index levels can be seen in Figure 20-1. Figure 20-2 shows how table of contents entry levels are designated. With table of contents entries, each additional colon indicates that the entry should be lowered another level. A printed and formatted table is shown in Figure 20-3.

For this entry	Type:
Automobile 100	Automobile

Automobile
  Engines 105
  Transmissions 110
	
	Automobile:Engines
	Automobile:Transmissions

Automobile
  Engines
    Block design 106
    Cylinders 108
	
	Automobile:Engines:Block design
	Automobile:Engines:Cylinders

Highlight the entries and use the Ctrl+I+E macro to designate them as index entries.

Figure 20-1.   Designating levels in index entries

Designating Entries That Contain Punctuation   Some entries may already contain punctuation marks such as quotation marks, colons, and semicolons. Simply surround these entries with an extra set of quotation marks.

```
.c.The Automobile Age
.c.:Men Creating Machines
.c.:Machines Moving Men
.c.:A Brief History
.c.::The Early Days
.c.::Consumer Demands
.c.:::The Production Line
```

Figure 20-2.   Codes for designating table of contents levels

Figure 20-3. A printed table of contents

Compiling the Entries

After adding the appropriate codes to the words and headings to be included in the index and table of contents, use the Library Index and Library Table commands to compile them. These procedures are covered next.

Compiling an Index   The Library Index command, shown here, is used to create an index from the designated entries. Because the command paginates a document to obtain correct page numbers, be sure that hidden text is made invisible so that it doesn't affect the page numbers.

```
LIBRARY INDEX entry/page # separated by: ███    cap main entries:(Yes)No
              indent each level: 0.2"           use style sheet: Yes(No)
```

Insert the index at the end of the document so that formatting changes can be made. The hidden text entries .Begin Index. and .End Index. are placed at the beginning and end of the compiled index.

If more than one file is to be compiled into an index, load the first file with the Transfer Load command, move to the bottom of the file with the CTRL+PGDN key combination, and then load the next file with the Transfer Merge command. Repeat these steps for each file to be included in the index. Finally, compile the file with the Library Index command.

Tip: *To compile a multiple-file index, use Transfer Merge to combine the files.*

You can use the Entry/Page Number Separated By field in the Library Index command to designate the character used to separate the index entry from its page number. In the Cap Main Entries field you can specify whether the first word of main entries is automatically capitalized. Use the Indent Each Level field to specify the amount of indents for each index level. In the Use Style Sheet field you can specify the use of a style sheet.

If you decide to use the style sheet, Word uses the formats assigned to the style's Index levels 1 through 4. Word ignores the Indent Each Level field when this option is selected because you can specify the indent of the level in the style sheet.

Compiling a Table of Contents

Word paginates the document before compiling the table of contents, so you must make sure that hidden text is invisible on the screen. Insert the table of contents at the end of the document and place the notation .Begin Table C. at the beginning of the table and .End Table C. at the end.

Use the Library Table command, shown here, to compile the table of contents. Word allows you to compile a table of contents from an outline or from the coded titles. Choose one of these selections in the From field.

```
LIBRARY TABLE from: Outline Codes       index code: C
        page numbers:(Yes)No            entry/page number separated by: ^t
        indent each level: 0.4"         use style sheet: Yes(No)
```

The Index Code field in the Library Table command allows you to specify the code of the table that you are compiling. Use this option if you want to compile a table other than the table of contents. For example, you could code illustrations and figure titles with the codes .l. and .t., respectively, and then compile these into separate tables by changing the contents of the Index Code field.

Use the Page Numbers field to specify compilation with or without page numbers.

In the Entry/Page Number Separated By field, designate the character used to separate the table entry from the page number. The default is ^t, which is a tab character. You can change this to a space character if you wish.

Use the Indent Each Level field to alter the amount of the indent and the Use Style Sheet field to specify use of a style sheet. If a style sheet is used, the Indent Each Level field is ignored. The Gallery Variants Table levels 1 through 4 are used to specify the formatting of the table entries based on their level.

Tips and Traps Summary

Hyphenation Techniques

Tip: Hyphenation is most useful when paragraphs are justified.

Trap: To delete hyphens, set the Options Visible field to Partial or Complete and then use the DEL key.

Trap: Hyphenation starts at the highlight location. Press CTRL+PGUP if you want to automatically hyphenate the whole document.

Tip: Place an optional hyphen at the end of a word to prevent it from being hyphenated.

The Spelling Checker

Tip: Think of the spelling checker as a tool that locates "unknown" words, rather than misspelled words.

Trap: Be careful when you correct repeated words. One of them may be the heading of a list that is repeated in the explanation.

Tip: SPELL remembers the actions taken on words in a spelling check session and repeats them for similar words.

Tip: Occasionally a single word will be mistakenly spaced and will appear as two words. Word finds each as a different word. You must mark the words and make the corrections in the edit window.

Tip: Build up a dictionary of words that you commonly use by using the Add command as much as possible. This will make future spelling checks run much faster.

Tip: If you have many specialized words that are not in Word's dictionary, set the Alternatives field to Manual.

Tips and Traps Summary (*continued*)

Trap: Word's asterisk marking character may interfere with other text in your documents. If necessary, change this character to fit your needs.

Trap: Setting Ignore All Caps on will cause SPELL to ignore all capitalized words, including titles and table entries.

Using the Thesaurus

Tip: It is sometimes useful to select a word from the thesaurus and then look that word up in the thesaurus to get closer to the word you want.

Working with Document Summaries

Tip: The Library Document Retrieval commands are used to locate documents whose contents have been forgotten.

Tip: The Options Summary Sheets field must be set to Yes to create document summaries.

Tip: You can update summary sheets by selecting the document in the Library Document Retrieval command and choosing Update.

Tip: Specifying specific groups of files within the Path field will cut down on the search time.

Tip: You can use logical operators to narrow a search among the files selected in the Path field.

Tips and Traps Summary (*continued*)

The Autosort Command

Tip: You may need to place temporary numbers in front of paragraphs and lines to sort them in the order that you want.

Tip: Use the column select mode (SHIFT+F6) to select and sort columns in tables.

Running External Programs

Tip: Diskette-based systems must have COMMAND.COM on the Word disk.

Trap: You may not be able to run memory-resident programs with the Library Run command. Such DOS commands as ASSIGN, GRAPHICS, MODE, and PRINT will also not run.

Trap: Never delete files that you are working on by using the Library Run command.

Word's Calculator

Tip: Calculation results are placed in the scrap, from which they can be inserted elsewhere in the text.

Trap: All numbers within a highlighted area are included in the calculations.

Tip: Be sure to include an operator symbol next to the number to indicate the type of calculation to be performed.

Trap: Use parentheses to alter the order of calculation. If an operator is not specified, the numbers are treated as negative.

Tips and Traps Summary (*continued*)

Indexing and Table of Contents

Tip: Use the codes .i. and .c. to designate index and table of contents entries, respectively. You can create other table entries by supplying your own codes.

Tip: Use the index and table of contents macros to designate entries.

Tip: To compile a multiple-file index, use Transfer Merge to combine the files.

IV

Automatic Word

You've already seen how glossaries and style sheets can make your job easier by retyping previously typed text or automatically formatting characters, paragraphs, and divisions. This section will introduce you to features that can further automate Word.

A *form letter* is a letter sent to many different people at once. Only the names, addresses, and other personal information change for each letter. The names and addresses are extracted from a separate file and are then inserted into the letter in a process called *merging*, which is discussed in Chapter 21.

Word can also help you manage the list of names and addresses used to create merged letters. A file that contains many different names and addresses is known as a *data file*. Such files can contain fields of information beyond the names and addresses of the people on your mailing list. They can also contain, for example, nicknames, or the balance of a customer's account, or the date of the last purchase from your business, including what was purchased.

Further, data files can go beyond your mailing list needs. You can create a data file to track the inventory of your business, and then use Word to report on that inventory. You can also use data files to collect and insert information into the forms used in your business. In this way data files can help automate *information collection*.

The material discussed in the next three chapters is closely related. Chapter 21 covers mail merging, while Chapter 22 covers the process for creating forms and filling out preprinted forms. Forms can be filled out either manually or automatically through the merge techniques discussed in Chapter 21.

Chapter 23 covers a special Word tool called *macros*. Macros can not only make mail merging and form generation easier; they can make just about any task performed in Word on a regular basis easier. The macro feature lets you record keystrokes and then "play them back" at another time.

21

Automatic
Document Preparation:
Merging

This chapter is divided into two parts. The first part will help you quickly create a letter and data document for mail merging. Through this process, you will be introduced to the concepts of merging. The second part will cover the extended features of Word's merging capabilities. There are special instructions that can be used in a merge to greatly increase its power and flexibility.

Part I: Quick Concepts Lesson

The process of merging a letter and data file is illustrated in Figure 21-1. The names and addresses that will make up your mailing list are collected and typed into a *data document*. An example data document can be seen in the top window

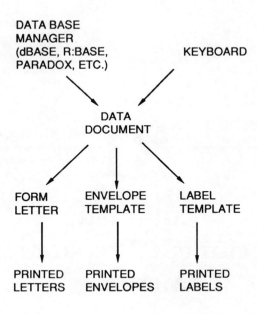

Figure 21-1.   The merging process

of Figure 21-2. The first line in the window assigns names to the individual fields of the data. The next three lines are the names and addresses of three different people or companies.

A document that contains the body text of a merged letter is known as the *main document*. An example of a main document can be seen in the bottom window of Figure 21-2. The top line of the window contains a filename between special chevron brackets. This filename specifies the data document from which the names and addresses will come. The next four lines contain field names surrounded by chevron brackets. These field names correspond to those in the data document. When the files are merged, these fields will be transferred from the data document to the main document.

```
1══[·········1·········2·········3·········4·········5·······6·········]···┐
  │ NAME,ADDRESS,CITY,STATE,ZIP,SALUTATION¶
  │ John·Jones,1345·First·St.,Lompoc,CA,93421,Mr·Jones¶
  │ Margo·Mars,85·South·State·St.,Nipoma,CA,93123,Margo¶
SP│ "Perform,·Inc.",654·Redgate·Dr.,National·City,CA,90124,art·lover◆
  │
  │                                                    MAILLIST.DOC═
2══[·········1·········2·········3·········4·········5···]···6·········7···┐
SP│ «DATA·MAILLIST.DOC»¶
  │
SP│ «NAME»↓
  │ «ADDRESS»↓
  │ «CITY»,·«STATE»·«ZIP»¶
  │
SP│ Dear·«SALUTATION»,¶
  │
SP│ We·are·pleased·to·announce·a·new·set·of·lithographs·by·
  │ artist·James·Brewster.··In·the·past,·you·have·requested·
  │ that·we·notify·you·when·the·artists·newest·works·would·
  │ be·available.··If·you·would·like·a·private·showing,·
  │ please·contact·us·at·the·number·on·our·letterhead.··We·
  │ hope·to·hear·from·you·soon.▯
  │                                                  ANNOUNCE.DOC═
```

Figure 21-2. A data document and a main document

When you merge a main document with a data document, Word extracts one name and address set at a time from the data document, merges it into the main document, formats, and then prints the letter. It then moves on to the next name and address in the data document and repeats the steps. This process is repeated until the last name and address set in the data document has been merged and printed.

An instruction called DATA is typed in the top of every main document to specify which data document is to be merged. Here, this command is shown with the filename MAILLIST.DOC as the file to merge.

```
▮DATA·MAILLIST.DOC»¶
```

Note that the filename MAILLIST.DOC is arbitrary. A data document can have any name that you prefer.

It's important to remember that the data document and the main document are two different files. You will usually create the data document first, saving it on disk with a name of your choice. Once typed, it can be used to create many different form letters. You can create as many different main documents as you like.

 Tip: *You can use a data document over and over again for many different types of letters and documents.*

For the most part, this chapter covers how to merge a mailing list with form letters, but that is only part of what you can do with the merging capabilities of Word. As you read through this chapter, keep in mind that a data file can hold other types of information, such as inventory part numbers, descriptions, and prices.

 Tip: *The merging process is not limited to creating form letters and mailing labels; other types of data files are possible.*

While this chapter discusses merging as a means to create numerous personalized letters, you must also think in terms of Word's ability to create just one document from a merge. For example, you can use merging to construct or build up a document from many smaller parts. These smaller parts are independent files that include often used text and are stored on the disk. A merge command called INCLUDE, followed by individual filenames, is typed in the main document for each file that you want to merge. In this way you can create contracts, proposals, and legal documents with little effort.

 Tip: *You can use a merge operation to create a single document from many smaller documents.*

Further evidence that merging is not just used to create multiple mail-merged documents can be seen in two commands that will be covered in the second part of this chapter. These commands—ASK and SET—can be used to obtain information such as the date or special text to be inserted in a letter that is typed often. Think in terms of a letter that you use every day. You type it once, save it on disk, and make minor changes each time you want to print it. You can use ASK and SET to automate the process of making the minor change by making Word ask you for the changes. Word then inserts them in the appropriate places before printing.

 Tip: *You can have Word ask for specific information to insert in a document before it is printed.*

Creating a Quick Data Document

This section will concentrate on the creation of a mailing list data document. A data document consists of records and fields. A *record* is an individual text block that contains all the information for a single person or company. Data documents can contain many such records. *Fields* are subsets of records and contain the individual components that make up each record, such as the name, address, city, and state.

 Tip: *Data documents consist of records that end with paragraph markers. Each record consists of fields, separated by commas.*

The file MAILLIST.DOC in the top window of Figure 21-2 illustrates a data document with three records. The top line, known as the *header record,* is always special because it gives the name of each field in each of the records that follow it. Each record has its own line that ends with a paragraph marker. The fields in each line are separated by a comma.

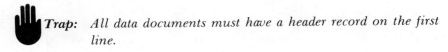

Trap: *All data documents must have a header record on the first line.*

Once the field names are described by the header record, the corresponding fields (separated by commas) in each record that follows it take on that field name. You must maintain the order described in the header file. For example, if the header record is NAME,ADDRESS,CITY,STATE,ZIP, the fields in each record must be typed with the name first, followed by the address and so on. Each field is separated by a comma.

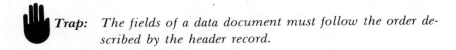

Trap: *The fields of a data document must follow the order described by the header record.*

Another way to look at a data record is shown in Figure 21-3. Tabs are used to present the mailing list in column format. Normally you will not include tabs in your data to separate fields because it can make the data too wide to view on the screen. However, you can use a technique described in the next section to temporarily convert data records to a column format so that you can select specific columns for sorting. In Figure 21-3 you select the ZIP column by using the

```
⊞═[·········1········L·······3········L········5·····L·6···L·····7L··┐
  NAME,→              ADDRESS,→        CITY,→          STATE,→ZIP,→  SAL│
  John·Jones,→        1345·First·St.,→ Lompoc,→        CA,→   93421,→Mr·│
  Margo·Mars,→        85·South·State·St.,→Nipoma,→     CA,→   93123,→Mar│
  "Perform,·Inc.",→   654·Redgate·Dr.,→ National·City,→ CA,→  90124,→art│
  :::::::::::::::::::::::::::::::::::::::::::::::::::::::::::::::::::::::│
  ═══════════════════════════════════════════════════════MAILLIST.DOC═┘
```

Figure 21-3.   Selecting a column for sorting in a data document

column select mode. By sorting on the ZIP column, a large mailing list can take advantage of presorted postal rates.

Type the Header Record

Before you start typing, determine exactly which fields you will need. The example file shown in the top window of Figure 21-2 uses a typical format that includes the fields NAME,ADDRESS,CITY,STATE,ZIP,SALUTATION.

You might want to add other fields to your mailing list. The following examples might give you some ideas.

FIRSTNAME	The first name is separated from the last name to help personalize the letter.
COMPANY	Company name field. In some cases you may need to use the company name and a personal name.
DATE	Date of first contact or purchase.
BALANCE	Current balance due.
INVOICE	Recent invoice number.
KIDS	In fields such as this the response might simply be Y for yes and N for no.

To type the header record, open a new file and type the fields exactly as they will appear in the main document. For example, if you create a field called LASTNAME, don't mistakenly use NAME in the main document. Remember to separate each field name with a comma. It helps to type the header record in all caps, but it is not essential.

 Trap: *If field names are not typed in the main document exactly as they appear in the data document, errors will occur.*

If the header records break to a second line, increase the width of the margins by specifying a larger paper width in the Format Division Margins Width field.

You can specify a width of up to 22 inches. This will give plenty of room for a typical mailing list record. Be sure to press ENTER at the end of the record. Do not use Space Before or Space After setting in the Format Paragraph command.

 Tip: *Increase the page width to display each record on one line. This does not pose a problem because data documents are not normally printed.*

Type the Data Records and Fields

Next, type in each name and address, making sure to follow the order described in the header record and to separate each field with a comma. If a field name already contains a comma, place quotation marks around the entire field, as shown in the company name in the third record in Figure 21-2. The quotation marks serve to block the text between as one field. If you fail to use them, the comma after the company name will be interpreted as a field separator, and the remaining fields will be printed out of synchronization.

 Trap: *Fields that already contain commas or quotation marks must be surrounded by a set of quotation marks; otherwise, Word will be confused by the field widths.*

You may sometimes need to have a field in a record blank because you don't have the information. For example, if you included a FIRSTNAME field and don't know the first name, you would need to leave the field blank. You must still type the comma for the field in order to maintain the field positions in relation to the header. In such a case two commas in a row will appear.

 Trap: *A comma is a placeholder for a field and must be typed even if the field is blank. In such a case two or more commas may appear in a row. This prevents Word from using the wrong fields in a merge.*

In the MAILLIST.DOC file of Figure 21-2, the last field, SALUTATION, is used to provide a personalized greeting. In the example the first record addresses

"Mr. Jones," while the second, more personal record addresses "Margo." The last record, "art lover," is more generic, and letters that use that salutation will begin with "Dear art lover."

After creating the data document, save it to the disk with an appropriate name. This name will be used in the DATA command at the top of the main document.

Creating a Quick Main Document

Type the main document just as you would type any other document, except that instead of typing actual names and addresses, you type the field names corresponding to the data document between chevron brackets. The example document in the bottom window of Figure 21-2 shows the field names from the data document inserted in the text at the places where they should be printed.

The first line of the file must be the statement ≪DATA *filename*≫, where filename is the name that you gave to the data document. Enter the fields of the letter and use CTRL+[and CTRL+] to type the left and right chevrons, respectively. Note that commas, spaces, and other punctuation are typed outside the chevrons in the same way that they will appear in the actual text. For example, a comma is typed after ≪CITY≫ in the address and also after the ≪SALUTATION≫ field. These punctuation marks are not included in the fields of the data document, only in the main document.

 Tip: *Type punctuation marks in the main document, not in the fields of the data document.*

If you want the inserted text to have character formats such as boldfacing, apply the formats to the bracketed fields just as you would format any other type of text. You can use a field more than once in any document. For example, you may want to include ≪NAME≫ in the address at the top of the document and somewhere in the middle of the text.

Merge and Print

Once the data document and main document are complete, they can be merged and then printed. The main document must be on the screen, but it is not essential to have the data document visible.

Before you print the merged files, you can send them to another document in order to review them for accuracy. Because it's possible that a field was left out or a comma not typed between fields in a data record, you can print to a file first to see the outcome of the merge. You can also make minor alterations to each of the merged documents by using editing keys or search and replace techniques before you print.

Printing to a file is also helpful if you want to print to the printer at a later time, say, after working hours. When you use the ASK instruction, printing to a file eliminates the need to wait until one document is printed before answering the questions for the next merge. You can quickly merge all of the documents to a file and then print them later. This is discussed in the second part of this chapter.

Tip: *Printing to a document file before printing to the printer can save time and help eliminate errors.*

Select the Print Merge command from the Word command menu. The following menu will appear.

PRINT MERGE: Printer Document Options

You can print directly to the printer, or you can print to a document for previewing, as just described. The Options command lets you pick specific records to print; for example, you could choose to print only records 1 and 3.

If you select Print Merge Printer, Word locates the data document and starts printing letters for each of its records. You will see the messages "Merging..." and then "Formatting page..." appear as the process continues.

Problems may occur if you have a field name in the main document that doesn't match a name in the data document. In addition, if you forgot to enter a comma or specified too many commas between a field, an error message will display. If a data document has blank paragraph markers, Word will attempt to create a letter for those markers, even though they do not have any fields. This often happens when you leave a few extra paragraph markers at the end of a data document. Be sure to remove them before using the file.

Trap: *Remove all blank paragraph markers from a data document to avoid errors.*

If you need to cancel printing at any time, press the ESC key.

Printing the Mailing List on Envelopes

To print on standard 9 1/2- by 4-inch business envelopes, set the paper size settings in the Format Division Margins menu to these sizes. Then include a DATA statement at the top of the screen and type the fields to include where you want them to print on the envelope.

Be sure to set Print Options Feed field to Manual so that you can insert your envelopes one at a time. If you need to print on labels, refer to the end of this chapter.

Quick Rules for Merging

The following quick-reference section is designed to help you set up a mail merge in as little time as possible. Follow the procedures in the order shown for best results. The first step is to create the data document. If a data document is already available, proceed to the section called "Creating the Main Document."

Creating the Data Document

1. Determine the data type and field names you will need, such as FIRST-NAME, LASTNAME, COMPANY, and so on.

2. Open a new document to hold the data. For better viewing, you can widen the margins by specifying a paper width of up to 22 inches. Remember, the data document is not printed, so it doesn't make any difference if the margins are wide.

3. Type in the special first-line header. The header assigns field names to each of the records that follow. The following example illustrates one way to set

up fields in a data document. Only two field names are used; the name, address, city, state, and ZIP are included in one field, surrounded by quotation marks.

```
ADDRESS,SALUTATION¶
"John Jones↓
Jones and Company↓
695 Randolf Road↓
Somerset, CA 91111",John¶
```

It is more practical, however, to type the fields separately so that they can be used individually in the main document. The example shown in Figure 21-4 illustrates this.

4. If you want to sort on a single field, make it the first field because the Library Autosort command sorts on the first character of a line.

5. Type the fields in each record in the same order that they appear in the header.

6. Separate fields with commas. If a field is blank, you must still insert a comma. In Figure 21-4 the ADDRESS2 field is blank in the first record. Two commas in a row are used to allocate the field.

7. End each record with a paragraph marker by pressing ENTER.

8. If a field includes a comma, as does the company name in Figure 21-4, surround it with quotation marks.

9. If a field is to include quotation marks, surround it with a double set of quotation marks, as can be seen in the SAL (salutation) field of Figure 21-4.

```
LAST,FIRST,COMPANY,ADDRESS1,ADDRESS2,CITY,STATE,ZIP,SAL,DATE¶
Cray,Robert,"JCR, Inc.",,24 Mill Rd,,Salinas,CA,95432,""Bob"",2/14/87¶
```

Figure 21-4. The field header and individual fields of a data document

10. Include spaces and punctuation marks in the main document, not in the fields of the data document.

11. Scan through the data document for errors, such as missing commas, field entries, or quotation marks.

12. Save the data document with an appropriate name.

Creating the Main Document

1. Open a new file. It is not necessary to have the data document loaded.

2. On the first line of the file, type the following command, replacing *file-name* with the name of the data document created earlier or with the name of any other data document. Press CTRL+[and CTRL+] to type the open and closed chevrons, respectively.

«DATA·*filename*»◆

3. Type the letter or other document as you normally would, with the exception of the fields from the data document. Type the field names surrounded by chevrons.

4. Type any commas, spaces, or other punctuation marks directly after the closing chevron, as required.

5. Save the file, if necessary.

Merging the Data and Main Documents

1. Load the main document if it is not already on the screen.

2. Select the Print Merge command and then select one of the following options:

- Select Printer if you are ready to begin printing.

- Select Document to send the merged letters to a file for previewing.

- Select Options to select a group or range of records to print from the data document.

Part II: Enhanced Merge Features

If you thought that merging letters with mailing lists was all you could do with Word's merging feature, you've underestimated Word's capabilities. For example, Word surpasses most other word processors on the market with its ability to perform conditional merges, which are merges that occur only if fields contain certain words or values.

Word also lets you merge several documents, or build letters that contain paragraphs, only if certain conditions are true (or false) about the person to whom you are sending a letter. You can also calculate numbers from fields in the letter they are merged with. Data files can be sorted in just about any order. You can sort on the ZIP code and then sort on the name or address. Sorting on the ZIP code lets you take advantage of cheaper postal rates.

Even though Word offers a number of features to manage data documents, you may find that programs such as dBASE, R:base, and Paradox are better tools for managing large data files. Word can use the data from these files in its merging facility.

Special Merge Instructions

Six special merge instructions are covered in this part of the chapter. The sections that follow explain these instructions based on what they are used for most often. The examples given here should not limit your creativity, however, because the commands are quite versatile. The special merge instructions are

IF and ELSE	The IF and ELSE instructions let you merge a field only under certain conditions. For example, you can print a statement such as "Your balance is overdue" if the date field is greater than a set date. The ELSE instruction lets you include a different statement if the first is not true. For example, if the balance is not overdue, the statement "Thank you for your immediate payment" could be typed.
SET	The SET instruction requests information from the operator at print time, such as the date. This information is then used in each merge.

ASK	ASK is similar to merge except that the information is requested for each record of the data file. Thus you can tailor each letter as the merge takes place.
SKIP	SKIP allows certain records to be skipped based on the contents of fields. For example, you could skip records with ZIP codes other than the one to which you want to send mail.
NEXT	The NEXT command is used to print fields from the next record in the data document on the same sheet. This command is used mainly for printing labels and data reports such as a listing of names and phone numbers in the data document.
INCLUDE	INCLUDE instructions can be placed in a document where text from other documents is to be inserted. INCLUDE instructions allow you to build up a large printed document while the main document remains small and easy to manage.

Working with Operators

Operators are used in most of the special merge instructions to make comparisons or establish relationships between fields, numbers, and dates. The most common operator, the equal sign, can be used to determine if a field is equal to a string that you specify. If equal, a specific action takes place, such as the printing of a message. The field operators are listed here:

=	Equal to
>	Greater than
<	Less than
<>	Not equal to
>=	Greater than or equal to
<=	Less than or equal to

An instruction that uses these operators is commonly called a *conditional instruction*. A conditional statement is executed only if the statement is true. That might involve a field being equal to another field or a number being greater than or less than another number. You'll see how to put these operators to use in the following sections.

 Tip: *You can use operators to perform actions based on the true or false outcome of an instruction.*

Using Math

Data documents may often contain fields with numbers. For example, a field called **BALANCE** might contain the most recent account balance for a customer. Another field might contain the price of a product or the salary of an employee. You can perform calculations on these fields during a merge. In this example calculations are performed on the **BALANCE** fields.

```
Your current balance is $«BALANCE», however, if you
feel you can't make payment at this time, three monthly
installments of $«(BALANCE+(BALANCE*.2))/3» may be
made.  A finance charge of $«BALANCE*.2» is included in
these payments.
```

In the next example a discount is deducted from the price of a product.

```
As one of our longtime customers, we can offer you a
20% discount on your new Turbo Wind Surfer.  Your price
with the discount will be $«PRICE*.8».
```

Notice that calculations within fields are performed directly on the field name, which will include the amount from the data document when merged. Use standard mathematical calculation order when brackets are included in the statements.

 Tip: *You can perform calculations on the values in fields as they merge into the main document.*

Typing Fields During a Merge

The SET and ASK instructions are used to insert fields into a document as a merge takes place. This allows you to supply information that changes every time you perform the merge, such as account balance or the current date. The data file holds more permanent information, such as names and addresses.

 Tip: You can use SET and ASK instructions to obtain information that is relevant only at the time of the merge.

Place the ASK and SET instructions at the top of the main document just under the DATA instruction. A SET or an ASK instruction usually includes a prompt, such as "ENTER THE ACCOUNT BALANCE" or "TYPE A PRODUCT NAME." This prompt will appear in the message line when Print Merge is executed. The prompt for a SET instruction will appear only once, at the beginning of the merge. The prompt for an ASK instruction will appear before Word merges each individual letter.

 Tip: Use SET to obtain information for all merged documents.
Use ASK to obtain information for each individual document.

Keep in mind that SET and ASK commands can be included in any document, not just in those where you are merging a mail list or another type of list. Simply place the SET or ASK instruction at the top of the document and print with the Print Merge command. A DATA instruction is not required. Word will prompt you for the information requested by the SET and ASK commands and then print one copy of the document. This is convenient for often typed documents where only certain parts, such as the date, change.

 Tip: You can use SET and ASK commands to automate any document, whether or not it is part of a mail merge.

The SET Instruction

There are three ways to build a SET instruction. You can have it set text included in the instruction, or you can have it ask the operator for the text, with or without a message prompt. Here is a SET instruction constructed in each of these ways.

```
«SET·DATE=2/23/89»¶
```

```
«SET·DATE=?»¶
```

```
«SET·DATE=?Enter·todays·date»¶
```

The instruction is typed between chevron brackets at the top of a document. SET is typed first, followed by the name of the field to receive it; then an equal sign is typed, followed by the text to insert in the field. If the instruction is to prompt the user, a question mark is typed. If you want a message with the prompt, type the message after the question mark.

A press release is a good place to use a SET instruction. It is a fairly standard-ized form that you can use over and over by simply inserting the name of new products. If you want to merge it with a mailing list, include the DATA instruction, as shown in Figure 21-5. Note that two SET instructions are used, one for the date and one for the new product.

Both SET instructions in Figure 21-5 use messages to prompt the operator for information. This message appears in the message line at the bottom of the screen. During a merge, nothing happens until the prompt is answered and ENTER is pressed.

 Tip: *Using message prompts with SET commands makes it easy to remember which information to type.*

In the case of the first SET instruction in Figure 21-5, "ENTER THE PRODUCT NAME" would appear in the command area when merging occurs. The response that you type would be placed in the variable PRODUCT. The same holds true for the next SET command, which obtains the current date. The prompt "ENTER THE DATE" would appear in the message line.

The prompt in a SET instruction is not essential; its main purpose is to remind the operator of the type of information needed by the SET command. If you do not include a prompt, "VALUE:" will appear in the message line during the merge.

```
1══[········1········2········3········4········5···]···6··
    «DATA·PRESS.DOC»¶
    «SET·PRODUCT=?ENTER·THE·PRODUCT·NAME»¶
    «SET·DATE=?ENTER·THE·DATE»¶
    ¶
    ¶
    TO:→ «NAME»¶
    →    «ADDRESS»¶
    →    «CITY»,·«STATE»·«ZIP»¶
    ¶
    ¶
              P·R·E·S·S··R·E·L·E·A·S·E¶
                        ¶
    Boston·(«DATE»).··Today,·the·Windham·Corporation·
    announced·its█newest·line·of·«PRODUCT»·at·the·Northeast·
    Trade·Show.··The·product·line·is·designed·to·provide·a·
```

Figure 21-5.   The SET command is used to obtain the date and product for a press release

You may want to include a message that appears in all documents for an extended period of time. You can use a nonprompted SET command to insert this message in all documents until you change the message by altering the main document. Here is an example:

`«SET·MESSAGE=Note:··Our·hours·will·be·9·to·5·until·further·notice.»¶`

The ASK Instruction

The main difference between SET and ASK is that SET obtains a single field response for a group of documents to be printed in a merge. ASK prompts for a different value just before printing each document. With ASK, you can tailor each letter to the person or business it is being sent to.

The ASK command is used in two ways and is set up much like SET. These examples show the ASK command with and without a prompt message.

```
«ASK·SALUTATION=?»¶

«ASK·SALUTATION=?Enter·a·salutation·for·this·letter»¶
```

Because ASK will prompt the operator for a response before printing each letter, unattended printing is impossible. You can, however, use the Print Merge Document command to print the documents to a file. In this way you can quickly supply the field text to each merged document without waiting for the printer to finish each one. When the merge is complete, you can print the document file to which the merged documents were sent while you go to lunch or take a coffee break.

 Tip: *When ASK is used, an operator must attend the merge to answer individual ASK instructions. You can speed the process by first printing to a file. Later, the document can be printed unattended.*

Remember that you can use ASK by itself in a document. You don't need to merge with a data document. This will produce only one letter, but you can use the instruction to supply information that changes in a document that is used often. Simply place the ASK command at the top of the document and then use the Print Merge command to print it.

Saving Merges to Files   The benefits of saving to a document file during a print merge, rather than printing, have already been covered to some extent. If you print to a file, you can open it and make minor changes or check for errors after the merge is complete. They will appear as individual pages, separated by the page break marker. Each page or group of pages will contain the inserted field text from the data document or other instructions, such as SET and ASK.

Embedding Fields in ASK Statements

It is often helpful to embed the NAME field from a mailing list in the message that appears for an ASK statement. Assume that you are merging from a list of customers. As each customer is merged, an ASK instruction prompts for an account balance. It would be helpful if the prompt displayed the customer's name so that you could verify that you are typing the correct account balance. The ASK instruction shown here includes the NAME field from the data document.

```
«ASK·BALANCE=?ENTER·«NAME»·ACCOUNT·BALANCE»¶
```

If the NAME field in the data document were Stargate Industries, you would see the message "ENTER Stargate Industries ACCOUNT BALANCE."

 Tip: *You can include name fields from the data document in prompt messages as an indicator of the current record being merged.*

Controlling Blank Lines

Each DATA, SET, ASK, and other special instruction adds a line to the top margin of your document. You can sometimes include these lines in the normal amount of space that you want to space down before typing the top of the letter. In most cases, however, these extra spaces are not desirable. If you had a DATA statement, two SET instructions, and an ASK instruction, four extra lines would be inserted at the top of your document.

You can solve this problem by replacing the ending chevron with a paragraph mark instead of typing a chevron and paragraph mark combination. To eliminate extra line feeds, construct your SET and ASK statements this way:

```
«DATA·MLIST.DOC¶
«SET·DATE=?ENTER·DATE¶
«ASK·BALANCE=?ENTER·«NAME»·ACCOUNT·BALANCE¶
¶
```

Merging Only Under Certain Conditions

Sometimes you will want to insert field text only if a certain condition is true. The IF and ELSE instructions are used for this purpose, as well as the special operators covered earlier. With IF and ELSE, Word moves into the realm of programming, but don't let that scare you. You're already familiar with how IF and

ELSE are used from everyday conversations. For example: "IF I have enough money, I'll buy this, ELSE I'll put it on layaway."

Another example would be: "IF the phone rings, don't answer it." There is no ELSE in this statement.

On the other hand, a statement may have several "ELSEs" (excuse the grammar): "IF the car breaks down, call Triple A, ELSE, IF you try to fix it yourself, make sure that you have the right tools, ELSE don't attempt it."

In this last statement there is a "nested" IF statement; in other words, there is a second IF inside the first IF. If you take out the words, it looks like this:

IF...ELSE IF...ELSE

As humans, we make IF ELSE decisions all the time. With Word, you can build up an instruction that lets Word make decisions on how to print your documents, depending on the contents of fields in the data document or fields that you supply with the SET and ASK commands.

Tip: *IF ELSE instructions are evaluated as either true or false. You can set up a resulting action for either condition.*

The decisions are always based on whether a statement is true or false. In this IF ELSE statement,

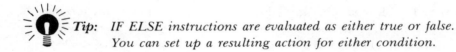

```
«IF·BALANCE·=·0»·Thank·you·for·your·prompt·payments,·«ELSE»·We've·
noticed·you·are·behind·on·your·payments,·«ENDIF»¶
```

the IF portion is performed or printed if the IF statement is true. If it is not true, the ELSE portion is performed or printed.

This statement is all one line. It starts out by determining whether the current balance is equal to 0. If the balance is 0, the "Thank you" statement is printed. If the balance is not equal to 0, the second text statement is printed instead of the first. The «ENDIF» at the end of the statement is equivalent to a period in a sentence. It ends the statement. Many levels of IF and ENDIF are possible, so it is important to end each one with an ENDIF instruction.

Trap: *All IF instructions must end with ENDIF.*

The Syntax of IF and ELSE Instructions

There are two forms of the IF instruction and a number of ways that it can control what is printed in your document. The first form of the IF instruction is illustrated here:

```
«IF A»B«ENDIF»
```

This statement is the simplest. If a condition placed in position A is true, the statement or command in position B is performed. B may contain text, data fields, or other instructions to be executed if the condition evaluates as true. Therefore, this portion of the statement is known as the *true* portion. If the condition in A is false, Word ignores the instruction and moves on.

The second form of the IF instruction includes the ELSE statement. This instruction can be read as "IF condition A is true, perform action B; ELSE, perform action C." ELSE is the same as saying "IF the condition is NOT true, then perform this action instead." In this instruction B is the *true* portion and C is the *false* portion.

```
«IF A»B«ELSE»C«ENDIF»
```

The IF instruction behaves in a number of ways, depending on whether fields are blank, fields are being compared, or numbers are being compared. The following sections cover these topics.

 Tip: *You can use an IF instruction to perform an action if a field is blank, has comparable text, or has numeric values.*

Printing Messages Based on Field Contents   The first condition to evaluate is a simple check to see if a field entry is blank. Blank spaces or blank lines may occur if a field specified in the main document is blank in one of the records of the data document. This might happen when the company name is known but not an individual within the company or when an individual does not have a company name. Your main document should check for all fields that might be blank with an IF instruction similar to the ones discussed in the next few paragraphs.

In the following instruction a message is inserted if a field has text in it.

```
«IF field name»message«ENDIF»¶
```

You can use this option to print messages based on data that you have for the names and companies in your mailing list. A field in a database might contain Yes responses. For example, a field might be called KIDS. If the KIDS field contains Yes, the following message would be inserted in the document: "We have a wide selection of children's clothes at discount prices."

If KIDS is blank, nothing is printed. You can, however, print an alternate message. The next example uses the ELSE instruction to print an alternate message if the field is empty.

```
«IF·field·name»message«ELSE»other·message«ENDIF»¶
```

In the following example an IF ELSE instruction controls the text used in a salutation.

```
«IF·SALUTATION»«SALUTATION»«ELSE»To·whom·it·may·concern«ENDIF»¶
```

If the SALUTATION field in the data document contains text, such as "Dear John" or "Dear Mr. Jones," it is printed because the instruction ≪IF SALUTATION≫ ≪SALUTATION≫ is true. If the SALUTATION field is blank, the message following the ELSE instruction is printed.

If you want to print a message when a field is blank, use this form of the IF statement:

```
«IF·field·name»«ELSE»Our·records·show·you·don't·have·
any·kids.··Perhaps·you·would·like·one·of·ours.«ENDIF»¶
```

In this example no message is supplied for the true portion of the statement; a message is supplied only for the false portion following the ELSE.

Controlling Extra Lines Produced by Blank Fields   In the next example blank lines are controlled for empty fields. Look at Figure 21-6. Two addresses are shown, one with a company name and one without. In the second an unwanted blank line where the company name usually prints has been omitted by using the form of the IF command shown here:

```
«IF·field·name»«field·name»¶
«ENDIF»«next·field»¶
```

```
John·T.·Webber¶
Webber·Industries¶
234·N.·Anderson·Rd.¶
Santa·Fe,·NM·78945¶
.................................
Allen·Doorman¶
75·Cattleman·Way¶
Lost·Wages,·NV·69834¶
```

Figure 21-6. Some records may have empty fields

The first line of the instruction determines if there is text in the field with the instruction "IF field name." If it is true (there is text in the field), the next portion of the command prints the field name. If it is not true (the field is blank), the ≪ENDIF≫ instruction is executed on the next line. This bypasses the carriage return of the first line. The next field is then typed on the line that was supposed to have the previous field.

Here are the instructions to type the names and addresses shown in Figure 21-6.

```
≪DATA·MLIST.DOC≫¶

≪NAME≫¶
≪IF·COMPANY≫≪COMPANY≫¶
≪ENDIF≫≪ADDRESS≫¶
≪CITY≫,·≪STATE≫·≪ZIP≫¶
```

Note that the next field after the ≪ENDIF≫ statement is the ≪ADDRESS≫ field, which prints on the line where the company name normally prints.

Printing Based on Field Comparisons   The second condition evaluates whether a field matches a string that you specify. You can use this form of the instruction to print messages only when a field contains specific text. This is the form of the command:

```
«IF·field·name·=·"text·string"»message«ENDIF»¶
```

A video store, for example, might use the following version of the instruction to print a special message to all of its customers who have a preference for westerns.

```
«IF·PREFERENCE·=·"WESTERNS"»We·have·just·stocked·a·
complete·line·of·old·John·Wayne·westerns·for·your·
enjoyment.··Call·us·if·you·would·like·to·reserve·any·of·
them.«ENDIF»¶
```

You can, of course, use this form of the command with an ELSE instruction, as shown here:

```
«IF·fieldname="text·string"»message«ELSE»alternate·message«ENDIF»¶
```

The video store might use this type of instruction in the following way:

```
«IF·CUSTSTATUS="PREFERRED"»As·a·preferred·customer,·
don't·forget·to·ask·for·your·free·monthly·movie·rental.·
«ELSE»You're·entitled·to·special·preferred·customer·
benefits·if·you·rent·more·than·two·movies·per·week.··
Call·us·for·details.«ENDIF»¶
```

This example assumes that the data document has a field called CUSTSTATUS that holds the status of a customer. If it is "PREFERRED," the first message prints; otherwise, the second message prints.

Printing Based on Numerical Comparisons   Most of the logical operators discussed earlier are used when you work with either numbers or dates in IF instructions. You can make comparisons between numbers and dates in fields and between numbers and dates that you specify at merge time with SET or ASK instructions. The format of the instruction is shown here:

```
«IF·fieldname·operator·number»message·or·instruction«ENDIF»¶
```

There are many ways to use this command. Here is a basic example:

```
«IF·BALANCE·>·$1000»You·have·exceeded·your·credit·limit.«ENDIF»¶
```

In this instruction the message is displayed if the account balance exceeds $1000.

The instruction can also be used to work with dates. In the next example the video store extends a welcome message to its newest customers and a thank you message to its longstanding customers.

```
«IF·JOINDATE·>·DATE»Welcome·to·our·video·club,·
«ELSE»Thanks·for·your·continued·support,··«ENDIF»¶
```

The message that is printed depends on the value of the DATE field, which you can set with the SET command at the beginning of the main document. The date set in DATE might not be the current date but a date of one or two months previous to the letter being sent. If the letter also requires a current date, you can enter it in another field, such as CURRENTDATE.

Use operators to make date comparisons based on older dates being less than newer dates. For example, January 15, 1988, is less than February 15, 1988.

Tip: *Actions can be performed based on comparisons between two dates.*

Nesting

You can nest commands to narrow down the response produced by an instruction. A nested command is illustrated here:

```
Welcome·to·our·club,··Under·the·«IF·AGE·<·13»kids«ELSE»«IF·AGE·<·
21»young·adult«ELSE»«IF·AGE·<·65»adult«ELSE»«IF·AGE·>=·65»senior·
citizens«ENDIF»«ENDIF»«ENDIF»«ENDIF»·program,·you·are·entitled·to·
the·following·benefits:¶
```

This long instruction, embedded within a sentence, prints one or two simple words. If, for example, the age of the person is over 65, the sentence would read "Under the senior citizen program, you are entitled to the following benefits:". The text "kids," "young adult," or "adult" also prints, depending on the age. In this example there are four IF instructions, three of which are nested. Figure 21-7 may help you see the nests within the instruction.

The letter from the video store shown in Figure 21-8 contains a nested paragraph that prints a message depending on the film preferences of the customers.

```
┌─IF AGE < 13
│ PRINT: "kids"
│ ELSE
│      ┌─IF AGE < 21
│      │ PRINT "young adult"
│      │ ELSE
│      │      ┌─IF AGE < 65
│      │      │ PRINT: "adult"
│      │      │ ELSE
│      │      │      ┌─IF AGE > = 65
│      │      │      │ PRINT "senior citizens"
│      │      │      └─ENDIF
│      │      └─ENDIF
│      └─ENDIF
└─ENDIF
```

Figure 21-7.   A nested IF...ELSE instruction

```
«DATA MLIST.DOC»¶
«NAME»¶
«ADDRESS»¶
«CITY», «STATE» «ZIP»¶
¶
«SALUTATION»¶
¶
     This is our chance to thank you for your continued support of our
video store.  We now have your name and personal preferences in our
computer system and will be able to automatically notify you when
special releases of interest to you are made available.¶
¶
«IF PREFERENCE = "SCI-FI"»We have just received several new science
fiction films.  Call us if you would like to reserve them.«ELSE»«IF
PREFERENCE = "WESTERNS"»We have just stocked a complete line of old
John Wayne westerns for your enjoyment.  Call us if you would like to
reserve any of them.«ELSE»«IF PREFERENCE = "MYSTERIES"»We now have the
complete series of "Mystery Theater" on tape, including the most
recent episodes.«ENDIF»«ENDIF»«ENDIF»▓
```

Figure 21-8.   A letter with a nested IF...ELSE instruction set

Three messages are nested, though more are possible. The nesting of the IF instructions can be seen in Figure 21-9.

 Tip: *You can nest merge instructions to save space and narrow down the action to be performed.*

Skipping Records in a Merge

The SKIP instruction offers you a way to ignore records in a data document based on the contents of certain fields. SKIP is usually combined with an IF instruction and its use is simple, as can be seen in the following command.

«IF SALES=0»«SKIP»«ENDIF»

This command is used to send thank you cards to customers. It skips all records with zero dollar sales. Place SKIP instructions at the top of a document because they don't insert text in a specific place.

You can use the mathematical operators to selectively ignore certain records. In the next example the not equal to operator is used to select only those records

```
┌IF PREFERENCE = "SCI-FI"
│ message
│ ELSE
│      ┌IF PREFERENCE = "WESTERNS"
│      │ message
│      │ ELSE
│      │      ┌IF PREFERENCE = "MYSTERIES"
│      │      │ message
│      │      └►ENDIF
│      └►ENDIF
└►ENDIF
```

Figure 21-9.   Levels of nesting in the letter of Figure 21-8

that match the given ZIP code. Any records that contain a ZIP code not equal to 93101 are ignored.

```
«IF ZIP <> 93101»«SKIP»«ENDIF»
```

In the example shown in Figure 21-10 an overdue notice is sent to customers with a balance due of over 90 days. Assume that an operator is merging letters from a standard mailing list that includes all customers. As the letters merge, the operator refers to an aged accounts receivable list that shows customer balances older than 90 days. The following steps occur:

1. The DATA instruction merges the mail list with the main document.

2. The SET instruction gets the current date and inserts it into all the overdue notices.

3. The ASK instruction asks the operator to enter the balance of accounts over 90 days. The message in the ASK instruction displays the customer name with the NAME variable so that the operator can validate the correct customer.

4. If the operator enters 0, the record is skipped. The operator can enter 0 for accounts that have a 0 balance as well as accounts that are not over 90 days. In this way one command can be used to skip over two types of unwanted records.

In the next example assume that the video store wants to send letters to specific customers.

```
«SET·SORT=?Preference·category?»¶
«IF·PREFERENCE<>SORT»«SKIP»«ENDIF»¶
```

The data document containing the video store's mailing list has a field called PREFERENCE that holds the type of film that the customer prefers, such as mysteries, westerns, or science fiction. A combination of SET, IF, and SKIP instructions can be used to extract records from the data document that match the preference. In this way the letter can list films and topics of interest to specific customers.

The SET command is placed at the top of the letter. Whenever the merge is executed, SET asks for a preference and makes it equal to the variable SORT. The operator can enter **mysteries**, **westerns**, or **science fiction**, depending on who is to receive the letter. The IF instruction then compares the PREFERENCE field in the data document to SORT. If they are not equal, the SKIP command skips over the record.

```
«DATA MLIST.DOC¶
«SET DATE=?ENTER DATE¶
«ASK BALANCE=?ENTER «NAME» ACCOUNT BALANCE¶
«IF BALANCE=0»«SKIP»«ENDIF»¶
¶
                O V E R D U E   N O T I C E¶
¶
¶
TO:  «NAME»¶
     «ADDRESS»¶
     «CITY», «STATE» «ZIP»¶
¶
     «DATE»¶
¶
Your current balance of $«BALANCE» has slipped past the
payment date. We would appreciate immediate payment. If
there are any problems, you may contact our credit office at
948-1285.¶
```

Figure 21-10.   A notice sent to customers with a balance greater than zero

Tip: *Use the SKIP instruction to selectively print certain records in a data document based on dates, numeric values, or values obtained with SET or ASK.*

Merging Several Documents

You may occasionally need to merge several smaller documents into one larger document. In fact, this is one way to create boilerplate letters, contracts, and proposals. You can place the INCLUDE instruction anywhere in a main document, and the contents of the file being merged will be placed in the location of the INCLUDE instruction. A contract or proposal might have standard text blocks that you use often. You can save the text blocks to separate files and then include them in new template-style documents.

Tip: *Use the INCLUDE instruction to construct a large printed document from small template-type documents.*

The letter shown in Figure 21-11 is partially taken from an earlier example that illustrates nested IF instructions. The first paragraph of the letter welcomes the new member. The nested IF instructions print an age description based on the member's age. The second paragraph uses INCLUDE statements to insert text from external document files based on the age of the new member. For example, if the age of the member is less than 13, the document KIDS.DOC, which contains member information relevant to kids, is included.

Notice that the top of the document contains commands that have already been covered. For example, the second and third lines contain SET and IF instructions that compare the date entered by the operator to the JOINDATE field in the data document. The operator should not type the current date, only a previous date, which could be a month or two previous to the current date. All members with join dates greater than this user-specified date will be included in the mailing. This record extraction is performed by the IF instruction in the third line.

```
«DATA·MLIST.DOC¶
«SET·DATE=?Enter·latest·date·to·include¶
«IF·JOINDATE<DATE»«SKIP»«ENDIF¶
«NAME»¶
«IF·COMPANY»«COMPANY»¶
«ENDIF»«ADDRESS»¶
«CITY», ·«STATE» ·«ZIP»¶
¶
Dear·new·member,¶

Welcome·to·our·club, ··Under·the·«IF·AGE·<·13»kids«ELSE»«IF·AGE·<·
21»young·adult«ELSE»«IF·AGE·<·65»adult«ELSE»«IF·AGE·>=·65»senior·
citizens«ENDIF»«ENDIF»«ENDIF»«ENDIF»·program,·you·are·entitled·to·the·
following·benefits:¶

«IF·AGE·<·13»«INCLUDE·KIDS.DOC»«ELSE»«IF·AGE·<·21»«INCLUDE·
YUNGADUL.DOC»«ELSE»«IF·AGE·<·65»«INCLUDE·ADULTS.DOC»«ELSE»«IF·AGE·>=·
65»«INCLUDE·SNRCITZ.DOC»«ENDIF»«ENDIF»«ENDIF»«ENDIF»¶
```

Figure 21-11. A customized letter based on the age of the recipient

Coding, Organizing, and Sorting Data Documents

Though Word's merging capabilities are powerful, the way it handles data is not so powerful when compared to such dedicated data base programs as dBASE and R:base. However, if you don't want to spend close to $500 and don't want to learn a completely new program to handle a fairly simple mailing list or other database, Word does an acceptable job. You can use a few tricks to code, organize, and report on the data in your data files. They are the subject of this section.

Sorting a Data Document

You can sort any data document with the Library Autosort command, but the sort can only be done on the first character of each line. Thus, you should place the field that you are most likely to sort on first in the paragraph. Using the column select mode (SHIFT+F6) and a special trick, you can sort on any other field of your data document. This technique is described next.

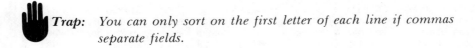 **Trap:** *You can only sort on the first letter of each line if commas separate fields.*

Consider the data document shown in Figure 21-12(a). It contains six common fields, each separated by a comma. You can sort on the first field by selecting the four records and using the Library Autosort command. To sort on other fields, you must line up the columns and use the column select mode (SHIFT+F6) to select the column to sort on. The trick is to line up the columns. First, set appropriate tab stops; then replace the comma separating each field with a comma and a tab. When you set tab stops, be sure to highlight the entire document so that all records are changed.

 Tip: *To sort on any column, align each to a tab stop; then use the column select mode (SHIFT+F6) to select the column to sort on.*

To set tab stops, press SHIFT+F10 to highlight the entire document; then press ALT+F1 to display the tab setting ruler. Set each tab a space or two over the maximum field width of each column. For example, the COMPANY column in Figure 21-12(b) is set at 1.6 inches. After setting the tabs, press ENTER. Next, use the Replace command, illustrated on the next page, to replace the commas with a comma and a tab.

```
═[········→·······1·········→·······2·······→········3·······→····4·······→····5·······→·····6·······→····]····→
NAME,COMPANY,ADDRESS,CITY,STATE,ZIP¶
John·T.·Webber,Webber·Industries,234·N.·Anderson·Rd.,Santa·Fe,NM,78945¶
Allen·Doorman,Doorman·&·Hope,75·Cattleman·Way,Lost·Wages,NV,69834¶
Jan·Hatch,Gravier·Co.,958·State·Rd.,Lambert,WA,98140¶
Tom·Hawks,SRT·Associates,1·W.·Manchester,Los·Angeles,CA,91200¶
```
(a)

```
═[········→·······1·········→·······2·······→········3·······→····4·······→····5·······→·····6·······→····]····→
NAME,→            COMPANY,→           ADDRESS,→           CITY,→          STATE
John·T.·Webber,→  Webber·Industries,→ 234·N.·Anderson·Rd.,→ Santa·Fe,→   NM,→
Allen·Doorman,→   Doorman·&·Hope,→    75·Cattleman·Way,→  Lost·Wages,→   NV,→
Jan·Hatch,→       Gravier·Co.,→       958·State·Rd.,→     Lambert,→      WA,→
Tom·Hawks,→       SRT·Associates,→    1·W.·Manchester,→   Los·Angeles,→  CA,→
```
(b)

```
═··2·······→·······3····L··4·······→·····5····L··6·········→····7L····L·8·········→····9···→
MPANY,→           ADDRESS,→          CITY,→           STATE,→ZIP¶
bber·Industries,→ 234·N.·Anderson·Rd.,→Santa·Fe,→    NM,→    78945¶
orman·&·Hope,→    75·Cattleman·Way,→ Lost·Wages,→    NV,→    69834¶
avier·Co.,→       958·State·Rd.,→    Lambert,→       WA,→    98140¶
T·Associates,→    1·W.·Manchester,→  Los·Angeles,→   CA,→    91200¶
```
(c)

```
═··2·······→·······3····7L··4·······→·····5····L··6·········→····7L····L·8·········→····9···→
MPANY,→           ADDRESS,→          CITY,→           STATE,→ZIP¶
orman·&·Hope,→    75·Cattleman·Way,→ Lost·Wages,→    NV,→    69834¶
bber·Industries,→ 234·N.·Anderson·Rd.,→Santa·Fe,→    NM,→    78945¶
T·Associates,→    1·W.·Manchester,→  Los·Angeles,→   CA,→    91200¶
avier·Co.,→       958·State·Rd.,→    Lambert,→       WA,→    98140¶
```
(d)

Figure 21-12. Steps in sorting a data document on a field other than the first

```
REPLACE text: ,                              with text: ,^t
       confirm: Yes No  case: Yes(No) whole word: Yes(No)
```

The tab must by typed as a caret and a *t*. It also helps to set the Confirm field to No.

When the replacement is done, the data file will look something like Figure 21-12(b). Some of the text may have scrolled out of view on the right, and the columns will look garbled if the lines of the records wrap to another line. You can increase the line width by adjusting the Width field in the Format Division Margins command.

> **Trap:** *Records may appear garbled after you set tabs if the margins are not wide enough. Enlarge the page width by using the Format Division Margins command.*

You can now easily select a column to sort on. In Figure 21-12(c) the ZIP code column has been selected with the column select mode. Place the cursor on the top left of the column, press SHIFT+F6, and scroll down the column. Do not select the header record; if you do, it will be sorted in with the rest of the records. The header record must be on the top line. After you select the column and execute the Library Autosort command, the records for this example should look like those shown in Figure 21-12(d).

> **Trap:** *Do not select the header record when you select a column; if you do, it will be sorted into the records.*

After sorting a data document, you must remove the tabs to be able to use it in a merge operation. Select the entire document with SHIFT+F10; then execute the Replace command as before, but in reverse. Type ,^t in the Text field and , in the With Text field. Don't forget to save the stored file.

> **Trap:** *Word cannot work with a data document that has fields separated by both tabs and commas. Be sure to convert a column-aligned data document back to normal comma-separated mode.*

Tip: *Word allows you to use tabs instead of commas to separate fields, thus allowing easy column sorts. However, tab separators make the record inordinately wide.*

Other Data Techniques: Coding and Searching

You can code a document to make it easier to handle. In the video store example the contents of the PREFERENCE field could be changed to M for mysteries, S for science fiction, W for westerns, and so on to save space. When you shorten fields, you might also want to shorten the header name to reduce the width of the entire column and make it fit better on the screen.

Tip: *You can code data to eliminate spelling errors, especially if several operators are entering data.*

Don't forget that you can use the search and replace commands in data documents just as you do in any other document. If you need to make address corrections or other changes to your data file, search for the customer name to locate the record for editing.

Tip: *Coded data in record fields is easier to search for and easier to extract when records must be skipped.*

Another technique is to use customer numbers, which can be printed on envelopes and labels. If you do a large mailing and a number of undeliverable pieces are returned, you can easily update your mailing list by using the customer numbers. Place the returned mailers in numeric order and simply scroll through the records to locate the ones that require deletion. The search commands are also easier to use when you are searching for numbers rather than names.

Tip: *Customer numbers make it easier to search and edit data documents.*

Listing Data Documents and Creating Reports

Occasionally you may need to print a list of the customers in your data document. Most of the merge instructions discussed so far treat each record as if it should be printed on a separate page. When you print data reports, however, you need to print as many records on one sheet as possible. You can do this with the NEXT command, which lets you print one record after another on the same sheet, without advancing to a new page.

 Tip: *The NEXT instruction allows you to print records one after the other on single sheets. It is used for labels and data reports.*

The NEXT command is usually used to print mailing labels, but this section will show you how to print reports of your data documents, while a later section will show you how to print mailing labels. Figure 21-13 shows a main document used to print a customer listing. Four fields are listed from the data document: NAME, PHONE, PREFERENCE, and JOINDATE. The video store might use this report at the front counter to verify customers.

The only problem with creating the main document for a report is that a line with fields, followed by a NEXT instruction, must be placed in the file for each record in the data document. Figure 21-13 has two of these lines; therefore, it will print only the first two records of the merged data document.

You can use the Insert command to create multiple copies of the lines that print the record fields. Use ALT+F3 to copy the line with fields plus the NEXT instruction to the scrap; then insert it for each record in your data document. Although this may seem like a lot of work, it does get the job done, and the alternative is to buy an expensive data management program.

Using Other Database Programs You can use other database programs with Word. Programs such as dBASE and R:base will *download* (export) their data into a format that Word can read. Downloading is a process that copies fields and records of a database program to another file in a format that can be read by another program, such as Microsoft Word. This data will be a file with fields separated by commas and surrounded by quotation marks. Recall that quotation marks and commas are acceptable field separators for Word.

```
«DATA·MLIST.DOC»¶
¶
                              C·U·S·T·O·M·E·R···L·I·S·T·I·N·G¶
    ¶
NAME→                    PHONE→      PREFERENCE→      YEAR·JOINED¶
    ¶
«NAME»→                  «PHONE»→    «PREFERENCE»→    «JOINDATE»¶
«NEXT»¶
«NAME»→                  «PHONE»→    «PREFERENCE»→    «JOINDATE»¶
«NEXT»¶
```

*Figure 21-13.   A report of customers and their phone numbers, preferences, and
year joined*

Tip: *Transferring data records from one program to another
involves downloading the records into a file. Each field of a
record is separated by a comma or quotation marks.*

It is often more beneficial to use Word to print reports from a database program such as dBASE rather than to use the facilities of dBASE itself. This is because you can more easily control the character formats, such as type fonts and styles, with Word than you can with the database program.

When downloading data from an external database program, you'll want to refer to the section in the owner's manual that refers to *exporting* to other programs or copying to ASCII files. There may be a section that describes how to export to Microsoft Word or WordStar (the process is the same). Follow the instructions in the section. You may need to specify that the data should be downloaded as ASCII-*delimited* data, which means that the fields will be separated by commas and quotation marks.

Tip: *To download data from other programs, refer to the section
in the owner's manual dealing with file export or copying
to ASCII files.*

Tip: *Word will only read data that has been delimited with
commas and quotation marks.*

To use the downloaded file in Word, simply load it. You may need to do some editing. For example, you may need to type a header record to describe each field in the first line of the file. In addition, you may need to remove extra spaces or lines with the Replace command, replacing space characters with no characters.

 Tip: *Some editing of a downloaded file may be necessary. You may need to remove extra lines and blank spaces.*

Mailing Labels

Mailing labels come either on continuous sheets, with tractor-feed holes at the side, or on single sheets. Tractor-fed labels are meant for pin-feed printers, while sheet labels are designed for laser printers, although they can be used in other printers with some effort.

Labels also come in different column types. You can buy labels that are "one-up" (one label wide) or "three-up" (three labels wide). Printing on these labels requires more tricks than a magician can shake a wand at, so this section is designed to give you the specification for printing without the theory.

Printing on Continuous Single-Wide Labels   First, set the page size with the Format Division Margins command so that Word thinks that pages are only 1 inch long. This is the length of the labels. Fill in the fields of the Format Division Margins command as shown in this illustration:

```
FORMAT DIVISION MARGINS top: 0      bottom: 0      left: .5     right: 0
                   page length: 1    width: 3.5█   gutter margin: 0"
```

Next, create a main document similar to this:

```
«DATA·MLIST.DOC»«NAME»¶
«IF·COMPANY»«COMPANY»¶
«ENDIF¶
«STREET»¶
«CITY»,·«STATE»·«ZIP»«IF·COMPANY=""»¶
«ENDIF»¶
¶
¶
```

Note that the first field from the data document is on the same line as the DATA instruction. This prevents the text from being printed too far down on the label.

There are some other important features in the label instructions. The second instruction is an IF instruction that prints the company name if it exists. But this presents a problem. If the company name doesn't exist, the remaining lines are shifted up, which will cause the rest of the labels to become out of synchronization. The instruction at the end of the fifth line solves this problem by adding an extra line if the COMPANY field in the data document is blank. Note also that the ENDIF instruction in the third line does not contain a closing chevron. Instead, a paragraph mark is typed to prevent a linefeed.

To start printing, choose the Print Merge Printer command.

Printing on Continuous Triple-Wide Labels   Printing on continuous triple-wide labels requires that you format the document in three-column mode with the Format Division Layout command. The trick is to fool Word into thinking that it is printing three columns on 1-inch-long paper, even though the sheets are continuous.

First, set up the margins and page size by entering the Format Division Margins menu and setting the page size and margins as shown here:

```
FORMAT DIVISION MARGINS top: 0      bottom: 0      left: .5      right: 0
                       page length: 1    width: 8"     gutter margin: 0"
```

Position the highlight above the division marker and select the Format Division Layout command. Type **3** in the Number of Columns field and **0** to **0.5** inch in the Space Between Columns field (you may have to try several values in this field to get the text to align horizontally where you want). In the Division Break field select column mode. Press ENTER.

Select all the fields and the division marker; then press ALT+F3 to copy them to the scrap. Press the INS key twice to insert two copies. In the second and the third copies, change the DATA field to the NEXT instruction. Your screen should look similar to that shown in Figure 21-14. Choose the Print Merge Printer command to start printing.

Printing on Triple-Wide Sheet Labels (Laser Printers)   This section describes how to print on sheet labels for laser printers. The labels described have three lines: one for the name; one for the address; and one for the city, state, and ZIP. Because laser printers force a page feed after every page, even if a division break is set to Continuous, it is necessary to work with the 11-inch length of the paper.

The process described here sets up three columns of labels with 11 labels down. You will create the left column first and then duplicate it to create the

```
«DATA·MLIST.DOC»«NAME»¶
«IF·COMPANY»«COMPANY»¶
«ENDIF¶
«STREET»¶
«CITY», ·«STATE»·«ZIP»«IF·COMPANY="""»¶
«ENDIF»¶
::::::::::::::::::::::::::::::::::::::::::::::::::::::::::::

«NEXT»«NAME»¶
«IF·COMPANY»«COMPANY»¶
«ENDIF¶
«STREET»¶
«CITY», ·«STATE»·«ZIP»«IF·COMPANY="""»¶
«ENDIF»¶
::::::::::::::::::::::::::::::::::::::::::::::::::::::::::::

«NEXT»«NAME»¶
«IF·COMPANY»«COMPANY»¶
«ENDIF¶
«STREET»¶
«CITY», ·«STATE»·«ZIP»«IF·COMPANY="""»¶
«ENDIF»⏷
::::::::::::::::::::::::::::::::::::::::::::::::::::::::::::
```

Figure 21-14. Layout for continuous triple-wide labels

middle and right columns. (Special thanks to Marty Matthews for working out the details of the label spacing.)

1. Type the DATA instruction using the name of your data file. Then type the first set of address field names, as shown in Figure 21-15.

2. Press ENTER twice to separate the first record from the second.

3. Move the highlight back up to the city/state/ZIP line of the first label. Choose the Format Paragraph command and type **3.6 pt** in the Space After field.

4. Move the highlight back down to the last line and type the field names for the second label. Type the NEXT command first to cause Word to advance to the next record in the database when merging.

```
«Data·data.txt»¶
«first»·«last»¶
«address»¶
«city»,·«st»··«zip»¶
¶
¶
«next»«first»·«last»¶
«address»¶
«city»,·«st»··«zip»¶
¶
¶
¶
```

Figure 21-15.   Header for triple-wide sheet labels used in sheet-fed laser printers

5. Press ENTER three times after this second label and each subsequent label. Only the first record in the column is followed by two paragraph markers.

6. Highlight the second label as shown in Figure 21-15, starting with the NEXT instruction and including the three paragraph markers following it. Press ALT+F3 to copy it to the scrap.

7. Place the highlight in the bottom line and press the INS key nine times.

8. Choose Format Division Margins. Set the top and bottom margins to 0.2 inch. Set the left and right margins to 0. Set the page length to 11 inches and the page width to 8 inches.

9. Position the highlight above the double dotted line and choose Format Division Layout. Set the Number of Columns field to 3, the Space Between Columns field to 0.35 inch, and the Division Break field to Column.

10. Select the entire document by pressing SHIFT+F10. Press ALT+F3 to copy it to the scrap.

11. Move the highlight below the double dotted division marker and press the INS key twice to insert the labels for the second and third columns.

12. Move to the top of the second and third columns and replace the DATA statement with a blank paragraph marker.

13. Choose Print Merge to start printing labels in the normal way.

Overall, the document should have three divisions with 11 labels in each division. The first label in each division or column is followed by two paragraph markers, and the last line is formatted with the Format Paragraph Space After field set to 3.6 points. All other labels are separated by three paragraph markers.

If the labels do not print in the exact location that you need, you may want to alter the Space Between Columns field or adjust the top and left settings slightly. In extreme cases you may want to adjust the Space After field of certain lines.

Tips and Traps Summary

Part I: Quick Concepts Lesson

Tip: You can use a data document over and over again for many different types of letters and documents.

Tip: The merging process is not limited to creating form letters and mailing labels; other types of data files are possible.

Tip: You can use a merge operation to create a single document from many smaller documents.

Tip: You can have Word ask for specific information to insert in a document before it is printed.

Creating a Quick Data Document

Tip: Data documents consist of records that end with paragraph markers. Each record consists of fields, separated by commas.

Trap: All data documents must have a header record on the first line.

Trap: The fields of a data document must follow the order described by the header record.

Trap: If field names are not typed in the main document exactly as they appear in the data document, errors will occur.

Tip: Increase the page width to display each record on one line. This does not pose a problem because data documents are not normally printed.

Tips and Traps Summary *(continued)*

Trap: Fields that already contain commas or quotation marks must be surrounded by a set of quotation marks; otherwise, Word will be confused by the field widths.

Trap: A comma is a placeholder for a field and must be typed even if the field is blank. In such a case two or more commas may appear in a row. This prevents Word from using the wrong fields in a merge.

Creating a Quick Main Document

Tip: Type punctuation marks in the main document, not in the fields of the data document.

Merge and Print

Tip: Printing to a document file before printing to the printer can save time and help eliminate errors.

Trap: Remove all blank paragraph markers from a data document to avoid errors.

Special Merge Instructions

Tip: You can use operators to perform actions based on the true or false outcome of an instruction.

Using Math

Tip: You can perform calculations on the values in fields as they merge into the main document.

Tips and Traps Summary (*continued*)

Typing Fields During a Merge

Tip: You can use SET and ASK instructions to obtain information that is relevant only at the time of the merge.

Tip: Use SET to obtain information for all merged documents. Use ASK to obtain information for each individual document.

Tip: You can use SET and ASK commands to automate any document, whether or not it is part of a mail merge.

Tip: Using message prompts with SET commands makes it easy to remember which information to type.

Tip: When ASK is used, an operator must attend the merge to answer individual ASK instructions. You can speed the process by first printing to a file. Later, the document can be printed unattended.

Tip: You can include name fields from the data document in prompt messages as an indicator of the current record being merged.

Merging Only Under Certain Conditions

Tip: IF ELSE instructions are evaluated as either true or false. You can set up a resulting action for either condition.

Trap: All IF instructions must end with ENDIF.

Tip: You can use an IF instruction to perform an action if a field is blank, has comparable text, or has numeric values.

Tip: Actions can be performed based on comparisons between two dates.

Tip: You can nest merge instructions to save space and narrow down the action to be performed.

Tips and Traps Summary (*continued*)

Skipping Records in a Merge

Tip: Use the SKIP instruction to selectively print certain records in a data document based on dates, numeric values, or values obtained with SET or ASK.

Merging Several Documents

Tip: Use the INCLUDE instruction to construct a large printed document from small template-type documents.

Coding, Organizing, and Sorting Data Documents

Trap: You can only sort on the first letter of each line if commas separate fields.

Tip: To sort on any column, align each to a tab stop; then use the column select mode (SHIFT+F6) to select the column to sort on.

Trap: Records may appear garbled after you set tabs if the margins are not wide enough. Enlarge the paper width by using the Format Division Margins command.

Trap: Do not select the header record when you select a column; if you do, it will be sorted into the records.

Trap: Word cannot work with a data document that has fields separated by both tabs and commas. Be sure to convert a column-aligned data document back to normal comma-separated mode.

Tip: Word allows you to use tabs instead of commas to separate fields, thus allowing easy column sorts. However, tab separators make the record inordinately wide.

Tip: You can code data to eliminate spelling errors, especially if several operators are entering data.

Tips and Traps Summary *(continued)*

Tip: Coded data in record fields is easier to search for and easier to extract when records must be skipped.

Tip: Customer numbers make it easier to search and edit data documents.

Tip: The NEXT instruction allows you to print records one after the other on single sheets. It is used for labels and data reports.

Tip: Transferring data records from one program to another involves downloading the records into a file. Each field of a record is separated by a comma or quotation marks.

Tip: To download data from other programs, refer to the section in the owner's manual dealing with file export or copying to ASCII files.

Tip: Word will only read data that has been delimited with commas and quotation marks.

Tip: Some editing of a downloaded file may be necessary. You may need to remove extra lines and blank spaces.

22

Automatic Forms Generation

Most offices use forms of one type or another. With Word, you can create your own forms or make the filling out of preprinted forms easier. When you create your own forms, both the titles and filled-in information are printed by your printer. On preprinted forms, only the filled-in information is printed.

The setup and use of forms, as discussed here, is very similar to the setup and use of merged documents, as covered in Chapter 21. You can use the Print Merge command to help fill out parts of the form from information that is already in a data document, such as names and addresses. You can then use the form techniques described in this chapter to fill out the rest of the form. Because the merge techniques discussed in Chapter 21 are used here, you should become familiar with them before proceeding.

When creating a form, you place special tab stops where information is to be filled in. In this way your forms can have text and fill-in areas at odd or irregular places. Two key combinations, CTRL+< and CTRL+>, make it easy to jump from one fill-in spot to another. The CTRL+< combination moves the insertion point back to a previous fill-in spot, while CTRL+> moves the highlight to the next spot.

Forms can contain boxes and lines created with the Format Border command and the vertical tab mark. Use the Format Border command to surround parts of your form with a box and the vertical tab mark to create divider lines within these boxes. You should place all titles and fill-in spots by using tab settings.

Form Types

There are several ways to create forms. These are related to how you intend to fill in the form after it is created and whether or not the form will print on preprinted forms. The various methods are described in the following sections.

Manual Forms

A manual form is one that is filled in on the screen and then printed. The CTRL+> and CTRL+< key combinations are used by the operator to jump from one field to the next. If the filled-in form is to be saved, it is saved under a different name because the original blank form must stay intact. The file protection techniques discussed in Chapter 5 can be used to force operators to save altered files under different names.

 Tip: *Once a form is created, use file-locking techniques to protect it from alteration.*

Merged Forms

Merged forms are not much different from mail-merged documents in the way they are created and filled in. A data document is used to collect data, which is then merged into the form. The form is printed as is with the titles as they appear on the screen, or the form is printed on preprinted form stock.

Merged and Manually Filled-in Forms

In many cases a form will be partially merged from a data document and then filled in manually. For example, the names and addresses in a data document may be merged with a form into a file. This file will then contain a set of partially filled-in forms for each name on the mailing list (or an extracted set, using the techniques discussed in Chapter 21). To fill in the remaining information manually, the operator opens the merged file and jumps to each remaining fill-in spot to finish filling in the forms.

Printing on Preprinted Forms

Any form can be printed as is on the screen or be printed on preprinted forms. When you print on a preprinted form, you must align the fill-in spots of your screen with those on the preprinted form. Techniques described later in this chapter make this relatively easy. The titles visible on the screen used to indicate the contents of a field are formatted as nonprinting hidden text when the form is printed. In this way only the contents of the fill-in fields are printed.

The Form Creation and Use Process

It is important to have a form design in hand before you create it in Word. This might be a preprinted form or one that you've drawn out on paper. Forms have *field titles, field marker characters,* and *merge fields,* as shown in the following illustration:

NAME: ··«NAME»→   TEST·SCORE: ··»→ ¶

In this example Name and Test Score are field titles. Name contains a merge field that will be filled in during a merge with a data document. As discussed in Chapter 21, it is surrounded by chevrons. Test Score contains a field marker character. The right-hand chevron is used alone to indicate the fill-in positions. It is usually formatted as hidden text and followed by a tab. The tab is important because it determines the character format of the inserted text.

 Tip: *Use only the right-hand chevron when you position field markers.*

 Tip: *You can add character formats to the tab following the field marker. The formats are applied to the fill-in text.*

Once the field names and positions have been determined, you type them into position by using tab settings. The use of tabs is important to forms because many of the fill-in entries must align. You can set the format of the characters for each field by formatting the tab characters.

When the file is complete, it can be saved to disk. Use the following command to protect the file from alteration and erasure.

Library Run ATTRIB +R *filename*

To fill in the form manually, use CTRL+< and CTRL+>. If the form is to be partially filled in by a merge, a DATA instruction must be at the top of the form, as described in Chapter 21. Once the document is filled in, it can be printed. The field names can be printed or formatted as hidden text so that they don't print on a preprinted form.

Quick Form Creation

This section will describe the steps and techniques used to create an interoffice memo. You can adapt them to create your own simple forms. The second half of this chapter covers additional techniques for those who wish to create forms with extended features.

Create the Initial Layout

Figure 22-1 illustrates an interoffice memo with a top centered heading and four field titles. The first thing to do with any form is to set up the tabs. You may need to divide forms into several sections, each with its own tab settings. In the memo in Figure 22-1 only one section requires special tab settings. A left tab is set at the 3.1-inch position.

The next step is to type in the heading and then the field titles. After each field title, type a space and then press CTRL+] to enter the right-hand chevron. Type a tab and then type in the next field name. Follow it with a space and a chevron; then proceed to the next field name and follow the same steps until the form is complete.

The space between the field names and chevrons is important because Word inserts text directly on the chevron. The space is used to separate the field name from the fill-in text. Note that you can place the space and chevron anywhere on

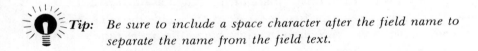

Figure 22-1.   Interoffice memo form fill-in positions

the line. They do not need to follow directly behind the field name.

> **Tip:** *Be sure to include a space character after the field name to separate the name from the field text.*

The last step is to highlight the chevrons and format them as hidden text. Place the highlight on the first chevron and press ALT+E twice (or ALT+X+E twice if a style sheet is attached). Alternatively, you can choose Yes in the Hidden field of the Format Character command. The chevron will become the double-arrow character that represents hidden text.

> **Trap:** *A direct format keystroke must be typed twice to format a single character.*

In the example memo of Figure 22-1 you may want to create one extra field marker at the beginning of the memo text. In this way you can easily jump to the position after the subject of the memo has been typed. Simply place a chevron before the paragraph marker where the body text begins and format it as hidden text, as just described.

The form should now look like the one shown in Figure 22-2.

```
2══[········1·········2·······3L·····4·········5·········]········7···]
       I·N·T·E·R·O·F·F·I·C·E···M·E·M·O¶
    From:·↔→              To:·↔→    ¶

    Date:·↔→             Subject:·↔¶

    ↔¶
```

Figure 22-2. Interoffice memo text typing point

Filling in the Form

Filling in the form is the easiest part. Place the highlight at the top of the form and press CTRL+> to move to the first field. Word highlights the tab stop of the field. Typing text will move the tab to the right but will not affect the next field unless too much text is typed.

When you finish typing the first field, press CTRL+> again to move to the next field. Type the text and continue on to the next fields in the same way. After filling out the memo completely, you can print it in the normal way.

Automatic Form Fill-in Macro

This section briefly jumps to topics covered in the next section to explain how you can make the form fill-in process easier. A macro is an automatic routine that is programmed into Word to make a particular task easier. The macro described here provides a set of instructions to make Word type the CTRL+> key combination automatically every time you press ENTER. In this way you can type the contents of a field and then press ENTER to automatically move to the next field. Macros will be covered in detail in Chapter 23, but you can create this simple macro now and begin using it to automate your forms.

 Tip: *You can use macros to automate keystrokes in Word.*

The macro contains the following instructions:

    REPEAT 30
      CTRL+>
      PAUSE
    ENDREPEAT

The REPEAT instruction repeats the CTRL+> and PAUSE commands 30 times. The CTRL+> is the keystroke command used to jump from field to field in a form, while the PAUSE command makes Word wait at a field so that you can type some text. When ENTER is pressed, Word executes the next repeat. The four commands form a loop that repeats 30 times, executing the two inner commands each time.

The number of repeats is arbitrary. You can change the number to match the number of fields in a form. The reason that 30 is used here is to make the macro useful for many different types of forms. One form may only have 4 fields to fill in, while another may have 25. When the number of repeats in a macro exceeds the number of fields in a form, simply press ESC twice to end the macro.

Creating the Form Fill-in Macro   Macros are stored in the glossary, just like any other glossary entry. You expand them from the glossary by typing the macro name and pressing the F3 (Glossary Expand) key. You can also execute Macros with a CTRL key combination if you assign a CTRL code to them. In the case of the macro covered here, CTRL+A+F will be assigned as the key combination that executes the macro. AF stands for AutoForm, which will be the name given to this macro. In addition to pressing CTRL+A+F to execute the macro, you can type **AUTOFORM** followed by the F3 (Glossary Expand) key.

Type the text shown in the following illustration anywhere on the current screen.

«REPEAT·30»<CTRL·.>«PAUSE»«ENDREPEAT»¶

First, press CTRL+[to create the left chevron; then type **REPEAT 30** followed by CTRL+] for the right chevron. Next, type the less than symbol (<), press CTRL, and type a space, a period, and the greater than symbol (>). Note that <CTRL.> is the same as CTRL+>. End the command by typing **PAUSE** and **ENDREPEAT** surrounded by chevrons.

When done, highlight the entire line and press ESC+C to execute the Copy command. Copy the highlighted macro into the glossary by typing its name as shown in the illustration on the next page.

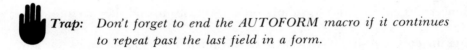

Type **AUTOFORM.MAC** and then type the caret symbol ($^$) by pressing SHIFT+6. Next, press CTRL+A, and type an **F** following the bracket. Word automatically inserts the brackets when CTRL+A is typed. Press ENTER to save the macro in the glossary.

Running the Macro   To run the macro, place the highlight at the top of the form and press the CTRL+A+F key sequence. The highlight will automatically jump to the first fill-in field. After typing the text, press ENTER and the highlight will jump to the next fill-in field. Continue in this way until the form is filled out. Note that even though the form is filled out, the macro will continue to repeat because the repeat number exceeds the number of fields in the form. Be sure to press ESC twice to end the macro. You can then print the form.

Trap: *Don't forget to end the AUTOFORM macro if it continues to repeat past the last field in a form.*

Right-Aligning the Field Names

You may sometimes want to right-align the field names to make the form look more organized or more visually appealing. The memo shown in Figure 22-3 illustrates this. Notice that the colons in the field names are aligned.

Figure 22-4 shows how the tabs were set to right-align the field names in the memo. First, highlight both paragraphs. Then place a right and left tab next to each other at the appropriate spots by using the ALT+F1 tab-setting command. After the tabs are set, press the TAB key before the From: and Date: field names and in between the colon and the space at the end of each field name.

Formatting the Form

Formatting the text of a form is no different than formatting any other document. In the form illustrated in Figure 22-5 the heading was formatted in 14-point Helvetica, the field names in 12-point bold Helvetica, and the fill-in text in 12-point Courier.

```
              I N T E R O F F I C E   M E M O

     From:   John Lockwood          To:   Morton Hamburg

     Date:   1/15/88           Subject:   New Financial Plan


  Hello Morton.  I've come up with some new ideas on how
  you might organize your finances.  You'll find the
  preliminary plan attached to this memo.

  Thanks
```

Figure 22-3. A completed interoffice memo

To give the fill-in text a format on any field, format the tab character that follows the field marker. In this case, this is easily done as part of formatting the entire section. First, highlight the two paragraphs that contain the field names and format them as Helvetica 12-point bold or any other typeface that you prefer or that your printer supports. Next, highlight each of the tabs after the field

```
2═[······RL·1·········2·········3··RL·····4·········5····]····6·········7···┐
 →From:→·•John·Lockwood→        To:→·•Morton·Hamburg→¶

 → Date:→·•1/15/88→        Subject:→·•New·Financial·Plan→¶
```

Figure 22-4. Aligning the text fields of the memo

INTEROFFICE MEMO

From: John Lockwood   **To:** Morton Hamburg

Date: 1/15/88   **Subject:** New Financial Plan

Hello Morton. I've come up with some new ideas on how
you might organize your finances. You'll find the
preliminary plan attached to this memo.

Thanks

Figure 22-5.   The completed interoffice memo with formatting and text alignment

markers and press ALT+SPACEBAR to revert them to normal text. The use of a normal Courier type font for the fill-in text produces a more natural appearance.

 Tip: *The tab character following a field marker determines the character format of the filled-in text.*

Adding Borders

Adding borders to a form will make it more readable and give it the look and feel of a form. In Figure 22-6 borders were added to the heading and the field titles by using the Format Border command. When adding borders, keep in mind that Word will place borders around each block of text that has a paragraph marker. In the interoffice memo the paragraph marker directly after the To: field was replaced with a soft carriage return (SHIFT+ENTER) to include it with the next paragraph. In this way the entire section was surrounded by one box.

 Trap: *You must format blocks of text to be surrounded by borders as a single paragraph by using soft carriage returns (SHIFT+ENTER).*

```
┌─────────────────────────────────────────────────────────┐
│  ╔═══════════════════════════════════════════════════╗  │
│  ║            I N T E R O F F I C E   M E M O         ║  │
│  ╚═══════════════════════════════════════════════════╝  │
└─────────────────────────────────────────────────────────┘

┌─────────────────────────────────────────────────────────┐
│  From:  John Lockwood        To:  Morton Hamburg         │
│                                                          │
│  Date:  1/15/88              Subject:  New Financial Plan│
└─────────────────────────────────────────────────────────┘

Hello Morton.  I've come up with some new ideas on how
you might organize your finances.  You'll find the
preliminary plan attached to this memo.

Thanks
```

Figure 22-6. Interoffice memo with borders

Merging Names from a List

In the revised interoffice memo (Figure 22-7), the data file MEMOLIST.DOC in the bottom window of the screen image will be merged into the Name and Department fields of the memo. In this way you can keep on file a list of people who normally receive your memos. (For more information on merging, refer to Chapter 21 or to the end of this chapter.)

Asking for Information

The ASK and SET instructions covered in Chapter 21 can also be used in the forms generation process. The interoffice memo illustrated in Figure 22-8 has been automated with these instructions. The instruction "SET FROM=Harry James" will place "Harry James" in the From field of all memos. In the next two SET commands a prompt is displayed at the bottom of the screen for the date and memo subject matter. The memo merges with the names and departments in the MEMOLIST file and is printed.

```
1══[·········1·········2·········3·········4·········5···]···6·········7···]
▌NP  «DATA·MEMOLIST.DOC»¶
▌   ┌─────────────────────────────────────────────────────────────────┐
▌   │ ║           I·N·T·E·R·O·F·F·I·C·E···M·E·M·O¶          ║ │
▌   └─────────────────────────────────────────────────────────────────┘
▌
▌   ┌─────────────────────────────────────────────────────────────────┐
▌   │ → From:→·→→              To:→·«NAME»→    ↓                        │
▌   │ →      →→          Department:→·«DEPARTMENT»↓                     │
▌   │ ↓                                                                 │
▌   │ → Date:→·→→            Subject:→·→→¶                              │
▌   └─────────────────────────────────────────────────────────────────┘
2══[·········1·········2·········3·········4·········5·········6·········]
▌NP  NAME,DEPARTMENT¶
▌NP  Tom·Higgins,Manufacturing¶
▌NP  Jim·Bradley,Distribution¶
▌NP  Alice·Kempf,Public·Relations¶
▌NP  June·Watson,Planning¶
```

Figure 22-7. A mailing list for the interoffice memo

```
1══[·········1·········2·········3L·······4·········5···]···6·········7···]
▌NP  «DATA·MEMOLIST.DOC»¶
▌NP  «SET·FROM=Harry·James»¶
▌NP  «SET·DATE=?Enter·the·date:·»¶
▌NP  «SET·SUBJECT=?Type·the·subject·matter·of·this·memo:·»¶
▌   ┌─────────────────────────────────────────────────────────────────┐
▌   │ ║           I·N·T·E·R·O·F·F·I·C·E···M·E·M·O¶          ║ │
▌   └─────────────────────────────────────────────────────────────────┘
▌
▌   ┌─────────────────────────────────────────────────────────────────┐
▌   │ → From:→«FROM»→          To:→·«NAME»→    ↓                       │
▌   │ →      →→          Department:→·«DEPARTMENT»↓                    │
▌   │ ↓                                                                │
▌   │ → Date:→«DATE»→        Subject:→·«SUBJECT»→¶                     │
▌   └─────────────────────────────────────────────────────────────────┘
```

Figure 22-8. Merge instructions for the interoffice memo

Printing a Blank Form

Keep in mind that you can print a form without filling in the fields. Thus, you can create forms that can be filled in by hand and then entered in the computer at a later time. You can create underlined fields by selecting the underline in the Leader Char field of the Format Tab Set menu.

 Tip: *Use underlined tab stops if you want to create blank forms that are filled in by hand.*

Enhanced Forms

The invoice illustrated in Figure 22-9 represents a more elaborate form than the memo discussed earlier, but it is just as easy to create. The invoice can be divided into nine sections, each with its own tab settings, borders, and fields. In the following discussion each of these sections will be covered individually. You can create the invoice shown here, or you can modify it to fit your needs. You can adapt each section to many other types of applications.

To create the invoice, perform the steps given in the following sections. Note that the Left and Right fields of the Format Division Margins command were set to 0.75 inch for this form.

The Header

There is nothing special about the header that hasn't already been covered in the formatting section of this book. Press ALT+C (or ALT+X+C) to center it; then format with an appropriate bold typeface. Note that each of the characters was separated by two or three spaces to give the header a wider appearance.

The INVOICE Block

Once again, the formatting for the INVOICE block is not new to you. The following illustration shows that soft carriage returns (SHIFT+ENTER) were used to space down one line and were used again after the word *INVOICE*. This produces a space around the paragraph for the double-line border. Use the Format Border command to produce the border. Seven spaces are used between each letter of the

S U R E F I R E   S U P P L I E S

P.O. Box 90524
Santa Barbara, CA 93190
(805) 687-0865

I N V O I C E

SHIP TO: Specialty Enterprises
CONTACT: Tim Johnson
ADDRESS: 265 N. Hagen Street
CITY: Wildwood   **STATE:** CA   **ZIP:** 93452
PHONE: (415) 654-1234

BILL TO: Specialty Enterprises
CONTACT: Accounts Payable
ADDRESS: P.O. Box 165
CITY: Wildwood   **STATE:** CA   **ZIP:** 93452

DATE: 1/2/88   **SALESPERSON:** AL
P.O. NUMBER: 83652   **ORDERED BY:** Shirley Ames

DESCRIPTION	ORDERED	SHIPPED	AMOUNT
Rotary Despatulator	1	1	37.50
Auxiliary Inhibitor	2	2	24.95

SUBTOTAL	62.45
CALIFORNIA SALES TAX	3.75
SHIPPING/HANDLING	3.00
TOTAL	69.20

CHECK NUMBER: 9385-4	**PREPAID AMOUNT**	69.20
	BALANCE DUE	0.00

Thank   you   for   your   order

Figure 22-9.   A completed invoice form with fill-in fields

word *INVOICE,* and it is formatted with a bold typeface.

```
I · · · · · N · · · · · U · · · · · ↓O · · · · · I · · · · · C · · · · · E↓
                                    ¶
```

The SHIP TO Block

The SHIP TO block, illustrated here, is formatted as a single paragraph, as indicated by the newline markers at the end of each line. In this way the single-line border can be applied to the entire block. Press ENTER in the last line of the block to insert a paragraph marker.

The ruler above the block in the illustration shows the tab settings used to align the field names and field markers.

```
[ · ·L · · · · ·1 · ·L · · · ·2 · · · · · · ·3 · · · · · ·RL · · · · · · ·5 · · ·RL · · ·6 · · · · ] · · · ·7 · · ·
  →  SHIP·TO:→  ↔→                              ↓
  →  CONTACT:→  ↔→                              ↓
  →  ADDRESS:→  ↔→                              ↓
  →  CITY:→     ↔→                  STATE:→↔→        ZIP:→↔↓
  →  PHONE:→    ↔→                       ↕
```

Remember, the double-arrow marks in the illustration represent hidden field marks. When you create this paragraph, press CTRL+] to create a field mark; then highlight it and press ALT+E (or ALT+X+E) twice to format it as hidden text.

The BILL TO Block

To create the BILL TO block, highlight the SHIP TO paragraph and copy it to the scrap with ALT+F3. Place the highlight on the paragraph mark below the SHIP TO paragraph and press the INS key to insert a copy of the block. Then alter the SHIP TO field title to BILL TO.

The INVOICE INFORMATION Block

To create the INVOICE INFORMATION block, make sure that the highlight is in the new paragraph marker. The border and tab formatting of the previous paragraph should be retained. For this block, however, you must alter the tab settings. Select the Format Division Tab Reset-All command. Then press ALT+F1 and set the tabs as shown here,

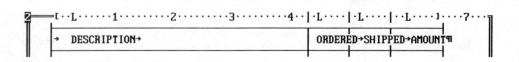

or alter the settings to fit your needs. Use CTRL+] to insert the field markers and then format them as hidden text.

The COLUMN HEADING Block

Make sure that the previous section ends with a paragraph marker and move to the next paragraph marker. The formats should be duplicated in this new paragraph. Retain the border format, but change the tab settings as shown in the ruler bar of the following illustration. Note that the vertical lines are created with the vertical line tab stops. Press ALT+F1, choose Vertical in the Alignment field, and then insert the tab stops in the positions shown. Also insert the left tabs as shown. Press ENTER when you are finished.

Next, type the column headings as shown. Note that the column headings on the right overlap the borders. This only occurs on the screen; it won't be a problem in the printout if you format the characters to a smaller type size. In the example of Figure 22-9 the 8-point LinePrinter font of the Hewlett-Packard LaserJet was used.

The INVOICE ITEM Block

The invoice items, quantities, and prices are typed in the INVOICE ITEM block. Notice that this section contains only field markers, not field names. Make sure that the previous section ends with a paragraph marker; then change the tab stops in the new paragraph as shown in the ruler of the following illustration. Note that the 4.3-, 5-, and 5.7-inch marks have vertical tabs. Also note that the 6.2-inch mark is a decimal tab.

After setting the tabs, press the TAB key to get to the first stop and insert a field mark by pressing CTRL+]. Tab to the next stop and repeat the process. At the end of the line, press SHIFT+ENTER to insert a newline character. Next, go back and format each field mark as hidden text. When the line is complete, highlight it as shown in the illustration and copy it to the scrap by using ALT+F3. Next, use the INS key to insert it up to 10 times or for as many line items as you need on your custom invoice. Press ENTER in the last block.

The TOTAL Block

Make sure that the highlight is on the new paragraph marker and change the tab settings as shown in the following illustration. Remove the first two vertical tabs and add the right tab and the decimal tab. Tab to each of the right tab markers and type the field titles. Be sure to end each line with SHIFT+ENTER to maintain paragraph integrity and the border around the block. The last line should end with a paragraph marker.

```
[··········1·········2·········3·········4·········5···R·|··6·D··]····7···]
  →                                         SUBTOTAL→       ↔↓
  →                              CALIFORNIA·SALES·TAX→       ↔↓
  →                              SHIPPING/HANDLING→          ↔↓
  →                                            TOTAL→       ↔▊
```

The PAYMENT RECEIVED Block

The last block, shown in the following illustration, is similar to the previous block except that a paragraph marker separates the two and forms a new box. Additional tabs are set for the Check Number field. A message is also shown at the bottom of the invoice.

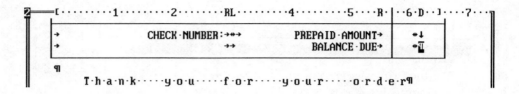

Save and Write-Protect the Form

Once the invoice is complete, be sure to save it and then write-protect it. Remember, write-protecting a file forces an operator to save it under a different filename if changes have been made, such as occurs when a form is filled out. To write-protect the form, issue the following command:

Library Run ATTRIB +R *filename*

Tip: *You can use the DOS ATTRIB command to write-protect forms from accidental alterations.*

Filling Out the Invoice

The invoice is filled out in the normal way as described in the first part of this chapter. Use the CTRL+> or CTRL+< key combination to move from one field to the next. You can also use the AUTOFORM macro discussed earlier to move from field to field rather than using the CTRL key combinations.

Using Merge Commands to Fill in Forms

Using merge commands to insert text from data files into a form was covered briefly earlier. There are several advantages to doing this. One is that you can save data such as names and addresses in a separate file, from which you can merge them into invoices, mailing labels, customer letters, notices, and newsletters. The Print Merge command also lets you use various conditionals in a field.

Tip: *Using data files allows you to keep a separate list of names and addresses for future use.*

The invoice shown in Figure 22-10 shows various alterations made to take advantage of the Print Merge command. Note that the header fields of the invoice have been removed for clarity and compactness. This invoice assumes that the customer names are entered into a data document as orders are taken. The data document has the following fields:

Ship to fields:

NAME
ADDRESS
CITY
STATE
ZIP
PHONE
CONTACT

Bill to fields:

NAME2
LOCATION
ADDRESS2
CITY2
STATE2
ZIP2

You might also want to collect other information in a data file of this sort, such as the order date, items ordered, and so on.

After the salesperson enters the names for their orders in the data document, it is merged with the invoice file. During the merge, the SET and ASK instructions in the top of Figure 22-10 obtain additional information. The SET instructions obtain the date and salesperson ID used on each invoice in the merge. The ASK instructions obtain information pertinent to each individual order, such as the purchase order number and the purchasing agent's name.

```
[·········1·········2·········3·········4·········5·······6····]···7···
«DATA·MAILLIST.DOC¶
«SET·DATE=?Enter·current·date¶
«SET·SP=?Enter·your·salespersons·ID¶
«ASK·PONUM=?Enter·purchase·order·number·for·«NAME»·order¶
«ASK·ORDPERSON=?Enter·order·person·for·«NAME»·order¶

→  SHIP·TO:→  «NAME»→                    ↓
→  CONTACT:→  «CONTACT»→                 ↓
→  ADDRESS:→  «ADDRESS»→                 ↓
→  CITY:→     «CITY»→          STATE:→«STATE»→ ZIP:→«ZIP»↓
→  PHONE:→    →                         ¶

→  BILL·TO:→  «IF·NAME2=""»Same«ELSE»«NAME2»«ENDIF»↓
→  LOCATION:→ «LOCATION»→                ↓
→  ADDRESS:→  «ADDRESS2»→                ↓
→  CITY:→     «CITY2»→         STATE:→«STATE2»→ZIP:→«ZIP2»¶

→  DATE:→     «DATE»→          SALESPERSON:→ «SP»→   ↓
→  P.O.·NUMBER:→ «PONUM»→      ORDERED·BY:→  «ORDPERSON»→ ¶
```

Figure 22-10. Invoice with fields to merge from a data document

After the merge is complete, the operator can use manual form fill-in techniques to supply the rest of the information for the invoice.

Note the BILL TO field in the invoice of Figure 22-10. It has an IF instruction that places the word *Same* in the field if the BILL TO fields in the data document are blank. If the fields are not blank, the ELSE portion of the instruction prints the field contents. This is one way that you can take advantage of conditionals in a merge.

Managing Collected Data

If names and addresses are collected in a data document on a daily basis, there must be a way to combine the daily data with a master list of customers. You can do this by merging the daily subfiles into a master list. The procedure is described here:

1. Open the master mailing list file. It can be called MASTLIST.DOC.

2. Use the Transfer Merge command to merge the subfile.

3. You must remove the header from the subfile because the master file already has one. Highlight the header and remove it, leaving the appended names and addresses intact.

Aligning Text to Print on Preprinted Forms

Word is an excellent tool to use when standard preprinted forms must be filled out. In fact all the fill-in information for the blanks of the form can be saved to a file for future use. You can also use the merge commands to obtain fill-in information from data files, as discussed previously.

The one problem with using preprinted forms is aligning the fields on your screen with the blank spaces on the form. This section will help you create a guide to make this task easier. Also, you'll see how to display titles to guide the operator who is filling out the form on the screen. These titles are not printed, however; only the text supplied in their fields is typed on the form.

 Tip: *You can create an alignment form to help determine field locations on preprinted forms.*

Creating an Aligment Guide

An alignment guide is simply a sheet of paper filled with numbers from 0 to 9 across and down the sheet. You then place the numbered sheet under the preprinted form so that you can easily determine the tab stops and line numbers for the fields on the form. Follow these instructions to create the form:

1. Measure the form's width and length and enter these numbers in the Page Length and Width fields of the Format Division Margins command.

2. If the form has margins, measure them exactly; then enter the numbers in the margin setting fields of the Format Division Margins command.

3. In the top-left corner of the new document type the numbers 1 through **9**; then type **0** to represent the tenth space, as shown in the following illustration. Make sure that the characters are formatted with a normal 12-point type such as Courier 12.

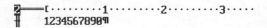

4. Next, highlight the characters and press ALT+F3 to copy them to the scrap.

5. Press the INS key until the characters reach the end of the line. The characters should fit exactly on the line and not word-wrap to the next line. You may need to remove a few numbers from the last insertion.

6. Highlight the entire line; then press ALT+F3 to copy it to the scrap.

7. Press the INS key for the number of lines that you have on your form. If you're not sure, try using the Print Repaginate command after inserting the number of lines that you think will fit on a page. You may need to execute Print Repaginate several times before you find the right number. If you overshoot, remove the excess lines.

8. The last step is to print the form.

You now have an alignment tool that you can use to find tab and line locations on the form. You might want to place a number to the left of every tenth line to make the line counting easier. You can also draw lines down the columns between the zeros and ones and then number the columns at the top.

Hiding Text for Preprinted Forms

The trick to printing on preprinted forms is to format the field names on the screen to hidden text. The hidden text is made visible to serve as a guide when you fill in the form. When the form is printed, the hidden text is suppressed.

To create such a form, you must format the field names and field markers as hidden text but format the tab as normal text. Remember that the tab determines the format of the filled-in text. Follow these steps to create a form with hidden field names.

1. Set the Window Options Show Hidden Text field to Yes to display hidden text fields on the screen.

2. Set the Print Options Hidden Text field to No to suppress hidden text printing.

3. Before typing each field name, press ALT+E (ALT+X+E if a style sheet is attached) to turn hidden text formats on.

4. Type the field name and the field marker (CTRL+]) in the positions determined by the alignment method described in the previous section.

5. Press ALT+SPACEBAR twice to return to normal typing mode; then press the TAB key.

6. Perform the steps starting with step 3 over again for each field in the form.

Fill out the form as you normally would, using CTRL+< or CTRL+> to jump between the fields or the macro described earlier under "Automatic Form Fill-in Macro."

Tips and Traps Summary

Form Types

Tip: Once a form is created, use file-locking techniques to protect it from alteration.

The Form Creation and Use Process

Tip: Use only the right-hand chevron when you position field markers.

Tip: You can add character formats to the tab following the field marker. The formats are applied to the fill-in text.

Tips and Traps Summary (*continued*)

Quick Form Creation

Tip: Be sure to include a space character after the field name to separate the name from the field text.

Trap: A direct format keystroke must be typed twice to format a single character.

Tip: You can use macros to automate keystrokes in Word.

Trap: Don't forget to end the AUTOFORM macro if it continues to repeat past the last field in the form.

Tip: The tab character following a field marker determines the character format of the filled-in text.

Trap: You must format blocks of text to be surrounded by borders as a single paragraph by using soft carriage returns (SHIFT+ ENTER).

Tip: Use underlined tab stops if you want to create blank forms that are filled in by hand.

Enhanced Forms

Tip: You can use the DOS ATTRIB command to write-protect forms from accidental alterations.

Using Merge Commands to Fill in Forms

Tip: Using data files allows you to keep a separate list of names and addresses for future use.

Aligning Text to Print on Preprinted Forms

Tip: You can create an alignment form to help determine field locations on preprinted forms.

23

Automating
with Macros

A *macro* is a series of keystrokes that can be reduced to a single CTRL key code. You can think of Word's macro feature as you would a tape recorder. Word records keystrokes as you type them and then plays them back at any time. In this way you can make any commonly performed or repetitive task as simple as pressing a key combination.

Many of Word's features are automated. For example, formatting is automated with style sheets, automatic typing can be performed by the glossary, and form letters can be easily created with the Print Merge command. Word's macro feature is just one more tool that you can use to make things easier.

You can record macros as you type keystrokes and commands, or you can create them manually by typing the commands of a macro as you would any other text. The full editing and command features of Word are available for writing and editing a macro. When you manually write a macro, keys on the keyboard or commands in Word have special names. The equivalent of a key press is performed when Word encounters these keynames while running the macro. For example, the ENTER key becomes <ENTER> in a macro.

Macros are given both a name and a CTRL key code so that you can start the macro by either typing its name or pressing the CTRL key code sequence.

You can automate many tasks in Word. The next section discusses a simple macro to reset tab stops. You can also create macros to perform such tasks as changing menu options, running DOS commands, saving text to other files, and searching and replacing text. Additionally, Word comes with its own set of macros, which are covered in the last section of this chapter.

A Simple Macro Example

A simple example is presented here to quickly acquaint you with the concepts and features of macros. Recall that tab settings made in one paragraph are repeated in the next if the ENTER key is pressed. Often, you may want to retain some formats of the previous paragraph, such as character formats and borders, but not the tab settings. To clear the tabs, you must press ESC and type **F**, **T**, and **R** for Format Tab Reset-all. You can make this procedure even simpler with the macro described in this section.

This example will show you how to record a macro by example. You will type the commands as you normally would with *macro record* on. Use SHIFT+F3 to turn the macro record mode on and off. Because the commands actually execute as part of the recording process, you'll want to make sure that the highlight is on a blank paragraph marker.

 Trap: *Actual keystrokes are executed while a macro records. Make sure that you want to perform the action before recording.*

Recording the Macro

Press SHIFT+F3 (Record Macro) to start recording the macro. Notice that the RM indicator appears in the status line to indicate that macro recording is on. Press CTRL+ESC to display the Word command menu. You press CTRL+ESC instead of ESC because it displays the command menu, even if it is already displayed. When recording macros, you must consider the status of the Word windows when the macro is run. For example, if the Word command menu is active and ESC is pressed, the menu is turned off or the highlight jumps out of the menu. The CTRL+ESC combination activates the menu no matter what.

 Tip: *When the menu must be accessed in a macro, use CTRL+ESC. This ensures that the menu stays active if it is already on.*

After pressing CTRL+ESC, select Format Tab Reset-all by typing **F**, **T**, and **R**. The tabs are reset in the current paragraph, and the keystrokes are recorded in the macro.

Saving and Naming the Macro

Next, press SHIFT+F3 to end macro recording. The Copy menu will immediately display. Word is asking for the name to give this macro. Type **TABRESET.MAC**, followed by a caret (SHIFT+6), and then press CTRL+R. Your display should look like the following:

```
COPY to: TABRESET.MAC^<ctrl R>█
```

TABRESET is the name that you can expand with the F3 (Glossary Expand) key to run the macro. Pressing CTRL+R will be the other way to run this macro. Press ENTER to save the macro. Macros are saved in the glossary, just like glossary entries, and one reason for supplying the .MAC extension in the macro name is to differentiate macro entries from normal entries in the glossary.

Running the Macro

The tab reset macro can be run in three different ways. The first is the easiest.

- Place the highlight on any paragraph that must have its tabs reset and press CTRL+R to run the macro.

- Alternatively, you can press ESC+INS and then F1 to get a list of macro names. Highlight TABRESET and press ENTER to run it. Use this method when you can't remember the name of the macro.

- Another way to run the macro is to type **TABRESET** in the text and press the F3 (Glossary Expand) key.

Looking at the Macro

To view the macro, perform the following steps:

1. Place the highlight in a blank part of the screen and press ESC+INS.

2. Press F1 to see a list of macros and glossary entries.

3. Highlight the TABRESET macro.

4. Type a caret by pressing SHIFT+6.

5. Press ENTER.

The following display will appear. The text mirrors the keystrokes that you typed earlier. The <CTRL ESC> text between the brackets is the CTRL+ESC key sequence. This is followed by "ftr," which represent the keystokes typed for the Format Tab Reset-all command.

```
<ctrl·esc>ftr▌
```

A Detailed Look at Macros

This section will look in more detail at how to create and use macros. The tab reset macro is only a small example of what can be done. There is a special macro language that includes instructions to make your macros even more powerful and sophisticated, as you'll see later.

How to Create a Macro

Macros are created in two ways. The *recording method* described earlier is the easiest, but it limits the power of macros to perform more sophisticated tasks, without further editing. The second method, called the *written method*, involves typing macro commands manually and then saving them to the glossary. This method is really an editing method. You can build up an entire macro by typing its commands, or you can add additional commands to a recorded macro by using the F3 (Record Macro) key.

 Tip: *The recording method is one way to create macros. Keystrokes are recorded as you type them in the normal way.*

Before recording a macro, determine what the macro will do and then plan out the commands and keystrokes that it will perform. You will usually know when a macro is needed because you have already repeated a certain set of keystrokes more than once and will need to do so again. Creating a macro in this case is as simple as turning macro record mode on and repeating the keystrokes just one more time.

You can also use a macro to make command execution easier for novice users. The macro language covered later allows you to display help messages and ask for information during a macro execution. This is especially useful when you are creating macros that other operators will use.

 Tip: *You can create macros to make complicated commands easier for novice users.*

If a macro is being written rather than recorded, it helps to write down each keystroke beforehand using the keynames shown in Table 23-1. These keynames are typed as shown and represent actual keystrokes when the macro runs. For example, if you need to move the highlight to the left, the keyname <LEFT> is used in the macro. Write down as much of the macro as possible, playing through the keystrokes in your head to make sure that all details have been considered; then type it on a blank screen.

After typing a macro, you can save it to the glossary under a macro name and then test it out.

Recording Macros

You've already seen how to record macros. This section will show you two more examples for reference. The second one is interesting because it includes, or nests, the first example in its keystrokes. In the first example a series of keystrokes is

Table 23-1.   Keynames Used in Macros

\<alt\>	ALT key
\<ctrl\>	CONTROL key
\<shift\>	SHIFT key
\<esc\>	ESC key
\<enter\>	ENTER key
\<tab\>	TAB key
\<del\>	DELETE key
\<ins\>	INSERT key
\<home\>	HOME key
\<end\>	END key
\<left\>	LEFT ARROW key
\<right\>	RIGHT ARROW key
\<down\>	DOWN ARROW key
\<up\>	UP ARROW key
\<pgdn\>	PAGE DOWN key
\<pgup\>	PAGE UP key
\<keypad*\>	Asterisk on keypad
\<keypad+\>	Plus symbol on keypad
\<keypad−\>	Minus symbol on keypad
\<space\>	SPACEBAR (when moving among menu commands)
\<backspace\>	BACKSPACE key
\<scroll lock\>	SCROLL LOCK key
\<numlock\>	NUMBER LOCK key
\<capslock\>	CAPS LOCK key

Note:
Function keys appear as: \<F1\>, \<F2\>, etc.
When used with other keys: \<SHIFT+F1\>, \<CTRL+F2\>, etc.
Number keys on the keypad appear as \<KEYPAD 5\>.

---

recorded to make the highlight jump to the periods at the end of sentences. This is accomplished through the Search command. Perform the following steps to record the macro:

1. Press SHIFT+F3 to turn the macro record mode on.
2. Press CTRL+ESC to display the Word command menu. Remember, using

ESC alone may cause the command menu to close if it is already open when the macro is executed.

3. Type **S** to select the Search command.

4. Type a period followed by a space in the Text field.

5. Tab to the Direction field and type **D** (for Down).

6. Press ENTER to execute the command.

7. Press SHIFT+F3 to turn macro record mode off.

8. In the Copy To field, type **JUMP-SENTENCE-END**, followed by a caret (SHIFT+6); then press CTRL+E and ENTER to save the macro.

You can try the macro by placing the cursor in any sentence and pressing CTRL+E. The macro name is long, but it helps describe what the macro does. Most macros are run using the CTRL keyname given to them. You will rarely type the descriptive name of a macro to run it.

To look at the macro just created, press ESC+INS, press F1, and then highlight the macro name. Type a caret (SHIFT+6) and press ENTER. The text of the macro will be inserted in the edit window at the location of the highlight. It should look like the following:

```
<ctrl·esc>s.<tab>d<enter>▯
```

Notice how the keystrokes are mirrored in the macro. The keynames can be found in Table 23-1.

You can create a macro just like the previous one to jump back to the period in the previous sentence. Record the macro in the same way, but type **U** (for Up) in the Direction field. Be sure to give the macro a different name when you save it. For example, type **JUMP-PREVIOUS-SENTENCE**, type a caret (SHIFT+6), and press CTRL+E.

In the next example the macro just created will be "nested." With this new macro, you will be able to place the highlight at a specific point in a sentence and highlight to the end of the sentence. This can be helpful when you are deleting or formatting the highlighted text.

1. Press SHIFT+F3 to turn macro record mode on.

2. Press F6 to turn the extend selection mode on.

3. Press CTRL+E to execute the sentence-end macro.

4. Press F6 again to turn off the extend mode.

5. Press SHIFT+F3 to turn macro record mode off.

6. The Copy command appears. Type **SELECT-SENTENCE-END**, followed by a caret. Next, press CTRL+S; then type **E** and press ENTER.

To execute this macro, press CTRL+S and type **E**. You will find that macro names, like style sheet names, should use two letters to increase the number of possibilities.

Display the contents of the macro so that you can see what the keystrokes look like. Press ESC+INS and then F1; then highlight the macro name. Type the caret (SHIFT+6) and press ENTER. You should see the following display. Notice how the previous macro is shown as <CTRL E> surrounded by the F6 key to turn the extend mode on and off.

`<f6><ctrl·E><f6>▯`

Writing Macros

In writing a macro you use the representations of the keystrokes shown in Table 23-1 instead of pressing the actual keys. Writing macros lets you tailor a macro in ways that are not possible in the record mode. For example, you can include the macro instructions discussed later in this chapter.

 Tip: *Writing macros instead of recording them allows you to use more features.*

When writing a macro, you must have a good idea of the keystrokes needed, which is why it is helpful to write down the keystrokes beforehand. You should "test run" the actual keystrokes on the keyboard before writing the macro to make sure that nothing has been left out.

 Trap: *It's a good idea to test run a macro before using it in a real situation.*

All the editing features of Word are available when you are writing a macro. You can place the highlight in any blank area of the screen to start. The following rules and features apply when you write macros:

- If you have a mouse, you cannot include its actions in a macro, so you will need to revert to keyboard commands.

- Page breaks, division breaks, paragraph marks, new line characters, and tab symbols are ignored in a macro when it is running. They can be used, however, to increase the readability of a long macro.

- You must surround macro instructions with chevrons, using the CTRL+[and CTRL+] key combinations.

- Always surround keynames with the greater than and less than brackets, for example, <ENTER> or <ESC>. See Table 23-1 for a complete list.

- To repeat any direction key in Table 23-1, follow it with the number of times it should repeat. For example, to repeat the LEFT ARROW key three times, type **<left 3>**.

- All alphanumeric keys on the keyboard are typed as they appear without brackets. These include the number and letter keys.

- If you need to include left chevron brackets or a caret in your macros, place a caret in front of them.

- When using search and replace commands, use two carets when typing search strings that include carets. For example, to search for tabs, type **^^t.**

- **Remember to use** <CTRL ESC> if you need to access a menu. If you need to make sure that edit mode is active, use <CTRL ESC ESC>.

To begin writing the macro, move to the blank area on the screen where you want to begin typing. Type the keystrokes that you planned out beforehand. When you are done typing, scan though the text of the macro and check for typing mistakes, unclosed brackets, and other possible problems. To save the macro, refer to the next section.

Naming Macros

Before you can save any macro, you must come up with a naming scheme. Because most macros are executed with the CTRL key rather than by typing their full names, you are limited to a one- or two-character naming scheme. As with styles, if you use a one-character name, you will unnecessarily limit the number of macros you can have. For example, the CTRL+E macro created earlier would cancel the use of any other macro starting with the letter *E* because this macro would always run first.

Tip: *Use two-character names for macros to maintain a large number of available names.*

When typing a macro name, always type the full name first, then the CTRL key code that you plan to use. You don't have to specify a CTRL code, but it is recommended. The caret is used to separate the two. You can type the full name using the underscore character, hyphen, or period to help separate the parts if you prefer to describe the macro in an English-like way. For example, a macro name such as DELETE-TO-END-OF-LINE perfectly describes what the macro does.

 Tip: *Use the macro name to describe the macro as much as possible.*

When typing the CTRL portion of the macro name, simply press the CTRL key and type the first character of the name. If the CTRL name has two characters, type the second character without holding down the CTRL key.

Keys that already have functions assigned to them by Word can also be used for macros, but this presents a particular problem however. For example, you can assign a macro to CTRL+F10, but this will alter the CTRL+F10 Save function assigned by Word. To use CTRL+F10 Save, you must press CTRL+X+F10, using *X* as you do for direct formatting keys when style sheets are attached. In general, you should avoid using preassigned keys.

 Trap: *When naming macros, avoid using existing CTRL keynames*
                 already assigned by Word.

Testing the Macro

Word provides a way to test your macros. Pressing CTRL+F3 before executing a macro will allow you to step through it to watch the effect of each keystroke, command, and instruction as they execute.

To test a macro, press CTRL+F3 and then start the macro in the normal way. Word will pause between each step of the macro until you press a key. The next step is then executed. Press ESC if you want to cancel the macro. Be sure to turn step mode off when you are finished testing a macro to avoid confusion.

 Trap: *Don't forget that macro step mode is on and that a macro is*
                 running. The key code indicator ST will appear at the
                 bottom of the screen.

Enhancing Macros

The remainder of this chapter discusses how you can enhance macros through the use of the macro instruction language and various programming techniques. You'll also see how to start a macro automatically and perform other tasks.

Macro Instructions

You can use macro instructions to control the flow of instructions while a macro runs or to display messages and collect information from the operator. Macro instructions can only be entered when you write a macro, not when you record one. However, you can edit a recorded macro, inserting the appropriate macro instructions where needed.

 Trap: *Macro instructions can only be written into a macro. They cannot be used when recording a macro.*

All macro instruction are included in a macro surrounded by chevrons. Type open and closed chevrons in the normal way by pressing CTRL+[and CTRL+], respectively. Remember that normal keys such as ENTER and TAB are surrounded by < and > in macro instructions.

The macro instructions are briefly described in the following list, followed by a more detailed discussion of their use, with examples.

ASK	The ASK instruction can be used to obtain a variable from the operator while the macro runs. ASK can include a message to prompt the operator to enter the variable.
COMMENT	The COMMENT instruction is used primarily to document the use and functions of a macro. Comments are typed as normal text but have no effect on the actual operation of the macro.
IF...ELSE...ENDIF	The IF and ELSE instructions cause macros to perform in specific ways under specific

conditions, which are based on true and false values.

MESSAGE	A message of up to 80 characters can be displayed on the edit window message line to explain the current status of a macro or describe a condition.
PAUSE	The PAUSE instruction will temporarily halt a macro so that text or other information can be typed by the operator. The macro resumes when ENTER is pressed.
QUIT	QUIT can be used to terminate a macro. It is primarily used when an IF or ELSE condition is evaluated as either true or false.
REPEAT...ENDREPEAT	The instruction between REPEAT and END-REPEAT is repeated the number of times specified.
SET	SET obtains information from the operator as well as parameters that are already set in Word, such as command field contents.
WHILE...ENDWHILE	WHILE performs a task until a specific condition is no longer true. The condition is tested before the next task is performed.

About the Examples

The examples discussed in the next sections are from a macro used to automate the calculation functions of the invoice described in Chapter 22. The macro adds up the figures in the AMOUNT column and places the result in the SUBTOTAL position. The operator is then asked whether the invoice is a California sale. If it is, the tax is calculated; if not, zeros are placed in the TAX position. The operator is then asked for shipping charges, which are added to the SHIPPING/ HANDLING position. From these amounts, the total is then calculated. If a check has been sent as prepayment, this is subtracted from the total due on the invoice.

The complete macro is shown in Figure 23-1. Parts of it will be discussed to explain the macro instruction language, and then the complete macro will be explained. Note how the macro is organized. Different parts are separated by blank lines, and each one is described with the COMMENT command. Because of the length and complexity of this macro, such an organization is essential.

 Tip: *Use blank lines and indents to make long macros easier to read and understand.*

The ASK Instruction

Use the ASK instruction to obtain information from the operator. This information may be evaluated with an IF instruction, become the contents of a field, or be used as text. The ASK instruction causes the macro to pause until the information is typed and ENTER is pressed.

 Tip: *Use the ASK instruction to obtain information from the operator.*

The instruction takes one of the following forms:

```
«ASK variable=?»

«ASK variable=?prompt»
```

The first version displays Word's prompt. The message "Enter text, press Enter when done." will appear when this version is used. The second version displays the prompt that you specify.

The variable name can be any combination of letters and numbers but cannot start with a number. Underscores, hyphens, and periods are not allowed in variable names when you use macros. The input supplied for an ASK instruction can be a date, numeric value, or text.

Word will treat numbers as a date if they are separated by a slash (/), hyphen, or period and are written in the format mm/dd/yy or mm/dd/yyyy. A sequence of

---

```
     «COMMENT»
 1   Before running this macro, place the highlight in the top left
     corner of the AMOUNT column. Press Ctrl+IC to start the macro
     «ENDCOMMENT»

 2   «COMMENT Highlight and add column»
     <shift f6><right 10><down 11><f2>

 3   «COMMENT Move to SUBTOTAL, insert scrap»
     <end><down 13><ins><down>

     «COMMENT calculate tax or print 0.00»
 4   «ASK CA=?Is this a California sale?»
     «IF CA="y"»«SET TAX=scrap *.06»«TAX»«ELSE»«0.00»
     «ENDIF»

 5   «COMMENT get shipping/handling charge»
     <DOWN>«ASK SH=?Enter shipping/handling charges: »«SH»

 6   «COMMENT add subtotal, tax, shipping/handling; place in total position»
     <shift f6><up 2><left 7><f2><end><down 3><ins>

 7   «COMMENT variable names TOTAL holds contents of scrap for future use»
     «SET TOTAL=SCRAP»

 8   «COMMENT get check number»
     <ctrl .>«ASK CKNUM=?What is the check number?»«CKNUM»

 9   «COMMENT get check amount»
     <ctrl .>«ASK PREPAID=?What is the check amount?»«PREPAID»

10   «COMMENT calculate and print amount due»
     <DOWN>«SET DUE=TOTAL-PREPAID»«DUE»
```

Figure 23-1.   A macro to calculate totals on the invoice form discussed in Chapter 22

digits is treated as a number, but a mathematical expression such as 5+2 is treated as a text string.

An example of the ASK instruction is shown here:

```
«ASK·DATE=?Enter·todays·date»¶
```

Section 4 of the macro in Figure 23-1 shows another example of an ASK instruction. The operator is asked whether the sale is a California sale. A **Y** response from the operator is placed in the CA variable. The IF instruction in the next line then evaluates CA. If it is **Y**, the tax is calculated; if not, zeros are placed in the TAX field of the invoice.

The COMMENT Instruction

Macros can often become quite complicated. You may need to include comments to remind you of what a particular instruction set does. In addition, you can document the macro for others who may need to alter it in the future. Use the COMMENT instruction for this purpose.

You can include text inside the chevrons of a COMMENT instruction, as shown here:

```
«COMMENT highlight to end of line»
```

If a description is long, place it between a COMMENT instruction and an ENDCOMMENT instruction, as shown here.

```
«COMMENT» This macro moves text formatted with the TP
style from the LEGAL.STY style sheet. «ENDCOMMENT»
```

Section 1 of the macro in Figure 23-1 contains a COMMENT...ENDCOMMENT instruction to explain the use and operation of the entire macro. Each of the other sections contains a separate COMMENT instruction.

 Tip: *Use the COMMENT instruction to document a macro for future reference or for other users.*

The IF...ELSE...ENDIF Instruction

The IF instruction performs an action if a conditional statement is true; then it ends. Alternatively, an IF...ELSE statement performs one action if the conditional statement is true and another if the statement is false. The two versions of the command are illustrated here. All IF and IF...ELSE instructions must end with the ENDIF instruction.

«IF condition»action«ENDIF»

«IF condition»action«ELSE»alternative action«ENDIF»

 Tip: *The IF...ELSE instruction performs conditional actions in a macro based on true and false statements.*

The IF Condition   The condition in an IF instruction is a comparative statement. It compares whether two numbers are the same, not equal, less or greater than the other, and so on. The condition can also test to see if two text strings are the same.

If a comparison is true, the action part of the IF instruction is executed; if not, the instruction either ends or performs the action following the ELSE instruction, which, by the way, can be another "nested" IF instruction.

In section 4 of the macro in Figure 23-1, an ASK instruction obtains a Yes response from the operator, which is evaluated by the IF instruction. The condition being evaluated is whether the variable CA is equal to *y*. It doesn't matter whether *y* is uppercase or lowercase.

Operators   Operators are used in the conditional parts of the IF instruction and in several other instructions to determine how the statement will be evaluated for true or false. The operators are listed here:

=	equal
<>	not equal
<	less than
>	greater than
<=	less than or equal to
>=	greater than or equal to

The Action   If the operator entered **y** or **Y** to the prompt "Is this a California sale?", then the IF condition is true and the action following it is executed. If the operator entered **n** or **N**, the alternative action is taken. This is the action following the ELSE instruction in the line. In many cases an alternative action will not be present. An IF instruction may only perform an action if the condition is true. If the condition is not true, Word goes to the next instruction.

Calculations can be performed as the action (or alternative action) of an IF instruction. In section 4 of the macro the tax is calculated from the contents of the scrap. Note that the word *scrap* is an actual reserved variable, the contents of which can be included in mathematical equations. (Reserved variables will be discussed shortly.) Also note that the scrap itself contains the subtotal because section 2 of the macro column-selected the invoice items and used the F2 key to calculate and place the result in the scrap.

Alternative Actions   Alternative actions are performed in an IF statement if the condition evaluates as false. These actions always follow the ELSE instruction in the statement. In section 5 of the macro in Figure 23-1 the alternative action is to print "0.00" in the TAX portion of the invoice.

Variables   *Variables* are names of memory locations that you create to store numbers, names, and other text that you may need later. In section 4 of the invoice macro the operator response is stored in the CA variable. It is then used in the conditional portion of the IF instruction in the next line. Variables are defined with the ASK instruction, as described earlier, or with the SET instruction, described later in the chapter.

Tip: *Variables hold temporary values or text strings for later use.*

Variables are grouped into two categories — text variables and numeric variables. The main difference between them is that calculations and comparisons can be performed on numeric variables, while only comparisons can be made on text variables. For example, SUBTOTAL*TAXRATE is a legal calculation if both SUBTOTAL and TAXRATE hold numeric values. In the invoice macro CA*.6 is not a valid calculation because CA holds a text response.

Trap: *Calculations can only be performed on variables that hold numeric values.*

Variables should not be confused with *constants*. A constant is anything enclosed in quotation marks, such as a text string or field input that is specified in an instruction. It does not change or represent other values; it only represents itself.

 Tip: *A constant only represents itself, never other values.*

Reserved Variables   Word reserves four variable names for its own use. They can be used in macros to perform specific actions or obtain information from specific locations in Word. These variables are listed here:

SELECTION   SELECTION allows you to perform operations on the text that is currently highlighted when a macro is running. For example, you could ask the user to highlight a specific portion of text and then move the text or duplicate it. If text is already highlighted before the macro starts, this text is the selection unless the macro moves the highlight elsewhere.

SCRAP   As you know, the scrap can be used to place text or numeric values. The reserved variable SCRAP lets you perform calculations on values placed in the scrap or perform operations on text in the scrap. Section 4 of the invoice macro calculates the tax from the subtotal in the scrap.

FIELD   FIELD (true or false) refers to the contents of the menu field currently selected in a Word command menu. The variable is numeric if the field contents are numeric. You can use this variable to determine what the current settings are in menu selections and then change them accordingly.

FOUND, NOTFOUND   These Boolean variables are used to test the results of a search. FOUND remains true until a search is unsuccessful. It then becomes false. The opposite holds for NOTFOUND. You can conditionally test FOUND and NOTFOUND with the IF and WHILE instructions.

The MESSAGE Instruction

Messages can be displayed while a macro is running to inform the user of its current status. The format of the instruction is shown here:

«MESSAGE text»

You can type any text of up to 80 characters. It will appear in the message line of the screen when the macro runs. Note that the messages are not displayed if the Word command menu is turned off. You may want to set it on before starting the macro or have the macro itself turn the menu on.

  Tip: *The MESSAGE instruction displays messages in the command line.*

Trap: *Messages will not display if the command menu is off.*

The PAUSE Instruction

The PAUSE instruction will temporarily interrupt a macro and wait for ENTER to be pressed. Alternatively, PAUSE can display a message and wait for input from the operator. The macro always resumes once ENTER is pressed. The two formats of the instruction are shown here:

«PAUSE»

«PAUSE prompt»

PAUSE is generally used to give the operator time to read text on the screen during a running macro. You can also use PAUSE to display a message informing the user of an action to be performed. For example, the instruction shown here opens the Transfer Save command and then pauses and displays the message shown. Once the operator enters the name of the file to save, the macro resumes when ENTER is pressed and saves the file.

```
<Esc>TS«PAUSE Enter filename»<Enter>
```

The next example, taken from Chapter 22, is used to jump from one field marker to the next when filling out a form. The REPEAT...ENDREPEAT instruction is used to repeat the <CTRL .> and PAUSE instruction 30 times. Note that <CTRL .> is the equivalent of the next field command, CTRL+>.

`«REPEAT 30»<CTRL .>«PAUSE»«ENDREPEAT»`

Almost any Word command or instruction can be performed when a macro is in pause mode. You can select text, scroll, switch modes, cut and paste, and use the mouse to select and edit or choose commands. The macro resumes when ENTER is pressed.

 Tip: *You can use the PAUSE instruction to temporarily stop a macro so that text can be read or commands can be executed manually.*

The QUIT Instruction

You can use the QUIT instruction to stop the execution of a running macro, usually as the result of an IF or END...WHILE evaluation. There is no special form of the instruction except that it must be enclosed within chevron brackets, as shown here:

`«QUIT»`

The following illustration shows how the QUIT instruction might be used. The code shown is part of a macro that expands glossary entries after a document has been typed. It will be discussed in detail later. Note that the code following the third line has been left out. It is the code that would execute if the operator pressed ENTER. If the operator types **Q** (for Quit) to the ASK instruction, the macro ends.

```
«ASK ANSWER=?This macro will expand glossary entries.
Type Q to quit or Enter to continue»
«IF ANSWER="Q"»«QUIT»«ENDIF»
```

Tip: You can use the QUIT instruction to stop a macro, usually after a condition tests false.

The REPEAT...ENDREPEAT Instruction

The REPEAT...ENDREPEAT instruction is used to repeat a series of keystrokes and macro instructions two or more times. The command is shown here, where *n* represents the number of times that the macro instructions between REPEAT and ENDREPEAT are repeated.

```
«REPEAT n» macro instructions «ENDREPEAT»
```

The number specified for *n* is often arbitrary. You may want to repeat a step but are not sure how often. You can specify a high number and then stop the macro when the correct number of repeats has been made. You've already seen this in the macro from Chapter 22 that jumps from one field to the next in a form. The instruction was discussed in the section on the PAUSE instruction.

The macro illustrated here copies the current file to the diskette in drive B three times. A PAUSE between saves lets you switch diskettes. You can use this macro to copy files on diskettes for other users.

```
«ASK FILENAME=?Type the name for this file: »
«REPEAT 3»
«PAUSE Insert diskette and press Enter»
<Ctrl Esc>TSB:«FILENAME»<Enter>
«ENDREPEAT»
```

Note that the fourth line first executes the Transfer Save command and then types **B:** in the Filename field, followed by the FILENAME variable specified by the ASK instruction in the first line of the macro.

Tip: You can use the REPEAT...ENDREPEAT instruction to repeat a macro a specified number of times.

The SET Instruction

The SET instruction, which is very similar to the ASK instruction, is used to define variables. The variable can be set inside the macro or from a response typed by the operator. The SET instruction has the forms illustrated here:

«SET variable=expression»

«SET variable=?»

«SET variable=?prompt»

 Tip: *The SET instruction obtains information from the operator and sets variable values.*

    The first form of the SET instruction is used to set a variable from inside the macro. For example, section 10 of the invoice macro of Figure 23-1 uses the SET instruction to set the variable DUE equal to TOTAL minus the PREPAID amount with the equation DUE=TOTAL−PREPAID.
    You could increment or decrement a value in a REPEAT...ENDREPEAT or WHILE...ENDWHILE loop. For example, the instruction SET COUNT= COUNT+1 could count the number of times an action was repeated or the number of loops in a WHILE...ENDWHILE loop. The file-saving macro discussed earlier is shown here with this modification. Note that the tab indents are not essential; they are used only to make the nested IF...ELSE...ENDIF instructions easier to read.

```
«SET COUNT=0»
«ASK FILENAME=?Type the name for this file: »
«REPEAT 3»
«SET COUNT=COUNT+1»
    «IF COUNT=1»«PAUSE Enter first disk and press Enter»
        «ELSE»
        «IF COUNT=2»«PAUSE Enter second disk and press Enter»
            «ELSE»
            «PAUSE Enter third disk and press Enter»
        «ENDIF»
    «ENDIF»
<Ctrl Esc>TSB:«FILENAME»<Enter>
«ENDREPEAT»
```

In this example the SET instruction first initializes the COUNT variable by making it equal to 0. In the fourth instruction it is incremented by 1 each time through the REPEAT loop. The value in COUNT then determines which message is displayed in the nested IF instructions.

You can also use SET to alter variables obtained from the operator with the ASK instruction. For example, ASK could obtain a discount percentage rate in whole numbers, such as 10 percent. This is placed in the variable DISCOUNT-RATE. The SET instruction could then convert this rate to a true percentage for future calculations with the instruction shown here:

```
«ASK DISCOUNTRATE=?Enter the rate of discount»
«SET DISCOUNTRATE=DISCOUNTRATE/100»
```

The WHILE...ENDWHILE Instruction

The WHILE...ENDWHILE instruction is used to perform a loop in a macro while a condition is true. The macro tells Word: "Repeat the following set of instructions while this condition is true. When it is no longer true, go to the next step." The format of the instruction is shown here:

```
«WHILE condition» instructions «ENDWHILE»
```

 Tip: *The WHILE...ENDWHILE instruction performs an instruction set over and over while a condition is true.*

As long as the condition is true, the instructions are repeated. The macro shown here illustrates the use of WHILE...ENDWHILE instructions. This macro is used to search through documents and expand glossary entries. The operator is asked for each glossary entry to expand, one after the other.

```
«ASK ANSWER=?This macro will expand glossary entries.
Type Q to quit or Enter to continue»
«IF ANSWER="Q"»«QUIT»«ENDIF»
«ASK GLOSSENTRY=?Type first glossary entry to convert:»
«WHILE GLOSSENTRY<>"Q"»
    <Ctrl PgUp><Ctrl Esc>S«GLOSSENTRY»<TAB>D<ENTER><F3>
        «WHILE FOUND»
        <Shift F4><F3>
        «ENDWHILE»
    «ASK GLOSSENTRY=?Type next name or Q to quit:»
«ENDWHILE»
```

Note that the macro has a nested WHILE...ENDWHILE instruction. The first set is used to ask the operator for another glossary entry, which is placed in the variable GLOSSENTRY. This WHILE...ENDWHILE loop will continue until the operator enters a **Q**. The fifth line of the macro instructs Word to repeat the macro while GLOSSENTRY is not equal to *Q*.

The parameters for the search are set up in the sixth line, which is followed by a second WHILE...ENDWHILE instruction. A loop is formed in the next three lines to repeat the Search command (SHIFT+F4) and expand the found entry (F3). This continues until FOUND is no longer true. Word sets FOUND equal to false when a search is finally unsuccessful.

When no more glossary entries can be found, the ENDWHILE instruction executes and the loop ends. The operator is then asked for the next glossary entry to search for in the second to last line. If the operator types **Q**, the WHILE instruction in the fifth line becomes false and the macro ends.

How To Automatically Start a Macro

A macro can start automatically, either when a glossary is merged or when Word starts. The reserved macro name AUTOEXEC is used. If you place the AUTO-EXEC macro in the NORMAL.GLY file, it will execute every time you start Word. As you'll see, you can use this macro to display a menu system on the screen.

The AUTOEXEC macro commands are no different than any other macro commands. If you place a control code behind the macro name when you save it, you can also start it at any time. For example, you could call the AUTOEXEC macro CTRL+A+X to start it whenever you want.

The AUTOEXEC macro will start if you execute the Transfer Clear All command, which means that the AUTOEXEC macro will start as if you had started Word from DOS. This can be a convenient feature if you create a menu like that shown in Figure 23-2 to list common file templates.

If you have a hard drive, you can create several directories in which to store your Word files. Each directory can have its own NORMAL.GLY file, each of which can have its own special AUTOEXEC macro. You could create directories for several users and then create a special log-on menu especially for each user.

```
┌──────────────────────────────────────────────────┐
│          J O E ' S   W O R D   M E N U            │
└──────────────────────────────────────────────────┘

     1)   BLOCK LETTER TEMPLATE

     2)   SEMI BLOCK LETTER TEMPLATE

     3)   MEMO TEMPLATE

     4)   WEEKLY REPORT TEMPLATE

     5)   BLANK SCREEN

┌──────────────────────────────────────────────────┐
│       T Y P E   A   S E L E C T I O N             │
└──────────────────────────────────────────────────┘
```

Figure 23-2.   A menu of template files

Macro Examples

The following examples should help you better understand the macro programming language. Each macro is useful on its own and can be modified to fit your needs, if necessary. The first one is the invoice calculation macro shown in Figure 23-1.

The Invoice Calculation Macro

The macro in Figure 23-1 is used to perform the calculations for the invoice discussed in Chapter 22. Each section of the macro contains its own COMMENT instructions to help define what it does. Remember that Word ignores page breaks, division breaks, paragraph marks, newline characters, and tab symbols in the text of a macro, so you can use them to make your macro easier to read, as was done in Figure 23-1.

Section 1   COMMENT and ENDCOMMENT instructions are used to document the macro for future reference.

Section 2   The column select mode (SHIFT+F6) is used to calculate the column of items. The highlight must first be placed in the upper-left corner of the column of numbers. You may need to select the tab in front of the number if the top number has fewer digits than other numbers in the column.

Section 3   After the column has been calculated, the results are placed in the scrap. The highlight is moved to the SUBTOTAL category, and the subtotal in the scrap is inserted.

Section 4   The operator is asked if this is a California sale. If true, the subtotal in the scrap is multiplied by the tax percentage and inserted in the TAX category. If not, "0.00" is inserted instead.

Section 5   This section asks for the shipping and handling charges and inserts them in the appropriate category.

Section 6   The previous three categories are added and placed in the TOTAL category.

Section 7   The total amount is assigned to the TOTAL variable for future use.

Section 8   The check number is obtained and inserted in the CHECK NUMBER INVOICE category.

Section 9   The prepaid amount is obtained in the PREPAID variable and is then placed in the PREPAID INVOICE category.

Section 10   The amount due is calculated by subtracting the PREPAID variable from the TOTAL variable and is then placed in the DUE category.

Creating Operator-Specified Hanging Indents

The macro illustrated here is extremely useful if you are creating hanging indented paragraphs with indents that do not fall on the normal 1/2-inch tab stops. The macro first asks for the desired indent. Then a tab stop is set, followed by the paragraph left indent and first-line indent. Note that INDENT is the variable used to hold the number specified. In the last line it is converted to a negative amount for the first-line indent.

```
«ASK INDENT=?Enter the amount of the hanging indent:»
<Ctrl Esc>fts«INDENT»<Enter>
<Ctrl Esc>fp<tab>«INDENT»
<TAB>«-INDENT»<Enter>
```

Compiling Titles

The macro illustrated here was actually used to compile the list of tips and traps of this book to a master list at the end of each chapter. You can use it to search for titles, illustration headings, and other formatted text and then copy that text to another window, which can be a window at the end of your document. The macro searches for the style name by using the Format sEarch Style Key Code field. The tips and traps in the book manuscript were given the style code name of TP.

```
«COMMENT Search for TP style code»
<ctrl esc>FESTP<enter>
«COMMENT Copy to scrap, jump to other window, insert
and jump back»
<alt f3><f1><ins><f1>
```

First, open a window to another document or at the end of your current document. Place the highlight at the top of the document in the top window and press the CTRL key code to start the macro. You can call it any name you want. The code CTRL+Z was used for the book because it was easy to type (rather than a two-character code). Note that the macro is executed for each search and copy. If you are copying the text to the end of your document, make sure that you don't "run" into it as you approach the bottom. This would cause already copied text to be copied again.

When the macro finds a block of text with the TP style code, it highlights it, copies it to the scrap (ALT+F3), moves to the other window, inserts it, and then moves back to the first window. You can then execute the macro again.

If you use many different style sheet codes to format different parts of your documents, you can use the style code search routines as described in this section. Style codes are often all that you can search for to locate common blocks of text such as titles and figure descriptions.

A Menu System

Because a macro can be created that executes every time you start Word, you can create a macro that displays a menu like the one shown in Figure 23-2. The AUTOEXEC macro shown in Figure 23-3 displays and automates the menu when Word is started. Note that each menu selection is a blank template file that the operator may need to use on a regular basis, except for the last selection, which displays a new, blank screen.

To create this menu system, you must first create a menu screen like that of Figure 23-2. You can name this file MENU.DOC. Be sure to create the menu file in the same directory as the macro file that displays it. Remember that each directory on your system can have its own NORMAL.GLY glossary file and thus its own AUTOEXEC macro and menu.

```
1 ──  <ctrl esc>tlMENU.DOC<Enter>
2 ──  «ASK OPTION=?Enter menu selection:»
3 ──  «IF OPTION=1»<ctrl esc>tcw<esc>tlBLOCKLET.DOC<Enter>
4 ──      «ELSE»
5 ──      «IF OPTION=2»<ctrl esc>tcw<esc>tlSEMIBLOK.DOC<Enter>
6 ──          «ELSE»
7 ──          «IF OPTION=3»<ctrl esc>tcw<esc>tlMEMOTEMP.DOC<Enter>
8 ──              «ELSE»
9 ──              «IF OPTION=4»<ctrl esc>tcw<esc>tlREPORT.DOC<Enter>
10 ──                  «ELSE»
11 ──                  «IF OPTION=5»<ctrl esc>tcw
12 ──                  «ENDIF»
13 ──              «ENDIF»
14 ──          «ENDIF»
15 ──      «ENDIF»
16 ──  «ENDIF»
```

Figure 23-3.   A macro to automate the menu shown in Figure 23-2

After creating the menu, you can create an AUTOEXEC macro similar to that shown in Figure 23-3. Type it in the normal way and then use the Copy command to place it in your glossary. Make sure that the name is AUTOEXEC only. Do not use the .MAC extension. The following list describes how the macro works.

Line 1	The first line displays the menu on the screen.
Line 2	The second line displays the "Enter menu selection:" message at the bottom of the screen and waits for the operator response. The response is placed in the variable OPTION.
Line 3	If OPTION is equal to 1, the window is cleared to remove the menu, then the template file BLOCKLET.DOC is loaded. The macro then ends.
Line 4	If the variable is not equal to 1, the instructions after this ELSE instruction are executed.
Lines 5-10	These lines perform a similar function to line 3. The file shown in line 5, 7, or 9 is loaded if one of the options is true.
Line 11	If OPTION is equal to 5, the window is cleared and the operator can create a new file.

A Log-On Macro

The log-on macro produces the display shown here when Word is first started. Its purpose is to change the default directory to the personal directory of the person currently logging on the system with the Transfer Options command. If Joe logs on, he types 1, and the default directory becomes C:\JOE. In this way Joe can access his own files from his personal directory and save to this directory. This helps keep the filing system organized and prevents duplicate files when more than one operator uses Word.

```
‖                                                              ‖

RESPONSE: ▮

Enter menu selection: 1) JOE  2) ALICE  3) FRANK  4) MARY
Pg1 Li1 Co1        {}               ?                   Microsoft Word
```

The log-on macro is shown in Figure 23-4. It should be named AUTOEXEC and saved in the glossary. If you are using the menu system discussed in the previous section, rename it MENU.MAC. You can then "chain" the menu to the bottom of the log-on macro. In this way the menu will display after a user logs in to his or her special directory. The description of the macro is listed here:

Line 1	The first line displays the list of users and obtains a response from the operator. The user's response is placed in the variable ID.
Line 2	This first IF statement evaluates whether ID is equal to 1. If it is, JOE is placed in the variable USER, and the macro continues execution in line 14.
Lines 3-8	These lines perform the same function as line 2, evaluating each possible response and setting the variable USER according to this response.
Line 9	If no response is given by the operator (ENTER is pressed), it is assumed that the user wants to use the current directory. This line displays the message shown, and the macro ends. Line 14 is not executed.
Line 14	This line changes the default directory based on the variable USER. The Transfer Options command is used to change the directory.

If you want to run a menu macro similar to that shown in Figure 23-3 and display a menu like that shown in Figure 23-2, you can add a line at the end of the log-on macro. Because the log-on macro must be named AUTOEXEC, rename the menu macro MENU.MAC and give it a CTRL code such as <CTRL M>U. At the end of the log-on macro, add the command <CTRL M>U to start the macro after the user directory has been set.

Word-Supplied Macros

Word 4 comes with its own set of macros. Before you can use them, however, you must first merge the MACRO.GLY glossary. You can merge these macros into the

```
 1 —  «ASK ID=?Enter menu selection: 1) JOE  2) ALICE  3) FRANK  4) MARY»
 2 —  «IF ID=1»«SET USER="JOE"»
 3 —        «ELSE»
 4 —     «IF ID=2»«SET USER="ALICE"»
 5 —           «ELSE»
 6 —         «IF ID=3»«SET USER="FRANK"»
 7 —               «ELSE»
 8 —             «IF ID=4»«SET USER="MARY"»
 9 —                     «ELSE»«MESSAGE Non-user directory in use»«QUIT»
10 —             «ENDIF»
11 —           «ENDIF»
12 —        «ENDIF»
13 —  «ENDIF»
14 —  <ctrl esc>toC:\«USER»<ENTER>
```

Figure 23-4. A log-on macro for four users

current glossary or clear the existing glossary before merging the new set. Because the macros are extremely useful, you may want to merge them with your existing NORMAL.GLY glossary so that you can use them at any time.

To merge the supplied macros, choose the Transfer Glossary Merge command. Type **Y** to save the current glossary. If you have a diskette system, type **macro** in the field. If you have a hard-drive system, type **c: \pathname \macro**, where *pathname* is the name of the directory where the file exists.

The following list provides a short description of each macro.

AUTHORITY—ENTRY.MAC. This macro is used first to mark a citation for inclusion in a table of authorities. The macro prompts you to highlight a citation and then select its scope from a list: previous case, constitution, statute, or other. The macro makes it an index entry and also prompts you to store it in a glossary name for the citation so that it can be easily inserted on another page.

AUTHORITY—TABLE.MAC. This macro generates and then titles an index (replacing an old index if necessary) with the name Table of Authorities. Ignore the "Search text not found" message.

BULLETED—LIST.MAC. This macro automatically inserts a hyphen at the specified indent and then lets you enter headings after each hyphen. Press ENTER between each heading. The headings are automatically formatted as modern i (Helvetica, 12-point type).

CHAINPRINT.MAC. This macro lets you print a list of documents and numbers the pages consecutively throughout the documents. It prompts you for the position of the page number.

COPY_TEXT.MAC. This macro prompts you to select the source text and then the destination; then it copies the text.

DCA_LOAD.MAC. This macro converts a DCA document with WORD... DCA.EXE and loads the output document into Word. It prompts for the input name and then gives the output document the same name with the .MSW extension.

DCA_SAVE.MAC. This macro converts the current document to the DCA format with the .DCA extension. The original documents remain unchanged in both cases.

FREEZE_STYLE.MAC. This macro transforms all formatting done with styles into direct formatting. It is useful with conversion utilities.

HP_LTR_ENV_MANUAL.MAC, HP_BUS_ENV_MANUAL.MAC, HP_LTR_ENV_TRAY.MAC, HP_BUS_ENV_TRAY.MAC. These macros are used to print envelopes on the Hewlett-Packard LaserJet Series II printer. The first two macros will use manual feeding, while the last two use the envelope tray. The TTYFF.PRD file must be used with this macro, and font selection must be done at the front panel of the printer. Type the desired label (including merge fields if desired); then move to the beginning of the document, run the macro, and choose the Print Printer command.

INDEX.MAC. This macro adds index codes to words in a document based on a list that you specify. It requires that the list of words be provided in a separate file, one word per line.

INDEX_ENTRY.MAC. This macro adds hidden index codes (.i. and ;) to selected hidden text.

MAILING_LABEL.MAC. This macro uses a label template with merge fields to print labels in one, two, or three columns. The macro prompts you for the name of the data file. The label template, stored in the glossary Label in this glossary file, can be customized to fit the field names of the data fields. The data and labels are merged into a document for future revisions. An 8.5-inch page width is assumed.

MEMO—HEADER. This macro creates a memorandum header with the From, To, and so on fields and then prompts you to fill them in.

MOVE—TEXT.MAC. This macro prompts you to select the source text and then the destination; then it moves the text.

NEXT—PAGE.MAC. This macro moves the highlight to the beginning of the next page. The document must have been previously printed or paginated with the Print Repaginate command.

PREV—PAGE.MAC. This macro moves the highlight to the beginning of the previous page. The document must have been previously paginated with the Print Repaginate command.

REPAGINATE.MAC. This macro removes all existing "hard" page breaks and repaginates with page break confirmation. It also removes all division breaks. Do not use this macro if you have division marks in your document.

REPLACE—WITH—GLOSSARY.MAC. This macro replaces specified search text with the contents of a specified glossary entry. (Note that a similar macro was described earlier in this chapter that allows multiple entries to be typed.)

REPLACE—WITH—SCRAP.MAC. This macro replaces specified search text with the current contents of the scrap.

RTF—LOAD.MAC and RTF—SAVE.MAC. These macros are the same as DCA—LOAD.MAC and DCA—SAVE.MAC covered earlier, except that the conversion is from and to the Rich Text Format (RTF), using WORD—RTF.EXE.

SAVE—ASCII.MAC This macro saves a document as an ASCII text file with carriage returns at the end of each line. You can then use the file with communication programs such as email or with other text editors that require carriage returns at the end of each line of text. PLAIN.PRD must be currently selected in the Printer field of the Print Options command.

SAVE—SELECTION.MAC. This macro saves selected text to a specified filename.

SIDEBYSIDE.MAC. This macro prompts for the number of paragraphs to position side by side on the same page, the desired space between paragraphs, and the desired alignment for each. The paragraphs are then formatted accordingly.

TABLE.MAC. This macro sets tabs for a table by prompting for the first tab position and the distance between consecutive tabs.

TABS.MAC. This macro sets tabs at positions that you specify; it prompts you for the desired alignment (left, centered, right, decimal, or vertical).

TABS2.MAC. This macro prompts you for the number of columns in a table, the position of the first column, and the desired alignment. The tabs are then set accordingly.

TOC_ENTRY.MAC. This macro creates table of contents entries by adding hidden table of contents codes (.c. and ;) to selected text.

Tips and Traps Summary

A Simple Macro Example

Trap: Actual keystrokes are executed while a macro records. Make sure that you want to perform the action before recording.

Tip: When the menu must be accessed in a macro, use CTRL+ESC. This ensures that the menu stays active if it is already on.

How to Create a Macro

Tip: The recording method is one way to create macros. Keystrokes are recorded as you type them in the normal way.

Tip: You can create macros to make complicated commands easier for novice users.

Tip: Writing macros instead of recording them allows you to use more features.

Trap: It's a good idea to test run a macro before using it in a real situation.

Tip: Use two-character names for macros to maintain a large number of available names.

Tip: Use the macro name to describe the macro as much as possible.

Trap: When naming macros, avoid using existing CTRL keynames already assigned by Word.

Trap: Don't forget that macro step mode is on and that a macro is running. The key code indicator ST will appear at the bottom of the screen.

Tips and Traps Summary (*continued*)

Macro Instructions

Trap: Macro instructions can only be written into a macro. They cannot be used when recording a macro.

Tip: Use blank lines and indents to make long macros easier to read and understand.

Tip: Use the ASK instruction to obtain information from the operator.

Tip: Use the COMMENT instruction to document a macro for future reference or for other users.

Tip: The IF...ELSE instruction performs conditional actions in a macro based on true and false statements.

Tip: Variables hold temporary values or text strings for later use.

Trap: Calculations can only be performed on variables that hold numeric values.

Tip: A constant only represents itself, never other values.

Tip: The MESSAGE instruction displays messages in the command line.

Trap: Messages will not display if the command menu is off.

Tip: You can use the PAUSE instruction to temporarily stop a macro so that text can be read or commands can be executed manually.

Tip: You can use the QUIT instruction to stop a macro, usually after a condition tests false.

Tip: You can use the REPEAT...ENDREPEAT instruction to repeat a macro a specified number of times.

Tip: The SET instruction obtains information from the operator and sets variable values.

Tip: The WHILE...ENDWHILE instruction performs an instruction set over and over while a condition is true.

A

Working at the DOS Level

This appendix provides tips and techniques for running Word in the DOS environment. Most of the topics covered here are meant for hard-drive systems. Floppy drive users will benefit from the discussion of startup batch files and RAM drives. Hard-drive users will benefit from the discussion of hard-drive organization techniques and startup batch files. Backing up document files is also covered.

Starting Word on a Floppy-Drive System

On a floppy-drive system with two drives, place the Word diskette in drive A and the data diskette in drive B. If the diskette in drive A has the DOS files on it, the system will start with that diskette. On systems other than those with 360K floppy drives, the Word program files can also be placed on this diskette. In this way Word can be started after the system boots. If both the DOS files and Word files will not fit on the diskette, you must first start DOS from a separate disk. You then place the Word disk in the drive and give the command to start Word.

The startup procedure discussed here is meant for diskettes that can hold both the DOS files and the Word program files. This eliminates diskettes formatted to 360K. Prepare the diskettes as covered in Chapter 1, using the command FORMAT B:/S. The /S parameter causes the DOS boot files to be placed on the formatted diskette. After the disk is formatted, proceed with the Word installation by using the SETUP program.

Create the Startup Batch File

To make Word start automatically from this new disk after DOS boots, you must place a file called AUTOEXEC.BAT on the disk. This file will contain the command to start Word and is special in that DOS always looks for and runs a batch file with this name whenever it boots. At the DOS prompt, type **COPY CON AUTOEXEC.BAT** to create the file. Press ENTER at the end of the command. The cursor will jump down to the next line. Type **WORD** and press ENTER. Next, press the F6 key (or CTRL+Z) and then ENTER again. The file will be written to the floppy disk. The disk is now prepared to start both DOS and Word whenever you boot the system with it.

Starting Word on a Hard-Drive System

Hard-drive systems use directories and subdirectories to store and separate different programs and files. When Word is copied to a hard drive with the SETUP program discussed in Chapter 1, the files are placed in a directory called WORD unless you specify another. You can use the batch file discussed next to switch to the WORD directory and then start Word.

Creating a Startup Batch File for Hard Drives

First, make sure that you are in the ROOT directory by typing **CD **. Place the file to start Word in the ROOT directory because it is the directory that DOS makes available after it boots unless an AUTOEXEC.BAT file, with alternate commands, has already been created in the ROOT directory.

The batch file to start Word will be called WORD.BAT. To create it, type **COPY CON WORD.BAT** at the DOS prompt. Press ENTER at the end of the line. The cursor will jump down to a new blank line on which you can type the following commands. Note that the first command changes directories to the WORD directory. If you are using another directory, type the name of that directory instead. Press ENTER at the end of each line.

```
CD WORD
WORD
```

After typing these two commands press F6, or CTRL+Z if your keyboard doesn't have an F6 key. This places an end-of-file marker at the end of the file. Press ENTER and DOS will write the file to disk.

To start Word after DOS boots, simply type **WORD** on the DOS command line. If you are using more than one directory or have more than one user, read further in this appendix to see how more advanced batch files can automate the log-on procedure.

Working with Multiple Directories

Hard-drive systems can hold hundreds or thousands of files. To help keep these files organized, directories can be created to separate them into groups and categories. The same can be done with Word. You can create a WORD directory to hold the Word program files and then create other directories to hold personal files, business files, or any other type of file.

The directories can branch from the WORD directory or from the ROOT directory. These two alternatives are shown in Figure A-1. The method you choose does not make much difference, though directories that branch from the ROOT directory tend to be easier to keep track of.

There are two ways to access the Word files in any of the directories. You can start Word in the normal way and then use the Transfer Options command to specify the name of the directory to use, or you can use the DOS CD (Change Directories) command to switch to the directory before starting Word. Either method is appropriate. If Word is started while you are in a directory other than the one that holds the Word program files, you will get an error unless you execute a PATH command to tell DOS where to find the Word files. This is covered next.

Starting Word from Other Directories

The example directories shown in Figure A-1 can be accessed from Word with the Transfer Options command, as discussed previously. Sometimes, however, you may want to start Word while you are logged into one of these directories. If other users are using the system, or if a temporary office person will be using the system, you may want to create a batch file that automatically places them in one of

Word: Secrets, Solutions, Shortcuts

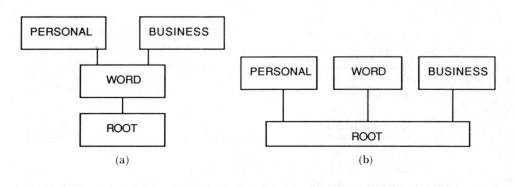

Figure A-1.   Examples of hard drive organization with Word (a) and (b)

these directories before starting Word.

The **DOS PATH** command specifies the location of the Word program files so that it can be started from other directories. You can type **PATH \WORD** at any time, or you can include it in the AUTOEXEC.BAT file or the batch file that is used to start Word from an alternate directory. Note that this example assumes that Word is stored in the WORD directory. If your AUTOEXEC.BAT file already has a PATH command, simply add **;\WORD** to the end of it.

The following example batch file can be created in the ROOT directory and used to start Word from a special directory once the PATH has been specified. Type the lines as shown and press ENTER at the end of each. This example assumes that Word is to be started from the PERSONAL directory, as shown in Figure A-1(b).

```
COPY CON WORDPERS.BAT
CD PERSONAL
WORD
```

After the last line, press F6 (or CTRL+Z) and then ENTER to write the file to the disk. Note that if your directory structure is like that shown in Figure A-1(a), replace the second line in the example with **CD \WORD\PERSONAL**. You can create similar files that you can use to log into any of your other directories before starting Word.

If your system is used by multiple users, you may want to create a directory for each user's files. When starting the system, a user would type a command to log into his or her special directory so that only the user's personal files are available, not those of other users. The following batch file commands can be used to log Joe into the JOE directory and then start Word. Note that Joe types **JOE** when he wants to start using Word.

```
COPY CON JOE.BAT
CD JOE
WORD
```

Type these commands as you did in the previous examples. Press F6 and then ENTER at the end of the file to write it to disk. This file should be created in the ROOT directory.

Using a Ram Drive

Recall from Chapter 1 that a RAM drive is a memory drive that simulates the function of a physical drive. RAM drives are used because the computer can access files in them at high speed. Access is not restricted by the moving parts that impede physical drives.

Because RAM drives exist in memory, they are lost whenever the system is shut down. Thus you must load any files that you want to access in the RAM drives every time you start the system. If the system accidentally shuts down, files will be lost. Therefore, only program files should be placed in RAM drives. Never place data files in RAM drives.

You must create a RAM drive in memory in order to use it. There are many sources of RAM drive programs. DOS version 3 and versions above it come with a VDISK command that is used to create a RAM drive. You must place the command in a file called CONFIG.SYS in the ROOT directory of your hard drive. (Refer to the VDISK section in your DOS manual or to the appropriate manual for the RAM drive program you have.) Note that the Word files listed in the following program may require as much as 450K of memory, which can be quite a chunk out of a normal 640K system. You may want to leave the help file out or add more memory to your system. If you have more than 640K of memory, be sure to specify that the RAM drive be placed in the extended memory above 640K, thus leaving normal memory free for Word.

You can add the following lines to the AUTOEXEC.BAT file or a Word startup batch file. They copy the important Word program files to the RAM drive, then switch access to that drive. Note that access to the data files is still retained on the floppy or hard drive. Assume that the name of the RAM drive is D.

```
COPY CON WORD.BAT
COPY \WORD\MW.PGM D:
COPY \WORD\MW.INI D:
COPY \WORD\WORD.COM D:
COPY \WORD\HYPH.DAT D:
COPY \WORD\MW.HLP D:
COPY \WORD\printername.PRD D:
PATH D:
CD C:\PERSONAL
WORD
```

The first line is the COPY CON command used to create the file. The next five commands copy the Word program files in the WORD directory to RAM drive D. In the sixth line replace the word *printername* with the name of the printer description file you use. The PATH command makes drive D the location where Word will execute. The next to last command ensures that the PERSONAL data directory is the location of retrieved and stored files. Any directory name can be substituted here. The last command starts Word. Be sure to press F6 and then ENTER to write the file to disk.

Backup Procedures

The following is a short discussion of techniques that you can use to back up your Word files. There are a number of ways to back up files on either a floppy-drive or hard-drive system. The idea is to keep duplicate copies of your files on hand in case something happens to your original diskette or the hard-drive equipment fails to operate. You can move backup diskettes to an offsite location for added security and protection.

You can make these duplicate copies as you save a file in Word. On a floppy-drive system this procedure could involve saving a file on one disk and then inserting the backup disk and saving the file again. On a hard-drive system you can first save a file to the hard drive and then use the Transfer Save command to save it again to a floppy disk.

Backup procedures can become more involved than simply saving each file as it is created. You may want to back up an entire floppy disk or hard-drive directory of files to another floppy disk, or even to a tape drive. Use the DOS COPY or DISKCOPY command to duplicate a floppy diskette. Use the DOS COPY or BACKUP command to copy a hard-drive directory to floppy disk.

A problem may occur with the BAK files that Word creates every time you save a file. Remember, these are the old versions of files that have been edited and saved. Word gives them the extension .BAK. BAK files may cease to be of use after a certain point and thus won't be desirable on the backup set. If you back up a diskette or a directory, you may want to first delete the BAK files to avoid cluttering the backup diskette.

If you use a hard-drive system, you can back up the individual directories used to hold your Word files. For example, if you use a PERSONAL directory to hold personal files and a BUSINESS directory to hold the files for your business, you may want to run a separate backup procedure for each one. You can use either the COPY command or the BACKUP command. The COPY command is best if you know that the files in the directory will fit on one diskette and if you want to be able to use these files on another system.

Use the BACKUP command if there are so many files that two or more diskettes will be needed. BACKUP automatically switches to additional diskettes. It also keeps track of the number of diskettes in a series and the order of the diskettes. The only problem with the BACKUP command is that it copies the files to the backup disk set in a "compressed" format. The files are not directly accessible; instead, you must use the RESTORE command to place them back on the hard drive for use.

B

ASCII Codes
for the IBM PC

Table B-1. *ASCII Codes for the IBM PC*

ASCII Value	Character	ASCII Value	Character
0	Null	12	Form-feed
1	☺	13	Carriage return
2	☻	14	♫
3	♥	15	☼
4	♦	16	►
5	♣	17	◄
6	♠	18	↕
7	Beep	19	‼
8	◘	20	¶
9	Tab	21	§
10	Linefeed	22	▬
11	Cursor home	23	↨

Table B-1.   *ASCII Codes for the IBM PC (continued)*

ASCII Value	Character	ASCII Value	Character
24	↑	59	;
25	↓	60	<
26	→	61	=
27	←	62	>
28	Cursor right	63	?
29	Cursor left	64	@
30	Cursor up	65	A
31	Cursor down	66	B
32	Space	67	C
33	!	68	D
34	"	69	E
35	#	70	F
36	$	71	G
37	%	72	H
38	&	73	I
39	'	74	J
40	(	75	K
41	)	76	L
42	*	77	M
43	+	78	N
44	,	79	O
45	-	80	P
46	.	81	Q
47	/	82	R
48	0	83	S
49	1	84	T
50	2	85	U
51	3	86	V
52	4	87	W
53	5	88	X
54	6	89	Y
55	7	90	Z
56	8	91	[
57	9	92	\
58	:	93	]

Table B-1. ASCII Codes for the IBM PC (continued)

ASCII Value	Character	ASCII Value	Character
94	^	129	ü
95	_	130	é
96	`	131	â
97	a	132	ä
98	b	133	à
99	c	134	å
100	d	135	ç
101	e	136	ê
102	f	137	ë
103	g	138	è
104	h	139	ï
105	i	140	î
106	j	141	ì
107	k	142	Ä
108	l	143	Å
109	m	144	É
110	n	145	ae
111	o	146	Æ
112	p	147	ô
113	q	148	ö
114	r	149	ò
115	s	150	û
116	t	151	ù
117	u	152	ÿ
118	v	153	Ö
119	w	154	Ü
120	x	155	¢
121	y	156	£
122	z	157	¥
123	{	158	Pt
124	¦	159	*f*
125	}	160	á
126	~	161	í
127	⌂	162	ó
128	Ç	163	ú

Word: Secrets, Solutions, Shortcuts

Table B-1.   ASCII Codes for the IBM PC (continued)

ASCII Value	Character	ASCII Value	Character
164	ñ	199	╟
165	Ñ	200	╚
166	ª	201	╔
167	º	202	╩
168	¿	203	╦
169	⌐	204	╠
170	¬	205	═
171	½	206	╬
172	¼	207	╧
173	¡	208	╨
174	«	209	╤
175	»	210	╥
176	░	211	╙
177	▒	212	╘
178	▓	213	╒
179	│	214	╓
180	┤	215	╫
181	╡	216	╪
182	╢	217	┘
183	╖	218	┌
184	╕	219	█
185	╣	220	▄
186	║	221	▌
187	╗	222	▐
188	╝	223	▀
189	╜	224	α
190	╛	225	β
191	┐	226	Γ
192	└	227	π
193	┴	228	Σ
194	┬	229	σ
195	├	230	μ
196	─	231	τ
197	┼	232	Φ
198	╞	233	θ

Table B-1.   *ASCII Codes for the IBM PC (continued)*

ASCII Value	Character	ASCII Value	Character
234	Ω	245	J
235	δ	246	$\div$
236	∞	247	$\approx$
237	$\varnothing$	248	$^\circ$
238	ϵ	249	$\bullet$
239	$\cap$	250	$\cdot$
240	$\equiv$	251	$\sqrt{}$
241	$\pm$	252	^{n}
242	$\geq$	253	^{2}
243	$\leq$	254	$\blacksquare$
244	$\lceil$	255	(blank 'FF')

C

Microsoft Pageview
and Windows

Two Microsoft programs — Microsoft Windows and Microsoft Pageview — add considerable features to Word, assuming that your system supports their use. Because Pageview comes with Windows and is best used with this program, both are covered here in the context of Pageview. As of this writing, Pageview is available as a separate program for about $50. Future versions of Word may include the modules as standard features.

Pageview allows page previewing of Word documents and allows pictures and graphs from other programs to be pasted into documents through use of the Windows clipboard. The graphics image needn't be created specifically for Windows; any graphics image can be captured by the clipboard and pasted into the document in Pageview, assuming that the application creating the image runs under Windows.

The view feature lets you view and change the layout of a document. The document appears in a window at a reduced page size, allowing you to see two entire pages side by side, as shown in Figure C-1. Because of the reduced size, text may not be legible. The idea is to view the blocks of text so that you can insert pictures and adjust margins, page numbers, headers, and footers.

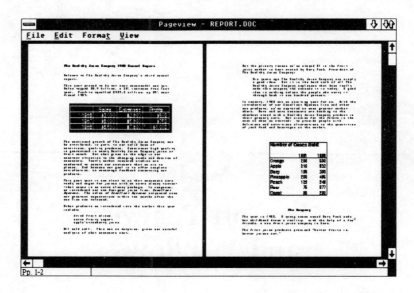

Figure C-1.   An example of a Microsoft Pageview screen (Courtesy of Microsoft Corporation)

The program is similar to desktop publishing programs in that its primary purpose is to help you lay out text and graphics on a sheet of paper. Word is still used for primary text editing.

Pageview requires two floppy-disk drives or a hard drive, DOS version 3.0 or higher, 512K or more of memory, Microsoft Word version 3 or higher, and a graphics screen. A mouse is also preferred for working in the Windows environment.

Basic Pageview Features and Commands

Pageview is used outside of Word. Documents are created, edited and saved in Word; then you return to DOS and start the Pageview program. You load the file into Pageview by using the Open command in the File menu.

Accessing Menus and Commands

Most of the commands to control Pageview are located along the menu selection bar at the top left of the screen. If you have a mouse, you can point to these options and press the mouse button to open the menu. Keyboard users can press the ALT key to jump to the menu area. You can press the underlined letter to choose a command, or move the highlight with the arrow keys. A control menu is displayed when you press ALT+SPACEBAR. Press ESC to return to the menu.

Scrolling Through Pages

Use the PGUP and PGDN keys to scroll through the document. As the keys are pressed, consecutive double pages of text are displayed in the window. The scroll bar can also be used to move between pages. A Jump command in the Edit menu allows you to move to a specific page.

Zooming Pages

Two pages of the document appear on the screen at once. One of them is always the active page. Initially the left page is active, but you can use the TAB key to change the active page or the mouse to point to the desired active page. The Single Page command in the View menu allows you to view a single page on the screen. The Zoom command in the View menu magnifies part of the active page. In this way exact spacing around inserted pictures and fonts, and font sizes can be seen in normal size.

Printing and Saving Documents

A Pageview document that has had pictures and graphs inserted must be printed from Pageview with the Print command in the File menu. You can select the number of copies, print quality, and page range in the menu. To save changes, choose the Save command in the File menu. If you want to save the document with a new name, choose the Save As command in the same menu.

Changing the Layout

You can change a document's layout in the Pageview window. You can adjust the margin and running head positions; change the page breaks; and add, change, or delete page numbers.

Changing Margin and Running Head Positions

Use the Margins command to adjust the left, right, top, bottom, and gutter margins, and the running head positions. When you select the Margins command, the pointer changes to a cross-hair-shaped pointer, and a grid appears on your document. Use the TAB key to move among the margin and running head positions. The status bar will indicate which is selected. Use the direction keys to adjust the margins or running head and press ENTER when you are finished.

Changing a Page Break

Choose the Page Breaks command in the Format menu. The pointer changes to a cross-hair shape and appears on the current page break. Use the UP and DOWN ARROW keys to adjust the page break. The measurement from the top of the page to the page break is displayed in the status bar. Press ENTER when the page break is in the desired position. To delete a page break, press DEL.

Adding or Changing Page Numbers

You can add page numbers or adjust their position with the Page Numbers command in the Format menu. After selecting the command, the pointer changes to a number 1 and is positioned on the current page. As you adjust the number with the mouse or direction keys, the measurement changes in the status bar. The first number indicates the distance from the left of the page; the second number indicates the distance from the top. Press ENTER when you are done. To delete a page number, simply press DEL after selecting the Page Numbers command.

Working with Pictures and Windows

You can copy pictures from other applications by using the Windows program. Programs such as Microsoft Excel, Chart, and Paint, as well as Lotus 1-2-3 and other graphics-capable software, can generate pictures that can be copied with Windows. Transferring the pictures is accomplished with the clipboard.

Pictures added to a Pageview document are inserted from the clipboard into a picture "frame," which you position in the text and then size to allow for the picture. The pictures are retained as disk files, so if you copy a Pageview document to another disk or directory, you must also copy the picture files. The pictures retain the name of the document file but are given the extensions P01, P02, P03, and so on, following the order in which they were inserted into the document.

Capturing Pictures

Not all applications work directly with Windows. You can capture pictures in one of two ways, depending on how well Windows and the application interface. If the application is compatible with Windows, start it and display the picture or other information to be copied. Select the picture and choose the program's Copy command to save the picture in the clipboard.

If the application is not directly compatible with Windows, you can display the picture that you want to capture on the screen and then press ALT+PRTSC. This saves the entire screen to the clipboard. You may need to crop part of the picture once it is inserted in Pageview.

Inserting a Picture in Pageview

You must create a picture frame in preparation for inserting a picture from the clipboard. Choose the Insert Picture command from the Edit menu. The pointer changes to a corner-shaped pointer that represents the upper-left corner of the picture frame. Use the UP or DOWN ARROW key to move the pointer to where you want the upper-left corner of the inserted picture to appear; then press ENTER to insert the picture frame.

Next, choose the Paste command from the Pageview Edit menu to insert the picture into the document.

Sizing and Moving a Picture

Use the Size Picture and Move Picture commands to position a frame on the page. The Size Picture command sizes the frame horizontally and vertically from the right margin, leaving the distance from the left margin unchanged. The Move Picture command moves the entire frame. Use the direction keys to both move and size the frame.

Clipping Pictures

Use the Clip Picture command in the Edit menu to clip the edges from pictures that contain undesirable parts. This command can be used when pictures are captured with ALT+PRTSC. Remember, this command captures an entire screen, which may contain undesirable parts.

First, select the frame or picture and choose the Clip Picture command in the Edit menu. The pointer changes to a cross-hair-shaped pointer. Use the TAB key to move the pointer to the corner that is to be adjusted. Use the direction keys to clip the picture and press ENTER when you are done. If you need to reset the picture, choose the Reset Clipping command from the Edit menu. To remove a picture, select it and press DEL.

Trademarks

AT and System/2™	International Business Machines Corporation
dBASE®	Ashton-Tate Corporation
Excel™	Microsoft Corporation
FX-80™	Seiko Epson Corporation
FX-86™	Seiko Epson Corporation
Hercules™	Hercules Computer Technology
HP™ LaserJet Series II™	Hewlett-Packard Company
Hewlett-Packard®	Hewlett-Packard Company
IBM®	International Business Machines Corporation
Lotus® 1-2-3®	Lotus Development Corporation
Microsoft®	Microsoft Corporation
Microsoft® Chart	Microsoft Corporation
MS-DOS®	Microsoft Corporation
Multiplan™	Microsoft Corporation
Operating System/2™ (DOS)	International Business Machines Corporation
Paradox®	Ansa, a Borland Company
PostScript®	Adobe Systems, Inc.
Quietwriter™	International Business Machines
R:base™	Microrim Inc.
WordStar®	MicroPro International Corporation

Index

Command Card

Function Key Assignments

F1 key only	Next window	F10 key only	Next paragraph
With SHIFT	Undo	With SHIFT	Whole document
With CTRL	Zoom window on/off	With CTRL	Save
With ALT	Set tab	With ALT	Record style
F2 key only	Calculate	F11 key only	Collapse heading
With SHIFT	Outline view on/off	With SHIFT	Collapse body text
With CTRL	Header		
With ALT	Footer	F12 key only	Expand heading
		With SHIFT	Expand body text
F3 key only	Expand glossary name		
With SHIFT	Record macro on/off	UP ARROW key only	Up one line
With CTRL	Step macro	With SHIFT	Extend up one line
With ALT	Copy to scrap	With CTRL	First char prev paragraph
F4 key only	Repeat last edit	Effect in menus	Up one line
With SHIFT	Repeat search	SCROLL LOCK on	Scroll up one line
With CTRL	Update list		
With ALT	Set margins	DOWN ARROW key only	Down one line
		With SHIFT	Extend down one line
F5 key only	Overtype on/off	With CTRL	First char next paragraph
With SHIFT	Outline organize		
With CTRL	Line draw	Effect in menus	Down one line
With ALT	Go to page	SCROLL LOCK on	Scroll down one line
F6 key only	Ext selection on/off	LEFT ARROW key only	Left one character
With SHIFT	Col selection on/off	With SHIFT	Extend left one char
With CTRL	Thesaurus	With CTRL	First char prev word
With ALT	Spell	Effect in menus	Left one command field
F7 key only	Previous word	SCROLL LOCK on	Left 1/3 window
With SHIFT	Previous sentence		
With CTRL	Load	RIGHT ARROW	
With ALT	Printer display on/off	key only	Right one character
		With SHIFT	Extend right one char
F8 key only	Next word	With CTRL	First char next word
With SHIFT	Next sentence	Effect in menus	Right one command field
With CTRL	Print		
With ALT	Font name	SCROLL LOCK on	Right 1/3 window
F9 key only	Previous paragraph	HOME key only	Start of line
With SHIFT	Current line	With SHIFT	Extend to start of line
With CTRL	Repaginate	With CTRL	Top of window
With ALT	Text/graphics toggle	Effect in menus	First command field

Microsoft® Word: Secrets, Solutions, Shortcuts

Function Key Assignments (*continued*)

END key only	End of line
With SHIFT	Extend to end of line
With CTRL	Bottom of window
Effect in menus	Last command field
PGUP key only	Up one window
With SHIFT	Extend up one window
With CTRL	Start of document
PGDN key only	Down one window
With SHIFT	Extend down one window
With CTRL	End of document
INS key only	Insert scrap
With SHIFT	Insert scrap/ replace selection
DEL key only	Delete to scrap
With SHIFT	Delete, not to scrap

Note: Press the following key codes with the ALT key. If a style sheet is attached, use ALT+X followed by the key code.

Character Formatting

B	Bold
D	Double underline
E	Hidden text
I	Italic
K	Small caps
S	Strikethrough
U	Underline
+,=	Superscript
−	Subscript
SPACEBAR	Return to normal

Paragraph Formatting

C	Centered
F	Indent first line to next tab
J	Justified
L	Left flush paragraph
M	Reduce left indent to previous tab
N	Increase left indent
O	Open paragraph spacing
P	Normal paragraph
R	Right flush paragraph
T	Hanging indent
2	Double-spaced paragraphs

Other Keyboard Actions

ESC	Move between document/menu
ENTER	New paragraph
SHIFT+ENTER	New line
CTRL+SHIFT+ENTER	New page
CTRL+ENTER	New division
CTRL+−	Optional hyphen
CTRL+SHIFT+−	Nonbreaking hyphen
CTRL+SPACEBAR	Nonbreaking space
CTRL+>	Next form field
CTRL+<	Previous form field
CTRL+ESC	Return to menu
ALT+H	Help

IF YOU ENJOYED THIS BOOK...

help us stay in touch with your needs and interests by filling out and returning the survey card below. Your opinions are important, and will help us to continue to publish the kinds of books you need, when you need them.

What brand of computer(s) do you own or use? _____ ☐ At work ☐ At school ☐ At home

Where do you use your computer the most? _____

What topics would you like to see covered in future books by Osborne/McGraw-Hill? _____

How many other computer books do you own? _____

Why did you choose this book?

☐ Best coverage of the subject.
☐ Recognized the author from previous work.
☐ Liked the price.
☐ Other

Where did you hear about this book?

☐ Book review.
☐ Osborne catalog.
☐ Advertisement in:
☐ Found by browsing in store.
☐ Found/recommended in library
☐ Other

Where did you find this book?

☐ Bookstore
☐ Computer/software store
☐ Department store
☐ Advertisement
☐ Catalog

☐ Required textbook
☐ Library
☐ Gift
☐ Other

Where should we send your FREE catalog?

NAME _____

ADDRESS _____

349-2 CITY _____ STATE _____ ZIP _____

BUSINESS REPLY MAIL

FIRST CLASS   PERMIT NO. 3111   Berkeley, CA

Postage will be paid by addressee

Osborne **McGraw-Hill**

2600 Tenth Street
Berkeley, California 94710

No Postage
Necessary
If Mailed
in the
United States

MICROSOFT® WORD
SECRETS, SOLUTIONS, SHORTCUTS

Microsoft® Word: Secrets, Solutions, Shortcuts puts all the power of this popular word processing software, up through version 4, at your fingertips.

With **Microsoft® Word: Secrets, Solutions, Shortcuts,** you'll not only learn how to perform Microsoft® Word procedures, but how and when to use these procedures more efficiently.

Sheldon leads you through all of Word's functions in a text that is generously sprinkled with helpful hints and tricks. Because the book is divided into four parts, each dealing with more advanced functions, you can quickly find the appropriate level of information that best applies to your work.

Some of the topics that Sheldon covers include

- Page setup
- Working with multiple windows
- Using math functions
- Running DOS
- Commands in Word
- Creating form letters

Special attention is focused on version 4's

- Powerful macro language
- Remappable function keys
- Redlining
- Paragraph borders

With **Microsoft® Word: Secrets, Solutions, Shortcuts,** greater performance is just a few keystrokes away.

Tom Sheldon is a consultant and trainer for ComputerLand who has taught Microsoft Word to hundreds of users. He is also the author of several acclaimed computer books and a software package on DOS. His "hands on" approach to understanding computer technology and software has been praised by many who have read his articles in such industry journals as *PC Magazine,* and *PC World.*

Microsoft is a registered trademark of Microsoft Corp.

ISBN 0-07-881349-2

$21.95